STRE   5

Camb   e

and Peterborough

First published in 2001 by

Philip's, a division of
Octopus Publishing Group Ltd
2-4 Heron Quays, London E14 4JP

Second edition 2005
Second impression with revisions 2006
CAMBB

ISBN-10   0-540-08736-X (pocket)
ISBN-13   978-0-540-08736-5 (pocket)

© Philip's 2006

Ordnance Survey®

This product includes mapping data licensed from
Ordnance Survey® with the permission of the
Controller of Her Majesty's Stationery Office.
© Crown copyright 2006. All rights reserved.
Licence number 100011710.

Printed by Toppan, China

Contents

III **Key to map symbols**

IV **Key to map pages**

VI **Route planning**

X **Administrative and Postcode boundaries**

1 **Street maps** at 2⅔ inches to 1 mile

208 **Street maps** at 1⅓ inches to 1 mile

239 **Street maps** at 2⅔ inches to 1 mile

246 **Street map of Cambridge city centre** at 5⅓ inches to 1 mile

247 **Index** of towns and villages

249 **Index** of streets, hospitals, industrial estates, railway stations, schools, shopping centres, universities and places of interest

Digital Data

The exceptionally high-quality mapping found in this atlas is available as digital data in TIFF format, which is easily convertible to other bitmapped (raster) image formats.

The index is also available in digital form as a standard database table. It contains all the details found in the printed index together with the National Grid reference for the map square in which each entry is named.

For further information and to discuss your requirements, please contact Philip's on 020 7644 6932 or james.mann@philips-maps.co.uk

Key to map symbols

III

Motorway with junction number (22a)	Ambulance station
Primary route – dual/single carriageway	Coastguard station
A road – dual/single carriageway	Fire station
B road – dual/single carriageway	Police station
Minor road – dual/single carriageway	Accident and Emergency entrance to hospital
Other minor road – dual/single carriageway	Hospital
Road under construction	Place of worship
Tunnel, covered road	Information Centre (open all year)
Rural track, private road or narrow road in urban area	Shopping Centre
Gate or obstruction to traffic (restrictions may not apply at all times or to all vehicles)	Parking, Park and Ride
Path, bridleway, byway open to all traffic, road used as a public path	Post Office
Pedestrianised area	Camping site, caravan site
Postcode boundaries DY7	Golf course
County and unitary authority boundaries	Picnic site
Railway, tunnel, railway under construction	Important buildings, schools, colleges, universities and hospitals
Tramway, tramway under construction	Built up area
Miniature railway	Woods
Railway station Walsall	Tidal water, water name
Private railway station	Non-tidal water – lake, river, canal or stream
Metro station South Shields	Lock, weir, tunnel
Tram stop, tram stop under construction	Non-Roman antiquity
Bus, coach station	Roman antiquity

Acad Academy · Allot Gdns Allotments · Cemy Cemetery · C Ctr Civic Centre · CH Club House · Coll College · Crem Crematorium · Ent Enterprise · Ex H Exhibition Hall · Ind Est Industrial Estate · IRB Sta Inshore Rescue Boat Station · Inst Institute · Ct Law Court · L Ctr Leisure Centre · LC Level Crossing · Liby Library · Mkt Market · Meml Memorial · Mon Monument · Mus Museum · Obsy Observatory · Pal Royal Palace · PH Public House · Recn Gd Recreation Ground · Resr Reservoir · Ret Pk Retail Park · Sch School · Sh Ctr Shopping Centre · TH Town Hall/House · Trad Est Trading Estate · Univ University · W Twr Water Tower · Wks Works · YH Youth Hostel

Adjoining page indicators and overlap bands 87 246
The colour of the arrow and the band indicates the scale of the adjoining or overlapping page (see scales below)

Enlarged mapping only

Railway or bus station building

Place of interest

Parkland

■ The small numbers around the edges of the maps identify the 1 kilometre National Grid lines
■ The dark grey border on the inside edge of some pages indicates that the mapping does not continue onto the adjacent page

The scale of the maps on the pages numbered in blue is 4.2 cm to 1 km • 2⅔ inches to 1 mile • 1: 23810

The scale of the maps on pages numbered in green is 2.1 cm to 1 km • 1⅓ inches to 1 mile • 1: 47620

The scale of the maps on pages numbered in red is 8.4 cm to 1 km • 5⅓ inches to 1 mile • 1: 11900

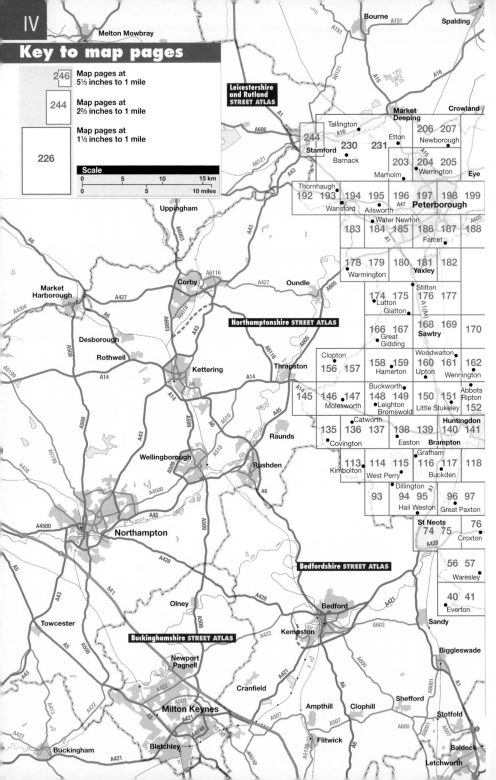

IV

Key to map pages

246	Map pages at 5⅓ inches to 1 mile
244	Map pages at 2⅔ inches to 1 mile
226	Map pages at 1⅓ inches to 1 mile

Scale

0   5   10   15 km

0   5   10 miles

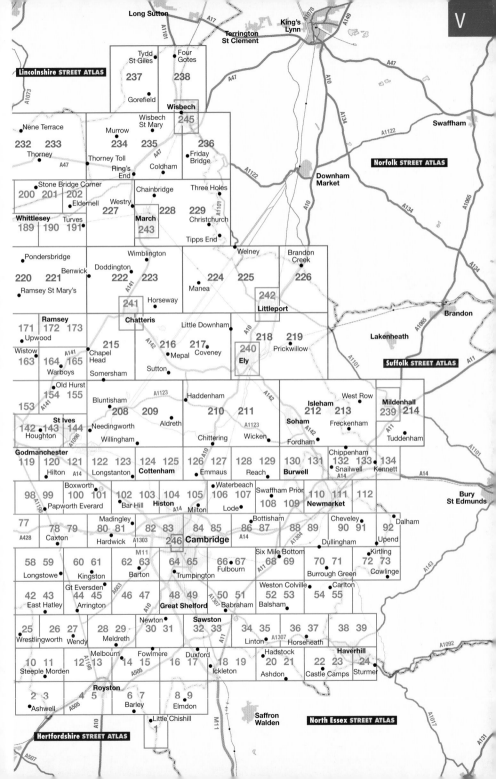

Long Sutton

A17

A1078

King's Lynn

A148

Terrington St Clement

A47

A1101

Lincolnshire STREET ATLAS

Tydd St Giles
Four Gotes

237
238

Gorefield

Wisbech

245

Swaffham

A1122

Norfolk STREET ATLAS

A134

A1085

A1073

Nene Terrace

Murrow
Wisbech St Mary

232 **233**
Thorney

234 **235**

236
Friday Bridge

A1065

A47

Thorney Toll
Ring's End

Coldham

A47

A1122

Downham Market

A10

Stone Bridge Corner

200 **201** **202**
Eldernell

Chainbridge

Three Holes

A1101

A134

Westry

Whittlesey

189 **190** **191**
Turves

227 **228**

March
243

229
Christchurch

Tipps End

Pondersbridge

Wimblington

Welney

Brandon Creek

220 **221**
Benwick

Doddington

222 **223**

224 **225**

226

Ramsey St Mary's

Manea

242

Littleport

Brandon

Horseway

241

Chatteris

Little Downham

A10

218 **219**
Prickwillow

Lakenheath

A1065

Ramsey

171 **172** **173**
Upwood

A141

Chapel Head

215

216 **217**
Mepal Coveney

240

Ely

West Row

Suffolk STREET ATLAS

A1101

A11

Wistow

163

164 **165**
Warboys

Somersham

Sutton

Isleham

212 **213**

Freckenham

Mildenhall

239 **214**

Old Hurst

A1123

Haddenham

A142

Soham

Tuddenham

153

154 **155**

A141

Bluntisham

208 **209**
Aldreth

210 **211**

A1123

Chippenham

Wicken

St Ives

142 **143** **144**
Houghton

Needingworth

Willingham

Chittering

Fordham

A1096

Godmanchester

119 **120** **121**
Hilton

A14

Longstanton

122 **123**

Cottenham

124 **125**

Emmaus

126 **127**

Reach

128 **129**

Burwell

130 **131**

Snailwell

132 **133** **134**
Kennett

A14

Bury St Edmunds

Boxworth

Waterbeach

Swaffham Prior

98 **99**

100 **101**
Papworth Everard

Bar Hill

102 **103**

Histon

104 **105**
Milton

Lode

106 **107**

108 **109**

110 **111**

Newmarket

112

A1198

Madingley

Bottisham

Cheveley

Dalham

77

78 **79**
Caxton

Hardwick

80 **81**

A1303

82 **83**

246

84 **85**

Cambridge

A14

86 **87**

Dullingham

88 **89**

90 **91**

Upend

92

A428

M11

Six Mile Bottom

Kirtling

A143

Longstowe

58 **59**

Kingston

60 **61**

Barton

62 **63**

Trumpington

64 **65**

Fulbourn

66 **67**

A11

68 **69**

Burrough Green

70 **71**

Carlton

Cowlinge

72 **73**

Gt Eversden

A603

Weston Colville

42 **43**
East Hatley

Arrington

44 **45**

A10

46 **47**

48 **49**

Great Shelford

A1307

Babraham

50 **51**

Balsham

52 **53**

54 **55**

Wrestlingworth

Wendy

Newton

Sawston

Haverhill

25

26 **27**

Meldreth

28 **29**

30 **31**

32 **33**

Linton

A1307

Horseheath

34 **35**

36 **37**

38 **39**

A11

A1092

Melbourn

Fowlmere

Duxford

Hadstock

10 **11**
Steeple Morden

A1198

12 **13**

14 **15**

Ickleton

16 **17**

Ashdon

18 **19**

20 **21**

Castle Camps

22 **23**

Sturmer

24

A505

A1017

Royston

2 **3**
Ashwell

A505

4 **5**

Barley

6 **7**

Elmdon

8 **9**

Little Chishill

M11

Saffron Walden

North Essex STREET ATLAS

A131

A10

A507

Hertfordshire STREET ATLAS

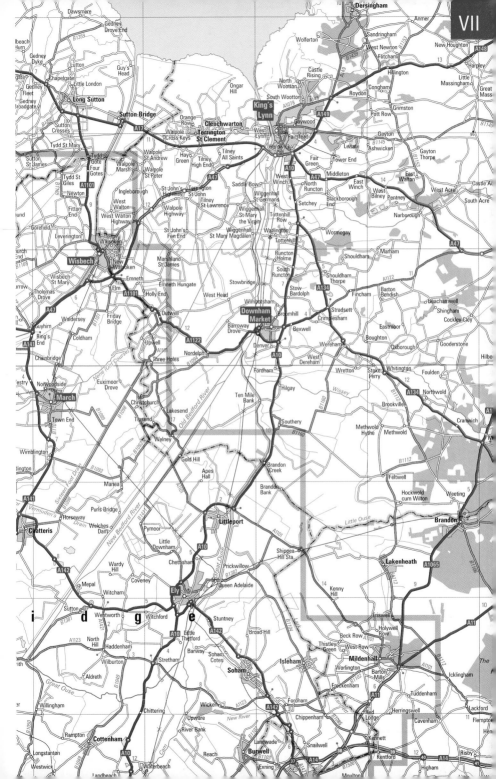

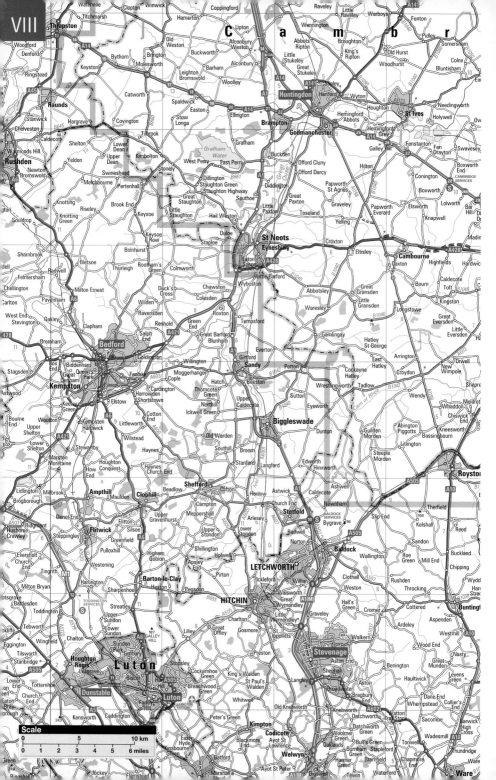

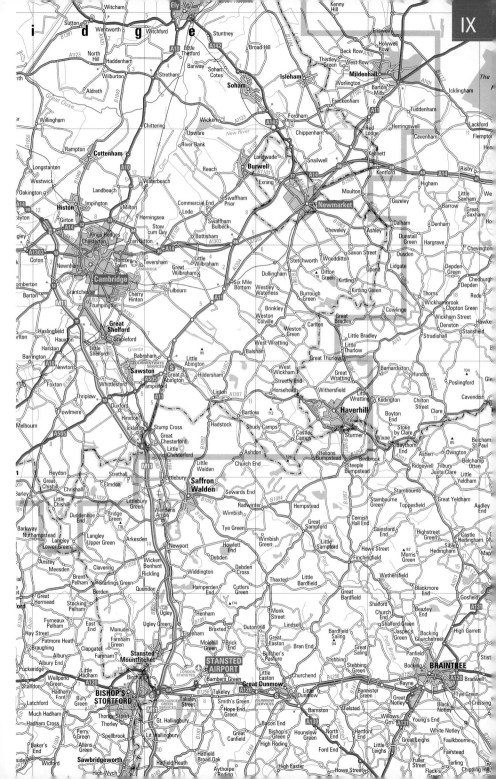

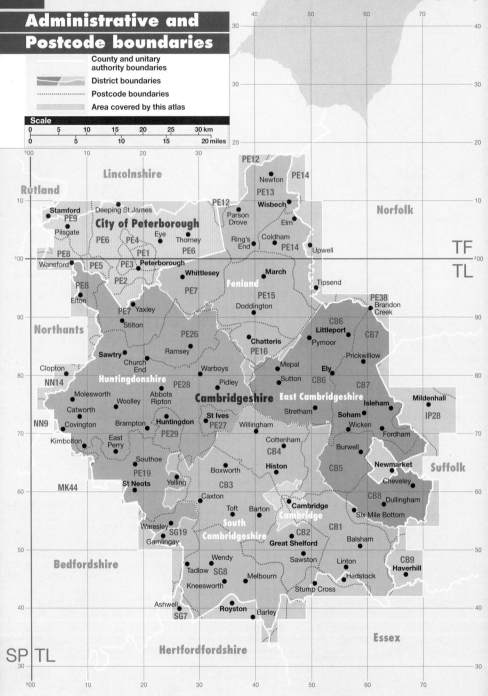

X

Administrative and Postcode boundaries

County and unitary authority boundaries
District boundaries
Postcode boundaries
Area covered by this atlas

Scale
| 0 | 5 | 10 | 15 | 20 | 25 | 30 km |
| 0 | 5 | | 10 | | 15 | 20 miles |

Lincolnshire

Rutland

Norfolk

PE12
Newton
PE14
PE13
Wisbech

Stamford
PE9
Deeping St James
PE12
Parson Drove
Elm

Pilsgate
City of Peterborough
Eye
Thorney
Ring's End
Coldham
PE14
Upwell

PE6
PE4
Thorney
PE6

PE8
Wansford
PE5
PE3 Peterborough
Whittlesey
March
Tipsend

PE8
Elton
PE2
PE7 Yaxley
Doddington
PE15

PE38
Brandon Creek

Northants
Stilton
PE26
Chatteris
PE16
Littleport
Pymoor
CB6
CB7
Prickwillow

Clopton
NN14
Sawtry
Church End
Ramsey
Warboys
Mepal
Sutton
Ely
CB7

Molesworth
Woolley
Abbots Ripton
PE28
Pidley
Cambridgeshire
Stretham
East Cambridgeshire
Isleham
Mildenhall

Catworth
NN9
Covington
Brampton
Huntingdon
PE27
St Ives
Willingham
Soham
Wicken
Fordham
IP28

Kimbolton
East Perry
PE29
Cottenham
CB4
Burwell

Southoe
PE19
Boxworth
Histon
CB5
Newmarket
Suffolk

MK44
St Neots
Yelling
CB3
Caxton
Cheveley

Waresley
SG19
Toft
Barton
Cambridge
CB8
Dullingham

Gamlingay
South Cambridgeshire
Great Shelford
CB2
Six Mile Bottom
Balsham

Bedfordshire
Wendy
Tadlow
SG8
Melbourn
Sawston
Linton
CB9
Haverhill

Kneesworth
Stump Cross
Hadstock

Ashwell
SG7
Royston
Barley

Hertfordshire
Essex

SP TL
TF
TL

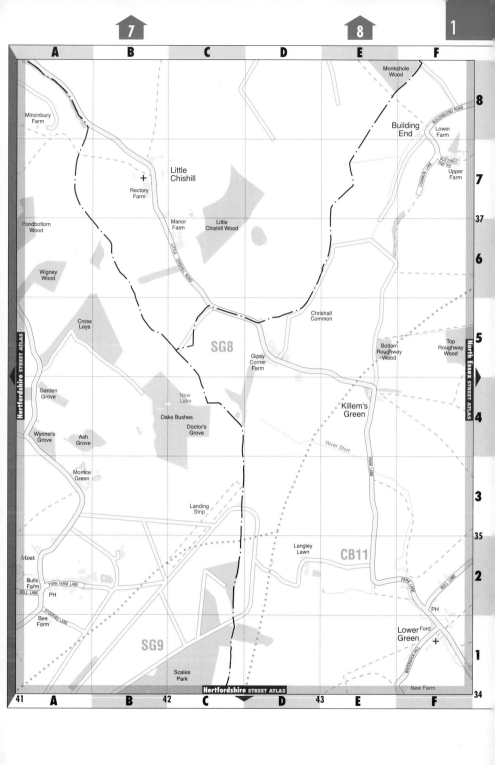

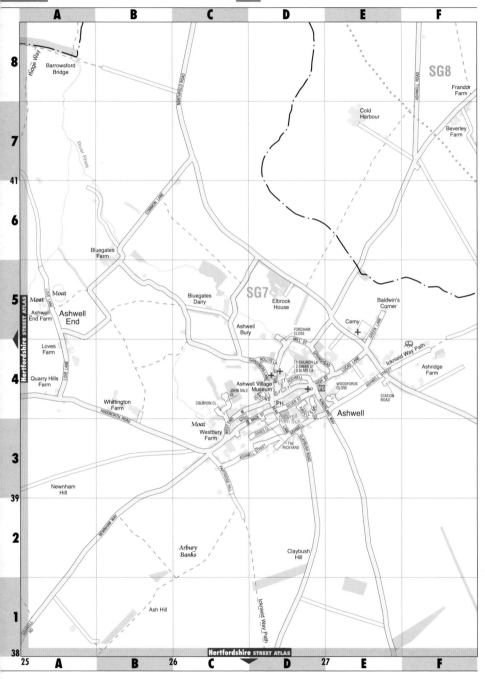

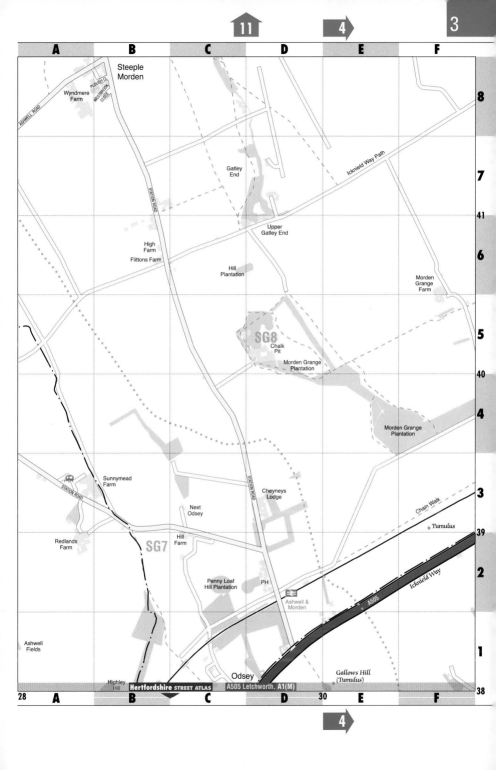

A B C D E F

8
7
41
6
5
40
4
3
39
2
1
38

Steeple
Morden

ASHWELL ROAD

Wyndmere
Farm

PLOUGH CL

WESTREVOOR
CLOSE

STATION ROAD

Gatley
End

Icknield Way Path

Upper
Gatley End

High
Farm

Flittons Farm

Hill
Plantation

Morden
Grange
Farm

SG8

Chalk
Pit

Morden Grange
Plantation

Morden Grange
Plantation

STATION ROAD

Cheyneys
Lodge

Chain Walk

STATION ROAD

Sunnymead
Farm

Tumulus

Next
Odsey

Redlands
Farm

SG7

Hill
Farm

Penny Loaf
Hill Plantation

PH

Ashwell &
Morden

A505

Icknield Way

Ashwell
Fields

Highley
Hill

Odsey

Gallows Hill
(Tumulus)

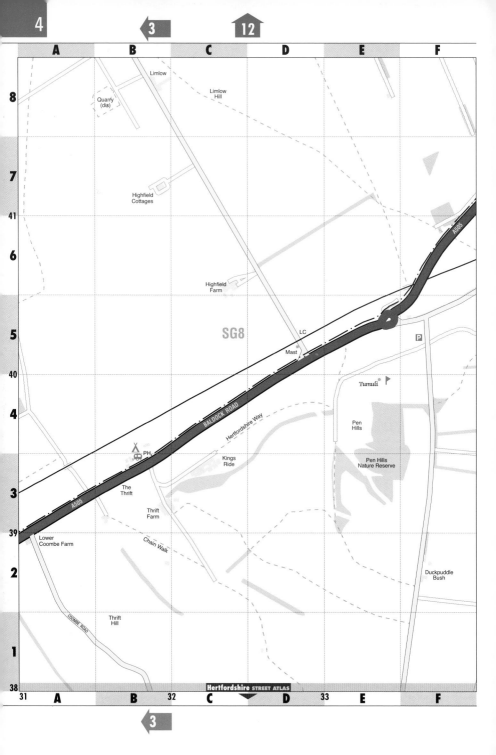

A B C D E F

8

7

41

6

5

40

4

3

39

2

1

38

Limlow

Quarry
(dis)

Limlow
Hill

Highfield
Cottages

Highfield
Farm

SG8

LC

Mast

A505

Tumuli

Pen
Hills

Pen Hills
Nature Reserve

P

BALDOCK ROAD

Hertfordshire Way

Kings
Ride

The
Thrift

PH

A505

Thrift
Farm

Lower
Coombe Farm

Chain Walk

Duckpuddle
Bush

COOMBE ROAD

Thrift
Hill

31 A 32 B C 33 D E F

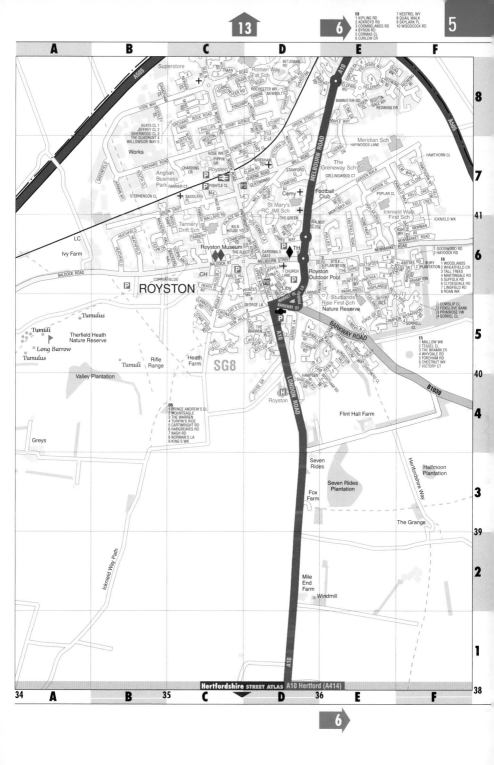

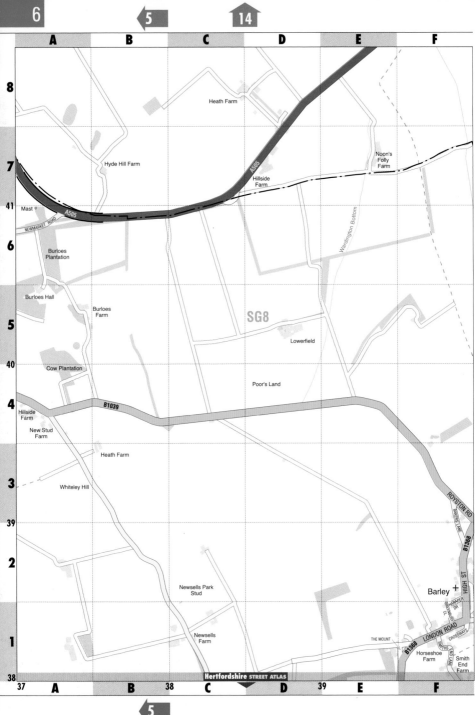

Heath Farm

Hyde Hill Farm

Noon's Folly Farm

A505

Hillside Farm

Mast

A505

NEWMARKET ROAD

Wardington Bottom

Burloes Plantation

Burloes Hall

Burloes Farm

SG8

Lowerfield

Cow Plantation

Poor's Land

B1039

Hillside Farm

New Stud Farm

Heath Farm

Whiteley Hill

ROYSTON RD

BACKER LANE

B1368

HIGH ST

Newsells Park Stud

Barley

SHRAMPER DR

PLUMMER D

THE MOUNT

CROSSWAYS

Newsells Farm

LONDON ROAD

B1368

SMITHS END LANE

Horseshoe Farm

Smith End Farm

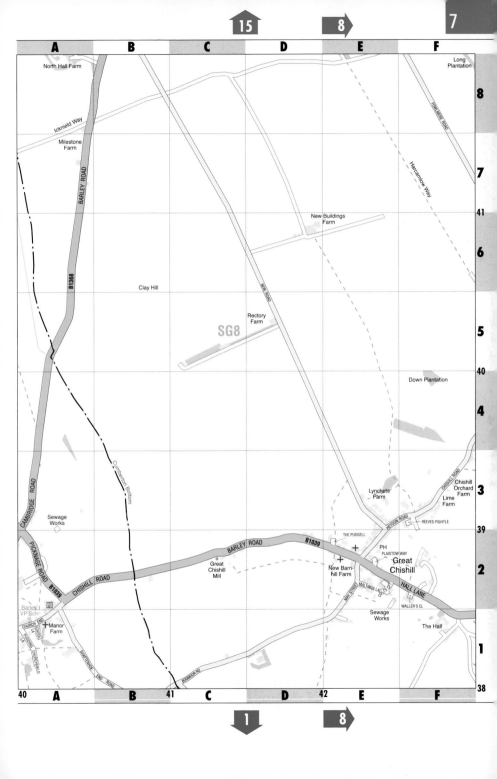

A   B   C   D   E   F

8   Long
    Plantation

    Anthonyhill   Anthony
    Plantation   Hill

                                           Redlands

7

41
                    • Strip
                      Lynchets
    Reeve
    Hill
6   Valley
                    Plantation

    Heydon
    Valley Farm   Pightle
5   Farm

    Heydon   Lane   MILL CAUSEWAY   SG8
                    Farm   Hillside Farm   CB11
                    HEYDON LANE
                                                Crawley
    HIGH   End
40 CL FOWMERE RD   Earthwork
                                          PISKENEYS
    +   ENGLERIC   Moat   Castle
    CHISHALL ROAD   Grove
4   Arrow   CRAWLEY END
    PH   Plantation   HEYDON LA
    PO   Wire
                                       Farm
    Woodgreen   Chrishall
    Animal Shelter   Martinholme   P
                    Broad   Farm
                    Green Farm   Broad
                                  Green
                                                            King's
3   PH   Grove
                                   PO
    Wisdom's   BRICK ROW
    Grove   Park
                                                 Farm   Ickmield Way Path
39   HIGH STREET
                                                            Park Wood
    Barnard's   Parsonage
2   Wood   Farm   CHALKY LANE
                                       Moat
                                                   Glebe
                                                   Farm   +
                                       HOLLOW ROAD
                                                BURY LANE
                                       New
                    New   Farm
1   B1039

                                   BUILDING END ROAD

38 Monkshole •
    Wood   North Essex STREET ATLAS

43 A   B   44   C   D   45   E   F

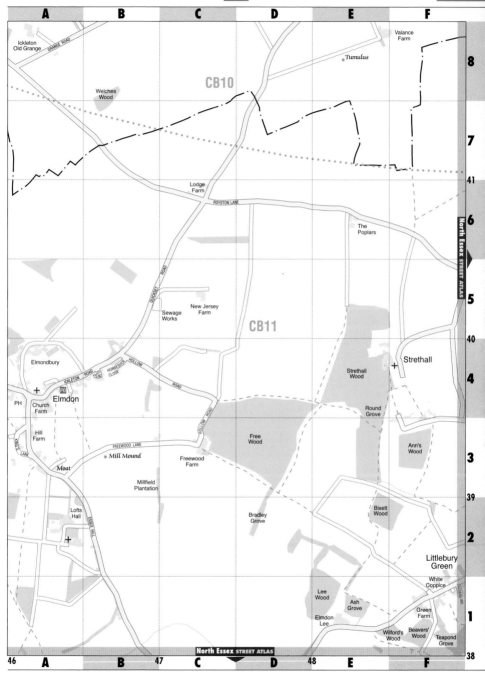

A B C D E F

Ickleton
Old Grange
GRANGE ROAD

Valance
Farm

Welches
Wood

CB10

Tumulus

8

7

41

Lodge
Farm
ROYSTON LANE

6

The
Poplars

QUICKSET ROAD

Sewage
Works

New Jersey
Farm

CB11

5

40

Elmondbury

ICKLETON ROAD
ELM CL
HORNBEAM CLOSE
HOLLOW

Strethall
Strethall
Wood

Strethall

4

PH

Church
Farm

PO

Elmdon

HOLLOW ROAD

Round
Grove

Ann's
Wood

Hill
Farm

KING'S LANE

FREEWOOD LANE

Mill Mound

Freewood
Farm

Free
Wood

3

Moat

39

Millfield
Plantation

Bixett
Wood

Lofts
Hall

ESSEX HALL

Bradley
Grove

2

Littlebury
Green

White
Coppice

Lee
Wood

Ash
Grove

Green
Farm

1

Elmdon
Lee

Wilford's
Wood

Beavers'
Wood

Teapond
Grove

38

46 A B 47 C D 48 E F

25

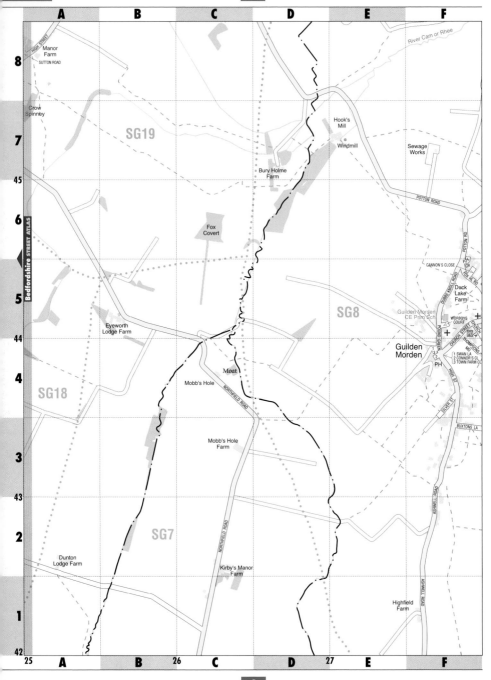

Manor Farm
HIGH STREET
SUTTON ROAD
Crow Spinney
SG19
Hook's Mill
Windmill
Sewage Works
Bury Holme Farm
POTTON ROAD
Fox Covert
Bedfordshire STREET ATLAS
CANNON'S CLOSE
Duck Lake Farm
SG8
Guilden Morden CE Prim Sch
WORBOYS COURT
Guilden Morden
1 SWAN LA
2 CONNOR'S CL
3 TOWN FARM CL
Eyeworth Lodge Farm
PH
Moat
Mobb's Hole
SG18
Mobb's Hole Farm
BUXTONS LA
NORTHFIELD ROAD
ASHWELL ROAD
SG7
SILVER ST
Dunton Lodge Farm
Kirby's Manor Farm
Highfield Farm
ASHWELL ROAD

2

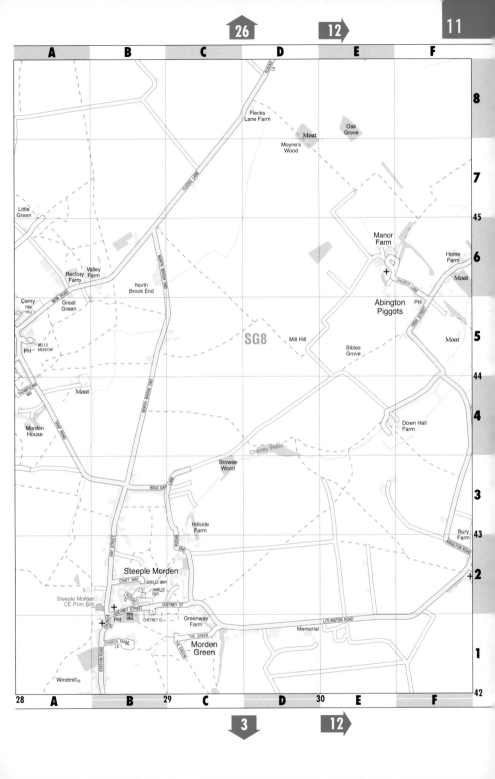

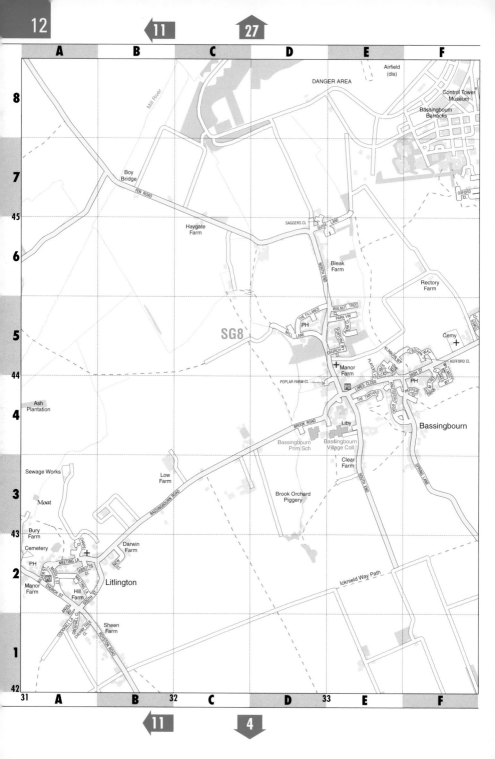

8

7

45

6

5

44

4

3

43

2

1

42

A   B   C   D   E   F

Sewage Works

Foxfield
Farm

Works

Meldreth
Prim Sch

THE GRANGE

BELL LA

FLAMBARDS CL

Meldreth

CH

Chiswick
End

WHITECROFT RD

HOWARD RD

DRAGS LA

CROSS LA

STATION ROAD

WOODLANDS DR

Meldreth

THE MOOR

A10

THE MOOR

Valley
Farm

St Johns
Farm

STATION ROAD

Moat

THATCHER STANFORDS

Melbourn
Village Coll

Swimming
Pool

Liby

The
Moor

BLACKTHORN

WINDMILL CL

THE MOOR

CAMBRIDGE ROAD

Melbourn
Science
Park

Solway
Farm

Tostock
Farm

FAIRBROOK

PORTWAY

MORTLOCK'S LANE

VICARAGE CL

ORCHARD CL

BARHAM CL

HALE ST

WORCESTER WAY

East Farm

Moat

Melbourn
Prim Sch

Melbourn

+

+

PO

LITTLE LANE

HIGH STREET

MALL WAY

DOLPHIN LANE

CHARLES WAY

GREENBANKS

THE LAWNS

BACK LANE

WATER LANE

GREENBANKS

CEDAR WAY

BECKWITH CL

BECKWITH CL

ELM WAY

SAXON WAY

SWAN ST

GREENBAGE CL

GREENBAGE DRI

CARLTON WE

CLEAR CRS

NEW ROAD

SG8

Windpump

Windpump

Bury Lane
Fruit Farm

Melda
Farm

BURY LANE

Melbourn
Bury

Long
Barrow

Greenlow

A10

Summer
House
Farm

Muncey's
Farm

Goffers Knoll
(Tumulus)

A505

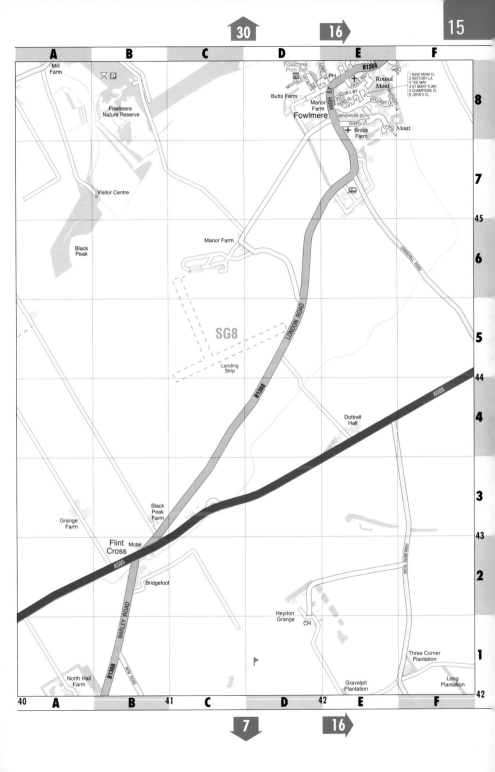

15 31

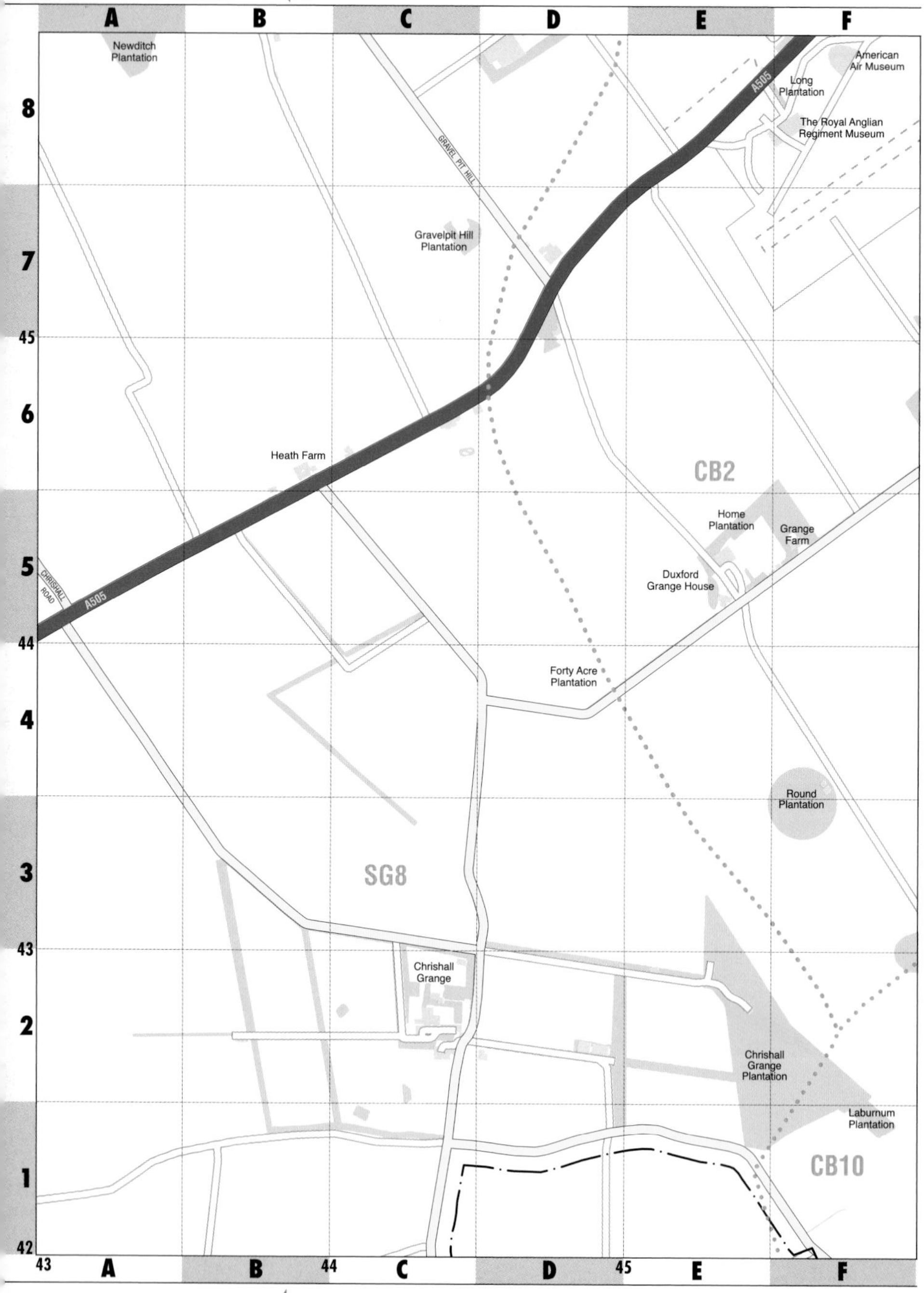
A
B
C
D
E
F
8
7
45
6
5
44
4
3
43
2
1
42
43
44
45
Newditch Plantation
American Air Museum
Long Plantation
The Royal Anglian Regiment Museum
A505
GRAVEL PIT HILL
Gravelpit Hill Plantation
Heath Farm
CB2
Home Plantation
Grange Farm
Duxford Grange House
CHRISHALL ROAD
Forty Acre Plantation
Round Plantation
SG8
Chrishall Grange
Chrishall Grange Plantation
Laburnum Plantation
CB10

15 8

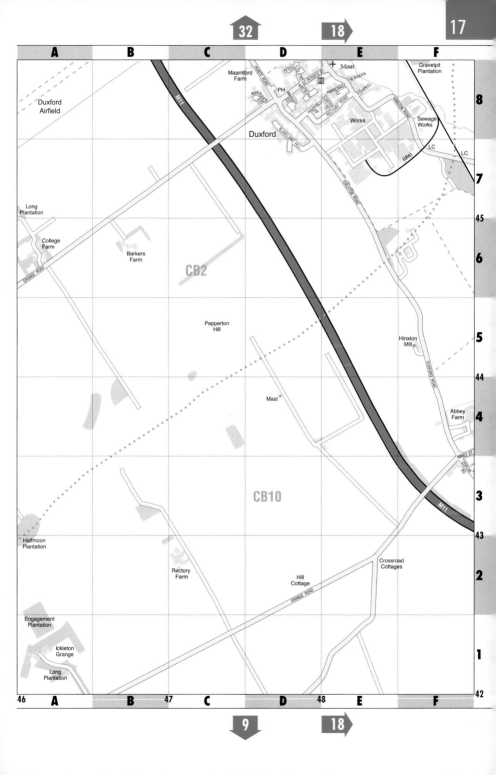

A   B   C   D   E   F

Duxford Airfield

Maarnford Farm

+ Moat

Gravelpit Plantation

PETER'S CL ST. PETER'S SC.

BUS TLES CL

PH

HINTS ROAD

MARKING

CL

PARSONAGE CL

THE BRIDGEN

FISHER CL

HINXTON ROAD

Duxford

Works

Sewage Works

HIGHFIELD

FACTORY ROAD

RECTORY ROAD

LAKELAND HILL

LC   LC

(dis)

Long Plantation

College Farm

Barkers Farm

GRANGE ROAD

CB2

ICKLETON ROAD

Pepperton Hill

Hinxton Mill

Mast

DUXFORD ROAD

Abbey Farm

CB10

ABBEY ST

CROFT RD

M11

Halfmoon Plantation

Rectory Farm

Crossroad Cottages

Hill Cottage

GRANGE ROAD

Engagement Plantation

Ickleton Grange

Long Plantation

M11

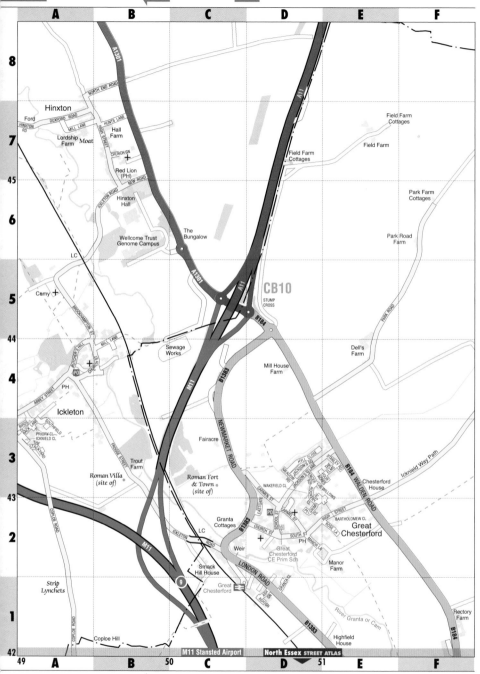

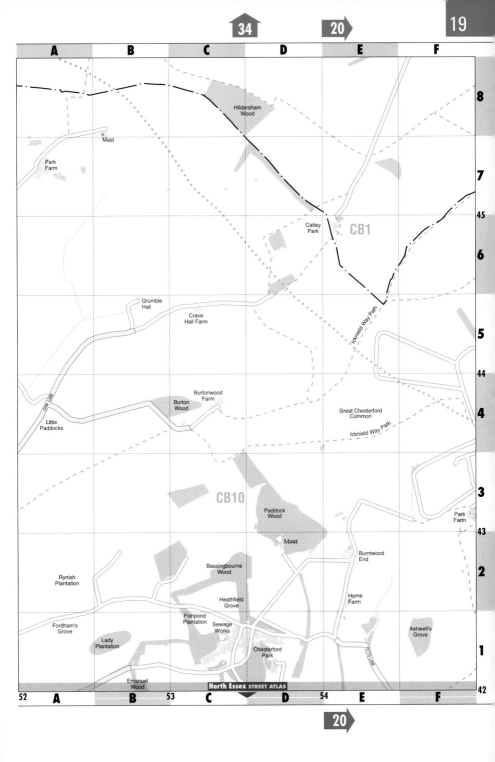

A B C D E F

8

Hildersham
Wood

Mast 7

Park
Farm 45

Catley
Park CB1 6

Grumble
Hall
Crave
Hall Farm

Icknield Way Path 5

44

Burtonwood
Farm
Burton
Wood Great Chesterford
Common 4

COW LANE

Little
Paddocks Icknield Way Path

3

CB10 Paddock
Wood
43

Park
Farm

Moat

Bassingbourne
Wood Burntwood
End 2

Rynish
Plantation
Heathfield
Grove Home
Farm

Fordham's
Grove
Fishpond
Plantation
Sewage
Works Ashwell's
Grove

Lady
Plantation Chesterford
Park

PETTS LANE

1

Emanuel
Wood

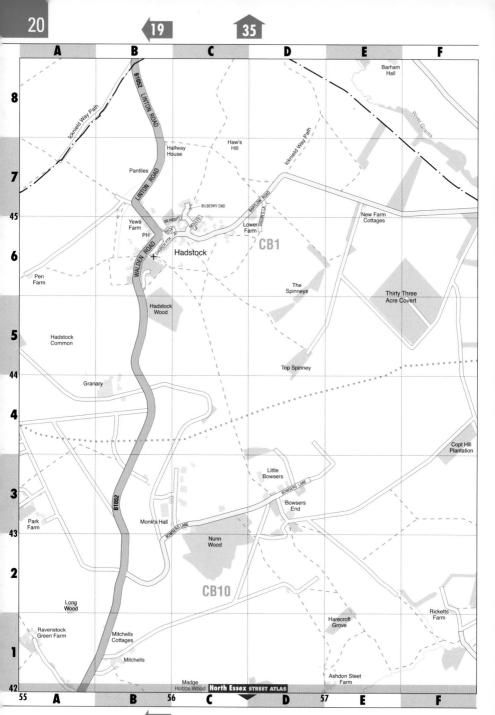

A B C D E F

8

Barham
Hall

River Granta

Icknield Way Path

B1052

LINTON ROAD

Haw's
Hill

Icknield Way Path

7

Halfway
House

Pantiles

LINTON ROAD

45

BILBERRY END

BARTLOW ROAD

New Farm
Cottages

Yews
Farm

DR PIGHTLE

MOLES
LA

SUDIN'S LA

Lower
Farm

CB1

PH

BACK

6

WALDEN ROAD

CHURCH PTH

Hadstock

Pen
Farm

The
Spinneys

Thirty Three
Acre Covert

Hadstock
Wood

5

Hadstock
Common

44

Top Spinney

Granary

4

Copt Hill
Plantation

B1052

Little
Bowsers

BOWSERS LANE

3

Bowsers
End

Monk's Hall

BOWSERS LANE

43

Nunn
Wood

2

CB10

Long
Wood

Ricketts
Farm

Park
Farm

Ravenstock
Green Farm

Harecroft
Grove

1

Mitchells
Cottages

Mitchells

Madge
Hobbs Wood

Ashdon Steet
Farm

42

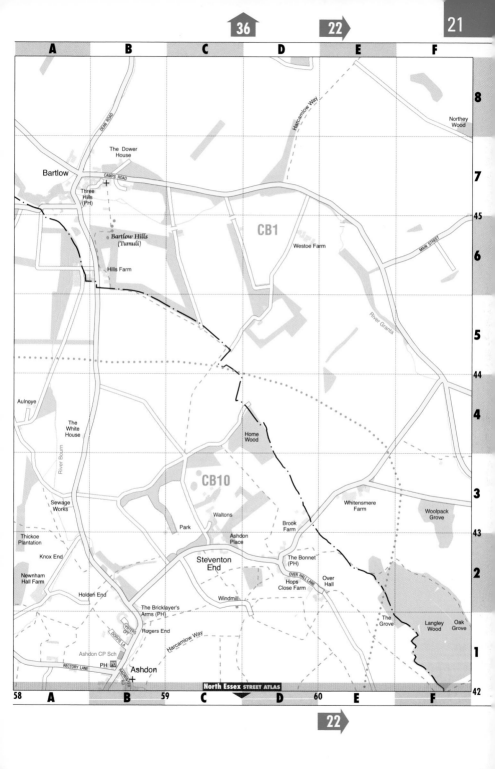

Northey Wood

Harcamlow Way

The Dower House

Bartlow

CAMPS ROAD

Three Hills (PH)

CB1

Bartlow Hills ('Tumuli)

Westoe Farm

MAIN STREET

Hills Farm

River Granta

Aulnoye

The White House

River Bourn

Home Wood

CB10

Whitensmere Farm

Woolpack Grove

Sewage Works

Waltons

Brook Farm

Thickoe Plantation

Park

Ashdon Place

Knox End

Steventon End

The Bonnet (PH)

Newnham Hall Farm

OVER HALL LANE

Over Hall

The Grove

Langley Wood

Oak Grove

Holden End

Hops Close Farm

The Bricklayer's Arms (PH)

Windmill

Ashdon CP Sch

Rogers End

Harcamlow Way

RECTORY LANE

PH

Ashdon

DEAN ROAD

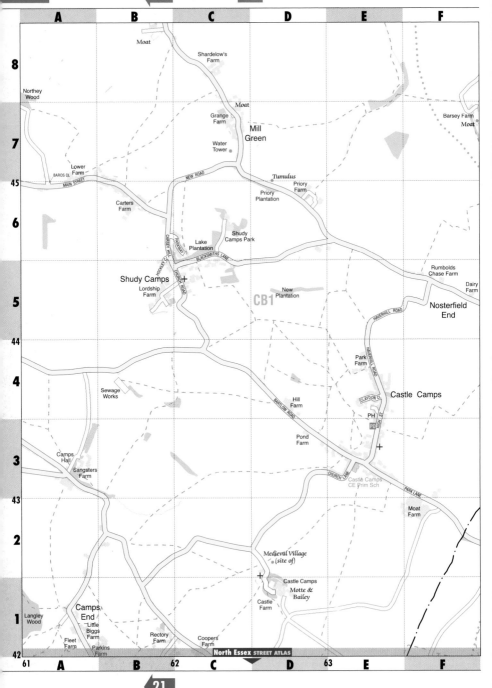

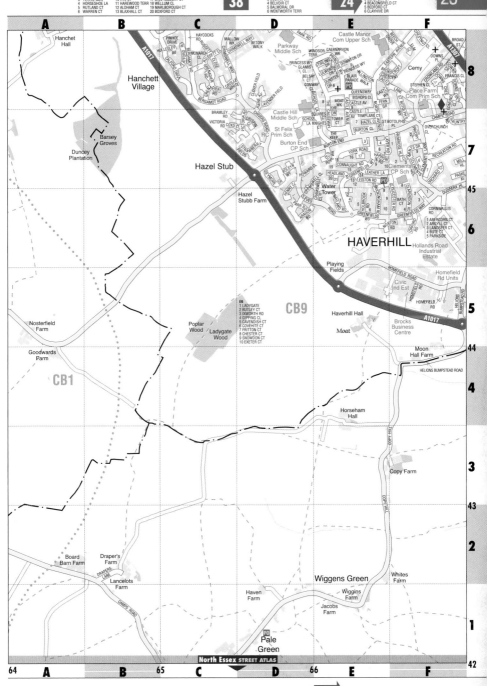

E7
1 GREENWOOD CL
2 PARSONAGE GDNS
3 YERRIL GDN
4 HORSESHOE LA
5 RUTLAND CT
6 WARREN CT

7 SHIRE CT
8 FALLOWFIELD CT
9 SHEPHERDS CT
10 RYE CT
11 HAREWOOD TERR
12 ALDHAM CT
13 BLAXHALL CT

14 BURES CT
15 WELLINGTON TERR
16 SOMERSET CT
17 SHAFTESBURY CT
18 WELLUM CL
19 MARLBOROUGH CT
20 BOXFORD CT

21 ALDEBURGH CL

38

E8
1 ARUNDEL WK
2 WARWICK CT
3 BODIAN WK
4 BELVOIR CT
5 BALMORAL CT
6 WENTWORTH TERR

7 QUEENS CT
8 BISHOPS CT
9 ST JAMES CT

24

F7
1 SALISBURY CT
2 TREFOIL CT
3 BEAUFORT CT
4 BEACONSFIELD CT
5 BEDFORD CT
6 CLAYHIVE DR

7 OLD CLEMENTS LA
8 BELMONT CT
9 MONTFORT CT

23

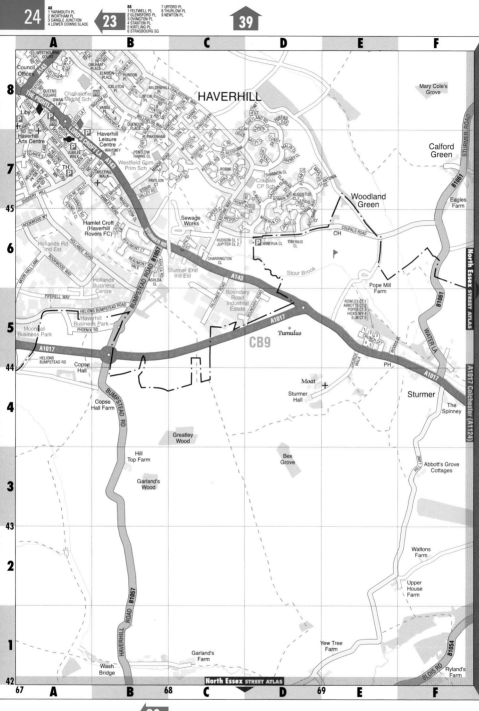

24
A8
1 YARMOUTH PL
2 WORTHAM PL
3 CANGLE JUNCTION
4 LOWER DOWNS SLADE

23

B8
1 FELTWELL PL
2 GLEMSFORD PL
3 OVINGTON PL
4 STANTON PL
5 KIRTLING PL
6 STRASBOURG SQ

7 UFFORD PL
8 THURLOW PL
9 NEWTON PL

39

HAVERHILL

Calford
Green

Woodland
Green

Sturmer

CB9

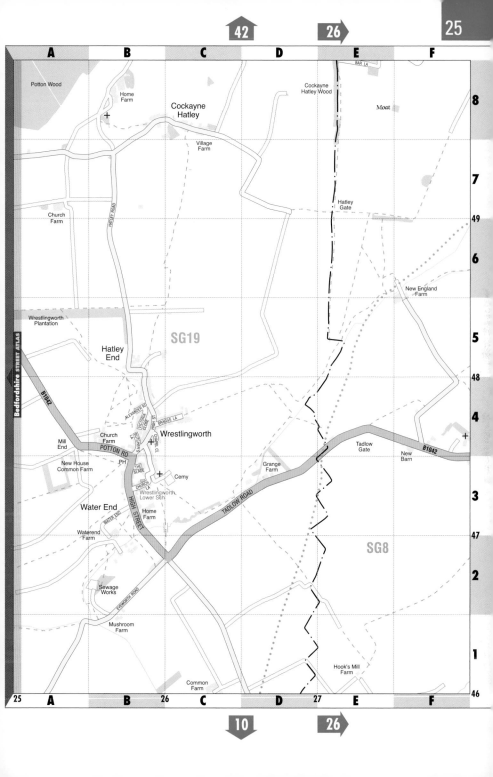

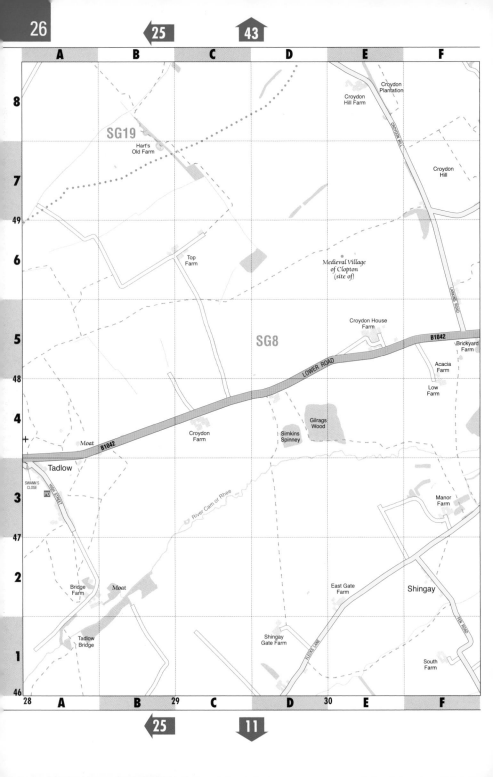

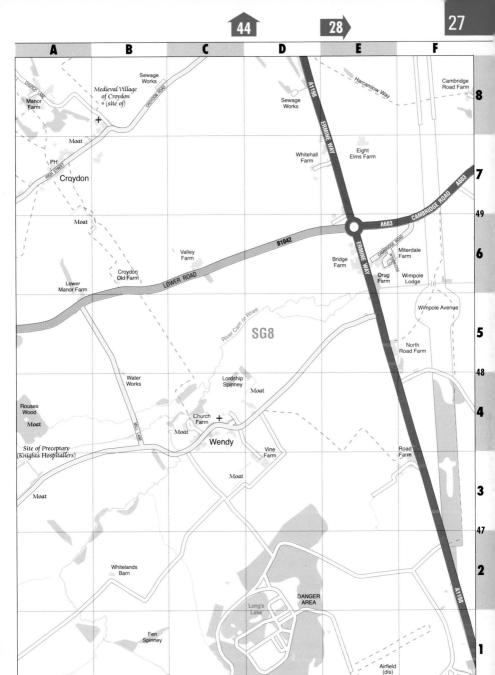

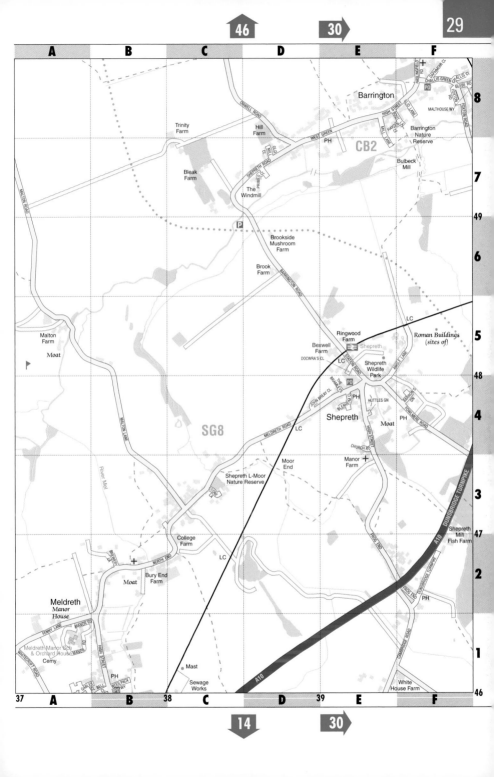

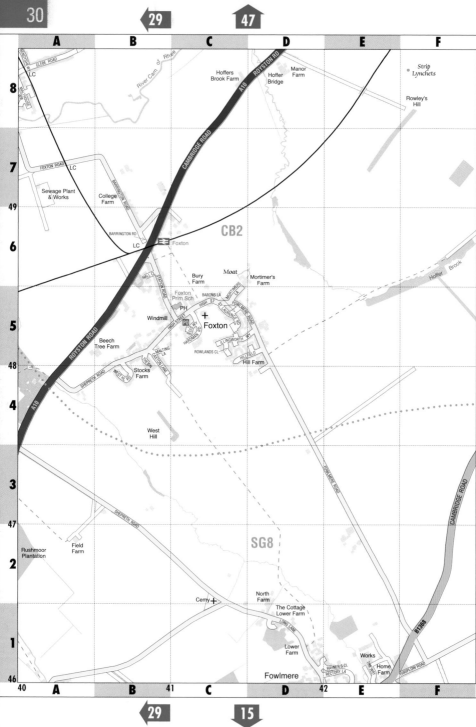

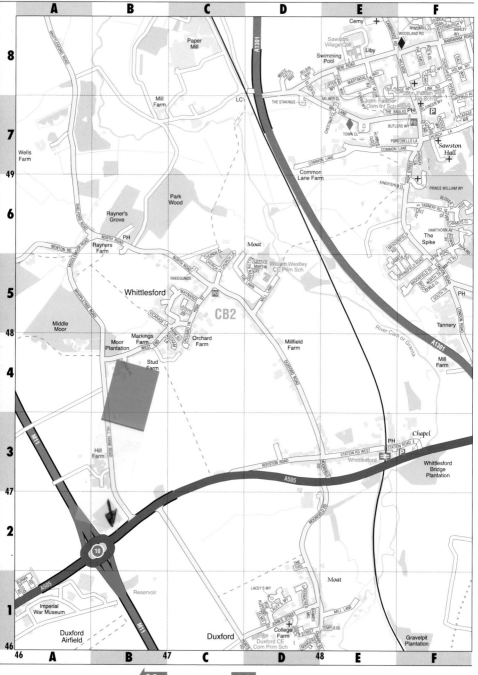

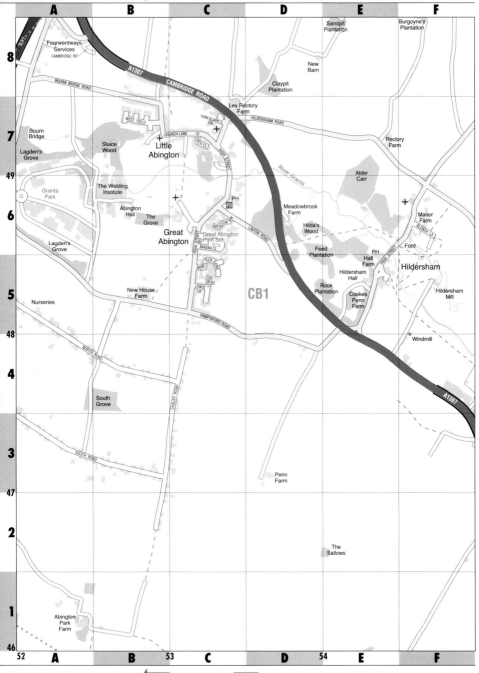

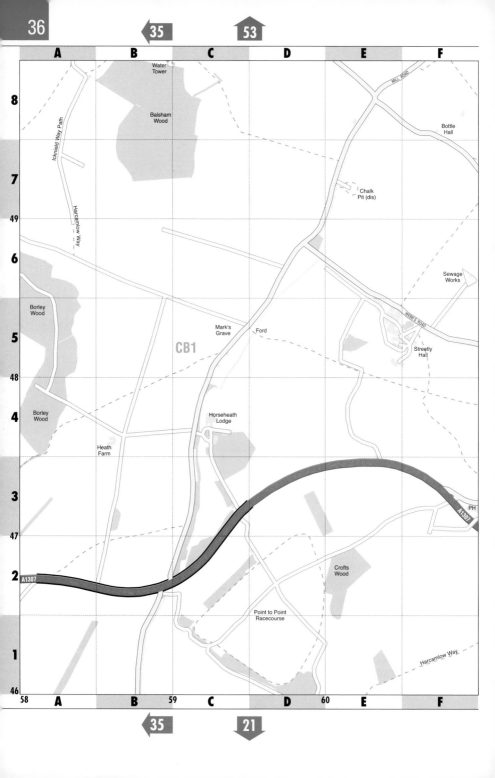

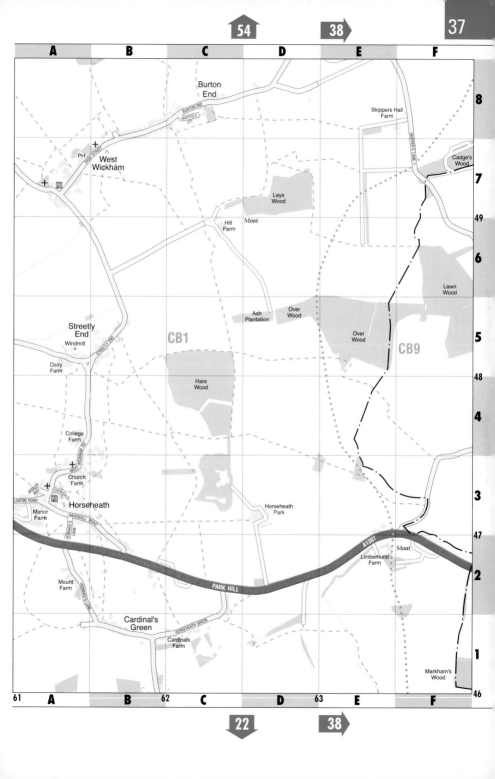

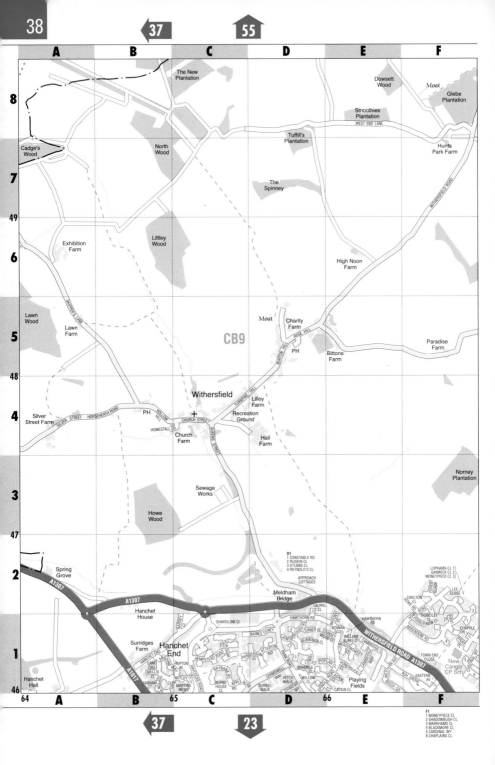

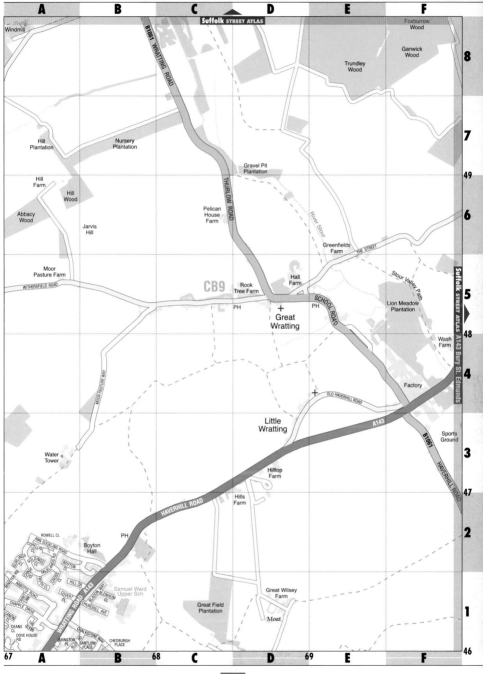

A   B   C   D   E   F

8

7

49

6

48

5

4

47

3

2

1

46

Windmill

Foxburrow Wood

Ganwick Wood

Trundley Wood

Hill Plantation

Nursery Plantation

Gravel Pit Plantation

Hill Farm

Hill Wood

Pelican House Farm

River Stour

Abbacy Wood

Jarvis Hill

Greenfields Farm

THE STREET

Moor Pasture Farm

Stour Valley Path

CB9

WITHERSFIELD ROAD

Rook Tree Farm

Hall Farm

Lion Meadow Plantation

PH

SCHOOL ROAD

PH

Great Wratting

Wash Farm

B1061 WRATTING ROAD

THURLOW ROAD

MOOR PASTURE WAY

Factory

OLD HAVERHILL ROAD

Little Wratting

A143

Sports Ground

Water Tower

B1061

HAVERHILL ROAD

HAVERHILL ROAD

Hilltop Farm

Hills Farm

ROWELL CL

ANN SUCKLING ROAD

COPELLS CL

Boyton Hall

GOLD DINGS

PALLARS

PH

Great Wilsey Farm

Great Field Plantation

Moat

WRATTING ROAD A143

HILL DR

BOYTON

FRY CL

BLENHEIM CL

Samuel Ward Upper Sch

CHURCHILL AVE

CHALKSTONE WAY

CHEDBURGH PLACE

ABINGTON PL

BARTLOW PLACE

DOVE HOUSE RD

DEANS CL

CANON

CHAPPLE DRIVE

ABBOTTS ROAD

COVERT CL

67   68   69

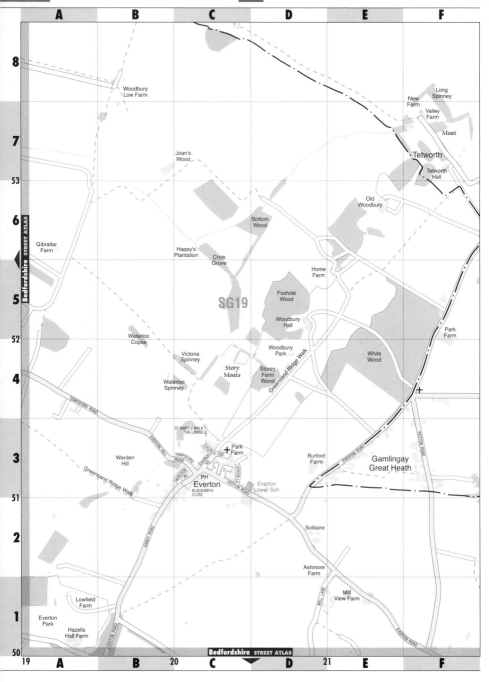

A **B** **C** **D** **E** **F**

Woodbury Low Farm

Long Spinney
New Farm
Valley Farm
Moat

Joan's Wood

Tetworth
Tetworth Hall

Old Woodbury

Bottom Wood

Gibraltar Farm

Happy's Plantation
Crow Grove

Home Farm

Foxhole Wood

SG19

Woodbury Hall

Waterloo Copse

Park Farm

Victoria Spinney

Woodbury Park

White Wood

Waterloo Spinney

Story Moats

Storey Farm Wood

Greensand Ridge Walk

TEMPSFORD ROAD

St Mary's Walk
THE LAWNS
Park Farm

Warden Hill

TEMPSFORD ROAD
CHURCH END
CHURCH HILL
EVERTON HILL

Burford Farm

EVERTON ROAD

Gamlingay Great Heath

Greensand Ridge Walk

PH
Everton
BLACKSMITH CLOSE
POTTER'S LANE
POTTON ROAD
WATERLOO HILL

Everton Lower Sch

POTTON ROAD

Solitaire

SANDY ROAD

Ashmore Farm

MILL LANE

Mill View Farm

EVERTON ROAD

Lowfield Farm

Everton Park
Hazells Hall Farm

POTTON ROAD

19 **A** **B** 20 **C** **D** 21 **E** **F**

8
7
53
6
52
5
4
3
51
2
1
50

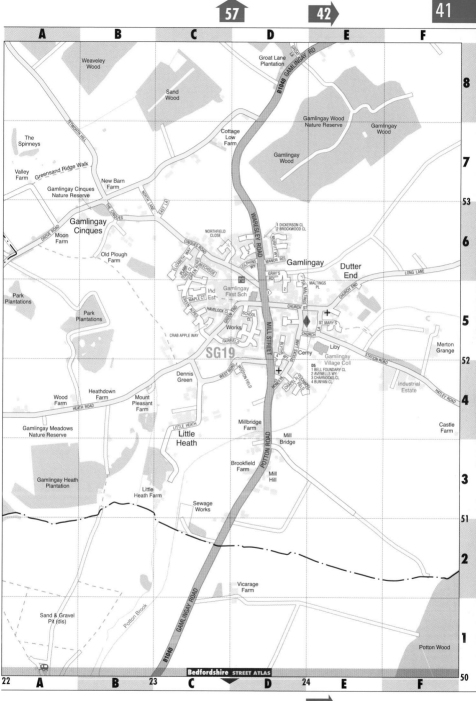

41
58

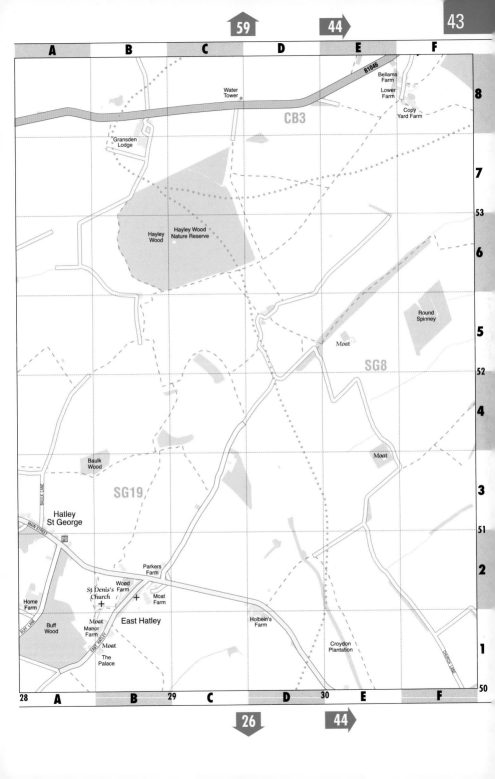

8
7
53
6
5
52
4
51
2
1
50

B1046

Bellams Farm
Lower Farm
Water Tower
Copy Yard Farm

CB3

Gransden Lodge

Hayley Wood

Hayley Wood Nature Reserve

Round Spinney

Moat

SG8

Moat

Baulk Wood

Moat

SG19

BAULK LANE

Hatley St George

MAIN STREET

PO

Parkers Farm

Wood Farm

St Denis's Church

Moat Farm

Home Farm

BUFF LANE

Buff Wood

Moat Manor Farm

East Hatley

EAST HATLEY

Moat

Holbein's Farm

Croydon Plantation

CHURCH LANE

The Palace

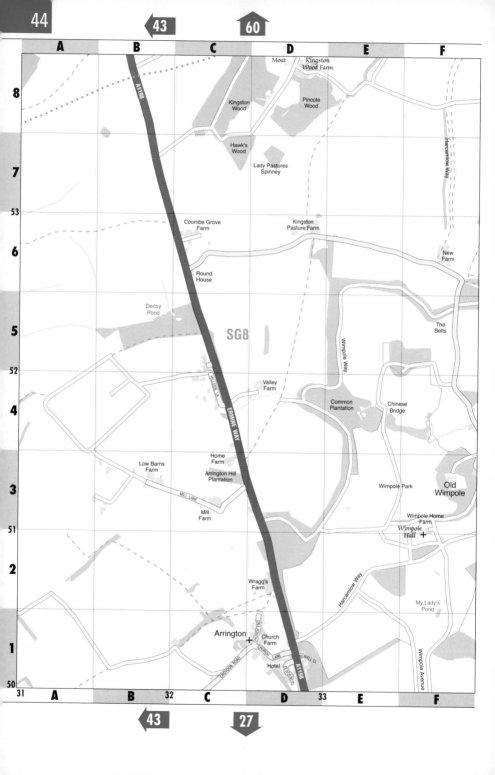

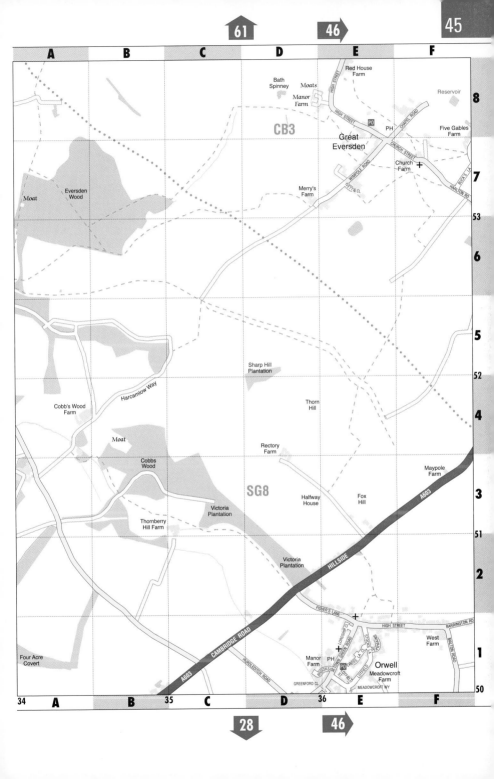

45
62

A **B** **C** **D** **E** **F**

8

A603

Travelling
Telescope
Lines

Radio Telescope

Radio Telescope

CAMBRIDGE ROAD

WASHPIT LANE

Travelling
Telescope
Lines

Mullard Radio
Astronomy
Observatory

LOWFIELDS

LEFFE'S LANE

CHURCH LA

7

Rectory
Farm

FINCH'S
RD

FINCH'S CL

FIELDS

Eversden
Church Sch

WHEELER'S WY

Little
Eversden

53

WHEELER'S CL

Moats

6

CB3

Poultry
Farm

WASHPIT LANE

PH

Butler's
Spinney

Manorial
Earthworks

Manor
Farm

COACH
LA

HASLINGFIELD ROAD

HARLTON ROAD

EVERSDEN ROAD

HIGH STREET

Harlton

PO

5

PH

52

4

A603

3

Lime
Quarry

51

Long
Plantation

CB2

Hill
Plantation

Wilsmere
Down Farm

2

Cracknow
Hill

Cement
Works

SG8

ORWELL ROAD

LC

BARRINGTON ROAD

HASLINGFIELD ROAD

1

Lilac
Farm

Moat

Church
Farm

Barrington
CE Prim Sch

50

37   **A**   **B**   38   **C**   **D**   39   **E**   **F**

45
29

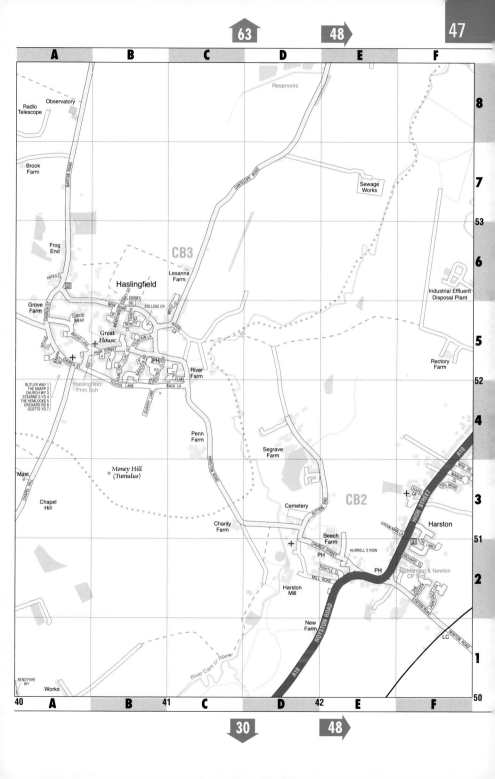

8

Radio Telescope
Observatory

Brook Farm

7

Reservoirs

CANTELUPE ROAD

Sewage Works

53

CB3

Frog End

PATES CL
PO

Lesanna Farm

6

Haslingfield

Industrial Effluent Disposal Plant

Grove Farm

CHURCH ST
BARTON ROAD

DODDS MEAD

NEW ROAD
MEADOWLANDS
SIDNEY GDS
TRINITY CL
COLLEGE CR
MICKS DR
RIVER

WELLS CL
ROAD LANE
Great House
HIGH STREET
HAZEL END
ELMS
FOUNTAIN LA

Rectory Farm

5

52

JPH
BADCOCK RD
CUTTER CL

River Farm

BUTLER WAY 1
THE KNAPP 2
CHURCH WY 3
STEARNE'S YD 4
THE HEMLOCKS 5
ORCHARD RD 6
SCOTTS YD 7.

Haslingfield Prim Sch

SCHOOL LANE
QUARRY LANE
BACK LA.

A10

4

Mast

Penn Farm

HARSTON ROAD

Segrave Farm

NEW RD
MANOR CL
HIGH MOW

CHAPEL LA.

Money Hill (Tumulus)

Cemetery

CB2

HIGH STREET

Harston

3

Chapel Hill

BUTTON END
GREEN MAN LA.

THE LIMES
PO
ORCHARD CL

51

CHURCH HILL

Charity Farm

Beech Farm
PH
CHURCH STREET

HURRELL'S ROW

PH
Harston & Newton CP Sch

THE NOOK
STATION ROAD
MANOR LA.

2

FIGHTLE CL
MILL ROAD

Harston Mill

ROYSTON ROAD

New Farm

LC

NEWTON ROAD

1

BENDYSHE WY

Works

River Cam or Rhee

A10

50

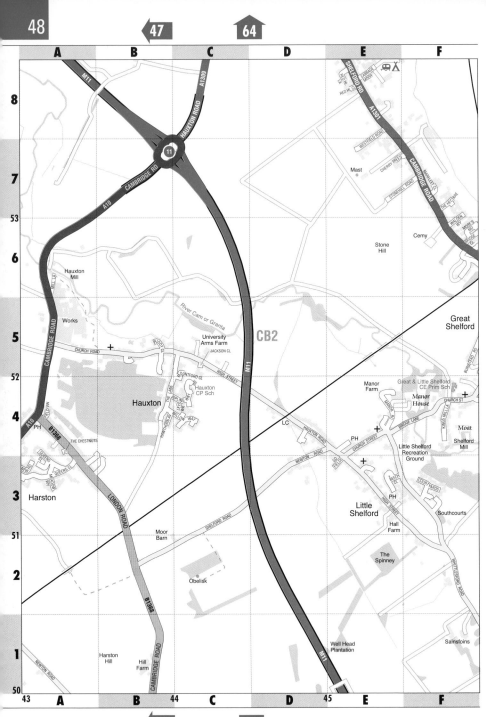

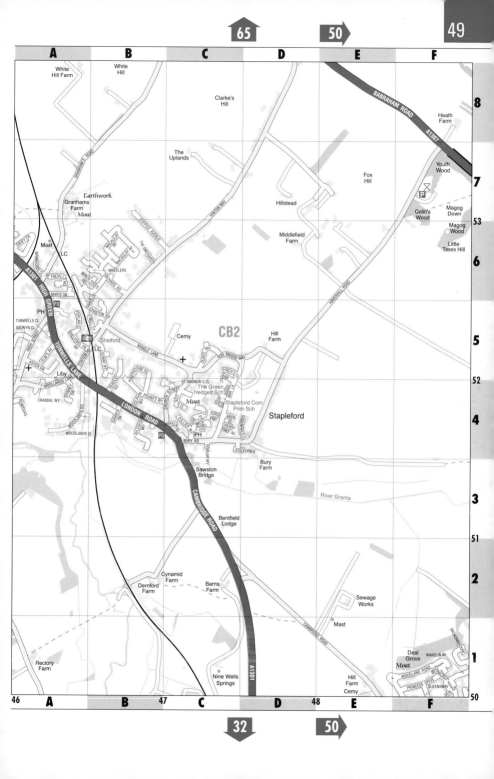

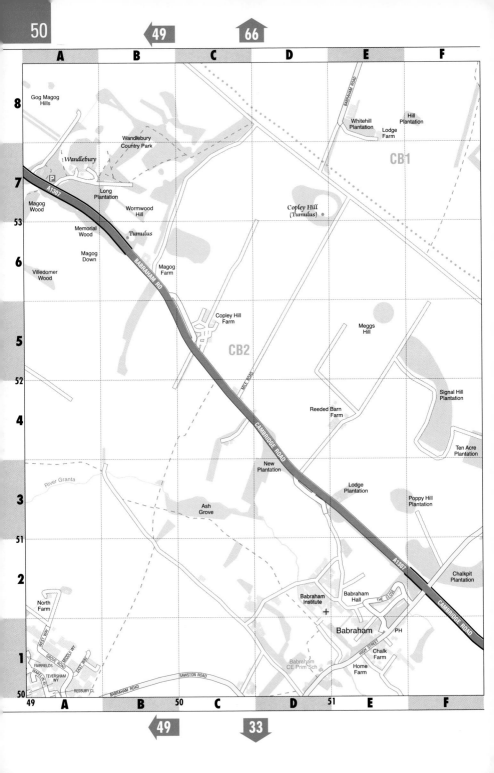

8

Gog Magog
Hills

Wandlebury
Country Park

Wandlebury

Whitehill
Plantation

Hill
Plantation

Lodge
Farm

CB1

7

P

A1307

Long
Plantation

Magog
Wood

Wormwood
Hill

Copley Hill
(Tumulus)

53

Memorial
Wood

Tumulus

BABRAHAM RD

6

Magog
Down

Magog
Farm

Villedomer
Wood

Copley Hill
Farm

Meggs
Hill

5

CB2

52

MILE ROAD

Signal Hill
Plantation

4

CAMBRIDGE ROAD

Reeded Barn
Farm

Ten Acre
Plantation

New
Plantation

Lodge
Plantation

Poppy Hill
Plantation

River Granta

3

Ash
Grove

51

A1307

Chalkpit
Plantation

2

North
Farm

Babraham
Institute

Babraham
Hall

THE CLOSE

CAMBRIDGE ROAD

WEST WAY

GROVE ROAD

MIDDLE WY

EAST WAY

Babraham

PH

HIGH STREET

Chalk
Farm

1

FAIRFIELDS

TEVERSHAM
WY

Babraham
CE Prim Sch

Home
Farm

BAXTER RD

RESBURY CL

BABRAHAM ROAD

SAWSTON ROAD

50

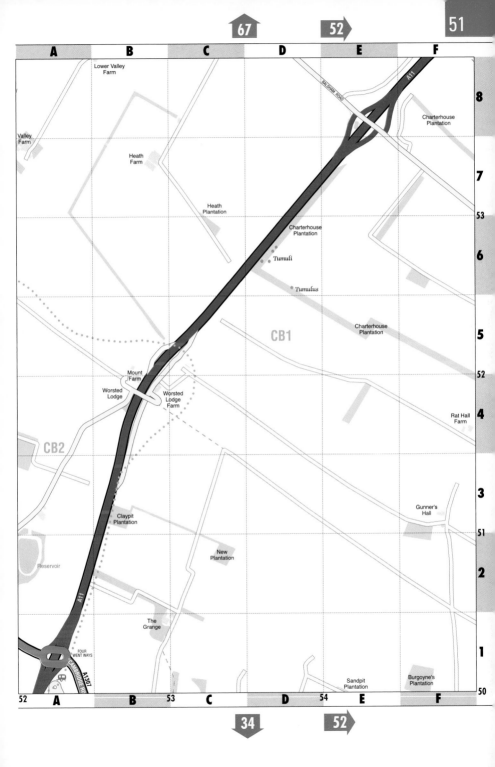

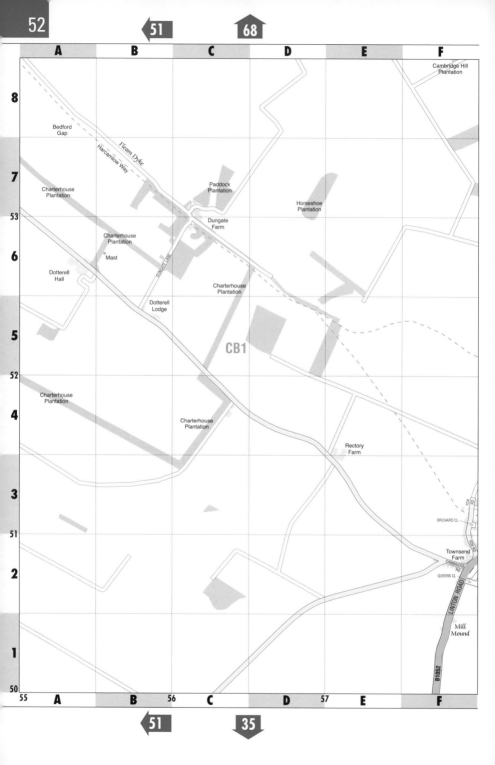

A B C D E F

8

Cambridge Hill
Plantation

Bedford
Gap

Fleam Dyke

Harcamlow Way

7

Charterhouse
Plantation

Paddock
Plantation

Horseshoe
Plantation

53

Dungate
Farm

Charterhouse
Plantation

6

Mast

DUNGATE LANE

Dotterell
Hall

Charterhouse
Plantation

Dotterell
Lodge

5

CB1

52

Charterhouse
Plantation

4

Charterhouse
Plantation

Rectory
Farm

3

FOX RD

FOX RD

ORCHARD CL

51

Townsend
Farm

CAMBRIDGE
RD

2

QUEENS CL

LINTON ROAD

Mill
Mound

1

B1052

50

55 A B 56 C D 57 E F

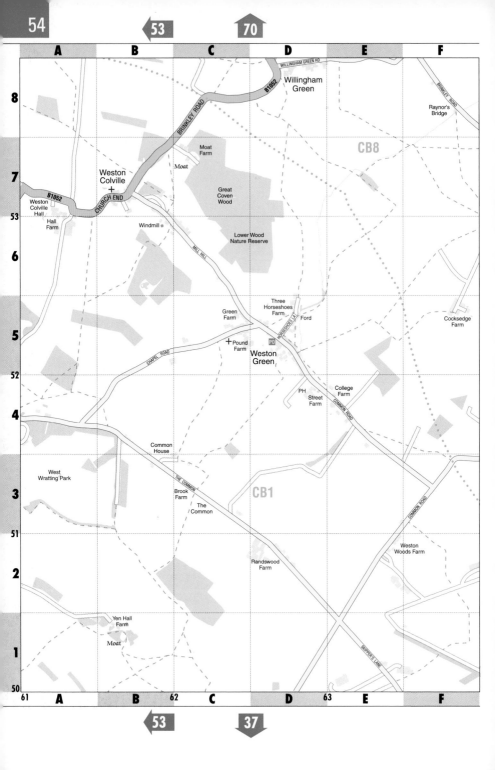

A B C D E F

8

Willingham Green
WILLINGHAM GREEN RD
B1052

Raynor's
Bridge

BRINKLEY ROAD

CB8

7

BRINKLEY ROAD

Moat
Farm

Moat

Weston
Colville

CHURCH END

B1052

Weston
Colville
Hall

Hall
Farm

53

Great
Coven
Wood

Windmill

Lower Wood
Nature Reserve

6

MILL HILL

Three
Horseshoes
Farm

Ford

Cocksedge
Farm

Green
Farm

5

CHAPEL ROAD

Pound
Farm

PO

Weston
Green

CROSSROADS LN

52

PH

Street
Farm

College
Farm

COMMON ROAD

4

Common
House

West
Wratting Park

THE COMMON

CB1

Brook
Farm

The
Common

COMMON ROAD

3

Weston
Woods Farm

51

Randswood
Farm

2

Yen Hall
Farm

SKIPPER'S LANE

Moat

1

50

61 A B 62 C D 63 E F

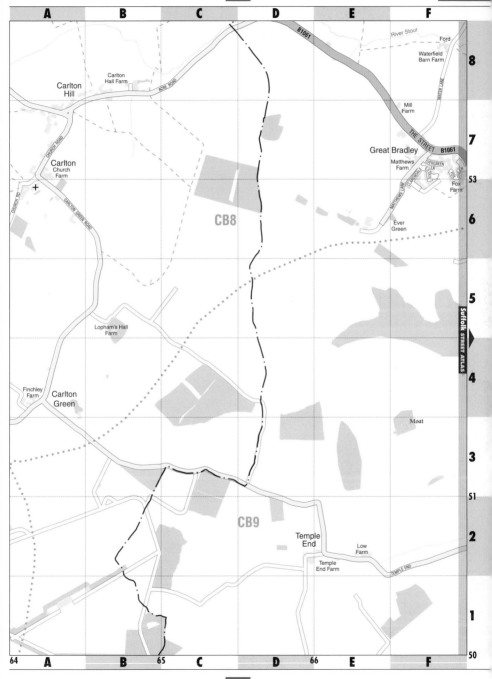

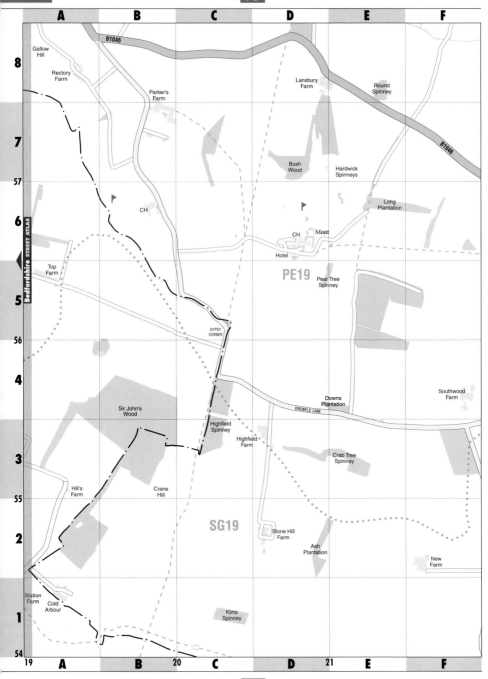

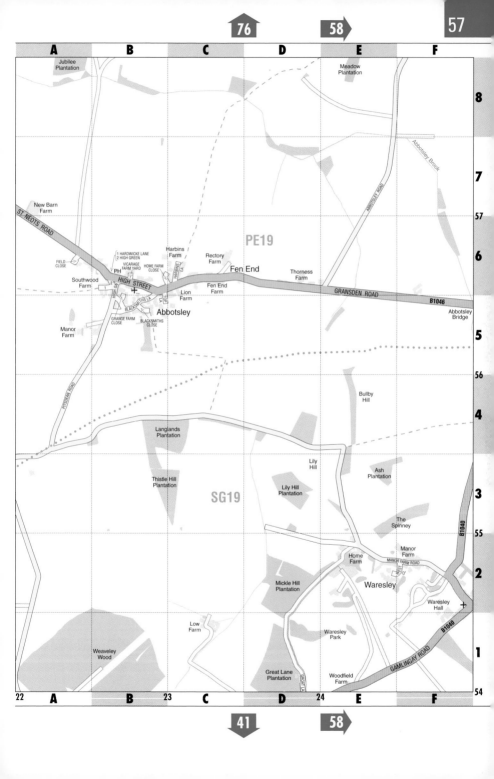

8

7

57

6

5

56

4

3

55

2

1

54

A B C D E F

25 26 27

B1040

North Farm

Leycourt Farm

PE19

ELTISLEY ROAD

Moor Farm

HARDWICKE ROAD

Tower Farm
Water Tower

Works

B1046

Kiln Farm

SG19

Woodhams Farm

Playing Field

CAXTON ROAD

Industrial Estate

SAND ROAD

MEADOW ROAD

Great Gransden

WANCHFT'S CL

AUDLEY CL

POPLAR

HALL CL

ST DUNWS

MANOR LA

B1046

FOLLY

GROVE

CHURCH ST

MANDENE RD

Mandean Bridge

Great Gransden Windmill

B1040

Moat

CROW TREE ST

WEBBS MD

CROW TREE ST

PH

1 LITTLE LA
2 WHITTETS CL

MILL ROAD

Rectory Farm

WARESLEY ROAD

LITTLE GRANSDEN LANE

MAIN RD

PRIMROSE HILL

WINDMILL CLOSE

Sewage Works

Little Gransden

CHURCH ST

PH

CHURCH LN

Sewage Works

Gransden Wood

THE LEYS

Waresley and Gransden Woods Nature Reserve

Elm Farm

MAIN ROAD

Hill Farm

Waresley Wood

PH

VICARAGE ROAD

Vicarage Farm

Cemy

Wood Farm

Moat

Chase Farm

B1046

A B C D E F

59 79

A B C D E F
8 7 57 6 5 56 4 3 55 2 1 54
31 32 33
BOURN RD
Amcotts
Bourn Lodge
Brooklands Farm
CAXTON END
CAXTON ROAD
Ford
BROADWAY
Rockery Farm
Sewage Works
Driftwood Farm
Chapmans Farm
Crow End Farm
Townsend Farm
Crow End
ALMS HILL
Moulton Hills
View Farm
Barrances Farm
MEADOW RI
KINGFISHER CL
WATER LANE
Manor Farm
Bourn
Bourn CE Prim Sch
RIDDY LANE
BALDWINS CL
PO
HIGH STREET
CHURCH ST
SHORT ST
HALL CL
PH
GILL'S HILL
Gill's Hill Farm
Bourn Hall
Hall Farm
FOX RD
CB3
GILL'S HILL
CH
West Grove
FOX ROAD
Golders Farm
A1198
Home Wood
Bourn Wood
Wysing Grange Farm
Beck Farm
Wysing Arts Centre
OLD NORTH ROAD
B1046
SCHOOL LANE
Fox Farm
New Farm
Moat
Beaconsfield House
Kingston Wood
A1198
Edgehill Farm
SG8
PH
Kingston Wood Farm

59 44

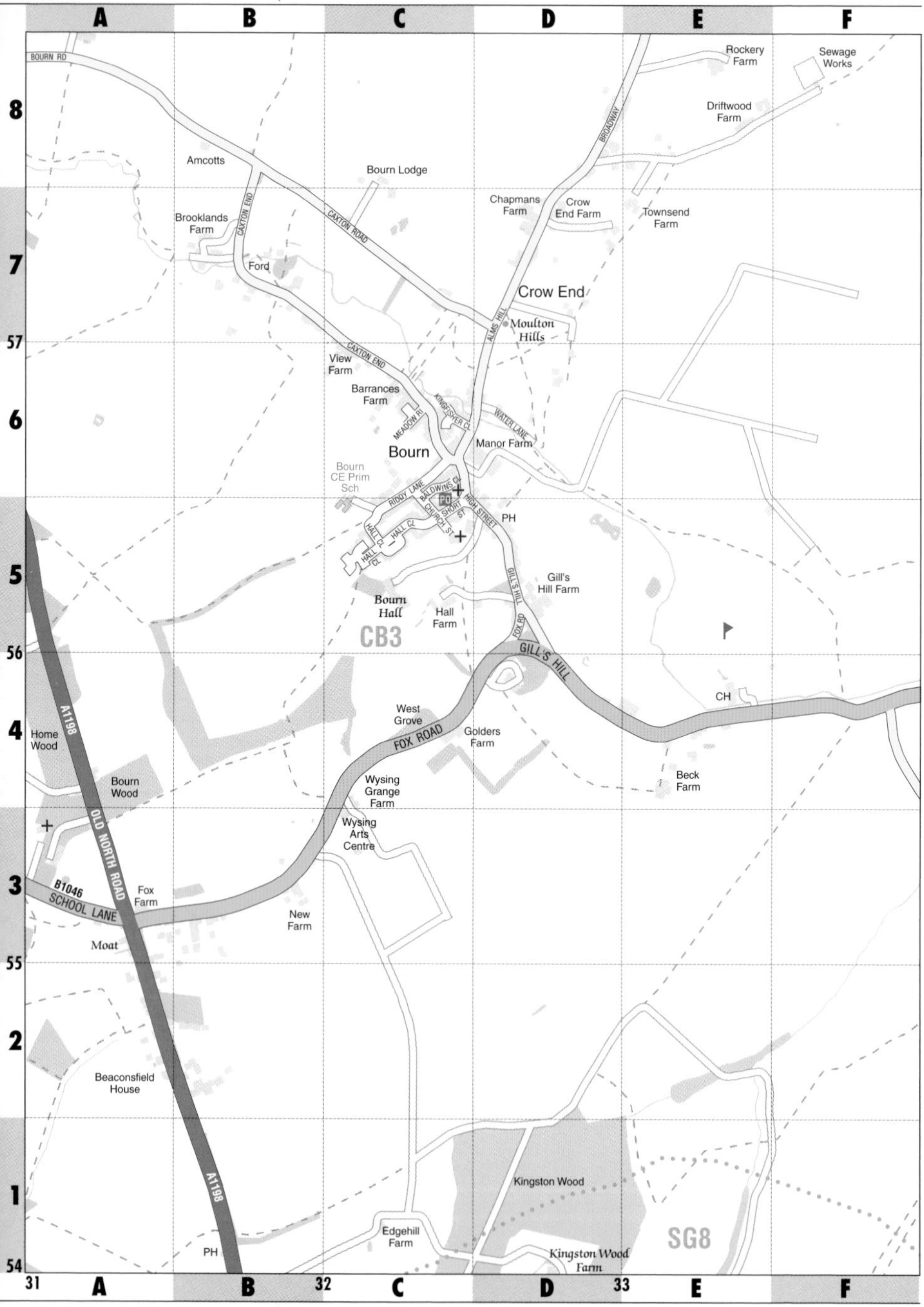

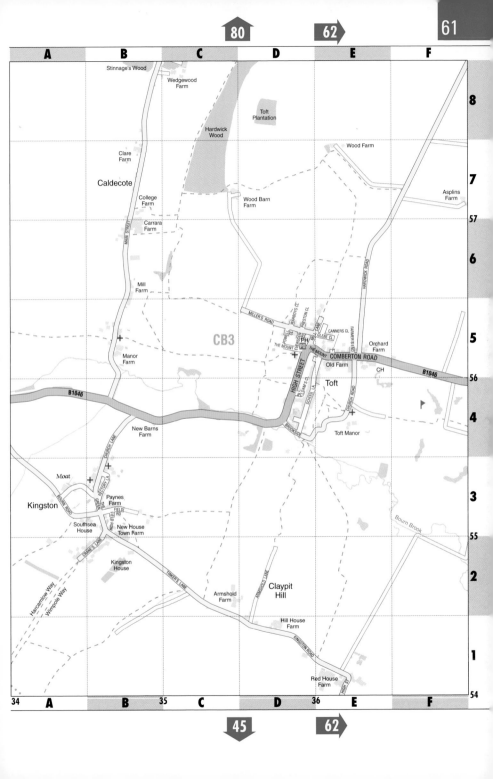

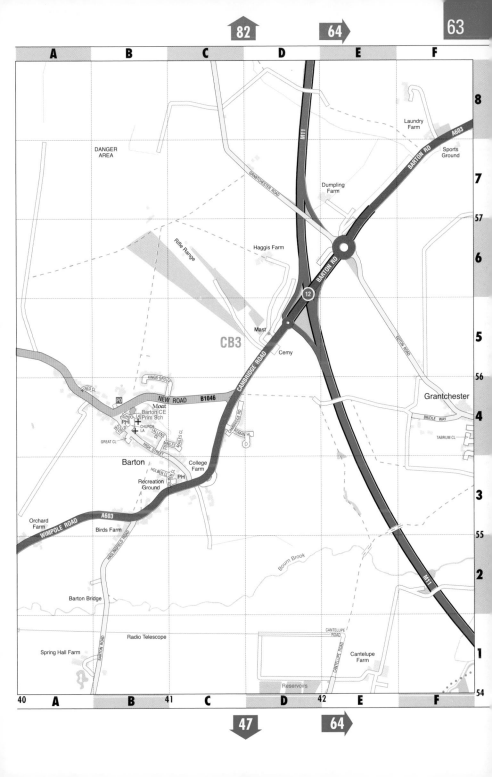

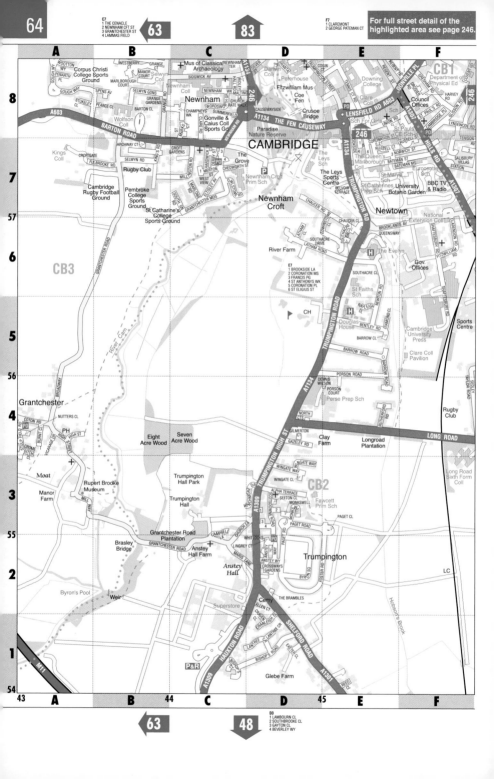

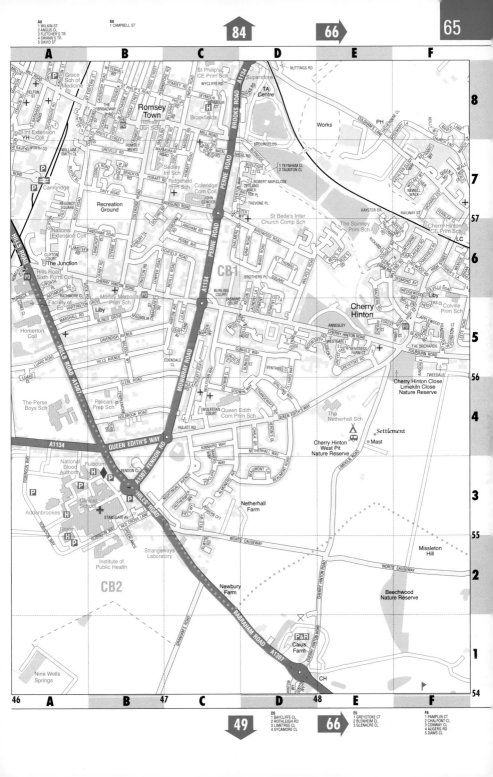

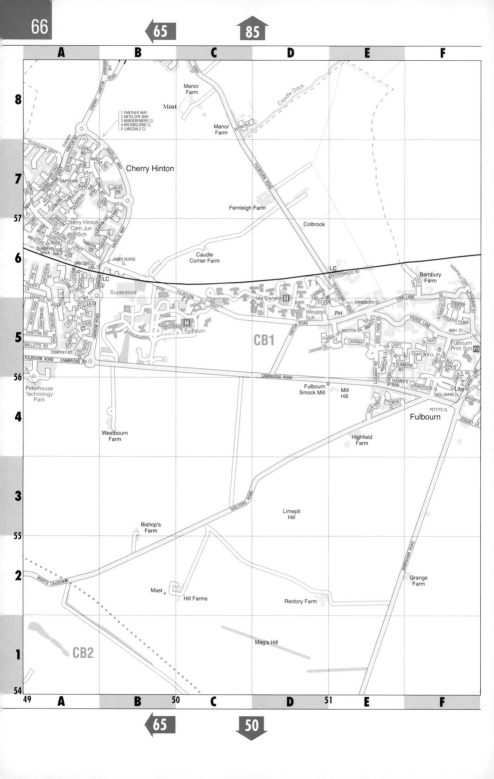

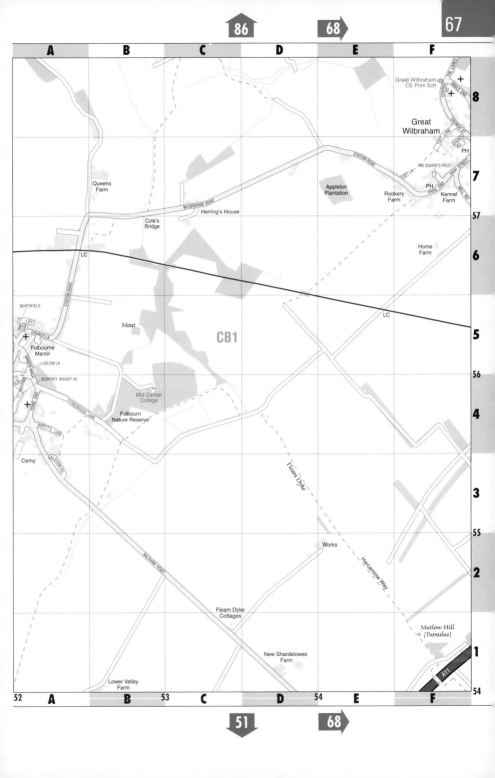

67 87

	A	B	C	D	E	F

8

Wilbraham Temple

Springs Plantation

The Vicarage

Coventry Farm

Bottisham Heath Stud

PO

RATFORDS YD
CHURCH ST

Great Wilbraham

Cedar Tree Stud

Streetways

Hotel

7

Six Mile Bottom

57

Sports Club

PH

LC

6

LC

CB8

Station Farm

A1304 LONDON ROAD

5

MILL ROAD

Lower Heath Farm

56

Upper Heath Farm

4

Lark Hall Heath Farm

3

CB1

Great Wilbraham Hall Farm

Middle Bit Plantation

55

2

The Lodge

Old Cambridge Road Plantation

A11

1

West Wratting Valley Farm

Cambridge Hill Plantation

54

55	A	B	56	C	D	57	E	F

67 52

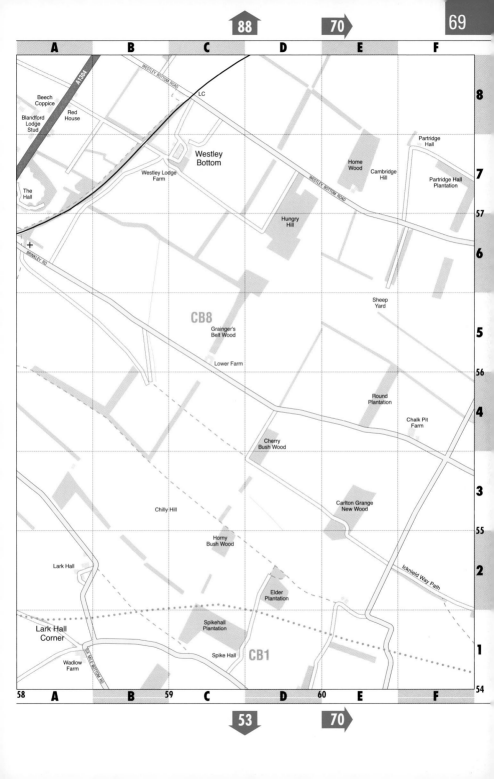

A   B   C   D   E   F

8
7
57
6
5
56
4
3
55
2
1
54

Beech
Coppice

Blandford
Lodge
Stud

Red
House

A1304

WESTLEY BOTTOM ROAD

LC

Westley
Bottom

Westley Lodge
Farm

The
Hall

BRINKLEY RD

Home
Wood

Cambridge
Hill

Partridge
Hall

Partridge Hall
Plantation

WESTLEY BOTTOM ROAD

Hungry
Hill

Sheep
Yard

CB8

Grainger's
Belt Wood

Lower Farm

Round
Plantation

Chalk Pit
Farm

Cherry
Bush Wood

Chilly Hill

Carlton Grange
New Wood

Horny
Bush Wood

Icknield Way Path

Lark Hall

Spikehall
Plantation

Elder
Plantation

Lark Hall
Corner

Wadlow
Farm

SIX MILE BOTTOM RD

Spike Hall

CB1

69
89

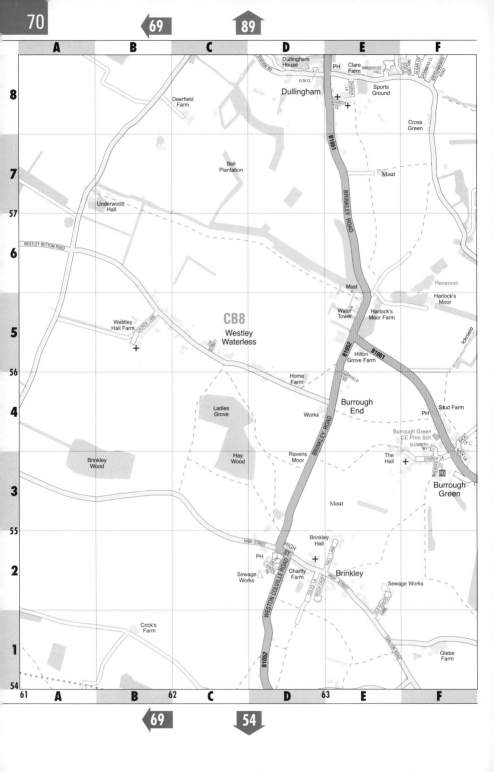

69
54

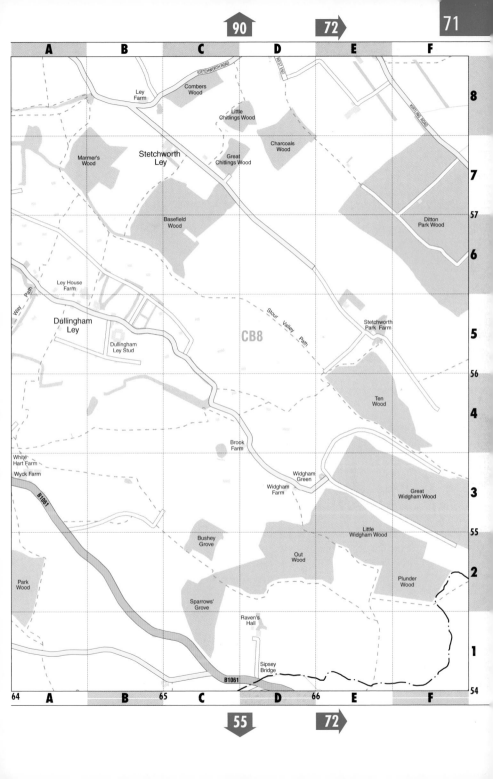

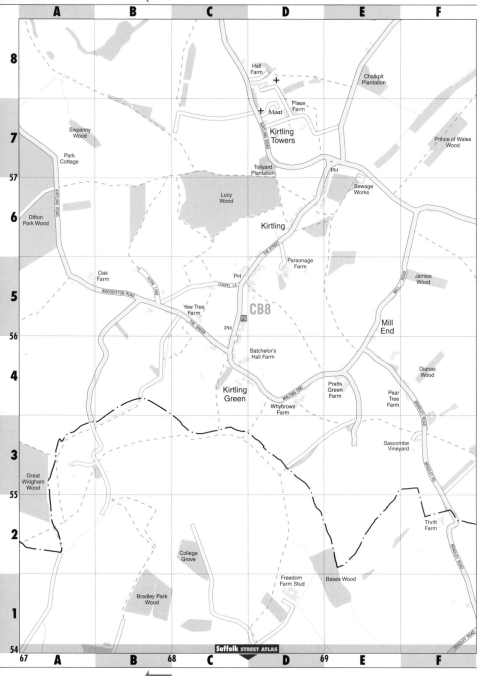

A B C D E F

8

Hall
Farm

Chalkpit
Plantation

Place
Farm

7

Sixpenny
Wood

Moat

Prince of Wales
Wood

Park
Cottage

Kirtling
Towers

KIRTLING ROAD

57

Toilyard
Plantation

PH

Sewage
Works

6

Ditton
Park Wood

Lucy
Wood

Kirtling

KIRTLING ROAD

THE STREET

Parsonage
Farm

Jamies
Wood

Oak
Farm

PH

CHAPEL LA.

MILL ROAD

5

WOODDITTON ROAD

ROUN LANE

Yew Tree
Farm

PH

PO

CB8

Mill
End

THE GREEN

56

PH

Batchelor's
Hall Farm

Dianas
Wood

4

Kirtling
Green

MALTING END

Whybrows
Farm

Pratts
Green
Farm

Pear
Tree
Farm

BRADLEY ROAD

3

Great
Widgham
Wood

Sascombe
Vineyard

55

Thrift
Farm

2

College
Grove

Freedom
Farm Stud

Bases Wood

BRADLEY ROAD

Bradley Park
Wood

1

54

BRADLEY ROAD

67 A B 68 C D 69 E F

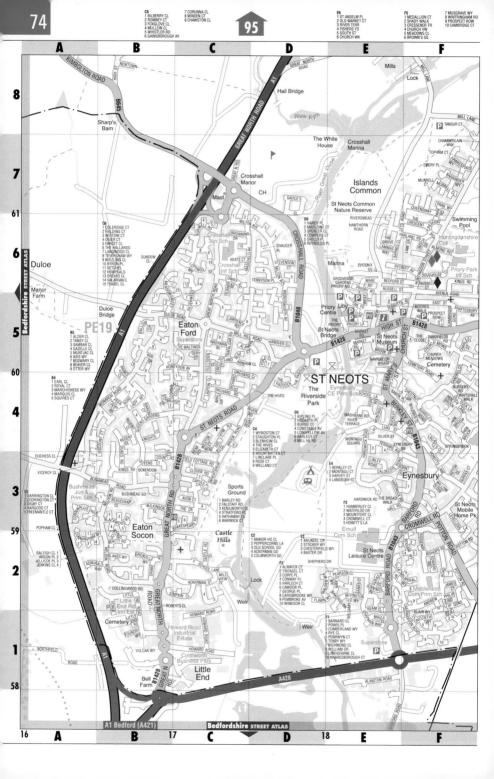

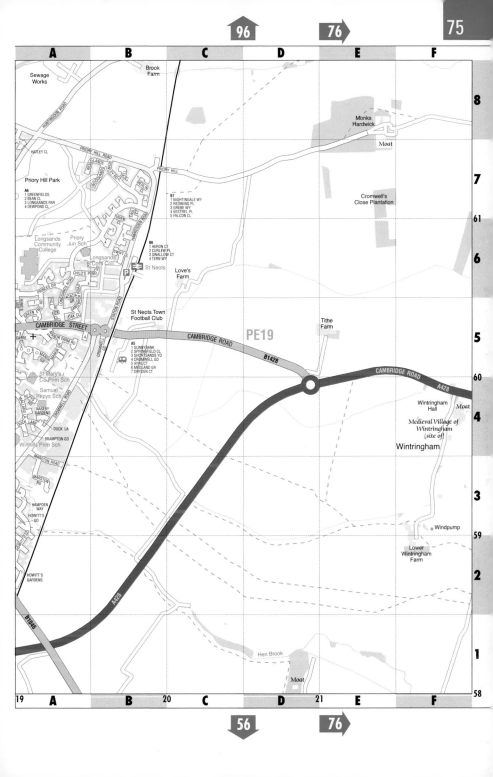

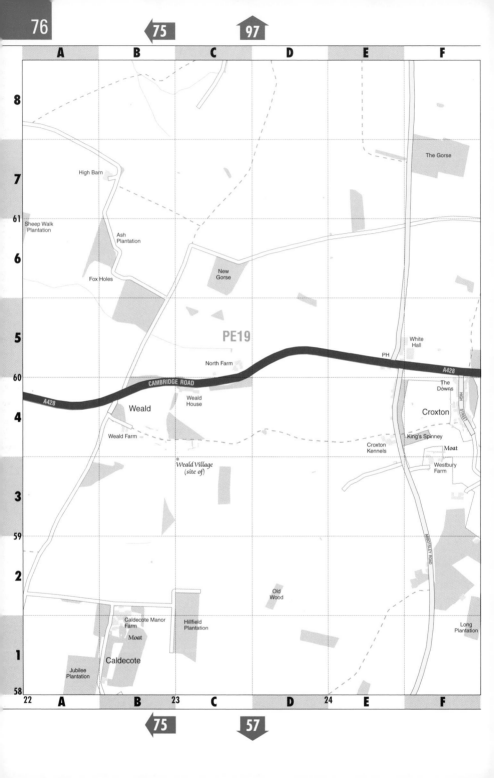

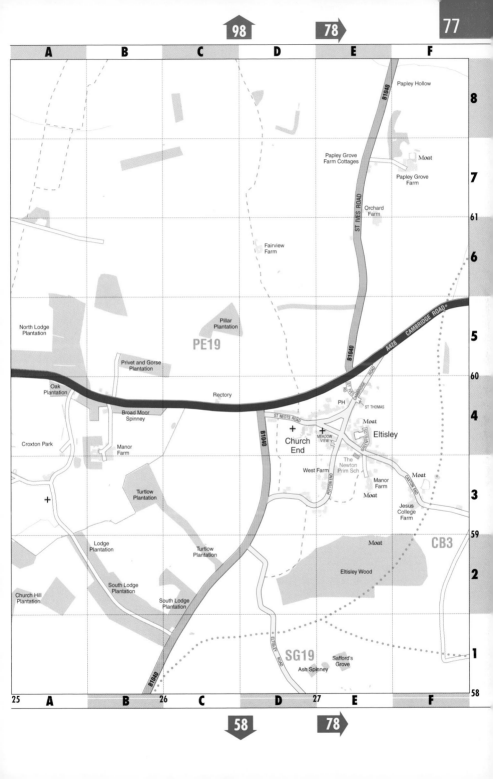

A **B** **C** **D** **E** **F**

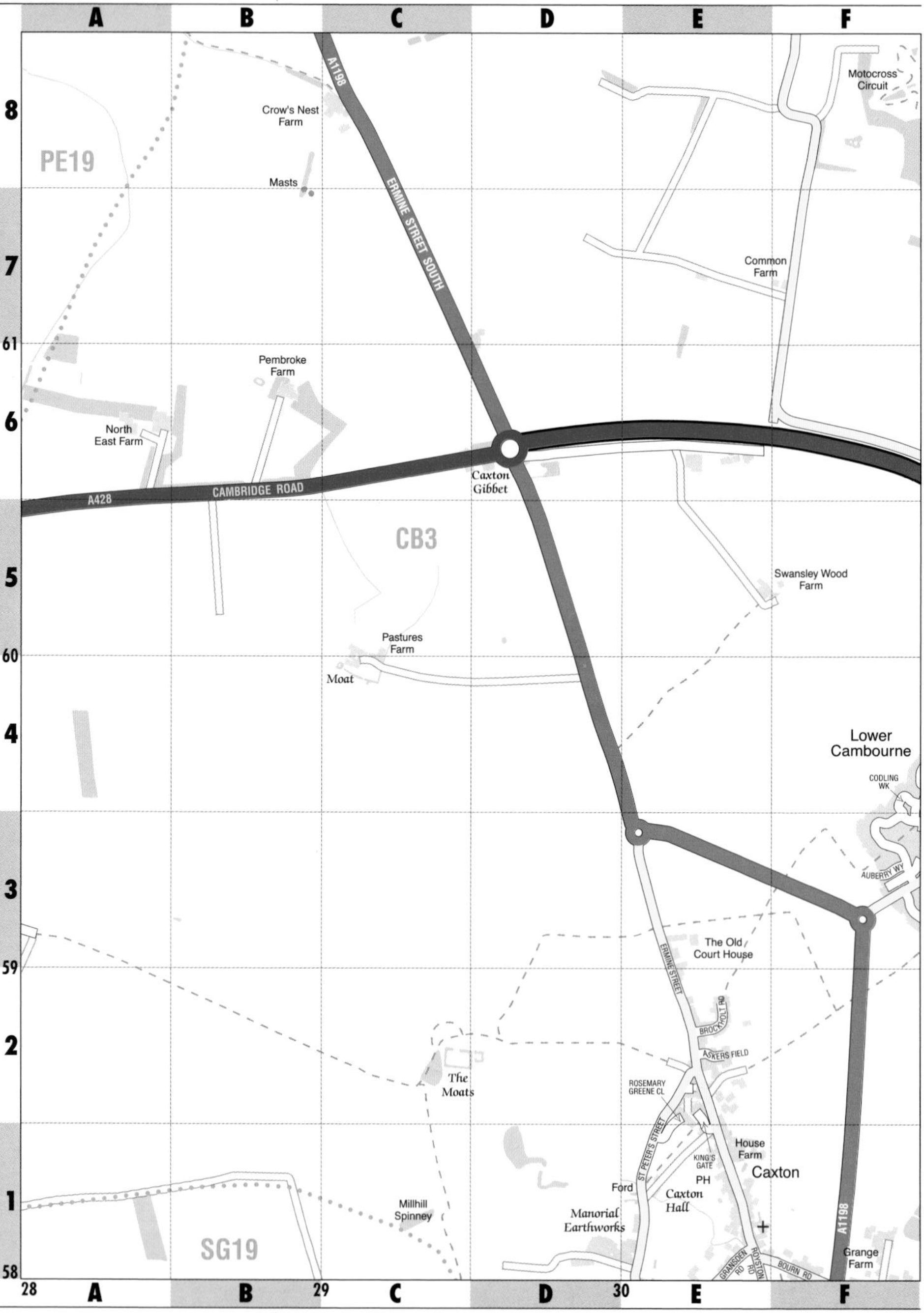

8

PE19

Crow's Nest Farm

Masts

ERMINE STREET SOUTH

A1198

Motocross Circuit

7

Common Farm

61

Pembroke Farm

North East Farm

6

A428 CAMBRIDGE ROAD

Caxton Gibbet

5

CB3

Swansley Wood Farm

60

Pastures Farm

Moat

4

Lower Cambourne

CODLING WK

AUBERRY WY

3

The Old Court House

59

ERMINE STREET

BROCK...

2

The Moats

ASKERS FIELD

ROSEMARY GREENE CL

House Farm

1

Millhill Spinney

SG19

ST PETER'S STREET

KING'S GATE

Ford

PH

Caxton Hall

Caxton

A1198

Grange Farm

Manorial Earthworks

GRANSDEN RD

BOURN RD

58

28 **A** **B** 29 **C** **D** 30 **E** **F**

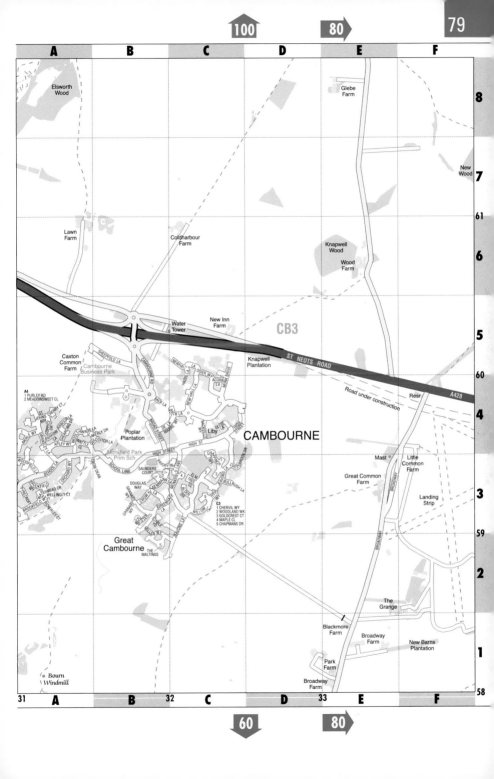

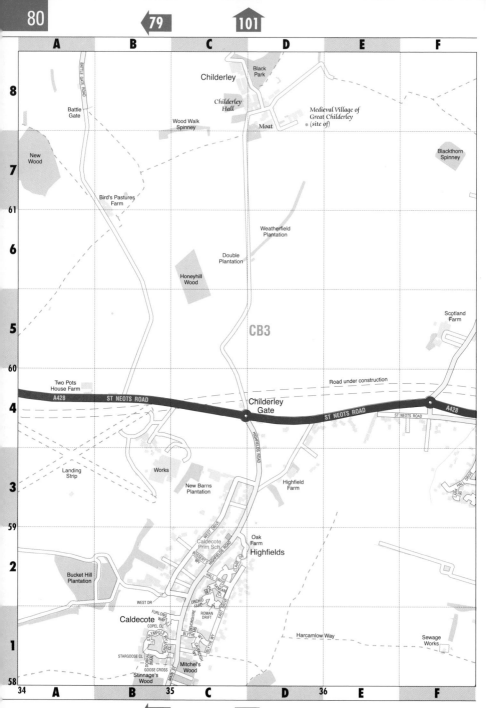

79
101

Childerley

Black Park

Childerley Hall

Medieval Village of Great Childerley
(site of)

Wood Walk Spinney

Moat

New Wood

Blackthorn Spinney

Battle Gate

BATTLE GATE ROAD

Bird's Pastures Farm

Weatherfield Plantation

Double Plantation

Honeyhill Wood

CB3

Scotland Farm

Two Pots House Farm

Road under construction

A428   ST NEOTS ROAD

Childerley Gate

ST NEOTS ROAD

ST NEOTS ROAD   A428

Landing Strip

Works

HIGHFIELDS ROAD

Highfield Farm

OAK HALL DRIVE

New Barns Plantation

WEST DRIVE

Caldecote Prim Sch

Oak Farm

Highfields

Bucket Hill Plantation

WEST DR

ORCHARD PARK

HALL DRIVE

CLARE DR

FURLONG WAY

COPEL CL

Harcamlow Way

Sewage Works

STARGOOSE CL

GOOSE CROSS

Caldecote

ROMAN DRIFT

BLYTHE

Mitchel's Wood

Stinnage's Wood

79
61

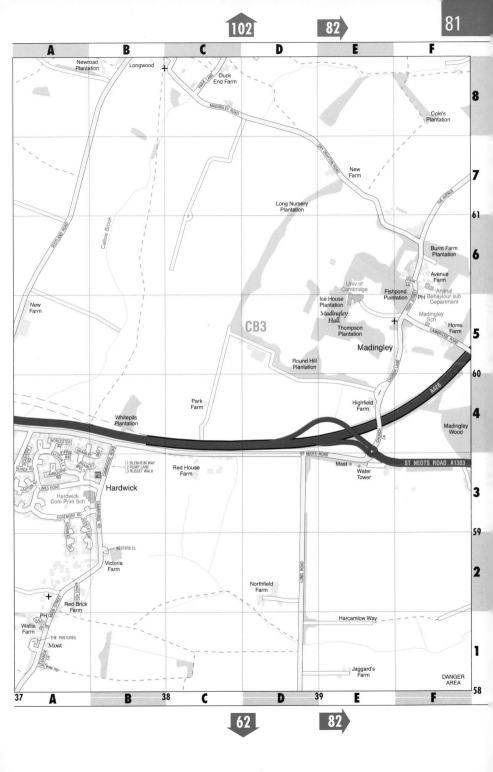

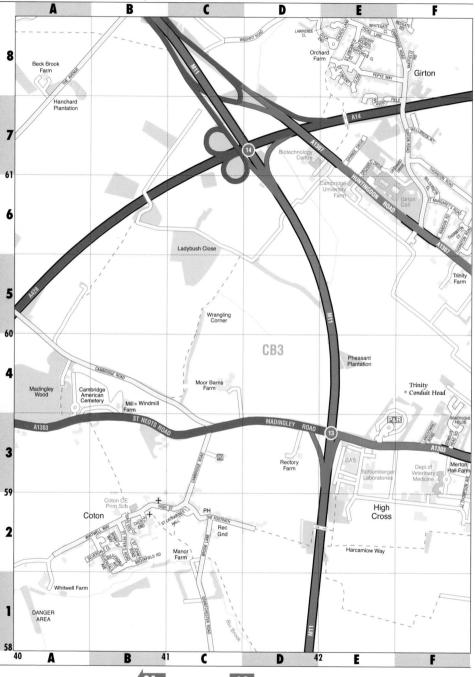

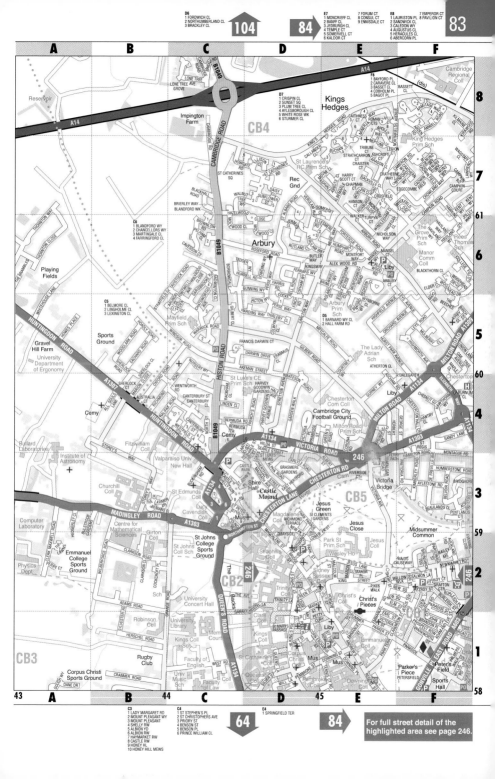

83
105

	A	B	C	D	E	F

Works
A14
Baits Bite Lock

St John's Innovation Centre
Sewage Works
Biggin Abbey

8

Cambridge Science Park
BIGGIN LANE

COWLEY ROAD
Northern Bridge Farm
Poplar Hall

MARKHAM CL
P&R Cambridge Business Park
Trinity Hall Farm Ind Est

7

HORNINGSEA ROAD
B1047

KENT
FIELD LANE

61

Works
CB4
Mast
Southgates Farm
MUSGRAVE WY

6

Chesterton
St Andrew's CE Com Jun Sch
RUSSET CT
Cemy
Fen Ditton CP Sch

A1309
Shirley Inf Sch
PH
Fen Ditton

PEARMAIN CT
Hall Farm
Musgrave Farm
HIGH ST
PH
Home Farm

5

SOUTHSIDE CT
LC
Stable Ind Est
HIGH STREET
SHEPHERD'S CL

MOSS BANK
Ditton Meadows

WHITEFRIARS
WATER LA
60

MALTSTERS WY
MISTY
HOWARD
HOWARD ROAD
DUNBAR
TIP TREE CL

Chesterton
HAIG COURT
Beadle Trading Estate
HEADINGLEY
EGERTON CL
DITTON LANE
FISON RD

4

CAMBRIDGE
Factory
HERBERT
DUDLEY RD
EGERTON CL
BRENTWOOD CL
E4
1 RACHEL CL
2 LEONARD CL
3 HELEN CL
4 BERGHOLT CL
5 COGGESHALL CL
6 BRENTWOOD CL
7 CHISWELL CT

A1134
Sports Club
Rec Gnd
ST BARTHOLOMEW'S CT
MERCERS ROW
SWANN'S RD
CB5
EKIN ROAD
HADLEIGH
ONGAR CT
JACK WARREN GN

3

ELIZABETH WAY
EAST ROAD
Mus of Technology
NEWMARKET ROAD
A1134
Cambridge United Football Club (Abbey Stadium)
QUAINTON RD
RAWLYN COURT
MALDEN CL
Cambridge Technopark
A1303
Liby
MEADOWLANDS RD
THE HOMING
NEWMARKET ROAD
Works

Cambridge Retail Park
ELFLEDA RD
STANESFIELD RD
RAYSON WAY
A1134
PEVEREL RD
Cambridge Airport

59

Coral Park Trading Estate
LC
GERARD CL
HORLEY CL
Works
Barnwell Business Park

2

Univ of Cambridge
SAVERWOOD
Beehive Centre Retail Park
WHITEHILL CL
Abbey Meadows Prim Sch
BARNWELL RD

NORFOLK PL
VICARAGE TR
Factory
GALFRID RD
Coldham's Common

EDWARD
MILFORD
CB1
STOURBRIDGE GR
BARNWELL ROAD
UPHALL RD

1

Cemy University
AINSWORTH
STONE TERRACE
Romsey Town
VINERY
COLDHAM'S GR
St Philip's CE Prim Sch
A1134
NOTTER
NORFOLK TR
BROAD ST
KERRIDGE CL
FAIRFAX RD
DANESBURY CT

	A	B	C	D	E	F
46 | | **47** | | **48** | |

83
65

A1
1 UPPER GWYDIR ST
2 FLOWER ST
3 BLOSSOM ST
4 AINSWORTH CT
5 MACKENZIE RD
6 ASHLEY CT
7 STAFFORDSHIRE GD
8 ATHLONE
9 BRAY

A2
1 SUN ST
2 PARKER'S TR
3 WELLINGTON CT
4 WELLINGTON ST
5 ST MATTHEW'S CT
6 HOLLYMOUNT
7 ENFIELD
8 FARRAN
9 CARLOW

A B C D E F

8

Quy Water

Hall Farm

Rookery Wood

St Ives Wood

Northfield Farm

QUY ROAD

7

B1102

COLLIERS LANE

Sewage Works

Potter's Plantation

Bottisham Park

Braddons Plantation

CB5

POUND

POUND

BEAN LANE

Tunbridge Hall

61

Bottisham Swimming Pool

Bottisham Village Coll

Liby

ABBEY CL

TUNBRIDGE LANE

Bottisham

6

Park Farm

PO

THE SQUARE

Stow cum Quy

COLLEGE CL 1
THE PIGHTLE 2
TUNBRIDGE CL 3
ROWLEY GD 4

PH

BECKWOOD AVE
WILLOW WY
SPRING LA
SPRING LA

WELBURY CL
ROWAN CL
CEDAR AVE

STOW RD

MAIN STREET

PH

BELL ROAD

HOPE CTE
WY

TRINITY CL
DOWNING CL

WEST WLK

MAPLE CL

MINTER CL

ALBERT ROAD

The Bury

WHEELWRIGHT WAY

STOCKS CL

Bottisham Com Prim Sch

HERRING'S CL

Dunsley Corner

PH

NEWMARKET ROAD

PETERFIELD STREET

Moat

Parsonage Farm

HIGH STREET

5

Parsonage Barns

A1303

60

A14

4

LITTLE WILBRAHAM ROAD

WILBRAHAM ROAD

3

CB1

59

Little Wilbraham River

Frog End

Primrose Farm

PRIMROSE FARM ROAD

Coville Farm

2

FEN ROAD

ORCHARD CL

PH

RECTORY FARM

Rectory Farm

GREAT WILBRAHAM ROAD

MANOR CL

HIGH ST

CHURCH RD

Windmill

MILL ROAD

Mill Road Farm

Little Wilbraham

1

Hawk Mill Farm

THE JAMES

58

52 **A** 53 **B** **C** 53 **D** 54 **E** **F**

A   B   C   D   E   F

8

Middle Hill
Plantations

SWAFFHAM HEATH ROAD

Park
End

Stone Bridge
Farm

Bottisham
Hall

Stone Bridge

Howe
Plantation

7

61

CB5

Bushmeadow
Wood

6

Chalk
Farm

5

A1303

PH

The
Grange

A1303

A14

A1303

60

Spring Hall

A14

4

A14

3

CB1

A11

59

CB8

2

Council
Farm

1

Bottisham
Heath Farm

58

55   A   B   56   C   D   57   E   F

87
109

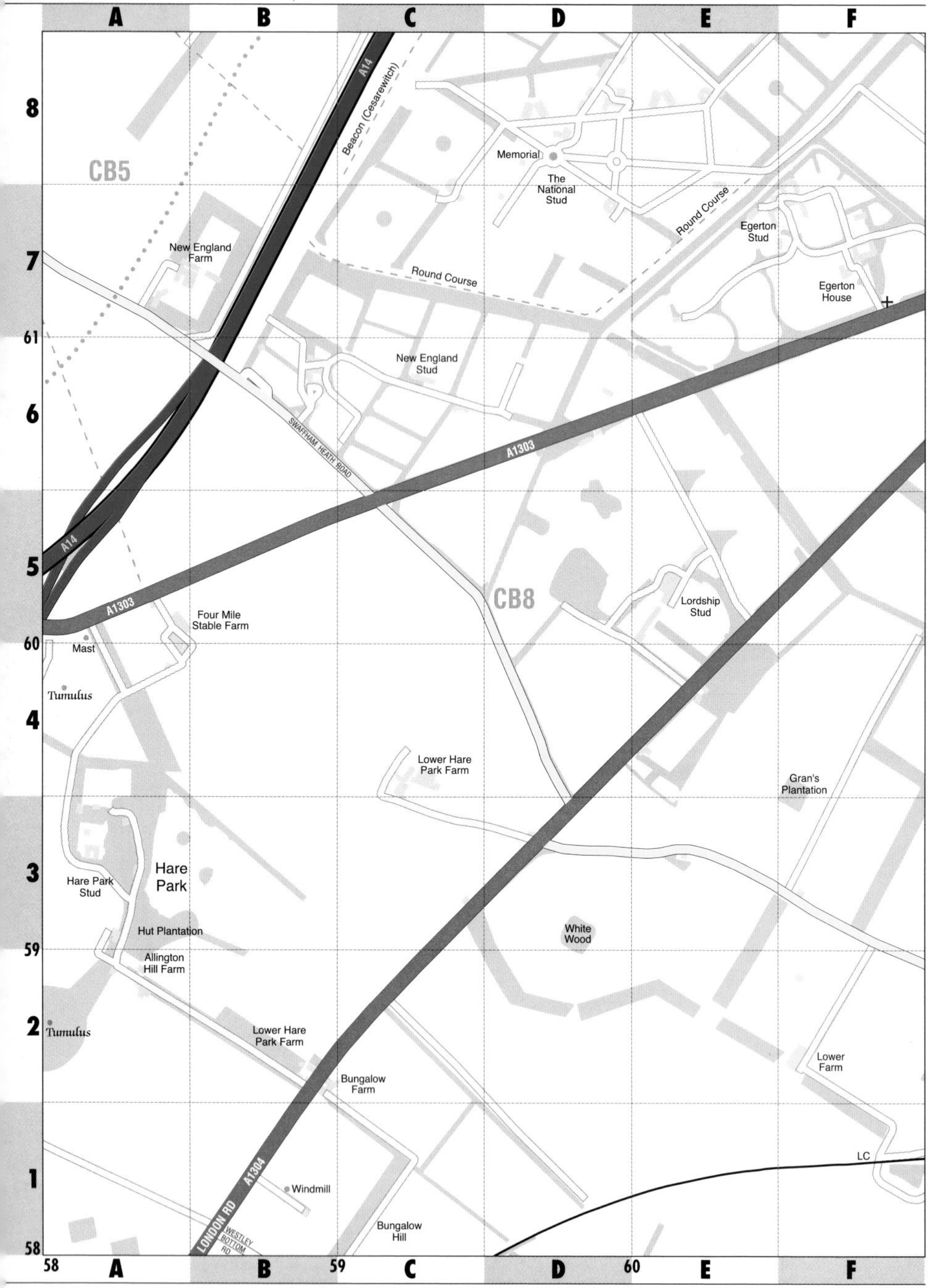

A B C D E F

8

CB5

New England
Farm

7

Beacon (Cesarewitch)

A14

Memorial

The
National
Stud

Round Course

Round Course

Egerton
Stud

Egerton
House

61

New England
Stud

6

SWAFFHAM HEATH ROAD

A1303

5

A14

A1303

CB8

Lordship
Stud

Four Mile
Stable Farm

60

Mast

Tumulus

4

Lower Hare
Park Farm

Gran's
Plantation

Hare Park
Stud

Hare
Park

3

Hut Plantation

White
Wood

59

Allington
Hill Farm

2

Tumulus

Lower Hare
Park Farm

Lower
Farm

Bungalow
Farm

LC

1

LONDON RD

A1304

BROSTLEY
BOTTOM
RD

Windmill

Bungalow
Hill

58

58 A 59 C 60 E F
B D

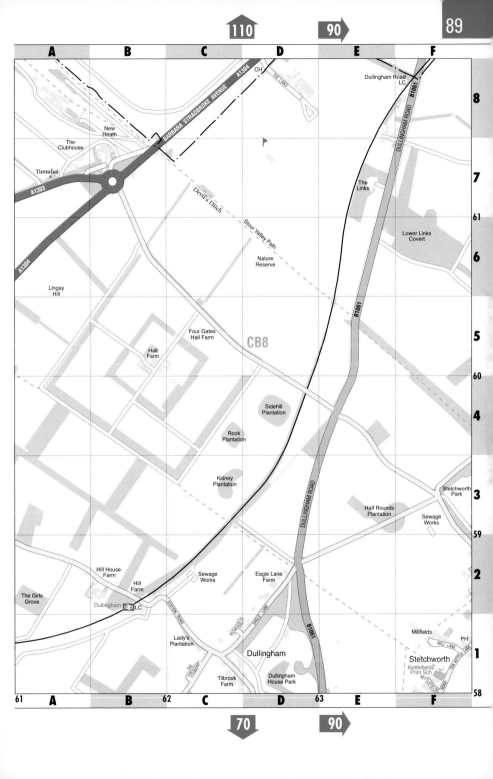

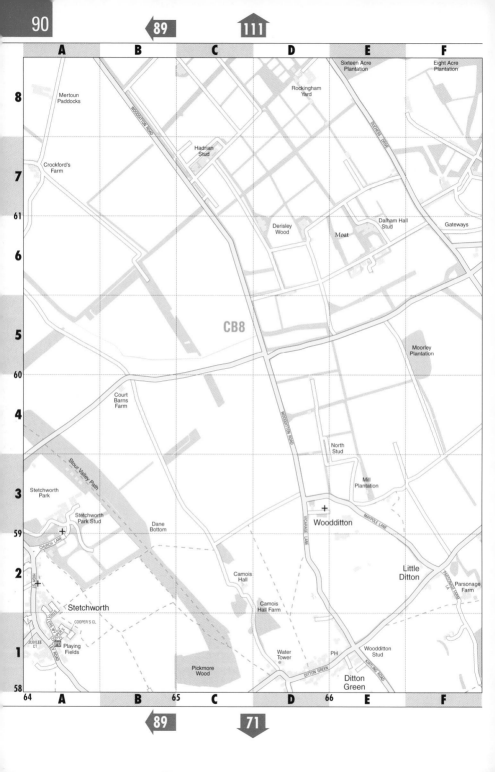

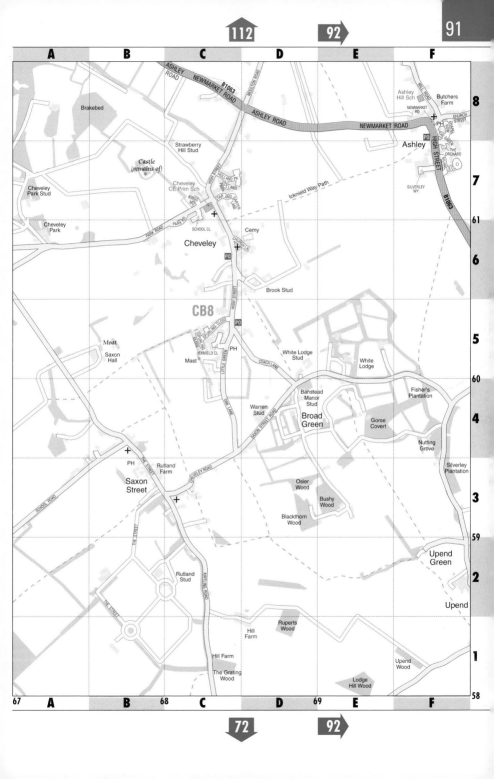

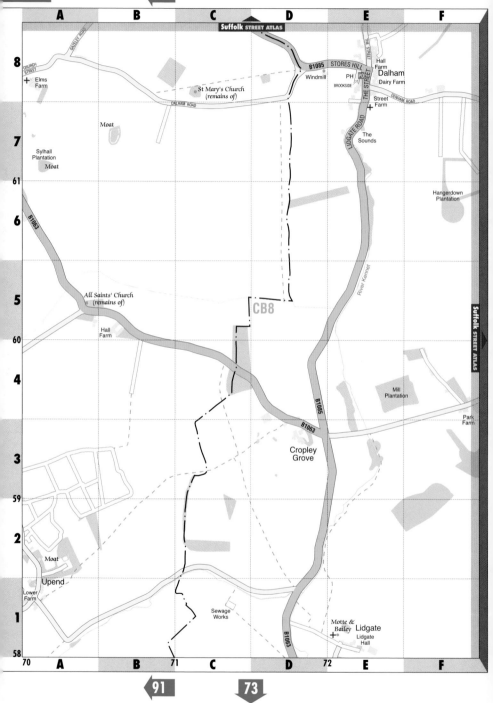

Suffolk STREET ATLAS

Suffolk STREET ATLAS

8

7

61

6

5

60

4

3

59

2

1

58

A B C D E F

CHURCH STREET

GAZELEY ROAD

+ Elms Farm

B1085

STORES HILL

Windmill

Hall Farm

Dalham

PH

Dairy Farm

BROOKSIDE

St Mary's Church (remains of)

DALHAM ROAD

DERHAM ROAD

+ Street Farm

THE STREET

Moat

LIDGATE ROAD

The Sounds

Sylhall Plantation

Moat

Hangerdown Plantation

B1063

River Kennet

All Saints' Church (remains of)

Hall Farm

CB8

Mill Plantation

B1085

Park Farm

B1063

Cropley Grove

Moat

Upend

Lower Farm

Sewage Works

Motte & Bailey

Lidgate

Lidgate Hall

B1063

70 A B 71 C D 72 E F

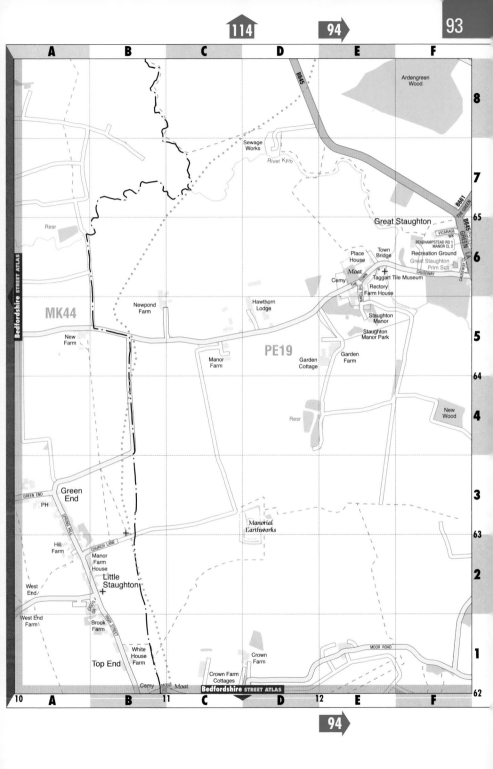

A B C D E F

8

Ardengreen
Wood

River Kym

Sewage
Works

7

B645

B661

65

Great Staughton

Resr

VICARAGE
WK

BEADHAMPSTEAD RD 1
MANOR CL 2

GREEN LA

THE GREEN

6

MK44

Newpond
Farm

Place
House

Town
Bridge

Recreation Ground

Great Staughton
Prim Sch

Moat

Taggart Tile Museum

Cemy

Rectory
Farm House

CAUSEWAY

THE TOWN

New
Farm

Hawthorn
Lodge

Staughton
Manor

Staughton
Manor Park

5

PE19

Manor
Farm

Garden
Cottage

Garden
Farm

64

Resr

New
Wood

4

Green End

GREEN END

PH

3

SPRING HILL

CHURCH LANE

Manorial
Earthworks

63

Hill
Farm

Manor
Farm
House

Little
Staughton

West
End

2

West End
Farm

Brook
Farm

HIGH STREET

Top End

White
House
Farm

Crown
Farm

MOOR ROAD

1

Cemy

MOOR
RD

Moat

Crown Farm
Cottages

62

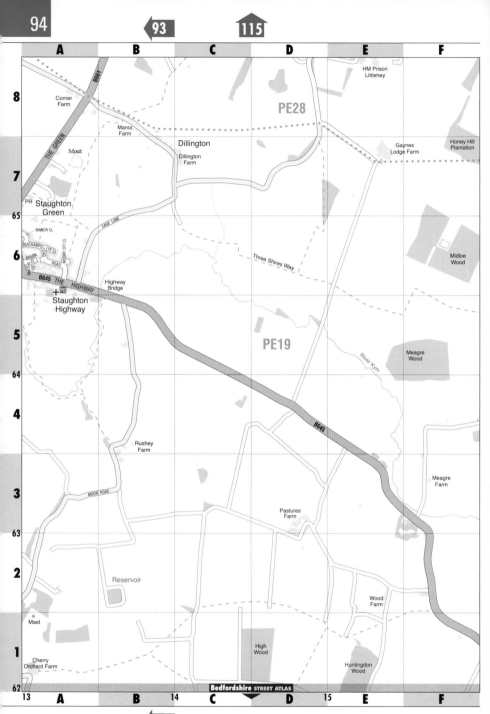

PE28

HM Prison
Littlehey

Corner
Farm

THE GREEN

B691

Manor
Farm

Dillington

Moat

Dillington
Farm

Gaynes
Lodge Farm

Honey Hill
Plantation

PH Staughton
Green

MANOR CL

CAGE LANE

BEACHAMPS

GREEN
SMITHS CL
LYE CL
MOOR CFT CL
ROAD

Three Shires Way

Midloe
Wood

B645 THE HIGHWAY

Highway
Bridge

Staughton
Highway

PE19

River Kym

Meagre
Wood

B645

Rushey
Farm

MOOR ROAD

Meagre
Farm

Pastures
Farm

Reservoir

Wood
Farm

Mast

High
Wood

Huntingdon
Wood

Cherry
Orchard Farm

95
117

Diddington

Home Farm

Manor Farm

Medieval Village (site of)

Boughton Village

Boughton Lodge Farm

Sand and Gravel Pit

Ouse Valley Way

LC

Bullens Farm

PE19

Manor Farm

Great Paxton CE Prim Sch

MOUNT PLEASANT

CHURCH LA

HIGH STREET

RECTORY CL

LUDDINGTON CL

LONGWOOD WY

MEADOW WY

CROSS KEYS WY

TRINITY CL 1
ST JOHNS MS 2

LONDON LA

ADAM'S LANE

Great Paxton

Paxton Pits Nature Reserve

Wray House

RIVER LANE

DOVECOTE RD

BROOKS

Low Farm

Paxton Pits Nature Reserve

LAKEFIELD AV
NURSERY GD
PIPISTRELLE CL
HIGH STREET
DAVIS CL
KINGFISHER

Visitor Centre

Pitt Farm
PH
Little Paxton

LAKESIDE CL

THE CROFTS

Ouse Valley Way

Harley Industrial Park

PAXTON HILL

HUNTINGDON ROAD

Paxton Hill House

Sewage Works

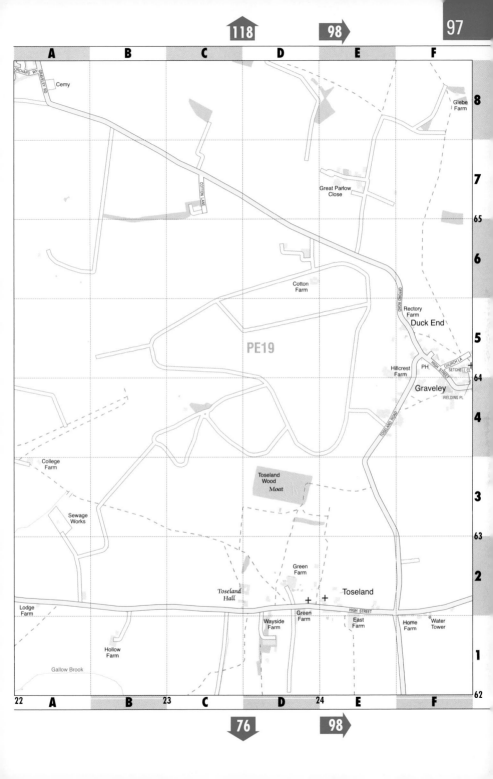

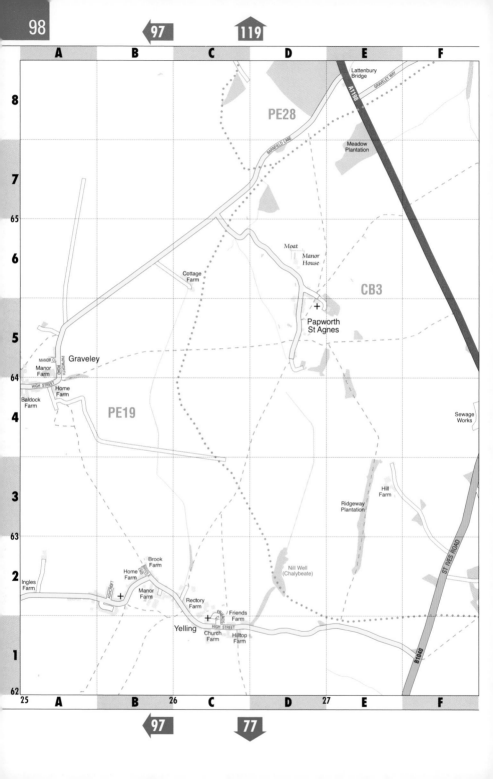

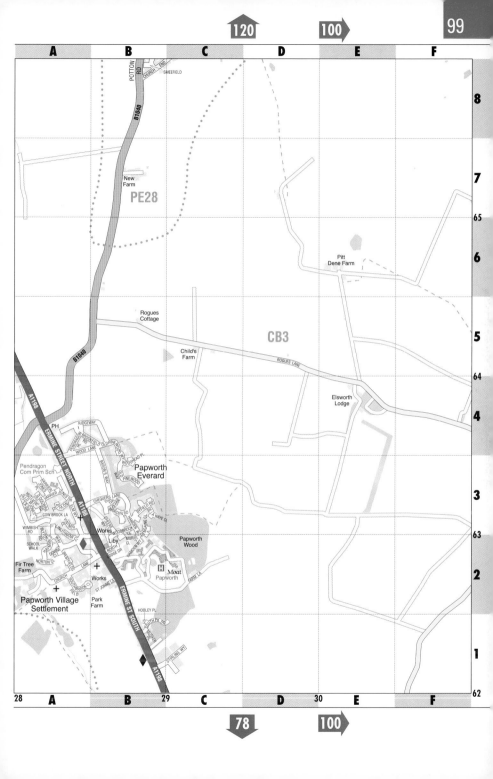

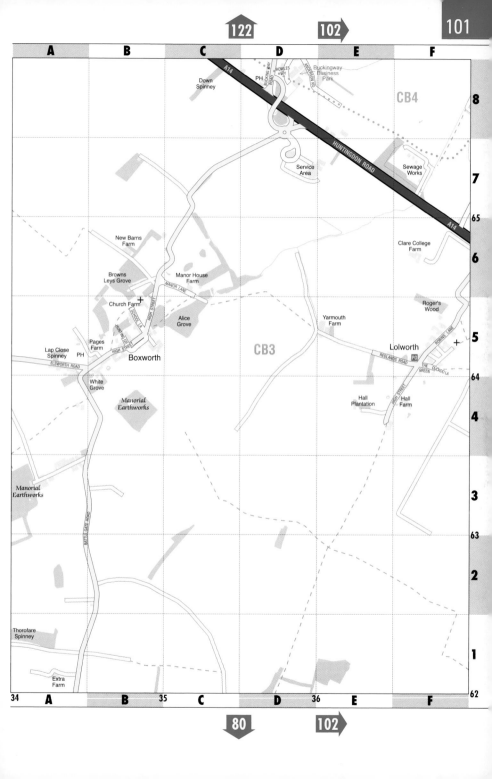

101
123

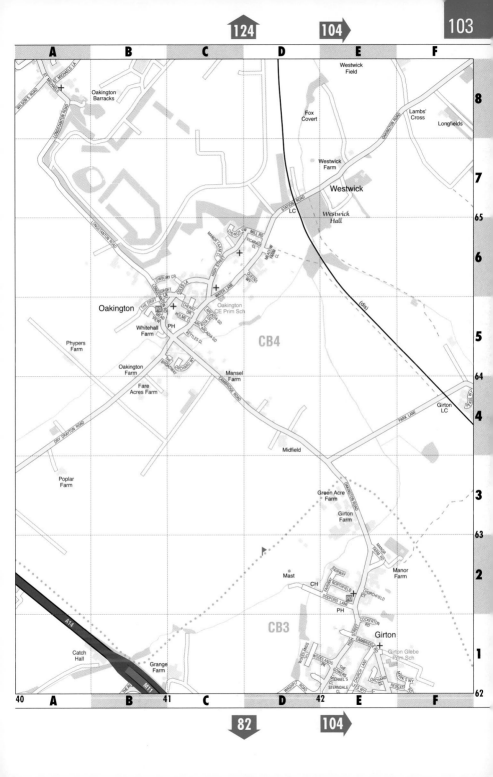

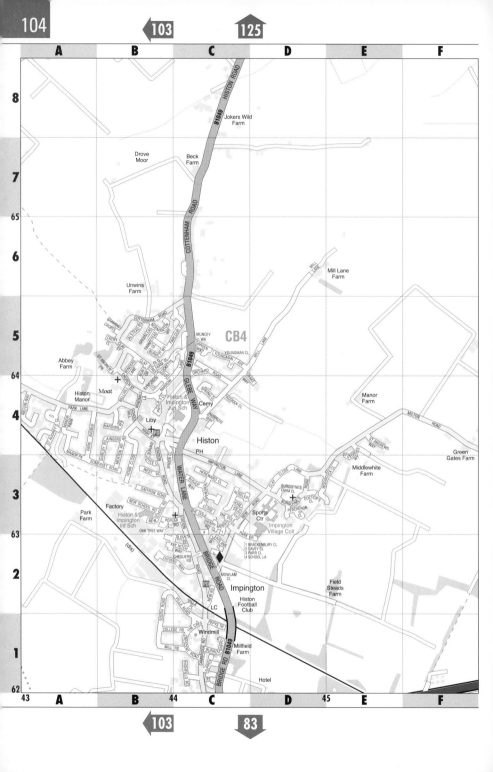

8

7

65

6

5

64

4

3

63

2

1

62

A B C D E F

43 44 45

B1049

HISTON ROAD

Jokers Wild Farm

Drove Moor

Beck Farm

COTTENHAM ROAD

Mill Lane Farm

MILL LANE

Unwins Farm

CB4

COTTENHAM ROAD

BARROWS CROFTS

ALSTEAD ROAD

NORMANTON WAY

GREENLEAS

CROFT CL

CLAY ST

FANSHAWE

ARDUCR CL

BRERETON CL

B1049

MUNCEY WK

GARDEN WK

YOUNGMAN

YOUNGMAN AVE

MILL WAY

Abbey Farm

ST ANDREWS PK

BILLING WAY

CLAY CL

WINDMILL CL

OLD FARM CL

HOLME CL

SYMONDS

ORCHARD

SPRING CL

PADDOCK CL

Manor Farm

Histon Manor

Moat

LANE

Histon & Impington Jun Sch

Cemy

PARK LANE

MANOR PK

HARDINGS

NEW RD

DWYER RD

AINGERS RD

Liby

PO

GLEBE WAY

AMBROSE WAY

Histon

PH

ST ANDREWS WAY

Green Gates Farm

MANOR PK AVENUE

PARK AVENUE

SHIRLEY RD

BURTON CL

STATION RD

SOMERSET ROAD

WEST RD

WATER LANE

IMPINGTON LANE

HEREWARD CL

BISHOP CLOSE

ROSE LA

OAK CLOSE

ST GEORGES WAY

WOODLACK CL

Middlewhite Farm

MILTON ROAD

Factory

Park Farm

NEW SCHOOL RD

SAFFRON ROAD

THE DOLE

CLOSE

THE DELL

ROAD

BURGOYNES FARM CL

DOCTOR'S CL

BURGOYNE

Histon & Impington Inf Sch

OAK TREE WAY

NEW RD

POPLAR RD

HENRY MORRIS

PERCHERON

Sports Ctr

Impington Village Coll

LOVE LA

KAY HITCH WAY

THE DOLE

PARK DR

THE LEA

1 BRACKENBURY CL
2 DAVEY CL
3 PARR CL
4 SCHOOL LA

CHIVERS WAY

CHEQUERS RD

BRIDGE ROAD

MOWLAM CL

PO

Impington

SOUTH RD

VILLA ROAD

GLEBE

LC

Histon Football Club

Field Steads Farm

COLLEGE RD

THE CRES

PEPYS TR

Windmill

MILL RD

CRESCENT RD

BURROW

B1049

Millfield Farm

THE CAMBRIDGE ROAD

HIGHFIELD RD

Hotel

(dis)

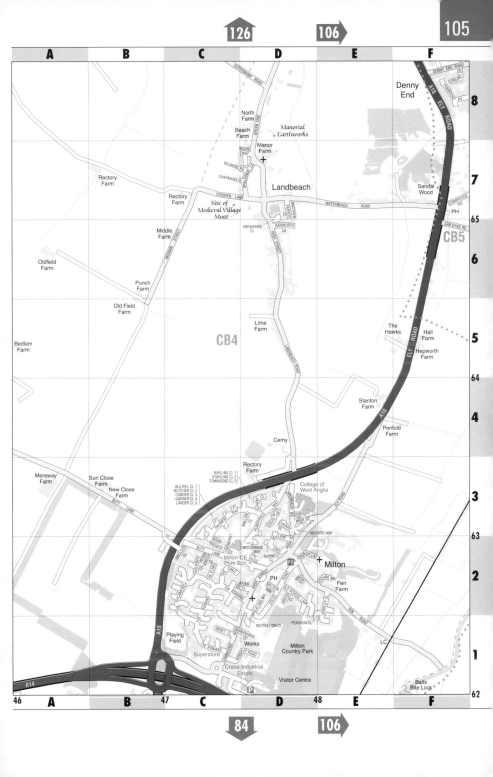

Denny
End

8

North
Farm

Beach
Farm

Manorial
Earthworks

BECHE
WAY

Manor
Farm

Rectory
Farm

REUBENS RD

CHAPMANS CL

SPALDINGS

7

Sandal
Wood

CAMBRIDGE
RD

Rectory
Farm

COCKFEN LANE

Landbeach

WATERBEACH   ROAD

PH

CAR DYKE RD

65

Site of
Medieval Village
Moat

BEDLAM STREET

Middle
Farm

ABRAHAMS
CL

BANWORTH
LA

MATTHEW
PARKER

HIGH STREET

CB5

6

Oldfield
Farm

Punch
Farm

Old Field
Farm

Bedlam
Farm

CB4

Lime
Farm

LANDBEACH ROAD

The
Hawks

Hall
Farm

ELY   ROAD

Hepworth
Farm

5

64

Stanton
Farm

A10

Penfold
Farm

4

Cemy

Rectory
Farm

BURLING CL 1
STARLING CL 2
TOWNSEND CL 3

College of
West Anglia

ELY ROAD

3

Mereway
Farm

Sun Close
Farm

New Close
Farm

BUTT   LANE

BULTEEL CL 1
BUTCHER CL 2
CONDER CL 3
GARNER CL 4
LANDER CL 5

LANDBEACH RD

WAY

BALLANT

HUMPHRIES

CHERRY

HIGH ST

KNIGHTS WAY

63

WOODMANS
WAY

WILLOW

GUNNELL
CL

CHURCH LA

PO

Milton

Fen
Farm

A10

Milton CE
Prim Sch

STREET

MILTON
WAY

OLD SCHOOL LANE

COLES RD

SHIRLEY CL

FEN
ROAD

2

THE SYCAMORES

THE ROWANS

BENET CL

Playing
Field

Superstore

RECREATION CL

Works

PEARSON CL

Milton
Country Park

LC

Baits
Bite Lock

1

Crane Industrial
Estate

Visitor Centre

P

62

A14

46

47

48

105
127

A B C D E F
8 7 65 6 5 64 4 3 63 2 1 62
49 50 51
Denny End
WATERBEACH
Waterbeach CP Sch
Liby
PO
Midlode Farm
Lock Farm
Bottisham Lock
Todds Farm
Hall Crest Farm
Frolic Farm
Hatley's Farm
Vicarage Farm
Northfields Farm
Waterbeach
ST JOHN'S CL
WHITMORE WAY
LC
Clayhithe
Clayhithe Farm
CB5
Queen's Fen
Queens Farm
River Cam
Grange Farm
Eye Hall Farm
CB4
Roman Pottery Kilns (site of)
CLAYHITHE ROAD
Harcamlow Way
Manor Farm
DOCK LANE
ST JOHN'S LA
Northgate Farm
Kings Farm
CHURCH END
PH
HIGH STREET
ABBOTS WY
PRIORY RD
Horningsea
HORNINGSEA ROAD
Stow cum Quy Fen
Allicky Farm
STATION RD
BANNOLD ROAD
CODY RD
LONG DROVE
BURGESS'S DROVE
LUG FEN DROVEWAY
STATION ROAD
CAR DYKE ROAD
CAMBRIDGE ROAD
GLEBE ROAD
CORONATION CL
HARDING CL 1
POORSFIELD RD 2
SAXON WAY 3
WILES CL
PRIMROSE LA
VICARAGE CL
CATTELL'S LA
BURGESS ROAD
ROSEMARY RD
PAYTON WAY
LODE AV
ADAMS CT
JOSIAH CT
SPURGEONS AV
PARK CR
FENLEIGH CL
PEMBROKE AVE

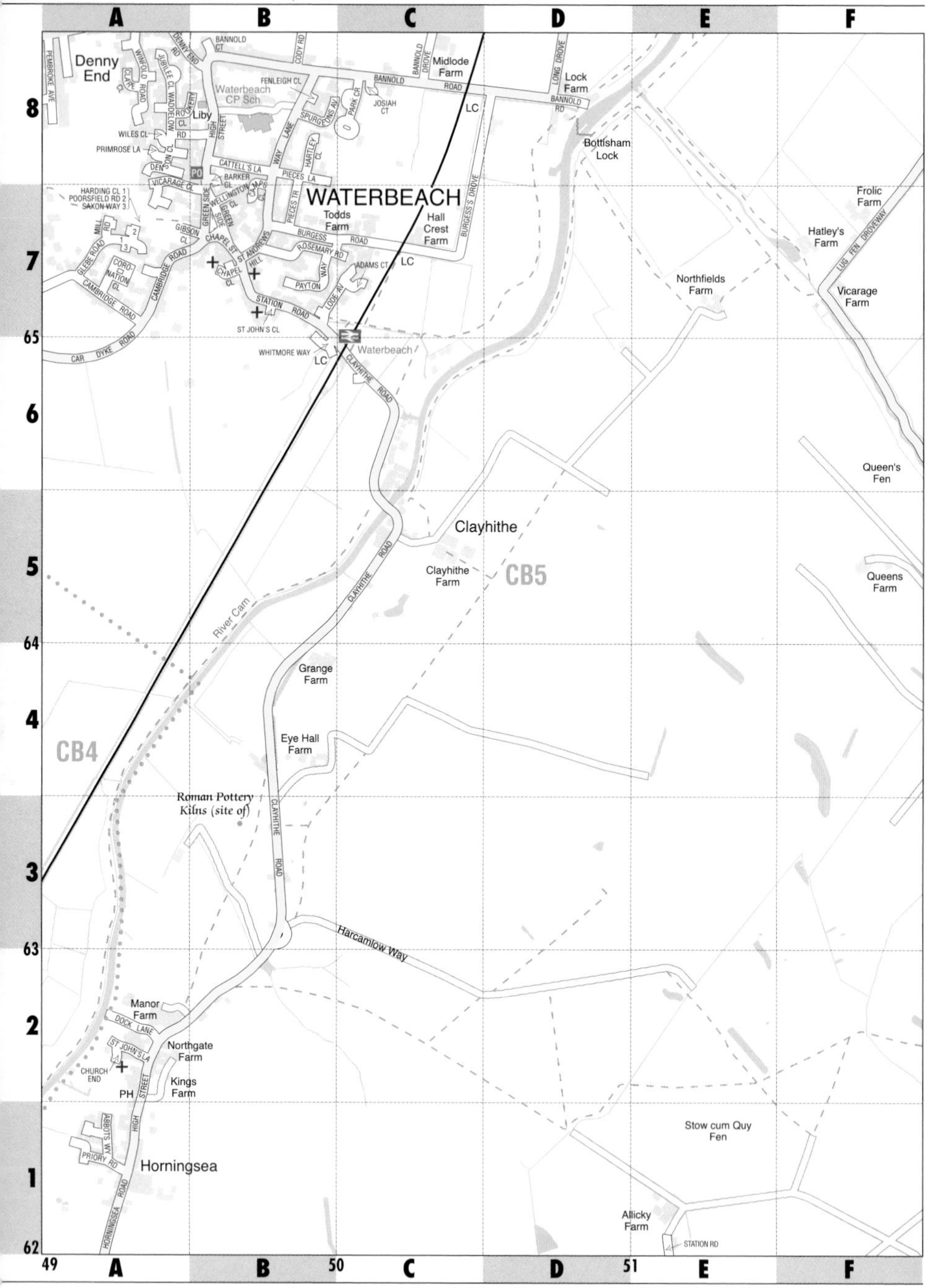

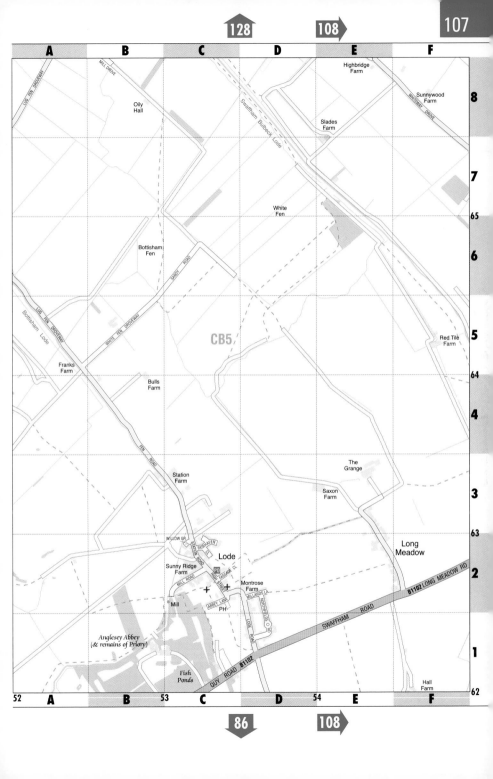

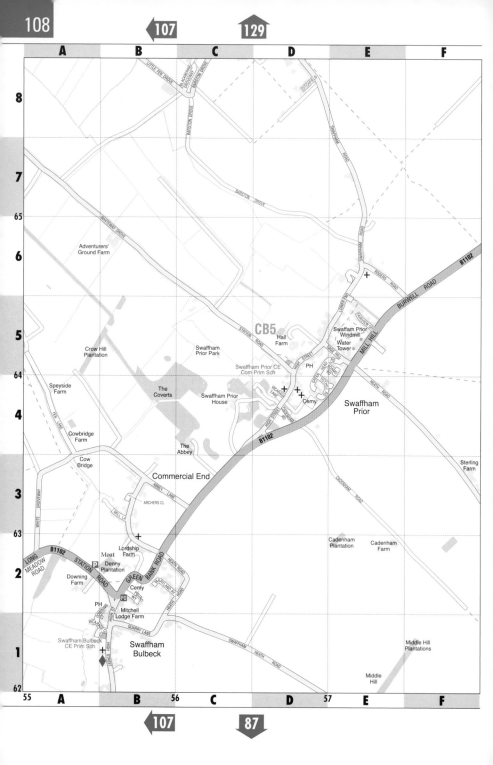

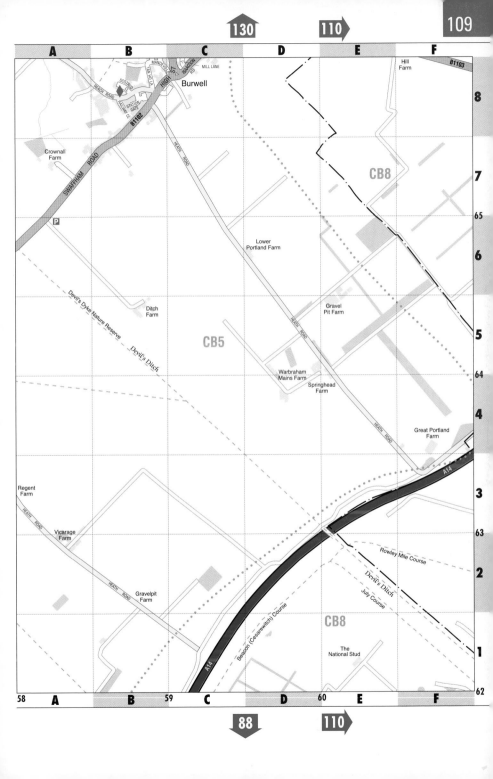

A B C D E F

MANOR CT
HIGH ST
JACKSON RD
MILL LANE

Burwell

SCOTRED
STATION
GATE
REACH ROAD
STATION CL
8

B1102

Hill
Farm

B1103

Crownall
Farm

CB8
7

65

SWAFFHAM ROAD

HEATH ROAD

P

6

Lower
Portland Farm

Devil's Dyke Nature Reserve

Ditch
Farm

Gravel
Pit Farm

5

Devil's Ditch

CB5

64

HEATH ROAD

Warbraham
Mains Farm

Springhead
Farm

4

Great Portland
Farm

A14

Regent
Farm

3

HEATH ROAD

Vicarage
Farm

63

Rowley Mile Course

2

Devil's Ditch

HEATH ROAD

Gravelpit
Farm

July Course

Beacon (Cesarewitch) Course

CB8

1

A14

The
National Stud

62

58 A B 59 C D 60 E F

109
131

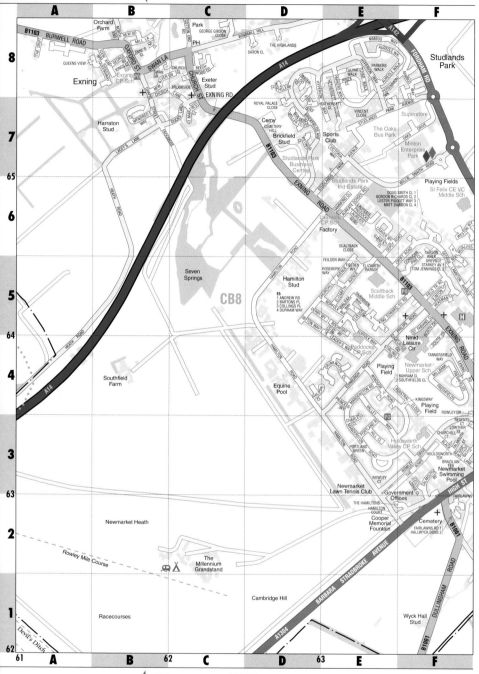

109
89

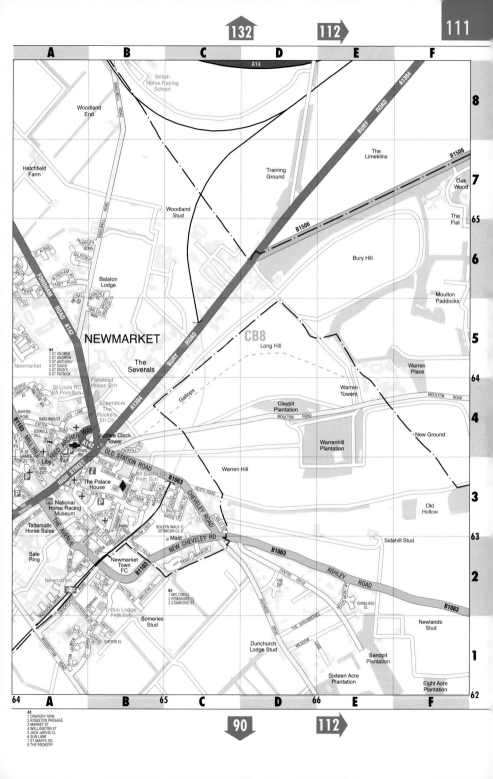

A B C D E F

8

British Horse Racing School

Woodland End

A14

BURY ROAD A1304

The Limekilns

B1506

7

Hatchfield Farm

Training Ground

Oak Wood

B1506

The Flat

65

Woodland Stud

B1506

Bury Hill

6

Balaton Lodge

FALMOUTH GDNS

SNAILWELL ROAD

FORDHAM ROAD A142

Moulton Paddocks

NEWMARKET

A4
1 ST GEORGE
2 ST ANDREW
3 ST ANTHONY
4 ST DAVID
5 ST DENYS
6 ST PATRICK

CB8

Long Hill

5

Newmarket

The Severals

BURY ROAD

Warren Place

St Louis RC WA Prim Sch

Fairstead House Sch

Warren Towers

MOULTON ROAD

64

Superstore
The Rookery Sh Ctr

A1304

Gallops

Claypit Plantation

MOULTON ROAD

New Ground

4

BAKERS ROW

BARLINGS CT

ICEWELL HILL

B1063

MILL HILL

FRED ARCHER WAY

Jubilee Clock Tower

OLD STATION ROAD

Warrenhill Plantation

Lib

A142

HIGH STREET

i

The Palace House

All Saints CE Prim Sch

B1063

Warren Hill

Old Hollow

3

63

National Horse Racing Museum

HEATH ROAD

CHEVELEY ROAD

Sidehill Stud

Tattersalls Horse Sales

THE AVENUE

P

Mast

BOLEYN WALK
SEYMOUR CL

NEW CHEVELEY RD

B1063

ASHLEY ROAD

2

Sale Ring

Newmarket Town FC

B1063

CRICKET FIELD

BARRY LYNHAM DR

CENTRE DRIVE

THE DIP

ISINGLASS CL

B1063

Ditton Lodge First Sch

B2
1 MELTON CL
2 PEMBROKE CL
3 STAMFORD ST

Someries Stud

THE SHRUBBERIES

MEADOW LANE

Newlands Stud

1

GIRTON CL

Dunchurch Lodge Stud

Sandpit Plantation

Sixteen Acre Plantation

Eight Acre Plantation

62

64 A 65 B C D 66 E F

A3
1 DRAPERY ROW
2 KINGSTON PASSAGE
3 MARKET ST
4 WELLINGTON ST
5 JACK JARVIS CL
6 SUN LANE
7 ST MARYS SQ
8 THE ROOKERY

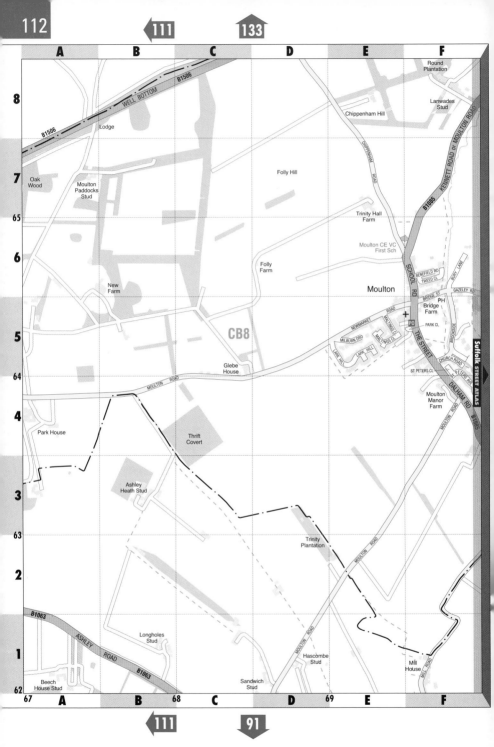

111
133

A **B** **C** **D** **E** **F**

8

7

65

6

5

64

4

3

63

2

1

62

Round
Plantation

B1506

WELL BOTTOM

B1506

Lanwades
Stud

B1506

Chippenham Hill

Oak
Wood

Moulton
Paddocks
Stud

Lodge

Folly Hill

CHIPPENHAM ROAD

KENNETT ROAD or MOULTON ROAD

B1085

Trinity Hall
Farm

Moulton CE VC
First Sch

Folly
Farm

BENEFIELD RD

BURY LANE

TWEED CL

New
Farm

Moulton

SCHOOL RD

GAZELEY RD

BRIDGE ST

PH
Bridge
Farm

NEWMARKET ROAD

MALTINGS CL

PARK CL

CB8

MILBURN DRO

LARK HILL

LARK HILL

MALTINGS CL

THE STREET

BROOKSIDE

CHURCH ROAD

ST PETERS CL

SEYERS AVE

Glebe
House

MOULTON ROAD

Moulton
Manor
Farm

DALHAM RD

B1085

Park House

Thrift
Covert

Ashley
Heath Stud

Trinity
Plantation

MOULTON ROAD

MOULTON ROAD

B1063

ASHLEY ROAD

Longholes
Stud

B1063

Hascombe
Stud

Mill
House

MILL ROAD

Beech
House Stud

Sandwich
Stud

67   **A**   **B**   68   **C**   **D**   69   **E**   **F**

111
91

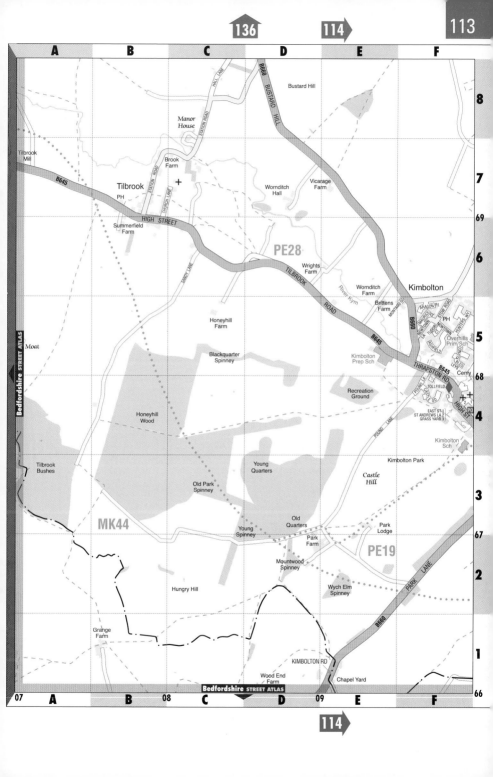

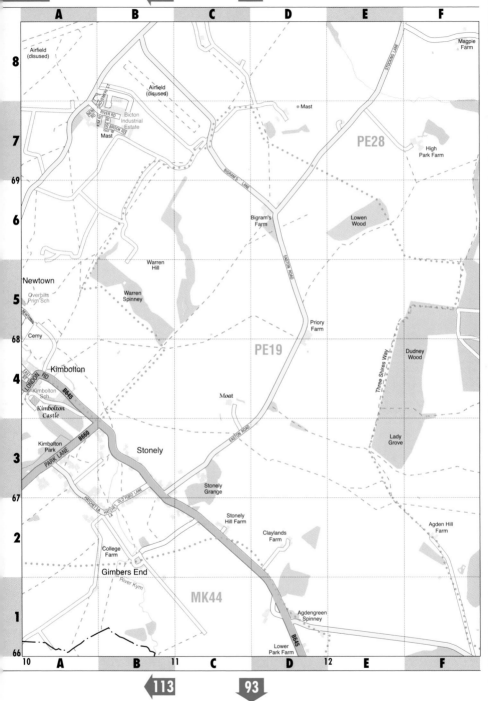

8   Airfield
(disused)

Magpie
Farm

Airfield
(disused)

RIVER RD   Bicton
Industrial
Estate

● Mast

PE28

STOCKING LANE

7   Mast

High
Park Farm

69

BIGRAM'S LANE

Bigram's
Farm

Lowen
Wood

6

Warren
Hill

Newtown

Overbills
Prim Sch

Warren
Spinney

EASTON ROAD

5

68   Cemy

Priory
Farm

PE19

Three Shires Way

Dudney
Wood

Kimbolton

4   LONDON RD   B645
Kimbolton
Sch

Moat

Lady
Grove

Kimbolton
Castle

B660

Kimbolton
Park   Stonely

EASTON ROAD

3   PARK LANE

HATCHET LA   TILTFORD LANE

Stonely
Grange

67
Stonely
Hill Farm

Agden Hill
Farm

2   College
Farm

Claylands
Farm

Gimbers End

River Kym   MK44

1   Agdengreen
Spinney

B645

66   Lower
Park Farm

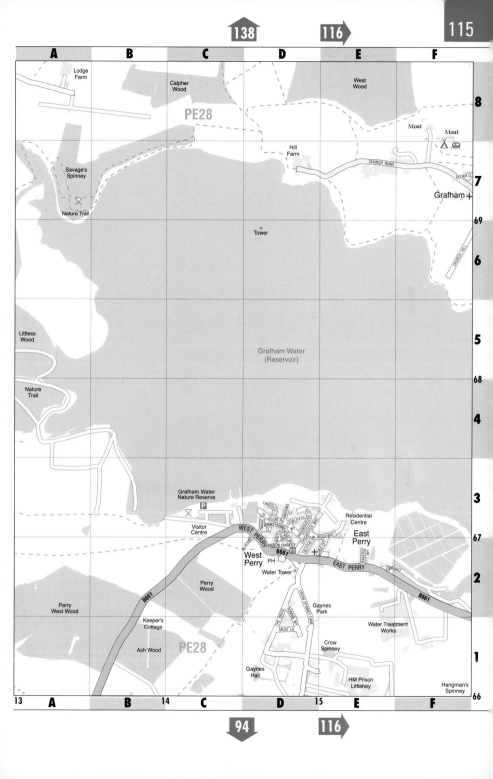

A B C D E F

Lodge Farm
Calpher Wood
West Wood

PE28

8

Moat
Moat

Hill Farm

CHURCH ROAD

CEDAR CL

Savage's Spinney

7

Grafham

Nature Trail

69

Tower

CHURCH HILL

6

Littless Wood

5

Grafham Water (Reservoir)

68

Nature Trail

4

3

Grafham Water Nature Reserve

LAKESIDE
GLEBE RD
ARMSTRONG WY
DUDLEY CL

Residential Centre

67

Visitor Centre

WEST PERRY

WY PERRY
HALL WY
HASTINGS

DUCHESTER WAY

RIDGEWAY

East Perry

West Perry

MANOR FARM CT
B661
PH

EAST PERRY

BAKERS WY

DUBERLY

2

Water Tower

Perry Wood

B661

B661

Perry West Wood

Keeper's Cottage

THE DRIVE
CROW SPINNEY LANE
CROW SPINNEY WY

Gaynes Park

Water Treatment Works

MOAT LA

Crow Spinney

Ash Wood

PE28

1

Gaynes Hall

HM Prison Littlehey

Hangman's Spinney

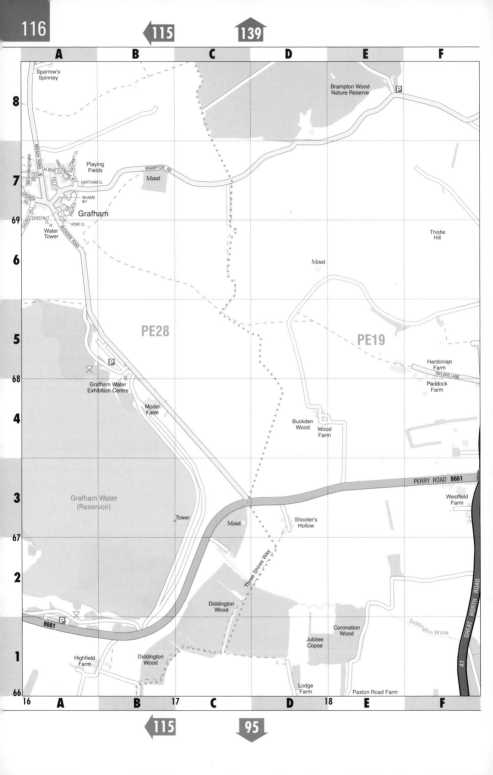

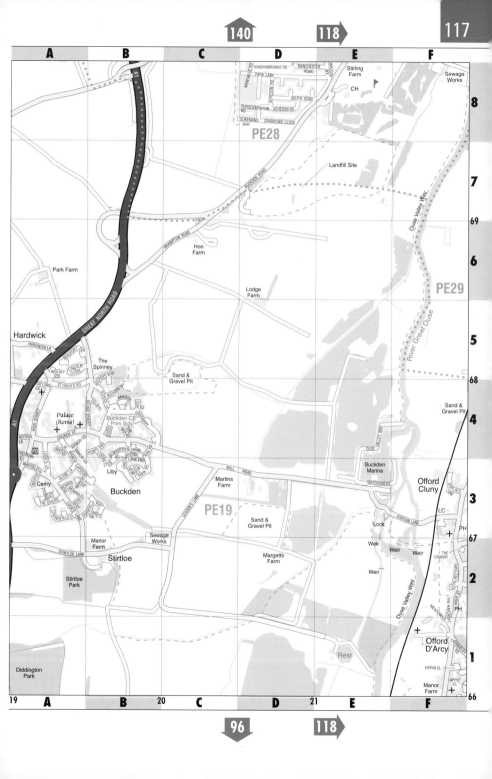

PE28

PE29

PE19

Hardwick

Park Farm

Hoo Farm

Lodge Farm

Landfill Site

Stirling Farm

CH

Sewage Works

HINCHINBROOKE RD
MONTAGUE RD
PARK LANE
MANCHESTER ROAD
WILSON WY
ACHESON RD
SOUTH ROAD
THROCKMORTON
ACHESON RD
SOKEMANS WAY
SPARROWS CLOSE

BUCKDEN ROAD

BRAMPTON ROAD

GREAT NORTH ROAD

A1

HARDWICK LA

The Spinney

Sand & Gravel Pit

Ouse Valley Way

River Great Ouse

Sand & Gravel Pit

Palace (Rems)

Buckden CE Prim Sch

Buckden

Liby

Cerny

Martins Farm

MILL ROAD

Buckden Marina

WATERSMEAD

VALLEY WAY

OUSE

Offord Cluny

STATION LANE

POPE IN S LANE

LC

PH

THE CRANNY

Lock

Weir

Weir

Weir

67

Manor Farm

Sewage Works

Stirtloe

STIRTLOE LANE

LEADEN'S LANE

Sand & Gravel Pit

Margetts Farm

Ouse Valley Way

THE RECTORY

RECTORY ST

THE HAVEN

MEADOW LA

PH

Stirtloe Park

Diddington Park

Resr

Offord D'Arcy

PIPPIN CL

APPLE CL

Manor Farm

CORNERS ST

66

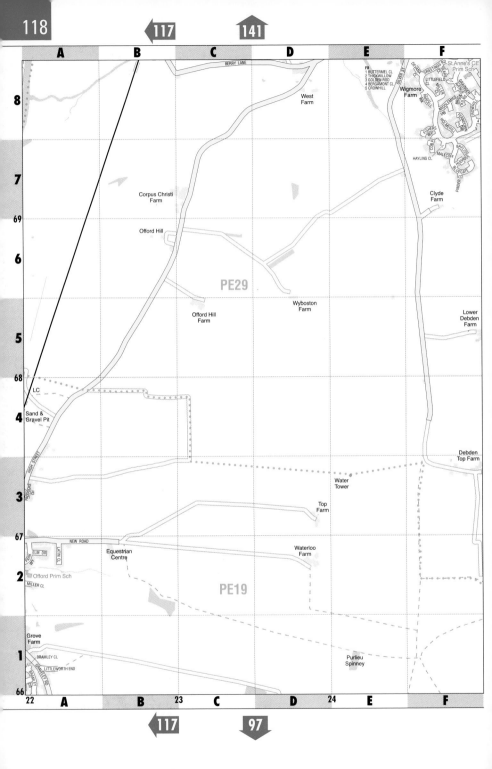

BERRY LANE

West Farm

F8
1 BUTTERMEL CL
2 THICKWILLOW
3 GOLDEN ROD
4 BERGAMONT CL
5 CROWHILL

St Anne's CE Prim Sch

GREETINGS RD

LITTLEFIELD

Wigmore Farm

HAYLING CL

Corpus Christi Farm

Clyde Farm

Offord Hill

PE29

Wyboston Farm

Lower Debden Farm

Offord Hill Farm

LC

Sand & Gravel Pit

HIGH STREET

Debden Top Farm

Water Tower

Top Farm

NEW ROAD

ELM DR

LATIN CL

Equestrian Centre

Waterloo Farm

Offord Prim Sch

MILLER CL

PE19

Grove Farm

BRAMLEY CL

LITTLEWORTH END

Purlieu Spinney

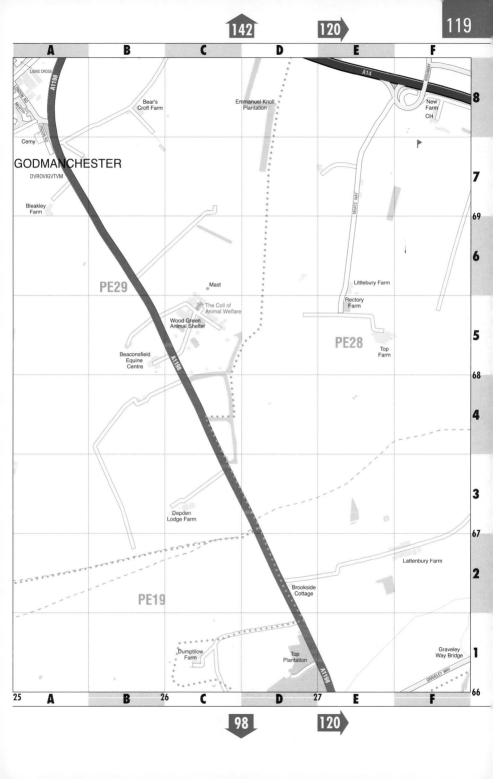

LIONS CROSS

Bear's
Croft Farm

Emmanuel Knoll
Plantation

A14

New
Farm
CH

Cemy

GODMANCHESTER

DVROVIGVTVM

Bleakley
Farm

PE29

Mast

Littlebury Farm

The Coll of
Animal Welfare

Rectory
Farm

Wood Green
Animal Shelter

PE28

Top
Farm

Beaconsfield
Equine
Centre

Depden
Lodge Farm

Lattenbury Farm

Brookside
Cottage

PE19

Dumptilow
Farm

Top
Plantation

Graveley
Way Bridge

GRAVELEY WAY

A1198

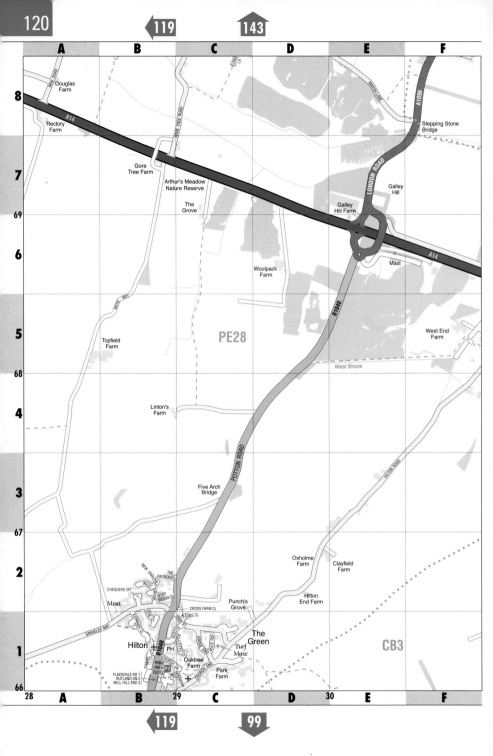

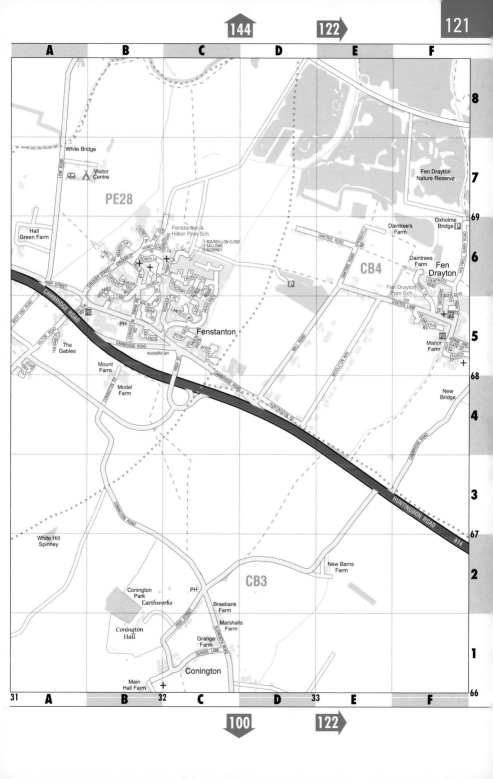

A B C D E F

8
7
69
6
5
68
4
3
67
2
1
66

White Bridge
Visitor Centre
PE28
Hall Green Farm

Fen Drayton Nature Reserve

Oxholme Bridge
Daintree's Farm
Daintrees Farm
Fen Drayton
CB4
Fen Drayton Prim Sch
OAKTREE ROAD

Fenstanton & Hilton Prim Sch
1 BOURDILLON CLOSE
2 SALLOWS
3 SCORNEY
HONEY SCHOOL LA
CHURCH LA
MANOR DR
MELT LA
CHEQUER ST
CHURCH ST
CHERRY TREE
CHURCH LE'S
SHAMBO
WALNUT
SWAN
HEADLANDS
LANCELOT
LOW ROAD

CHEQUER STREET
WEST END ROAD
HIGH STREET
CAMBRIDGE ROAD
PH
The Gables
HILTON ROAD
CODDINGTON RD
PEAR TREE
Mount Farm
CAMBRIDGE ROAD
ROOKERY WY
PITCH CL
Fenstanton

Manor Farm
HORSE AND GATE ST
CHURCH ST
ABOVE DOTE
THE ORCHARD
HOLYWELL FERRY ROAD
DAINTREES
IVES RD
HIGH ST
DRAYTON WY

Model Farm
CODDINGTON RD

P
COOTES LANE
OAKTREE ROAD
DRINGHILL
MILL ROAD
MIDDLETON WY

New Bridge
HUNTINGDON RD
CAMBRIDGE ROAD

White Hill Spinney
CONINGTON ROAD

HUNTINGDON ROAD
A14

New Barns Farm
CB3
Conington Park Earthworks
PH
Braebank Farm
Marshalls Farm
Grange Farm
HIGH STREET
ELSWORTH ROAD
SCHOOL LANE
Conington Hall
Main Hall Farm
Conington

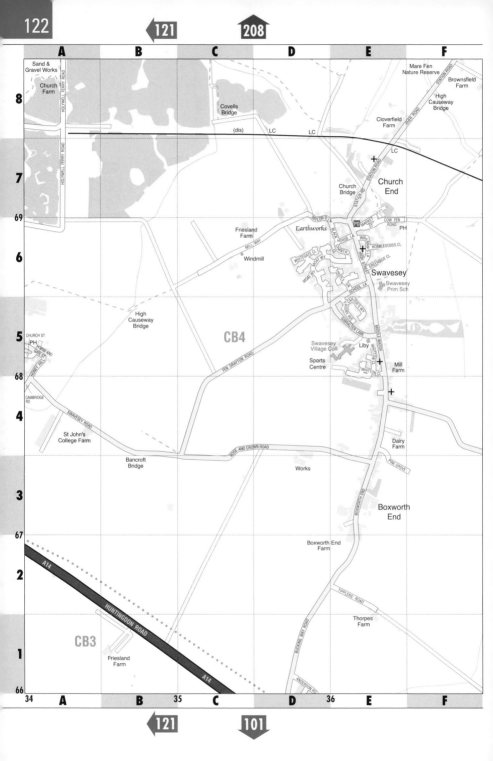

121
208

A **B** **C** **D** **E** **F**

Sand & Gravel Works

Church Farm

HOLYWELL FERRY ROAD

8

Covells Bridge

Mare Fen Nature Reserve

Brownsfield Farm

High Causeway Bridge

Cloverfield Farm

STATION ROAD

(dis) LC LC

LC

7

Church Bridge

Church End

HOLYWELL FERRY ROAD

69

Friesland Farm

Earthworks

TAYLOR'S

PO MARKET ST

COW FEN ROAD

PH

BLACK HORSE LA

HIGH STREET

WALNUT LA

HOBBLEDODDS CL

GREENSIDE CL

MILL WAY

6

Windmill

WHITEGATE CL

BOAT WY

MOAT WY

Swavesey

Swavesey Prim Sch

SCHOOL LA

CAXTER'S WY

PLOUGH LA

High Causeway Bridge

CB4

FEN DRAYTON ROAD

Swavesey Village Coll

Liby

MIDDLE WATCH

WHITTON CL

Mill Farm

CHURCH ST

PH

HICKMAN AND PETTIT CLOSE

HONEY HILL

5

Sports Centre

WHITTON CL

CAMBRIDGE RD

68

St John's College Farm

SWAVESEY ROAD

Dairy Farm

4

Bancroft Bridge

ROSE AND CROWN ROAD

Works

BOXWORTH END

PINE GROVE

Boxworth End

3

67

Boxworth End Farm

A14

TIPPLERS ROAD

2

HUNTINGDON ROAD

Thorpes Farm

CB3

Friesland Farm

A14

BLOCKING WAY ROAD

AMUSCROFT RD

1

66

34 **A** **B** 35 **C** **D** 36 **E** **F**

121
101

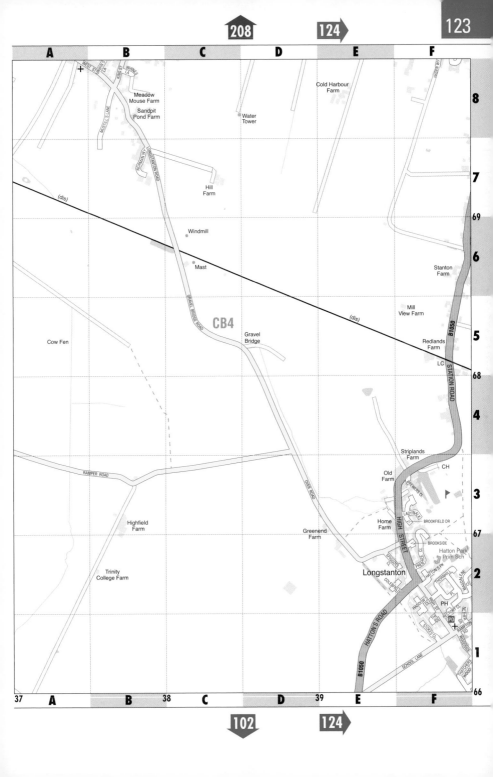

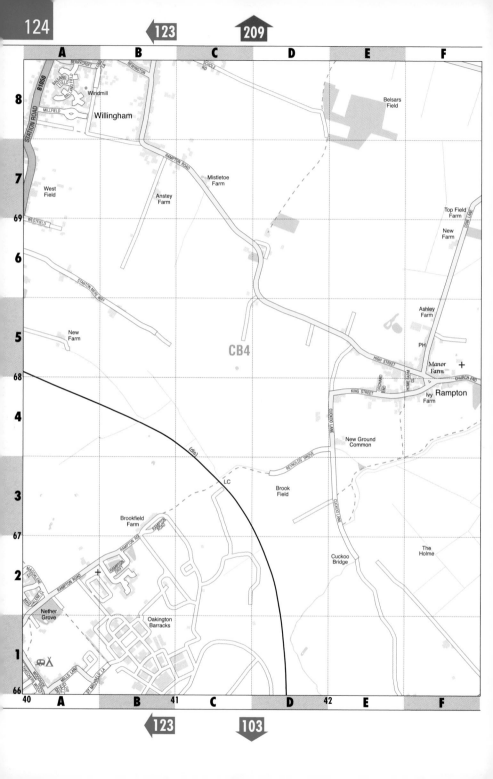

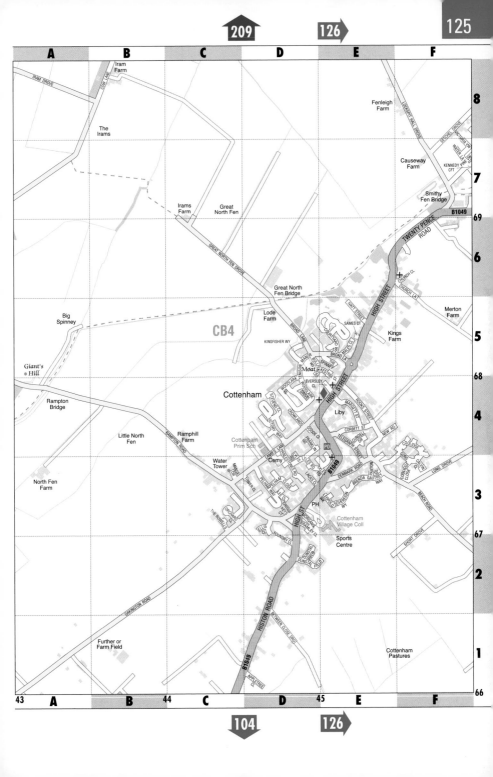

125
210

| | A | B | C | D | E | F |

8

Chestnut Farm

Mitchell Hill Farm

Elm Farm

Gravel Diggers Farm

College Farm

B1049

The Lots

7

PINE VIEW
KENNEDY DRIVE
WATER LANE
SETCHEL DRIVE

Cottenham Lode

TWENTY PENCE ROAD

Lodge Farm

Church End Cow Pastures

Sand & Gravel Pits

LONG DRIVE

Alboro House Farm

69

B1049

6

Top Moor

A10

Two Bit Farm

Top Moor

5

Church Field

Church Farm

Albrough Farm

LONG DRIVE

CB4

Green End Cow Pastures

Northerwood Farm

68

Ashton Farm

Hedge Rose Farm

Cambridge Research Park

4

LONG DRIVE

CB5

3

Mason's Pastures

Beach Ditch

Goose Hall

FLINT LA

Flint House

67

Point to Point Race Course

ELY ROAD

2

BEACH ROAD

Overbrook Farm

Car Dyke

GREEN END

Emmaus

New Farm

Cardyke Farm

1

Elm Tree Farm

COTTENHAM ROAD

A10

66

| 46 | A | B | 47 | C | D | 48 | E | F |

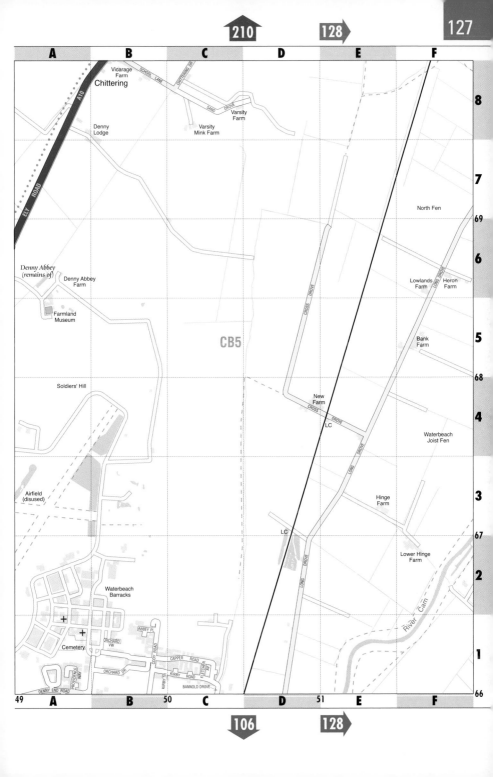

127
211

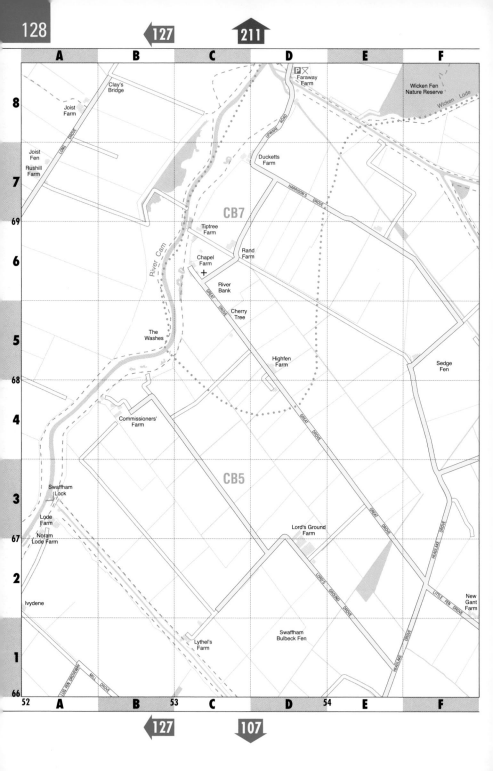

127
107

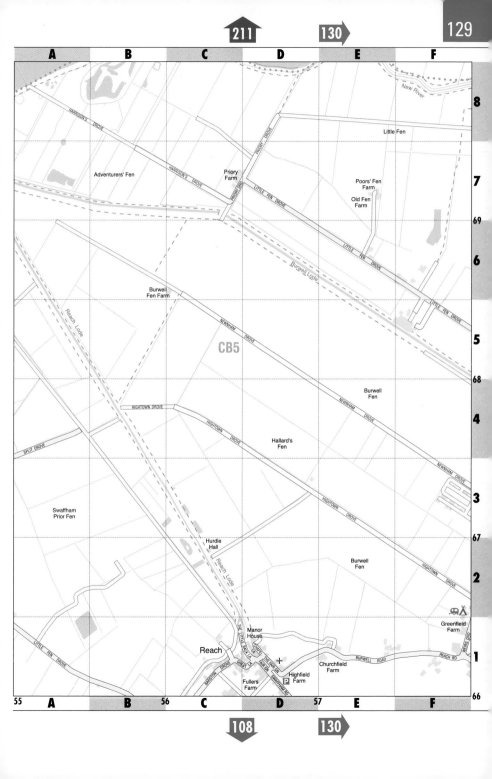

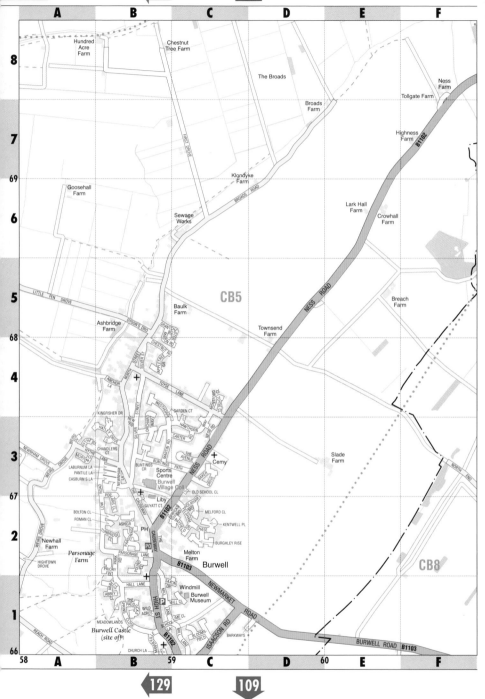

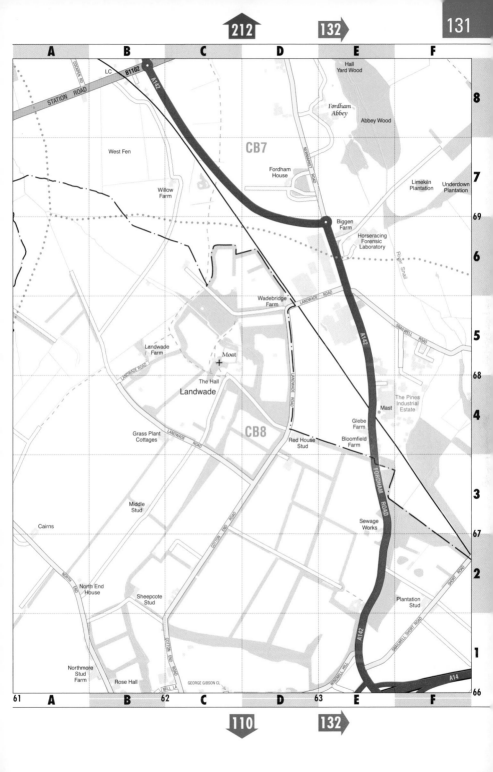

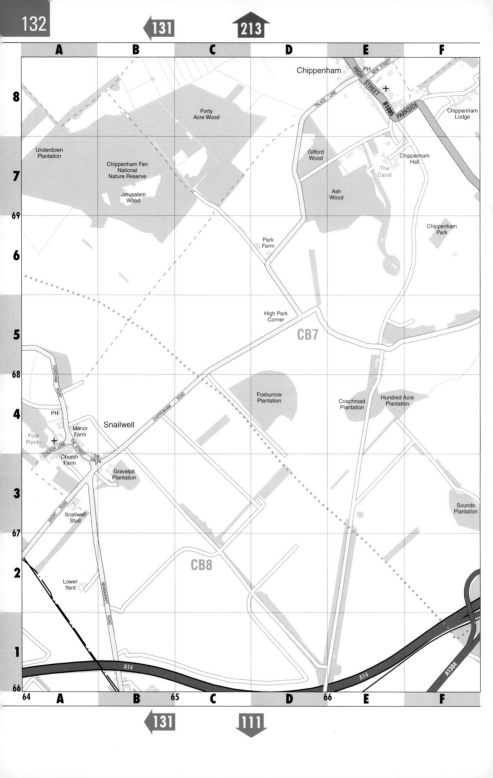

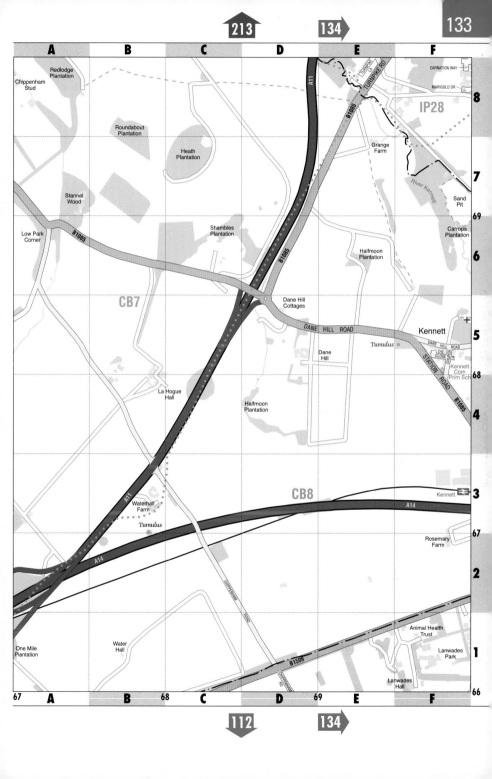

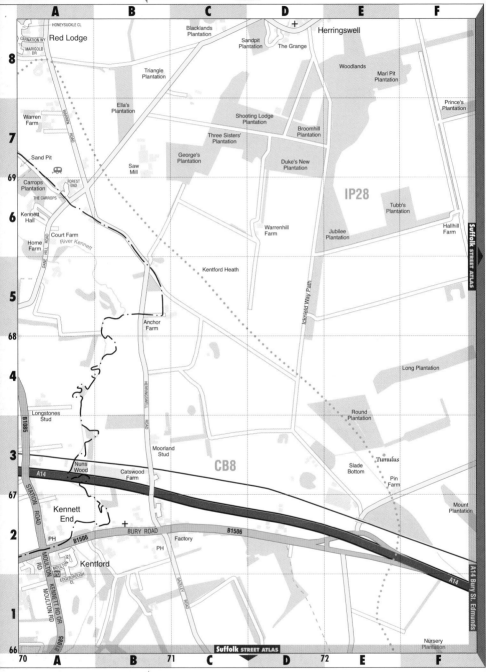

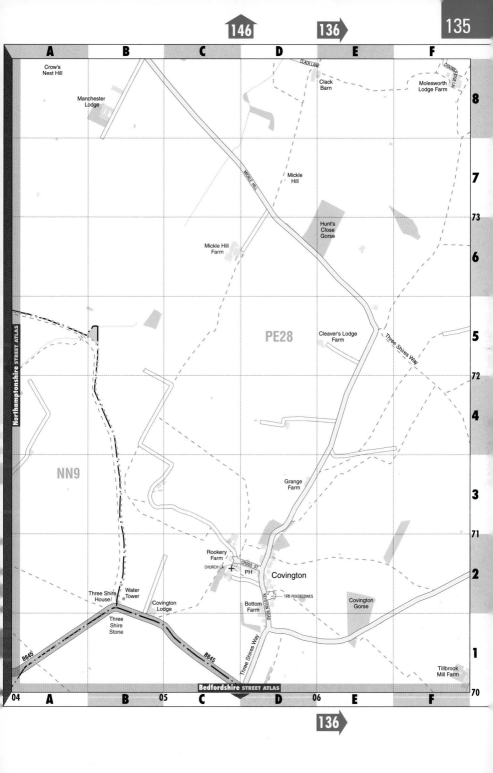

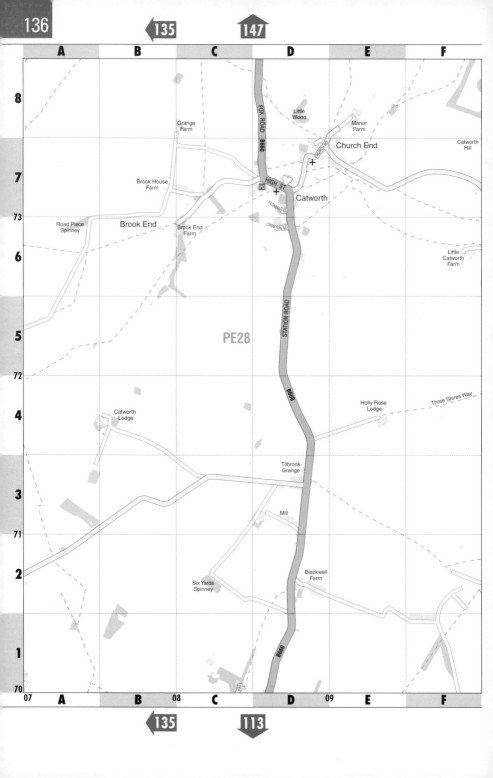

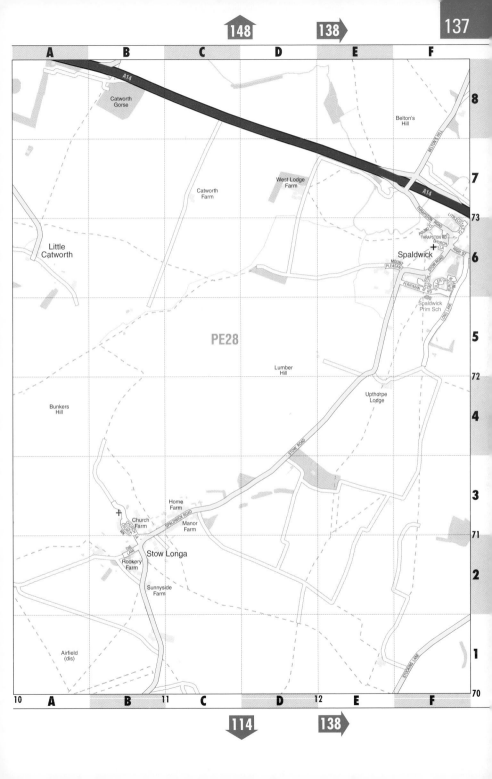

A   B   C   D   E   F

A14

Catworth
Gorse

Belton's
Hill

8

West Lodge
Farm

A14

7

Catworth
Farm

BELTON HILL

73

THRAPSTON ROAD

LITTLE COURT

Little
Catworth

POUND CL ROAD
THRAPSTON RD
CHURCH LA

Spaldwick

HIGH ST

STOW ROAD

6

MOUNT
PLEASANT

FERRIMAN RD

BUSTLER CL
ER CLOSE
BELTON
RD

LONG LANE

PE28

Spaldwick
Prim Sch

5

Lumber
Hill

72

Upthorpe
Lodge

Bunkers
Hill

4

STOW ROAD

Home
Farm

3

Church
Farm

SPALDWICK ROAD

Manor
Farm

71

THE LANE

Stow Longa

Rookery
Farm

2

Sunnyside
Farm

Airfield
(dis)

STICKING LANE

1

70

10   A   B   11   C   D   12   E   F

8

7

73

6

Woolley
Hill

Coton
Barn

WOOLLEY HILL

Whitleather
Lodge

PH +
HIGH STREET
IVY WAY

Spaldwick

Willow
House

Mad
Bridge

5

Wayside

PE28

Brook
Farm

A14

72

West
Farm

BROADWAY
THE LANE
BROADWEIR

HILL SIDE CL

GRAFHAM RD   PH

CHURCH LA
GREEN LA

GRAHAM ROAD

4

CHAPEL LANE

Easton

CHURCH RD

WINDMILL CL
WINDMILL CL

SPINNEY
FIELD

Hill
Farm
+

Grange
Farm

3

71

2

Sewell's
Barn

Moat

Thorpe Lodge
Farm

THREE SHIRES WAY

1

West Wood

Ellington
Hill

70

13   **A**   **B**   14   **C**   **D**   15   **E**   **F**

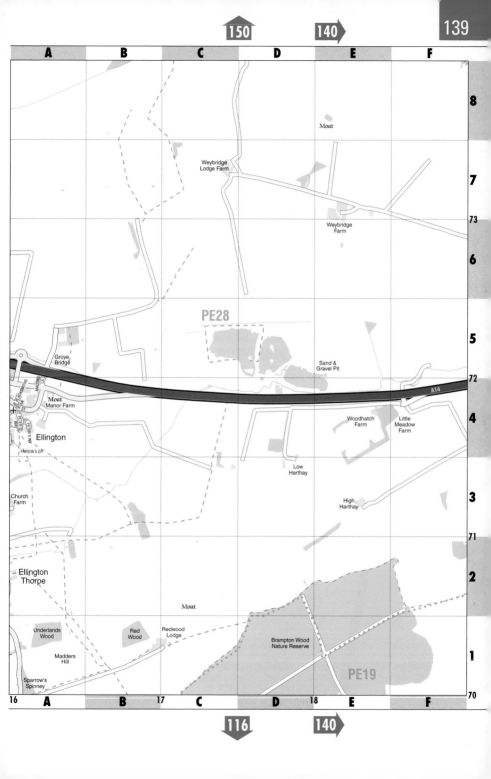

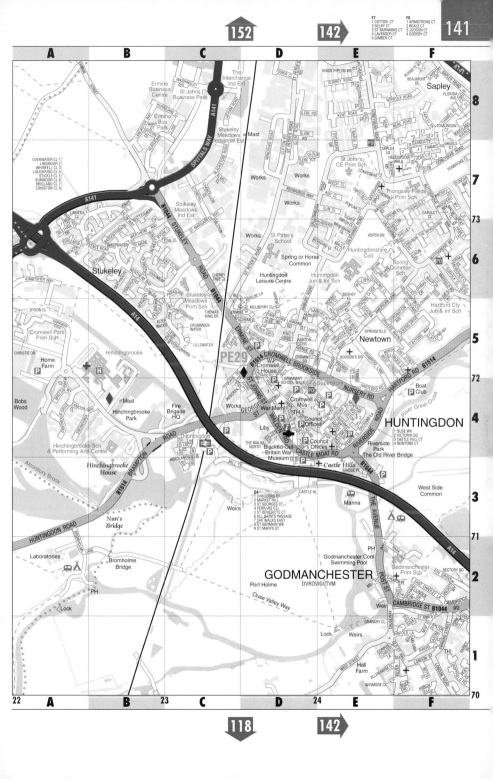

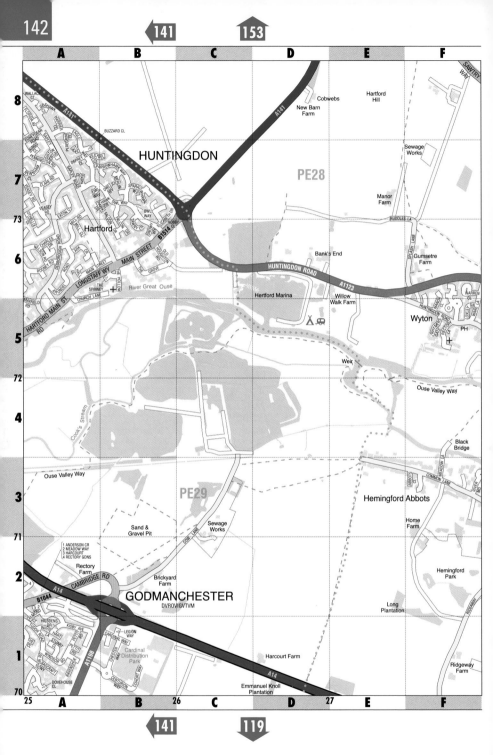

141
153

HUNTINGDON

PE28

New Barn Farm

Cobwebs

Hartford Hill

Sewage Works

Manor Farm

BUZZARD CL

WALLACE CT

Hartford

Bank's End

Gumsetre Farm

HUDDLES LA

SPLASH LANE

HUNTINGDON ROAD

A1123

Hertford Marina

Willow Walk Farm

Wyton

PH

River Great Ouse

THE SPINNEY

CHURCH LANE

MAYFIELD RD

HARTFORD MAIN ST

LONGSTAFF WY

MAIN STREET

MAIN STREET

Weir

Ouse Valley Way

WARREN

Cook's Stream

Black Bridge

Ouse Valley Way

PE29

Hemingford Abbots

Sand & Gravel Pit

Sewage Works

COB LANE

Home Farm

1 ANDERSON CR
2 MEADOW WAY
3 HARCOURT
4 RECTORY GDNS

Rectory Farm

CAMBRIDGE RD

A14

Brickyard Farm

Hemingford Park

B1044

GODMANCHESTER

DVROVIGVTVM

Long Plantation

HILSDENS

KISBY AVE

LEGION WAY

CARDINAL WAY

A1198

Cardinal Distribution Park

Harcourt Farm

A14

Ridgeway Farm

DOVEHOUSE CL

Emmanuel Knoll Plantation

SAWTRY WAY

141
119

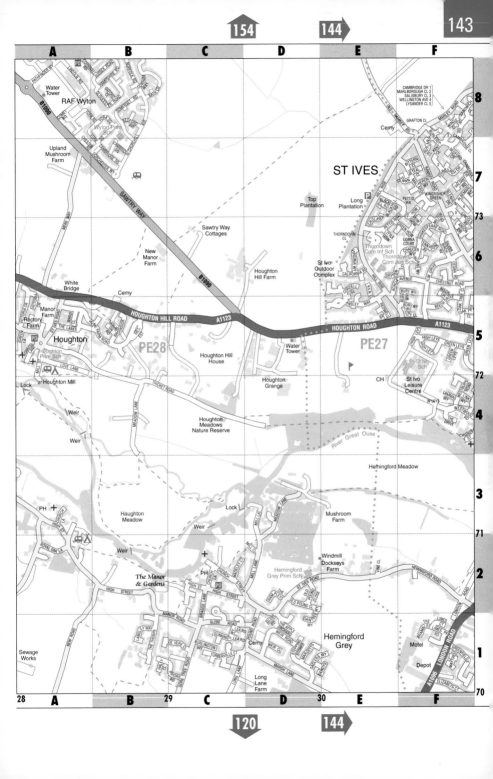

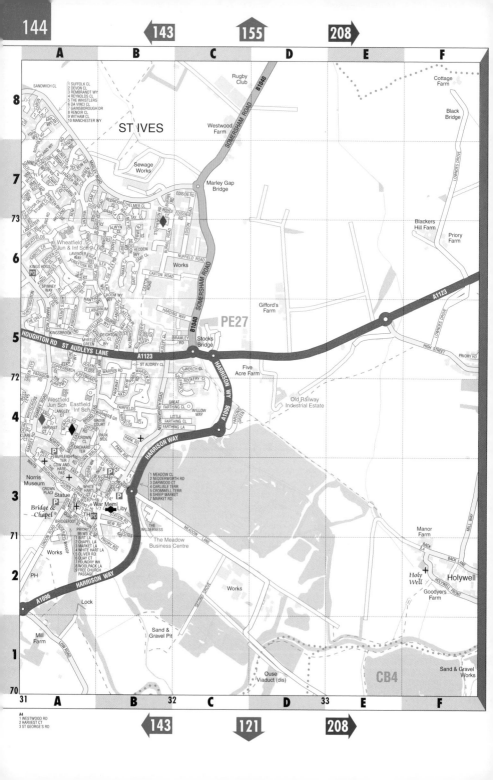

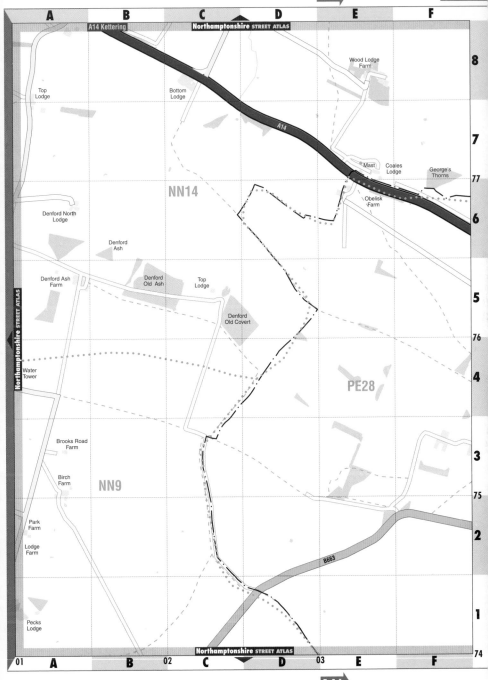

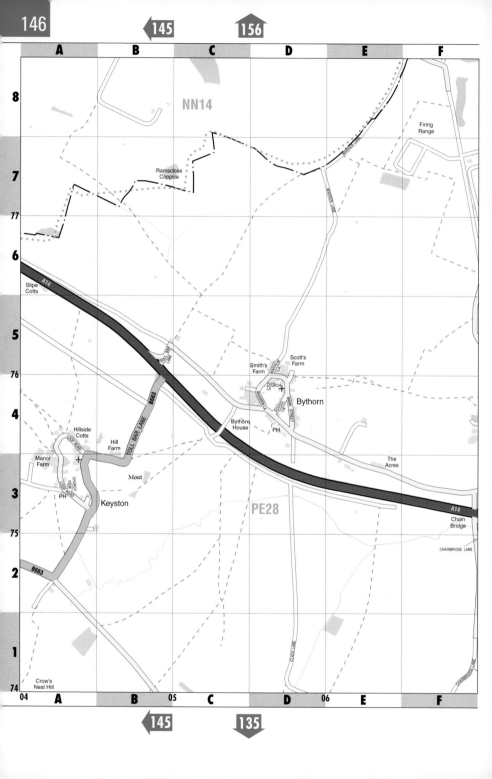

NN14

8

7

77

6

5

76

4

3

75

2

1

74

A

B

C

D

E

F

Ramsclose
Coppice

Firing
Range

WARREN LANE

WARREN LANE

A14

Slipe
Cotts

TOLL BAR
LANE

B663

TOLL BAR LANE

Smith's
Farm

Scott's
Farm

CHURCH
LA

Bythorn

MAIN STREET

WARREN LA

SCHOOL LA

Hillside
Cotts

Hill
Farm

Bythorn
House

PH

The
Acres

LOOP ROAD

Manor
Farm

CHURCH
VIEW ROAD

LOOP ROAD

PH

Keyston

Moat

PE28

A14

Chain
Bridge

CHAINBRIDGE LANE

B663

CLOCK LANE

CHAINBRIDGE LANE

Crow's
Nest Hill

04

A

B

05

C

D

06

E

F

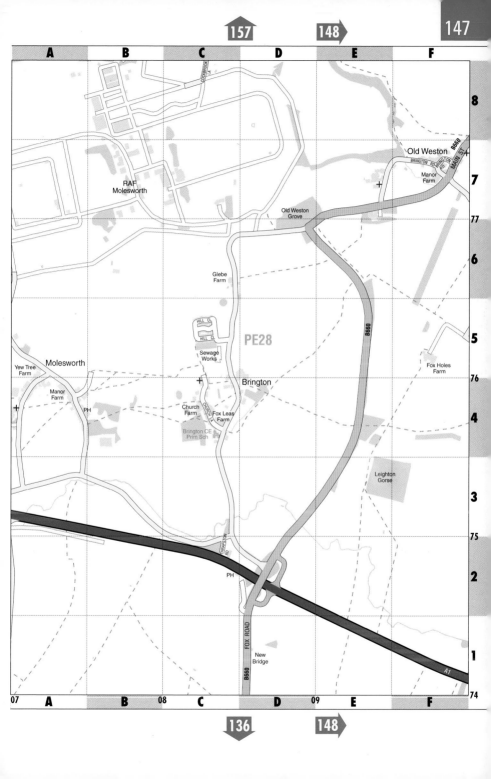

A B C D E F

8

COGBROOK LA

RAF
Molesworth

7

Old Weston

BRINGTON RD

BRISTOL CL

B660

MAIN ST

Manor
Farm

77

Old Weston
Grove

6

Glebe
Farm

B660

HILL CL

HILL CL

PE28

5

Molesworth

Yew Tree
Farm

Sewage
Works

Fox Holes
Farm

76

Manor
Farm

Brington

PH

Church
Farm

Fox Leas
Farm

CHURCH ST

4

Brington CE
Prim Sch

Leighton
Gorse

3

THRAPSTON RD

75

PH

2

FOX ROAD

New
Bridge

B660

A1

1

74

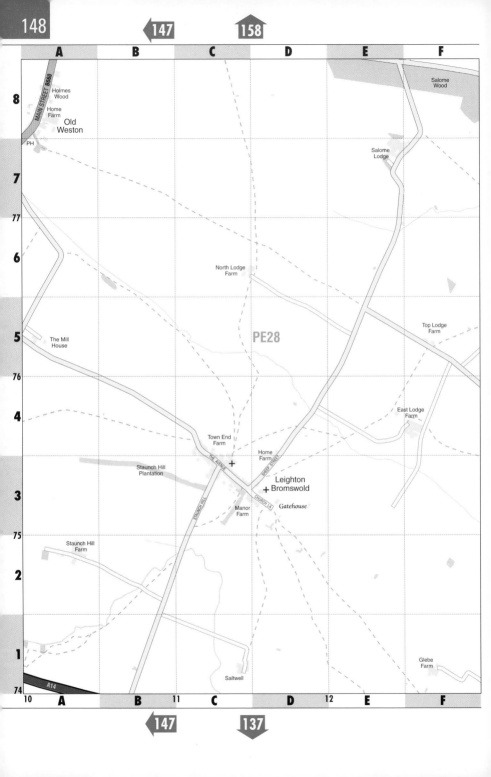

147
158

A **B** **C** **D** **E** **F**

MAIN STREET B660

Holmes
Wood

Home
Farm

Old
Weston

PH

Salome
Wood

Salome
Lodge

8

7

77

North Lodge
Farm

Top Lodge
Farm

6

PE28

The Mill
House

East Lodge
Farm

5

76

4

Town End
Farm

Home
Farm

THE AVENUE

STAUNCH HILL

SHED STREET

Staunch Hill
Plantation

Leighton
Bromswold

Gatehouse

3

Manor
Farm

CHURCH LA

75

Staunch Hill
Farm

2

1

Saltwell

Glebe
Farm

A14

74

10 **A** **B** 11 **C** **D** 12 **E** **F**

147
137

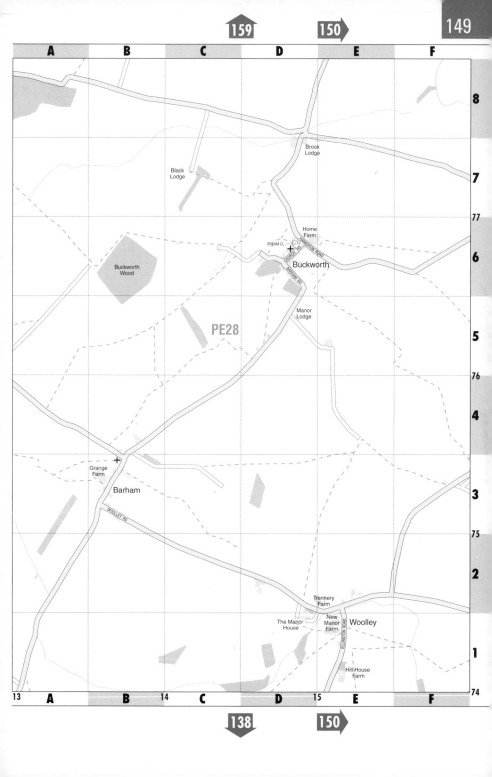

A   B   C   D   E   F

8

Brook
Lodge

7

Black
Lodge

77

Home
Farm

BRAM CL

CHURCH RD

ELLINGTON ROAD

Buckworth

6

Buckworth
Wood

BARHAM RD

Manor
Lodge

PE28

5

76

4

Grange
Farm

Barham

3

WOOLLEY RD

75

2

Trennery
Farm

New
Manor
Farm

Woolley

The Manor
House

Hill House
Farm

ELLINGTON ROAD

1

74

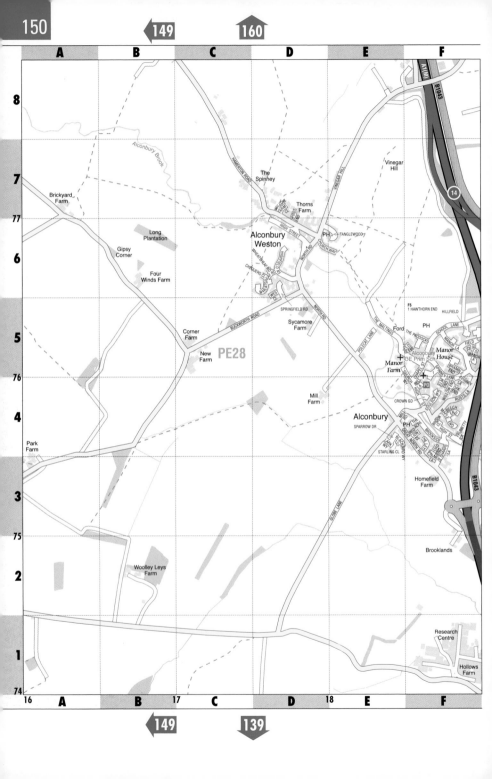

8

A B C D E F

7

Alconbury Brook

Brickyard
Farm

77

Hampton Road

The
Spinney

Thorns
Farm

Vinegar
Hill

14

Long
Plantation

Alconbury
Weston

PH TANGLEWOOD

6

Gipsy
Corner

WILLOW
ROAD

HIGH STREET

NORTH RD

CHURCH WAY

Four
Winds Farm

WHEATSHEAF CLOSE

CHEQUERS CLOSE

CLEAVERS WAY

WEST
CL

F5
1 HAWTHORN END HILLFIELD

SPRINGFIELD RD

Corner
Farm

BUCKWORTH ROAD

Sycamore
Farm

THE MALTINGS

Ford

PH

THE PADDOCKS

SCHOOL LANE

BRAMBLE

Manor
House

FIELD

MARSH

5

New
Farm

PE28

Alconbury
CE Prim Sch

Manor
Farm

SPINEY LANE

POLECAT LANE

NORTH RD

COLLEGE WY

CROWN GD

BRIDGE RD

BEECH

RUSSET RD

76

Mill
Farm

Alconbury

PH

SPARROW DR

BLACKBIRD WY

GREAT NORTH RD

STARLING CL

4

Park
Farm

Homefield
Farm

B1043

3

75

Brooklands

2

Woolley Leys
Farm

GLOBE LANE

1

Research
Centre

Hollows
Farm

74

16 A B 17 C D 18 E F

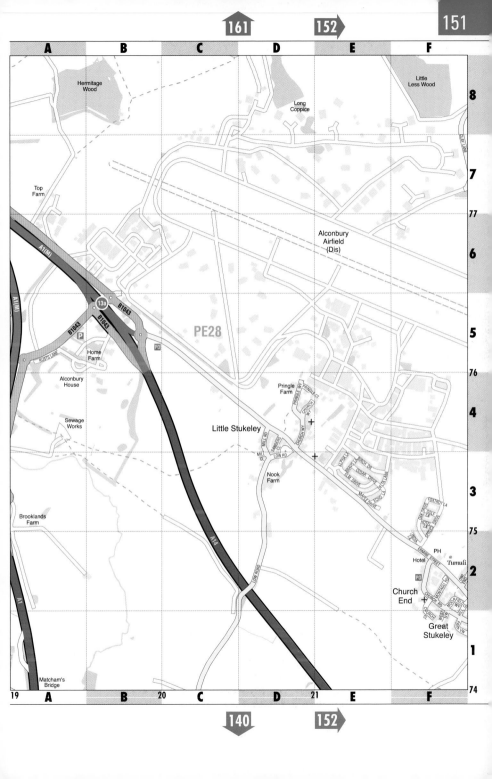

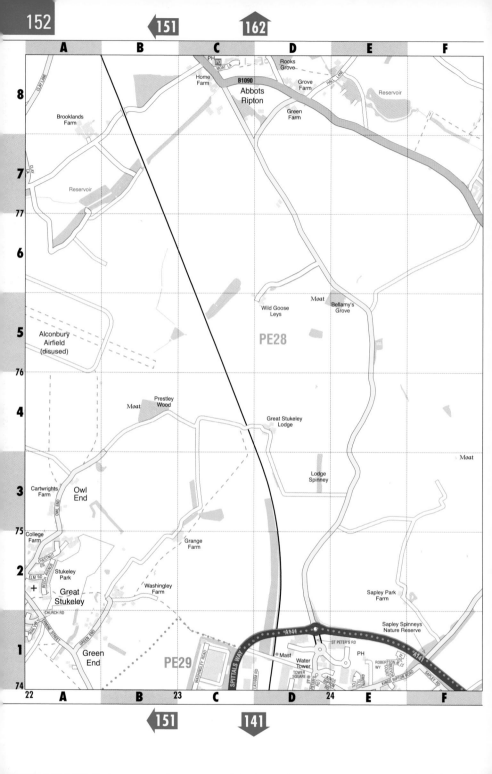

A B C D E F

8

7

77

6

5

76

4

3

75

2

1

74

Cliff Lane

Brooklands
Farm

Reservoir

OLIN

Alconbury
Airfield
(disused)

Cartwrights
Farm

Owl
End

OWL END

College
Farm

CHESTNUT
DR

ELM RD
BEECH DRIVE

+

Stukeley
Park

Great
Stukeley

CHURCH RD

PRESTON LANE STREET

GREEN RD

Green
End

PE29

PH
PO
MOAT LA.

Home
Farm

B1090

Abbots
Ripton

Rooks
Grove

Grove
Farm

Green
Farm

HALL LANE

Reservoir

Moat

Wild Goose
Leys

Bellamy's
Grove

PE28

Prestley
Wood

Moat

Great Stukeley
Lodge

Lodge
Spinney

Moat

Grange
Farm

Washingley
Farm

SPITTALS WAY

WASHINGLEY ROAD

LATHAM RD

A141

Sapley Park
Farm

Sapley Spinneys
Nature Reserve

A141

A1141

Mast

Water
Tower

TOWER
SQUARE

ST PETER'S RD

ST PETER'S RD

KINGS
RD

GREEN
END

ROBERTSON
WY

PH

KING RIPTON ROAD

SAPLEY RD

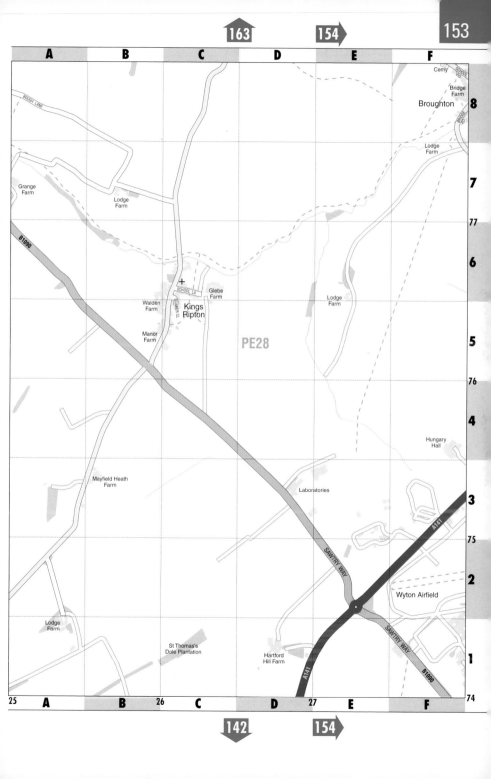

A B C D E F

BOUGH LANE

Cemy
SCHOOL LA

Bridge
Farm

Broughton 8

Lodge
Farm

7

Grange
Farm

Lodge
Farm

77

6

School La

+

Glebe
Farm

Lodge
Farm

Walden
Farm

**Kings
Ripton**

QUAKER CL

Manor
Farm

PE28 5

76

4

Hungary
Hall

Mayfield Heath
Farm

Laboratories

3

A141

75

SAWTRY WAY

2

Wyton Airfield

Lodge
Farm

SAWTRY WAY

St Thomas's
Dole Plantation

Hartford
Hill Farm

B1090

A141

1

25 A B 26 C D 27 E F 74

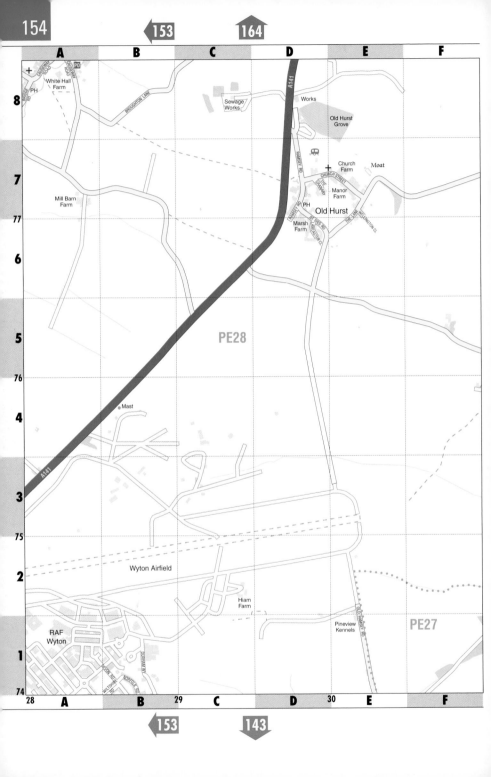

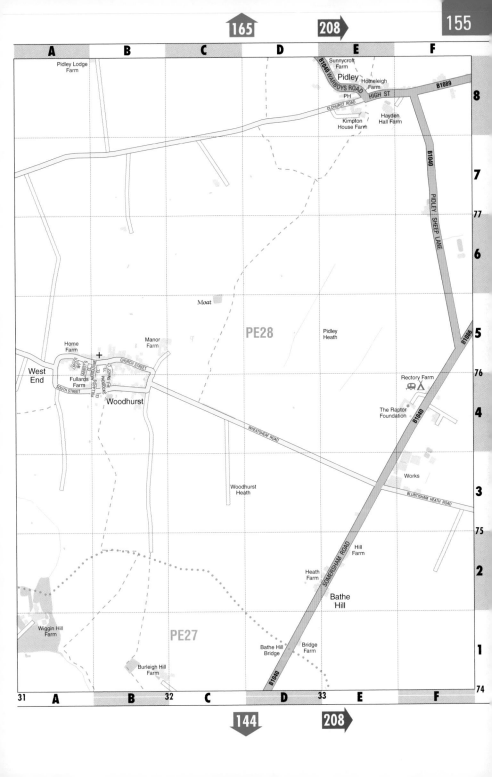

A   **B**   **C**   **D**   **E**   **F**

Pidley Lodge Farm

Sunnycroft Farm

Pidley

Homeleigh Farm

B1040 WARBOYS ROAD

HIGH ST

PH

OLDHURST ROAD

Kimpton House Farm

Hayden Hall Farm

B1089

B1040

8

7

77

PIDLEY SHEEP LANE

6

Moat

PE28

Pidley Heath

5

B1088

Home Farm

Manor Farm

CHURCH STREET

LAMBS LANE

THE PADDOCKS

LIONS CL

West End

Fullards Farm

SOUTH STREET

Woodhurst

Rectory Farm

The Raptor Foundation

B1040

76

4

WHEATSHEAF ROAD

Works

Woodhurst Heath

BLUNTISHAM HEATH ROAD

3

75

Hill Farm

SOMERSHAM ROAD

Heath Farm

Bathe Hill

2

Wiggin Hill Farm

PE27

Bathe Hill Bridge

Bridge Farm

Burleigh Hill Farm

B1040

1

74

31   **A**   **B**   32   **C**   **D**   33   **E**   **F**

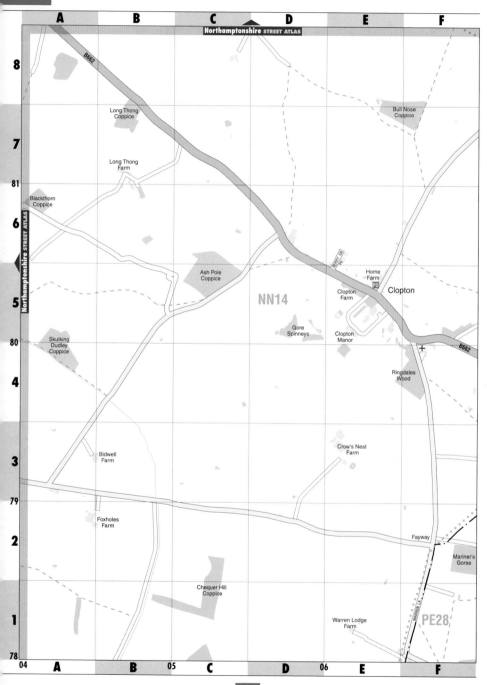

B662

Long Thong
Coppice

Bull Nose
Coppice

Long Thong
Farm

Blackthorn
Coppice

Ash Pole
Coppice

NN14

Home
Farm

Clopton

Clopton
Farm

Gore
Spinneys

Clopton
Manor

Skulking
Dudley
Coppice

Ringdales
Wood

B662

Bidwell
Farm

Crow's Nest
Farm

Foxholes
Farm

Fayway

Mariner's
Gorse

Chequer Hill
Coppice

PE28

Warren Lodge
Farm

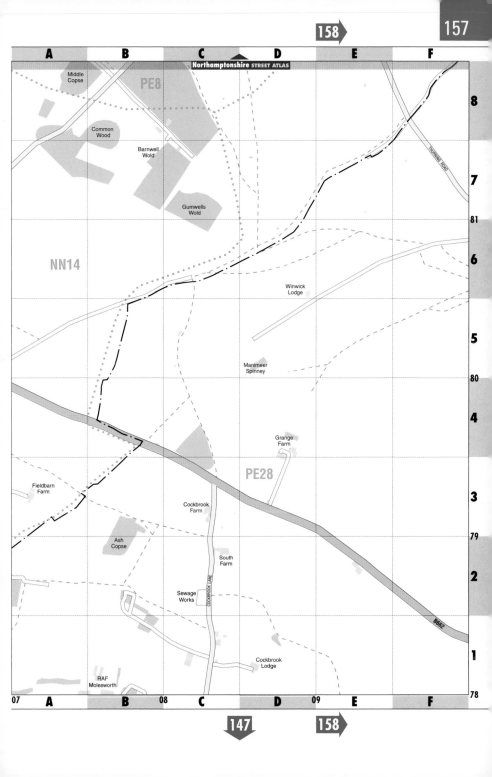

158

Northamptonshire STREET ATLAS

Middle Copse

PE8

Common Wood

Barnwell Wold

Gumwells Wold

NN14

Winwick Lodge

Manimeer Spinney

Grange Farm

PE28

Fieldbarn Farm

Cockbrook Farm

Ash Copse

South Farm

COCKBROOK LANE

Sewage Works

Cockbrook Lodge

RAF Molesworth

THRAPSTON ROAD

B662

147
158

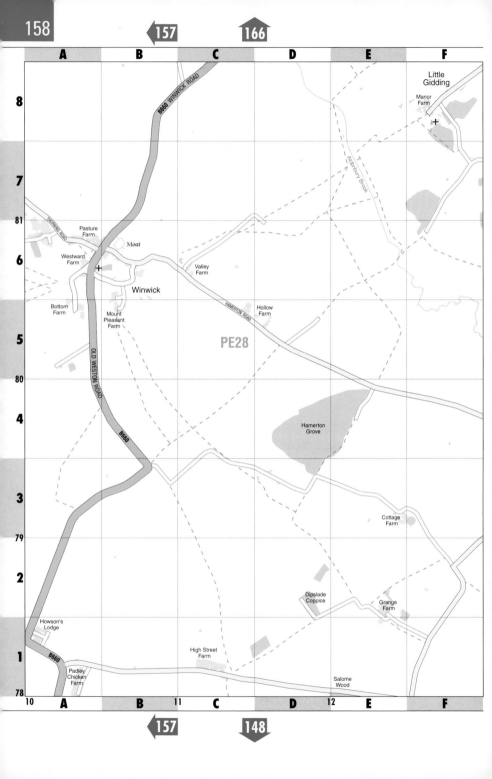

157
166

Little Gidding

Manor Farm

B660 WINWICK ROAD

Alconbury Brook

PASTURE ROAD

Pasture Farm

Moat

Westward Farm

Winwick

Valley Farm

HAMERTON ROAD

Hollow Farm

Bottom Farm

Mount Pleasant Farm

PE28

OLD WESTON ROAD

Hamerton Grove

B660

Cottage Farm

Dipslade Coppice

Grange Farm

Howson's Lodge

B660

High Street Farm

Padley Chicken Farm

Salome Wood

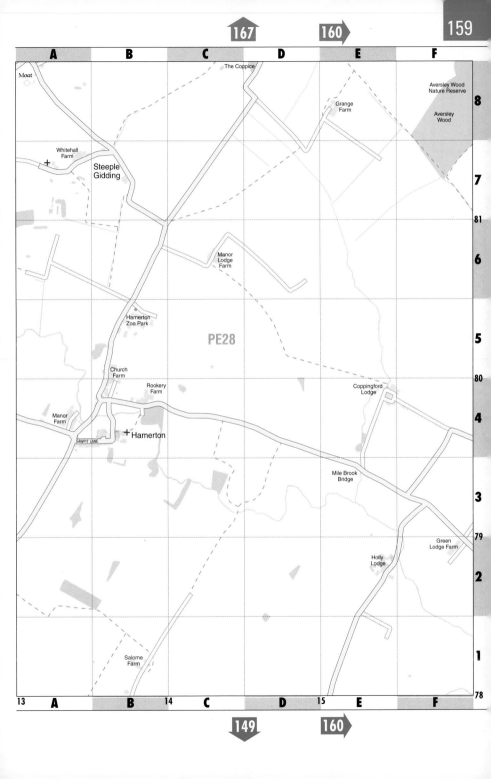

Moat

The Coppice

Aversley Wood
Nature Reserve

8

Grange
Farm

Aversley
Wood

Whitehall
Farm

Steeple
Gidding

7

81

Manor
Lodge
Farm

6

Hamerton
Zoo Park

PE28

5

80

Church
Farm

Coppingford
Lodge

Rookery
Farm

4

Manor
Farm

SAWPIT LANE

Hamerton

Mile Brook
Bridge

3

79

Green
Lodge Farm

Holly
Lodge

2

Salome
Farm

1

78

A B C D E F

8

Aversley
Wood

Whitehall

Whitehall
Farm

ST JUDITH'S LANE

B1043

A1(M)

B1090

7

Manorial
Earthworks

Brickyard
Farm

Archers Wood
Farm

Archers Wood
Nature Reserve

81

Archer's
Wood

ST JUDITH'S LANE

6

Hill
Top Farm

Hermitage
Grove

Motel

PE28

5

Mast

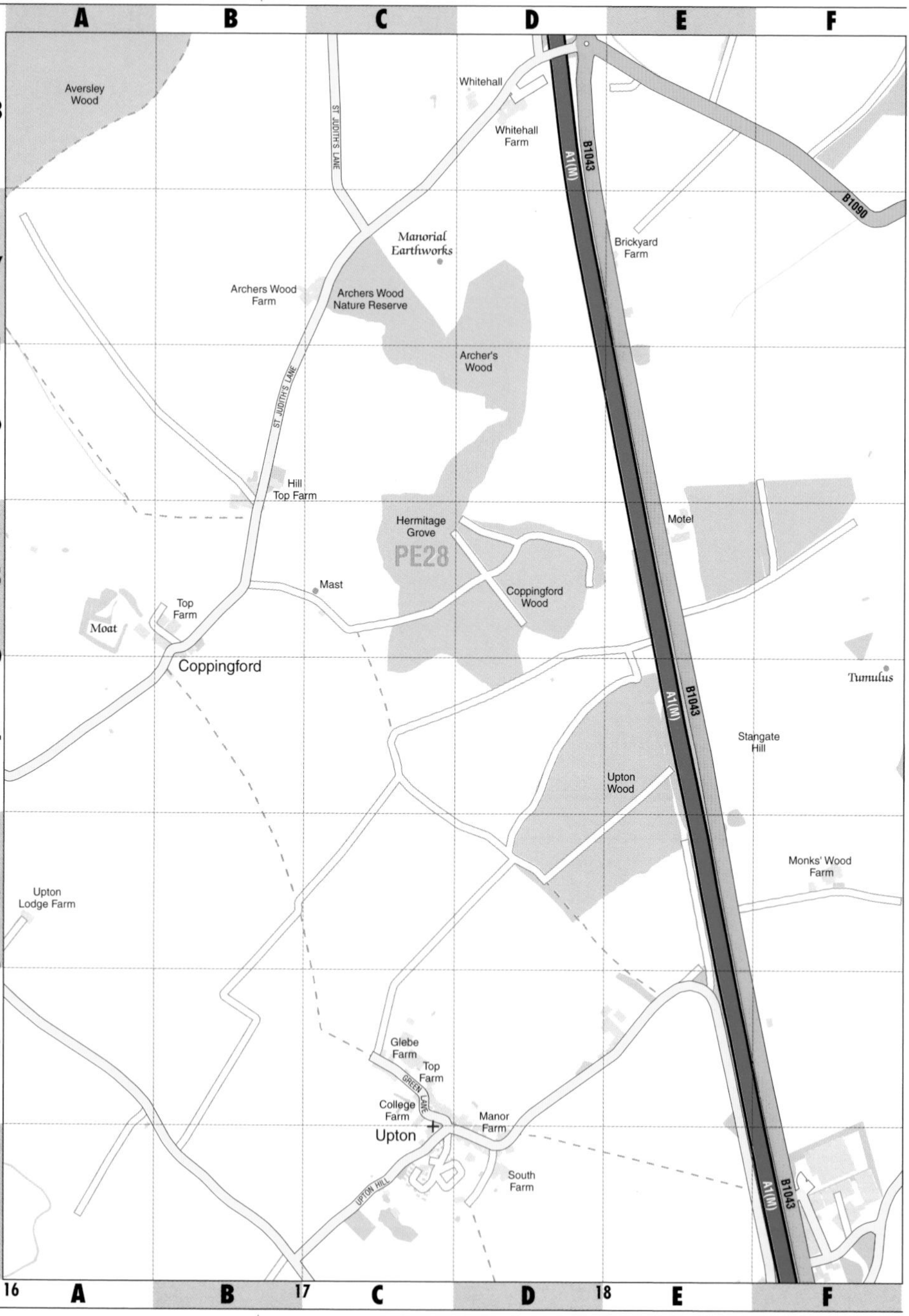

Coppingford
Wood

Top
Farm

Moat

80

Coppingford

Tumulus

A1(M) B1043

4

Stangate
Hill

Upton
Wood

3

Upton
Lodge Farm

Monks' Wood
Farm

79

2

Glebe
Farm

Top
Farm

GREEN LANE

College
Farm

Manor
Farm

Upton

South
Farm

UPTON HILL

A1(M)

B1043

1

78

16   **A**   **B**   **17**   **C**   **D**   **18**   **E**   **F**

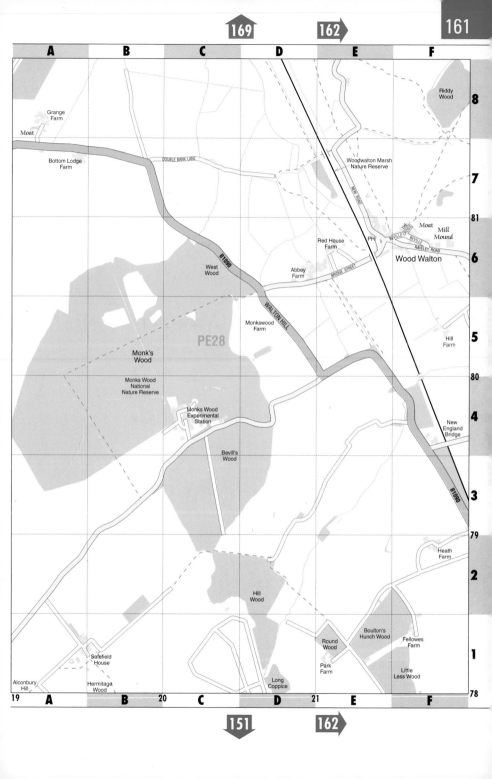

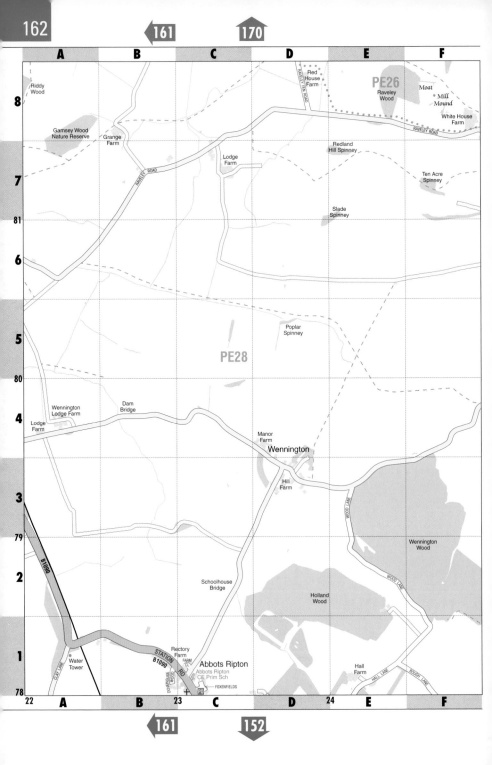

161
170

PE26

Riddy Wood

Moat

Mill Mound

Gamsey Wood Nature Reserve

Grange Farm

Raveley Wood

White House Farm

RAVELEY ROAD

Red House Farm

Redland Hill Spinney

Ten Acre Spinney

RAVELEY ROAD

Lodge Farm

Slade Spinney

Poplar Spinney

PE28

Wennington Lodge Farm

Dam Bridge

Lodge Farm

Manor Farm

Wennington

Hill Farm

WOOD LANE

Wennington Wood

B1090

Schoolhouse Bridge

Holland Wood

WOOD LANE

CLAY LANE

Water Tower

STATION RD

B1090

Rectory Farm

FARM

Abbots Ripton

Abbots Ripton CE Prim Sch

DOVEHOUSE WOOD

PO

FOXENFIELDS

Hall Farm

HALL LANE

BOUGH LANE

161
152

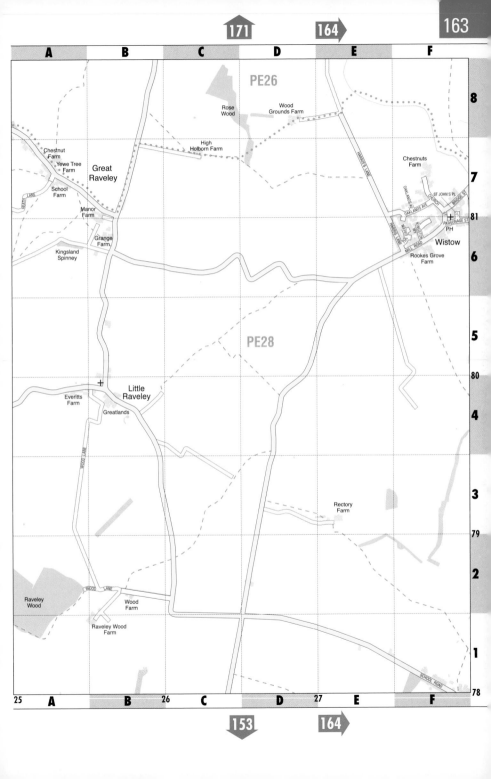

163
172

A **B** **C** **D** **E** **F**

8

Hill
Farm

Wistow Wood
WISTOW FEN LANE

Warboys
Wood

B1040

Toll
Farm

7

The
Spinney

Humbrill's
Farm

STATION ROAD

BRIDGE ST

Manor
Farm

MANOR ST

81

Fenside
Farm

6

Wiggs
Farm

ST MARY'S GN

RAMSEY ROAD

JUBILEE AVE

SECOND AV

THIRD AV

5

Pelican
Farm

PE28

KNOWLES
AV

GARNER
AV

Warboys
CP Sch

SCHOOL ROAD

GEORGE LN

SPINNEY CL

B1040

HUMBERDALE WAY

MEADOW WY
CLACK LN

FELT LN

SOLD PITS

HIGH STREET

THROCKMORTON

+ Library

PH

FARRIERS
WY

80

Manor
Farm +

Sports
Ground

WELLINGTON WY

CHURCH RD

WK BECKS

STIRLING WY

LEA BROOKS
CL

LANCASTER CL

4

Cemy

3

Tithe
Farm

B1040

Water
Tower

79

2

Mast

Ballantines
Farm

Oakleigh
Farm

Warboys Airfield
Industrial Estate

NEW RD

1

Moat

Manor
Farm

Illings
Farm

+

LUMB'S LA

LUMB'S LANE LA

Bull
Bridge

A141

Holborn
Farm

BROUGHTON LANE

78

28 A B 29 C D 30 E F

163
154

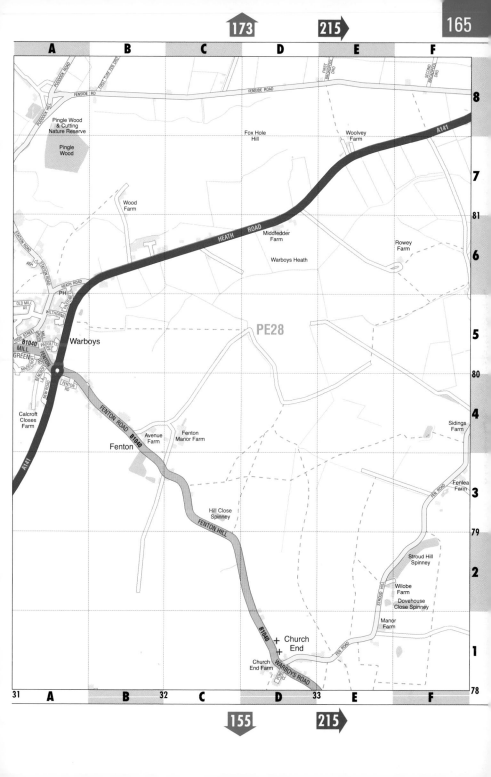

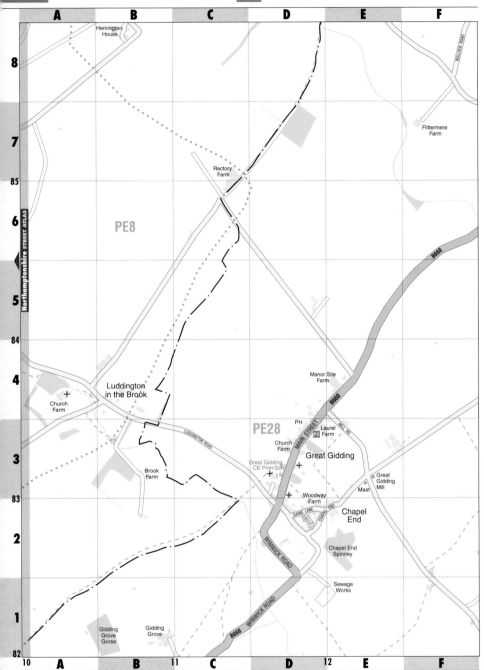

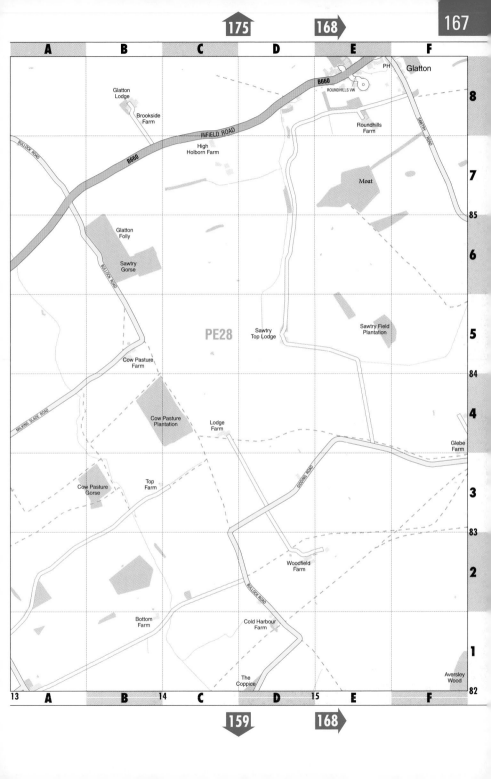

	A	B	C	D	E	F	

Glatton Lodge

Brookside Farm

B660

Glatton

PH

ROUNDHILLS VW

B660

INFIELD ROAD

High Holborn Farm

Roundhills Farm

8

BULLOCK ROAD

SAWTRY ROAD

7

Moat

85

Glatton Folly

Sawtry Gorse

BULLOCK ROAD

6

PE28

Sawtry Top Lodge

Sawtry Field Plantation

5

Cow Pasture Farm

84

MILKING SLADE ROAD

Cow Pasture Plantation

Lodge Farm

4

Glebe Farm

Cow Pasture Gorse

Top Farm

GROOME ROAD

3

83

Woodfield Farm

2

BULLOCK ROAD

Bottom Farm

Cold Harbour Farm

1

The Coppice

Aversley Wood

82

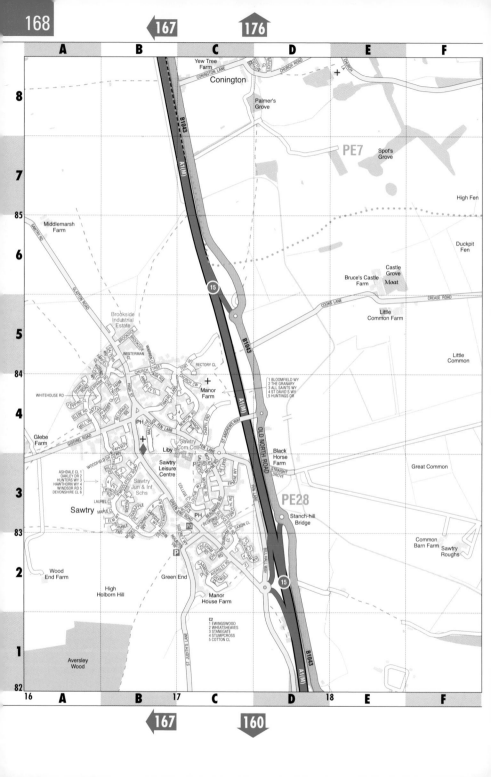

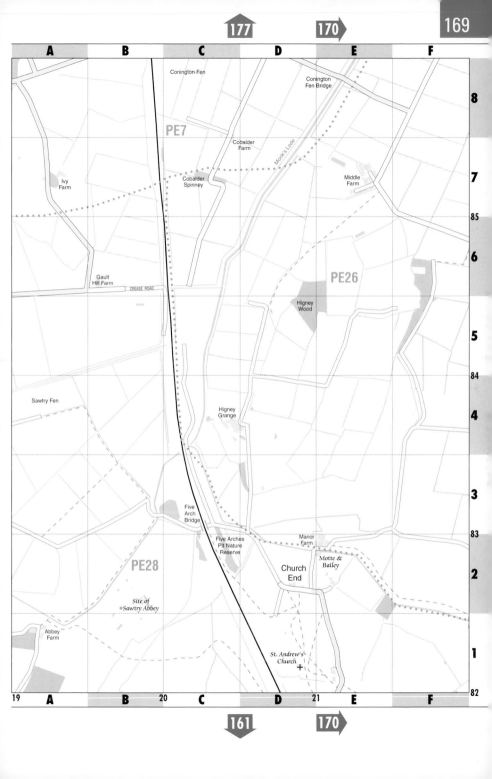

A   B   C   D   E   F

8

Conington Fen

Conington
Fen Bridge

PE7

Cobalder
Farm

7

Ivy
Farm

Cobalder
Spinney

Monk's Lode

Middle
Farm

85

6

Gault
Hill Farm

CREASE ROAD

PE26

Higney
Wood

5

84

Sawtry Fen

Higney
Grange

4

3

Five
Arch
Bridge

83

Five Arches
Pit Nature
Reserve

Manor
Farm

PE28

Motte &
Bailey

Church
End

2

Site of
Sawtry Abbey

Abbey
Farm

1

St. Andrew's
Church

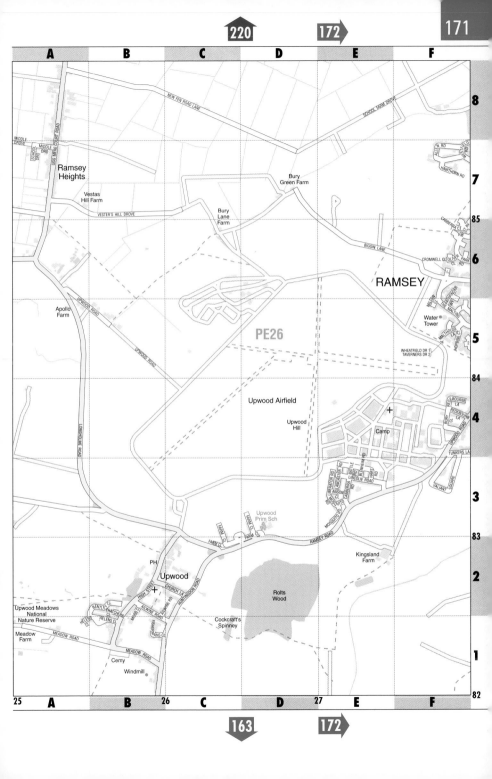

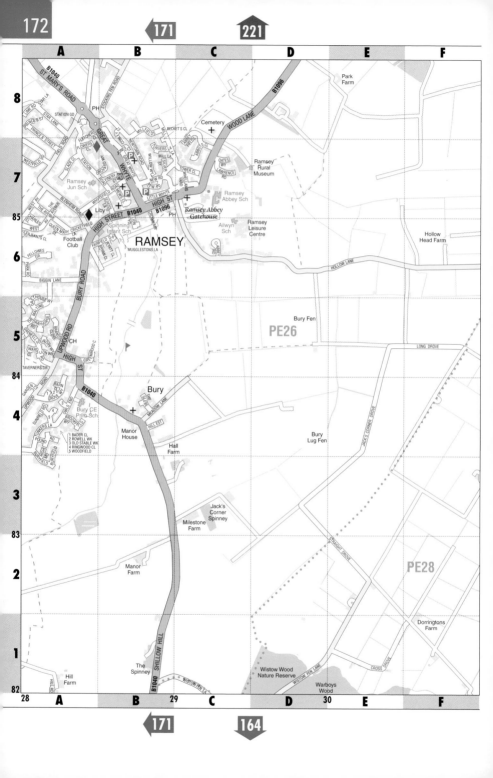

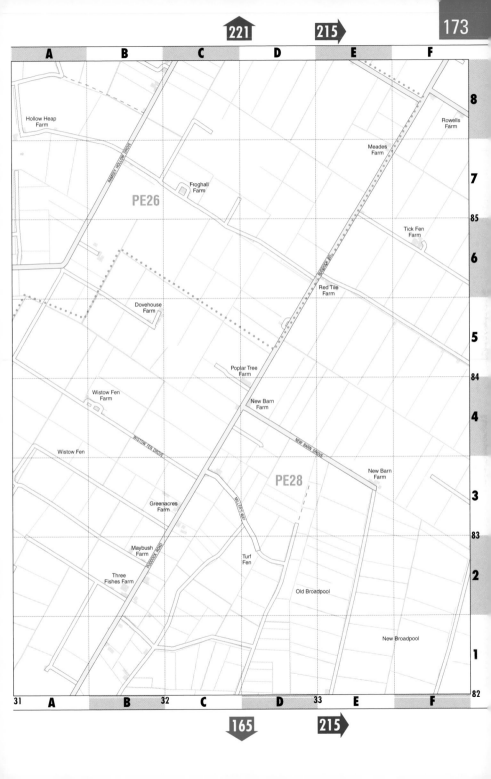

Hollow Heap Farm

Rowells Farm

Meades Farm

RAMSEY HOLLOW DROVE

PE26

Froghall Farm

Tick Fen Farm

Dovehouse Farm

Red Tile Farm

BIDDOCK RD.

Poplar Tree Farm

New Barn Farm

Wistow Fen Farm

Wistow Fen

WISTOW FEN DROVE

NEW BARN DROVE

New Barn Farm

PE28

Greenacres Farm

MILLERS WAY

Maybush Farm

PUDDOCK ROAD

Three Fishes Farm

Turf Fen

Old Broadpool

New Broadpool

8 7 85 6 5 84 4 3 83 2 1 82

A B C D E F

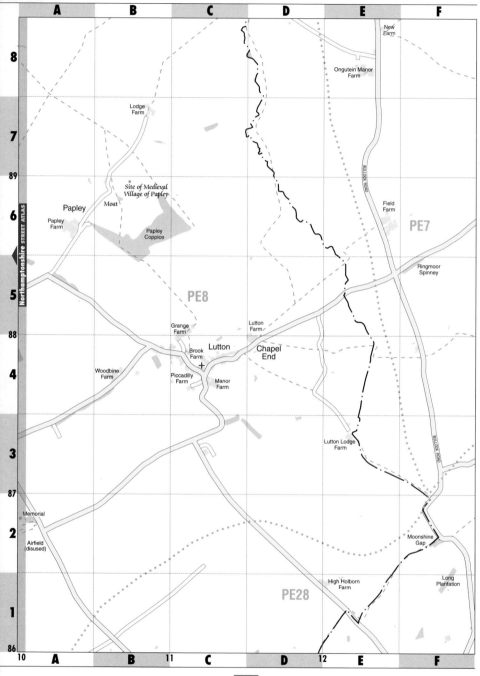

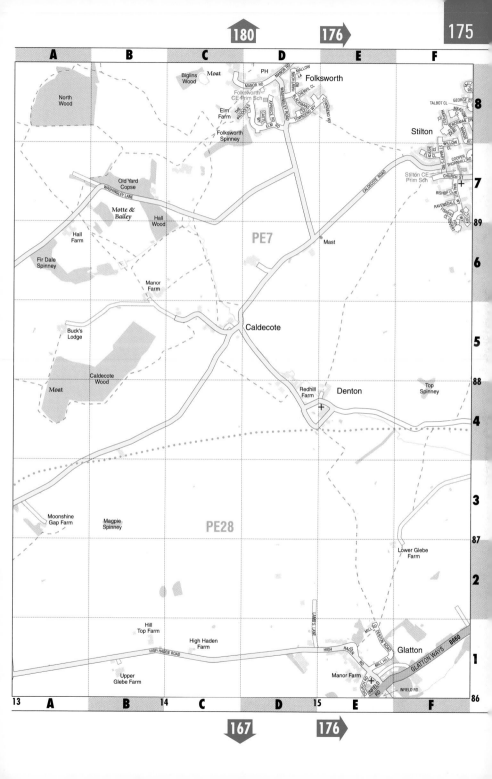

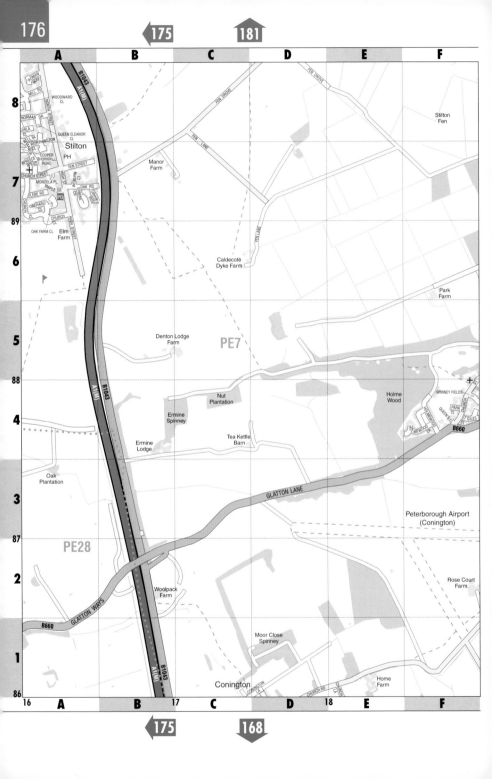

175
181

A   B   C   D   E   F

8

Stilton
PH

7

89

Oak Farm Cl   Elm Farm

6

5

PE7

88

4

3

PE28

87

2

1

86

16   **A**   **B**   17   **C**   **D**   18   **E**   **F**

B1043
A1(M)

WOODWARD CL
NORTH STREET
MILL RD
GALA CL
BELL CL
NORMAN DR
QUEEN ELEANOR CL
WORTHINGTON CL
COOPER THORNHILL ROAD
FEN STREET
CHURCH STREET
MONDELA PL
MAPLE DR
GLEBE RD
OAK RD
CR DHAPPING
OAK FARM CL
CHURCH CL
CHURCH
ORCHARD CL
HIGH STREET

Manor Farm

FEN DROVE
FEN LANE
FEN LANE

Stilton Fen

Caldecote Dyke Farm

Park Farm

Denton Lodge Farm

Nut Plantation

Ermine Spinney

Holme Wood

SPINNEY FIELDS
PARK CL
HOLBROOK DR
MEWBURN DR
QUEEN'S CL
CHURCH
ST GILES
B660

Ermine Lodge

Tea Kettle Barn

Oak Plantation

GLATTON LANE

Peterborough Airport (Conington)

GLATTON WAYS

Woolpack Farm

Rose Court Farm

B660

Moor Close Spinney

A1(M)
B1043

LORINGTON

CHURCH RD
CHURCH RD

Home Farm

Conington

175
168

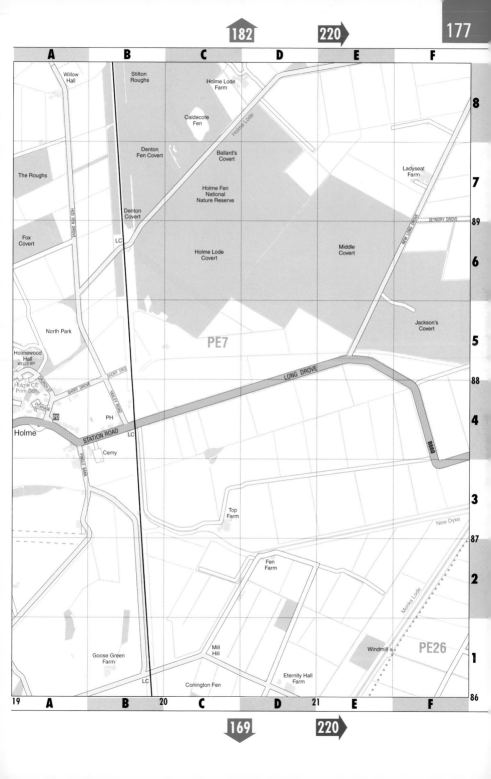

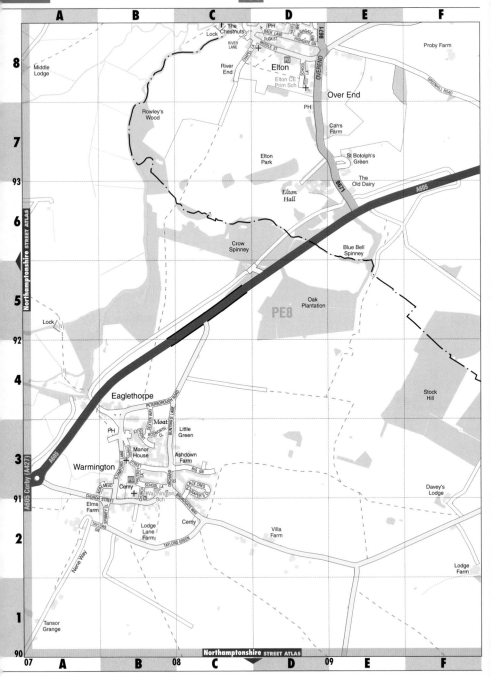

183

A   B   C   D   E   F

Middle
Lodge

Lock
The
Chestnuts

RIVER
LANE

PH
BACK LANE
HIGHGATE GN
DUCK ST
MIDDLE ST
PO

Proby Farm

OVEREND

GREENHILL ROAD

B671

River
End

Elton

Elton CE
Prim Sch

Over End

Rowley's
Wood

PH

Carrs
Farm

Elton
Park

St Botolph's
Green

B671

The
Old Dairy

A605

Elton
Hall

Crow
Spinney

Blue Bell
Spinney

PE8

Oak
Plantation

Stock
Hill

Lock

Eaglethorpe

PETERBOROUGH ROAD

Moat

PH

Manor
House

Little
Green

BUNTING'S LANE

Ashdown
Farm

Warmington

BIG GN

Davey's
Lodge

PO

Cemy

SCHOOL LA

ORCHARD

Warmington
Sch

CHURCH STREET

Elms
Farm

Cemy

Villa
Farm

Lodge
Lane
Farm

TAYLORS GREEN

Nene Way

Lodge
Farm

Tansor
Grange

Northamptonshire STREET ATLAS

A605 Corby (A427)

Northamptonshire STREET ATLAS

8

7

93

6

5

92

4

3

91

2

1

90

07   A   B   08   C   D   09   E   F

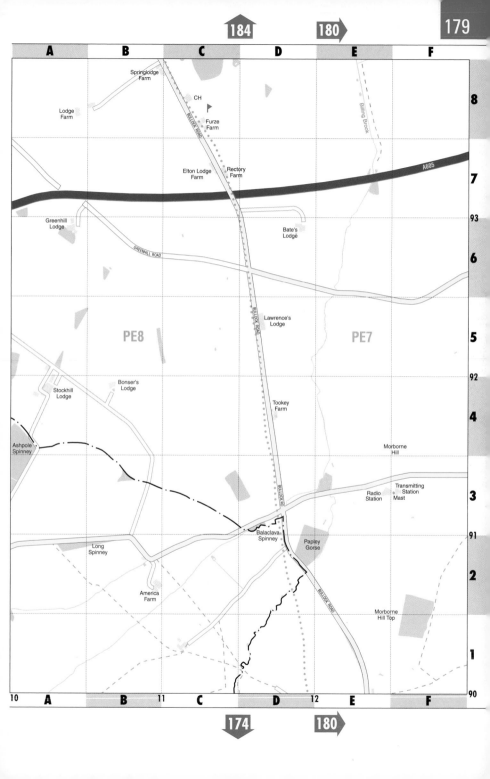

179
185

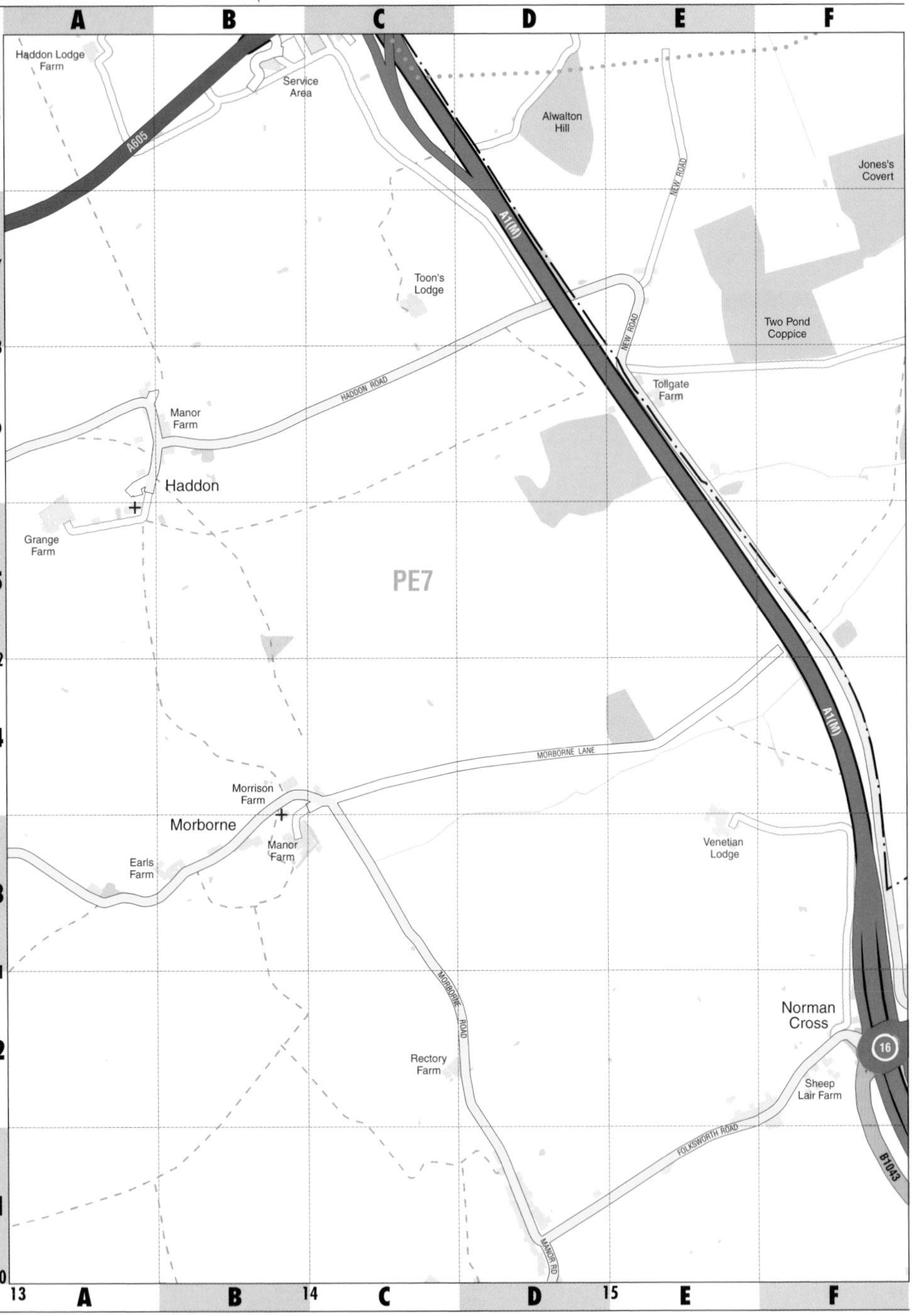

	A	B	C	D	E	F

8

Haddon Lodge Farm

Service Area

A605

Alwalton Hill

Jones's Covert

A1(M)

7

Toon's Lodge

NEW ROAD

Two Pond Coppice

93

HADDON ROAD

Manor Farm

Tollgate Farm

6

Haddon +

Grange Farm

PE7

5

92

A1(M)

4

MORBORNE LANE

Morrison Farm

Morborne +

Earls Farm

Manor Farm

Venetian Lodge

3

91

MORBORNE ROAD

Norman Cross

16

2

Rectory Farm

Sheep Lair Farm

FOLKSWORTH ROAD

B1043

90

MANOR RD

1

13	A	B	14	C	D	15	E	F

179
175

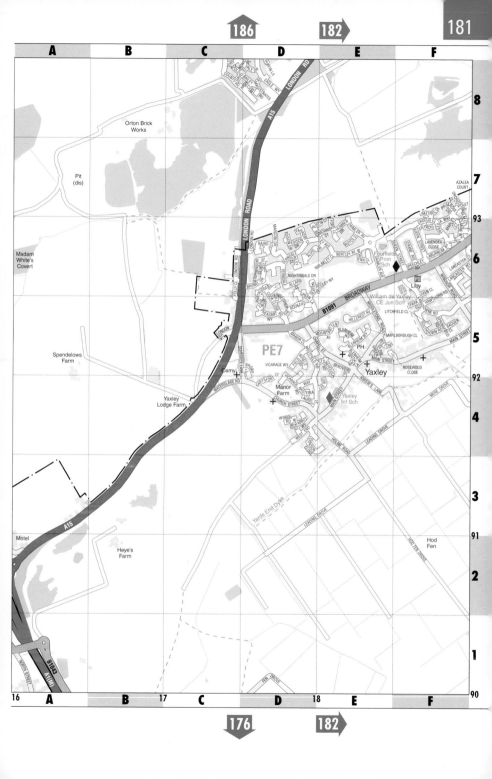

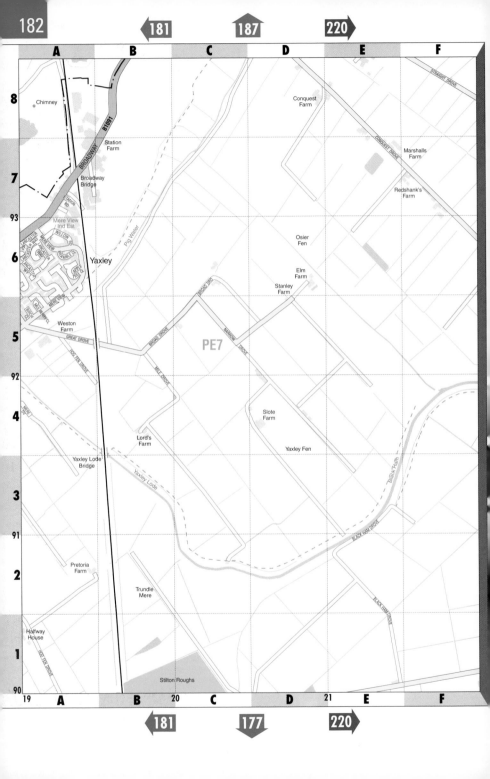

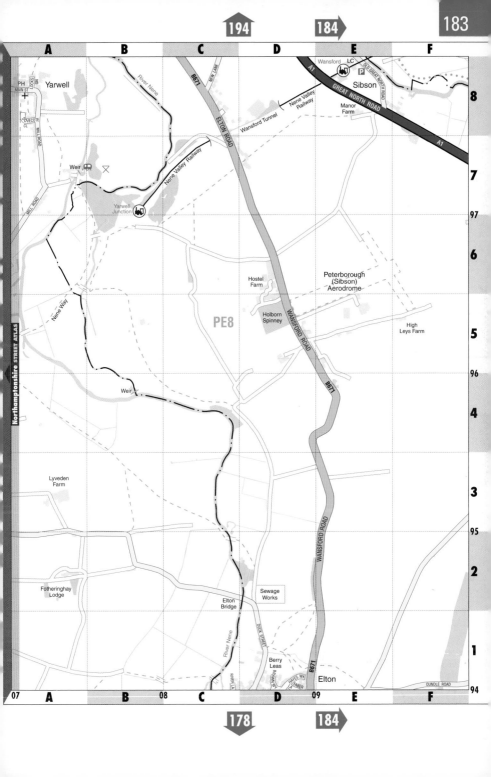

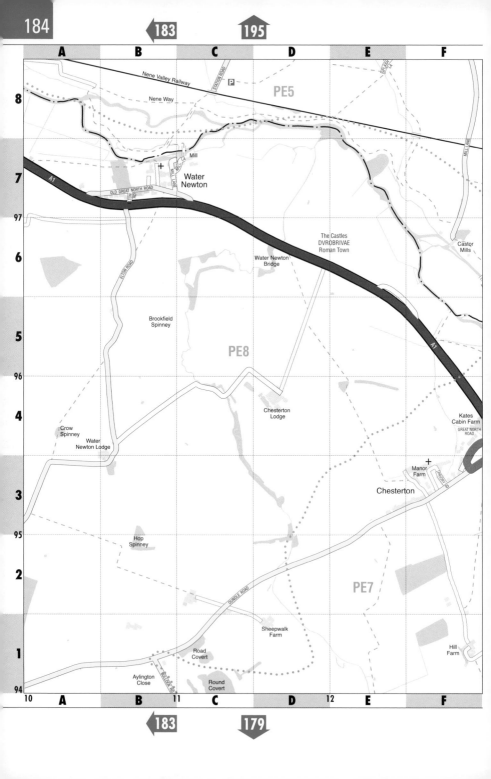

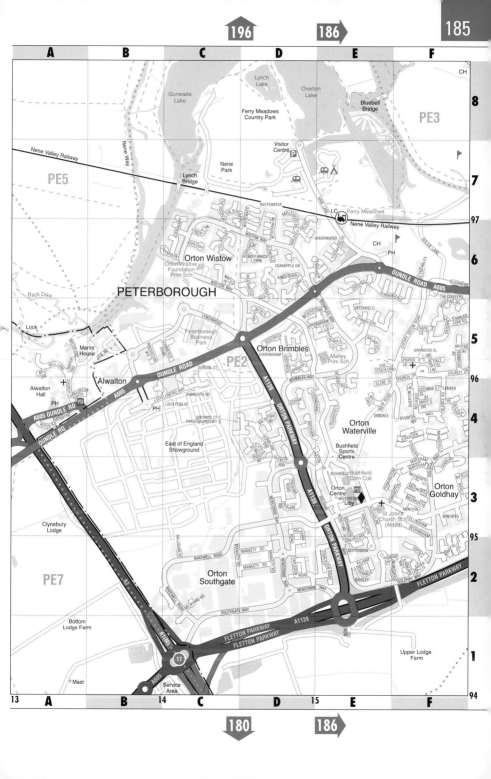

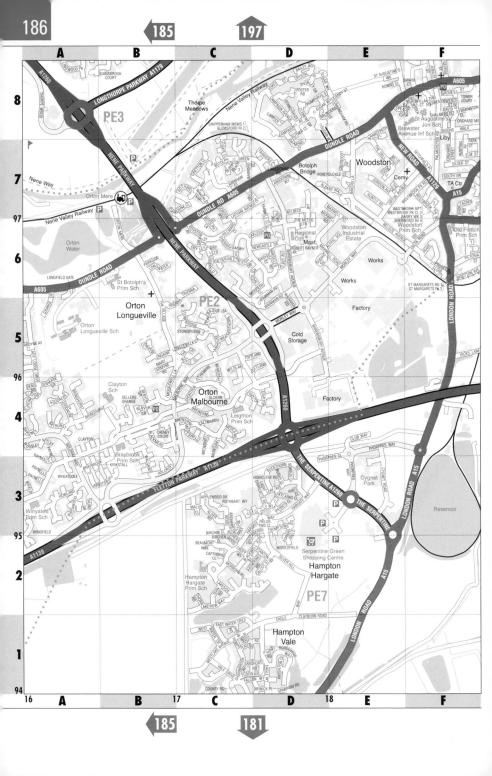

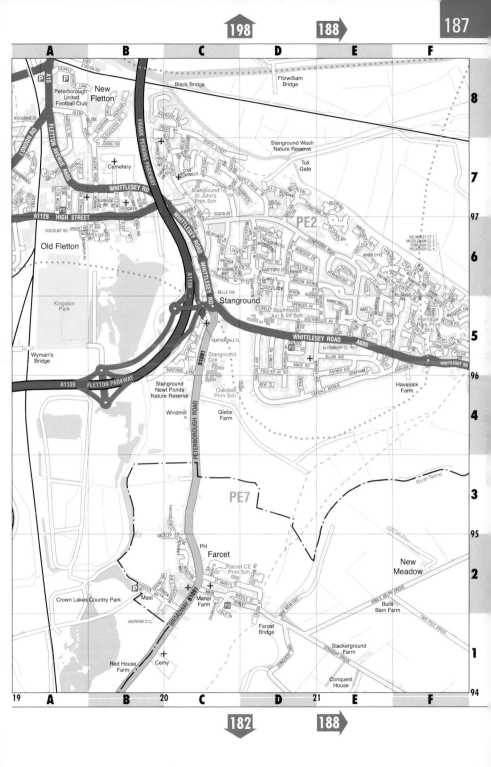

A B C D E F

8

New Fletton

P A15 P CRIPPLE SIDINGS LANE
EAST STATION RD
Black Bridge
Fitzwilliam Bridge

Peterborough United Football Club
WOODBINE ST

GLEB2

FRANK PERKINS PARKWAY

RIVERSIDE ROAD
RIDGE WY
NORTH STREET
Stanground Wash Nature Reserve

Toll Gate

7

LONDON RD
FLETTON AVENUE A605
FAIRFIELD RD
GLEBE RD
SLOUGHTON DRIVE
SLOUGHTON RD
ST JOHNS RD
Cemetery
BEECH
CHURCH
STAN DOWLING CT.
THISTLE DRIVE
CURLEW
MERGAN CL BECK CL
REDWIN
LONGTOWNE WAY
CELT

WHITTLESEY RD
QUEENS ROAD
KINGS RD
Stanground St John's Prim Sch
SOUTH ST

97

A1129 HIGH STREET
VISCOUNT RD
KNIGHT MS
MONARCH
FLEET
TUCKER'S YD
WHITTLESEY ROAD
STUART CL
DEXTON
WOODHURST PL
WOODGATE CL
WINDSOR DR
CONEYGREE ROAD
KINGS DYKE
HEMINGFORD CL
NENE

PE2

HELMSLEY CT 1
MIDDLEHAM CL 2
OXBURGH CL 3
PECKOVER CL 4

6

Old Fletton

WHITTLESEY ROAD
A1139
BELLE VUE
ANDREA CL
BYTHORN WAY
THRAPLING
HARTFORD CT
SHELTON RD
HERON CL
ST WELLS CT 1
Liby
Stanground
SPENCER AV
MARY WALSHAM CL
DECOY CL
EASTREA CL
Heritage Park Prim Sch

HEATHERDALE CL
STUKELEY CL
BYRON CL
SOUTHFIELDS AV
HARL
FRAMLINGHAM CL

5

Kingston Park

A1139 FLETTON PARKWAY
BUNTINGS LANE
B1091
Stanground Coll
Southfields Jun & Inf Sch
SYDNEY RD
CENTRAL
PO 1
ALCONBURY CL
MACE RD
ALLAN AVE
RAYNER AVE
GRAHAM
WHITTLESEY ROAD A605
Havelock Farm

Wyman's Bridge
Stanground Newt Ponds Nature Reserve
Oakdale Prim Sch
OAKDALE AVE
POULTER RD
BEW CL
OAKDALE AVENUE

96

Windmill
PETERBOROUGH ROAD
Glebe Farm

4

PE7
River Nene

3

95

THROSTLE NEST
GAZELEY
LAWRENCE
PH
Farcet

New Meadow

2

P
BROADWAY B1091
THROSTLE NEST WY
ST MARY'S CL
ST MARY'S ST
Farcet CE Prim Sch
MAIN
MIDDLE ST
STREET
KINGS DELPH DRIVE
TWO POLE DROVE

Crown Lakes Country Park
Mast
Manor Farm
CHURCH RD
PO
FIELD TR
Bulls Barn Farm

ANDREWE'S CL
Farcet Bridge
NEW MOW DRO
Slackerground Farm
STRAIGHT DROVE

1

Red House Farm
Cemy
CONQUEST
Conquest House

19 A B 20 C D 21 E F 94

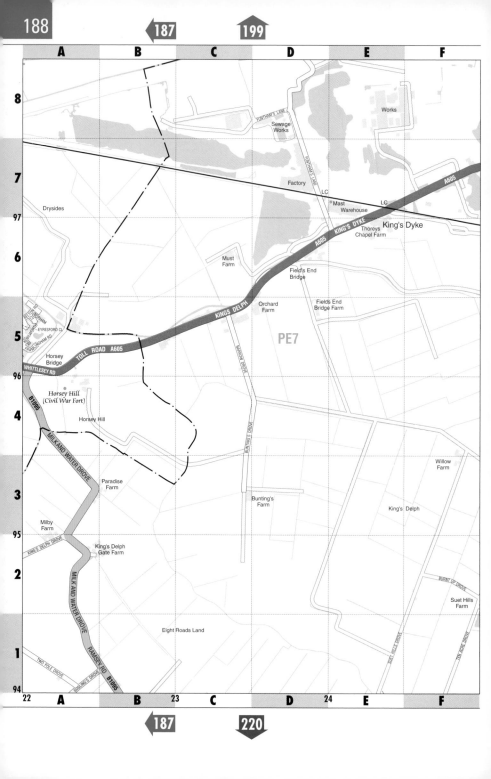

A B C D E F

8

7

97

6

5

96

4

3

95

2

1

94

22 23 24

Works

FUNTHAM'S LANE

Sewage Works

Factory

LC

Mast Warehouse

LC

A605

King's Dyke

KING'S DYKE

Thoreys Chapel Farm

King's Dyke

Drysides

Must Farm

Field's End Bridge

KINGS DELPH

Orchard Farm

Fields End Bridge Farm

PE7

TOLL ROAD A605

Horsey Bridge

BECTON GINGHAM
NEW DOVE
EYRESFORD CL
PEARL
GINGHAM RD

WHITTLESEY RD

NARROW DROVE

Horsey Hill (Civil War Fort)

B1095

Horsey Hill

MILK AND WATER DROVE

BUNTING'S DROVE

Willow Farm

Paradise Farm

Bunting's Farm

King's Delph

Milby Farm

KING'S DELPH DROVE

King's Delph Gate Farm

MILK AND WATER DROVE

BURNT UP DROVE

Suet Hills Farm

Eight Roads Land

SUET HILLS DROVE

TEN ACRE DROVE

TWO POLE DROVE

RAMSEY RD B1095

GOSLING'S DROVE

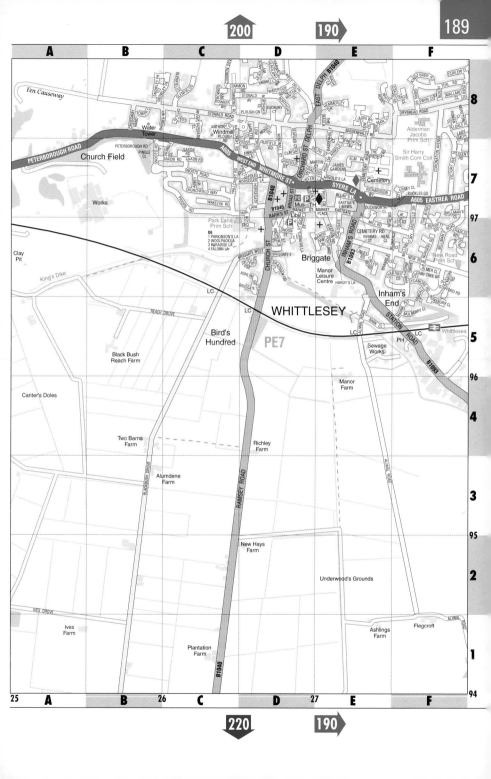

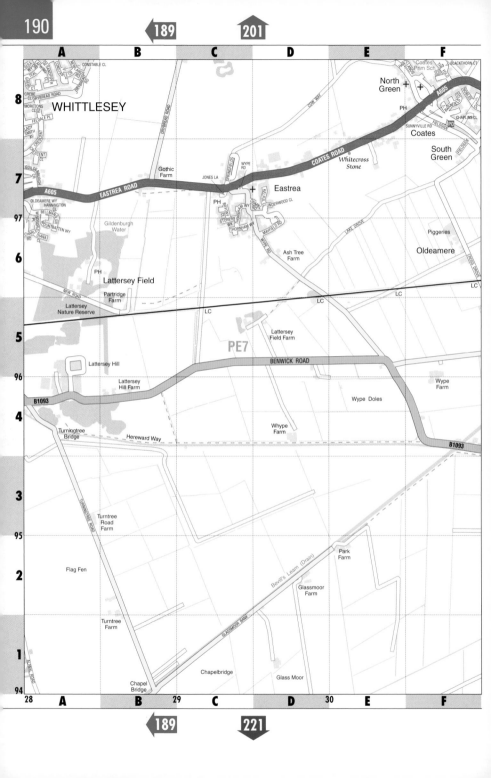

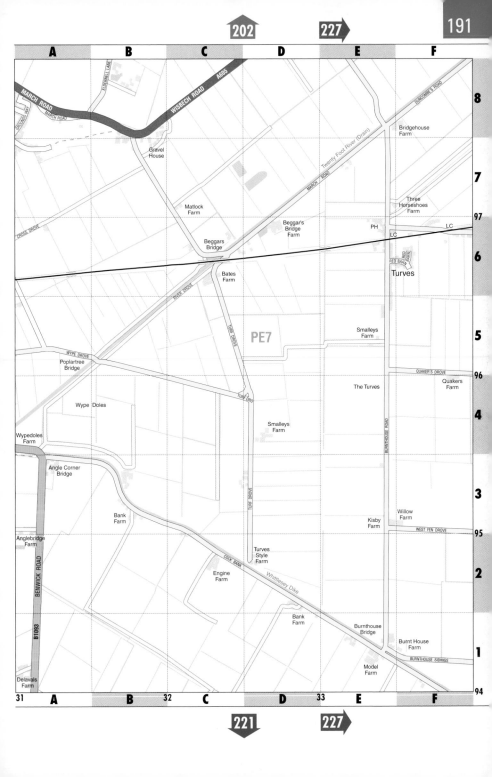

A B C D E F

8
7
97
6
5
96
4
3
95
2
1
94

MARCH ROAD
GROUNDS LANE
MARCH ROAD
ELDERNELL LANE
WISBECH ROAD A605
Gravel House
Matlock Farm
CROSS DROVE
Beggars Bridge
Beggar's Bridge Farm
Twenty Foot River (Drain)
MARCH ROAD
Bridgehouse Farm
DUNCOMBE'S ROAD
Three Horseshoes Farm
PH
LC
LC
RED BARN
RED BARN
Turves
Bates Farm
RIVER DROVE
TURF DROVE
PE7
Smalleys Farm
WYPE DROVE
Poplartree Bridge
TURF DRO
The Turves
QUAKER'S DROVE
Quakers Farm
BURNTHOUSE ROAD
Wype Doles
Wypedoles Farm
Smalleys Farm
Angle Corner Bridge
TURF DROVE
Willow Farm
WEST FEN DROVE
Kisby Farm
Bank Farm
Anglebridge Farm
BENWICK ROAD
Turves Style Farm
LOCK BANK
Engine Farm
Whittlesey Dike
Bank Farm
Burnthouse Bridge
Burnt House Farm
BURNTHOUSE SIDINGS
B1093
Model Farm
Delavals Farm

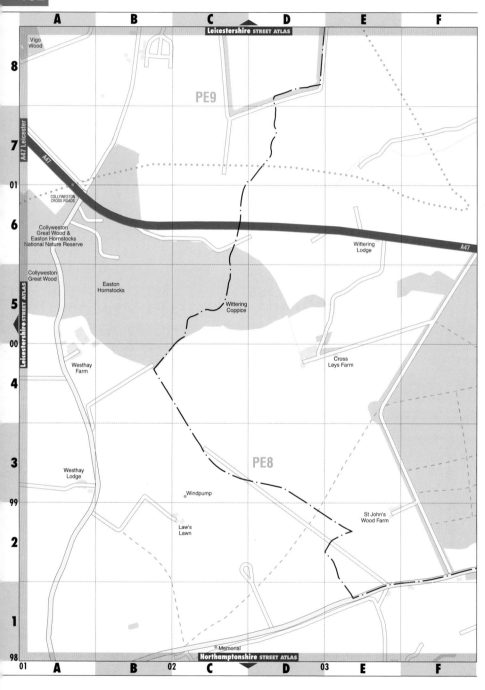

PE9

A47 Leicester

A47

COLLYWESTON
CROSS ROADS

Collyweston
Great Wood &
Easton Hornstocks
National Nature Reserve

Collyweston
Great Wood

Easton
Hornstocks

Wittering
Lodge

Wittering
Coppice

Westhay
Farm

Cross
Leys Farm

Vigo
Wood

A47

Westhay
Lodge

PE8

Windpump

Law's
Lawn

St John's
Wood Farm

Memorial

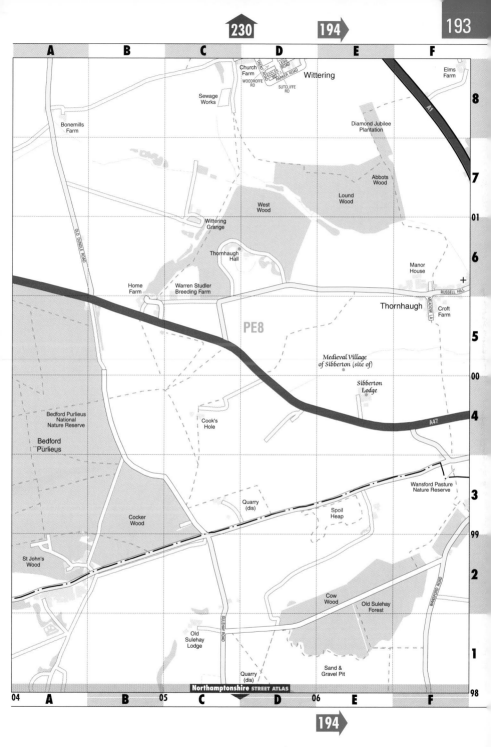

A B C D E F

8

Church
Farm
WOODROFFE
RD
TRENT RD
ECCLES WY
EGG ROAD
PARKER ROAD
Wittering
SUTCLIFFE
RD
Elms
Farm

A1

Sewage
Works

Bonemills
Farm

Diamond Jubilee
Plantation

7

01

Abbots
Wood

Lound
Wood

West
Wood

OLD DUMBLE ROAD

Wittering
Grange

Manor
House

6

Thornhaugh
Hall

+

RUSSELL HILL

Home
Farm

Warren Studler
Breeding Farm

Thornhaugh

MEADOW LA

Croft
Farm

PE8

5

Medieval Village
of Sibberton (site of)

00

Sibberton
Lodge

Bedford Purlieus
National
Nature Reserve

Cook's
Hole

A47

4

Bedford
Purlieus

Wansford Pasture
Nature Reserve

3

Quarry
(dis)

Spoil
Heap

Cocker
Wood

99

St John's
Wood

2

Cow
Wood

Old Sulehay
Forest

SULEHAY ROAD

WANSFORD ROAD

Old
Sulehay
Lodge

1

Quarry
(dis)

Sand &
Gravel Pit

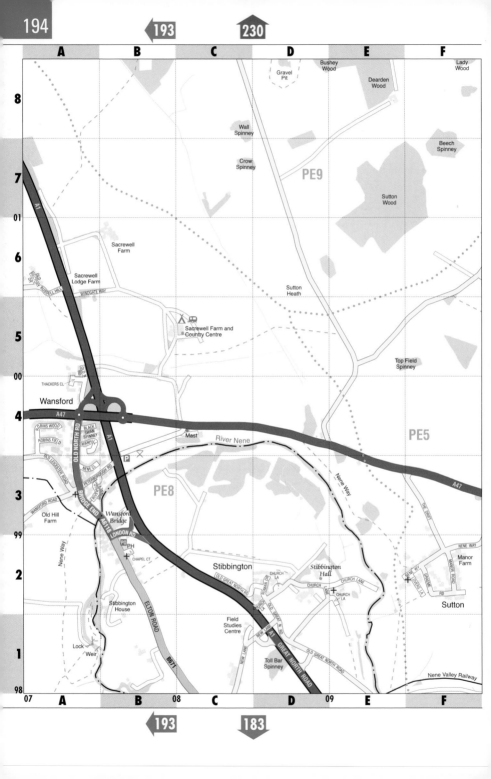

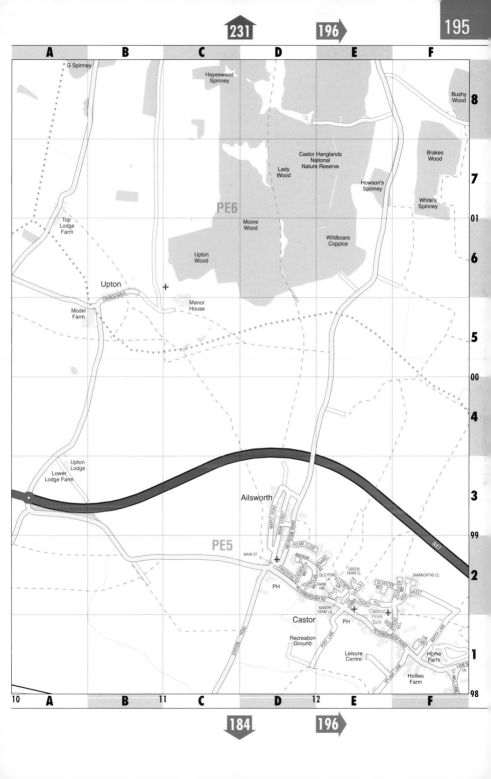

A B C D E F

8

G Spinney

Hayeswood
Spinney

Bushy
Wood

Castor Hanglands
National
Nature Reserve

Lady
Wood

Brakes
Wood

7

01

PE6

Howson's
Spinney

White's
Spinney

Top
Lodge
Farm

Moore
Wood

6

Wildboars
Coppice

Upton
Wood

Upton

CHURCH WALK

Manor
House

Model
Farm

5

00

4

Upton
Lodge

Lower
Lodge Farm

3

99

Ailsworth

A47

2

PE5

MAIN ST

MAFFIT ROAD

MAIN STREET

HELPSTON ROAD

HOLME CLOSE

ANDREW
CLOSE
HILL

LINDISFARNE CLOSE

SOUTH VIEW

REMANS

THORNEY
CLOSE

OLD POND
LANE

FARM
VW

AILSWORTH
LANE

GREEN
FARM CL

CALLET

SILVESTER
RD

SAMWORTHS CL

SILVESTER RD

STOCKS HILL

STEELS

LANGLEY

CHURCH HILL

PETERBOROUGH ROAD

PH

PETERBOROUGH RD

MANOR
FARM LA

Castor

PORT LANE

PH

Castor
Prim
Sch

PETERBOROUGH ROAD

STOCKS HILL

SILVESTER STREET

THE
LIMES

WATER LANE

Recreation
Ground

STANMIRE ROAD

Leisure
Centre

SPLASH LANE

Home
Farm

LOVES
HILL

MILL LANE

Hollies
Farm

1

98

10 A 11 B C 12 D E F

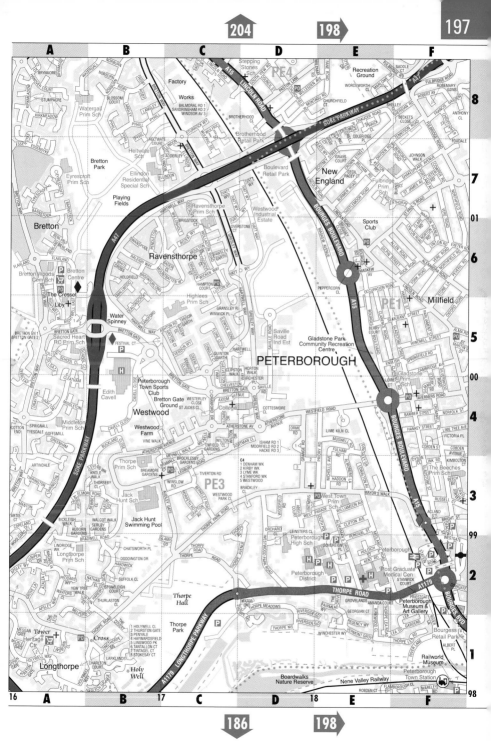

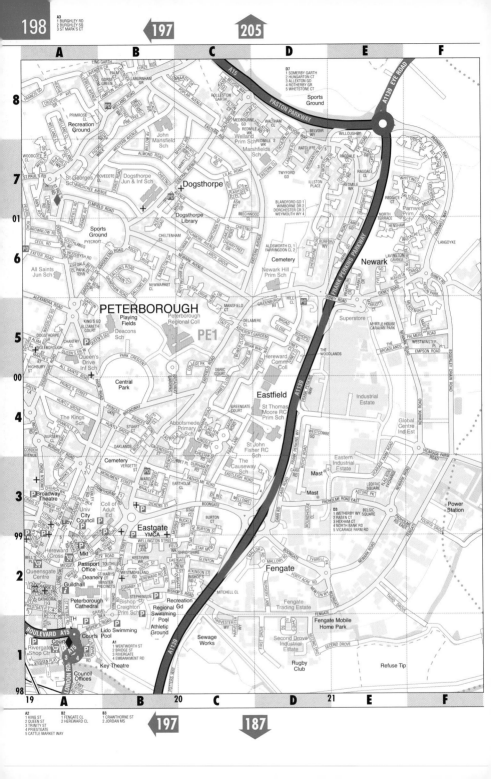

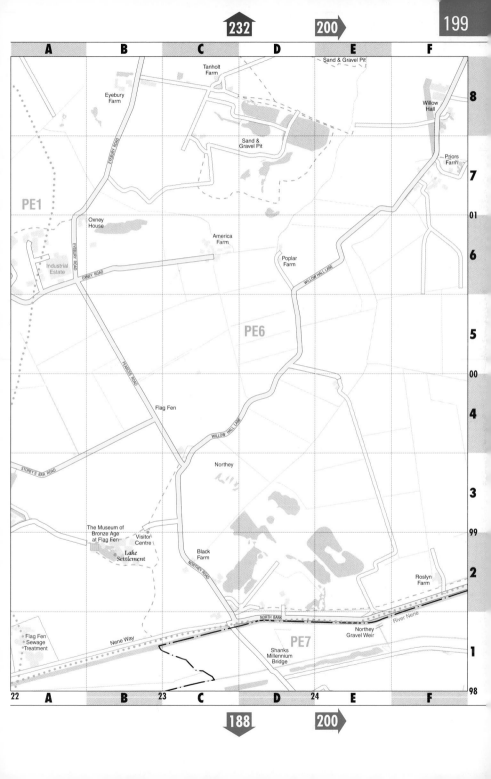

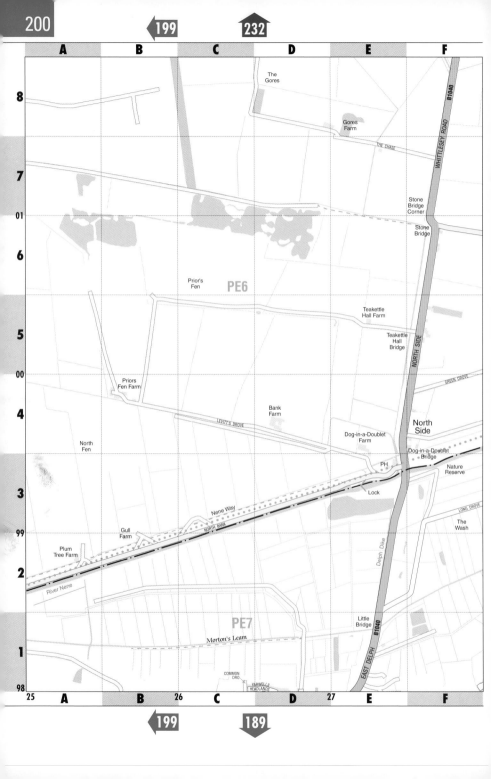

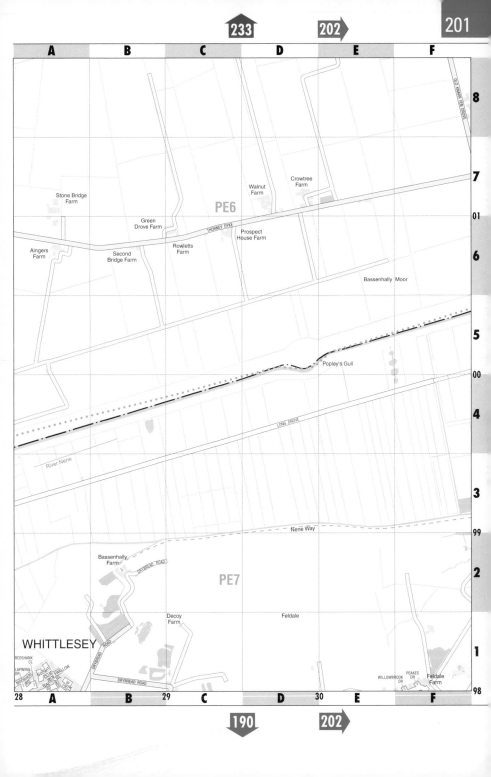

A B C D E F

8

7

01

6

5

00

4

3

99

2

1

98

Stone Bridge
Farm

PE6

Green
Drove Farm

Aingers
Farm

Second
Bridge Farm

Rowletts
Farm

THORNEY DYKE

Walnut
Farm

Crowtree
Farm

Prospect
House Farm

Bassenhally Moor

Popley's Gull

River Nene

LONG DRIVE

Nene Way

Bassenhally
Farm

DRYBREAD ROAD

PE7

Decoy
Farm

Feldale

WHITTLESEY

REDSHANK
CL

LAPWING
DR.

MOORHEN
AVE.

SWALLOW

DRYBREAD ROAD

DRYBREAD ROAD

WILLOWBROOK
DR

PEAKES
DR

Feldale
Farm

OLD KNARR FEN DROVE

28 29 30

A B C D E F

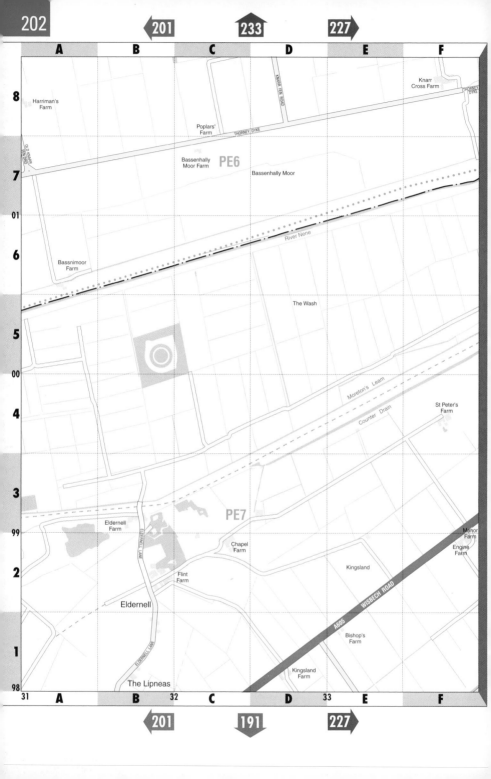

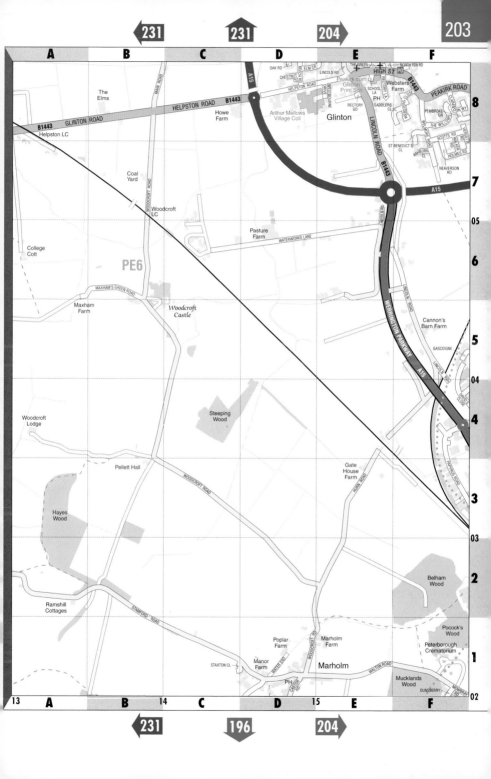

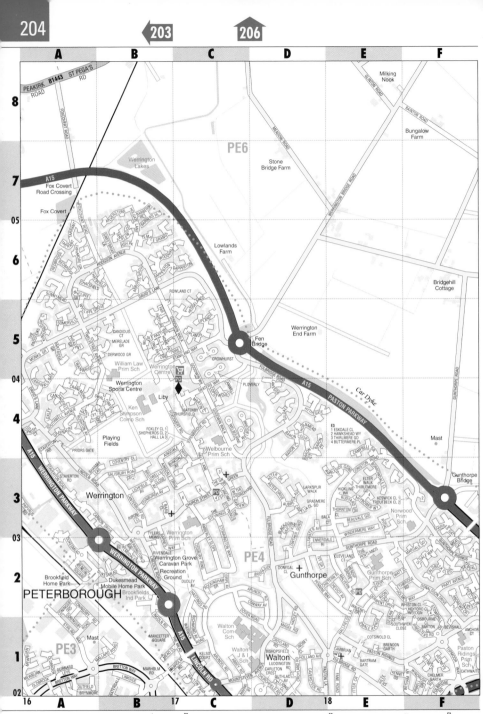

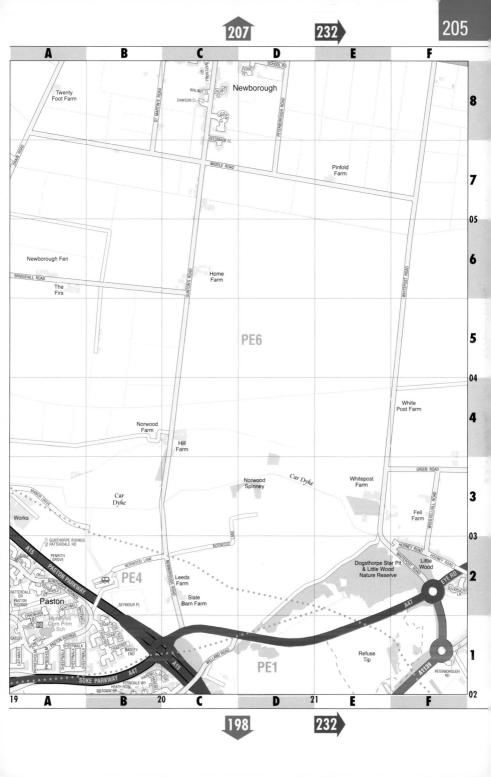

231

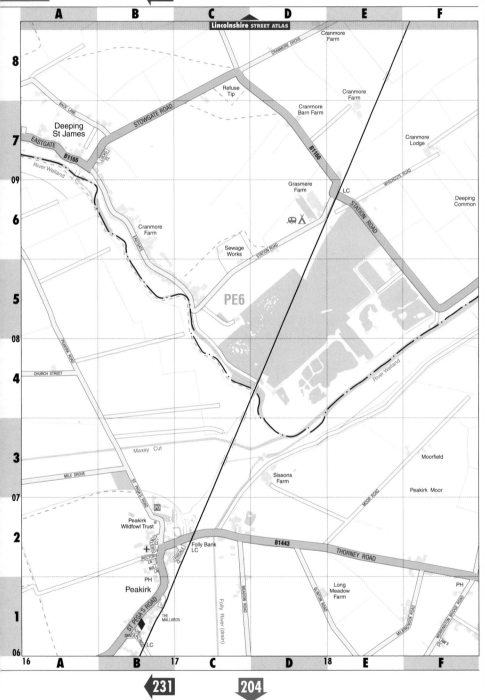

Lincolnshire STREET ATLAS

PE6

Deeping
St James

EASTGATE

B1166

River Welland

BACK LANE

STOWGATE ROAD

Refuse
Tip

Cranmore Farm

CRANMORE DROVE

Cranmore
Farm

Cranmore
Barn Farm

B1166

Cranmore
Lodge

WITHCOTE ROAD

Deeping
Common

Grasmere
Farm

LC

STATION ROAD

Cranmore
Farm

EASTGATE

Sewage
Works

STATION ROAD

River Welland

PEAKIRK ROAD

CHURCH STREET

Maxey Cut

MILE DROVE

ST PEGA'S ROAD

Moorfield

Peakirk Moor

Sissons
Farm

MOOR ROAD

PO

Peakirk
Wildfowl Trust

RECTORY
LA

BULL
LA

FERNDALE

Folly Bank
LC

B1443

THORNEY ROAD

Long
Meadow
Farm

GUNTHORPE ROAD

PH

MEADOW ROAD

Folly River (drain)

MILKING NOOK DROVE

WORBRIDGE BRIDGE ROAD

PH

Peakirk

ST PEGA'S ROAD

THE
MALLARDS

THE
SANDERS

LC

ST LAW'S

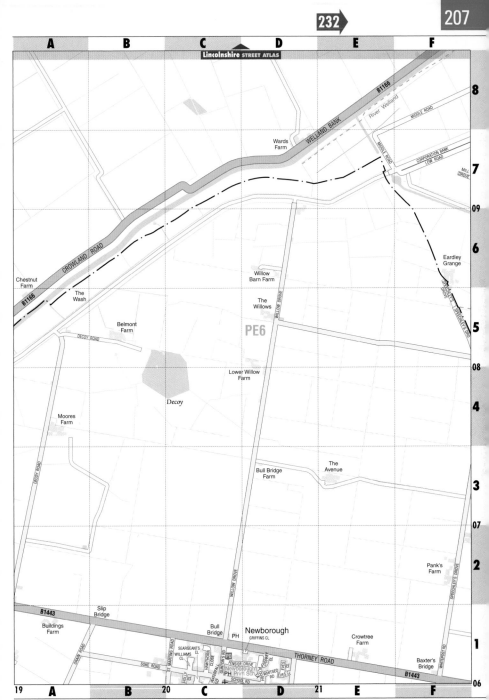

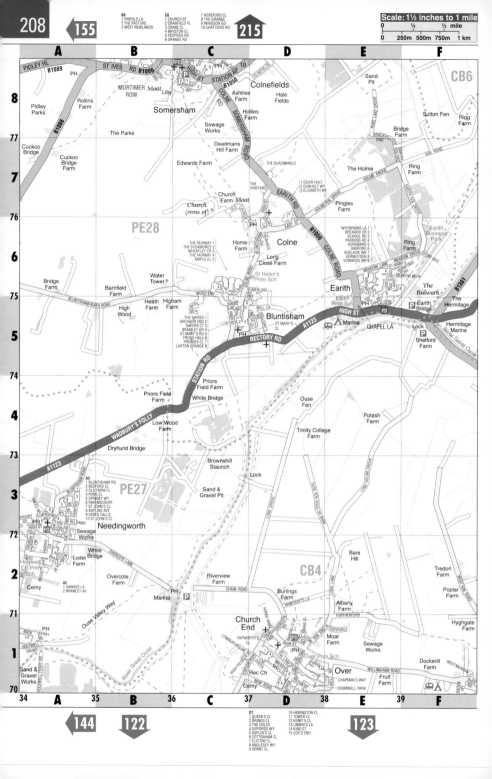

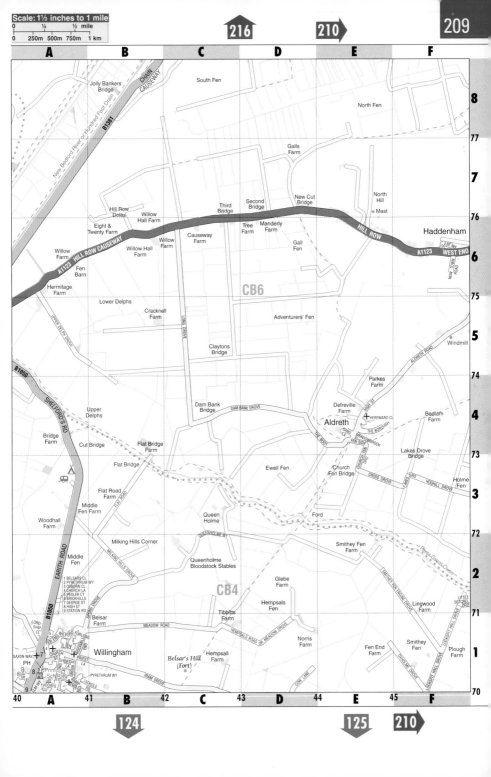

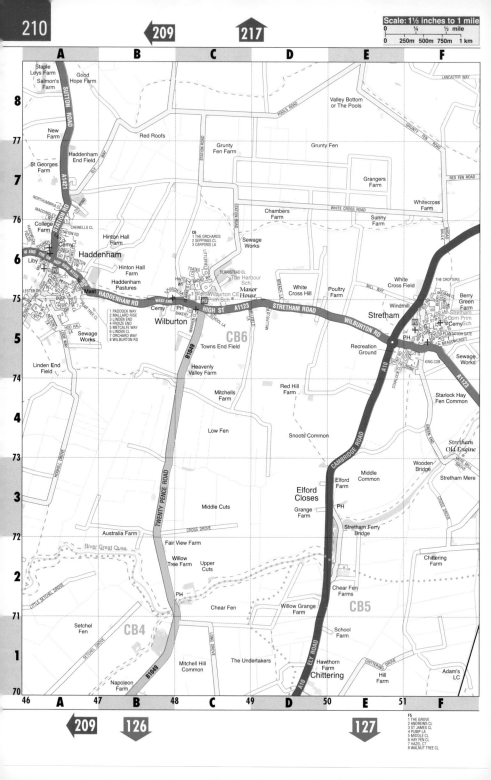

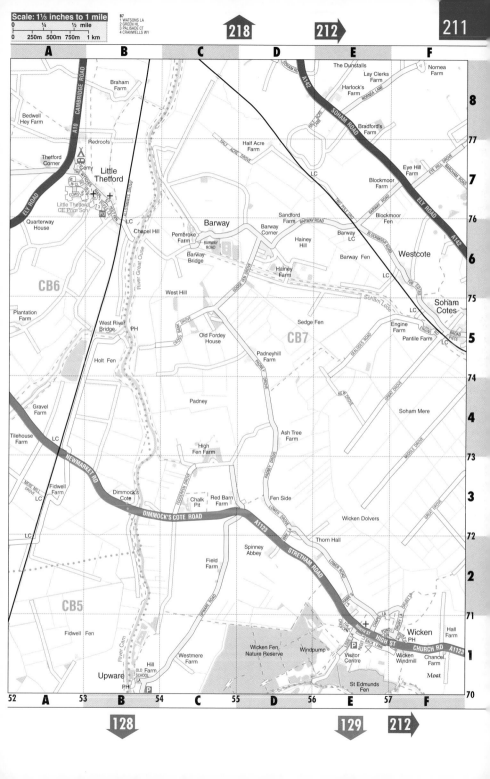

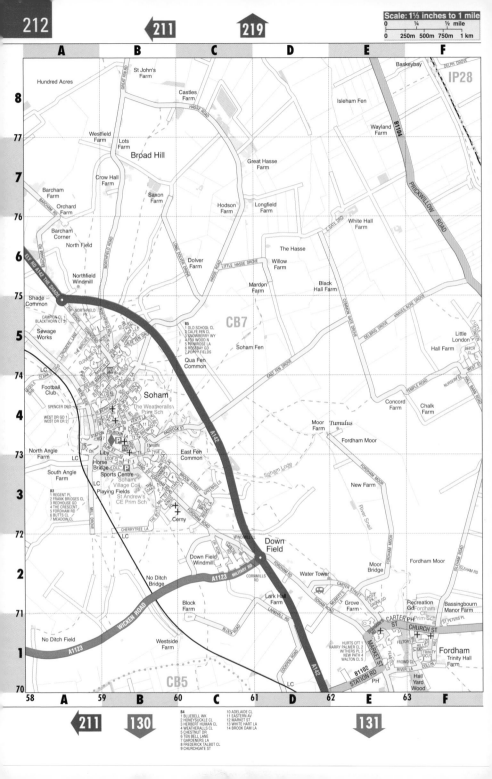

212

211

219

Scale: 1⅓ inches to 1 mile
0   ¼   ½ mile
0   250m 500m 750m 1 km

IP28

Baskeybay

St John's Farm

Castles Farm

Isleham Fen

Hundred Acres

Hasse Road

Westfield Farm

Lots Farm

Wayland Farm

Broad Hill

Great Hasse Farm

Crow Hall Farm

Saxon Farm

Barcham Farm

Orchard Farm

Hodson Farm

Longfield Farm

White Hall Farm

Barcham Corner

North Field

Dolver Farm

The Hasse

Northfield Windmill

Little Hasse Drive

Willow Farm

Mardon Farm

Black Hall Farm

Shade Common

CB7

Sewage Works

B5
1 OLD SCHOOL CL
2 CALFE FEN CL
3 SNOWBERRY WY
4 FOX WOOD N
5 PRIMROSE LA
6 ROSEBAY GD
7 POPPY FIELDS

Little London

Hall Farm

Soham Fen

Qua Fen Common

Football Club

Soham

Concord Farm

Chalk Farm

North Angle Farm

The Weatheralls Prim Sch

East Fen Common

Moor Farm

Tumulus

Fordham Moor

South Angle Farm

Liby

Horse Bridge

Sports Centre

Ennion

Cerny

New Farm

B3
1 REGENT PL
2 FRANK BRIDGES CL
3 REDHOUSE GD
4 THE CRESCENT
5 FORDHAM RD
6 BUTTS CL
7 MEADOW CL

Soham Village Coll

Playing Fields

St Andrew's CE Prim Sch

Soham Lode

River Snail

Cherrytree La

Down Field

Windmill La

Down Field Windmill

Moor Bridge

Fordham Moor

No Ditch Bridge

A1123   Military Rd

Cornmills Rd

Water Tower

Carter Street

Block Farm

Lark Hall Farm

Grove Farm

Recreation Gd

Bassingbourn Manor Farm

Wicken Road

No Ditch Field

A1123

Westside Farm

Cooper Road

B1102

Station Rd

Church St

Fordham

Trinity Hall Farm

CB5

Hall Yard Wood

B4
1 BLUEBELL WK
2 HONEYSUCKLE CL
3 HERBERT HUMAN CL
4 WEATHERALLS CL
5 CHESTNUT DR
6 TEN BELL LANE
7 GARDENERS LA
8 FREDERICK TALBOT CL
9 CHURCHGATE ST
10 ADELAIDE CL
11 EASTERN AV
12 MARKET ST
13 WHITE HART LA
14 BROOK DAM LA

HURTS CFT 1
HARRY PALMER CL 2
WITHERS PL 3
NEW PATH 4
WALTON CL 5

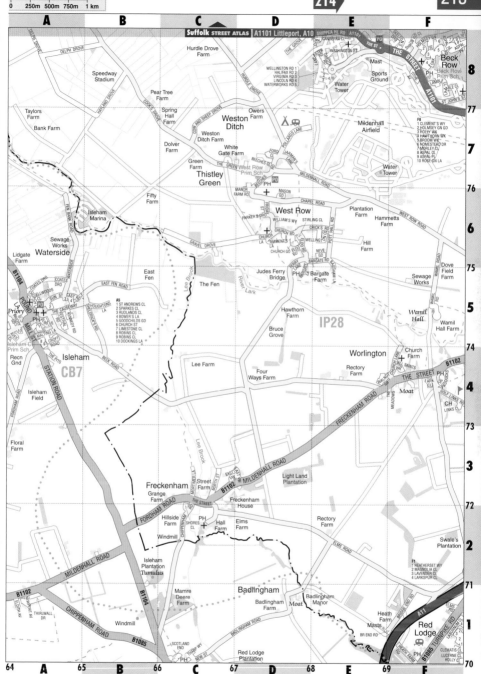

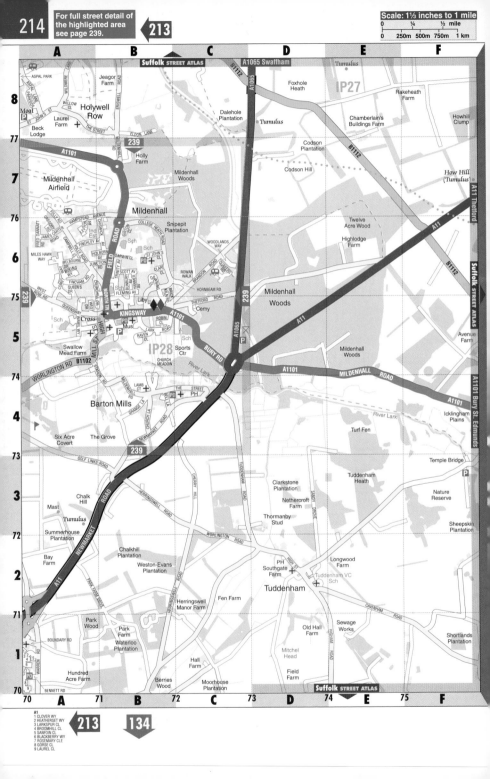

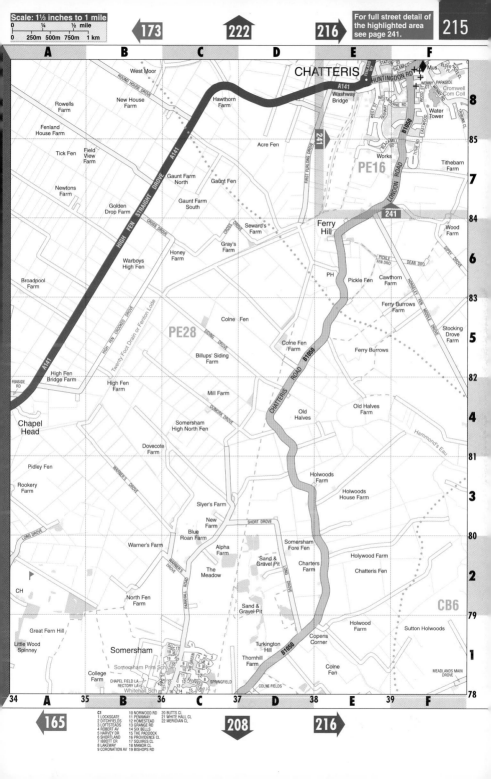

216

For full street detail of the highlighted area see page 241.

← 215

223↑

Scale: 1⅓ inches to 1 mile
0   ¼   ½ mile
0 250m 500m 750m 1 km

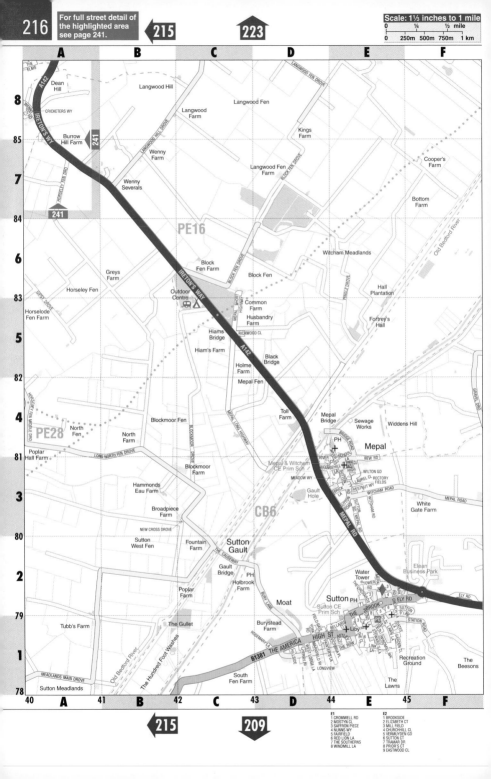

E1
1 CROMWELL RD
2 MOSTYN CL
3 SAFFRON PIECE
4 NUNNS WY
5 FAIRFIELD
6 RED LION LA
7 THE SOUTHERNS
8 WINDMILL LA

E2
1 BROOKSIDE
2 ELIZABETH CT
3 MILL FIELD
4 CHURCHILL CL
5 VERMUYDEN GD
6 SUTTON CT
7 TRAMAR DR
8 PRIOR'S CT
9 EASTWOOD CL

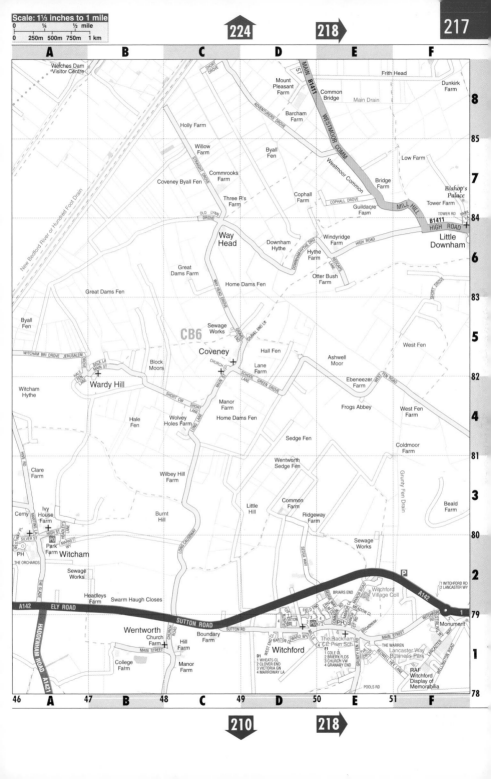

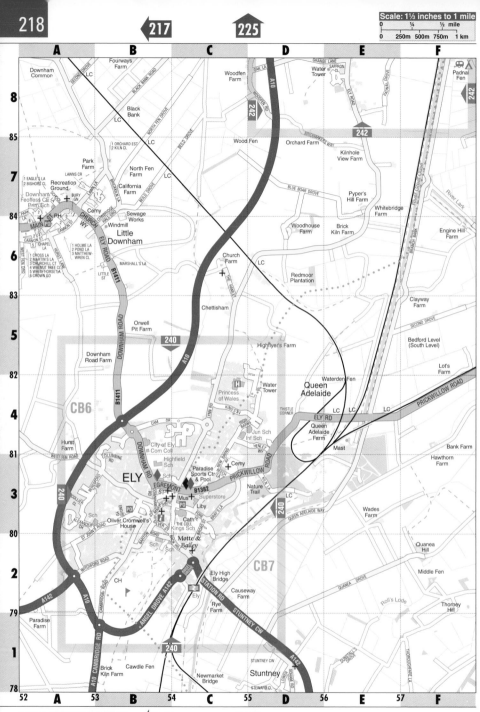

217
225

Scale: 1⅓ inches to 1 mile

0   ¼   ½   mile
0   250m 500m 750m 1 km

8
85
7
84
6
83
5
82
4
81
3
80
2
79
1
78

A   B   C   D   E   F

Downham Common

Fourways Farm

BLACK BANK ROAD
SECOND DROVE
LC

Black Bank
LC

Park Farm
1 ORCHARD EST
2 KILN CL

North Fen Farm

Woodfen Farm

OAK LA
A10

Water Tower
GRANGE LANE
SAFFRON CL

Padnal Fen

242

WOODFEN RD

242

Wood Fen

Orchard Farm
BRICKMAKERS WAY

242

Kilnhole View Farm

River Lark

LAWNS CR
California Farm

1 EAGLE'S LA
2 BISHOPS CL

Recreation Ground
Downham Feoffees CE Prim Sch

BURY LGN
BRACKEN LA
LAWN LA

BLUE BOAR DROVE

Pyper's Hill Farm

Whitebridge Farm

Engine Hill Farm

Cemy

CHURCH WY
ELY ROAD

Windmill

Little Downham

1 HOLME LA
2 POND LA
3 MATTHEW-WREN CL

MARSHALL'S LA

Sewage Works

Woodhouse Farm

Brick Kiln Farm

MAIN COM
ST PH
CANNON ST

PARK CL
CHAPEL LA
CROWN GD

1 CROSS LA
2 MARTIN'S LA
3 CHURCHILL CT
4 WALNUT TREE CL
5 WHITE HORSE LA
6 CROWN GD

LITTLE ST
B1411

Church Farm
LC

Redmoor Plantation

Clayway Farm

WEST FEN DRIV
HURST LANE

Chettisham

Bedford Level (South Level)

Lot's Farm

DOWNHAM ROAD
B1411

Orwell Pit Farm

240
A10

Highflyer's Farm

Waterden Fen

Queen Adelaide

CB6

Downham Road Farm

Water Tower

THISTLE CORNER

ELY RD
LC   LC   LC

PRICKWILLOW ROAD

Hurst Farm

WEST FEN ROAD

COLUMBINE RD

CAM DR

Princess of Wales

KING'S AV

LYNN RD

HIGH BARNS

Jun Sch
Inf Sch

Queen Adelaide Farm

Mast

Bank Farm

Hawthorn Farm

DOWNHAM RD

City of Ely Com Coll

Highfield Sch

Sch

HENLEY WY

PRICKWILLOW ROAD

ELY

ALEXANDER
ST JOHN'S ROAD

EGREMONT ST

Mus

Liby

B1382

Superstore

Nature Trail

QUEEN ADELAIDE WAY

240
LC

Wades Farm

Oliver Cromwell's House

PO

Cath'l
The Coll
Kings Sch

Sch

Motte & Bailey

Sch

Paradise Sports Ctr & Pool
Cemy

Quanea Hill

MITCHFORD ROAD

CH

Ely High Bridge

CB7

Middle Fen

A142
A10

CAMBRIDGE ROAD

ANGEL DROVE A142

STATION RD

Ely

Causeway Farm

QUANEA DRIVE

Roll's Lode

Thorney Hill

Paradise Farm

240

Rye Farm

STUNTNEY CW

DUNTZEL'S DROVE

THORNQUIRE LA

Brick Kiln Farm

Cawdle Fen

Newmarket Bridge

Stuntney

STEWARD CL

STUNTNEY CW

A142

A   B   C   D   E   F

52   53   54   55   56   57

217
211

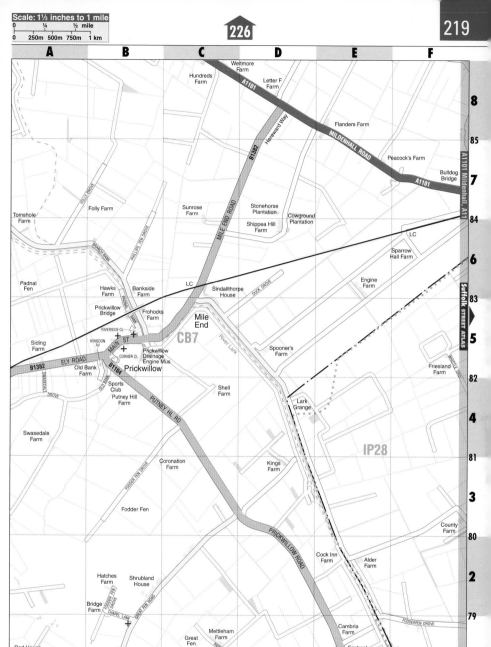

Scale: 1⅓ inches to 1 mile

| 0 | ¼ | ½ mile |
| 0 | 250m 500m 750m | 1 km |

A B C D E F

Weltmore Farm
Hundreds Farm
Letter F Farm
A1101
Hereward Way
MILDENHALL ROAD
Flanders Farm
Peacock's Farm
A1101
Bulldog Bridge
A1101 Mildenhall, A11

B1382

Tomshole Farm
Folly Farm
FOLLY DRIVE
Sunrose Farm
MILE END ROAD
Stonehorse Plantation
Shippea Hill Farm
Cowground Plantation
LC
Sparrow Hall Farm
Suffolk STREET ATLAS

Padnal Fen
BRANCH BANK
PHILLIPS FEN DRIVE
Hawks Farm
Bankside Farm
Prickwillow Bridge
PADNAL BANK
Frohocks Farm
LC
Sindallthorpe House
DUCK DROVE
Engine Farm

Siding Farm
RIVERSIDE CL
KINGDON AV
MAIN ST
CORNER CL
Mile End
CB7
River Lark
Spooner's Farm
Friesland Farm
WHITTLE DRIVE

B1382 ELY ROAD
Old Bank Farm
B1104
Prickwillow
Prickwillow Drainage Engine Mus
SWASEDALE DROVE
OLD BANK
Sports Club
Putney Hill Farm
PUTNEY HL RD
Shell Farm
Lark Grange

Swasedale Farm
FODDER FEN DRIVE
Coronation Farm
Kings Farm
IP28

Fodder Fen

County Farm

PRICKWILLOW ROAD
Cock Inn Farm
Alder Farm

Hatches Farm
Shrubland House
FODDER FEN DRIVE
GREAT FEN ROAD
Cambria Farm
FODDERFEN DROVE

Bridge Farm
CHAPEL LANE
Mettleham Farm
PARISH BUSH DROVE
Fenbank Farm

Red House Farm
Great Fen
B1104

8
85
7
84
6
83
5
82
4
81
3
80
2
79
1
78

58 A 59 B 60 C 61 D 62 E 63 F

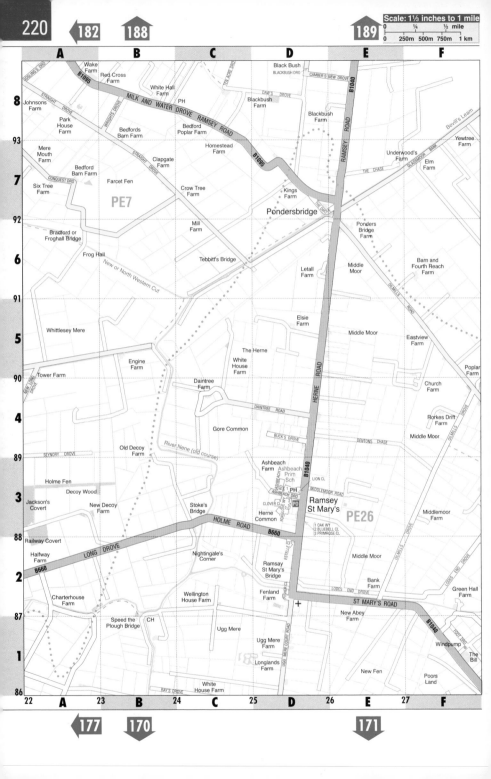

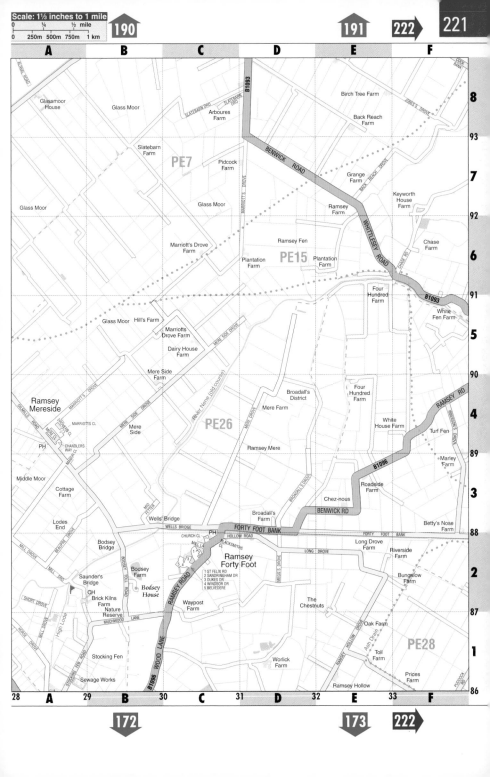

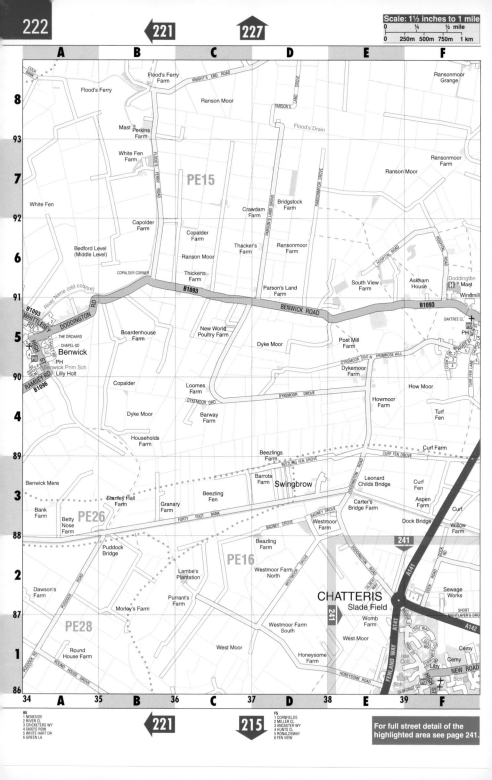

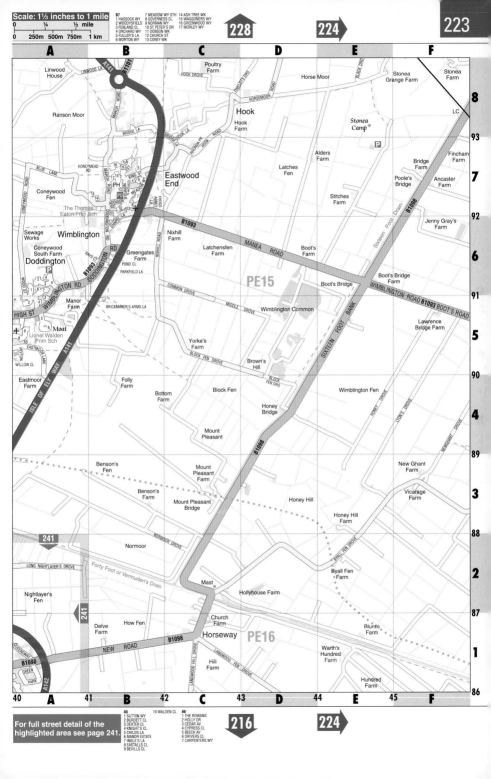

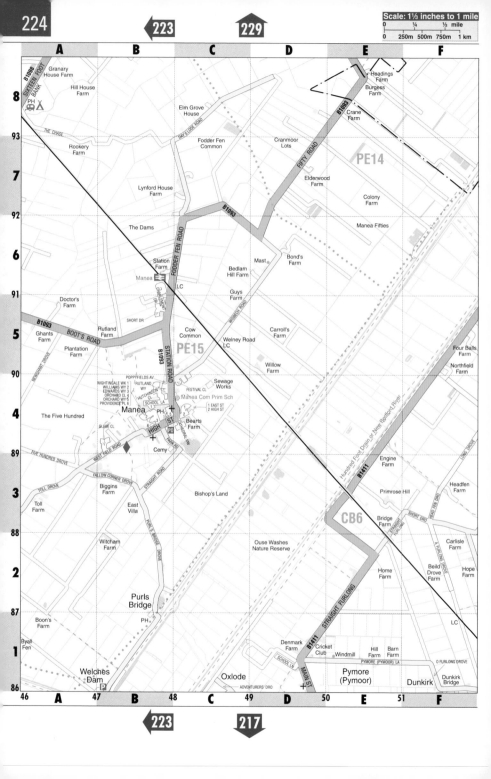

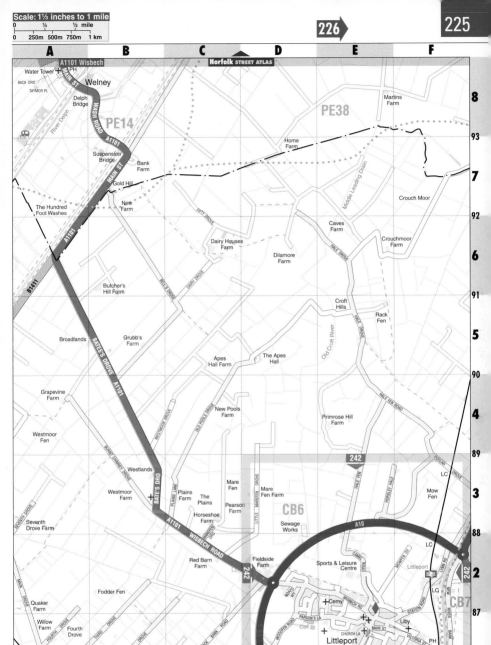

Norfolk STREET ATLAS

A1101 Wisbech

Water Tower
PH
BACK DRO
MAIN ST
TAYMOR PL
Welney
Delph
Bridge
WASH ROAD
A1101
PE14
River Delph

PE38

Martins
Farm

Home
Farm

93

Suspension
Bridge
MAIN ST
Bank
Farm
Gold Hill
A1101
New
Farm
The Hundred
Foot Washes

Crouch Moor

7

Middle Leading Drain

TIFTY DROVE

Caves
Farm

92

Crouchmoor
Farm

Dairy Houses
Farm
DAIRY DROVE
BELL'S DROVE

Dilamore
Farm

B1411
A1101

Butcher's
Hill Farm

HALE DROVE

Croft
Hills

91

Rack
Fen

Broadlands
BATE'S DROVE A1101
Grubb's
Farm

Apes
Hall Farm
The Apes
Hall

Old Croft River

HALE DROVE

5

90

Grapevine
Farm

OLD POOLS DROVE
WESTMOOR DROVE

New Pools
Farm

Primrose Hill
Farm

HALF FEN ROAD

4

Westmoor
Fen

BURNT CHIMNEY DROVE

89

242

Westlands
BATE'S DRO

Mare
Fen
LITTLE WARFEN DROVE
Mare
Fen Farm

HALF FEN

WISBECH HALE

POPLAR DROVE
LC

Mow
Fen

3

Westmoor
Farm
Plains
Farm
PLAINS LANE
The
Plains
Pearson
Farm

CB6

Horseshoe
Farm
A1101
WISBECH ROAD
242

Sewage
Works

A10

88

LC

SEVENTH DROVE

Seventh
Drove Farm

Red Barn
Farm
242
Fieldside
Farm

Sports & Leisure
Centre

CAMEL ROAD
MONTS WY

Littleport
LC

242
CB7

2

MAIN DROVE

Fodder Fen
BLACK BANK ROAD

A10

Cemy
PARSON'S LA
Coll
MAIN ST
WISBECH RD
WOLSELEY ROAD
CHURCH LA
VICTORIA ST
STATION ROAD
Liby
PH
BANK
LC
ELY ROAD

87

Quaker
Farm
Willow
Farm
FOURTH DROVE
Fourth
Drove
THIRD DROVE
SECOND DROVE

Littleport

Highfield
Farm
EASTFIELDS

Sandhill
Bridge

Laurel
Farm
Second
Drove

Wood
Fen Farm

Highfield
Farm
Millfield CP Sch
WIGFEN ROAD
ELY ROAD
PADNAL
HAWKINS DRIVE
Sandhill

1

Gravel
Head Farm
LC

86

52 A 53 B 54 C 55 D 56 E 57 F

◄218   226 ►

For full street detail of the
highlighted area see page 242.

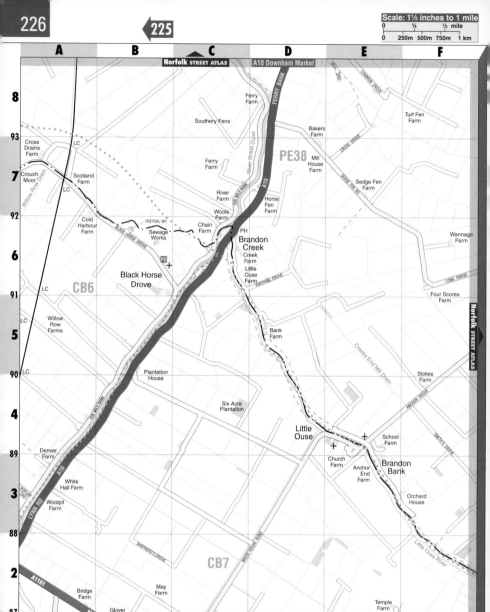

Scale: 1⅓ inches to 1 mile

0   ¼   ½   mile
0   250m 500m 750m 1 km

Norfolk STREET ATLAS

A10 Downham Market

Ferry
Farm

FERRY BANK

Southery Fens

River Great Ouse

Bakers
Farm

COMMON DRIVE

Turf Fen
Farm

CROSS DRIVE

PE38

Ferry
Farm

Mill
House
Farm

SEDGE FEN RD

Sedge Fen
Farm

River
Farm

Cross
Drains
Farm

LC

Scotland
Farm

LC

Crouch
Moor Farm

Willow Row Drain

A10

TEN MILE BANK

Wools
Farm

Horse
Fen
Farm

Cold
Harbour
Farm

BLACK HORSE DROVE

FESTIVAL WY

Sewage
Works

Chain
Farm

PH

Wannage
Farm

Brandon
Creek

Creek
Farm

Little
Ouse
Farm

FARTHING DROVE

LONG DROVE

Four Scores
Farm

PO

CB6

Black Horse
Drove

LC

LC

Willow
Row
Farms

LC

Bank
Farm

Creeks End Mill Drain

Stokes
Farm

ANCHOR DROVE

LC

Plantation
House

TEN MILE BANK

Six Acre
Plantation

Little
Ouse

SMITH'S DROVE

Denver
Farm

A10

White
Hall Farm

Church
Farm

Anchor
End
Farm

School
Farm

Brandon
Bank

LYNN RD

Woolpit
Farm

Orchard
House

A1101

SHEPHERD'S DROVE

CB7

WHITE HOUSE ROAD

Little Ouse River

Bridge
Farm

May
Farm

Temple
Farm

Old Bank
Farm

CROSS DROVE

Glover
Farm

MILDENHALL   ROAD

White
House

HAWKINS'S DRO.

Hill
Farm

A1101

Burnt Fen

Wesleyan
Farm

Norfolk STREET ATLAS

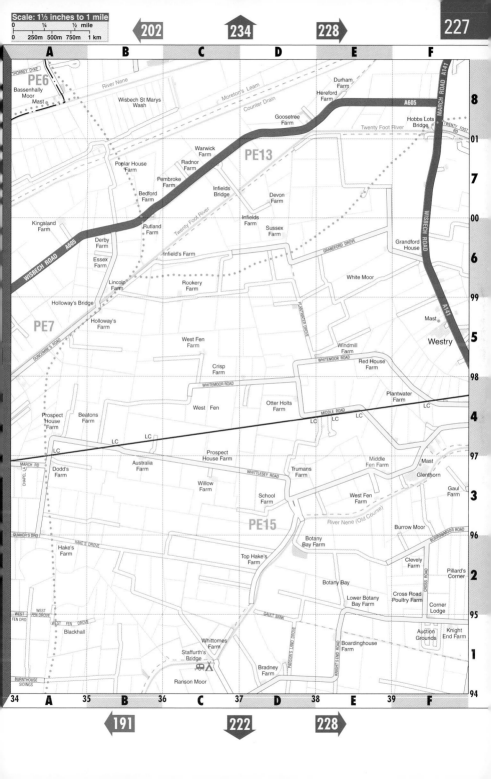

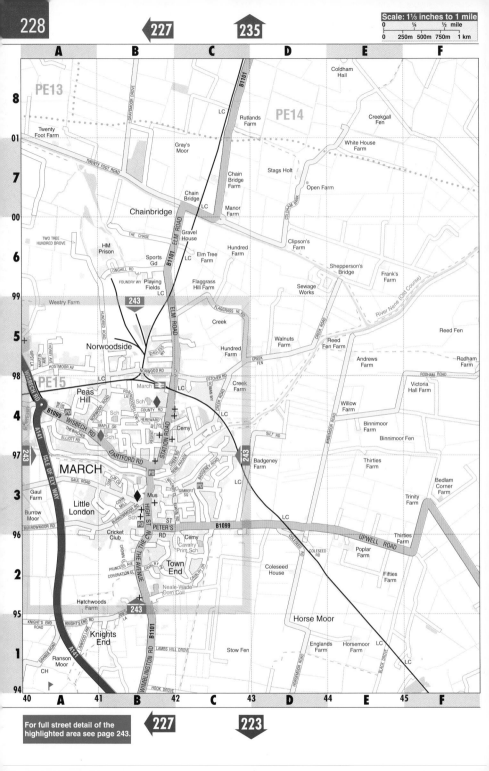

Scale: 1⅓ inches to 1 mile

0 ¼ ½ mile
0 250m 500m 750m 1 km

PE13

8

01

Twenty
Foot Farm

TWENTY FOOT ROAD

Gray's
Moor

Coldham
Hall

PE14

Rutlands
Farm

LC

Creekgall
Fen

White House
Farm

Chain
Bridge
Farm

Stags Holt

7

00

THE CHASE

Chainbridge

Chain
Bridge

LC

Manor
Farm

Open Farm

6

HM
Prison

Sports
Gd

LONGHILL RD

FOUNDRY WY

Playing
Fields

TWO TREE
HUNDRED DROVE

Gravel
House

Elm Tree
Farm

LC

Hundred
Farm

Clipson's
Farm

Shepperson's
Bridge

Frank's
Farm

Westry Farm

LC

243

Flaggrass
Hill Farm

FLAGGRASS HILL RD

Sewage
Works

River Nene (Old Course)

99

Norwoodside

HUNDRED ROAD

ELM ROAD

Creek

Walnuts
Farm

Reed
Fen Farm

CREEK ROAD

Reed Fen

5

GIPSY LA

HORSEY AV

MILTON
AV

HOSTMOOR AV

Hundred
Farm

Andrews
Farm

Rodham
Farm

DAGLES
WY

CREEK
FEN

RODHAM ROAD

98

PE15

WISBECH RD

NORWOOD RD

March

Creek
Farm

Victoria
Hall Farm

Peas
Hill

B1099

ROOKWOOD ROW

ESTOVER RD

NUNMAN WY

CREEK ROAD

Willow
Farm

4

A141

243

B1099

THE BRIDGES

ELLIOTT RD

DARTFORD RD

WISBECH RD

ROOKWOOD ROAD

Sch

MAPLE GR

Sch

Sch

HEREWARD

STATION ROAD

COUNTY RD

REGENT

Cemy

BADGENEY ROAD

LC

SILT RD

Binnimoor
Farm

BINNIMOOR ROAD

Binnimoor Fen

97

243

ISLE OF ELY WAY

GAUL ROAD

CROWN

DILY WY

NENE PARADE

LIMBERT'S
SQ

PO

Badgeney
Farm

Thirties
Farm

3

Gaul
Farm

Burrow
Moor

BURROWMOOR RD

MARCH

Little
London

CORN MILL

HIGH ST

Mus

ST
PETER'S
RD

Cavalry
Prim Sch

Trinity
Farm

Bedlam
Corner
Farm

2

Cricket
Club

PRINCESS AVE

CORONATION CL

THE AVENUE

CAVALRY

Cemy

Town
End

CAUSEWAY

B1099

Coleseed
House

COLESEED RD

UPWELL ROAD

COLESEED
RD

Poplar
Farm

Thirties
Farm

Fifties
Farm

96

Hatchwoods
Farm

243

Neale-Wade
Com Coll

95

Knights
End

KNIGHT'S END
ROAD

KNIGHT'S END LANE

LINKSFIELD LANE

B1101

WIMBLINGTON RD

LAMBS HILL DROVE

Stow Fen

HORSEMOOR ROAD

Horse Moor

Englands
Farm

Horsemoor
Farm

LC

BLACK DROVE

LC

1

GRANGE ROAD

A141

Ranson
Moor

CH

94

HOOK DROVE

40 A 41 B 42 C 43 D 44 E 45 F

For full street detail of the
highlighted area see page 243.

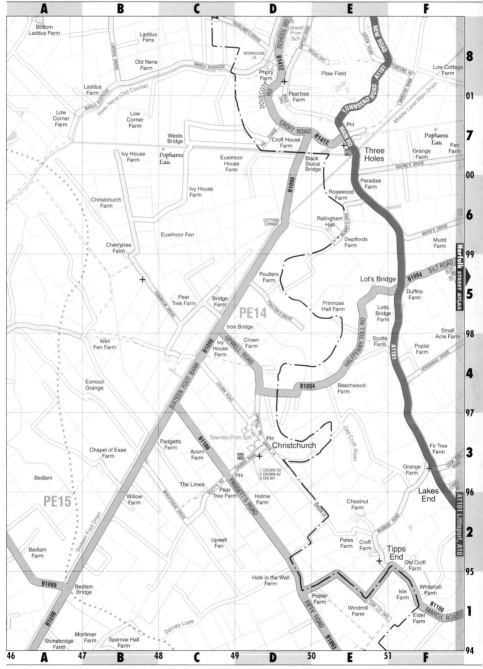

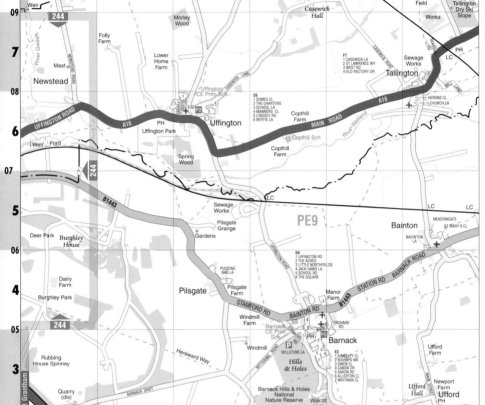

Lincolnshire STREET ATLAS

For full street detail of the highlighted area see page 244.

193

194

B1
1 GLEN RD
2 NENE CL
3 CHATER RD
4 HARVEY CL
5 THE LIMES
6 BROWNES RD
7 EXETER RD
8 THE HOLT
9 BURGHLEY AV

10 FREEMANS CL
11 MANOR CL
12 ST MICHAEL'S RD
13 ST JOHN'S RD
14 ST GEORGE'S RD
15 BROADHURST RD
16 NEWMAN CL
17 MALTBY CL
18 CARNEGIE RD
19 EMBRY RD

20 HALL LA
21 LEGG RD
22 JEFFERSON CL

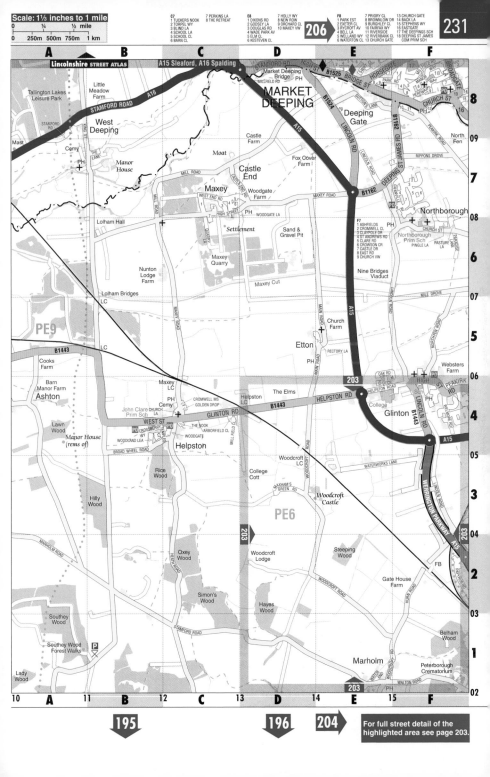

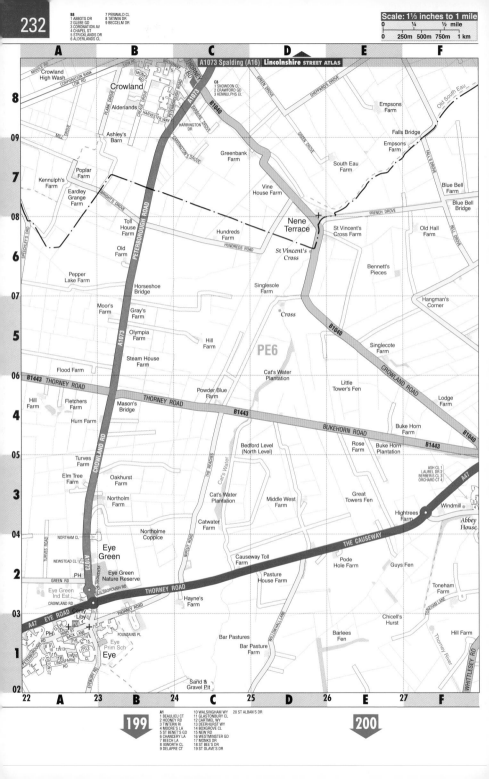

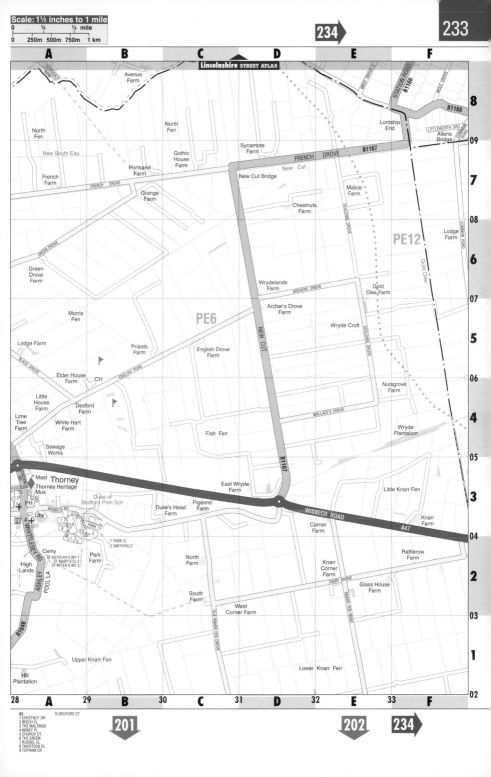

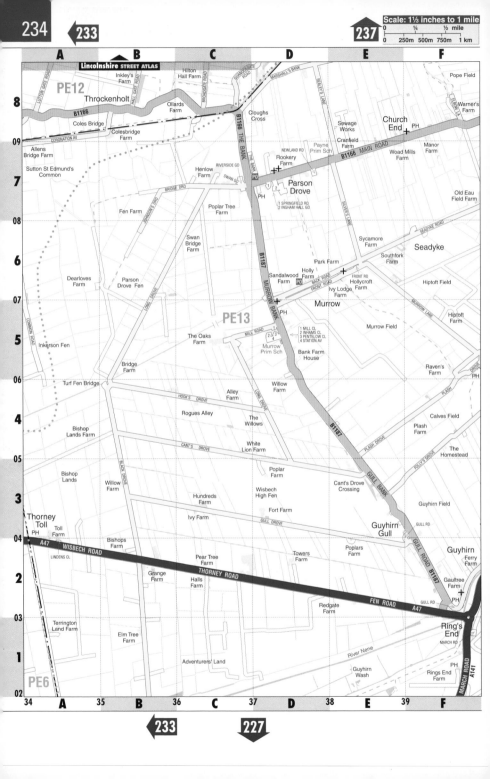

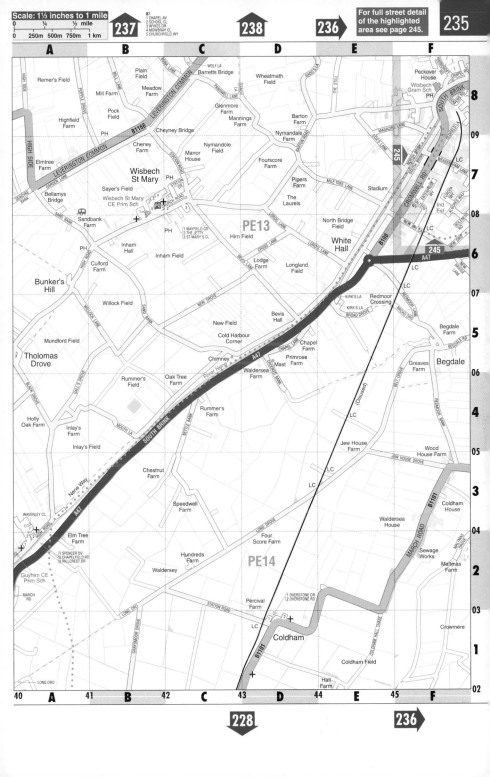

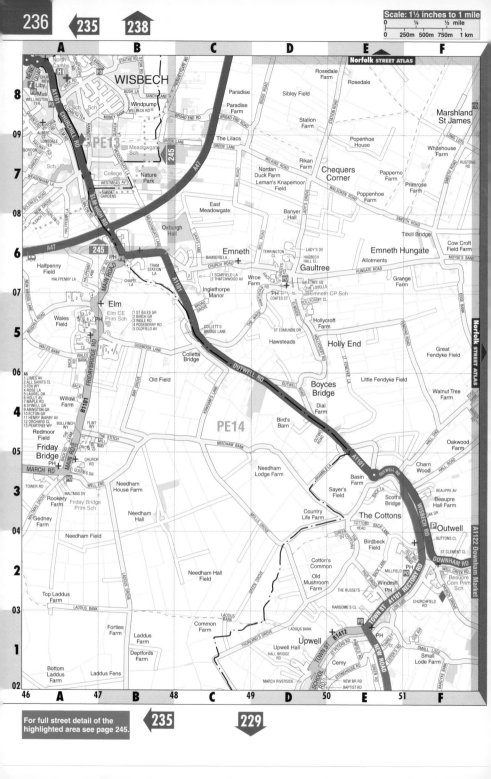

236   ◀ 235   ▲ 238

Scale: 1⅓ inches to 1 mile
0   ¼   ½ mile
0   250m   500m   750m   1 km

Norfolk STREET ATLAS

WISBECH

PE13

PE14

Marshland St James

Rosedale Farm
Rosedale
Sibley Field
Station Farm
Popenhoe House
Whitehouse Farm
Rikan Farm
Nordan Duck Farm
Leman's Knapmoor Field
Chequers Corner
Papperno Farm
Primrose Farm
Paradise
Paradise Farm
The Lilacs
Windpump
Meadowgate Sch
East Meadowgate
Banyer Hall
Oxburgh Hall
Emneth
Terrington CL
Gaultree
Emneth Hungate
Titkill Bridge
Cow Croft Field Farm
Allotments
Grange Farm
Halfpenny Field
Elm
Wales Field
Inglethorpe Manor
Wroe Farm
Emneth CP Sch
Hollycroft Farm
Holly End
Great Fendyke Field
Collett's Bridge
Hawsteads
Willow Farm
Old Field
Boyces Bridge
Little Fendyke Field
Walnut Tree Farm
Redmoor Field
Friday Bridge
Bird's Barn
Dial Farm
Oakwood Farm
Charn Wood
Rookery Farm
Friday Bridge Prim Sch
Needham House Farm
Needham Lodge Farm
Sayer's Field
Basin Farm
Scott's Bridge
Beaupre Av
Beaupre Hall Farm
Gedney Farm
Needham Hall
Country Life Farm
The Cottons
Outwell
Needham Field
Cotton's Head
Birdbeck Field
Suttons CL
St Clement CL
Top Laddus Farm
Needham Hall Field
Cotton's Common
Old Mushroom Farm
Windmill PH
Millfield
Beaupre Com Prim Sch
Laddus Bank
Forties Farm
Laddus Farm
Common Farm
The Russets
Ransome's CL
Churchfield Rd
Deptfords Farm
Laddus Bank
Upwell Hall
Hall Bridge Rd
Upwell
Small Lode Farm
Bottom Laddus Farm
Laddus Fens
March Riverside
Cemy
New Br Rd
Baptist Rd

For full street detail of the highlighted area see page 245.

◀ 235   ▼ 229

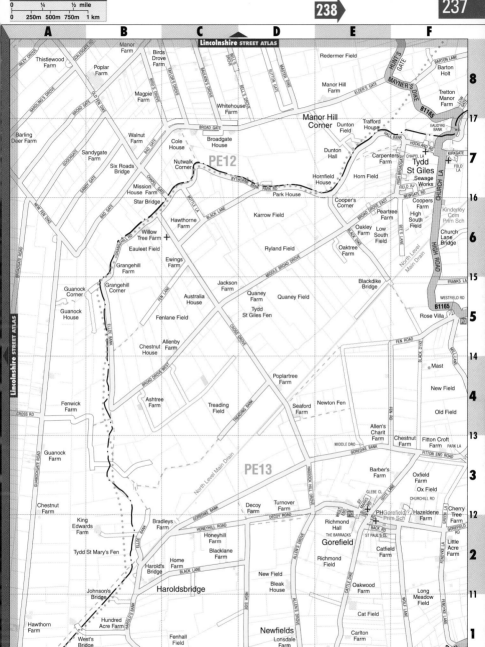

Scale: 1⅓ inches to 1 mile

0   ¼   ½ mile
0   250m 500m 750m 1 km

Lincolnshire STREET ATLAS

	A	B	C	D	E	F	

Lincolnshire STREET ATLAS

Thistlewood Farm
Manor Farm
Birds Drove Farm
Redermer Field
Barton Lane
Barton Holt

Poplar Farm
Tretton Manor Farm

Barling Deer Farm
Magpie Farm
Whitehouse Farm
Manor Hill Farm
Elder's Gate

Sandygate Farm
Walnut Farm
Cole House
Broadgate House
Manor Hill Corner
Dunton Field
Trafford House
EAUDYKE BANK
KIRKGATE

Six Roads Bridge
Nutwalk Corner
PE12
Dunton Hall
Carpenters Farm
Tydd St Giles
FOLD LA

Mission House Farm
Star Bridge
Hornfield House
Horn Field
Sewage Works
Kinderley Cem Prim Sch

Willow Tree Farm
Hawthorne Farm
Black Lane
Karrow Field
Cooper's Corner
Peartree Farm
Coopers Farm
High South Field
Church Lane Bridge

Eauleet Field
Oakley Farm
Low South Field

Grangehill Farm
Ewings Farm
Ryland Field
Oaktree Farm

Grangehill Corner
Jackson Farm
Quaney Farm
Quaney Field
Blackdike Bridge
WESTFIELD RD
FRANKS LA

Guanock Corner
Australia House
Tydd St Giles Fen
Rose Villa

Guanock House
Fenlane Field
Mast

Chestnut House
Allenby Farm
B1165
New Field

Fenwick Farm
Ashtree Farm
Treading Field
Poplartree Farm
Seaford Farm
Newton Fen
Old Field

Guanock Farm
Allen's Charit Farm
Chestnut Farm
Fitton Croft Farm
Fitton End Road

Chestnut Farm
MIDDLE DRO
GOREDIKE BANK
Barber's Farm
Oxfield Farm
Ox Field

King Edwards Farm
Bradleys Farm
Decoy Farm
Turnover Farm
PE13
Richmond Hall
Gorefield Prim Sch
Hazeldene Farm
Cherry Tree Farm

Tydd St Mary's Fen
Honeyhill Farm
THE BARRACKS
Gorefield
Catfield Farm
Little Acre Farm

Harold's Bridge
Home Farm
Blacklane Farm
Richmond Field

Johnson's Bridge
Haroldsbridge
New Field
Bleak House
Oakwood Farm
Long Meadow Field

Hawthorn Farm
Hundred Acre Farm
Fenhall Field
Newfields
Lonsdale Farm
Cat Field
Carlton Farm

West's Bridge
The Sycamores
CHALK ROAD
BONA LANE
LEVERINGTON COMMON
B1169

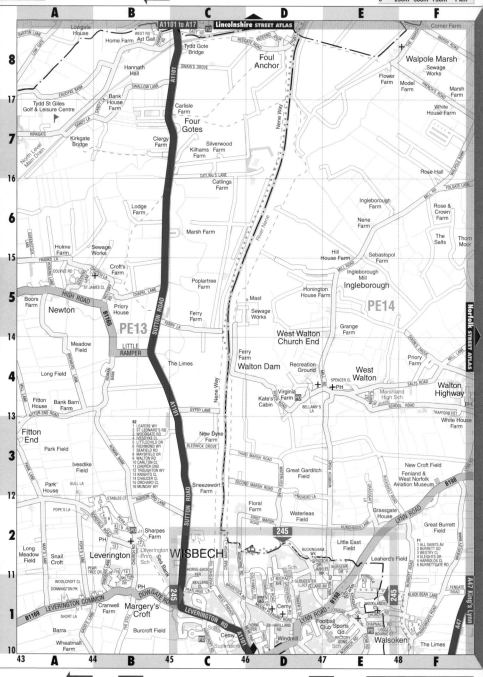

Scale: 1⅓ inches to 1 mile

0   ¼   ½ mile

0   250m 500m 750m 1 km

A **B** **C** **D** **E** **F**

Corner Farm

Lowgate House

Barton Lane

LOW GATE

WEST RD

Home Farm

Art Gall

Lincolnshire STREET ATLAS

EAST RD

PO

REDGATE ROAD

BEDFORD ROW

Walpole Marsh

MARSH ROAD

Hannath Hall

Tydd Gote Bridge

SWAIN'S DROVE

Foul Anchor

Flower Farm

Model Farm

Sewage Works

FRENCH'S RD

Marsh Farm

8

SWALLOW LANE

Carlisle Farm

17

EAUDYKE BANK

SANDY LANE

Bank House Farm

Tydd St Giles Golf & Leisure Centre

KIRKGATE

SANDY LANE

Kirkgate Bridge

Clergy Farm

Four Gotes

Silverwood Farm

Kilhams Farm

Nene Way

White House Farm

Rose Hall

HECKLES DRIVE

7

North Level Main Drain

CATLING'S LANE

Catlings Farm

River Nene

MILL RD

FOLGATE LANE

Rose & Crown Farm

16

Lodge Farm

Ingleborough Farm

The Salts

Thorn Moor

GREENSTOCK LANE

Holme Farm

Sewage Works

Marsh Farm

Nene Farm

6

Croft's Farm

Poplartree Farm

Hill House Farm

Sebastopol Farm

Ingleborough Mill

Ingleborough

FRANK'S LA

COLVILLE RD

CHURCH LA

ST JAMES CL

CHAPEL LANE

Honington House Farm

MILL DROVE

PE14

15

Boors Farm

HIGH ROAD

Newton

B1165

Priory House

SUTTON ROAD

FERRY LA

Mast

Sewage Works

West Walton Church End

Grange Farm

DOCKING DROVE

Priory Farm

5

PE13

LITTLE RAMPER

Meadow Field

The Limes

Ferry Farm

Nene Way

Ferry Farm

Walton Dam

Recreation Ground

SPENCER CL

PH

West Walton

SALTS ROAD

Walton Highway

14

Long Field

BREVERNS LANE

RAMPER BANK

A1101

GYPSY LANE

Kate's Cabin

Virginia Farm

PO

BELLAMY'S LA

Marshland High Sch

SCHOOL ROAD

TRAFFORD EST

White House Farm

4

Fitton House

Bank Barn Farm

FITTON END ROAD

MILL LANE

Fitton End

B2
1 LEAFERE WY
2 ST LEONARD'S RD
3 WOODGATE RD
4 IVESDYKE CL
5 LITTLECHILD DR
6 RICHMOND WY
7 SEAFIELD RD
8 MAYSFIELD DR
9 WALTON RD
10 CARLTON CL
11 CHURCH END
12 TROUGHTON WY
13 KNIGHTS CL
14 CHAUCER CL
15 ORCHARD CL
16 MUNDAY WY

New Dyke Farm

BLEDWICK DROVE

THIRD MARSH ROAD

Great Garditch Field

New Croft Field

Fenland & West Norfolk Aviation Museum

B198

3

Park Field

Ivesdike Field

PARSON'S LANE

Sneezewort Farm

SECOND MARSH ROAD

GRASSGATE LA

Grassgate House

Great Burrett Field

BLACKSMITH DROVE

13

PARK LANE

ROMANS BANK

GULL LA

Park House

STABLES CT

SUTTON ROAD

Floral Farm

FIRST MARSH ROAD

Waterleas Field

HUNCHBACK LANE

LYNN ROAD

F1
1 ALL SAINTS AV
2 BURRETT GD
3 WESTRY CL
4 SLEIGHTS DR
5 HARROLDS CL
6 BURRETTGATE RD

12

Long Meadow Field

POPE'S LANE

Snail Croft

PH

POPE'S LANE

PO

Sharpes Farm

Leverington Prim Sch

Sea Bank

WISBECH

245

Buckingham WK

WINDSOR DR

Little East Field

Leaherd's Field

245

2

B1169

MAY'S LANE

PEAR TREE CR

Leverington

MILTON CL

PH

HORSE-SHOE TER

BRIDGSTOCK RD

KEILLER'S CL

ST MICHAEL AV

GLOUCESTER JCT

NURSERY DR

PENDLE RD

WOODLANDS

CHURCH RD

FENGATE ROAD

A47 King's Lynn

11

LEVERINGTON COMMON

WOOLCROFT CL

DONNINGTON PK

Cranwell Farm

Margery's Croft

DOWGATE ROAD

245

PEATLINGS LA

SOUTHWELL RD

BATH ROAD

ST PETER'S RD

MOUNT PLEASANT RD

Cemy

LYNN ROAD

B198

Football Club Sports Gd

CHAPNALL RD

LEGGE ST

BOURNE CT

Walsoken

The Limes

A47

1

Barra

SHORT LA

GADE'S LANE

Burcroft Field

LEVERINGTON RD

A1101

PO

York Row

CRAB MARSH

DE-HAVILLAND RD

Windmill

Cemy

Superstore

PO

10

43   **A**   44   **B**   45   **C**   46   **D**   47   **E**   48   **F**

For full street detail of the highlighted area see page 245.

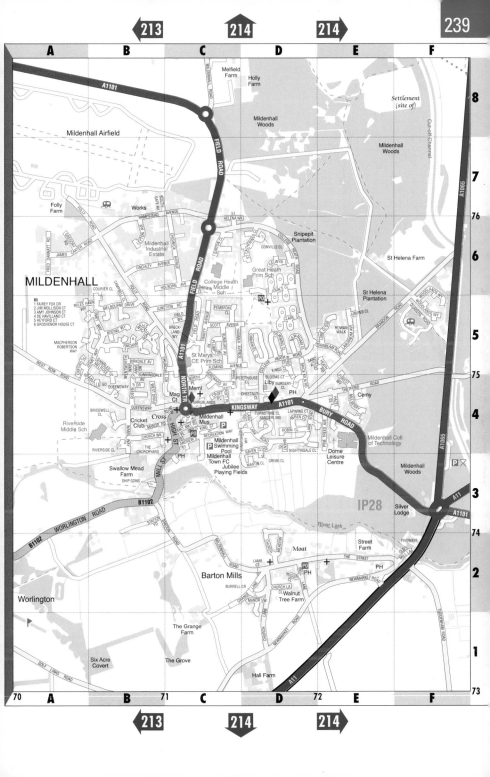

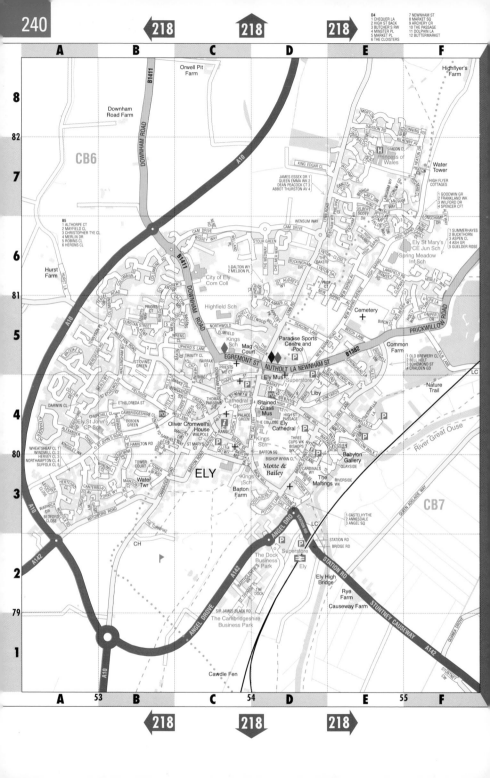

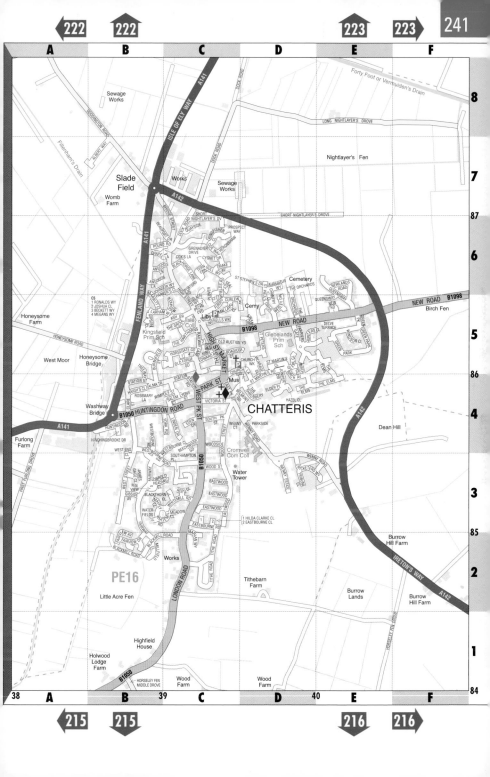

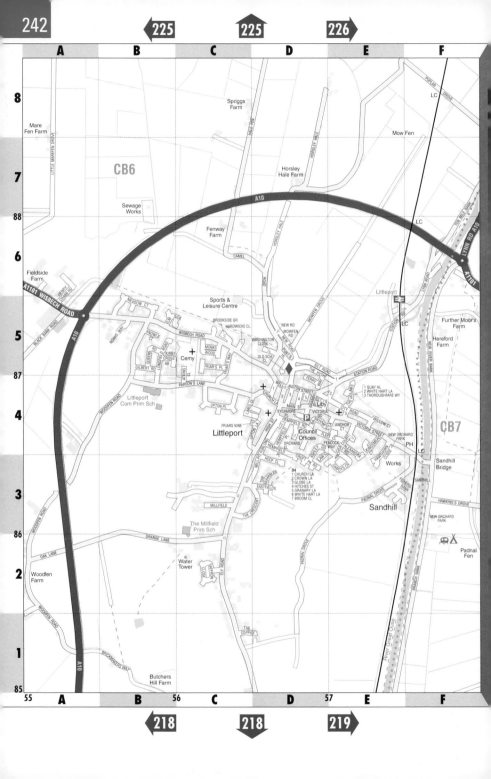

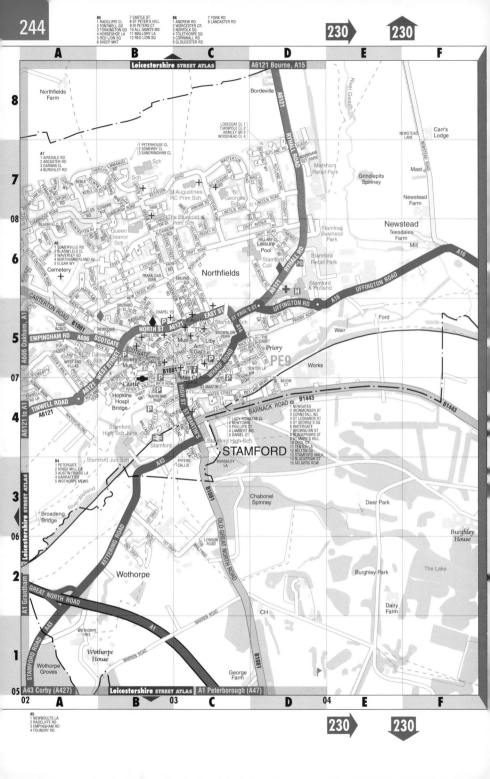

230 230

B5
1 RADCLIFFE CL
2 FONTWELL GD
3 TORKINGTON GD
4 HORSESHOE LA
5 RED LION SQ
6 SHEEP MKT

7 CASTLE ST
7 CASTLE ST
8 ST PETER'S HILL
9 ST PETERS CT
10 ALL SAINTS MS
11 MALLORY LA
12 RED LION SQ

B6
1 ANDREW RD
2 WORCESTER CR
3 NORFOLK SQ
4 TOLETHORPE SQ
5 CORNWALL RD
6 GLOUCESTER RD

7 YORK RD
7 YORK RD
8 LANCASTER RD

Leicestershire STREET ATLAS

A6121 Bourne, A15

Northfields Farm

Bordeville

River Gwash

NEWSTEAD LANE

Carr's Lodge

LOSECOAT CL 1
TURNPOLE CL 2
ARMLEY GR 3
WOODHEAD CL 4

Mast

A7
1 AIREDALE RD
2 ANCASTER RD
3 DARWIN CL
4 BURGHLEY RD

1 PETERHOUSE CL
2 SOMERBY CL
3 SANDRINGHAM CL

MARKHAM
RET PARK

Markham Retail Park

Grindlepits Spinney

Newstead Farm

St Augustines RC Prim Sch

St Georges Sch

Newstead

Teesdales Farm

Mill

A6
1 SOMERVILLE RD
2 BLASHFIELD GD
3 WAVERLEY GD
4 NORTHUMBERLAND AV
5 ELGAR WY

Queen Eleanor Sch

The Bluecoat Print Sch

Stamford Business Park

Stamford Leisure Pool

Stamford Coll

Cemetery

Northfields

Stamford Retail Park

Stamford & Rutland

H

A16

Ford

UFFINGTON ROAD

Weir

NORTH ST
EAST ST

ST PAUL'S ST

UFFINGTON RD

The CROFT

Priory

PE9

Works

CASTERTON ROAD

B1081

EMPINGHAM RD A606

SCOTGATE

WEST STREET

St Gilberts Sch

Brewery

Mus

Liby

Arts

Priory Road

Axiom CT

A6121 to A1

Castle

Hopkins Hospl

Bridge

Warrene Keep

BARNACK ROAD

B1443

B1443

C5
1 NEWGATES
2 IRONMONGER ST
3 CORNSTALL BG
4 ST LEONARDS ST
5 ST GEORGE S SQ
6 WATERGATE
7 BROWNLOW ST
8 BLACKFRIARS ST
9 ST MARY S HILL
10 CECIL PL
11 TENTER LA
12 BELTON GD
13 STAMFORD WALK
14 BLACKFRIARS ST
15 MILNERS ROW

TINWELL ROAD

A6121

Stamford High Sch Juns

Stamford High Sch

Stamford

B4
1 PETERGATE
2 KINGS MILL LA
3 AUSTIN FRIARS LA
4 GARRATT RD
5 WOTHORPE MEWS

1 LADY ROMAYNE CL
2 NEWTOWN
3 PHILLIPS CT
4 LAMBERT MS
5 DANIEL CT

STAMFORD

Stamford Jun Sch

FRYERS CALLIS

BURGHLEY LA

Broadeng Bridge

River Welland

KETTERING ROAD

Chabonel Spinney

Deer Park

Burghley House

OLD GREAT NORTH ROAD

B1081

LONDON ROAD

Wothorpe

WARREN ROAD

CH

Burghley Park

The Lake

GREAT NORTH ROAD

A1 Grantham

A43

Wothorpe Ho.

Wothorpe Groves

Wothorpe House

WARREN ROAD

George Farm

Dairy Farm

STAMFORD ROAD

A43 Corby (A427)

Leicestershire STREET ATLAS

A1 Peterborough (A47)

A5
1 NEWBOULTS LA
2 RADCLIFFE RD
3 EMPINGHAM RD
4 FOUNDRY RD

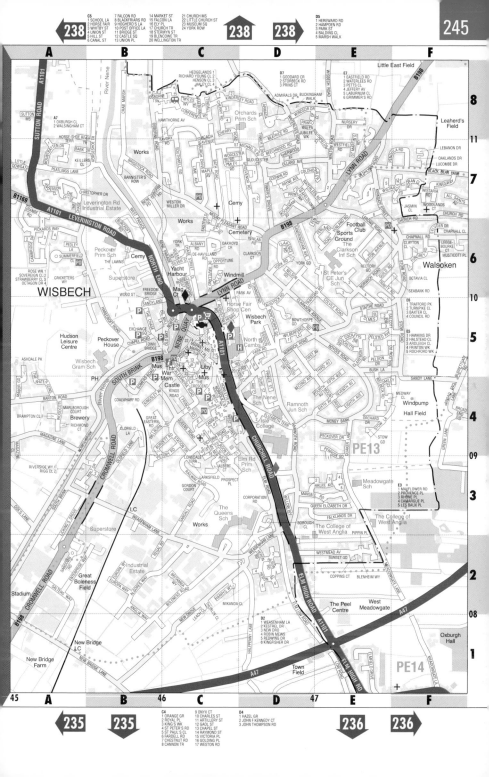

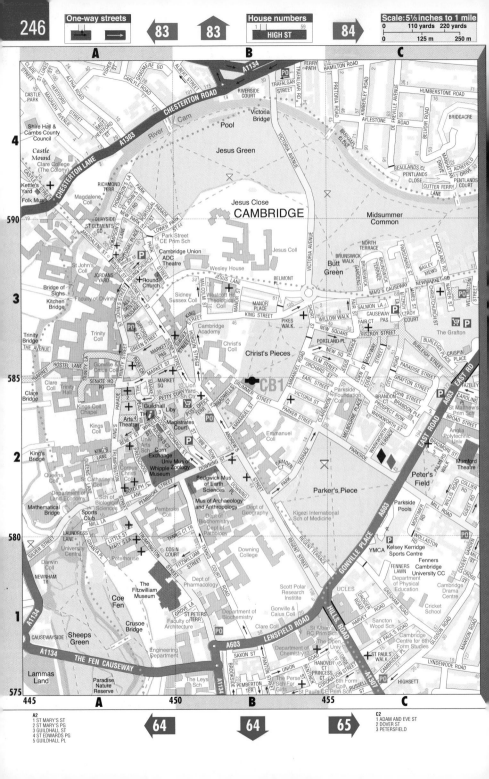

Index

Church Rd **6** Beckenham BR2.......... **53** C6

Place name	**Location number**	**Locality, town or village**	**Postcode district**	**Page and grid square**
May be abbreviated on the map	Present when a number indicates the place's position in a crowded area of mapping	Shown when more than one place has the same name	District for the indexed place	Page number and grid reference for the standard mapping

Public and commercial buildings are highlighted in magenta   **Places of interest** are highlighted in blue with a star★

Abbreviations used in the index

Acad	**Academy**	Comm	**Common**	Gd	**Ground**	L	**Leisure**	Prom	**Promenade**
App	**Approach**	Cott	**Cottage**	Gdn	**Garden**	La	**Lane**	Rd	**Road**
Arc	**Arcade**	Cres	**Crescent**	Gn	**Green**	Liby	**Library**	Recn	**Recreation**
Ave	**Avenue**	Cswy	**Causeway**	Gr	**Grove**	Mdw	**Meadow**	Ret	**Retail**
Bglw	**Bungalow**	Ct	**Court**	H	**Hall**	Meml	**Memorial**	Sh	**Shopping**
Bldg	**Building**	Ctr	**Centre**	Ho	**House**	Mkt	**Market**	Sq	**Square**
Bsns, Bus	**Business**	Ctry	**Country**	Hospl	**Hospital**	Mus	**Museum**	St	**Street**
Bvd	**Boulevard**	Cty	**County**	HQ	**Headquarters**	Orch	**Orchard**	Sta	**Station**
Cath	**Cathedral**	Dr	**Drive**	Hts	**Heights**	Pal	**Palace**	Terr	**Terrace**
Cir	**Circus**	Dro	**Drove**	Ind	**Industrial**	Par	**Parade**	TH	**Town Hall**
Cl	**Close**	Ed	**Education**	Inst	**Institute**	Pas	**Passage**	Univ	**University**
Cnr	**Corner**	Emb	**Embankment**	Int	**International**	Pk	**Park**	Wk, Wlk	**Walk**
Coll	**College**	Est	**Estate**	Intc	**Interchange**	Pl	**Place**	Wr	**Water**
Com	**Community**	Ex	**Exhibition**	Junc	**Junction**	Prec	**Precinct**	Yd	**Yard**

Index of localities, towns and villages

A

Abbotsley 57 C5
Abbots Ripton 162 C1
Abington Piggots 11 E5
Ailsworth 195 D3
Alconbury 150 E4
Alconbury Weston 150 D6
Aldreth 209 E4
Alwalton 185 B4
Arbury 102 C3
Arrington 44 C1
Ashdon 21 B1
Ashley 91 F7
Ashton 231 A4
Ashwell 2 E4
Ashwell End 2 A5

B

Babraham 50 E1
Badlingham 213 D1
Bainton 230 F5
Balsham 53 A2
Barham 149 B3
Bar Hill 102 C3
Barley 6 F2
Barnack 230 E3
Barrington 29 E8
Bartlow 21 A7
Barton 63 B3
Barton Mills 239 C2
Barway 211 C6

Bassingbourn 12 F4
Beck Row 213 F8
Begdale 235 F5
Benwick 222 A5
Bird's Hundred 189 C5
Blackhall 227 A1
Black Horse Drove 226 B6
Bluntisham 208 D5
Bordeville 244 D8
Bottisham 86 F6
Bourn 60 C6
Boxworth 101 B5
Boxworth End 123 E3
Boyces Bridge 236 D4
Brampton 140 C2
Brampton Lodge 140 A1
Brampton Park 140 D1
Brandon Bank 226 E3
Brandon Creek 226 D6
Bretton 197 A6
Briggate 189 E6
Brington 147 D4
Brinkley 70 E2
Broad Green Newmarket . .91 D4
Broad Green Royston 8 C3
Brook End 136 B6
Broughton 153 F8
Buckden 118 B3
Buckworth 149 E6
Bunker's Hill 235 A6
Burrough End 70 E4
Burrough Green 70 F3
Burton End 37 C8
Burwell 130 C2
Bury 172 B4

Bythorn 146 D4

C

Caldecote Highfields 61 B7
Caldecote Highfields 80 B1
Caldecote Stilton 175 D5
Caldecote St Neots 76 B1
Calford Green 24 F7
Cambourne 79 D4
Cambridge 246 A2
Camps End 22 A1
Cardinal's Green 37 B1
Carlton 55 A7
Carlton Green 55 A4
Carlton Hill 55 A8
Castle Camps 22 F4
Castle End 231 D7
Castor 195 D1
Catworth 136 D7
Caxton 78 F1
Chainbridge 228 B7
Chapel End 174 D4
Chatteris 241 D4
Cherry Hinton 65 F5
Chesterford Park 19 D1
Chesterton Cambridge ...84 A6
Chesterton Peterborough .184 E3
Cheveley 91 C6
Childerley 80 C8
Childerley Gate 80 D4
Chippenham 133 D8
Chittering 127 B8
Chrishall 8 D4

Christchurch 229 D3
Church End Catworth ...136 E7
Church End Eltisley 77 D4
Church End Great Stukeley 151 F2
Church End Over 208 C1
Church End Pidley 165 D1
Church End Swavesey ...122 E7
Church End Woodwalton .169 D2
Church Field 189 B7
Clayhithe 106 D5
Claypit Hill 61 D2
Clopton 156 E5
Coates 190 F8
Cockayne Hatley 25 C8
Coldham 235 D1
Coldham Hall 228 E8
Coldham's Common 84 D2
Coleseed House 228 D2
Colne 208 D6
Colnefields 208 D8
Comberton 62 C5
Commercial End 108 C3
Conington Fenstanton ..121 C1
Conington Sawtry 168 C8
Corner Lodge 227 F2
Coton 82 B2
Cottenham 126 C3
Coveney 217 C5
Covington 135 D2
Cowlinge 73 D1
Crawley End 8 D5
Cropley Grove 92 D3
Crow End 60 D7
Crowland 232 B8
Croxton 76 F4

Croydon 27 A7

D

Dalham 92 E8
Deeping Gate 231 E8
Deeping St James 206 A7
Denny End 105 F8
Denton 175 E4
Diddington 96 A8
Dillington 94 C7
Ditton Green 90 E1
Doddington 223 A6
Dogsthorpe 198 C2
Down Field 212 D2
Downham Hythe 217 D6
Dry Drayton 102 C1
Duck End 97 F5
Duckpuddle Bush 4 F2
Dullingham 71 A5
Dullingham Ley 71 A5
Duloe 74 A6
Dunkirk 224 F1
Duxford 17 D8
Dyer's Green 13 C8

E

Eaglethorpe 178 A4
Earith 208 E6
Eastfield 198 D4
Eastgate 198 B2
East Hatley 43 B1

Easton ...138 C4
East Perry ...116 E3
Eastrea ...190 D7
Eaton Ford ...74 C5
Eaton Socon ...74 B3
Eldernell ...202 B2
Ellington ...139 A4
Ellington Thorpe ...139 A2
Elm ...236 B5
Elmdon ...9 A4
Elsworth ...100 C4
Eltisley ...77 C4
Elton ...178 D8
Ely ...240 C1
Emmaus ...127 E2
Emneth ...236 C6
Emneth Hungate ...236 E6
Etton ...231 D5
Everton ...40 C3
Exmoor Grange ...229 B4
Exning ...110 A8
Eye ...232 B1
Eye Green ...232 B2
Eynesbury ...74 F3

F
Farcet ...187 C2
Fen Ditton ...84 F5
Fen Drayton ...122 F6
Fen End ...57 D6
Fengate ...198 D2
Fenstanton ...122 C5
Fenton ...165 B4
Fitton End ...238 A3
Flint Cross ...15 B2
Folksworth ...175 D8
Fordham ...212 F1
Fowlmere ...15 D8
Foxton ...30 C5
Freckenham ...213 C3
Friday Bridge ...236 A4
Fulbourn ...66 F4

G
Gamlingay ...41 D5
Gamlingay Cinques ...41 B6
Gamlingay Great Heath ...40 E3
Garden Cottage ...93 D5
Gatley End ...3 C7
Gaultree ...236 D6
Gimbers End ...115 B2
Girton ...82 F8
Glatton ...175 F1
Glenthorn ...227 F3
Glinton ...203 E8
Godmanchester ...141 E2
Gorefield ...237 E2
Grafham ...116 A7
Grandford House ...227 F6
Grantchester ...64 A4
Graveley ...97 F4
Gravel House ...228 C6
Great Abington ...34 C6
Great Bradley ...55 F7
Great Cambourne ...79 B2
Great Chesterford ...18 D2
Great Chishill ...2 A7
Great Eversden ...45 E8
Great Gidding ...166 E3
Great Gransden ...58 D5
Great Paxton ...96 E4
Great Raveley ...163 B7
Great Shelford ...48 F5
Great Staughton ...93 F6
Great Stukeley ...152 A2
Great Wilbraham ...68 A7
Great Wratting ...39 D5
Green End Comberton ...62 B6
Green End Great Stukeley ...152 A1
Green End Little Staughton ...93 A3
Guilden Morden ...10 E4
Gunthorpe ...204 D2
Guyhirn ...234 F2

H
Haddenham ...210 B6
Haddon ...180 B6
Hadstock ...20 C6
Hail Weston ...95 B1
Hamerton ...139 D2
Hampton Hargate ...186 D2
Hanchet End ...38 C1
Hanchet Village ...23 B8
Hardwick Buckden ...117 A5
Hardwick Cambridge ...81 B3
Hare Park ...88 A3
Harlton ...46 D5
Haroldsbridge ...237 C2
Harston ...48 A3

Hartford ...142 A6
Haslingfield ...47 B6
Hatley End ...25 B5
Hatley St George ...43 A3
Hauxton ...48 B4
Haverhill ...24 C8
Hawthorn Lodge ...93 D5
Hazel Stub ...23 C7
Heydon ...8 A5
Helpston ...231 C4
Hemingford Abbots ...142 E3
Hemingford Grey ...143 E1
Herringswell ...113 E8
Heydon ...8 A5
High Cross ...82 E2
Highfields ...80 D2
High Harthay ...139 E3
Hildersham ...34 F5
Hilton ...121 B1
Hinton ...18 A7
Hinxton ...104 C4
Histon ...104 C4
Holly End ...236 E5
Holme ...177 A4
Holywell ...144 F2
Holywell Row ...214 A8
Hook ...223 D8
Horningsea ...106 A1
Horseheath ...37 A3
Horse Moor ...228 D1
Houghton ...143 A5
Huntingdon ...141 F4

I
Ickleton ...18 A4
Impington ...104 C2
Ingleborough ...238 E5
Inham's End ...189 F6
Islands Common ...74 E7
Isleham ...213 A5

K
Kennett ...134 F5
Kennett End ...113 A2
Kentford ...113 B2
Keyston ...146 B3
Kimbolton ...113 F6
King's Dyke ...188 E6
Kings Hedges ...83 E7
Kings Ripton ...153 C5
Kingston ...61 B3
Kingswood Park ...243 B2
Kirtling ...72 D6
Kirtling Green ...72 C4
Kirtling Towers ...72 D7
Knapwell ...100 E1
Kneesworth ...13 A6
Knights End ...228 A1

L
Laddus Fens ...236 B1
Lakes End ...229 F3
Landbeach ...105 D7
Landwade ...132 C4
Lark Hall Corner ...69 A1
Lattersea Field ...190 B6
Leighton Bromswold ...148 D3
Leverington ...238 B2
Lidgate ...73 E8
Linton ...35 E3
Litlington ...12 B2
Little Abington ...34 B7
Littlebury Green ...9 F2
Little Catworth ...137 A6
Little Chishill ...1 C7
Little Ditton ...90 F2
Little Downham ...218 B6
Little End ...74 C1
Little Eversden ...46 A7
Little Gidding ...158 F8
Little Gransden ...58 D3
Little Green ...178 C3
Little Heath ...41 C4
Little Linton ...35 B3
Little London ...243 C4
Little Ouse ...226 D4
Little Paxton ...96 B2
Littleport ...242 C4
Little Raveley ...163 B4
Little Shelford ...48 E3
Little Staughton ...93 B2
Little Stukeley ...151 C4
Little Thetford ...211 B7
Little Wilbraham ...86 E1
Little Wratting ...39 D3
Lode ...107 C2
Lolworth ...101 F5
Long Meadow ...107 F2
Longstanton ...124 E2
Longstowe ...59 F3
Longthorpe ...197 A1

Lower Cambourne ...78 F4
Luddington in the Brook 166 B4
Lutton ...174 C4

M
Madingley ...81 E5
Manea ...221 B4
March ...243 B4
Margery's Croft ...238 B1
Marholm ...203 E1
Market Deeping ...231 D8
Marshland St James ...236 F8
Maxey ...231 C7
Melbourn ...14 C5
Meldreth ...29 A2
Mepal ...216 E4
Mildenhall ...239 A6
Mile End ...219 C5
Mill End ...72 E5
Millfield ...197 E2
Mill Green ...22 D7
Milton ...105 E2
Molesworth ...147 A5
Morborne ...180 B3
Morden Green ...11 C1
Moulton ...112 E6
Murrow ...234 D5

N
Needingworth ...208 B3
Nene Terrace ...232 D6
Newark ...198 E6
Newborough ...207 D1
New England ...197 E2
Newfields ...237 D1
New Fletton ...187 B8
Newmarket ...111 B5
New Meadow ...187 F2
Newnham ...64 C8
Newnham Croft ...64 D7
Newstead ...244 E6
Newton Harston ...31 C8
Newton Wisbech ...238 A5
Newtown Cambridge ...64 E7
Newtown Kimbolton ...114 A5
New Wimpole ...28 B8
Norman Cross ...180 F2
Northborough ...231 F7
Northfields ...241 C6
North Green ...190 E8
North Side ...200 F4
Norwoodside ...243 C7
Nosterfield End ...22 F5

O
Oakington ...103 B5
Odsey ...3 C1
Offord Cluny ...118 F3
Offord D'Arcy ...118 F1
Old Fletton ...187 A6
Old Hurst ...154 E7
Old Weston ...148 A8
Old Wimpole ...44 F3
Orton Brimbles ...185 D5
Orton Goldhay ...185 F3
Orton Longueville ...186 B5
Orton Malbourne ...186 C4
Orton Southgate ...185 C2
Orton Waterville ...185 E4
Orton Wistow ...185 C6
Orwell ...45 E1
Outwell ...236 F3
Over ...208 E1
Over End ...178 E7
Owl End ...152 A3
Oxlode ...224 C1

P
Pale Green ...23 D1
Pampisford ...33 B5
Papley ...174 A6
Papworth Everard ...99 B3
Papworth St Agnes ...98 D5
Papworth Village Settlement ...99 A2
Parson Drove ...234 D7
Paston ...205 A1
Peakirk ...206 B1
Peas Hill ...243 B6
Peterborough ...197 D5
Pidley ...155 E8
Pilsgate ...230 C4
Place House ...93 E6
Pondersbridge ...220 D7
Prickwillow ...219 B5
Pymore (Pymoor) ...224 E1

Q
Queen Adelaide ...218 D4

R
Ralingham Hall ...229 E6
Rampton ...125 F4
Ramsey ...172 B6
Ramsey Forty Foot ...221 C2
Ramsey Heights ...171 A7
Ramsey Mereside ...221 A4
Ramsey St Mary's ...220 D3
Ravensthorpe ...197 C6
Reach ...130 C1
Red Lodge ...213 F1
Ring's End ...234 F1
Romsey Town ...65 B8
Royston ...5 B6

S
St Ives ...143 E7
St Neots ...74 E4
Sandhill ...242 E3
Sapley ...33 A7
Sawston ...33 A3
Sawtry ...168 A3
Saxon Street ...91 B3
Seadyke ...234 F6
Sewell's Barn ...138 A2
Shepreth ...29 E4
Shingay ...26 F2
Shudy Camps ...22 B5
Sibson ...183 E8
Six Mile Bottom ...68 F7
Slade Field ...241 B7
Snailwell ...133 B4
Soham ...212 B4
Soham Cotes ...211 F5
Somersham ...215 B1
Somersham Park ...208 C8
South Green ...190 F7
Southoe ...95 E5
Southorpe ...230 D2
Spaldwick ...137 F6
Stags Holt ...228 D7
Stamford ...244 D4
Stanground ...187 C5
Stapleford ...49 D4
Staughton Green ...94 A6
Staughton Highway ...94 A5
Steeple Gidding ...159 B7
Steeple Morden ...11 B2
Stetchworth ...90 A2
Stetchworth Ley ...71 A7
Steventon End ...21 C2
Stibbington ...194 C2
Stilton ...176 A7
Stirtloe ...118 B2
Stonely ...115 B3
Stourbridge Common ...84 B4
Stow Cum Quy ...86 A6
Stow Longa ...137 C2
Streetly End ...37 A5
Strethall ...9 F4
Stretham ...210 E6
Studlands Park ...110 F8
Stukeley ...141 B6
Stuntney ...218 D1
Sturmer ...24 F4
Sutton Ailsworth ...194 F2
Sutton Ely ...216 E2
Sutton Gault ...216 C2
Swaffham Bulbeck ...108 B1
Swaffham Prior ...108 E4
Swavesey ...123 E6
Swingbrow ...222 D3

T
Tadlow ...26 A3
Tallington ...230 E7
Temple End ...55 D2
Tetworth ...40 F7
Teversham ...85 C1
The Cottons ...236 E3
The Green ...121 D1
The Limes ...229 C3
The Lipneas ...202 B1
The Meadow ...215 C2
The Severals ...111 B5
Thistley Green ...213 C7
Tholomas Drove ...235 A5
Thorney ...233 A3
Thorney Toll ...234 A3
Thornhaugh ...193 F5
Three Holes ...229 E7
Thriplow ...31 C2
Throckenholt ...234 B8
Tilbrook ...114 B7

Tipps End ...229 F2
Toft ...61 E4
Top End ...93 B1
Toseland ...97 D2
Town End ...243 D1
Trumpington ...64 E2
Tuddenham ...214 D2
Turves ...191 F6
Tydd St Giles ...237 F7

U
Uffington ...230 C6
Ufford ...230 F3
Upend ...92 A1
Upend Green ...91 F2
Upton Ailsworth ...195 B6
Upton Alconbury ...160 C1
Upware ...211 B1
Upwell ...236 D1
Upwood ...171 C2

W
Walpole Marsh ...238 F8
Walsoken ...245 F6
Walton ...204 D1
Walton Dam ...238 D4
Walton Highway ...238 F4
Wansford ...194 A4
Warboys ...165 A5
Wardy Hill ...217 B4
Waresley ...57 F2
Warmington ...178 A3
Waterbeach ...106 C7
Water End ...25 B3
Water Newton ...184 C7
Waterside ...213 A6
Way Head ...217 C6
Wayside ...138 C5
Weald ...76 B4
Welches Dam ...224 A1
Welney ...225 B8
Wendy ...27 C4
Wennington ...162 D4
Wentworth ...217 B1
Werrington ...204 B3
Westcote ...211 F6
West Deeping ...231 B8
West End ...155 A5
Westley Bottom ...69 C7
Westley Waterless ...70 C5
Weston Colville ...54 B7
Weston Ditch ...213 C7
Weston Green ...54 D5
West Perry ...116 D2
West Row ...213 D6
Westry ...227 F5
West Walton ...238 E4
West Walton Church End ...238 D5
Westwick ...103 E7
West Wickham ...37 B7
Westwood ...197 B4
West Wratting ...53 E5
Whaddon ...28 C1
White Hall ...235 E6
Whittlesey ...189 D5
Whittlesford ...32 B5
Wicken ...211 F1
Wiggens Green ...23 E2
Wilburton ...210 B5
Willingham ...209 B1
Willingham Green ...54 D8
Wimblington ...223 A6
Wintringham ...75 F4
Winwick ...158 B6
Wisbech ...245 A6
Wisbech St Mary ...235 C6
Wistow ...163 F6
Witcham ...217 A2
Witchford ...217 D1
Withersfield ...38 C4
Wittering ...230 C1
Wooddition ...90 E3
Woodhurst ...155 B4
Woodland Green ...24 E7
Woodston ...186 E7
Wood Walton ...161 F6
Woolley ...149 E1
Worlington ...214 B2
Wothorpe ...244 E4
Wrestlingworth ...25 C4
Wyton ...142 F5

Y
Yarwell ...183 A4
Yaxley ...181 F4
Yelling ...98 C1

A

A Furlong Dro CB6 ....224 F2
Abbey Cl Burwell CB5 .....130 B1
  Sawtry PE28 ....168 B4
Abbey Fields PE26 ....172 C7
Abbey La Lode CB5 ....107 C2
  Swaffham Bulbeck CB5 .....108 B3
Abbey Mdws Prim Sch
  CB5 ....84 D2
Abbey Pl 4 Thorney PE6 ...233 A3
  Waterbeach CB5 ....127 B1
Abbey Rd
  Cambridge CB5 ....84 A3
  Peterborough PE4 ....204 C1
  Ramsey PE26 ....172 C6
Abbey St Cambridge CB1 ...84 A2
  Ickleton CB10 ....17 E3
Abbey Way PE7 ....189 C7
Abbey Wlk CB1 ....84 A2
Abbot Thurston Ave
  CB6 ....240 E6
Abbot Way PE7 ....181 D4
Abbot's Cl PE28 ....155 A5
Abbots Cl
  Cambridge CB4 ....83 E7
  Hemingford Abbots
  PE28 ....142 F3
  Ramsey PE26 ....172 C7
Abbots Cres PE27 ....144 A6
Abbots Dr 1 PE6 ....232 B8
Abbots Ripton CE Prim Sch
  PE28 ....162 C1
Abbots Way Ely CB6 ......240 B5
  Horningsea CB5 ....106 A1
Abbotsbury PE2 ....186 A3
Abbotsley Rd PE19 ....57 E8
Abbotsmede Prim Sch
  PE1 ....198 C4
Abbott Cl PE28 ....140 C3
Abbott's Ct PE9 ....244 D4
Abbott's Gr Cotts CB9 ...24 F3
Abbotts Cl SG8 ....12 A2
Abbotts Ct 2 CB1 ....24 E5
Abbotts Gr PE4 ....204 B6
Abbotts Rd CB9 ....39 A1
Abercorn Ct CB9 ....23 F6
Abercorn Pl 6 CB4 ....83 C7
Abington Gr 4 PE14 ......236 A5
Abington Rd SG8 ....11 F2
Aboyne Ave PE2 ....185 F5
Abrahams Cl CB4 ....105 D6
Abram's La SG8 ....8 C4
Acacia Ave
  Peterborough PE1 ....198 B8
  St Ives PE27 ....143 E6
  Wisbech PE13 ....245 C8
Acacia Gr March PE15 ....243 C5
  St Neots PE19 ....75 A6
Acer Rd PE1 ....198 B6
Acheson Rd PE28 ....117 D8
Ackerman Gdns 4 PE19 ...74 C2
Ackerman St PE14 ....74 C2
Ackroyd Rd 2 SG8 ....5 E8
Acland St PE17 ....197 F3
Acorn Ave CB3 ....102 C4
Acorn La CB3 ....79 C4
Acre Rd Carlton CB8 ......55 B8
  March PE15 ....243 D4
Acre The PE28 ....150 F4
Acrefield Dr CB4 ....246 C4
Acremead PE8 ....178 A3
Acres The 2 PE9 ....230 D4
Acton Way CB4 ....83 D5
Adam and Eve St 1
  CB1 ....246 C1
Adam's La PE19 ....96 E4
Adams Ct CB5 ....106 C7
Adams Rd
  Cambridge CB3 ....83 B2
  Swaffham Prior CB5 ....108 D5
Adastral Cl PE28 ....110 E4
Addenbrookes Hospl
  CB2 ....65 A3
Adderley PE3 ....197 C7
Addington Way 1 PE4 ....204 C3
Addison Rd PE15 ....223 B7
Adelaide Cl 10 CB7 ......212 B4
Adelaide Pl PE15 ....243 C4
Adelaide St PE9 ....244 C5
Adelaide Wlk PE28 ......208 E6
Admirals Dr PE13 ....245 D8
Admirals Way PE19 ......74 A2
Adventurers' Dro CB6 ....224 C1
Ailwine Rd PE28 ....171 B2
Ailwyn Sch PE26 ....172 C6
Aingers Rd CB4 ....104 B4
Ainsdale CB1 ....65 F5
Ainsdale Dr PE4 ....204 B4
Ainsworth Cl 4 CB1 ......84 A1
Ainsworth Pl CB1 ....84 B1
Ainsworth St CB1 ....84 A1
Aintree Rd SG8 ....5 D8
Aireside Cl PE1 ....198 A6
Airedale Rd 1 PE2 ....244 A7
Airport Way CB1 ....85 B2
Akeman Cl CB6 ....210 F6
Akeman St
  Cambridge CB4 ....83 C5
  Landbeach CB4 ....105 C6
Akerly Dr CB3 ....79 A4
Alan Ct PE19 ....74 C5
Albany Rd PE13 ....245 C6
Albany Wlk PE2 ....186 D7
Albemarle Rd PE27 ......143 F7
Albemarle Way CB4 ......83 E7

Albert Ct PE13 ....245 C3
Albert Pl PE3 ....197 F1
Albert Rd Stamford PE9 ..244 C5
  Stow cum Quy CB5 ....86 A5
Albert St CB4 ....246 B4
Albert Way PE16 ....241 B7
Alberta Cres PE29 ....141 E5
Albert's Dr PE15 ....243 F3
Albion Row 6 CB4 ....83 C3
Albion Yd 5 CB3 ....83 C3
Alconbury CE Prim Sch
  PE28 ....150 F5
Alconbury Cl PE2 ....187 E5
Alde Rd CB9 ....39 A1
Aldeburgh Cl 2 CB9 .....23 E7
Aldreth Rd CB6 ....209 F5
Alder Cl 1 PE19 ....74 B5
Alder Dr Bourn CB3 ......79 C3
  Peterborough PE29 ....141 D5
Alder Rd PE7 ....186 C3
Alderlands PE6 ....232 B8
Alderlands 5 PE6 ....232 B8
Alderman Jacobs Prim Sch
  PE7 ....189 F8
Alderman's Dr PE3 ......197 E3
Aldham Ct 12 CB9 ....23 E7
Aldreth Rd CB6 ....209 F5
Aldsworth Cl PE1 ....198 D6
Alec Rolph Cl CB1 ....66 D5
Alex Wood Rd CB4 ....83 E6
Alexander Chase CB6 ....240 A4
Alexander Rd SG19 ......25 B4
Alexandra Rd
  Littleport CB6 ....242 E4
  Peterborough PE1 ....197 F6
  Stamford PE9 ....244 B6
  Wisbech PE13 ....245 C5
Alfric Sq PE2 ....186 D6
Alfruda Cl PE15 ....243 C6
Algar Dr CB8 ....70 F8
Algores Way PE13 ....245 B2
Alington Rd PE19 ....74 E1
Aliwal Rd PE7 ....189 F1
Alix Way CB7 ....240 F7
All Saints Ave CB1 ......245 F7
All Saints CE Prim Sch
  CB8 ....111 B3
All Saints Cl
  St Ives PE27 ....144 A6
  2 Wisbech PE14 ....236 A5
All Saints Gn PE27 ......144 A6
All Saints IC Prim Sch
  PE15 ....243 D6
All Saints Jun Sch
  PE1 ....198 A6
All Saints Mews 10 PE9 ..244 B5
All Saints Pas
  Cambridge CB2 ....246 A3
  6 Huntingdon PE29 ......141 D4
All Saints Rd
  Fulbourn CB1 ....66 F5
  Newmarket CB8 ....111 A3
All Saints' Rd PE1 ....198 A5
All Saints' St PE9 ....244 B5
All Saints Way CB8 ......168 C4
All Souls La CB3 ....83 B4
Allan Ave PE27 ....187 E5
Allard Cl PE7 ....181 D6
Allen Ct CB2 ....64 D2
Allen Farm Cl PE29 ......141 E1
Allen Rd
  Peterborough PE1 ....197 E6
  Ramsey PE26 ....171 F7
Allen's Dro PE13 ....237 D1
Allen's Orch PE28 ....140 E1
Allens Cl CB3 ....63 B4
Allerton Cl 6 PE9 ....230 D3
Allerton Garth PE7 ......185 A4
Allexton Gdns 3 PE1 ....198 D7
Allington Wlk CB9 ....23 E8
Allotment La PE15 ......195 E2
Allotments Dro CB6 ......211 B7
Alma Rd PE1 ....197 F5
Alma Terr PE16 ....241 B4
Almond Cl PE29 ....142 A1
Almond Dr PE15 ....243 C3
Almond Gr CB3 ....102 C4
Almond Rd
  Peterborough PE1 ....198 B7
  St Neots PE19 ....74 F6
Almoners' Ave CB1 ......65 C3
Almoners La PE3 ....197 E3
Alms Cl PE29 ....141 C7
Alms Hill CB3 ....60 D7
Alms La SG7 ....2 D4
Alnwick Ct 1 PE19 ......74 C5
Alpha La PE28 ....151 E3
Alpha Rd CB4 ....246 A4
Alpha St PE15 ....243 D5
Alpha Terr CB2 ....64 D3
Alstead Rd CB4 ....104 B5
Alsyke Cl PE28 ....116 A7
Althorpe St 1 CB6 ....240 B5
Alvis Dr PE7 ....181 D6
Alwin Cl PE28 ....168 B3
Alwyn D PE27 ....144 B8
Alwyne Rd CB1 ....65 C2
Amanda Ct PE3 ....197 E2
Amberley Slope PE4 .....204 C3
Ambleside Gdns PE4 .....204 D3
Ambrose Way CB4 ....104 C4
Ambury Hill PE29 ....141 E5
Ambury Rd PE29 ....141 D5
Ambury Rd S 2 PE29 ....141 D5
Amcotts CB3 ....60 B8
America The CB6 ....216 D1
American Air Mus* CB2 ..16 F8
American La PE29 ....141 E5

Amwell Rd CB4 ....83 F8
Amy Johnson Ct 3
  IP28 ....239 B5
Ancaster Rd 2 PE9 ......244 A7
Ancaster Way
  Cambridge CB1 ....65 C7
  3 Doddington/Wimblington
  PE15 ....222 F5
Anchor Ct
  Littleport CB6 ....242 E3
  Peterborough PE4 ....205 F1
Anchor Dro PE38 ....226 F4
Anchor La CB5 ....130 B4
Anderson Cl PE13 ....245 A7
Anderson Cres PE29 .....142 A2
Anderson Rd
  Boxworth CB4 ....101 D8
  Swavesey CB4 ....122 D1
Andrea Cl PE2 ....187 C6
Andrews Cres PE4 ....204 F2
Angel Dro CB7 ....240 D2
Angel Sq CB7 ....240 D3
Angell's Mdw SG7 ....2 D4
Angle End CB1 ....67 F8
Angle La SG8 ....29 E5
Anglers Cl PE15 ....243 A5
Anglers Way CB4 ....84 C5
Angles Theatre The*
  PE13 ....245 C5
Anglesey Abbey & remains
  of Priory)* CB5 ....107 B1
Anglesey Way 8 CB4 ....208 D1
Anglia Polytechnic Univ
  CB1 ....246 C2
Anglia Way PE13 ....245 B2
Anglian Bsns Pk SG8 ....5 B7
Anglian Ct PE2 ....187 D6
Angoods La PE16 ....241 B6
Angus Cl 2 CB1 ....65 A8
Angus Ct PE3 ....197 D3
Ann Suckling Rd CB8 ....39 A2
Anne Rd PE9 ....244 A6
Anne's Cl CB8 ....144 A6
Annesdale CB7 ....240 D3
Annesley CB1 ....65 E5
Annesley Cl PE28 ....168 B4
Annington Cres SG8 .....13 A8
Ann's Rd CB5 ....84 E4
Ansley Way PE27 ....143 E5
Anson Cl PE26 ....171 E3
Anson Dr PE27 ....143 F6
Anson Pl PE19 ....74 A2
Anstey Way CB2 ....64 D2
Antelope Way CB4 ....66 A7
Anthony Cl
  Peterborough PE1 ....197 F8
  Whittlesey PE7 ....189 C8
Antonia Cl CB4 ....24 E7
Anvil Cl CB2 ....49 C4
Apeldoorn Wlk PE13 .....245 D7
Apley Way CB3 ....79 A4
Apollo Way CB4 ....83 E8
Apple Acre Rd CB9 ......38 C1
Apple Cl PE19 ....96 F8
Apple Gr PE19 ....74 C4
Apple Orch The PE28 ....143 D2
Apple Tree Cl PE7 ......182 A6
Appleby Pk CB6 ....240 D5
Appletree Cl CB4 ....125 D1
Appletree Gr CB5 ....130 B4
Appletrees CB3 ....102 C3
Applewood Cl CB1 ....65 F5
Applewood Dr PE7 ....186 C3
Appleyard PE2 ....187 C6
Approach Cotts CB9 .....38 D2
Apreece Rd PE7 ....175 D8
Apreece Way PE7 ....176 A7
Apsley Way PE7 ....197 A2
Apthorpe St CB1 ....66 F6
Apthorpe Way CB4 ....84 A7
Aragon Cl
  Buckden PE19 ....117 B4
  Cambridge CB4 ....83 E7
Aragon Pl PE28 ....113 F5
Aragon Rd CB2 ....23 D6
Arber Cl CB5 ....86 E6
Arborfield Cl PE6 ....231 C4
Arbour La CB3 ....79 A4
Arbroath Gdns PE2 ......185 C4
Arbury Banks* SG7 ......2 C2
Arbury Cl PE13 ....197 A3
Arbury Ct CB4 ....83 E6
Arbury Prim Sch CB4 ....83 E6
Arcadia Gdns CB4 ....103 C5
Archers Cl CB5 ....108 B3
Archers Dro PE6 ....233 D6
Archers Wood Rd PE7 ...186 C3
Archers Wood Nature
  Reserve* PE7 ....160 C7
Archery Cres 9 CB7 ....240 D4
Archway Ct CB3 ....64 B7
Arden Rd CB4 ....83 F8
Ardleigh Cl 3 PE13 .....245 E5
Ardross Ct CB4 ....68 F6
Argyle St CB1 ....66 B2
Argyll Ct CB3 ....23 F6
Arles Ave PE13 ....245 E3
Armada Cl PE13 ....245 D8
Armingford Cres SG8 ....14 E7

Armitage Way CB4 ....83 F8
Armley Gr PE9 ....244 D7
Armshold La CB3 ....61 D2
Armstrong Cl
  Newmarket CB8 ....111 B3
  Perry PE28 ....115 D3
Armstrong Ct 1 PE29 ....141 F8
Arnhem Ct PE19 ....74 C5
Arnold's La PE7 ....189 E7
Arran Cl CB1 ....65 F6
Arran Way PE27 ....144 A8
Arrendene Rd CB9 ......38 F1
Arthur Mellows Village Coll
  PE6 ....203 D8
Arthur St CB4 ....83 C4
Arthur's Mdw Nature
  Reserve* PE26 ....120 C7
Artillery St 11 PE13 ....245 C4
Artindale PE3 ....197 E3
Artis Ct PE3 ....197 A3
Arundel Ct CB4 ....83 C5
Arundel Cres PE19 ......74 E2
Arundel Rd
  Huntingdon PE29 ....142 A6
  Peterborough PE4 ....204 C1
Arundel Wlk 1 CB9 ......23 E8
Arundell CB6 ....240 C5
Ascham La CB2 ....32 B4
Ascham Rd CB4 ....83 D5
Ascot Dr PE1 ....198 B6
Ascot Rd SG8 ....5 F6
Ash Cl Huntingdon PE29 ..141 E7
  Peterborough PE1 ....198 C7
  Thorney PE6 ....232 F3
  Warboys PE28 ....165 A6
Ash Ct Brampton PE28 ..140 C3
  Peterborough PE1 ....198 C7
Ash Gn Burwell CB5 ....130 B2
  Chatteris PE16 ....241 C5
  Ely CB7 ....240 E1
  Haverhill CB9 ....38 E1
  March PE15 ....243 C5
  Melbourn SG8 ....14 C5
Ash Pk PE4 ....204 B6
Ash Tree 14 PE15 ....223 B7
Ash Way SG8 ....5 F6
Ashbeach Dro PE26 .....220 D3
Ashbeach Prim Sch
  PE26 ....220 D3
Ashburn Cl PE26 ....203 F7
Ashbury Cl CB1 ....65 B6
Ashcroft PE19 ....98 B2
Ashcroft Ct CB4 ....83 E7
Ashcroft Gdns PE1 ......198 C5
Ashdale Cl PE28 ....168 B3
Ashdale Pk PE13 ....245 A5
Ashdon CP Sch CB10 ....21 B1
Ashdon Pl CB10 ....21 C2
Ashen Gn CB2 ....49 A5
Ashfield PE28 ....113 F5
Ashfield Rd CB4 ....84 B5
Ashfields 1 PE6 ....231 F7
Ashlea Cl CB9 ....24 B6
Ashlea Rd CB9 ....24 B6
Ashleigh PE2 ....185 C6
Ashley Cl CB5 ....84 A1
Ashley Gn CB6 ....242 D3
Ashley Hill Sch CB8 ....168 B8
Ashley Pool La PE6 .....233 A2
Ashley Rd
  Cheveley CB8 ....112 A1
  Newmarket CB8 ....111 E2
Ashley Way CB2 ....32 F8
Ashline Gr PE7 ....189 D6
Ashmead Dr CB3 ....81 A3
Ashton Cl PE27 ....208 A2
Ashton Gdns PE7 ....141 D5
Ashton Rd PE13 ....197 B5
Ashvale CB4 ....83 D7
Ashwell & Morden Sta
  SG7 ....3 D2
Ashwell Bury SG7 ....2 C5
Ashwell Prim Schol SG7 ..2 D4
Ashwell Rd
  Guilden Morden SG8 .....10 F2
  Newnham SG7 ....2 A1
  Bassingbourn cum Kneesworth
  SG8 ....13 A3
Ashwell Village Mus*
  SG7 ....3 D2
Askers Field CB2 ....78 E2
Askew's La PE7 ....181 E4
Aspal Cl 3 IP28 ....213 F8
Aspal Hall Rd IP28 .....213 F8
Aspal La IP28 ....214 A8
Aspal Pk
  Beck Row, Holywell
  Row & Kenny Hill IP28 ..214 A8
  Mildenhall IP28 ....213 F8
Aspal Pl 9 IP28 ....213 F8
Aspen Cl Ely CB7 ....240 E5
  Haverhill CB9 ....38 E1
Aspen Gn PE29 ....141 E6
Asplin Ave PE15 ....243 A5
Asplin's Cl 5 CB4 ......208 D1
Asplins La PE17 ....117 F3
Asplins Ave 8 PE27 ....208 A3
Aster Dr PE4 ....204 D3
Astile La PE29 ....141 D5
Astley Cl CB6 ....216 E1

Astore Pk PE1 ....198 E3
Atherstone Ave PE3 .....197 B4
Atherton Cl CB4 ....83 E5
Athlone 7 CB1 ....84 A1
Athlone Cl CB3 ....99 A3
Atkins Cl Cambridge CB4 ..84 A7
  Littleport CB6 ....242 C5
Atkinson St PE1 ....198 C2
Atlantic Cl PE15 ....243 B6
Atterton Rd CB9 ....38 D1
Auberry Way CB3 ....78 F3
Auborn Gdns PE3 ....197 A3
Aubretia Ave PE4 ....204 D3
Auckland Rd CB5 ....246 C3
Audley Cl SG19 ....58 E4
Audley Gate PE3 ....197 C3
Audley Way CB1 ....37 A3
Augers Rd 4 CB1 ....65 F6
Augusta Ct PE1 ....198 E6
Augustus Cl
  4 Cambridge CB4 ....83 E8
  Haverhill CB9 ....24 D7
Augustus Way PE16 .....241 D6
Aureole Wlk CB8 ....110 E8
Austin Ct PE7 ....181 D6
Austin Friars La 3 PE9 ..244 B4
Austin St PE9 ....244 B4
Australia Ct CB3 ....83 B4
Avenells Way 2 SG19 ...41 D5
Avenue Rd
  Peterborough PE1 ....141 D5
  St Neots PE19 ....74 F6
Avenue The
  Borough Fen PE6 ....207 E3
  Burwell CB5 ....130 C3
  Cambridge CB3 ....246 A3
  Girton CB3 ....103 B1
  Godmanchester PE29 .....141 E3
  Leighton PE28 ....148 C3
  Madingley CB3 ....81 F7
  March PE15 ....243 D2
  Newmarket CB8 ....111 A3
  Ramsey PE26 ....172 A7
Aversley Rd PE28 ....168 C2
Aversley Wood Nature
  Reserve* PE28 ....159 F8
Aves Cl CB7 ....213 A5
Avon Ct
  Eaton Socon PE19 ....74 C3
  Peterborough PE4 ....204 E2
Avro Ct PE29 ....141 B8
Axiom Ave PE3 ....197 C4
Axiom Ct PE9 ....244 D4
Axis Way 6 PE19 ....74 B5
Aydon Rd PE7 ....187 F6
Aylesborough Cl 4 CB4 ..83 D7
Aylesford Way CB2 ......49 B4
Aylestone Rd CB4 ......246 C4
Aylington Ct PE8 ....184 B1
Ayre Ct 5 PE19 ....75 A4
Ayres Dr PE2 ....187 C6
Azalea Cl PE3 ....197 A3
Azalea court 181 F6

B

Babble Cl PE15 ....243 C4
Babraham CE Prim Sch
  CB2 ....50 D1
Babraham Institute
  CB2 ....50 D2
Babraham Rd
  Babraham CB2 ....50 B1
  Cambridge CB2 ....65 C2
  Fulbourn CB1 ....50 E8
  Great Shelford CB2 ....49 E8
  Sawston CB2 ....32 F8
Babylon Gaol* CB7 ......240 E3
Back Dro Upwell PE14 ..229 D8
  Welney PE14 ....225 A8
Back Hill Ely CB7 ....240 D3
  Hadstock CB1 ....20 B4
Back La Bourn CB3 ......79 B4
  Burrough Green CB8 ......70 F4
  Cambourne CB3 ....79 C4
  Coveney CB6 ....217 B5
  10 Deeping St James PE6 ..231 F8
  Elton PE8 ....178 D8
  Ely CB7 ....240 D4
  Eye PE6 ....232 A1
  Haslingfield CB3 ....63 A8
  Holywell-cum-Needingworth
  PE27 ....144 F2
  Ickleton CB10 ....18 A3
  Market Deeping PE6 ....206 A7
  Melbourn SG8 ....14 C4
  Outwell PE14 ....236 E3
  Stamford PE9 ....244 C5
  Wicken CB7 ....211 E1
  Yaxley PE7 ....181 E5
Back Reach Dro PE15 ..221 E7
Back St SG7 ....2 D4
Bacon's Yd SG7 ....2 D4
Bad Gate PE12 ....47 B5
Badcock Rd CB3 ....47 B5
Bader Cl
  Peterborough PE3 ....197 B6
  Ramsey PE26 ....172 A4

Badgeney Rd PE15 ....243 E4
Badger Cl PE7 ....181 F5
Badinton La PE9 ....230 F5
Badlingham Rd CB7 .....213 C1
Badminton Cl CB4 ....83 C6
Badney Dro PE16 ....222 D3
Bagley End PE4 ....205 B1
Bagot Pl **9** CB4 ....83 F8
Bagsham La IP28 ....213 E6
Bahram Cl CB8 ....110 E4
Bailey Cl CB9 ....24 D7
Bailey Mews CB5 ....246 C3
Bailey Way PE2 ....186 D8
Bain Cl PE9 ....244 C7
Bainton Coney CB9 ....38 D1
Bainton Rd
  Barnack PE9 ....230 D4
  Newborough PE6 ....204 F8
Baird Cl PE7 ....181 D6
Bakehouse Hill CB8 ....70 E8
Baker Dr CB5 ....130 C3
Bakers Cl CB3 ....62 D6
Bakers Field CB5 ....102 C1
Bakers La Barley SG8 ....9 A7
  Linton CB1 ....35 D2
  Peterborough PE2 ......186 E7
Bakers Link PE11 ....74 E2
Bakers Row CB8 ....111 A4
Bakers Sq IP28 ....115 E2
Bakery Cl Fen Ditton CB5 .84 E5
  Wilburton CB6 ....210 C5
Bakewell Rd PE2 ....185 C2
Bala Ct PE4 ....204 E3
Balaton Pl CB8 ....111 A6
Balding Cl **4** PE13 .....245 D5
Baldock Rd SG8 ....4 C4
Baldock Way CB11 ....65 B5
Baldwin Cl CB1 ....230 C1
Baldwins Cl CB3 ....60 C5
Baldwin's Cnr SG7 ....2 E5
Baldwins Manor SG19 ....58 D4
Balingdon La CB1 ....35 D3
Balintore Rise PE2 ....185 D4
Balland Field CB4 ....124 A8
Ballard Cl CB4 ....105 D3
Balmoral Dr **5** CB9 .....23 E8
Balmoral Rd PE4 ....197 C8
Balmoral Way PE12 ......74 E2
Balsham Rd
  Fulbourn CB1 ....67 B2
  Linton CB1 ....35 D3
Bamber St PE1 ....197 F4
Bambers La PE14 ....236 C6
Bancroft Cl CB1 ....65 B6
Bancroft La CB7 ....212 B5
Bandon Rd CB3 ....82 F6
Banff Cl **2** CB4 ....83 E7
Banhams Cl CB4 ....246 C4
Bank Ave PE28 ....208 C8
Bank Cl PE7 ....189 E5
Bank Dr PE13 ....245 A7
Bank The PE13 ....234 C7
Bankes Mead CB2 ....32 D1
Banks Cnr CB6 ....240 C4
Banks Ct PE19 ....74 E2
Bank's End PE28 ....142 D6
Bannister Gdns SG8 .....5 E8
Bannister's Row PE13 ...245 B7
Bannold Ct CB5 ....106 B8
Bannold Dro CB5 ....106 C8
Bannold Rd CB5 ....106 D8
Banworth La CB4 ....105 D6
Baptist Rd PE14 ....229 D8
Bar Cl CB2 ....49 C5
Bar Dro PE14 ....236 B4
  Bar Hill Prim Sch CB4 ..102 B4
Bar La Hatley SG19 ....42 E2
  Stapleford CB2 ....49 C4
  Tadlow SG19 ....25 E8
Barbara Stradbroke Ave
  CB8 ....89 B7
Barber Cl PE2 ....187 C7
Barbers Dro PE6 ....232 C8
Barbers Hill PE4 ....204 B7
Barcham Rd CB7 ....211 F7
Barding's Dro PE12 ......237 A8
Bardney PE2 ....186 A4
Bardyke Bank PE14 ....74 F1
Baretts Cl PE7 ....189 D8
Barford Cl PE2 ....186 C7
Barford Rd PE19 ....74 E2
Bargate La IP28 ....213 D5
Bargate Rd IP28 ....213 D6
Barham Cl PE2 ....187 F5
Barham Ct SG8 ....14 D6
Barham Rd PE28 ....149 D6
Barker Cl
  Hail Weston PE19 ....95 A1
  Waterbeach CB5 ....106 B8
Barker's La PE15 ....243 D1
Barkham Cl CB6 ....242 D4
Barkston Dr PE1 ....198 B6
Barkway Rd SG8 ....5 E5
Barkway St SG8 ....5 D5
Barkways CB5 ....130 C1
Barleuy Ct **6** PE19 ....74 D5
Barley Rd
  Eaton Socon PE19 ......74 C3
  Great & Little Chishill SG8 7 A7
Barley VP Sch SG8 ....7 A2
Barley Way CB1 ....35 D2
Barlings Ct CB4 ....111 A4
Barn Cl
  Huntingdon PE29 ....142 A2

Barn Cl continued
  6 Maxey PE6 ....231 C7
  Peterborough PE4 ......204 B3
  Ramsey PE26 ....172 A4
  Stilton PE7 ....175 F8
Barn Hill PE9 ....244 B5
Barnabas Ct CB4 ....105 D1
Barnabas Oley CE Prim Sch
  SG19 ....58 E4
Barnack CE Prim Sch
  PE9 ....230 D4
Barnack Drift PE9 ....230 B3
Barnack Hills & Holes
  National Nature Reserve*
  PE9 ....230 D3
Barnack Rd
  Bainton PE9 ....230 E4
  St Martins Without PE9 244 C4
Barnard Cl **1** PE19 ....74 F1
Barnard Way
  1 Cambridge CB4 .....83 D5
  Peterborough PE3 ......196 F3
Barnes Cl
  Cambridge CB5 ....84 D2
  St Neots PE19 ....74 E6
Barnes Way
  Peterborough PE4 ......204 B3
  Whittlesey PE7 ....189 B8
Barnfield Gdns PE7 ......190 F8
Barnfield La PE28 ....98 D7
Barns Cl CB4 ....208 D1
Barns The PE19 ....117 B4
Barnstock PE3 ....197 A7
Barnwell Dr CB1 ....84 E2
Barnwell Rd CB1 ....84 D1
Barnt Ct
  Eaton Socon PE19 ......74 B4
  Peterborough PE4 ......204 D4
Baron's Way CB3 ....99 B3
Barons La CB2 ....30 C5
Baros Cl CB1 ....22 A7
Barrasdale Cl CB4 ....238 A1
Barracks The PE13 ....237 E2
Barringer Way PE19 .....74 F7
Barrington CE Prim Sch
  CB2 ....46 F1
Barrington Nature Reserve*
  CB2 ....29 F8
Barrington Rd
  Orwell SG8 ....45 F1
  Shepreth SG8 ....29 D6
Barrons Way **1** CB3 ...62 C5
Barrow Cl CB2 ....64 E5
Barrow La CB3 ....79 A4
Barrow Rd CB2 ....64 E5
Barrowcrofts CB4 ....104 B5
Barrowfield PE1 ....198 E7
Barry's St PE7 ....189 D7
Barry Lynham Dr CB8 ...111 C2
Barry Wlk PE2 ....186 F7
Barsey Cl CB9 ....38 C1
Barston Dro CB5 ....108 C7
Bartholomew's Wlk
  CB7 ....240 C2
Bartholomew Cl CB10 ...18 E2
Bartlow Hills (Tumuli)*
  CB1 ....21 B6
Bartlow Pl CB9 ....39 B1
Bartlow Rd
  Castle Camps CB1 ......22 D4
  Hadstock CB1 ....20 D7
  Linton CB1 ....35 E2
Barton CE Prim Sch
  CB3 ....63 B4
Barton Cl Cambridge CB3 ..64 B8
  Peterborough PE4 ......204 F1
  Witchford CB6 ....217 D1
Barton Holt PE13 ....237 F8
Barton La PE13 ....237 F8
Barton Mews CB7 ....240 C4
Barton Rd
  Cambridge CB3 ....64 B8
  Comberton CB3 ....62 D5
  Ely CB7 ....240 C3
  Haslingfield CB3 ....47 A7
  Wisbech PE13 ....245 A4
Barton Sq CB7 ....240 D4
Bartons Cl CB1 ....53 B2
Bartons Pl CB8 ....110 E5
Bartram Gate PE4 ....204 E1
Barway Cnr CB7 ....211 D6
Barway Rd CB7 ....211 E7
Bascraft Way PE29 ......142 A1
Basil Gn PE2 ....186 D6
Bassenhally Ct PE7 ......189 E7
Bassenhally Rd PE7 ......189 E8
Bassenthwaite PE29 ....141 B6
Basset Cl **3** CB8 ....111 D6
Bassett Cl CB4 ....83 F8
Bassingbourn Barracks
  SG8 ....12 F8
Bassingbourn Prim Sch
  SG8 ....12 D4
Bassingbourn Rd SG8 ...12 D4
Bassingbourn Village Coll
  SG8 ....12 E4
Bateman Mews CB2 .....64 E7
Bateman St CB2 ....64 E7
Bate's Dro CB6 ....225 B3
Bateson Rd CB4 ....83 D4
Bates's Dro CB6 ....225 B6
Bath Cres PE28 ....143 B8
Bath Rd PE13 ....245 C7
Bath Row PE7 ....244 B4
Bathurst PE2 ....186 A4
Battle Gate CB3 ....80 A8
Battle Gate Rd CB3 ......80 A8

Battle Rd PE26 ....171 E3
Baulk La SG19 ....43 A3
Baulk The Thriplow SG8 ..31 B2
  Whittlesey PE7 ....189 E8
Baulkin's Dro PE12 ......237 C8
Baulks The CB2 ....32 E7
Bawtree Cres CB1 ....35 E3
Baxter Cl **3** PE13 .....245 E6
Baxter Dr **7** PE19 .....74 E2
Baycliffe Cl **1** CB1 ....65 D5
Bayfield Dr CB1 ....130 C2
Bayford Pl **1** CB4 ......83 F8
Bayliss PE29 ....118 F7
Beach Rd CB4 ....125 F3
Beachampstead Rd 1
  PE19 ....93 F6
Beacon Cl PE7 ....141 A6
Beaconsfield Ct **4** CB9 .23 F7
Beaconsfield Terr CB4 ...83 D4
Beald Way CB6 ....240 B4
Beale Ct **2** PE29 ....141 F8
Beales Way CB4 ....84 A7
Bean Cl **2** PE19 ....75 A6
Bear La SG7 ....2 D4
Beatrice Rd PE13 ....241 B6
Beatty Rd PE7 ....74 B2
Beauchamp Cl PE19 .....74 B3
Beaufort St **3** CB9 ....83 F7
Beaufort Dr
  Chatteris PE16 ....241 B6
  Hardwick PE19 ....117 A5
Beaulands Cl CB4 ....246 C4
Beaulieu Ct **1** PE6 ....232 F5
Beaumaris Rd PE28 .....168 C3
Beaumont Cl PE29 ....141 F8
Beaumont Cres CB1 .....65 D3
Beaumont Rd CB8 ....24 B6
Beaumont Rd CB1 ....65 D3
Beaumont Vale CB9 ......24 B6
Beaumont Way PE7 ......186 C2
Beaupre Ave PE14 ....236 F3
Beaupre Com Prim Sch
  PE14 ....236 F2
Beaupre Dro PE26 ....221 A2
Beauvale Gdns PE4 ......204 E3
Beauvoir Pl PE7 ....181 E5
Beaver Cl **8** PE19 .....74 B5
Bec Rd PE19 ....74 E5
Beccelm Dr **9** PE6 ....232 D8
Beche Rd CB5 ....84 A2
Beche Way CB4 ....105 C7
Beck Rd CB7 ....213 B4
Beck Row Prim Sch
  IP28 ....213 F8
Becket's Cl PE26 ....172 B8
Beckets Cl PE1 ....197 F8
Beckett Way **3** PE16 ..241 C5
Beckingham PE2 ....185 F3
Bede Pl PE1 ....198 A6
Bedford Ave PE28 ....143 B8
Bedford Cl CB4 ....240 A3
  2 Needingworth PE27 208 A3
  St Ives PE27 ....143 F7
Bedford Ct
  5 Haverhill CB9 ....23 F7
  10 Thorney PE6 ....233 A3
Bedford Purlieus National
  Nature Reserve*
  PE8 ....193 A4
Bedford Row PE13 ....238 D8
Bedford St
  Peterborough PE1 ......198 B4
  St Neots PE19 ....74 E7
  Wisbech PE13 ....245 C6
Bedford Way PE28 ....168 C3
Bedwell Hey La CB6 .....217 E1
Beech Ave
  7 Doddington/Wimblington
  PE15 ....223 A6
  Little Stukeley PE28 ...152 A2
  Peterborough PE1 ......197 F3
Beech Cl
  Great Shelford CB2 .....48 E3
  Huntingdon PE29 ....141 E7
  Isleham CB7 ....212 F5
  2 Thorney PE6 ....233 A3
  Warboys PE28 ....164 E4
Beech Croft CB8 ....70 D2
Beech Dr PE27 ....143 F5
Beech End PE28 ....150 F4
Beech Gr Haverhill CB9 ..23 E8
  March PE15 ....243 C5
  St Neots PE19 ....74 F6
Beech La Ely CB7 ....240 E5
  7 Eye PE6 ....232 A1
  Pampisford CB2 ....33 B5
Beech Rd PE6 ....203 D8
Beech Way CB6 ....240 B4
Beeches The CB4 ....83 F5
Beechside CB6 ....41 C6
Beechwood Ave
  Bottisham CB5 ....86 F6
  Melbourn SG8 ....14 C5
Beechwood Cl
  Exning CB8 ....110 C8
  Peterborough PE1 ......198 C7
Beechwood Gdns
  PE16 ....241 C4
Beechwood Nature Reserve*
  CB1 ....65 F2

Beeston Dr PE7 ....187 F5
Beeton Cl SG8 ....14 C6
Beetons Cl PE7 ....181 E5
Beevor Ct PE29 ....152 E1
Beezling Cl **9** PE19 ...74 C6
Beezling Fen Dro
  PE26 ....222 D3
Begdale Rd PE14 ....235 F5
Begbroke Way **7** PE19 .74 B5
Beild Dro CB6 ....218 B7
Belbin Way CB2 ....32 D8
Beldam Ave SG8 ....5 E5
Beldam's Cl CB3 ....61 D4
Beldams PE27 ....208 A3
Belgic Sq PE2 ....198 E3
Belgrave Rd CB1 ....65 C8
Belgrave Sq PE28 ....168 B4
Belham Rd PE1 ....197 E7
Bell Cl Ely CB6 ....240 D5
  Meldreth SG8 ....14 A8
  Stilton PE7 ....176 A7
Bell Dro PE6 ....232 F6
Bell Foundry Cl **1** SG19 .41 D5
Bell Gdns
  Haddenham CB6 ....210 A6
  Soham CB7 ....212 B4
Bell Hill CB4 ....104 B4
Bell Holt CB7 ....240 E4
Bell La Alconbury PE28 ..150 F4
  Barton Mills IP28 ....239 D2
  Fenstanton PE28 ....121 B5
  4 Market Deeping PE6 .231 F8
  Nuthampstead SG8 .....1 A2
  Southoe & Midloe PE19 ..95 E6
Bell Rd CB5 ....86 E5
Bellairs CB6 ....216 E1
Bellamy Cl PE19 ....74 E2
Bellamy's La PE14 ....238 D4
Bell's Dro
  Littleport CB6 ....225 B6
  Sutton St James PE12 ..237 C8
Bell's Pl PE1 ....198 A2
Belle Isle Cres PE28 ....140 B3
Belle Isle Cres PE28 ....140 B3
Belle Vue PE7 ....187 C6
Bellman's Cl PE7 ....189 F7
Bellman's Rd PE7 ....189 F6
Bellmans Gr PE7 ....190 A7
Bells Mdw SG19 ....41 A5
Belmont Cl **3** CB9 .....23 F7
Belmont Gdns PE16 .....241 C4
Belmont Pl CB5 ....246 B3
Belmont Rd PE15 ....243 D5
Belmore Cl **1** CB4 .....83 C5
Belsar's Hill (Fort)*
  CB4 ....209 C1
Belsars Cl CB4 ....209 A1
Belsay Ct CB9 ....23 D8
Belsay Pr PE2 ....187 F5
Belsize Ave PE2 ....186 E6
Belt Dro PE14 ....235 F4
Belt The CB8 ....73 D8
Belton Rd PE7 ....187 F5
Belton St PE9 ....244 C5
Belton's Hill PE28 ....137 D7
Belvedere PE26 ....221 C2
Belvoir Ct **4** CB9 ......23 E8
Belvoir Rd CB4 ....246 C4
Belvoir Terr CB7 ....64 E7
Belvoir Way PE1 ....198 C8
Benams CB11 ....195 E2
Bencroft La PE28 ....165 A4
Bendysbe Way
  Barrington CB2 ....30 A8
  Harston CB2 ....47 A1
Benedict Sq PE4 ....204 A2
Benedict St CB8 ....240 B5
Benefield Rd CB8 ....112 F6
Benet Cl CB4 ....105 C1
Bene't St CB2 ....246 A2
Benians CB1 ....83 B3
Benland PE3 ....214 A1
Bennett Rd PE28 ....219 E8
Benny's Way CB3 ....82 B2
Benson Pl **5** CB4 ......83 C4
Benson St **4** CB4 ......83 C4
Benstead PE2 ....185 E3
Bensteads End CB1 ......68 A8
Bentham Way CB6 ......240 B4
Bentinck St CB4 ....246 B1
Bentley Ave PE7 ....181 E6
Bentley Cl PE26 ....171 B2
Bentley Rd CB2 ....64 E5
Bentley St PE9 ....244 C5
Benwick Prim Sch
  PE15 ....222 A5
Benwick Rd
  Doddington PE15 ....222 D5
  Ramsey PE26 ....221 E3
  Whittlesey PE7 ....221 D7
Benyon Gr PE2 ....186 B4
Berberis Cl PE6 ....232 F3
Beresford Rd CB6 ....240 A5
Bergamont Cl **5** PE29 .118 F8
Bergamot Rd CB9 ....23 E8
Bergholt Cl **4** CB5 ....84 E4
Berkeley Rd PE3 ....197 C3
Berkley St **1** PE11 ....74 E4
Berkley St PE11 ....74 E4
Bermuda Rd CB4 ....83 D4
Bermuda Terr CB4 ......83 C4
Bernard Rd PE28 ....140 D3
Bernard St CB4 ....240 B4
Berristead Cl CB6 ....210 C6
Berry Cl CB6 ....210 F5
Berry Ct PE1 ....197 E5
Berry Gn CB6 ....210 F5

Berry Gn Pk NN14 ....156 E5
Berry La CB6 ....118 C8
Berry Leas PE8 ....183 D1
Berrybut Way PE9 ....244 D7
Berrycroft Soham CB7 ...212 B4
  Willingham CB4 ....124 A8
Berryfield PE15 ....243 E7
Bertie La **8** PE9 ....230 C6
Betjamin Rd SG8 ....5 D8
Betjeman Rd SG8 ....13 D1
Betony Vale SG8 ....5 E5
Betony Wlk CB9 ....23 D8
Bettles Cl PE1 ....198 A6
Betts Cl PE29 ....141 F1
Between Cl Dro CB4 .....125 D2
Bevan Cl PE29 ....141 E6
Beverley Cl SG8 ....5 B8
Beverley Gdns PE9 ......244 A6
Beverley Way **4** CB2 ..64 D3
Beverstone PE2 ....185 D5
Beville PE28 ....161 F6
Bevills Cl **10** PE15 ....223 A5
Bevills Pl PE15 ....243 D3
Bevington Way PE3 .....196 A1
Bevis La PE13 ....235 C6
Bevishall PE4 ....204 F1
Bew Cl PE2 ....187 D4
Bewick Pl PE7 ....181 D8
Bewicks Mead PE3 ......130 C2
Bickerley Ct CB3 ....79 A3
Bickleigh Wlk PE3 ....197 A3
Bicton Ind Est PE28 .....114 B7
Bifield PE2 ....185 F3
Biggin Gn PE8 ....178 C3
Biggen The CB2 ....17 E8
Biggin Abbey* CB5 .....84 F8
Biggin La Fen Ditton CB5 ..84 F8
  Ramsey PE26 ....171 E6
Biggs Rd PE14 ....236 D8
Bigram's La PE13 ....114 C7
Billberry Cl **3** PE19 ...74 C5
Bilberry End CB1 ....20 C7
Bill Hall Way PE28 ......168 D2
Bill Rickaby Dr CB8 .....111 A5
Binnimoor Rd PE15 .....228 E4
Biotechnology Ctr CB3 ..82 D7
Birch Ave PE16 ....241 D5
Birch Cl Cambridge CB4 ..83 F5
  Chatteris PE16 ....241 D5
  Ely CB7 ....240 E5
  Yaxley PE7 ....182 A5
Birch Dr PE28 ....151 E3
Birch Gr PE14 ....236 B5
Birch Trees Rd CB3 .....49 A6
Birchen Cl PE7 ....186 C3
Birches The CB7 ....212 A5
Birchin Cl PE7 ....186 C3
Birchtree Ave PE1 ....198 A7
Birchwood PE2 ....186 A3
Birchwood Ave PE15 ....243 B2
Bird Farm Rd PE28 ......96 B6
Bird La PE19 ....95 A1
Bird's Dro
  Gorefield PE13 ....237 D3
  Sutton St James PE12 ..237 B8
Birds Cl CB10 ....18 A3
Birdwood Rd CB1 ....65 D6
Birkdale Ave
  Mildenhall IP28 ....239 B5
  Peterborough PE4 ......204 B3
Birt La PE27 ....144 A3
Biscay Cl CB9 ....24 C7
Bishop Dr PE7 ....175 F7
Bishop Creighton Prim Sch
  PE1 ....198 B2
Bishop Laney Dr CB6 ....240 F2
Bishop Way CB4 ....104 C3
Bishop Wynn Cl CB7 ....240 F3
Bishop's Ct CB2 ....64 C1
Bishop's Rd
  Cambridge CB2 ....64 D1
  Peterborough PE1 ......198 A1
Bishops Cl Haverhill CB9 ..23 E8
  Little Downham CB6 ...218 A7
  Peterborough PE1 ......198 D5
Bishops Ct **8** CB9 .....23 E8
Bishops Rd
  St Neots PE19 ....74 F2
  5 Somersham PE28 ..215 C1
Bishops Way
  Buckden PE19 ....117 B4
  Great Paxton PE19 ....96 E4
Bishops Wlk
  2 Barnack PE9 ....230 D3
  Ely CB7 ....240 D4
Bishopsfield PE4 ....204 D1
Bittern Cl PE27 ....143 F7
Bittern Way PE15 ....243 F5
Black Bank CB6 ....218 B8
Black Bank Rd CB6 ......218 B8
Black Bear La
  Leverington PE13 ....245 E7
  Newmarket CB8 ....110 F3
  Walsoken PE14 ....245 F8
Black Dike PE13 ....237 E6
Black Dro March PE15 ..233 A5
  Thorney PE6 ....233 A5
  Wisbech St Mary PE13 ..234 F8
Black Dyke CB3 ....237 F4
Black Ham Dro PE7 .....182 E2
Black Hill Rd PE27 ......143 E6
Black Horse Dro CB6 ...226 D6
Black Horse La
  Chatteris PE16 ....241 C6
  Swavesey CB4 ....143 B5
Black La Gorefield PE13 ..237 C2
  Tydd St Giles PE13 ....237 C6

Black Swan Spinney
PE8 ....194 A4
Blackberry Droveway
CB5 ....108 C8
Blackberry Way 6 IP28 .214 A1
Blackbird Way PE28 ...150 E4
Blackbush Dro PE7 ....220 D8
Blackdown Garth PE4 .204 D3
Blacked-Out Britain War
Mus* PE29 ....141 D4
Blackfriar St 4 PE9 ..244 C5
Blackfriars Rd 8 CB3 .245 C5
Blackfriars St 8 PE9 ..244 C5
Blackhall Rd CB4 ......83 C7
Blackmans Rd PE7 ....175 D8
Blackmead PE2 ....186 B4
Blackmill Rd PE16 ....241 B2
Blackmore Cl 4 CB7 ..38 F1
Blacksmith Cl SG19 ...40 C3
Blacksmiths Cl
Abbotsley PE19 ....57 B5
Ramsey Forty Foot PE26 .221 C2
Blacksmiths La
Abbotsley PE19 ....57 B5
Ellington PE28 ....139 A4
Shudy Camps CB1 .....22 C5
Blackstone Rd PE29 ..141 C7
Blackthorn Cl
Cambridge CB4 ....83 F6
Chatteris PE16 ....241 C3
Blackthorn Ct
Coates/Eastrea PE7 ..190 F8
Soham CB7 ....212 A6
Blackwell Rd PE4 .....186 C2
Blackwood Rd PE19 ...74 B3
Bladon Way CB9 ....39 B1
Blair Par CB9 ....23 E8
Blair Way PE19 ....74 E2
Blake Cl SG8 ....13 D1
Blakeland Hill CB2 ...17 D8
Blakes Way PE14 ......198 E2
Blandford Gdns PE1 ..198 F7
Blandford Wlk 4 CB4 ..83 C6
Blanford Wlk CB4 .....83 C7
Blashfield Cl 2 PE9 ..244 A6
Blaxhall Ct 16 CB9 ...23 F1
Blea Wr PE29 ....141 B6
Bledwick Dro PE13 ...238 C3
Blench La CB1 ....34 F6
Blencowe Terr 11 PE13 .145 C5
Blenheim Cl
2 Cambridge CB1 .....65 E5
8 Eaton Socon PE19 ..74 C4
Haverhill CB9 ....39 B1
Shepreth SG8 ....59 F4
Blenheim Dr PE27 ....143 F7
Blenheim Gr PE19 ....96 F8
Blenheim Rd
Ramsey PE26 ....172 A4
Upwood PE26 ....171 E3
Blenheim Way
Enneth PE14 ....245 E2
1 Hardwick CB3 ......81 A4
Yaxley PE7 ....181 E5
Blethan Dr PE29 .....141 A6
Blinco Gr CB1 ....65 B5
Blind La 3 Maxey PE6 .231 C7
Sawtry PE28 ....168 C3
Bliss Way CB1 ....66 A6
Block Fen Dro
Chatteris PE16 ....216 C6
Wimblington PE15 ....223 C5
Block Rd CB7 ....216 C4
Blockmoor Dro CB6 ..216 C4
Blockmoor Rd CB7 ...211 E6
Blois Rd CB9 ....24 F1
Bloomfield Cl PE19 ...95 E1
Bloomfield Way PE28 .168 E4
Blooms Ct IP28 ....239 D4
Bloomsfield CB5 .....130 C1
Blossom Ct PE3 ......197 B8
Blossom Dr 3 CB1 ....84 A1
Blue Boar Dro PE6 ...218 D7
Blue La PE13 ....223 A7
Blue Ridge Gdns PE15 .243 E5
Bluebell Cl 4 PE14 ...198 A8
Bluebell Cl PE26 .....220 D3
Bluebell Wlk 1 CB7 ..212 B4
Bluecoat Prim Sch The
 ....244 B6
Bluegate PE29 ....118 F7
Bluntisham Heath Rd
PE28 ....155 F3
Bluntisham Rd
Bluntisham/Colne PE28 .208 D6
1 Needingworth PE27 .208 A3
Blunt's La PE7 ....189 E7
Blythe Gn PE28 ......115 D2
Blythe Way
Caldecote CB3 ....80 C1
Gamlingay SG19 .....41 D5
Blyton Rd CB3 ....99 A3
Boadicea Ct PE16 ...241 C5
Boardman Cl PE19 ...95 F7
Boardwalks Nature Reserve*
 ....197 D1
Bodiam Way PE19 ...111 F6
Bodiam Wlk 3 CB9 ...23 E8
Bodsey Toll Rd PE26 .221 B2
Boeing Way IP28 .....239 B5
Bogmoor Rd SG8 .....7 C1
Bogs Gap La SG8 ....11 B3
Bohemond St CB7 ...240 E5
Bohemore Rd PE13 ..245 C2
Boleyn Ave PE29 ....118 F7
Boleyn Way CB9 .....23 D7
Boleyn Wlk CB8 .....111 C3
Bolton Cl CB5 ....130 A2
Bonga La PE13 ......235 B8

Boongate PE1 ....198 C3
Boot La CB2 ....29 E8
Boot The CB6 ....209 D4
Booth Way PE19 .....95 F1
Boot's Rd PE15 ......223 F6
Boretree Way PE29 .141 A7
Borough Cl PE13 ....245 D3
Borough The CB6 ....209 E4
Borrowdale CB4 .....83 C6
Borrowdale Cl PE4 ..204 E3
Borthwick Pk PE7 ...125 D8
Borthwick Pl PE2 ...185 D6
Bossert's Way CB5 ...80 C2
Boswell Cl PE8 ......197 E8
Bosworth Cl PE8 ....178 B3
Bosworth Rd PE7 ...175 D8
Bosworth Way 2 PE15 .243 D2
Botolph Gn PE2 .....186 C7
Botolph La CB2 .....246 A2
Bottels Rd PE28 ....164 E5
Bottisham Com Prim Sch
 CB5 ....86 F5
Bottisham Pk* CB5 ..86 F7
Bottisham Swimming Pool
 CB5 ....86 F5
Bottisham Village Coll
 CB5 ....86 E6
Bottle La PE13 ......237 C7
Bough La PE28 .....162 F1
Boulevard Ret Pk PE1 .197 D7
Boundary Dr PE13 ..243 C3
Boundary Rd
Haverhill CB9 ....24 D5
Red Lodge IP28 ....186 C4
Boundary Rd Ind Est
CB3 ....24 C5
Bourdillon Cl 1 PE28 .121 B6
Bourges Bvd PE1 ...197 D7
Bourges Ret Pk PE1 .197 E5
Bourn Bridge Rd CB1 .34 A8
Bourn CE Prim Sch
CB3 ....59 F8
Bourn Rd
Cambridge CB4 .....84 C5
Haverhill CB9 ....24 B8
Bourns The CB1 ....67 A4
Bower Cl PE14 ......198 C5
Bower's La 4 CB7 ..213 A5
Bowers Croft CB1 ..65 C3
Bowker Way PE7 ....198 A3
Bowlings Ct PE27 ..144 A3
Bowness Way 2 PE4 .204 F2
Bowsers Cl CB10 ...20 D3
Bowsers La CB10 ...20 B2
Bowthorpe Gdns
PE13 ....245 D5
Boxer Rd PE8 ......230 B1
Boxford Cl 20 CB9 ..23 E7
Boxgrove Cl 14 PE6 .232 A1
Boxworth End CB4 .122 E3
Boxworth Rd CB3 ..100 C4
Boyce Cl PE7 ......189 D7
Boyces Rd PE13 ...245 E5
Boyton Cl CB9 .....39 A2
Bozeat Way PE3 ...197 C6
Brackenbury Cl CB4 .104 C3
Brackenwood PE2 ..185 D6
Brackhill Fen Dro
PE28 ....208 E8
Brackley Cl
3 Cambridge CB4 ...83 D6
Peterborough PE3 ..197 D3
Brackwood PE2 ....185 D6
Brackyn Rd CB1 ...197 C6
Bradden St PE3 ...197 C6
Bradegate Dr PE1 .198 E7
Bradford's Cl CB5 .86 E6
Bradley Rd CB8 ....72 F1
Bradmore St CB1 ..246 C2
Bradrushe Fields CB3 .82 F3
Bradshaw Cl PE29 ..118 A7
Bradshaw Ct PE15 .243 C2
Bradwell Rd PE3 ...197 A2
Bradwells Ct CB1 ..246 B2
Braeburn Ave PE14 .245 C8
Braemar Gdns PE7 .189 D6
Braggs La
Hemingford Grey PE28 .143 C1
Wrestlingworth SG19 ..25 A4
Brailsford Cl PE3 ..197 A4
Bramall Ct PE7 ....197 C3
Bramble Cl
Haverhill CB9 ....38 D1
Whittlesey PE7 ....189 E6
Yaxley PE7 ....182 A6
Bramble Ct 2 PE28 .140 C3
Bramble End
Alconbury PE28 ...150 F5
Sawtry PE28 ......168 B3
Bramble La PE14 ..236 D3
Brambles Wlk PE15 .243 E7
Brambles The
Balsham CB1 ......53 C1
Bar Hill CB23 .....102 D3
Cambridge CB4 ....64 D2
Girton CB3 ....83 A6
Hemingford Grey PE27 .143 F1
Littleport CB6 .....242 D3
7 Royston SG8 .....5 C1
Bramley Ave
Melbourn SG8 ......14 D6
Needingworth PE27 ..208 A2
Bramley Cl
Cottenham CB4 ...125 D3
Offord Cluny PE19 .118 A1
Bramley Ct CB4 ...84 B6

Bramley Dr PE19 ...118 A1
Bramley Gr PE28 ..208 C5
Bramley Rd
Hardwick CB9 ....23 C7
St Ives PE27 ....144 B5
Wisbech PE13 .....245 C7
Bramley Way CB3 ...81 A4
Bramleys The
March PE15 ....243 D1
Shepreth SG8 .....29 E4
Brampton Cl PE13 ..245 A4
Brampton Cr PE2 ..187 D6
Brampton Gdns PE19 .75 A4
Brampton Inf Sch
 ....140 C2
Brampton Jun Sch
 ....140 C2
Brampton Rd
Buckden PE19 ......117 C6
Cambridge CB1 ....84 B1
Graham PE28 ......116 B7
Huntingdon PE29 ..141 B3
Royston SG8 ......5 F6
Brampton Wood Nature
 Reserve* PE28 ...139 D1
Branceth Pl PE2 ...186 E7
Branch Bank Ely CB7 .218 F6
Branch Rd CB2 ....62 C7
Brandon Cl CB1 ...246 C2
Brandon Pl CB1 ...246 C2
Brandon Rd IP28 ..239 E5
Brands Cl PE26 ....172 A5
Brangehill La CB6 ..216 D3
Brassey Cl PE7 ....197 C6
Bravo La PE28 .....151 E3
Braybrook Rd PE13 .197 C6
Bray 6 CB1 ....84 A1
Braybrooke PE2 ...186 A3
Braybrook Prim Sch
 ....186 B4
Brays La CB7 ......240 C4
Brazilian Terr CB8 .110 F3
Breach La CB6 .....210 D6
Breach Rd PE28 ...116 A7
Bream Cl PE28 ....149 D6
Breamore Gdns PE3 .197 B3
Breckenwood Rd CB1 .66 E6
Breckland Way IP28 .239 C5
Brecon Way PE29 ..141 A4
Brenda Gautrey Way
 CB4 ....125 C3
Brendon Garth PE4 .204 E1
Brent Cl PE28 .....239 D4
Brentwood Cl 6 CB5 .84 E4
Brentwood Ct CB5 .84 E4
Breton Ave PE15 ..243 E2
Bretton Ctr PE3 ..197 A5
Bretton Gate PE3 .197 A5
Bretton Gn PE3 ..197 A5
Bretton Way
Bretton PE3 ....197 A7
Peterborough PE3 .196 F7
Bretton Woods Com Sch
PE3 ....197 A6
Brewerne PE2 .....186 C4
Brewers Cl CB4 ...123 D3
Brewers La PE13 ..238 A4
Brewery La SG8 ..29 B2
Brewery Rd CB2 ...33 A5
Brewhouse La CB7 .212 B4
Brewin Ave CB7 ..243 B3
Brewin Chase The
PE15 ....243 D4
Brewster Ave PE2 .186 F8
Brewster Ave Inf Sch
PE2 ....186 B8
Briar Way PE1 ....198 C5
Briars End CB7 ....217 E2
Briars The PE28 ..168 B3
Briary La SG8 .....5 C5
Brick Kiln Rd IP28 .239 D5
Brick Kilns PE29 ..118 E8
Brick La CB6 ......216 E3
Brick Row SG8 ....8 D3
Brickberry Cl PE7 .186 C2
Brickfields Ave CB8 .110 D7
Brickhills CB1 .....209 A1
Brickkiln La CB4 ..123 B3
Brickmaker's Arms La
PE15 ....223 B5
Brickmakers Way CB6 .242 B1
Bridewell Cl IP28 ..239 B4
Bridewell Rd CB1 ..66 A5
Bridgacre PE28 ....246 C4
Bridge Cl CB2 .....48 F6
Bridge Dro PE13 ..234 B7
Bridge End Earith PE28 .208 E5
 Wansford PE8 ....194 A3
Bridge End Rd PE28 .213 E1
Bridge La
Great Shelford CB2 .48 E4
Wimblington PE15 ..223 B8
Bridge of Sighs* CB3 .246 A3
Bridge Pl PE29 ....141 E3
Bridge Rd
Broughton PE28 ...153 F8
Ely CB7 ....240 E2
Histon CB4 ....104 C2
Impington CB4 ....83 C8
Mepal PE15 ....216 E4
Bridge St
Cambridge CB2 ...246 A3
Chatteris PE16 ...241 B7
Market Deeping PE6 .231 E8
Moulton CB8 .....57 E8
2 Peterborough PE1 .198 A1
St Ives PE27 .....144 A3

Bridge St continued
Whaddon SG8 ....13 B8
11 Wisbech PE13 ...245 C5
Wistow PE28 ....163 F7
Wood Walton PE28 .161 E6
Bridgefoot
Great & Little Chishill SG8 ..15 B2
St Ives PE27 ....144 A3
Bridgehill Rd PE6 ..205 A6
Bridle End PE19 ....98 B2
Bridle Way CB3 ....63 F4
Brierley Wlk CB4 ..83 C2
Briery Fields 2 CB6 .217 E1
Briggate Cres PE7 .189 C6
Briggate E PE7 ....189 D6
Briggate W PE7 ...189 C6
Bright St PE1 .....197 F3
Brigland Ct PE29 ..141 B6
Brigstock Ct PE3 ..197 C6
Brigstock Rd PE13 .245 B7
Brimbles Way PE7 .185 E5
Brimley Rd CB4 ...83 D6
Brinhurst PE2 .....186 A4
Brington CE Prim Sch
 PE28 ....147 C4
Brington Rd PE28 .147 F7
Brinkley Rd Brinkley CB8 .46 F1
Carlton CB8 ....54 F8
Westley Waterless CB8 .70 D3
Weston Colville CB1 .54 C8
Brinkman Rd CB1 .35 D3
Bristol Ave PE14 ..204 B3
Britannia Way PE13 .245 C2
Britannic Way CB1 .65 F7
British Antarctic Survey
CB3 ....82 E3
British Horse Racing Sch
CB8 ....111 B8
Britten Pl CB1 ....65 D7
Broad Baulk CB6 ..210 F6
Broad Cl PE1 .....198 D5
Broad Dro
Enneth PE14 .....236 C5
Upwell PE14 .....229 D8
Wisbech PE14 ....235 F5
Yaxley PE7 ....182 B5
Broad Dro E PE13 .237 E6
Broad Dro W PE13 .237 B4
Broad End CB3 ...100 A4
Broad End La PE14 .245 F4
Broad End Rd PE14 .245 E4
Broad Gate PE12 .237 A8
Broad Hill CB7 ...212 B7
Broad La
Cottenham CB4 ..125 E5
Haslingfield CB3 ..47 A5
Broad Leas PE27 .144 A4
Broad Piece CB7 ..211 F5
Broad St Bourn CB23 .59 F8
Cambridge CB1 ...246 C2
Ely CB7 ....240 D3
Haverhill CB9 .....23 F8
March PE15 ......243 D4
Stamford PE9 ...244 B5
Whittlesey PE7 ..189 D7
Broad Way CB6 ..210 C6
Broad Wheel Rd PE6 .211 B8
Broad Wlk The PE6 .74 E3
Broadall's Dro PE26 .221 D3
Broadcroft Cres CB9 .23 E8
Broadgate La CB6 .231 F8
Broadgate Rd PE12 .234 C8
Broadgate Way PE7 .178 B3
Broadhurst Rd 18 PE6 .230 B1
Broadlands CB6 ..210 C6
Broadlands The PE14 .198 E5
Broadmeadow CB2 .49 F1
Broads Rd CB5 ...130 C6
Broadway Bourn CB3 .60 D8
Cambourne CB3 ..79 E3
Crowland PE6 ....232 B8
Farcet PE7 ....187 C1
Grantchester CB3 .84 C6
Witchford CB6 ....217 E1
Yaxley PE7 ....181 E5
Broadway Gdns PE1 .198 B5
Broadway The
Oakington/Longstanton
CB4 ....103 B5
Romsey Town CB1 .65 B8
St Ives PE27 .....144 A3
Broadway Theatre*
PE1 ....197 F3
Brockenden PE28 .138 C4
Brockholt Rd CB3 ..78 E2
Brocklesby Gdns PE3 .197 C3
Brockley Rd CB3 ..100 B4
Brocks Bsns Ctr CB9 .23 F5
Brockwood Cl 2 SG19 .41 D6
Brodsworth Rd PE7 .187 F5
Bromholme La PE28 .141 A3
Brook Cl
Alconbury PE28 ...150 F4
Histon CB4 ....243 C4
Brook Dam La 14 CB7 .212 B4
Brook End CB8 ...82 C2
Brook La Coton CB3 .187 B2
Farcet PE7 ....187 B2
Stretham CB6 ....210 F5
Brook Rd
Bassingbourn cum Kneesworth
SG8 ....12 D4
Eaton Socon PE19 .74 C4
Kimbolton PE28 ..113 B7
Newton CB2 ....31 B6
Brook Service Rd CB9 .24 A8
Brook St Elsworth CB3 .100 B3

Brook St continued
Peterborough PE1 ..198 A2
St Neots PE19 .....74 E5
Soham CB7 ....212 C3
Brook The CB6 ....216 E1
Brook's Rd PE15 ..243 D4
Brookdale CB3 ....102 C3
Brooke Gr CB6 ....240 A5
Brooke Rd SG8 ....5 D8
Brookfield Cl CB2 .32 F5
Brookfield Dr CB4 .123 F3
Brookfield Home Pk
PE4 ....204 B2
Brookfield Rd
Coton CB3 ....82 B2
Papworth Everard CB3 .99 A4
Sawston CB2 ......32 F5
Brookfield Way
Cambourne CB3 ..79 A3
Ramsey PE26 .....172 A4
Brookfields CB1 ..65 D7
Brookfields CB3 ..111 B5
Brookfields Hospl CB1 .65 C8
Brookfields Ind Pk
PE4 ....204 B2
Brookfurlong PE3 .197 B6
Brookhampton St CB10 .18 A5
Brooklands PE28 ..150 F2
Brooklands Ave CB2 .64 E6
Brooks Rd CB1 ....65 D8
Brookside
Alconbury PE28 ...150 F4
Cambridge CB2 ...246 B1
Dalham CB8 ....92 E8
Exning CB8 ....110 C8
Great Paxton PE19 .96 D4
Huntingdon PE29 .141 D5
Moulton CB8 ......112 F5
Oakington/Longstanton
PE28 ....168 B5
Brookside Gr CB6 .242 C5
Brookside Ind Est
PE28 ....168 B5
Brookside La 11 CB2 .64 E7
Broom Cl
7 Littleport CB7 ..242 D4
Peterborough PE1 .198 A8
Broom Way PE27 ..144 A5
Broom Wlk 5 IP28 .213 F8
Broomhill Cl 4 IP28 .214 A1
Brotherhood Ret Pk PE4 .197 D8
Brotherhood Ret Pk
PE4 ....197 D8
Brothers Pl CB1 ..65 D6
Broughton House Gall*
CB1 ....246 B3
Broughton La PE28 .154 B8
Brownes Rd 6 PE8 .230 B1
Browning Dr PE19 .74 F4
Brownlow Dr 8 PE6 .231 F8
Brownlow Quay PE9 .244 C5
Brownlow Rd
Cambridge CB4 ...83 C6
Peterborough PE1 .198 A6
Brownlow St 7 PE9 .244 C5
Brownlow Terr PE9 .244 C5
Brown's Sq PE7 ..74 F5
Brownshill Staunch
PE27 ....208 C3
Broxbourne Rd CB6 .66 A7
Bruces Cl PE7 ....145 D8
Brudenell PE2 ....185 E2
Brunel Dr PE7 ....181 D6
Brunswick Cl CB1 ..65 E5
Brunswick Gdns CB5 .246 C3
Brunswick Terr CB5 .246 C3
Brunswick Wlk CB1 .246 C3
Bryan Cl PE26 ....172 B6
Brybank Rd CB9 ..38 C1
Brynmore PE2 ....185 E2
Bryony Cl
Coates/Eastrea PE7 .190 C7
Haverhill CB9 .....38 E1
Buchan St CB4 ...83 B7
Buckden CE Prim Sch
 ....117 B4
Buckden Marina PE19 .117 E3
Buckden Rd
Brampton PE28 ...117 D7
Buckden Way PE13 .101 E8
Buckingham Dr CB6 .240 D6
Buckingham Rd
Cambridge CB3 ...83 C3
Haverhill CB9 .....23 E7
Buckingham Way
PE28 ....168 C2
Buckingway Bsns Pk
CB4 ....101 E8
Buckle St PE1 ....198 C5
Buckles Gdns PE7 .189 F7
Buckley Rd PE19 .74 E4
Buck's Dro PE26 .172 D2
Buck's La CB2 ....45 F7
Buckshott Rd PE14 .238 E3
Buckthorn CB7 ...240 F6

Buckthorn Rd PE7 ....186 D3
Buckworth Rd PE28 ....150 C5
Budge Cl PE28 ....140 E2
Budleigh Cl CB1 ....65 D7
Buff La SG19 ....43 A1
Buffalo Way CB1 ....66 A7
Building End SG8 ....1 F8
Building End Rd CB1 .....1 F7
Bukehorn Rd PE6 ......232 D4
Bulbeck Mill CB1 ....29 F7
Bull La Broughton PE28 ..164 A1
  Langley CB11 ....1 F2
  Peakirk PE6 ....206 B2
  West Wratting CB1 ....53 F6
Bullard Laboratories
  CB3 ....83 A4
Bullen Cl CB1 ....65 D5
Bullfinch Way
  Cottenham CB4 ....125 D5
  Friday Bridge PE14 ....44 C8
Bullock Rd Elton PE8 ...184 B1
  Folksworth & Washingley
  PE7 ....174 E7
  Great Gidding PE28 ....167 B6
  Little Gidding PE28 ...167 D2
Bullrush La CB3 ....79 C3
Bulstrode Gdns CB3 ......83 A2
Bulteel Cl CB4 ....105 C3
Bumpstead Rd CB9 ......24 B5
Bunbury Ave IP28 ......239 C5
Bunting's Dro PE7 .....188 C4
Buntings La PE8 ....178 B3
Buntings Cres CB5 .....130 B3
Buntings La PE7 ....187 B5
Buntings Path CB5 .....130 B3
Bunyan Cl 4 SG19 ....41 D5
Burberry Rd PE19 ....117 B3
Burcroft Rd PE13 ......245 B6
Burdett Cl 3 PE15 .....223 A5
Burdett Gr PE7 ....189 F6
Burdett Rd PE13 ....245 B4
Bure Cl PE27 ....144 B6
Bures Ct 14 CB9 ....23 E7
Burford Way PE1 ....198 D6
Burgess Rd CB6 ....106 B7
Burgess's Dro CB5 .....106 C7
Burghley Ave 9 PE8 ....230 B1
Burghley Cl 3 PE6 .....231 F8
Burghley Ct PE9 ....244 E3
Burghley House* PE9 ...244 F3
Burghley La PE9 ....244 C3
Burghley Rd
  1 Peterborough PE1 ...198 A3
  4 Stamford PE9 ....244 A7
Burghley Rise CB5 .....130 C2
Burghley Sq 2 PE1 .....198 A3
Burgynes Farm Cl
  CB4 ....104 D3
Burgoyne's Rd CB4 .....104 D3
Buristead Rd CB2 ....48 F5
Burkett Way CB4 ....104 B5
Burleigh Pl CB1 ....246 C3
Burleigh Way CB2 ......147 B7
Burleigh St CB1 ....144 C3
Burleigh Terr PE27 ....144 A3
Burling Ct CB1 ....65 C6
Burling Wlk CB1 ....105 D3
Burlington Way PE28 ...143 C1
Burma Rd CB2 ....32 A1
Burmer Rd PE1 ....197 E2
Burmoor Cl PE29 ......141 B6
Burn St PE15 ....243 D5
Burnaby Cl PE28 ....140 C3
Burnet Gdns PE15 .....243 E7
Burnett Way PE29 .....141 F8
Burnham Cl CB1 ....66 A6
Burns Cl PE1 ....197 F7
Burns Ct 3 PE19 ....74 D5
Burns Rd SG8 ....5 C8
Burns Way PE27 ....143 F6
Burnsfield St PE16 ....241 B5
Burnside CB1 ....65 D7
Burnt Chy Dro CB6 ....225 B4
Burnt Cl
  Grantchester CB3 ......64 A4
  St Neots PE19 ....74 E3
Burnt House Cl CB1 .....38 C1
Burnt Up Dro PE7 .....188 F2
Burnthouse Rd PE7 ....191 E4
Burnthouse Sidings
  PE7 ....191 F1
Burntwood End CB10 ....19 E2
Burrel Rd PE27 ....144 B6
Burrell Cres IP28 .....239 C2
Burrell Way CB1 ....53 B2
Burrett Gdns 2 PE14 ..238 F1
Burrett Rd PE14 ....238 F1
Burrettgate Rd
  6 Leverington PE14 ...238 F1
  Walsoken PE13 ....245 F5
Burrough Field CB4 ....104 C1
Burrough Gn Endowed CE
  Prim Sch CB8 ....70 F4
Burrowmoor Prim Sch
  PE15 ....243 C3
Burrowmoor Rd PE15 ...243 C3
Burrows Dr PE29 ......141 C3
Burstellars PE27 ......144 A6
Burswood PE2 ....185 F2
Burton Cl CB9 ....23 E7
Burton Cl PE1 ....198 C3
Burton End
  Haverhill CB9 ....23 E7
  West Wickham CB1 ......37 C8

Burton End CP Sch
  CB9 ....23 D7
Burton Hill CB9 ....38 D5
Burton St PE1 ....198 C3
Burton Way PE28 ......137 F6
Burwell Castle (site of)*
  CB5 ....130 B1
Burwell Mus* CB5 .....130 C1
Burwell Rd
  Eaton Socon PE19 ......74 C6
  Exning CB8 ....110 A8
  Reach CB5 ....129 E1
  Swaffham Prior CB5 ...108 E5
Burwell Reach PE2 ....186 C7
Burwell Village Coll
  CB5 ....130 B3
Bury CE Prim Sch
  PE26 ....172 A4
Bury Cl Ramsey PE26 ..172 A4
  St Ives PE27 ....143 F5
Bury Gn CB6 ....218 A7
Bury La Chrishall SG8 ...8 D1
  Haddenham CB6 ....210 A5
  Lidgate CB8 ....73 F8
  Meldreth SG8 ....14 A5
  Moulton CB8 ....112 F6
  Sutton CB6 ....216 D2
Bury Plantation SG8 .....5 F6
Bury Rd
  Great Shelford CB2 .....49 C4
  Kentford CB8 ....134 B2
  Mildenhall IP28 ......239 E4
  Newmarket CB8 ....111 C5
  Ramsey PE26 ....172 A5
  Snailwell CB8 ....111 B3
Bury The CB5 ....86 C5
Bury Way PE27 ....143 F5
Buryfield PE26 ....172 A4
Burystead PE2 ....187 B8
Bush Cl CB3 ....62 D5
Bush La PE13 ....245 E5
Bushel La CB7 ....212 B4
Bushey Cl PE29 ......141 E5
Bushfield PE2 ....185 E3
Bushfield Com Coll
  PE2 ....185 E3
Bushfield Sports Ctr
  PE2 ....185 E4
Bushmead Gdns PE19 ...74 B3
Bushmead Jun Sch
  PE19 ....74 A3
Bushmead Prim Sch
  PE19 ....74 A3
Bushmead Rd PE19 .....74 A3
Bushy Cl PE7 ....186 D3
Bustard Hill PE28 ....113 D8
Butler's Rise CB2 .....17 D8
Butcher Cl CB4 ....105 C3
Butcher's Hill CB10 ..118 A4
Butcher's La SG19 .....25 B4
Butcher's Row 3 CB7 ..240 C4
Bute Ct CB7 ....23 F6
Butler Way
  Cambridge CB4 ....83 D6
  Haslingfield CB3 ......47 A5
Butlers Way CB2 ....32 F7
Butt Ave PE15 ....243 B2
Butt La
  Great Wilbraham CB1 ...68 A7
  Milton CB4 ....105 B3
Butt's La CB7 ....211 F1
Buttermarket CB6 .....240 D4
Buttermel Cl 1 PE28 ..118 F8
Buttermere PE29 ......141 B6
Buttermere Pl 2 PE4 ..204 E3
Button End CB2 ....47 D4
Butts Cl 8 Soham CB7 .212 B3
  20 Somersham PE28 ...215 C1
Butts The Fowlmere SG8 .15 B4
  Soham CB7 ....212 B3
Buttsgrove Way PE29 ..141 F7
Buxtons La SG8 ....10 F3
Buzzard Cl PE28 ......142 B8
Byall Fen Dro PE15 ...223 E2
Bydand La PE19 ....95 F2
Byfield Rd CB3 ....99 B3
Byng Cl PE19 ....74 B2
Byres The PE7 ....189 F7
Byron Cl
  Huntingdon PE29 .....141 F6
  Peterborough PE7 ....187 D6
Byron Pl 10 PE19 ......74 C6
Byron Rd 4 SG8 ....5 E8
Byron Sq CB2 ....64 D2
Bythorn Rd PE1 ....187 C6
Bythorn Way PE13 ....187 C6
Bythorne Bank PE13 ..237 C7

C

Cabbage Moor CB2 ......48 E8
Cadenham Rd CB5 .....108 E3
Cadwin Field CB4 ......83 F7
Caernarvon Rd PE19 ...74 F2
Caernarvon Wlk CB9 ...23 E8
Cage Hill CB8 ....108 D5
Cage La
  Great Staughton PE19 ..94 B6
  Stretham CB6 ....210 F5
Cairns CB8 ....131 A3
Caithness Ct CB4 ......83 E8
Calcot St PE7 ....186 D2
Calcot St PE2 ....204 F2
Caldecote Cl PE2 .....187 E6
Caldecote Prim Sch
  CB3 ....80 C2

Caldecote Rd
  St Neots PE19 ....74 E3
Calderside PE2 ....175 E7
Caldervale PE2 ....186 C6
Caledon Way 3 CB4 ....83 E8
Calfe Fen Cl 2 CB7 ...212 B5
Calfe Fen Dro CB7 ....212 B5
Calford Dr CB4 ....23 C8
California Rd
  Huntingdon PE29 .....141 E6
  St Ives PE27 ....143 E6
Callander Cl CB4 ......83 D7
Calvin Cl CB4 ....125 F3
Cam Cl PE27 ....144 A7
Cam Cswy CB4 ....84 B6
Cam Rd CB6 ....240 C6
Camargue Dr PE15 ....243 D2
Camargue Pl 4 PE13 ..245 E3
Cambanks CB4 ....84 A4
Camber's New Dro
  PE7 ....220 D8
Cambourne Bsns Pk
  CB3 ....79 B5
Cambourne Rd CB3 .....79 B5
Cambrian Way PE4 ....204 E1
Cambridge & Cty Folk Mus*
  CB3 ....246 A4
Cambridge Acad CB1 ..246 B3
Cambridge Airport CB1 .84 F2
Cambridge Ave CB6 ...240 A3
Cambridge Bsns Pk
  CB4 ....84 C7
Cambridge Cl
  St Neots PE19 ....38 E1
  St Ives PE27 ....143 F8
Cambridge Cres SG8 ...13 A8
Cambridge Ct 10 PE13 .245 A6
Cambridge Drama Ctr
  CB1 ....246 C1
Cambridge Gdns PE19 ..74 F5
Cambridge Pl CB1 ....246 C1
Cambridge Rd
  Babraham CB2 ....50 D4
  Balsham CB1 ....52 F2
  Barley SG8 ....7 A3
  Barton CB3 ....62 E1
  Ely CB7 ....240 B3
  Eynesbury Hardwicke
  PE19 ....76 B4
  Fenstanton PE28 .....121 A6
  Foxton CB22 ....30 C7
  Fulbourn CB1 ....66 A5
  Girton CB3 ....82 E8
  Godmanchester PE29 ..141 C4
  Great Shelford CB2 .....48 F7
  Hardwick CB23 ....81 B3
  Hauxton CB2 ....48 A5
  Histon CB4 ....83 C8
  Madingley CB3 ....81 F5
  Melbourn SG8 ....14 E7
  Meldreth SG8 ....14 A6
  Milton CB4 ....105 C1
  Newton CB22 ....31 B8
  Oakington/Longstanton
  CB4 ....103 C4
  Orwell SG8 ....45 C1
  St Neots Rural PE19 ...75 C5
  Sawston CB2 ....32 E8
  Stamford PE9 ....244 A6
  Stretham CB6 ....210 E3
  Thetford CB6 ....29 F7
  Thriplow SG8 ....30 F3
  Waterbeach CB5 ....105 F7
  Wimpole SG8 ....27 F6
Cambridge Regional Coll
  CB4 ....83 F8
Cambridge Ret Pk CB4 ..84 B3
Cambridge Science Pk
  CB4 ....84 B8
Cambridge Sp CB28 ...143 B7
Cambridge St
  Godmanchester PE29 ..141 F2
  St Neots PE19 ....75 A5
Cambridge Sta CB1 ....65 A7
Cambridge Summer Sch of
  Tech CB3 ....84 B7
Cambridge Univ Botanic
  Gdn* CB2 ....64 F7
Cambridge Univ Ctr
  CB2 ....246 A1
Cambridge Univ Press
  CB2 ....246 A1
Cambridge Way CB1 ....38 E1
Cambridgeshire Cl
  CB6 ....240 B4
Camden Ct CB4 ....246 B2
Camel Rd CB6 ....242 C6
Camelia Cl PE4 ......204 D3
Cameron Rd CB4 ....83 E7
Campaign Ave PE2 ....186 D8
Campbell Dr IP28 ....239 B6
Campbell Dr PE4 .....204 D2
Campbell La CB2 ....64 C2
Campbell St 1 CB1 .....65 B8
Campbell Way PE15 ...243 D7
Camping Cl CB6 ......210 A6
Campion Cl CB7 ......212 A5
Campion Rd PE1 ......198 B8
Campion Way SG8 ....5 E5
Campkin Cl CB4 ....83 F7
Campkin Rd CB4 ....83 F7
Camps Cl CB5 ....106 B7
Camps Rd Bartlow CB1 ..21 B7
  Haverhill CB9 ....23 F7

Camps Rd continued
  Helions Bumpstead CB9 ..23 B1
Camside CB4 ....84 A4
Canal St 8 PE15 ......245 C5
Canberra Cl
  Bassingbourn SG8 ......13 B5
  Mildenhall IP28 ......213 E8
Canberra Ct PE26 ....171 F7
Canberra Dr PE27 ....143 C7
Canberra Rd PE27 ....171 E7
Candidus Ct PE4 .....204 B5
Candy St PE2 ....186 E8
Cangle Junc CB4 ....24 A8
Canmore Ct PE28 .....168 C2
Canners Cl CB3 ....61 E5
Cannon St
  Little Downham CB6 ...218 A6
  Wisbech PE13 ....245 C4
Cannon Terr 8 PE13 ...245 C4
Cannon's Cl SG8 ......10 F5
Canon Cl CB9 ....39 A1
Canon Dr 4 PE9 ......230 D3
Canonsfield PE4 .....204 A4
Cantelupe Rd CB7 .....47 C7
Canterbury Ave CB6 ..240 A3
Canterbury Cl CB4 ....204 B3
Canterbury St CB4 ....83 C4
Cant's Dro PE13 .....234 C4
Canute Cres CB8 .....240 E7
Canwell PE4 ....204 C4
Capper Rd CB5 ....127 C1
Capstan Cl CB4 ....84 A3
Capthorne Cl PE7 ....186 C2
Capuchin Cl CB1 ....66 A4
Capulet Cl PE19 ....74 C3
Capulet Ct PE29 .....141 F7
Car Dyke Rd
  Landbeach CB5 ....105 F6
  Waterbeach CB5 ......106 A6
Caravere Cl 2 CB4 .....83 F8
Caraway Rd CB1 ....66 E5
Cardiff Pl SG8 ....13 A8
Cardigan St CB8 .....111 A3
Cardinal Distribution Pk
  PE29 ....142 B1
Cardinal Way
  Godmanchester PE29 ..142 B1
  5 Haverhill CB9 ....38 F1
Cardinals Gate PE4 ..204 A5
Cardinals Way CB7 ...240 D4
Carey Cl CB7 ....240 F6
Caribou Way CB1 ......66 A7
Carisbrook Ct PE3 ...186 B8
Carisbrooke Rd CB4 ...83 C5
Carisbrooke Way 8
  PE19 ....74 F2
Carlcton Crest PE4 ...204 D1
Carlisle Terr PE27 ..144 B3
Carlow Cl CB1 ....84 A2
Carlton Cl Haverhill CB9 ..38 F2
  10 Leverington PE13 ..238 B2
Carlton Gn Rd CB8 ....55 A6
Carlton Rd CB8 ....70 E1
Carlton Rise SG8 ....14 D5
Carlton Way CB4 .....83 D5
Carlyle Rd CB4 ......246 A4
Carmel St CB10 ....18 D2
Carmen St CB10 ......18 D3
Carnation Way IP28 ..133 F8
Carnegie Rd 18 PE8 ..230 B1
Caroline Cl PE1 .....246 C2
Carpenters Way 9
  PE15 ....223 A6
Carpol La 3 CB6 .....210 C6
Carr Rd PE1 ....198 D3
Carradale PE2 ....185 D5
Carrick Cl CB1 ....66 A4
Carrier Cl PE1 ......186 D8
Carrington Pl PE28 ..140 C3
Carrington's Dro PE6 .232 B8
Carron Dr PE4 ....204 A3
Carrps The CB8 ......134 A6
Carr's Lodge PE4 ....244 F8
Carsey Hill CB1 ......22 B6
Carson Wlk CB1 ......110 F6
Carter Cl
  Brampton PE28 ....140 C3
  Duxford CB2 ....17 E8
Carter Rd CB5 ....130 C4
Carter St CB7 ....212 E1
Carter's Way CB4 ....122 E5
Carters Cl PE3 ......196 F3
Carters Croft CB10 ...21 B1
Cartmel Way PE6 .....232 A1
Cartwright Rd 5 SG8 ...5 D5
Caryer Cl PE2 ....186 D6
Carysfort Cl PE7 ....187 C6
Casburn's La CB5 ....130 A3
Casewick La 1 PE9 ..230 F7
Casewick Rd PE4 ....230 E7
Castel Way PE7 .....175 D8
Castellhythe CB7 ....240 D3
Casterton Rd PE4 ...244 A6
Castle Ave CB9 ....23 E7
Castle Camps CB1 .....22 D1
Castle Camps CE Prim Sch
  CB1 ....22 E3
Castle Dyke PE9 .....244 B5
Castle End Rd PE6 ...231 C7
Castle Gdns CB6 .....113 F4
Castle Hill PE29 ....141 D3
Castle Hill CB3 ......83 A3
Castle Hill Gall* CB3 .83 C4
Castle Hill Mid Sch
  CB9 ....23 D7

Castle La CB9 ....23 E8
Castle Manor Com Upper Sch
  CB9 ....23 E8
Castle Moat Rd PE1 ..141 D4
Castle Pk CB1 ....246 A4
Castle Row 8 CB3 .....83 C3
Castle Sq 12 PE13 ...245 C5
Castle St
  7 Stamford PE9 ......244 B5
Castle Wlk CB9 ....23 E8
Castor Hanglands National
  Nature Reserve*
  PE6 ....195 E7
Castor Mills PE8 ....184 F6
Castor Prim Sch PE5 ..195 E2
Castor Rd Castor PE6 .196 C6
  Marholm PE6 ....203 D1
  Sacworth Way PE15 ...195 D2
Cat Field PE13 ....237 E1
Catharine St CB1 ......65 B8
Cathedral Sq PE3 ....198 A2
Cathedral View PE15 .224 C4
Catherine Ct PE2 ....186 B7
Cathwaite PE4 ....204 F1
Catkin Cl CB9 ....38 E1
Catley Ct PE4 ....205 A1
Catley Pk CB1 ....19 D6
Catling's La PE13 ...238 C7
Cattell's La CB7 ....106 B8
Cattle Dike PE13 ....237 E2
Cattle Mkt CB7 ......240 D3
Cattle Mkt 6 PE4 ....198 A2
Causeway
  Godmanchester PE29 ..141 E1
  Great Staughton PE19 ..93 F6
  Pampisford CB2 ....33 C5
Causeway Cl
  Great Staughton PE19 ..93 F6
  March PE15 ....243 C2
Causeway Gdns PE15 ..243 D3
Causeway Pas CB1 ....246 C3
Causeway Rd PE28 ...154 A8
Causeway Sch The
  PE1 ....198 C3
Causeway The
  Bassingbourn SG8 .....13 A5
  Burwell CB5 ....130 B2
  Elsworth CB3 ....100 B4
  Haverhill CB9 ....23 E8
  Isleham CB7 ....213 A5
  March PE15 ....243 D2
  Soham CB7 ....212 B4
  Sutton CB6 ....216 C2
  Thorney PE6 ....232 E2
  West Wratting CB1 ....53 E5
Causewayside CB1 ....246 A1
Cavalry Dr PE15 ....243 E2
Cavalry Prim Sch
  PE15 ....243 E2
Cavell Ct 3 PE1 .....197 B4
Cavendish Ave CB1 ....65 B5
Cavendish Ct PE28 ..168 C3
Cavendish Cl 3 CB9 ...23 E6
Cavendish Rd CB1 .....84 B1
Cavendish St PE1 ...198 B4
Cavendish Way CB5 ...80 C1
Cavenham Rd PE28 ...214 E2
Caverstede Rd PE4 ..204 D1
Cavesson Ct CB4 ......83 C6
Caville White CB9 ....23 C8
Cawdor Pl 6 PE19 .....74 F2
Cawood Cl PE15 .....243 E6
Caxton Cl Bourn CB3 ..60 E7
  Eltisley PE19 ....77 F3
Caxton La CB2 ....30 B5
Caxton Rd Bourn CB3 .60 C7
  Great Gransden SG19 ..58 E5
  St Ives PE27 ....144 B6
Cecil Ct 10 PE9 .....244 C5
Cecil Lodge Cl CB8 ..110 F3
Cecil Pacey Ct PE1 ..197 E7
Cecil Rd PE1 ....198 A6
Cedar Ave 6 PE15 ...223 A6
Cedar Ct Grafham PE28 .115 F7
  March PE15 ....243 E5
  Melbourn SG8 ....14 C5
Cedar Cres SG8 ....14 E7
Cedar Dr CB4 ....242 D4
Cedar Dr PE28 ....151 E3
Cedar Gr PE1 ....198 B8
Cedar Rd PE27 ....143 F6
Cedar Wlk PE15 .....243 E6
Celta Rd PE2 ....186 F6
Celtic Cl PE2 ....187 D7
Cemetery Hill CB8 ...110 D7
Cemetery Rd
  St Neots PE19 ....74 F5
  Whittlesey PE7 ......189 E6
Cenacle The 1 CB8 ...64 C2
Centenary Way PE28 ..140 C2
Central Ave
  Brampton PE28 ....140 D1
  Peterborough PE1 ....197 D5
Central Sq PE1 ......187 D5
Central Sta CB1 .....111 D2
Centre for Mathematical
  Sciences CB3 ....83 B2
Centre Rd CB7 ....212 C4
Centurion Way PE29 ..142 B1
Century Way PE15 ...243 C7
Cerris Rd PE1 ....198 B7
Chadburn PE4 ....205 A1
Chadley La PE29 .....141 F2
Chadwell Way CB3 ....79 C4
Chain Cl PE1 ....198 B6
Chain Cswy CB6 .....209 B8

Chain Rd CB4 ....208 C2
Chainbridge La PE28 ...135 F8
Chalfont Cl 2 CB1 ......65 F6
Chalk Gr CB1 ....65 D4
Chalk Rd PE13 ....237 D1
Chalkhill Barrow SG8 ...14 C4
Chalklands CB1 ....35 C3
Chalkstone Mid Sch
CB9 ....24 A8
Chalkstone Way CB9 ....39 A1
Chalky La SG8 ....8 D2
Chalky Rd CB1 ....34 C3
Challis Cl CB2 ....29 F8
Challis Gn CB2 ....29 F8
Chalmers Rd CB1 ....65 C6
Chamberlain Way PE19 ..74 F7
Chamois Cl CB2 ....32 F6
Champions Cl SG8 .....15 E8
Champneys Wlk CB3 ....64 C8
Chancellor Cl PE29 .....141 C7
Chancellors Wlk CB4 ...83 C6
Chancery La 6 PE6 ....232 A1
Chandler's Way PE15 ...243 D2
Chandlers CB2 ....185 E5
Chandlers Ct CB5 ......130 B3
Chandlers Way PE26 ...221 A4
Chantry Cl
Cambridge CB4 ....83 F4
Chatteris PE16 ....241 D6
Peterborough PE1 ......198 A5
Swavesey CB4 ....122 E6
Chantry The CB1 ....67 A5
Chapel Ave 1 PE13 ....235 B7
Chapel Cl Hilton PE28 ..120 B1
Litlington SG8 ....12 A2
Needingworth PE27 ....208 A3
Waterbeach CB5 ....106 B7
Wrestlingworth SG19 ...25 B4
Chapel Ct PE8 ....194 B2
Chapel End
Great Gidding PE28 ....166 D2
Sawtry PE28 ....168 C4
Chapel Field SG19 .....41 D4
Chapel Field La PE28 ...215 B1
Chapel Gate PE12 .....237 B7
Chapel Gdns
Benwick PE15 ....222 A5
Coates/Eastrea PE7 ...190 C7
Chapel Hill CB2 ....47 A3
Chapel La
Chatteris PE16 ....241 B6
Downham CB6 ....218 A6
Easton PE28 ....138 B4
Elm PE14 ....236 B6
Elton PE8 ....178 C8
Fowlmere SG8 ....15 E8
Harston CB2 ....47 F3
Kirtling CB8 ....72 C5
Melbourn SG8 ....14 C6
Newton PE13 ....238 B5
Alwalton PE2 ....185 F5
4 Peterborough PE4 ..204 C3
Reach CB5 ....129 D1
Houghton PE28 ....143 A5
St Ives PE27 ....144 A3
Soham CB7 ....219 B2
Tydd St Giles PE13 ...237 F7
Whittlesey PE7 ....227 A3
Wicken CB7 ....211 E1
Willingham CB4 ......208 E5
Wimblington PE15 ....223 B6
Wisbech PE14 ....235 D5
Chapel Rd
Beck Row, Holywell
Row & Kenny Hill IP28 ..213 D6
Earith PE28 ....208 E5
Great Eversden CB3 ...45 F8
Weston Colville CB1 ...54 B5
Wisbech PE13 ....245 B5
Chapel Row CB8 ....91 F8
Chapel St
Alconbury PE28 ....150 F4
Cambridge CB4 ....84 A4
4 Crowland PE6 ......232 B8
Duxford CB2 ....32 D1
Ely CB6 ....240 C4
Exning CB8 ....110 B8
March PE15 ....243 D3
Stanground PE2 ......187 C7
Peterborough PE1 ....198 B3
Stretham CB6 ....210 F5
Warmington PE8 .....178 B3
Waterbeach CB5 .....106 B7
13 Wisbech PE13 ....245 C4
Yaxley PE7 ....181 D5
Chapel Yd
Kimbolton MK44 .....113 E1
Sawtry PE28 ....244 C5
Chapelfield Rd PE13 ...235 A2
Chapelfield Way CB2 ...32 F8
Chaplains Cl 6 CB9 ...38 F1
Chaplin's Cl CB1 ....66 F5
Chaplins Cl PE7 ....190 F8
Chapman Cl CB4 ......83 E7
Chapman Way PE19 ...74 E1
Chapman's Cl CB4 ....105 C7
Chapman's Way CB4 ..208 E1
Chapmans Cl CB4 ....105 C7
Chapmans Dr 5 CB3 ..79 C3
Chapnall Cl PE13 .....245 F6
Chapnall Rd PE13 ....245 F6
Chapple Dr CB9 ......38 F1
Charcoal La PE28 ....140 C3
Charding Cres SG8 ...5 C7
Charlemont Dr PE15 ..224 B5
Charles Cl
Newmarket CB8 ......110 E3
Ramsey PE26 ....172 A7

Charles Cope Rd PE2 ..185 F5
Charles Dr PE29 ....142 A6
Charles Melrose Cl
IP28 ....239 B5
Charles Rd
Stamford PE9 ....244 A7
Whittlesey PE7 ......189 F6
Charles St
Cambridge CB1 ......65 B7
Peterborough PE1 ....198 B3
Charles' St PE19 .....74 F5
Charles St 10 PE13 ..245 C4
Charlton Cl PE3 .....197 B1
Charnocks Cl 3 SG19 .41 D5
Charnwood Cl PE2 ...187 A7
Charrington Cl CB9 ...24 C6
Charters The 2 PE9 ..230 C6
Chartfield Rd CB1 ....65 F6
Chase Cl CB9 ....39 A1
Chase Rd PE15 ......221 F6
Chase St PE13 ......245 C6
Chase The Ely CB6 ..240 B4
March PE15 ....243 C4
Thorney PE6 ....200 E7
Upwell PE14 ....229 D7
Whittlesey PE7 .....220 E7
Whittlesey PE7 .....224 A8
Wisbech PE13 ......245 A7
Chaston Rd CB2 .....49 A5
Chater Rd 8 PE8 ....230 B1
Chatsfield PE6 ......204 A6
Chatsworth Ave CB4 .83 C5
Chatsworth Pl PE3 ..197 B2
Chatteris Mus* PE16 .241 C4
Chatteris Rd
Chatteris PE16 .....215 D4
10 Somersham PE28 ..208 C8
Chaucer Cl
Cambridge CB2 ....64 E6
14 Wisbech PE13 ...238 B2
Chaucer Pl PE19 ...74 D6
Chaucer Rd
Cambridge CB2 ....64 D7
Peterborough PE1 ..197 E8
Royston SG8 ......5 C8
Chaucer Way PE27 .143 F6
Chauntry Rd CB9 ...23 F7
Chawston Cl 9 PE19 .74 C5
Chedburgh Pl PE9 ..39 B1
Cheddars La CB5 ...83 B3
Chedworth St CB3 ..64 C7
Cheere Way CB3 ...99 B3
Chelmer Cl PE27 ...144 B7
Chelmer Garth PE4 .204 F1
Chelmer Rd CB9 ....24 B8
Chelmer Way CB6 ..240 D6
Cheltenham Cl PE1 .198 B6
Chelveston Way PE3 .197 C5
Chelwood Rd CB1 ..65 F6
Cheney Ct PE2 .....186 C4
Cheney Way CB4 ..83 C5
Chequer La 1 CB7 ..240 C4
Chequer St PE28 ...121 B6
Chequers Cl
Alconbury Weston PE28 ..150 C6
Cambridge CB1 .....65 F5
Fenstanton PE28 ...121 B6
Chequers Cnr PE14 .236 E7
Chequers Croft PE28 .120 B2
Chequers Ct 1 PE29 .141 D4
Chequers La CB3 ..99 B3
Chequers Rd CB4 ..104 C2
Chequers Way PE29 .141 C4
Cherry Bounds Rd CB3 ..82 E8
Cherry Cl Cambridge CB1 ..65 E5
Linton CB1 ....35 B3
Milton CB4 ....105 D3
Cherry Ct CB3 .....79 A4
Cherry Hill PE28 ...214 C3
Cherry Hinton CE Inf Sch
CB1 ....65 F6
Cherry Hinton Cl Limekiln
Close Nature Reserve*
CB1 ....65 F4
Cherry Hinton Com Jun Sch
CB1 ....66 A6
Cherry Hinton Rd
Cambridge CB1 ....65 B6
Great Shelford CB2 ..65 D1
Teversham CB1 ....66 A8
Cherry Hinton W Pit Nature
Reserve* CB1 ....65 E4
Cherry Holt La PE9 .244 D5
Cherry Orch
Fulbourn CB1 ......66 D5
Haddenham CB6 ...210 A5
Oakington/Longstanton
CB4 ....103 C5
Cherry Orton Rd PE7 .185 F5
Cherry Rd PE13 ...245 C8
Cherry Rise CB6 ..216 D1
Cherry Tree CB7 ..128 C5
Cherry Tree Ave CB2 ..49 C4
Cherry Tree Cl
Huntingdon PE29 ..141 C6
Litlington SG8 .....12 A1
Cherry Tree Gr PE7 .189 F6
Cherry Tree Way PE28 .121 B6
Cherry Trees CB2 ..48 E7
Cherryfields PE2 ...185 E6
Cherryholt Ave PE5 ..243 B3
Cherryholt Rd PE9 ..244 D5
Cherrytree Cl CB2 ..49 C4
Cherrytree La CB7 ..212 B3
Cherrywood Ave PE15 .243 B3
Cherrywood Gn PE15 .243 B3
Chervil Cl PE7 ....175 D8

Chervil Way 1 CB3 ...79 C3
Cherwell Ct CB3 .....64 C7
Chesham Rd PE28 ...168 C2
Chesnut Gr CB4 ....83 F4
Chester Cl CB9 .....23 E6
Chester Ct 8 CB9 ..23 C6
Chester Rd
Peterborough PE1 ..198 C3
Wyton Airfield PE28 .143 B7
Chester Way PE29 ..142 B1
Chesterfield Rd CB4 .84 A6
Chesterfield Way 9
PE19 ....74 E2
Chesterton Com Coll
CB4 ....83 E4
Chesterton Gr PE2 .187 D6
Chesterton Hall Cres
CB4 ....83 E4
Chesterton Hospl CB4 .83 F4
Chesterton La CB4 ..246 A4
Chesterton Rd CB4 .246 A4
Chestnut Ave PE1 ..198 C5
Chestnut Cl
Brampton PE28 ...140 D2
Glinton PE6 ....203 D8
Grafham PE28 .....116 A7
Haslingfield CB3 ..47 B4
Haverhill CB9 .....23 F8
Huntingdon PE29 ..141 E7
Mildenhall IP28 ...239 D4
Peakirk PE6 ....206 B2
Sawston CB2 ....32 E7
Sawtry PE28 ......168 B4
Chestnut Cres
March PE15 ....243 B3
Whittlesey PE7 ...189 E6
Chestnut Dr
6 Soham CB7 ....212 B4
1 Thorney PE6 ..233 A3
Chestnut Gr
Cambridge CB4 ..83 F4
Little Shelford PE28 .152 A2
St Neots PE19 ...74 F4
Chestnut La SG8 ..13 B6
Chestnut Rd
St Ives PE27 .....143 F6
7 Wisbech PE13 .245 C4
Chestnut Rise
Bar Hill CB3 .....102 D3
Burwell CB5 .....130 B4
Chestnut Way CB6 .216 E3
Chestnut Wlk 6 SG8 ..5 E5
Chestnuts The
Elton PE8 ....178 C8
Harston CB2 .....48 A4
Chettisham CB6 ..218 C5
Cheveley CE Prim Sch
CB8 ....91 C7
Cheveley Rd
Newmarket CB8 ..111 C3
Woodditton CB8 ..91 C3
Cheviot Ave PE4 .204 E2
Chewells Cl CB6 ..210 A6
Chewells La CB6 ..210 A6
Cheyney Cl SG8 ..11 B1
Cheyney St SG8 ..11 B1
Chichester Way CB2 .115 D2
Chicks St CB6 ....240 C4
Chigwell Ct 7 CB5 .84 E4
Chilcourt SG8 .....5 C6
Childerley Hall* CB3 .80 D8
Childers St PE7 ...189 C8
Childs La 12 PE15 .223 A5
Child's Pond Rd PE7 .75 A6
Chilford Hall Vineyard*
CB1 ....35 D6
Chiltern Rise PE4 .204 D2
Chimswell Way CB9 .23 C8
Chippenham Fen National
Nature Reserve*
CB7 ....132 B7
Chippenham Mews
PE2 ....186 C7
Chippenham Rd
Chippenham CB8 .133 C2
Fordham CB7 ....213 A1
Moulton CB8 ....133 D1
Chisenhale PE2 ..185 E6
Chishill Rd Barley SG8 ..7 A2
Great & Little Chishill SG8 ..7 B3
Heydon SG8 ....8 A4
Chishill Windmill* SG8 ..7 C2
Chiswick Ave CB1 .239 C6
Chiswick End SG8 ..14 A7
Chittering Dro CB5 .127 C8
Chivers Rd CB9 ..23 D7
Chivers Way CB4 .104 B2
Chrishall Rd SG8 ..14 A7
Christ Church Cl PE7 .244 B6
Christchurch St CB1 .246 C3
Christie Dr PE29 ..141 A5
Christopher Cl PE1 .197 F8
Christopher Dr PE13 .245 A7
Christopher Tye Cl 3
CB6 ....240 B5
Church Cl
Bassingbourn SG8 ..12 E5
Cottenham CB4 ...125 F6
Coveney CB6 .....217 C5
Dullingham CB8 ..70 E8
Exning CB8 ....110 C8
Great & Little Abington
CB1 ....34 C7
Great Wilbraham CB1 .67 F7
Newborough PE6 ..205 C8
Ramsey PE26 ....221 C2
Stilton PE7 ......176 A3
Church Rd
Brampton PE28 ..140 E2

Church continued
Whittlesford CB2 ...32 C5
Church Cswy PE28 .168 C4
Church Dr PE2 ....185 F5
Church Dro PE14 ..236 F2
Church End
Arrington SG8 ....44 D1
Barley SG8 ....7 A1
Cambridge CB1 ...65 F8
Coton CB3 ....64 A2
Everton SG19 ....40 C3
Gamlingay SG19 .41 E5
Hilton PE28 ......99 B8
Horningsea CB5 .106 A2
11 Leverington PE13 ..238 E2
Over CB4 ....208 D1
Parson Drove PE13 .234 E8
Rampton CB4 ....84 D8
Weston Colville CB1 .54 A7
Whaddon SG8 ...28 B2
Church Farm La SG8 ..11 B1
Church Fen Dro CB6 .209 E3
Church Gate 18 PE6 .231 F8
Church Gdns IP28 ..213 D6
Church Gn CB10 ..18 B7
Church Hill Castor PE5 .195 E2
Grafham PE28 ...115 F6
Church Hill Cl PE7 .187 C1
Church La
Abington Pigotts SG8 ..11 F6
Arrington SG8 ...44 D1
Ashwell SG7 .....2 D4
Balsham CB1 ....53 B2
Barton CB3 ......63 B4
Barton Mills IP28 .239 D1
Beck Row, Holywell
Row & Kenny Hill IP28 ..213 D6
Brington & Molesworth
PE28 ....147 C4
Burwell CB5 ....130 B1
Cambridge CB2 .64 C2
Castle Camps CB1 ..22 E3
Chatteris PE16 ..241 C4
Cheveley CB8 ...91 C6
Comberton CB3 .62 C3
Conington PE7 ..168 E8
Cottenham CB4 .125 F6
Covington PE28 .135 C2
Croydon SG8 ....27 A8
Doddington/Wimblington
PE15 ....222 F5
Ellington PE28 ..138 F4
Elsworth CB3 ...100 B4
Ely CB7 ....240 C4
Exning CB8 .....110 C8
Fenstanton PE28 .121 B6
Fulbourn CB1 ...66 C4
Gamlingay SG19 .41 D5
Girton CB3 .....82 E8
Graveley PE19 ..97 F5
Great & Little Abington
CB1 ....34 B7
Great Paxton PE19 .96 D5
Guilden Morden SG8 ..10 F5
Haddenham CB6 .210 A6
Hemingford Abbots
PE28 ....143 A3
Hemingford Grey PE28 .143 C2
Huntingdon PE29 .120 B1
Isleham CB7 ....213 A5
Kennett CB8 ....133 F5
Kingston CB3 ...61 B3
Leighton PE28 ..148 D3
Linton CB1 .....35 C2
Little Eversden CB3 ..46 A7
Little Staughton MK44 ..93 B2
1 Littleport PE28 .242 D4
Madingley CB3 ..81 E4
Milton CB4 .....111 A3
Newmarket CB8 ..111 C3
Newton PE13 ...238 A5
Pampisford CB2 .33 B5
Papworth Everard CB3 .99 A2
Peterborough PE2 .187 B7
Ramsey PE26 ..171 B2
Royston SG8 ...5 D6
Sawston CB2 ...32 F7
Sibson cum Stibbington
PE8 ....194 E2
Snailwell CB8 ..132 A3
Spaldwick PE28 .137 F6
Stamford PE9 ..244 C4
Stetchworth CB8 ..90 A2
Stow Longa PE28 .137 B3
Sutton CB6 ....241 B8
Tallington PE9 .230 F6
Tilbrook PE28 .113 B7
Tydd St Giles PE13 .237 F6
Warmington PE8 .178 B2
Westley Waterless CB8 ..70 B5
Whittlesford CB2 ..32 C5
Wilburton CB6 ..220 A4
Willingham CB4 .209 A1
Worlington PE28 .213 F4
Wrestlingworth SG19 ..25 B3
Church La Cl IP28 .239 D2
Church Leys PE28 .121 C6
Church Mdw IP28 .239 D2
Church Mdws PE19 ..74 F5
Church Mews 21 PE13 ..245 C5
Church Path CB1 ..66 C4
Church Pl PE29 ...141 E2
Church Rate Wlk CB4 ..64 C8
Church Rd
Brampton PE28 ..140 E2

Church Rd continued
Buckworth PE28 ..149 D6
Carlton CB8 .....55 A6
Catworth PE28 ..136 D7
Chrishall SG8 ...8 D3
Christchurch PE14 ..229 E2
Conington PE7 ..168 D8
Easton PE28 ....138 B4
Everton SG19 ...40 C3
Glatton PE28 ...175 E1
Grafham PE28 ..115 E7
Great Wilbraham CB1 ..67 F8
Hauxton CB2 ...48 A5
Leverington PE13 ..245 F7
Little Stukeley PE28 ..151 F2
Little Wilbraham CB1 ..86 F2
Moulton CB8 ....112 F5
Shepreth SG8 ..29 E4
Shudy Camps CB1 ..22 C5
Stow cum Quy CB5 ..85 F4
Teversham CB1 ..85 B2
Thistley Green IP28 ..28 D3
Toft CB3 ....61 E4
Warboys PE28 ..164 E4
Wentworth CB6 .217 C1
Wicken CB7 ....211 F1
Friday Bridge PE14 ..236 A3
Wisbech PE13 ..238 B1
Wisbech St Mary PE13 ..235 B7
Wittering PE8 ..230 B1
Church Side Ashley CB8 ..91 F8
Bourn CB3 .....60 C5
Buckden PE19 ..117 A4
Cambridge CB4 ..84 A4
12 Doddington/Wimblington
PE15 ....223 B7
Exning CB8 ....110 C8
Fen Ditton CB5 .84 E6
Fen Drayton CB4 ..121 F5
Fenstanton PE28 .121 B6
Fordham CB7 ...212 F1
Gamlingay SG19 .41 D5
Great Chesterford CB10 ..18 D2
Great Eversden CB3 ..45 E7
Great Gransden SG19 ..58 E4
Great Shelford CB2 ..49 C4
Great Wilbraham CB1 ..67 F8
Guilden Morden SG8 ..10 F4
Harston CB2 ....47 D2
Haslingfield CB3 ..47 A5
Hemingford Grey PE28 ..143 C2
Histon CB4 .....104 B5
Holme PE7 .....176 D2
6 Ickleton CB10 .18 A4
6 Isleham CB7 ..213 A5
Litlington SG8 ..12 A2
Little Gransden SG19 ..58 E3
March PE15 ....243 C1
Market Deeping PE6 ..231 F8
Needingworth PE27 ..208 A2
Northborough PE6 ..174 D7
Old Hurst PE28 .154 D7
Alwalton PE2 ..185 A4
Stanground PE2 .187 C7
Peterborough PE1 ..198 A2
Werrington PE4 ..204 C3
St Ives PE27 ...143 F4
St Neots PE19 .74 F5
Sawtry PE28 ...244 C5
1 Somersham PE28 ..208 C8
Stamford PE9 ..244 B4
Steeple Morden SG8 ..11 B1
Stilton PE7 ....175 F7
5 Thorney PE6 ..233 A3
Thriplow SG8 ..31 C1
Warmington PE8 ..178 A3
Whaddon SG8 ..28 A3
Whittlesey PE7 ..189 D6
Wilingham CB4 ..209 A1
Wistow PE28 ...163 F7
Withersfield CB9 ..38 C4
Woodhurst PE28 ..155 B5
Yaxley PE7 ....181 D4
Church Terr 17 PE13 ..245 C5
Church View
Keyston PE28 ..146 A3
9 Northborough PE6 ..231 F7
Oakington/Longstanton
CB4 ....103 C6
2 St Neots PE19 ..74 F5
3 Witchford CB6 ..217 E1
Church View Cl PE2 ..187 B7
Church Wlk
Chatteris PE16 ..241 D5
Little Gransden SG19 ..58 E3
Mildenhall IP28 ..239 B6
Peterborough PE1 ..198 A3
6 St Neots PE19 ..74 E5
Stow Longa PE28 ..137 B3
Sturmer CB9 ...24 E5
Upton PE28 ....195 B5
Churchfield SG8 ..7 A1
Churchfield Ave CB2 ..32 F8
Churchfield Ct
Girton CB3 .....103 E2
6 Peterborough PE4 ..197 E8
Churchfield Rd
Peterborough PE4 ..197 D8
Upwell PE14 ...236 F2

Churchfield Way
Whittlesey PE7 .189 C7
5 Wisbech St Mary PE13 .235 B7
Churchgate St 9 CB7 .212 B4
Churchill Cl 4 CB6 .216 E2
Churchill Ave
Haverhill CB9 .39 B1
Houghton & Wyton PE28 .143 B7
Newmarket CB8 .110 D5
Churchill Cl CB6 .240 A4
Churchill Coll CB3 .83 B3
Churchill Ct
Little Downham CB6 .218 A6
Newmarket CB8 .110 F3
Churchill Dr IP28 .239 B5
Churchill Rd
Gorefield PE13 .237 F3
Stamford PE9 .244 B7
Wisbech PE13 .245 D4
Churchyard The IP28 .239 B4
Cinques Rd SG19 .41 C6
Cinques The SG19 .41 B6
Cissbury Ring PE4 .204 C2
City of Ely Com Coll
CB6 .240 C6
City Rd Cambridge CB1 .246 C2
Littleport CB6 .242 E4
March PE15 .243 D4
Peterborough PE1 .198 A2
Civic Ind Est CB9 .23 F5
Clack La PE28 .135 D8
Clare Cl
Mildenhall IP28 .239 D5
Stamford PE9 .244 A5
Waterbeach CB5 .106 A8
Clare Coll (The Colony)
CB4 .246 A4
Clare Coll CB2 .246 A2
Clare Coll Pavilion CB2 .64 F5
Clare Ct PE27 .144 A4
Clare Dr CB3 .80 C2
Clare Pl CB8 .111 B2
Clare Rd Cambridge CB3 .64 C8
Huntingdon PE29 .142 A7
5 Northborough PE6 .231 F7
Peterborough PE1 .197 F6
Clare St Cambridge CB4 .246 A4
Chatteris PE16 .241 B4
Claremont 1 CB1 .64 F7
Claremont Rd PE13 .245 E5
Clarence Rd
Peterborough PE1 .197 E5
Wisbech PE13 .245 D6
Clarendale Est CB8 .55 F6
Clarendon Rd
Cambridge CB2 .64 F6
Haverhill CB9 .23 F7
Clarendon St CB1 .246 B2
Clarendon Way PE6 .203 F8
Clark Rd SG8 .5 D7
Clark's Dro CB7 .212 A4
Clarke's La CB6 .210 C5
Clarkes Way SG8 .12 F5
Clarkson Ave PE13 .245 D5
Clarkson Cl CB3 .83 B2
Clarkson Ct PE13 .245 D6
Clarkson Inf Sch The
PE13 .245 E6
Clarkson Rd CB3 .83 B2
Claudian Cl CB9 .24 D7
Clay Cl La CB4 .104 D3
Clay La
Abbots Ripton PE28 .162 A1
Castor PE5 .195 E2
Little Stukeley PE28 .151 F7
Clay St Histon CB4 .104 B5
Soham CB7 .212 B4
Clayburn Rd PE7 .186 C1
Claybush Rd SG7 .2 D3
Claydon Cl CB1 .22 E4
Claygate PE7 .189 D7
Claygate Rd CB1 .65 F6
Clayhithe Rd CB5 .106 C5
Clayhive Dr 6 CB9 .23 F7
Claypole Dr 3 PE6 .231 F7
Clayton PE2 .186 A4
Clayton Cl PE13 .245 F6
Clayton Sch PE2 .186 B4
Claytons Way PE29 .141 F5
Clayway CB7 .240 E6
Clear Cres SG8 .14 D5
Cleatham PE3 .197 A4
Clematis Cl IP28 .213 F1
Clement Dr PE2 .186 D8
Clement's La CB9 .23 F7
Clement's Way 1 IP28 .213 F8
Clements Cl CB9 .23 F7
Clements CP Sch CB9 .23 F7
Clements Dr CB9 .23 F7
Clerk Maxwell Rd CB3 .83 A2
Cleve Pl PE6 .232 A1
Cleveland Bay PE15 .243 E2
Cleveland Ct PE4 .204 E2
Cleves Rd CB9 .23 D6
Cley Ct CB9 .38 C1
Clifden Cl SG8 .44 D1
Cliff Cres PE9 .244 B5
Cliff Rd PE9 .244 B5
Clifton Ave PE3 .197 E3
Clifton Ct CB1 .65 A6
Clifton Rd
Cambridge CB1 .65 A6
Huntingdon PE29 .141 D7
Clipston Wlk PE3 .197 C5
Clive Hall Dr CB4 .124 A1
Cliveden Cl CB4 .83 C5
Cloisters The 6 CB7 .240 D4
Close The Babraham CB2 .50 E2
Godmanchester PE29 .142 A1
Kennett CB8 .133 F5
Papworth Everard CB3 .99 B3
Royston SG8 .5 F7
St Neots PE19 .74 E6
Sutton CB6 .216 E1
Close Victoria SG19 .25 B4
Cloughs Cross PE13 .234 D8
Clover Cl PE26 .220 D3
Clover Ct Cambridge CB1 .66 A5
Linton CB1 .35 D2
Clover End 2 CB6 .217 D1
Clover Field CB9 .23 D8
Clover Rd PE19 .74 C3
Clover Way 1 IP28 .214 A1
Cloverfield Dr CB7 .212 A5
Club Way PE7 .186 E4
Clydesdale Cl PE15 .243 E2
Clydesdale Rd 6 SG8 .5 E6
Coach Dr CB3 .46 D5
Coach House La CB2 .31 B7
Coach La CB8 .91 D5
Coalwharf Rd PE13 .245 B4
Coates Ct PE14 .236 D6
Coates Dro CB7 .213 A5
Coates Prim Sch PE7 .190 F8
Coates Rd PE7 .190 D7
Cob Pl PE29 .118 F7
Cobbet Pl PE1 .198 B3
Cobble Yd CB1 .246 C3
Cobden Ave PE1 .197 F4
Cobden St PE1 .197 F4
Cobholm Pl 4 CB4 .83 F8
Cobwebs PE28 .142 D8
Cock Bank PE7 .191 C2
Cock Fen Rd PE14 .229 F3
Cockbrook La
Brington & Molesworth
PE28 .147 C8
Old Weston PE28 .157 C2
Cockburn St CB1 .65 B8
Cockcroft Pl CB3 .83 B2
Cockerell Rd CB4 .83 D5
Cockerton Rd CB3 .103 E1
Cocketts Dr PE13 .245 E5
Cockfen La CB4 .105 C7
Cockhall Cl SG8 .12 A1
Cockhall La SG8 .12 A1
Cockle Cl CB2 .31 C7
Cockpen Rd CB7 .131 A8
Codling Wlk CB3 .78 F4
Codrington Ct 2 PE19 .74 B3
Cody Rd CB5 .127 B1
Coggeshall Cl 5 CB5 .84 E4
Cohort Way PE29 .142 B1
Colbron Cl SG7 .2 C4
Colbrook CB1 .66 D6
Cold Arbour SG19 .56 A1
Cold Harbour SG7 .2 E7
Cold Harbour Cnr
PE13 .235 C5
Coldham Bank PE15 .228 D6
Coldham Hall Chase
PE14 .235 E1
Coldham's Gr CB1 .84 C1
Coldham's La CB1 .84 C2
Coldham's Rd CB1 .84 B2
Coldhams Cres PE29 .141 F6
Coldhams N PE29 .141 F6
Coldhams S PE29 .141 F5
Coldhorn Cres PE13 .245 D7
Cole Cl 1 CB6 .217 D1
Coleridge Com Coll
CB1 .65 C7
Coleridge Ct 1 PE19 .74 C6
Coleridge Pl PE1 .197 E8
Coleridge Rd CB1 .65 B6
Coles La Brinkley CB8 .70 D2
Linton CB1 .35 C2
Oakington/Longstanton
CB4 .103 C6
Coles Rd CB4 .105 D2
Coleseed Rd PE15 .228 D2
Colesfield CB4 .123 E2
Coll of Animal Welfare The
PE29 .119 C5
Coll of W Anglia CB4 .105 D3
College Cl CB5 .86 E6
College Cres CB3 .47 B5
College Ct PE28 .168 C3
College Fields CB4 .83 F6
College Gdns PE15 .243 E7
College Heath Mid Sch
IP28 .239 C6
College Heath Rd
IP28 .239 D6
College Pk PE1 .198 C5
College Rd Histon CB4 .104 B1
Soham CB7 .212 B3
College The CB7 .240 D4
Collett's Bridge La
PE14 .236 C5
Collier Rd CB1 .246 C2
Collier Way CB2 .49 C4
Colliers La CB5 .86 A6
Collingham PE2 .185 F3
Collings Pl CB8 .110 E5
Collingwood Ave
PE15 .243 E3
Collingwood Ct SG8 .5 E7
Collingwood Rd PE19 .74 B2
Collin's Hill CB7 .212 F1
Collyweston Great Wood &
Easton Hornstocks National
Nature Reserve*
PE8 .192 A6
Collyweston Rd PE9 .230 B2
Colmworth Bsns Pk
PE19 .74 C1
Colmworth Gdns 5 PE19 .74 C2
Colne Fields
Colne PE28 .215 D1
Somersham PE28 .208 D8
Colne Rd
Bluntisham PE28 .208 C6
Colne PE28 .208 C8
Earith PE28 .208 D6
Colne Valley Rd CB9 .24 A7
Colour Ct PE29 .141 D7
Colts Croft SG8 .7 E2
Coltsfoot Cl CB1 .66 A5
Coltsfoot Dr
Peterborough PE2 .186 E7
Royston SG8 .5 E6
Columbine Rd CB6 .240 B6
Colvile Rd
Newton PE13 .238 A5
Wisbech PE13 .245 E5
Colville Prim Sch CB1 .65 F5
Colville Rd CB1 .65 F6
Colwyn Cl CB4 .83 D5
Comberton Rd
Barton CB3 .62 F5
Little Eversden CB3 .46 C8
Toft CB3 .61 E5
Comberton Village Coll
CB3 .62 A4
Comet Rd PE29 .143 A8
Comet Way
Mildenhall IP28 .239 B5
St Ives PE27 .144 A7
Comfrey Ct CB1 .66 A5
Commerce Rd PE2 .185 C5
Commercial Rd PE15 .243 C7
Common Acre La CB6 .225 D6
Common Dro
Southery PE38 .226 E8
Whittlesey PE7 .189 C8
Wimblington PE15 .223 C6
Common Gate Dro
CB7 .212 E5
Common La Ashwell SG7 .2 B6
Chrishall SG8 .1 F7
Hemingford Abbots
PE28 .142 F3
Sawston CB2 .32 D7
Common Rd
Parson Drove PE12 .233 F7
West Wratting CB1 .54 E2
Weston Colville CB1 .54 E4
Whittlesey PE7 .189 C8
Witchford CB6 .217 E1
Common The CB1 .53 F4
Commons Rd PE7 .189 C8
Compton Fields CB7 .240 E7
Computer Laboratory
CB3 .83 A3
Conder Cl CB4 .105 C3
Conduit Head Rd CB3 .82 F3
Conduit Rd PE9 .244 C6
Coneygear Ct PE29 .141 E7
Coneygear Rd PE29 .141 E8
Coneygree Rd PE2 .187 D6
Coneywood Rd PE15 .223 A7
Conference Way PE13 .245 C8
Conifers The PE2 .185 F6
Coningsby Rd PE3 .204 A2
Conington La PE7 .168 C8
Conington Rd CB3 .121 B3
Coniston Cl PE29 .141 B6
Coniston Rd
Cambridge CB1 .65 B6
Peterborough PE4 .204 E3
Conley Cl PE26 .172 B7
Connaught Rd CB9 .23 E7
Connor's Cl SG8 .10 F4
Conquest Dro PE7 .187 D1
Constable Ave 4 PE19 .74 D5
Constable Cl PE7 .190 A8
Constable Cres PE7 .190 A8
Constable Rd
1 Haverhill CB9 .38 D1
St Ives PE27 .144 A7
Constables Leys PE28 .113 F5
Consul Ct 8 CB4 .83 E7
Control Twr Mus* SG8 .12 F8
Convent Dr CB5 .105 F8
Conway Ave PE4 .204 C2
Conway Cl
3 Cambridge CB1 .65 F6
Haverhill CB9 .23 D8
March PE15 .243 B3
Conway Pl 4 PE19 .74 F2
Cook Cl CB4 .84 B6
Cook Cl Rd PE7 .181 D6
Cook's Dro
Beck Row, Holywell
Row & Kenny Hill IP28 .213 B8
Earith PE28 .208 E6
Cook's Gn PE15 .222 F5
Cook's Hole PE8 .193 C4
Cooks La PE28 .168 D5
Cookson Cl PE7 .181 D4
Coolidge Gdns CB4 .125 F4
Coombe Rd SG8 .4 A1
Coombelands SG8 .13 E1
Coombelands Rd 3 SG8 .5 E8
Cooper Thornhill Rd 1
PE7 .175 F7
Cooper's Cl CB8 .90 A1
Cootes La CB4 .121 E5
Cootes Mdw PE27 .144 B3
Copalder Cnr PE15 .222 B6
Copel Cl CB3 .80 B1
Copeland PE3 .197 A3
Copellis Cl CB9 .39 A2
Copes Cl PE19 .117 B4
Cophall Dro CB6 .217 E7
Coploe Rd CB10 .17 F3
Copper Beech Way
PE2 .187 B7
Copperbeech Cl PE27 .144 A5
Copperfields SG8 .5 B6
Coppice Ave CB2 .49 B6
Coppice Dr CB3 .79 A4
Coppice The
Histon CB4 .104 C1
Littleport CB6 .242 C1
Coppingford Cl PE2 .187 D6
Coppins Cl PE28 .168 A4
Coppins Ct PE14 .245 E2
Copsewood PE4 .204 C4
Copy Hill CB9 .23 E3
Coral Pk Trading Est
CB1 .84 B2
Corbett St CB4 .125 E4
Cordell Cl PE27 .143 E6
Cordon St PE13 .245 C4
Coree Cl CB2 .65 A5
Corfe Ave PE4 .204 C2
Corfe Pl 3 PE19 .74 F2
Cormas Cl 5 SG8 .5 E8
Corn Exchange St
CB2 .246 A2
Corn Mill PE15 .243 C3
Corner Cl CB7 .219 B5
Cornfields 1 PE15 .222 F5
Cornish Cl CB1 .37 A3
Cornmills Rd CB7 .212 D2
Cornstall Bldgs 3 PE9 .244 C5
Cornwall Ct PE19 .74 B4
Cornwall Rd
6 Stamford PE9 .244 B6
Wyton Airfield PE28 .143 A8
Cornwallis Dr PE19 .74 A3
Cornwallis Rd CB9 .23 F6
Corona Rd CB4 .83 E4
Coronation Ave
3 Crowland PE6 .232 B8
Huntingdon PE29 .141 E5
Parson Drove PE12 .234 A7
Royston SG8 .5 C5
9 Somersham PE28 .215 C1
Warboys PE28 .164 F6
Whittlesey PE7 .189 F7
Coronation Cl
March PE15 .243 C2
Waterbeach CB5 .106 A7
Coronation Mews 2 CB2 .64 E7
Coronation Pl CB2 .64 E7
Coronation St CB2 .246 B1
Corporation Bank PE6 .207 F7
Corporation Rd PE13 .245 D3
Corpus Christi Coll
CB2 .246 A2
Corpus Christi La
PE29 .141 E1
Corrie Rd CB1 .65 B7
Corsican Pine Cl CB8 .110 F5
Corunna Cl 7 PE19 .74 C5
Corvus Cl SG8 .5 E8
Cosgrove Cl PE3 .197 C6
Cosin Ct CB1 .246 A1
Cotes The CB7 .211 F6
Coton CE Prim Sch
CB3 .82 B2
Coton Rd CB3 .63 E5
Cotswold Cl
March PE15 .243 E4
Peterborough PE4 .204 E1
Cottenham Cl 6 CB4 .208 D1
Cottenham Prim Sch
CB4 .125 D4
Cottenham Rd
Histon CB4 .104 B5
Landbeach CB4 .126 B1
Cottenham Village Coll
CB4 .125 E3
Cottesmore Cl PE3 .197 D4
Cotton Cl
Conington PE7 .168 C8
5 Sawtry PE28 .168 C2
Cotton Ct 1 PE29 .141 F7
Cotton End PE3 .197 A4
Cotton End Rd CB8 .110 C8
Cotton La PE19 .97 C7
Cotton's Field CB3 .102 B1
Cottons Cnr PE14 .229 D6
Cottons Head PE14 .236 E3
Cottons The PE14 .236 E2
Cottrell's La CB3 .100 B4
Coulson Cl CB4 .105 C2
Coulson Way PE28 .150 F4
Council Rd 4 PE13 .245 E6
Council St PE4 .197 D8
Countess Cl PE19 .74 B3
County Rd
Hampton Vale PE7 .181 C8
March PE15 .243 D6
Coupals Cl CB9 .24 C6
Coupals CP Sch CB9 .24 D7
Coupals Rd CB9 .24 E6
Courier Cl IP28 .239 B6
Courtland Ave CB1 .65 C5
Courtney Way CB4 .83 E4
Courtyard Way CB4 .125 E5
Courtyards CB2 .48 F3
Cousins Cl PE15 .243 C4
Covehite Ct 6 CB9 .23 E6
Covent Gdn CB1 .246 C1
Covent Gdns CB4 .209 A1
Coventry Cl PE4 .204 B3
Covert Cl CB9 .39 A1
Covert The
1 Comberton CB3 .62 D6
Peterborough PE3 .197 B1
Cow and Hare Pas
PE27 .144 A3
Cow and Sheep Dro
IP28 .213 C7
Cow Brook La CB3 .99 A3
Cow Fen Rd CB4 .122 E6
Cow La Fulbourn CB1 .66 E5
Godmanchester PE29 .142 C2
Great Chesterford CB10 .19 A4
Rampton CB4 .124 F6
Cow Way PE7 .190 D8
Cowbridge Hall Dro
CB6 .218 B6
Cowdell End CB3 .100 B4
Cowgate PE1 .197 F2
Cowley Cl PE28 .115 D3
Cowley Pk CB4 .84 B7
Cowley Rd CB4 .84 C7
Cowlinge Cnr CB8 .73 D8
Cowper Rd
Cambridge CB1 .65 B6
Huntingdon PE29 .141 D5
Peterborough PE1 .197 F7
Cowpers Ct 4 PE19 .74 D6
Cowslip Cl SG8 .5 F5
Cowslip Dr CB6 .211 A7
Cox's Cl CB2 .49 C4
Cox's Dro CB1 .66 F6
Cox's End 15 CB4 .208 D1
Cox's La Chatteris PE16 .241 C6
Wisbech PE13 .245 A3
Coxons Cl PE29 .141 E5
Coxs Cl CB1 .23 C7
Crab Apple Way SG19 .41 C5
Crab Marsh PE13 .245 B8
Crabapple Cl PE28 .168 B3
Crabapple Gdns PE2 .185 D6
Crabtree PE4 .205 B1
Crabtree Croft CB1 .35 B3
Craft Way SG8 .11 B2
Crafts Way CB3 .102 C3
Craig St PE1 .197 F3
Craister Ct CB4 .83 E7
Cramswell Cl CB1 .23 E6
Crandal Way CB2 .49 A4
Crane Ave PE7 .181 F6
Crane Cl 3 PE28 .208 C8
Crane St PE28 .140 C3
Cranemore PE4 .204 A4
Crane's La CB3 .61 A2
Cranfield Pl 2 PE28 .208 C8
Cranfield Way
Brampton PE28 .140 D2
Buckden PE19 .117 A3
Cranford Dr PE3 .197 C4
Cranleigh Cl CB2 .64 D1
Cranmer Rd CB3 .83 B1
Cranmore Dro PE6 .206 D8
Cranny The PE19 .117 F2
Cranwells Way 4 CB6 .211 B7
Crathern Way CB4 .83 F7
Cratherne Way CB4 .83 F7
Crauden Gdns CB7 .240 E5
Craven Cl CB2 .64 D2
Craven Way CB8 .110 E6
Crawford Gdns 2 PE6 .232 C8
Crawley End SG8 .8 D4
Crawthorne Rd PE1 .198 A3
Crawthorne St 1 PE1 .198 B3
Crease Dro PE6 .232 B8
Crease Rd
Conington PE28 .168 F5
Sawtry PE28 .169 B6
Crecy Ct PE19 .74 C5
Creek Fen PE15 .228 D5
Creek Rd PE15 .243 D4
Crescent Cl PE7 .190 A7
Crescent Rd
Histon CB4 .104 C1
Whittlesey PE7 .189 F7
Crescent The
Cambridge CB3 .83 B3
Dullingham CB8 .89 C1
Eaton Socon PE19 .74 C3
Eye PE6 .232 A1
Impington CB4 .104 C1
Littleport CB6 .242 C3
Peterborough PE2 .186 E7
St Ives PE27 .144 A5
St Neots PE19 .74 F6
4 Soham CB7 .212 B3
Wicken CB7 .211 E1
Wisbech PE13 .245 C4
Cressbrook Dr CB3 .79 C3
Cressener Terr 3 PE19 .74 F5
Cresset The PE3 .197 A6
Cresswells La CB7 .240 E4
Crester Dr 3 PE4 .204 C3
Criccieth Way PE19 .74 F1
Cricket Field Rd CB8 .111 B2
Cricket Sch CB1 .246 C1
Cricketers Cl PE15 .243 C3
Cricketers Way
3 Benwick PE15 .222 A5
Chatteris PE16 .241 D3
Wisbech PE13 .245 A6
Cricketfield La PE26 .172 A6
Crick's Rd IP28 .213 D6
Cripple Sidings La
PE2 .187 A8

Crishall CE Prim Sch
SG8 ....8 C3
Crispin Cl Haverhill CB9 ....23 D7
🇮 Impington CB4 ....83 D7
Crispin Pl CB1 ....246 C3
Crockfords Rd CB8 ....111 A2
Crocus Cl PE7 ....181 F6
Crocus Gr PE1 ....198 A8
Croft Cl Brampton PE28 ...140 D2
  Histon CB4 ....104 B5
Croft Gdns CB3 ....64 C7
Croft La Haverhill CB9 ...24 B6
  Oakington/Longstanton
  CB4 ....103 B6
Croft Pk Rd CB6 ....242 D3
Croft Pl IP28 ....239 C4
Croft Rd Isleham CB7 ....213 A5
  Newmarket CB8 ....110 E5
  Outwell PE14 ....229 D7
Croft The Fulbourn CB1 ...66 E5
  Stamford PE9 ....244 D5
Croft Way PE7 ....186 C2
Crofters The CB6 ....210 F6
Croftfield Rd PE29 ....141 F1
Croftgate CB3 ....64 A7
Crofts The PE19 ....95 F1
Cromwell Cl
  🇮 Northborough PE6 ......231 F7
  Ramsey PE26 ....171 F6
Cromwell Com Coll
  PE16 ....241 C4
Cromwell Ct 🇮 PE19 ....74 F3
Cromwell Gdns 🇮 PE19 ....75 A5
Cromwell House*
  PE29 ....141 D5
Cromwell Mews PE26 ......231 C4
Cromwell Mus* PE29 ......141 D4
Cromwell Pk CB4 ....208 E1
Cromwell Pk Prim Sch
  PE29 ....141 A5
Cromwell Pl PE27 ....144 B3
Cromwell Rd
  Cambridge CB1 ....84 B1
  Ely CB6 ....240 C4
  March PE15 ....243 D6
  Peterborough PE1 ....197 F4
  St Neots PE19 ....74 F3
  🇮 Sutton CB6 ....216 E1
  Wisbech PE13 ....245 B3
Cromwell Sq PE29 ....141 D5
Cromwell Terr PE27 ....144 B3
Cromwell Way PE28 ....168 B3
Cromwell Wlk PE29 ....141 D5
Crooked Bank PE14 ....235 D6
Croots Cl PE28 ....140 B2
Cropston Rd PE1 ....198 E7
Crosfield Ct CB4 ....83 E7
Cross Bank Dro CB7 .....211 C5
Cross Cl CB9 ....39 A1
Cross Dro
  Haddenham CB6 ....209 E3
  Littleport CB7 ....226 A1
  Southery PE38 ....226 E7
  Stretham CB6 ....210 F3
  Tydd St Giles PE13 ......237 C5
  Warboys PE28 ....215 C6
  Waterbeach CB5 ....127 D4
  Whittlesey PE7 ....190 F6
  Wilburton CB6 ....210 C3
  Wistow PE28 ....172 E1
Cross Farm Cl PE28 ......120 C2
Cross Gn CB8 ....70 F8
Cross Hall Rd PE19 ....74 D6
Cross Keys Ct CB4 ....125 D3
Cross La
  Little Downham CB6 .....218 A6
  Melbourn SG8 ....14 C6
  Wisbech PE13 ....235 D6
Cross La CB SG8 ....45 E1
Cross Rd March PE15 .....227 F2
  Sutton St Edmund PE12 ..237 A4
  Whittlesey PE7 ....189 C7
Cross St
  Cambridge CB1 ....246 C1
  Covington PE28 ....135 D2
  Farcet PE7 ....187 D1
  Huntingdon PE29 ....141 E5
  Peterborough PE1 ....198 A2
Cross The PE28 ....161 F6
Crossberry Way PE6 .....231 B4
Crosshall Inf Sch PE19 ...74 C6
Crosshall Jun Sch
  PE19 ....74 C6
Crosshall Marina*
  PE19 ....74 E7
Crosshall Rd PE19 ....74 D6
Crossroad Cotts CB10 ....17 E2
Crossway Hand PE7 ......189 B8
Crossways Barley SG8 ....6 F1
  Linton CB1 ....35 D2
Crossways Gdns CB2 .....64 D2
Crow Dean CB3 ....79 A3
Crow Hill La CB7 ....79 B3
Crow Spinney La
  PE28 ....115 D2
Crow Tree St SG19 ....58 D4
Crowhill 🇮 PE20 ....118 F8
Crowhurst PE4 ....204 C5
Crowland Rd
  Deeping St James PE6 ...207 A6
  Eye PE6 ....232 A3
  Haverhill CB9 ....23 F8
  Newborough PE6 ....232 E5
  Thorney PE6 ....232 E5
Crowland Way CB4 ....83 F7
Crowlands CB4 ....125 D4
Crown Ave PE14 ....229 D3

Crown Cl
  Hail Weston PE19 ....95 A1
  March PE15 ....243 C2
  St Ives PE27 ....144 A4
Crown Gdns
  Alconbury PE28 ....150 E4
  Little Downham CB6 .....218 A6
Crown La 🇮 CB6 ....242 D4
Crown Lakes Ctry Pk*
  PE7 ....187 B2
Crown Mews PE26 ....172 B7
Crown Pl PE27 ....144 A3
Crown Rd PE14 ....229 D3
Crown St
  Peterborough PE1 ....197 E7
  St Ives PE27 ....144 A3
  Stamford PE9 ....244 B5
Crown Wlk
  Newmarket CB8 ....111 A4
  St Ives PE27 ....144 A3
Crowson Cres 🇮 PE6 .....231 F7
Crowthorne Cl CB1 ....65 F6
Croxton Gdns PE28 ......136 D6
Croydon Hill SG8 ....26 E8
Croydon Rd
  Arrington SG8 ....44 C1
  Croydon SG8 ....27 B8
Croyland Rd PE4 ....204 D1
Crummock Wr PE29 .....141 C5
Crunch Croft PE19 ....24 E5
Crystal Dr PE2 ....186 D8
Cuckoo La
  Lolworth CB3 ....101 F5
  Rampton CB4 ....124 E3
Culloden Cl PE19 ....74 C5
Cumberland Way 🇮
  PE19 ....73 F1
Cundell Dr CB4 ....125 E4
Cunningham Cl CB4 ......231 E8
Cunningham Rd PE2 .....186 E8
Cunningham Way PE19 ..74 A2
Curf PE16 ....222 F3
Curf Fen Dro PE16 ....222 E4
Curlew Ave PE16 ....241 C5
Curlew Cl PE7 ....189 F8
Curlew Cres 🇮 SG8 ....5 E8
Curlew Gr PE2 ....187 D7
Curlew Pl 🇮 PE19 ....75 B6
Cutter Ferry Cl CB4 .....241 C6
Cutter Ferry La CB4 .....246 C4
Cutter Dr PE16 ....241 C6
Cygnet Dr PE2 ....186 E3
Cygnet Rd PE7 ....186 E3
Cypress Cl
  🇮 Doddington PE15 ......223 A6
  Peterborough PE2 ....197 A2
Cyprus Rd CB1 ....65 C7

D

Da Vinci Cl PE27 ....144 A7
Dacre Gn SG8 ....5 F6
Daffodil Gr PE2 ....187 C7
Dagless Way PE15 ....243 D7
Daimler Ave PE7 ....181 E6
Daintree PE27 ....208 A3
Daintree Rd PE26 ....220 D4
Daintree Way PE28 .....143 D1
Daintrees Rd CB4 ....121 F6
Dairy Dro
  Littleport CB6 ....225 C6
  Thorney PE6 ....233 E2
Daisy Cl CB4 ....83 D7
Dakota Rd IP28 ....213 E8
Dalby Ct PE1 ....198 C8
Dale Cl PE2 ....185 F5
Dale The CB4 ....123 F1
Dale Way CB2 ....32 F8
Dalegarth CB4 ....83 F4
Dales Way PE27 ....208 A3
Dalham Pl PE19 ....24 B8
Dalham Rd Ashley CB8 ..97 B7
  Moulton CB8 ....112 F4
Dalton St CB4 ....84 B5
Dalton Way CB6 ....240 D6
Dam Bank Dro CB6 .....209 C4
Dane Dr CB3 ....83 A1
Dane Hill CB8 ....133 E5
Dane Hill Rd CB8 ....133 D5
Dancis Cl PE1 ....198 C4
Danesbury Ct CB1 ....84 C1
Daniel Ct PE9 ....244 C4
Danish Ct PE4 ....204 A4
Daphmoir Cl CB2 ....29 F8
Darford PE28 ....208 E6
Darley Cl PE4 ....230 C1
Darrington Cl 🇮 PE19 ...74 B3
Dart Cl PE27 ....144 B6
Dartford Rd PE15 ....243 C4
Darthill Rd PE15 ....243 D5
Dartmoor Dr PE29 .....141 A4
Darwin Cl Ely CB6 ....240 A4
  Mildenhall IP28 ....239 C6
  🇮 Stamford PE9 ....244 A7
Darwin Coll CB3 ....246 A1
Darwin Dr CB4 ....83 D5
Darwin Pl CB8 ....111 B1
Darwood Cl PE27 ....144 B3
Daules Rd PE28 ....140 E1
Davey Cl CB4 ....104 C3
Davey Cres CB2 ....49 A6
David Bull Way CB4 .....105 D3
David Chalmers Cl
  PE4 ....186 F8
David St 🇮 CB1 ....65 A8
David's Cl PE4 ....203 F4
David's La PE4 ....244 B6

Davie La PE7 ....201 A1
Davis Cl PE7 ....96 A2
Davison Rd CB6 ....240 E8
Davy Rd CB1 ....65 B7
Daw's Dro PE7 ....220 D8
Daws Cl 🇮 CB5 ....65 F6
Dawson Cl PE4 ....205 C8
Daymond St PE2 ....186 D7
Day's St 🇮 CB5 ....5 C5
Day's Lode Rd PE15 ....224 C7
De Bec Cl PE1 ....198 C3
De Freville Ave CB4 ....246 C4
De Freville Rd CB2 ....49 A6
De Havilland Cl 🇮 PE28 .223 A6
De Havilland Rd PE13 ...245 C6
De La Haye Cl CB3 ....99 B3
De La Warre Way CB3 ...79 B4
De Vere Cl PE28 ....143 B1
Deacon St PE1 ....197 F3
Deacons La CB7 ....240 D5
Deacons Sch PE1 ....198 B5
Deaconscroft PE2 ....197 B5
Deal Cl PE29 ....141 E8
Deal Gr CB2 ....32 F8
Dean Dr CB1 ....65 B4
Dean Dro PE16 ....215 F6
Dean Peacock Ct CB6 ..240 E6
Dean Rd CB1 ....241 A5
Deans Cl CB9 ....39 A1
Debdale Rd PE7 ....185 E4
Debdale Ct PE7 ....189 F5
Debden Gn CB6 ....240 B4
Debden Ave PE27 ....144 A7
Debden Cl PE15 ....243 B5
Debden Rd CB9 ....24 B8
Decoy Rd
  Borough Fen PE6 ....207 A3
  Gorefield PE13 ....237 D2
Deene Ct PE7 ....197 D3
Deeping St James Com Prim
  Sch 🇮🇸 PE6 ....243 B6
Deeping St James Rd
  PE6 ....231 E7
Deepings Sch The 🇮🇷
  PE6 ....231 B8
Deerfield Rd PE15 ......243 E6
Deerhurst Way 🇮🇸 PE6 ...232 A1
Deerleap PE5 ....197 A5
Deerpark Rd PE28 ......168 A4
Degas Dr PE27 ....144 A7
De-Havilland Rd PE13 ...245 C6
Deighton Cl PE27 ....144 B5
Delamere Cl
  Little Wilbraham CB8 .....68 F6
  Peterborough PE7 ....198 C5
Delapre Ct 🇮 PE6 ....232 A1
Delbrig Dro CB7 ....212 E5
Dell The
  Peterborough PE2 ....186 E7
  Royston SG8 ....5 C5
Dells Cl PE28 ....166 D2
Delph PE7 ....189 D7
Delph Ct PE7 ....187 F6
Delph Dro IP28 ....212 F8
Delph St PE7 ....189 D7
Delta La PE28 ....151 E3
Delve Terr PE16 ....241 C5
Dendys PE28 ....143 D1
Dengaine Cl CB3 ....99 B2
Denham Rd CB8 ....92 E8
Denham Wlk 🇮 PE1 .....197 C4
Denis Dr PE2 ....186 A4
Denmark Dr PE2 ....186 A4
Denmark Rd CB4 ....125 E3
Dennis Gn SG19 ....41 C4
Dennis Rd CB5 ....84 F4
Dennis Wilson Ct CB2 ...64 D4
Denny Abbey* CB5 ......127 A6
Denny End Rd CB5 ......105 F8
Denson Cl CB5 ....106 A8
Denton Rd
  Glatton PE28 ....175 E1
  Peterborough PE7 ....187 C6
Dentons Chase PE26 ...220 E4
Depot Rd CB8 ....110 E6
Deptford Cl PE15 ....243 B3
Derby Dr PE1 ....198 C6
Derby Rd CB1 ....65 B6
Derby St CB3 ....64 C7
Derby Way CB8 ....110 D5
Derwent Cl
  Cambridge CB1 ....65 D5
  Huntingdon PE29 ....141 B5
  St Ives PE27 ....144 B6
Derwent Dr PE4 ....204 E2
Derwood Gr PE4 ....204 B5
Desborough Ave PE2 ...187 D5
Desborough Rd PE29 ...142 A6
Desmond Ave CB1 ......241 A6
Devana Cl PE7 ....118 F8
Devils Pl PE16 ....243 D4
Devil's Dyke Nature
  Reserve* CB5 ....109 B5
Devoke Ct PE2 ....141 B6
Devon Cl PE27 ....144 A8
Devon Rd PE28 ....154 A1
Devonshire Cl PE28 ....168 B3
Devonshire Mews CB1 ..80 C1
Devonshire Rd CB1 .....65 A8
Dewpond Cl 🇮 PE19 .....75 A6
Dexter Cl 🇮🇸 PE15 .....223 A5
Dexter Way PE4 ....178 B3
Dial Cl PE19 ....95 F2
Diamond Cl CB2 ....64 C3
Dickasons SG8 ....14 D7
Dickens St PE1 ....198 B3

Dickerson Cl 🇮 SG19 ....41 D6
Digby Ct 🇮 PE8 ....74 B3
Dimmock's Cote CB6 ...211 B3
Dimmock's Cote Rd
  CB7 ....211 B3
Dingley Ct PE3 ....197 C5
Dip The CB8 ....111 D2
Ditchburn Pl CB1 ....84 A1
Ditchfield CB5 ....108 D8
Ditchfields 🇮 PE28 .....215 C1
Ditton Cl CB6 ....111 A1
Ditton Fields CB4 ......84 C3
Ditton Gn CB8 ....90 D1
Ditton La CB5 ....84 E4
Ditton Lodge Fst Sch
  CB8 ....111 B2
Ditton Wlk CB4 ....84 C4
Dixies Cl SG7 ....2 D3
Dixon's Dro PE14 ....238 F5
Dixons Rd 🇮 PE6 ....231 E8
Dobson Wlk 🇮🇸 PE15 ...223 B7
Dock Bsns Pk The
  CB7 ....240 D2
Dock La CB5 ....106 A2
Dock Rd PE16 ....241 C6
Dock The CB7 ....240 D2
Dockings La CB8 🇮🇰 CB7 ...213 A5
Doctor's Cl CB4 ....104 D3
Docwra Rd CB3 ....99 A3
Docwra's Cl SG8 ....29 D5
Doddington Dr PE3 .....197 B2
Doddington Hospl
  PE15 ....222 F6
Doddington Rd
  Benwick PE15 ....222 A5
  Chatteris PE16 ....241 A8
  Doddington/Wimblington
  PE15 ....223 B6
Dodds Mead CB3 ....47 A5
Dodford La CB3 ....103 E2
Dog Kennel La SG8 .....5 D6
Dogget Cl CB1 ....66 F4
Doggett Rd CB1 ....84 A1
Dogsthorpe Gr PE1 ....198 A5
Dogsthorpe Jun & Inf Sch
  PE1 ....198 B7
Dogsthorpe Rd PE1 .....198 A5
Dogsthorpe Star Pit & Little
  Wood Nature Reserve*
  PE6 ....205 E2
Dole The CB4 ....104 C3
Doles The 🇮 CB4 ....208 D1
Dolls Cl CB1 ....53 C1
Dolphin Cl
  Cambridge CB1 ....66 A7
  Linton CB1 ....35 D7
Dolphin La 🇮 Ely CB7 ...240 D4
  Melbourn SG8 ....14 B6
Dolphins Way SG19 .....41 D6
Dome Leisure Ctr
  IP28 ....239 E4
Donaldson Dr 🇮 PE4 ....204 E2
Donegal 🇮 CB1 ....84 A2
Donegal Cl PE4 ....204 D2
Donne Cl SG8 ....5 F8
Donnington Pk PE13 ....245 C6
Dorchester Cres 🇮 PE1 .198 D7
Dorchester Way PE28 ..143 B7
Doris St CB5 ....110 F3
Dorling Way PE28 ......140 B3
Dorral Dean CB3 ....80 B1
Dorvis La CB10 ....21 B1
Double Bank La PE28 ..161 B7
Doug Smith Cl CB8 .....110 F6
Doughty St PE9 ....244 D7
Douglas House Hospl
  CB2 ....64 E5
Douglas Rd 🇮 PE6 ......231 E8
Douglas Way CB3 ....79 B3
Dove Cl CB4 ....121 C5
Dove Cote Cl CB4 ......121 F5
Dove House Rd CB9 ....24 A8
Dovecote Cl
  Peterborough PE1 ......198 A3
  Yarwell PE8 ....183 A8
Dovecote La PE7 ....181 C5
Dovecote Rd
  Great Paxton PE19 .....96 D3
  Upwell PE14 ....229 D7
Dovehouse Cl Ely CB7 ..240 D3
  Fowlmere SG8 ....15 E8
  Godmanchester PE29 ..142 A1
  St Neots PE19 ....74 F6
Dovehouse Wood
  PE28 ....162 B1
Dover Cl PE29 ....141 E8
Dover Rd PE4 ....204 C2
Dover St 🇮 CB1 ....246 C2
Dovey Cl PE27 ....144 B6
Dowding Way CB4 ......83 D6
Dowgate Rd PE13 ......238 B1
Dowland Cl CB4 ....104 A3
Down Gate PE1 ....197 A1
Downe Cl CB3 ....99 A2
Downham Feoffees CE Prim
  Sch CB6 ....218 A7
Downham Hythe Dro
  CB6 ....217 D6
Downham Rd Ely CB6 ..240 B7
  Outwell PE14 ....236 F2
Downham's La CB4 ....84 A6
Downing Cl
  Bottisham CB5 ....86 E6
  Mildenhall IP28 ....239 D5
  Newmarket CB8 ....111 B3
Downing Coll CB2 ......246 B1
Downing Cres PE9 .....143 B8
Downing Ct CB5 ....108 A1

Downing Pl 246 B2
Downing St CB2 ....246 B2
Downlands SG8 ....5 C6
Downs Cres CB9 ....23 F8
Downs Pl CB9 ....23 F8
Downton Dr CB9 ....23 E8
Dowsdale Bank PE6 ...233 A8
Dragoon Dr 🇮 PE15 ....243 D2
Drain Rd PE6 ....205 A7
Drake Ave PE16 ....241 C6
Drake Cl PE29 ....141 F6
Drake Rd PE19 ....74 B2
Drake Way CB4 ....104 C5
Draper's Cl PE8 ....178 C3
Drapers La CB9 ....23 B2
Drapery Row 🇮 CB8 ....111 A3
Drayhorse Rd PE26 ....172 A5
Drayton PE3 ....197 A4
Drayton Cl CB1 ....66 A5
Drayton Rd CB1 ....66 A5
Drewels La PE19 ....56 D4
Drift Ave PE9 ....244 D7
Drift Gdns PE9 ....244 D7
Drift Rd PE19 ....244 C6
Drift The Elsworth CB3 ..100 B4
  Exning CB8 ....110 A8
  Oakington/Longstanton
  CB4 ....103 B5
  Sutton PE5 ....194 F3
Drings Cl 🇮 CB4 ....208 D1
Drinkwater Cl CB8 .....110 E4
Drive The Perry PE28 ..115 D1
  Peterborough PE3 .....197 E2
  St Ives PE27 ....143 F4
Drivers Ave PE29 .....141 E5
Drivers Cl 🇮 PE15 .....223 A6
Drosier Rd CB2 ....246 C1
Drove Rd SG19 ....41 A6
Drove The Farcet PE26 ..220 D7
  Witchford CB6 ....217 E1
Drovers Cl PE26 ....221 A4
Drummer St 🇮 CB1 .....246 B2
Drury La
  Bluntisham/Colne PE28 ..208 D7
  Melbourn SG8 ....14 D6
  Wicken CB7 ....211 F2
Dry Drayton CE Prim Sch
  CB3 ....102 C1
Dry Drayton Rd
  Madingley CB3 ....81 D7
  Oakington & Westwick
  CB4 ....103 A4
Dry Leys PE2 ....186 C6
Drybread Rd PE7 ......189 F8
Dryden Cl PE27 ....144 A7
Dryden Ct 🇮 PE19 .....75 A5
Dryden Rd PE1 ....197 F7
Dubbs Knoll Rd SG8 ...10 F5
Duberly Cl PE28 ....115 E2
Duchess Cl PE19 ......74 A3
Duchess Dr
  Newmarket CB8 ....111 D2
  Woodditton CB8 ....90 C8
Duck Dro CB7 ....219 D5
Duck End Girton CB3 ..82 D8
  Godmanchester PE29 ..141 F1
Duck La
  Haddenham CB6 ....210 A6
  St Neots PE19 ....74 F4
Duck St PE28 ....178 D8
Ducks La CB8 ....110 C7
Duckworth Cl PE7 ....189 E7
Duddery Hill CB9 ......23 F6
Duddery Rd CB9 ......24 A7
Dudley Ave PE4 ....204 C2
Dudley Rd CB5 ....84 E4
Duke of Bedford Prim Sch
  PE6 ....233 B3
Duke St
  Peterborough PE1 .....187 A7
  Wisbech PE13 ....245 D4
Dukes Dr PE26 ....221 C2
Dukes Mdw CB2 ......49 C5
Dukes Rd PE19 ....74 B4
Dukesmead PE4 ....204 A2
Dukesmead Mobile Home Pk
  PE4 ....204 B2
Dullingham Sta CB8 ...89 B2
Duloe Rd PE19 ....74 F4
Dunblane Dr PE2 ......185 D4
Duncan Way PE29 ....141 F7
Dunnock La CB3 ......100 B4
Duncombe's Rd PE7 ..191 F8
Dundee Cl CB4 ....84 A5
Dundee Ct PE2 ....185 C5
Dungate La CB1 ....52 B6
Dunholt Way PE28 ....206 D6
Dunkirk Dro PE28 ....215 C4
Dunmowe Way CB1 ..66 E5
Dunsberry
  Marholm PE5 ....203 F1
  Peterborough PE3 .....196 F8
Dunsbridge Turnpike
  SG8 ....29 F2
Dunsey Wood Cl SG9 ..38 E1
Dunsmore Cl CB5 .....84 E4
Dunstal Field CB4 .....103 C2
Dunstall's Dro CB7 ...218 E1
Dunstan St CB4 ....240 B5
Dunster Dr CB9 ....23 E8
Durham Cl PE28 ......168 C2

Durham Rd PE1 ....198 C3
Durham Way
Newmarket CB8 ......110 E5
Wyton Airfield PE28 ....143 B8
Durnford Way CB4 ......83 E5
Duxford Airfield CB2 .....17 A8
Duxford Camp CB2 .....31 F1
Duxford CE Com Prim Sch
CB2 ....32 D1
Duxford Rd
Hinxton CB10 ....18 A7
Ickleton CB10 ....17 F5
Whittlesford CB2 ....32 D4
Dwyer-joyce CI CB4 ...104 B4
Dykemoor Dro PE15 ...222 C4
Dykemoor Dro N PE15 .222 E5
Dyson CI
Peterborough PE1 ......197 F3
The Stukeleys PE29 ....141 A3
Dyson's Dro CB5 ......130 B5

E

Eachard Rd CB3 ....83 B5
Eagle Ct PE19 ....75 B7
Eagle La CB8 ....89 D1
Eagle Way PE29 ....142 A8
Eagle's La CB6 ....218 A7
Eaglesthorpe PE1 .....197 E7
Eames Gdns PE1 ......198 E6
Eardley Grange PE6 ...207 F6
Earith Bsns Pk PE28 ..208 F6
Earith Fen Dro PE28 ..208 F6
Earith Prim Sch PE28 .208 E5
Earith Rd
Bluntisham/Colne PE28 .208 D7
Willingham CB4 ....209 A2
Earl CI ■ PE19 ....74 B4
Earl Spencer Ct PE2 ..186 E8
Earl St CB1 ....246 B2
Earls CI PE2 ....187 B6
Earls Hill Gdns SG8 .....5 C6
Earlswood PE2 ....185 E5
Earning St PE29 ......141 F1
Earith CI PE2 ....187 E5
East Chadley La PE1 ..141 F2
East CI PE15 ....243 B6
East Delph PE7 ....189 E8
East Dr Caldecote CB3 .80 C1
March PE15 ....243 F4
East Fen Comm CB7 ..212 C4
East Fen Dro CB7 ....212 D4
East Fen Rd CB7 .....213 B5
East Hatley SG19 ....43 A1
East Hertford St CB4 ..246 A4
East La SG19 ....41 C6
East Meadowgate
PE14 ....236 C7
**East of England
Showground*** PE2 ..185 C4
East Perry PE28 ....115 E2
East Pk St PE16 ......241 C4
East Rd Cambridge CB1 .246 C2
Isleham CB7 ....213 A5
■ Northborough PE6 ..231 F7
Tydd St Mary PE13 ...238 C8
East St
Bluntisham/Colne PE28 .208 C5
Great Gransden SG19 ...58 E4
Huntingdon PE29 ......141 F5
■ Kimbolton PE28 ....113 F4
Manea PE15 ....224 C4
St Ives PE27 ....144 A3
St Neots PE19 ....74 F5
Stamford PE9 ....244 C5
East Sta Sta Rd PE2 ...187 B8
East View IP28 ....213 C3
East Villa PE15 ....224 B3
East Way CB2 ....50 A1
East Wr Cres PE7 .....186 C1
Eastalls CI ■ PE15 ...223 A5
Eastbourne CI ■ PE1 .241 C3
Eastbourne Rd PE16 ..241 C3
Eastern Ave
Haverhill CB9 ....23 E8
Peterborough PE1 .....198 C8
■ Soham CB7 ....212 B4
Eastern CI PE1 ....198 D7
Eastern Ind Est PE1 ..198 E3
Eastfield CB4 ....84 A5
Eastfield Dr PE7 .....189 F6
Eastfield Gr CB1 .....198 B4
Eastfield Inf Sch PE27 .144 A4
Eastfield Rd
Peterborough PE1 .....198 C4
Royston SG8 ....5 E6
■ Wisbech PE13 .....245 E7
Eastfield Way PE13 ..245 C6
Eastfields CB4 ....242 C3
Eastgate
Great Chesterton CB10 ..18 D2
■ Market Deeping PE6 .231 F8
Peterborough PE1 .....198 B2
Whittlesey PE7 ....189 E7
Eastgate Mews PE7 ..189 E7
Eastholm CI PE1 ......198 C3
Eastholm City Sch PE1 198 C4
Eastleigh Rd PE1 .....198 C2
Eastmoor La PE15 ....223 A5
Easton Rd PE19 ......114 C3
Eastrea Ct PE2 ....187 E6
Eastrea Rd PE7 ....189 F7
Eastwood PE6 ....241 C3
Eastwood Ave PE15 ..243 E3

Eastwood CI CB6 .....216 E2
Eastwood End PE15 ..223 C7
Eaton CI Cambridge CB4 .84 A6
Huntingdon PE29 .....142 A7
Eaton Est PE15 ....223 B7
Eaudyke Bank PE13 ..237 F7
Eayre Ct PE19 ....75 A5
Eccles Rd PE8 ....193 D8
Echo Hill SG8 ....5 C5
Echo La PE28 ....151 E3
Ecton Gr ■ PE14 ....236 A5
Eden Cres PE16 ......241 C4
Eden Rd CB9 ....24 A7
Eden St CB1 ....246 C3
Eden St Backway CB1 .246 C2
Edendale CI CB1 ......65 C5
Edenfield PE2 ....186 C6
Edgcote CI PE3 ......197 C5
Edge Bank PE14 .....236 F6
Edgeborough CI CB8 .134 A1
Edgecombe CB4 ......83 F7
Edgerley Drain Rd
PE1 ....198 F5
Edinburgh Ave
Peterborough PE4 ....204 B3
Sawston CB2 ....32 F8
Edinburgh Dr
Eaton Socon PE19 .....74 B4
St Ives PE27 ....143 F7
Wisbech PE13 ....245 C8
Edinburgh Rd
Cambridge CB4 ....84 A5
Newmarket CB8 ......110 E4
Stamford PE9 ....244 B7
Edis Way CB2 ....30 C5
Edison Dr PE7 ....181 D6
Edison Rd PE7 ......144 C6
Edith Cavell Hospl
PE3 ....197 B4
Edmonds CI PE9 .....244 D6
Edmund CI Haverhill CB9 .23 F7
Milton CB4 ....105 C2
Edwalton Ave PE1 ....197 E3
Edward Rd
St Neots PE19 ....74 F2
Stamford PE9 ....244 B7
Edward St CB1 ....84 A1
Edwards Way PE15 ..224 B4
Edwards Wlk PE28 ..208 E6
Edwinstowe CI CB2 ...64 E6
Egar Way PE3 ....196 F2
Egerton CI CB5 ....84 D4
Egerton Rd CB5 ......84 E4
Egremont Rd CB3 .....81 A3
Egremont St PE28 ...240 C5
Eight Acres PE9 .....244 A5
Eighth Ave PE13 ....245 E4
Ekin Rd CB5 ....84 D4
Ekin Wlk CB5 ....84 D3
Eland Way CB1 ....66 A7
Elbourn Way SG8 .....12 F5
Elbow La PE13 ....234 F8
Elder CI Cambridge CB4 .83 F6
Sawston CB2 ....32 D8
Elder PI PE16 ....241 D4
Eldern PE2 ....186 C4
Eldernell La PE7 ....191 B8
Elder's Gate PE12 ...237 E8
Eldith Ave CB7 ......213 A1
Eldo Gdns IP28 .....213 D6
Eldo Rd IP28 ....213 D6
Eldon La IP28 ....214 B8
Elean Bsns Pk CB6 ..216 F2
Eleanor CI PE9 .....244 A6
Elecks La SG8 ....11 D8
Elfleda Rd CB5 ....84 C3
Elford Closes CB6 ..210 E3
Elgar Way ■ PE9 ....244 A6
Elin Way SG8 ....14 B8
Elizabeth Ave CB8 ..110 E5
Elizabeth Ct
■ Eaton Socon PE19 ..74 C4
Hemingford Grey PE27 .143 F1
Peterborough PE1 ....198 A5
■ Sutton CB6 ....216 E2
Elizabeth Dr PE29 ..142 B6
Elizabeth Par CB8 ..110 E5
Elizabeth Rd PE9 ....244 A6
Elizabeth Terr PE13 ..245 D4
Elizabeth Way
Bluntisham/Colne PE28 .208 D7
Burrough Green CB8 ..70 F4
Cambridge CB4 ....83 F4
Gamlingay SG19 ......41 C6
Elsworth St St John's CP Sch
CB7 ....240 A4
Ely St Mary's CE Jun Sch
CB7 ....240 F6
Ely Way CB6 ....210 A7
Embankment Rd ■ PE1 .198 A1
Embry Rd ■ PE6 ....230 B1
Emery CI PE28 ....140 C3
Emery PI PE19 ....74 F2
Emery Rd CB1 ....84 A1
Emery St CB1 ....84 A1
Emlyns Gdns PE9 ....244 C6
Emlyns St PE9 ....244 C6
Emmanuel CI IP28 ..239 D5
Emmanuel Coll CB1 ..246 B2
Emmanuel Rd
Cambridge CB1 ......246 B2
Sawston CB2 ....32 D7
Stamford PE9 ....244 B7
Emmanuel St CB1 ...246 B2
Emneth CP Sch PE14 ..236 D6
Emperor St ■ CB4 ...83 E8
Empingham Rd PE9 ..244 A5

Elm CI continued
March PE15 ....243 D7
■ Market Deeping PE6 ..231 E8
Stilton PE7 ....175 F7
Witchford CB6 ....217 E2
Yaxley PE7 ....181 F7
Elm Cres PE6 ....203 D8
Elm Croft PE19 ....95 F3
Elm Ct Elmdon CB11 ...9 B4
■ Sturmer CB9 ....24 E5
Elm Dr
Little Stukeley PE28 ...151 E3
Offord Cluny PE19 ...118 A2
St Ives PE27 ....143 F6
Elm End PE28 ....150 F4
Elm High Rd PE14 ...245 E8
Elm Low Rd PE14 ...245 D2
Elm Pk PE7 ....189 F7
Elm Rd Folksworth PE7 .175 D8
Little Stukeley PE28 ..152 A2
March PE15 ....243 D8
Wisbech PE13 ....245 D3
Elm Rd Prim Sch
PE13 ....245 D4
Elm Side CB6 ....242 B5
Elm St Cambridge CB1 .246 B3
Peterborough PE2 ....186 F7
Stamford PE9 ....244 C5
Elm Tree CI CB3 ....79 C3
Elm Tree Dr SG8 .....12 F4
Elm Way Melbourn SG8 ..14 C5
Papworth Everard CB3 ..99 A3
Sawtry PE28 ....168 B3
Willingham CB4 ......209 A1
Elm Wlk SG8 ....5 F7
Elmdon Lee CB11 ......9 E1
Elmdon PI CB9 ....24 B8
Elmfield CB6 ....240 C5
Elmfield Dr PE14 ....245 E1
Elmfield Rd
Cambridge CB4 ....84 A5
Peterborough PE1 ....198 A7
Elmhurst CI CB9 ....24 B7
Elmondbury CB11 ......9 A4
Elmore Rd PE3 ......197 A3
Elm's Ave CB2 ....49 A5
Elms CI CB2 ....32 D1
Elms Rd
Freckenham IP28 ....213 E2
Red Lodge IP28 .....213 F1
Elms The
Chatteris PE16 ....241 E4
Great Chesterford CB10 ..18 E3
Haslingfield CB3 ......47 C5
Milton CB4 ....105 C2
Elmside PE14 ....236 D5
Elsie's Way PE28 ....141 F6
Elstone PE2 ....186 A4
Elstow ■ CB4 ....208 D1
Elstone PE2 ....186 A4
Elsworth CE Prim Sch
CB3 ....100 A4
Elsworth CI PE27 ....144 C5
Elsworth PI CB1 .....65 A6
Elsworth Rd
Boxworth CB3 ....101 A5
Conington CB3 ....100 C8
Elter Wlk PE4 ....204 E3
Eltisley Ave CB3 ......64 C7
Eltisley Rd SG19 ......58 E6
Elton CE Prim Sch
PE8 ....178 D8
Elton Hall* PE8 ....178 D6
Elton Rd
Sibson cum Stibbington
PE8 ....183 C8
Water Newton PE8 ...184 B7
Elvedon Way CB8 ....110 E5
Elwyn Ct PE15 ....243 D3
Elwyn Rd PE15 ......243 D4
Elwyndene Rd PE15 ..243 D3
Ely Cath CB7 ....240 D4
Ely CI PE4 ....204 B3
Ely Mus* CB7 ....240 D4
Ely PI ■ PE13 ....245 C5
Ely Rd Downham CB6 .218 B6
Ely CB7 ....240 D4
Landbeach CB5 ......105 F8
Littleport CB6 ....242 C2
Milton CB4 ....105 E3
Soham CB7 ....211 F7
Stretham CB6 ....210 F5
Sutton CB6 ....216 F2
Waterbeach CB5 .....106 B3
Wentworth CB6 .....217 A2

Empire Theatre*
PE13 ....245 C5
Empress Swimming Pool
PE16 ....241 C4
Empson Rd PE1 .....198 F5
Emson's CI CB1 ....35 D2
Enderbys Wharf PE27 .144 A3
Enfield ■ CB1 ....84 A2
Enfield Gdns PE2 ....197 C4
Engaine PE2 ....186 B5
Engine Rd CB7 ......211 F5
Engine Yd CB6 ......240 B4
Engleric SG8 ....8 D4
English Rd PE6 ......233 B4
English St PE1 ....197 E5
Ennerdale CI PE4 ...141 B6
Ennerdale Rise PE4 ..204 D2
Ennion CI CB7 ......212 B3
Ennisdale CI CB4 ......83 E7
Enniskillen Rd CB4 ...84 B5
Enterprise Way PE13 ..245 A2
Erasmus CI CB4 ....83 D5
Erica Rd PE27 ....144 A6
Eriswell Rd
Bow & Kenny Hill IP28 .214 B8
Haverhill CB9 ....24 B8
Ermine Bsns Ctr PE29 .141 B6
Ermine Bsns Pk PE29 .141 B8
Ermine CI March PE15 ..243 C2
Royston SG8 ....5 D8
Ermine Cres PE7 ....176 A7
Ermine Ct PE29 .....141 C5
Ermine St Caxton CB3 ..78 C2
Huntingdon PE29 ....141 C5
Little Stukeley PE28 ..151 F2
The Stukeleys PE28 ..141 A8
Ermine St N CB3 ......99 A4
Ermine St S CB3 ......78 C8
Ermine Way
Arrington SG8 ....44 C4
Sawtry PE28 ....168 C3
Erratts Hill CB8 ......73 D1
Eskdale CI ■ PE4 ...204 E3
Essendyke PE3 ......197 A4
Essex CI CB4 ....83 E5
Essex Hill CB11 ....9 B2
Essex Rd
Huntingdon PE29 ....141 E8
■ Stamford PE9 ....244 B6
Estelle CI PE26 .....220 D2
Estover Rd PE15 ....243 E6
Etheldreda St CB4 ...240 B4
Eurocentre Sch CB2 ..64 F7
Europa Way PE13 ....245 B2
Euston St PE29 .....141 E4
Euximoor Dro PE14 ..229 B5
Evans CI
Brampton PE28 ......140 D3
Royston SG8 ....5 D7
Evans Way CB2 ....32 E8
Evelyn Hospl The CB2 ..64 A8
Ever Gn CB8 ....55 F6
Everdon Way PE3 ...197 C5
Evergreen La CB8 .....55 F7
Evergreens CB4 ......84 B5
Everingham PE2 ....185 D5
Eversden Church Sch
CB3 ....46 A7
Eversden CI CB3 ......61 D5
Eversden Rd CB3 ......46 A7
Eversley CI CB4 ......125 D4
Everton Hill SG19 ....40 B3
Everton Lower Sch
SG19 ....40 D3
Everton Rd
Gamlingay Great Heath
SG19 ....40 E3
Sandy SG19 ....40 B1
Ewin CI PE6 ....207 D1
Ewingswood ■ PE28 .168 C2
Exchange Sq PE13 ..245 B5
Exchange St PE1 ....197 A2
Exeter CI Cambridge CB2 .64 D1
■ Market Deeping PE6 ..231 F8
Exeter Ct ■ CB9 .....23 E6
Exeter Rd
Newmarket CB8 .....111 A4
Peterborough PE1 ...197 F6
■ Wittering PE8 .....230 B1
Exmoor CI PE29 ....141 A4
Exning CP Sch CB8 ..110 B8
Exning Rd CB8 ......110 D6
Eye Gn Ind Est PE6 ..232 A2
Eye Gn Nature Reserve*
PE6 ....232 B2
Eye Hill Dro CB7 ....211 F7
Eye Prim Sch PE6 ...232 B1
Eye Rd PE1 ....198 E7
Eyebury Rd PE6 ....199 A6
Eyeworth Rd SG19 ...25 B2
Eynesbury CE Prim Sch
PE19 ....74 E4
Eynesbury Gn PE19 ..74 F4
Eynesford CI PE7 ...188 A5
Eyrescroft PE3 ....197 A7
Eyrescroft Prim Sch
PE3 ....197 A7
Eyresford CI PE7 ....188 A5

F

Faber La PE8 ....183 D3
Fair Ct CB1 ....246 C3
Fair Gn The CB5 ....129 D1
Fair St CB1 ....246 C3
Fairacre CB1 ....18 C3

Fairbairn Rd CB4 .....84 C5
Fairchild Way PE1 ...198 A7
Fairey Ave PE29 .....141 C6
Fairey Fox Dr ■ IP28 .239 B5
Fairfax Ct Ely CB6 ...240 C4
St Neots PE19 ....74 F3
Fairfax Rd CB1 ....84 B1
Fairfax Way
March PE15 ....243 E1
■ Market Deeping PE6 ..231 F8
Fairfield Gamlingay SG19 ..41 C5
■ Sutton CB6 ....216 E1
Fairfield Dr PE26 ...172 A6
Fairfield Rd PE2 ....187 A8
Fairfield Way CB1 .....35 D3
Fairfields St Ives PE27 ..144 B4
Sawston CB2 ....32 E8
Fairfields Cres PE27 .144 B4
Fairhaven CI CB5 ....107 C2
Fairhaven Way CB8 ..110 E5
Fairlawns CB8 ....110 E5
Fairlawns Rd CB8 ...110 F2
Fairmead Way PE3 ..197 E2
Fairstead House Sch
CB8 ....111 A4
Fairview Ave PE16 ...241 B2
Fairview Dr PE16 ....241 B2
Fairview Gr CB5 ....108 E5
Fairway Chatteris PE16 .241 B3
Girton CB3 ....103 E2
Fairway The
Bar Hill CB3 ....102 D3
Bluntisham/Colne PE28 .208 C6
Falcon CI Haverhill CB9 ..24 C8
■ St Neots PE19 .....75 B7
Falcon Dr PE29 .....142 B7
Falcon La
■ Whittlesey PE7 ...189 D6
■ Wisbech PE13 ...245 C5
Falcon Mews CB6 ...240 B5
Falcon Rd ■ PE13 ..245 C5
Falcon Way
Buckden PE19 ....117 B3
Peterborough PE7 ...186 C1
Falconer Rd CB9 .....24 C5
Falklands Dr PE13 ..245 E3
Falklands Rd CB9 ....39 A1
Fallodan Rd PE2 ....185 A3
Fallow Cnr Dro PE15 .224 A3
Fallow Dr PE19 ....74 B5
Fallowfield
Cambridge CB4 ....84 B5
Peterborough PE2 ...185 D5
Fallowfield CI ■ CB9 ..23 E7
Fall's Dro PE6 ....232 C8
Falmouth Ave CB8 ..110 F3
Falmouth Gdns CB8 .111 A6
Falmouth St CB4 ....110 F3
Falstaff Rd PE19 ......74 C3
Fane Cl PE9 ....244 B7
Fane Rd PE4 ....197 E8
Fanshawe Rd CB1 ....65 A6
Far Pasture PE4 ....204 B5
Faraday CI PE7 ....181 D6
Farcet CE Prim Sch
PE7 ....187 C2
Farcet CI ■ PE19 .....74 C6
Fardell Rd ■ PE13 ..245 C4
Fardell's La CB3 ....100 A3
Farendon Rd PE28 ..140 E1
Farfield CI PE28 ....168 A3
Farleigh Fields PE2 ..185 D7
Farm CI
Abbots Ripton PE28 ..162 C1
Ramsey PE26 ....171 C3
Sawtry PE28 ....168 B4
Farm La
Papworth Everard CB3 ..99 C2
Thriplow SG8 ....11 F5
Farm Rise CB2 ....32 C5
Farm View PE5 .....195 E2
Farmer's End CB3 ....61 E5
Farmer's Row CB1 ...66 E4
Farmland Mus* CB5 ..127 A3
Farmstead CI CB4 ..104 B5
Farrier Ct SG8 ....5 C7
Farriers Ct PE2 .....186 D7
Farriers Gate PE16 ..241 D5
Farriers Way PE28 ..164 F5
Farringdon CI PE1 ..198 D6
Farringford CI ■ CB4 ..83 C6
Farthing Dro PE8 ...226 D6
Farthing La PE27 ....144 B4
Fassage CI CB5 ....107 C2
Fastnet CI CB9 ....24 D8
Faulkner CI CB4 ....105 C2
Fawcett Prim Sch CB2 ..64 E3
Fawsley Garth PE3 ..197 C5
Fayway NN14 ....156 F2
Fazeley CB1 ....246 C2
Feast CI CB7 ....212 E1
Feilden Way CB8 ....110 E5
Felbrigg Wlk PE2 ...187 B6
Feldale PI PE7 ......189 F8
Fellowes Dr PE26 ..172 A6
Fellowes Gdns PE1 ..187 A7
Fellowes Rd PE2 ....187 A7
Felsham Chase CB5 .130 C2
Felsted PE9 ....245 E5
Felton CI CB1 ....65 A8
Felton Way CB7 ....240 C6
Feltons CB7 ....212 B3
Feltwell PI ■ CB9 ....24 B8
Fen Bank Rd CB7 ...213 A6
Fen CI PE13 ....245 E6
Fen Cswy* CB7 .....189 A8
Fen Cswy The CB3 ..246 A1

Fen Ditton CP Sch CB5 . . .84 F5
Fen Drayton Nature
 Reserve* CB4 . . . . . . .121 F7
Fen Drayton Prim Sch
 CB4 . . . . .121 F6
Fen Drayton Rd CB4 . . .122 C5
Fen Dro PE7 . . . . .176 C8
Fen End Over CB4 . . . . .208 D1
 Willingham CB4 . . . . . .209 A1
Fen La Sawtry PE28 . . . .168 C3
 Stilton PE7 . . . . .176 C8
 Swaffham Bulbeck CB5 . . .108 A4
 Tydd St Giles PE13 . . . .237 B5
Fen Rd
 Bassingbourn cum Kneesworth
 SG8 . . . . .12 B7
 Little Wilbraham CB1 . . . .86 D2
 Lode CB5 . . . . .107 B4
 Milton CB4 . . . . .84 D6
 Newton PE13 . . . . .237 E4
 Pidley cum Fenton PE28 . . .165 E1
 Shingay cum Wendy SG8 . . .26 F1
 Wisbech St Mary PE13 . . .234 E2
Fen Side
 Haddenham CB6 . . . . . .209 E4
 Wicken PE7 . . . . .211 D3
Fen St PE7 . . . . .176 A7
Fen The PE28 . . . . .121 B6
Fen View
 Chatteris PE16 . . . . . . .241 B3
 Christchurch PE14 . . . . .229 D3
 6 Doddington/Wimblington
 PE15 . . . . .222 F5
 Peterborough PE2 . . . . . .187 F6
Fen Way **8** CB4 . . . . . .236 A5
Fenbridge Rd PE4 . . . . .204 C4
Fendon Cl CB1 . . . . .65 B3
Fendon Rd CB1 . . . . .65 B3
Fendyke La PE13 . . . . . .237 F1
Fendyke Rd PE14 . . . . . .236 E5
Fengate PE1 . . . . .198 D1
Fengate Cl **1** PE1 . . . .198 B2
Fengate Mobile Home Pk
 PE1 . . . . .198 D1
Fengate Rd PE14 . . . . . .238 F1
Fengate Trad Est PE1 . . .198 D2
Fenhall Field PE13 . . . . .237 C1
Fenland & W Norfolk
 Aviation Mus* PE14 . . .238 F3
Fenland Cl **3** PE15 . . .223 B7
Fenland Rd PE13 . . . . . .245 E6
Fenland Way PE15 . . . . .241 B5
Fenland Wlk PE15 . . . . .243 D4
Fenleigh Cl CB5 . . . . . . .106 B8
Fennec Cl CB1 . . . . .66 B6
Fennells Cl CB9 . . . . .24 A7
Fenners Lawn CB1 . . . . .246 C1
Fenny La SG8 . . . . .24 A7
Fenside Dr PE6 . . . . . . .207 C1
Fenside Rd PE8 . . . . . . .165 D8
Fenstanton & Hilton Prim
 Sch PE28 . . . . .121 C6
Fenton Hill PE28 . . . . . .165 C3
Fenton Rd Haverhill CB9 . .24 B8
 Warboys PE28 . . . . . . .165 A4
FeoFfees Rd **6** PE28 . . .208 C8
Fern Gr CB9 . . . . .23 E8
Ferndale Teversham CB1 . . .66 C8
 Yaxley PE7 . . . . .181 D6
Ferndale Cl PE1 . . . . . . .111 B5
Ferndale Rise CB5 . . . . .84 C4
Ferndale Way PE1 . . . . .205 B1
Ferndown Dr PE29 . . . . .118 F8
Ferne Cl PE6 . . . . .205 D8
Fernlea Cl CB1 . . . . .66 C5
Ferrars Ave PE19 . . . . . .74 E4
Ferrars Rd PE29 . . . . . .141 D4
Ferrars Rd **4** PE29 . . .141 D5
Ferrars Way CB4 . . . . . .83 D6
Ferriman Rd PE38 . . . . .137 F6
Ferry Bank PE38 . . . . . .226 D8
Ferry Cutter La CB4 . . . .196 D4
Ferry Dr PE6 . . . . .196 D3
Ferry Hill Castor PE5 . . .196 B1
 Chatteris PE16 . . . . . . .215 E6
Ferry La
 Beck Row, Holywell
 Row & Kenny Hill IP28 . . .213 D5
 Cambridge CB4 . . . . . . .84 B4
 Newton PE13 . . . . .238 B5
Ferry Mdw PE27 . . . . . .185 D8
Ferry Mdws Ctry Pk*
 PE2 . . . . .185 D8
Ferry Path PE1 . . . . . . .246 B4
Ferry Way CB6 . . . . . . .242 D4
Ferryview PE2 . . . . .185 E6
Festival Cl PE15 . . . . . .224 C4
Festival Ct PE3 . . . . . . .197 B5
Festival Rd CB7 . . . . . . .213 A5
Festival Way CB6 . . . . . .226 B6
Fews Cl **4** PE27 . . . . .208 A3
Field Ave PE13 . . . . .237 F7
Field Baulk PE15 . . . . . .243 D2
Field Bell PE28 . . . . . . .140 F3
Field Cl Abbotsley PE19 . .57 A6
 Alconbury PE28 . . . . . .150 F5
 Buckden PE19 . . . . . . .117 B4
 Grafham PE28 . . . . . . .116 A7
 Linton CB1 . . . . .35 B2
 Little Paxton PE19 . . . .95 F2
 Warboys PE28 . . . . . . .164 F5
Field Cottage Rd PE19 . . .74 C3
Field Cres SG8 . . . . .5 F7
Field End Balsham CB1 . . .60 B3
 Witchford CB6 . . . . . . .217 D2
Field Farm Cotts CB10 . .18 F7
Field Gate CB5 . . . . . . .216 D2
Field La CB5 . . . . .84 E6

Field Rd Kingston CB3 . . .61 B3
 Mildenhall IP28 . . . . . .239 C5
Field Rise PE7 . . . . .172 A7
Field Row CB3 . . . . .61 B3
Field Terr PE7 . . . . .187 C2
Field Terr Rd CB10 . . . .110 F5
Field View Bar Hill CB3 . .102 B2
 Harston CB2 . . . . .48 A4
Field Way CB1 . . . . .65 C3
Field Wlk
 Mildenhall IP28 . . . . . .239 C5
 Peterborough PE1 . . . . .198 B2
Fielden Way CB8 . . . . . .110 E5
Fieldfare Dr PE2 . . . . . .187 E6
Fieldfare Way **10** SG8 . .5 E8
Fielding Cl **2** PE19 . . .74 C6
Fielding Pl PE19 . . . . . . .97 F4
Fields End Cl PE7 . . . . .186 D3
Fieldside Ely CB6 . . . . .240 B4
 Stretham CB6 . . . . . . .210 E5
 Whittlesey PE7 . . . . . . .190 F8
Fifth Ave PE13 . . . . . . .245 E4
Fifty Dro CB6 . . . . .225 C7
Fifty Rd
 Christchurch PE14 . . . . .229 D1
 Manea CB6 . . . . .224 D7
Figtree Wlk **4** PE1 . . .198 B8
Fillance The SG8 . . . . . .102 D5
Finch Rd CB4 . . . . .83 D5
Fincham Rd IP28 . . . . . .239 B5
Fincham's Cl CB1 . . . . . .35 D2
Finchfield PE1 . . . . .198 F7
Finchley Ave IP28 . . . . .239 B6
Finchley Gn PE3 . . . . . .197 E4
Finch's Cl CB2 . . . . .49 C5
Finch's Field CB1 . . . . . .46 A7
Finch's Rd CB3 . . . . . . .46 A6
Finkle La PE7 . . . . .189 D7
Firdale Cl PE6 . . . . .206 C2
Firelots Dro PE15 . . . . .223 C8
Firs The CB2 . . . . .32 D2
First Ave Warboys PE28 . .164 E6
 Wisbech PE13 . . . . . . .245 D5
First Broadpool Dro
 PE28 . . . . .165 E8
First Drift PE9 . . . . .244 B2
First Dro Burwell CB5 . . .130 C7
 Peterborough PE1 . . . . .198 D1
First Furlong Dro
 PE16 . . . . .241 A3
First Marsh Rd PE14 . . .238 D2
First Turf Fen Dro
 PE28 . . . . .165 B8
Fish Hill SG8 . . . . .5 D6
Fisher Cl Duxford CB2 . . .17 E8
 Haverhill CB9 . . . . .24 D7
 Ramsey St Mary's PE26 . .220 D2
Fisher St CB4 . . . . .84 C6
Fisher's La
 Cambridge CB1 . . . . . . .65 F6
 Orwell SG8 . . . . .69 A5
Fishermans Cl PE26 . . . .171 B1
Fishermans Dr PE15 . . .243 A5
Fishers Bank CB6 . . . . .242 E3
Fishers Cl PE7 . . . . .175 F7
Fishers Way PE29 . . . . .118 F8
Fishers Yd **4** PE19 . . .74 E5
Fison Rd CB5 . . . . .84 E4
Fitton End Rd PE13 . . . .237 F3
Fitzgerald Cl CB4 . . . . .240 E8
Fitzroy Cl CB1 . . . . .246 C3
Fitzroy La CB1 . . . . .246 C3
Fitzroy St
 Cambridge CB1 . . . . . . .246 C3
 Newmarket CB8 . . . . . .111 A3
Fitzwilliam Coll CB3 . . . .83 B4
Fitzwilliam Hospl PE6 . . .196 E2
Fitzwilliam Mus The*
 CB2 . . . . .246 A1
Fitzwilliam Rd
 Cambridge CB2 . . . . . . .64 F6
 Stamford PE9 . . . . . . .244 A7
Fitzwilliam St
 Cambridge CB2 . . . . . . .246 B1
 Peterborough PE1 . . . . .198 A3
Five Arches PE2 . . . . . .185 C6
Five Hundred Dro
 PE15 . . . . .224 A4
Fiveways PE28 . . . . . . .239 F2
Flackdale Rd PE28 . . . .120 B1
Flag Bsns Exchange
 PE1 . . . . .198 B3
Flag Fen Rd PE1 . . . . . .198 C4
Flaggrass Hill Rd
 PE15 . . . . .243 E8
Flambards Cl SG8 . . . . .14 B8
Flamborough Cl PE2 . . .197 E1
Flamsteed Dr PE29 . . . .140 F5
Flamsteed Rd CB1 . . . . .65 A6
Flat Rd CB4 . . . . .209 B3
Flat The CB8 . . . . .111 F7
Flatford Rd CB9 . . . . . .32 E4
Flavian Cl CB9 . . . . .24 D7
Flawn Way PE19 . . . . . .74 D2
Flaxfields CB1 . . . . .35 C3
Flaxland PE3 . . . . .197 A6
Fleam Dyke Cotts CB1 . . .67 C2
Flecks La
 Shingay cum Wendy SG8 . .26 D1
 Steeple Morden SG8 . . .11 D8
Fleet Cl CB6 . . . . .242 D4
Fleet The SG8 . . . . .4 C4
Fleet Way PE2 . . . . . . .187 B6
Fleetwood CB6 . . . . . . .240 C5
Fleetwood Cl PE15 . . . .243 D2

Flegcroft PE7 . . . . .189 F1
Fleming Ave PE28 . . . . .239 C5
Fleming Ct CB1 . . . . . . .24 D7
Fletcher Ave CB5 . . . . .127 C1
Fletcher's Terr **3** CB1 . .65 A8
Fletchers Cl PE26 . . . . .172 A7
Fletton Ave PE2 . . . . . .187 A8
Fletton Fields PE2 . . . . .187 A7
Fletton Parkway PE2 . . .185 F2
Flint Cl PE28 . . . . .140 C2
Flint House Rd PE14 . . .229 F5
Flint La CB5 . . . . .126 E3
Flint Way Elm PE14 . . . .236 A4
 St Neots PE19 . . . . . . .74 E2
Flood's Ferry PE15 . . . .222 A8
Flood's Ferry Rd PE15 . .222 B7
Flore Cl PE3 . . . . .197 C5
Florence Cl PE7 . . . . . .189 F6
Florida Ave PE10 . . . . .161 F8
Flower St **3** CB1 . . . .84 A1
Flowers Cl PE28 . . . . . .172 A7
Flowmere Rd SG8 . . . . .8 A5
Fodder Fen Dro CB7 . . .212 B5
Fodder Fen Rd PE15 . . .224 C6
Fodderfen Dro
 Beck Row, Holywell
 Row & Kenny Hill IP28 . .219 F1
 Wicken CB7 . . . . .211 C3
Fold La PE13 . . . . .237 F7
Fold The PE7 . . . . .190 F8
Folgate La PE14 . . . . . .238 F6
Folk Mus* CB1 . . . . . . .246 A4
Folksworth CE Prim Sch
 PE7 . . . . .175 D8
Folksworth Rd PE7 . . . .180 E1
Folly Cl PE7 . . . . .181 C5
Folly Dro CB7 . . . . .219 A7
Folly Rd IP28 . . . . .239 B6
Folly's Dro PE13 . . . . . .234 F3
Fontwell Ave CB4 . . . . .83 C5
Fontwell Gdns **2** PE9 . .244 B5
Foot Dro PE26 . . . . . . .220 F1
Football The CB3 . . . . . .82 C2
Ford Cl
 Beck Row, Holywell
 Row & Kenny Hill IP28 . .213 D7
 Eaton Socon PE19 . . . .74 D5
 Yaxley PE7 . . . . .181 C6
Ford End
 Alconbury PE28 . . . . . .150 F4
 Hail Weston PE19 . . . . .95 B1
Fordham Abbey*
 CB7 . . . . .131 D8
Fordham CE Prim Sch
 CB7 . . . . .212 F1
Fordham Cl SG7 . . . . . .2 D5
Fordham Moor CB7 . . . .212 E1
Fordham Rd
 Exning CB8 . . . . .131 C3
 Freckenham IP28 . . . . .213 B2
 Isleham CB7 . . . . .213 A4
 Newmarket CB8 . . . . . .110 F8
 5 Royston SG8 . . . . .5 C5
 Snailwell CB8 . . . . . . .132 A5
 5 Soham CB7 . . . . .212 B3
Fordham Way SG8 . . . .5 C5
Fordwich Cl **1** CB4 . . .83 D6
Fore Hill CB7 . . . . .240 D4
Foreman's Rd CB1 . . . .50 B2
Forest End CB8 . . . . . .134 A6
Forest Glade CB9 . . . . .38 F2
Forest Rd CB1 . . . . . . .65 E5
Forest Way IP28 . . . . . .239 E4
Forge Cl PE19 . . . . . . .74 B2
Forge End
 Great Shelford CB2 . . . .49 C4
 Peterborough PE7 . . . . .185 A4
Forge Way PE28 . . . . . .164 F5
Forster Rd PE28 . . . . . .140 E1
Forsythia Rd PE27 . . . .144 A6
Fortescue Rd CB4 . . . . .83 E6
Forties Cl CB9 . . . . . . .24 D8
Fortune Way SG8 . . . . .8 A5
Forty Acre Rd PE1 . . . .198 D2
Forty Foot Bank
 Doddington PE26 . . . . .222 C3
 Ramsey PE26 . . . . .221 C3
Forum Ct **7** CB4 . . . .83 E7
Foster Ct PE29 . . . . . . .141 F7
Foster Rd
 Cambridge CB2 . . . . . . .64 D2
 Peterborough PE2 . . . . .186 D8
Foster Way CB3 . . . . . .79 B3
Foul Anchor PE13 . . . . .238 D8
Foundry Cl CB4 . . . . . .125 D3
Foundry Rd PE9 . . . . . .244 A5
Foundry Way
 Eaton Socon PE19 . . . .74 B1
 March PE15 . . . . .228 B6
 Ramsey PE26 . . . . .221 B4
Foundry Wlk PE27 . . . .144 A3
Fountain La
 Haslingfield CB3 . . . . . .47 B5
 Soham CB7 . . . . .212 B4
Fountains Pl PE6 . . . . .232 B1
Four Acres
 Fenstanton PE28 . . . . .121 B6
 Great Chesterford CB10 . .18 D3
Four Gotes PE13 . . . . .238 C6
Four Went Ways CB1 . . .51 A1
Fourfields Prim Sch
 PE7 . . . . .181 E6
Fourth Ave
 Downham CB6 . . . . . . .225 A4
 Peterborough PE1 . . . . .198 A3

Fowlmere Nature Reserve*
 SG8 . . . . .15 B8
Fowlmere Prim Sch
 SG8 . . . . .15 D8
Fowlmere Rd
 Foxton SG8 . . . . .30 D3
 Heydon SG8 . . . . .7 F8
 Newton CB2 . . . . .31 B6
 Shepreth SG8 . . . . . . .29 F4
 Thriplow SG8 . . . . .31 A2
Fox Cl PE19 . . . . .75 A8
Fox Cnr SG8 . . . . .10 F5
Fox Covert PE7 . . . . . .175 F7
Fox Gn CB8 . . . . .55 F7
Fox Gr PE29 . . . . .141 F2
Fox Hill SG8 . . . . .11 A5
Fox Hill Rd SG8 . . . . . .10 F5
Fox Hollow CB3 . . . . . .102 C4
Fox Rd Balsham CB1 . . .82 B3
 Bourn CB3 . . . . .60 D5
 Catworth PE28 . . . . . .136 D8
Fox St SG19 . . . . .58 E5
Fox Wood N **4** CB7 . . .212 B5
Fox Wood S CB7 . . . . .212 B4
Foxburrow Cl CB9 . . . .38 F1
Foxcovert Rd
 Peakirk PE6 . . . . .204 A8
 Werrington PE4 . . . . . .204 B4
 Peterborough PE4 . . . .204 A7
Foxdale PE1 . . . . .197 F7
Foxenfields PE28 . . . . .162 C1
Foxglove Bank SG8 . . .5 F7
Foxglove Cl **3** PE19 . .74 C5
Foxglove Way PE26 . . .220 D3
Foxley Cl PE4 . . . . .204 C4
Fox's Cl CB4 . . . . .105 D2
Fox's Way CB3 . . . . . . .62 D6
Foxton Prim Sch CB2 . . .30 C5
Foxton Rd
 Barrington CB2 . . . . . .29 F8
 Foxton CB2 . . . . .30 A7
 Foxton Sta CB2 . . . . . .30 B5
Foxton Rd La PE13 . . . .151 F3
Framlingham Rd PE7 . . .187 F5
Francis Cl CB9 . . . . . . .23 F8
Francis Darwin Ct CB4 . .83 C5
Francis Gdns PE1 . . . . .197 F8
Francis Pas **3** CB2 . . .64 E7
Frank Bridges Cl **2**
 CB7 . . . . .212 B3
Frank Perkins Parkway
 PE2 . . . . .187 B8
Frank Perkins Way
 CB1 . . . . .198 D4
Frankland Wlk CB4 . . . .240 F6
Franklin Cres PE1 . . . . .198 E6
Franklin Gdns CB4 . . . .125 D4
Frank's La CB4 . . . . . . .83 C3
Franks La PE13 . . . . . .237 F5
Fraser Dr PE27 . . . . . .144 A7
Fraser Rd CB4 . . . . . . .84 A6
Fraserburgh Way **2**
 PE2 . . . . .185 C4
Freckenham Rd IP28 . . .213 E3
Fred Archer Way CB8 . .111 A3
Fred Dannatt Rd IP28 . .239 A6
Frederick Talbot Cl **3**
 CB7 . . . . .212 B4
Free Church Pas PE7 . .144 A3
Free Sch La CB2 . . . . .246 A2
Freedom Bridge PE13 . .245 B6
Freeman Cl **10** PE8 . .230 B1
Freemantle Ct **5** PE19 . .74 B3
Freesia Way PE7 . . . . .181 F6
Freewood La CB11 . . . .9 B3
French Dro PE6 . . . . . .232 E7
French's Rd
 Cambridge CB4 . . . . . . .83 D4
 Walpole PE14 . . . . . . .238 F8
Freshfields CB8 . . . . . .110 F4
Freston CB4 . . . . .204 F2
Friar Cl PE13 . . . . .65 F5
Friars Cl CB3 . . . . .242 C5
Friar's Pl CB6 . . . . .242 C5
Friar's Way CB6 . . . . . .242 C5
Friars Nine CB2 . . . . . .242 C4
Friday Bridge Prim Sch
 PE14 . . . . .236 A3
Friday St IP28 . . . . . . .213 D6
Fridaybridge Rd PE14 . .236 A4
Friends Cl PE9 . . . . . . .212 A4
Frinton Way **7** PE13 . .245 E5
Fritton Ct **7** CB9 . . . .23 E6
Frobisher Cl PE29 . . . .141 F6
Frog End
 Great Wilbraham CB1 . . .67 F7
 Haslingfield CB3 . . . . . .47 A6
 Little Wilbraham CB1 . . .86 C2
 Shepreth SG8 . . . . . . .18 B3
Frogge St CB10 . . . . . .18 B3
Froggs Abbey CB6 . . . .217 A5
Frogs Abbey La PE15 . .223 B7
Frogs Hall PE28 . . . . . .208 C5
Froize End CB6 . . . . . .210 A5
Froment Way CB4 . . . . .83 E6
Fromont Ct CB1 . . . . . .66 E4
Front Rd Murrow PE13 . .234 D6
 Tydd St Giles PE13 . . . .238 D8
Frowd Cl CB7 . . . . .212 A4
Frumetty La PE7 . . . . .150 F4
Fryers Callis PE9 . . . . .39 A1
Fryth Cl CB7 . . . . .212 B5
Fulbourn Hospl
 Cambridge CB2 . . . . . . .65 B3
 Fulbourn CB1 . . . . . . .66 C5
Fulbourn Nature Reserve*
 CB1 . . . . .67 B4

Fulbourn Old Drift CB1 . .66 A6
Fulbourn Prim Sch CB1 . .66 F5
Fulbourn Rd
 Cambridge CB1 . . . . . . .65 F5
 Fulbourn CB1 . . . . . . .66 D7
Fulbridge Prim Sch
 PE1 . . . . .197 F7
Fulbridge Rd PE1 . . . . .197 F8
Fulbrooke Rd CB3 . . . . .64 A7
Fulham Rd PE3 . . . . . . .197 E4
Fullards Cl PE29 . . . . . .155 B4
Fuller Cl PE28 . . . . .137 F6
Fuller's La **5** PE15 . . .223 B7
Fundrey Rd PE13 . . . . .245 F6
Furlong Ave PE14 . . . . .188 D7
Furlong Way CB3 . . . . .80 B1
Furlongs The PE27 . . . .208 A2
Furrells The CB1 . . . . . .35 C3
Furrowfields Rd PE16 . .241 C5
Furrows The PE27 . . . . .144 A4
Furtherford CB4 . . . . . .208 E1
Furze Gr SG8 . . . . .5 E8
Furze Ride PE1 . . . . . . .198 B8
Fydell Ct PE19 . . . . . . .75 B7

G

Gables Cl SG8 . . . . .29 A1
Gables The PE28 . . . . . .121 A5
Gadd's La PE13 . . . . . . .235 D8
Gage Cl SG8 . . . . .5 D8
Gains La PE28 . . . . . . .166 D2
Gainsborough Ave **6**
 PE19 . . . . .74 C5
Gainsborough Cl CB4 . . .84 B6
Gainsborough Dr
 PE27 . . . . .144 A7
Gainsborough Rd CB9 . .38 D1
Gala Cl PE7 . . . . .176 A8
Galfrid Rd CB5 . . . . . . .84 D2
Gallery The CB4 . . . . . .240 D4
Gallions Cl PE4 . . . . . . .204 C4
Gallows Hill (Tumulus)*
 SG7 . . . . .3 E1
Gall's Dro PE13 . . . . . . .235 A4
Gamlingay Cinques Nature
 Reserve* SG19 . . . . .41 A7
Gamlingay Fst Sch
 SG19 . . . . .41 D5
Gamlingay Mdws Nature
 Reserve* SG19 . . . . .41 A4
Gamlingay Rd
 Gamlingay SG19 . . . . .41 D8
 Potton SG19 . . . . .41 C1
 Waresley SG19 . . . . . .57 E1
Gamlingay Village Coll
 SG19 . . . . .41 E5
Gamlingay Wood Nature
 Reserve* SG19 . . . . .41 E8
Gamsey Wood Nature
 Reserve* PE28 . . . . .162 A8
Gannet Cl CB9 . . . . . . .24 C8
Gannocks Cl PE7 . . . . .185 F5
Gannocks The PE2 . . . .185 F5
Ganwick Cl CB3 . . . . . .38 F2
Gaol St **12** PE13 . . . .245 C4
Garden Cl Royston SG8 . .5 E7
 St Ives PE27 . . . . .144 A6
 Sutton CB6 . . . . .216 E1
Garden Ct Burwell CB5 . .130 C4
 Ramsey PE26 . . . . . . .172 A4
Garden End SG8 . . . . . .14 D5
Garden End Rd PE1 . . . .198 B6
Garden Fields CB2 . . . . .48 E3
Garden La Royston SG8 . .5 D5
 Wisbech St Mary PE13 . .235 A7
Garden Rd PE1 . . . . . . .198 A6
Garden Wlk
 Cambridge CB4 . . . . . . .83 D4
 Histon CB4 . . . . .104 C5
 Royston SG8 . . . . .5 E7
Gardeners La **7** CB7 . .212 B4
Gardens The PE15 . . . .243 A6
Gardiners La SG7 . . . . .2 D4
Garlic Row CB5 . . . . . . .84 B3
Garner Ave PE28 . . . . .121 A6
Garner Cl CB4 . . . . . . .105 C3
Garner Ct PE29 . . . . . .141 F7
Garratt Rd **4** PE9 . . .244 B4
Garret Hostel La CB2 . . .246 A2
Garrick Wlk PE7 . . . . . .187 B7
Garry Dr CB4 . . . . .84 A7
Garton St PE1 . . . . . . .198 A1
Garton Cl CB9 . . . . . . .24 D7
 Stamford PE9 . . . . . . .244 C5
Gas Rd PE15 . . . . .243 D3
Gas St PE9 . . . . .244 C5
Gascoigne Pl PE6 . . . . .203 F5
Gatenby PE4 . . . . .204 C4
Gateways CB8 . . . . . . .90 F6
Gault Bank PE15 . . . . . .243 B4
Gaultree Sq PE14 . . . . .236 D6
Gavel St PE7 . . . . .181 C8
Gayton Cl **3** CB2 . . . .64 D3
Gayton Ct PE3 . . . . . . .197 C5
Gazeley Gdns PE7 . . . .187 B2
Gazeley Rd Ashley CB8 . .92 A8
 Cambridge CB2 . . . . . .112 A2
 Kentford CB8 . . . . . . .134 C1
 Moulton CB8 . . . . .112 F6
Gazelle Cl **4** PE19 . . .74 B5
Gazelle Way CB1 . . . . . .66 B7

Geneva St PE1 ....198 A3
Geoffrey Bishop Ave
 CB1 ....67 A4
George Campbell Leisure Ctr
 PE15 ....243 C4
George Gibson Cl
 CB8 ....110 C8
George IV St CB2 .....246 C1
George La
 Buckden PE19 ....117 A4
 Royston SG8 ....5 D5
 Warboys PE28 ....164 E5
George Lambton Ave
 CB8 ....110 F6
George Nuttall Cl CB4 ..84 A6
George Pateman Ct **2**
 CB1 ....64 F7
George Pl **7** PE19 ....74 F2
George St
 Cambridge CB4 ....83 F4
 Huntingdon PE29 ....141 D4
 March PE15 ....243 D4
 Peterborough PE2 ...186 F8
 Stilton PE7 ....175 F8
 Willingham CB4 ......209 A1
Georgian Ct PE3 ......197 E2
Gerard Cl CB5 ....84 C2
Gerard Rd CB5 ....84 D3
Gery Ct PE19 ....74 C5
Giant's Hill* CB4 ....125 A5
Gibraltar La CB4 ......122 E5
Gibside Ave PE16 .....241 B3
Gibson Cl CB5 ....106 A7
Gidding Gr PE28 ......166 B1
Gidding Rd PE28 ......167 D3
Giddings Cl PE2 ......185 F4
Gifford Pl CB2 ....246 A3
Gifford's Cl CB3 ....82 E8
Giffords Way **4** CB4 ..208 D1
Gilbert Cl CB4 ....83 C5
Gilbert Rd
 Cambridge CB4 ....83 D5
 Littleport CB6 ....242 B5
Gilbert Scott Dr CB6 ..240 E7
Gildale PE4 ....204 D4
Gildenburgh Ave PE1 .198 D5
Gill's Hill CB3 ....60 D5
Gilmerton Ct CB2 ......64 D4
Gilmorton Dr PE1 ....198 D7
Gilpin St PE1 ....197 E6
Gilvan Cl PE19 ....95 E1
Gimber Ct **5** PE29 ..141 F7
Gimber Rd CB7 ....212 B4
Gimbert Sq PE15 .....243 E4
Gipping Cl **4** CB9 ....23 E6
Gipsey Cnr PE19 ....56 C5
Gipson Cl PE16 ....241 B5
Gipsy Dro PE16 ....215 F6
Gipsy La PE15 ....243 A7
Girton
 Mildenhall IP28 .....239 C6
 Wooddltton CB8 .....111 B1
Girton Coll
 Cambridge CB3 ....83 B2
 Girton CB3 ....82 F6
Girton Cres PE29 ....142 A7
Girton Glebe Prim Sch
 CB3 ....103 E1
 Haverhill CB9 ....24 B7
Girton Way PE9 ......244 A7
Gisborne Rd CB1 .....163 C6
Gladeside CB3 ....102 C4
Glebe Ave PE2 ....185 E4
Glebe Cl
 Chatteris PE16 ....241 D5
 Gorefield PE13 ....237 E3
 Great Paxton PE19 ....96 E4
 Toft CB3 ....61 E5
 Wimblington PE15 ....224 B4
Glebe Cres CB2 ....33 B4
Glebe Ct PE2 ....187 A8
Glebe Gdns **2** PE6 ..232 B8
Glebe La Buckden PE19 .117 A3
 Cambourne CB3 ....79 C4
Glebe Rd Barrington CB2 ..79 B8
 Brampton PE28 ....140 E2
 Cambridge CB1 ....65 B4
 Hemingford Grey PE28 .143 D1
 Huntingdon PE29 ....141 D7
 Perry PE26 ....115 D3
 Peterborough PE2 ....187 A8
 Sawtry PE28 ....168 A4
 Stilton PE7 ....176 A7
 Waterbeach CB5 ......204 E7
Glebe The Haverhill CB9 ..39 A1
 Ramsey PE26 ....172 B4
Glebe Way
 Haddenham CB6 ......209 F6
 Histon CB4 ....104 C4

Glebelands Prim Sch
 PE16 ....241 D5
Glemsford Pl **2** CB9 ...24 B8
Glemsford Rise PE2 ...186 C7
Glen Cres PE9 ....244 C2
Glen Rd **1** PE8 ......230 B1
Glen The PE2 ....187 B7
Glenacre Cl **8** CB1 ....65 E5
Glencoe Way PE2 .....185 D3
Glendale PE2 ....185 D6
Gleneagles PE2 ....185 D4
Glenfields PE7 ....189 C8
Glenmere Cl CB1 ....65 D5
Glenton St PE1 ....198 C2
Glenville Cl CB1 ....85 B1
Glinton Rd
 Helpston PE6 ....203 A8
 Newborough PE6 .....204 E8
Glisson Rd CB1 ....246 C1
Global Cnr Ind Est PE1 .198 E4
Globe La
 Alconbury PE28 ....150 E3
 3 Littleport CB6 ...242 D4
Gloucester Ct PE13 ..245 D7
Gloucester Rd
 Brampton PE28 ....140 D1
 Haverhill CB9 ....23 F7
 Peterborough PE2 ....187 B7
 Sawtry PE28 ....168 C3
 7 Stamford PE9 ....244 B6
 Wyton Airfield PE28 ..143 B8
Glover Cl CB2 ....32 F6
Glover St CB4 ....208 D1
Goddard Cres **1** PE13 ..245 D7
Godeby Ct **4** PE29 ....65 F1
Godesdone Rd CB5 .....84 A3
Godfrey Cl PE6 ....207 D1
Goding Way CB4 ......105 E2
Godmanchester Com
 Swimming Pool
 PE29 ....141 E2
Godmanchester Prim Sch
 PE29 ....141 F2
Godric Sq PE2 ....186 D6
Godsey La **2** PE6 ....231 E8
Godwin Cl CB1 ....65 C4
Godwin Rd PE13 .....245 D7
Godwin Way CB1 ....65 C4
Godwit Cl PE7 ....201 A1
Goffers Knoll (Tumulus)*
 SG8 ....14 E1
Goffsmill PE3 ....197 A4
Gog Magog Way CB2 ...49 C5
Gold St PE15 ....243 C7
Goldcrest Ct **3** CB3 ...79 C3
Golden Drop PE6 .....231 C4
Golden Miller Cl CB8 ..110 D7
Golden Rod **3** PE29 ..118 F8
Goldhay Way PE2 ....185 C2
Goldie La PE2 ....185 F6
Golding Pl **15** PE13 ..245 C4
Golding Rd CB1 ....65 B6
Goldings Cl CB9 ....39 A2
Goldpits PE28 ....164 F5
Golf La PE28 ....151 F3
Golf Links Rd
 Barton Mills IP28 ....214 A3
 Worlington IP28 .....239 A1
Gonville & Caius Coll
 CB2 ....246 B1
Gonville Cl IP28 .....239 D6
Gonville Pl CB1 ......246 C1
Goochgate PE12 ......237 A7
Goodacre PE2 ....186 A4
Goodchilds Gdns **5**
 CB7 ....213 A5
Goode Cl CB4 ....125 D4
Goodens La CB13 ....238 A5
Goodliffe Ave CB11 ...53 C2
Goodwin Gr CB7 .....240 F7
Goodwin Wlk PE4 ...204 C4
Goodwood Rd
 Peterborough PE3 ...196 F3
 Royston SG8 ....5 F6
Goose Cross CB8 ......80 B1
Goose Fen Dro CB7 ..211 C6
Gordon Ave
 March PE15 ....243 D4
 Peterborough PE2 ...186 E7
Gordon Cl PE19 ....95 F1
Gordon Cr PE13 .....245 C3
Gordon Fendick Sch
 PE13 ....245 D8
Gordon Rd PE19 ......95 F1
Gordon Richards Cl
 CB8 ....110 F6
Gordon Way PE2 .....186 C7
Gore Tree Rd PE28 ..120 C7
Goredike Bank PE13 ..237 E3
Gorefield Prim Sch
 PE13 ....237 E2
Gorefield Rd PE13 ...237 F2
Gorse Cl **8** IP28 ....214 A1
Gorse Gn PE1 ....198 B8
Gorse Way PE27 .....144 B5
Goshawk Cl PE29 ....142 A8
Gosling Cl CB4 ....123 A3
Gosling's Dro PE7 ...220 A8
Gosmoor La PE14 ....236 B5
Gosselan Cl PE2 .....144 A6
Gostwick PE2 ....185 D5
Gote La PE13 ....237 E3
Gough Way CB3 ....64 A8
Governess Cl **8** PE15 ..223 B7
Gower Rd SG8 ....5 C7
Gowers The CB1 .....103 E1
Grace Sch of Medicine
 CB1 ....65 A8

Gracious St PE7 ......189 D7
Graeme Rd PE5 ......194 F2
Grafham Cl PE2 ......187 E4
Grafham Rd PE28 ...138 F4
Grafham Wr Ex Ctr*
 PE28 ....116 B5
Grafham Wr Nature
 Reserve* PE28 ......115 C3
Grafton Ave PE3 ....197 C3
Grafton Ct PE27 ....143 F8
Grafton Cr CB1 ......246 C3
Grafton St CB1 ......246 C2
Grain Cl CB2 ....49 A5
Grainger Ave PE29 ..118 F8
Grammar Sch Wlk
 PE29 ....141 D4
Granary Cl PE29 .....141 E1
Granary End **4** CB6 ..217 E1
Granary La **5** CB6 ...242 D4
Granary Rd CB8 .....111 B2
Granary The
 Old Hurst PE28 ......154 D7
 Sawtry PE28 ....168 B4
Granary Way CB3 ....79 B3
Granby St
 Littleport CB6 ....242 D4
 Newmarket CB8 .....111 B3
 Peterborough PE1 ...198 B2
Grandford Dro PE15 ..227 E6
Grandridge Cl CB1 ....66 F4
Grange Ave PE1 .....198 A6
Grange Bottom SG8 ...5 E5
Grange Cl PE28 ....168 C2
Grange Cres PE2 ....186 A5
Grange Ct CB3 ....64 B8
Grange Dr CB3 ....82 E7
Grange Farm Cl PE19 ..57 B5
Grange Farm The
 IP28 ....239 C1
Grange La
 Barton Mills IP28 ...239 C2
 Littleport CB6 ....242 B2
Grange Rd
 Cambridge CB3 ....64 B8
 Duxford CB2 ....17 A6
 Ickleton CB10 ....9 A8
 March PE15 ....228 A1
 Peterborough PE3 ...197 D4
 6 Somersham PE28 ..208 C8
 Wisbech PE13 ....245 A7
Grange The
 Meldreth SG8 ....14 B8
 8 Somersham PE28 ..208 C8
Grangehill Rd PE13 ..237 B6
Granham's Rd
 Cambridge CB2 ....65 C1
 Great Shelford CB2 ...49 A7
Granhams Cl CB2 .....49 A6
Gransden Rd
 Abbotsley PE19 ....57 E6
 Caxton CB3 ....59 D8
Gransley Rise PE3 ...197 C5
Granta Cl
 Great Chesterford CB10 ..18 D1
 St Ives PE27 ....144 B7
 Witchford CB6 ....217 D1
Granta Cotts CB10 ...18 D2
Granta Leys CB11 ....35 B3
Granta Pk CB1 ....34 A6
Granta Pl CB2 ....246 A1
Granta Rd CB2 ....32 E5
Granta Terr CB2 ....49 B4
Granta Vale CB11 ....35 D2
Grantchester Mdws
 CB3 ....64 C7
Grantchester Rd
 Barton CB3 ....63 D7
 Cambridge CB3 ....64 B2
 Coton CB3 ....82 C1
 Grantchester CB3 ....64 B4
Grantchester Rise
 CB5 ....130 B5
Grantchester St **3** CB3 ..64 C7
Grantham Cl SG8 ....5 B8
Granville Ave PE16 ..231 F7
Granville Gdns IP28 ..239 A4
Granville St PE1 .....198 A4
Grasmere PE29 ......141 B6
Grasmere Gdns
 Cambridge CB1 ......246 A4
 Peterborough PE4 ...204 D3
Grass Plant Cotts CB8 .131 B4
Grass Yd **8** PE26 ....113 F4
Grassgate La PE14 ...238 E3
Gravel Bridge Rd CB4 ..123 C6
Gravel Dro
 Beck Row, Holywell
 Row & Kenny Hill IP28 ..213 C6
 Witcham CB6 ....216 F4
Gravel End CB6 ....217 C5
Gravel End La CB6 ...217 D5
Gravel Pit Hill SG8 ...16 C8
Gravel Wlk PE1 ......198 A2
Graveley Rd PE19 .....97 A8
Graveley Way PE28 ...98 E8
Gray Ct PE1 ....197 E8
Gray's Cl CB8 ....50 D6
Gray's Rd SG19 ....41 D6
Grayling Cl CB4 ....84 A4
Grays Cl SG8 ....5 C8
Grays Gr MK44 ....93 B2
Grays La Emneth PE14 ..236 C6
 March PE15 ....243 D4
Graysmoor Dro PE14 ..228 B8
Great & Little Shelford CE
 Prim Sch CB2 ....48 F4
Great Abington Prim Sch
 CB1 ....34 C5

Great Chesterfield CE Prim
 Sch CB10 ....18 D2
Great Chesterford Sta
 CB10 ....18 C1
Great Cl CB3 ....18 C1
Great Dro Soham CB7 ..211 F3
 Swaffham Prior CB7 ..128 C6
 Yaxley PE7 ....182 A5
Great Eastern Rd
 March PE15 ....243 D7
 Wisbech PE13 ....245 B4
Great Eastern St CB1 ...65 B8
Great Farthing Cl
 PE27 ....144 B4
Great Fen Rd CB7 ....212 B8
Great Gidding CE Prim Sch
 PE28 ....166 D3
Great Gn SG8 ....5 D6
Great Heath Prim Sch
 IP28 ....239 D6
Great How PE27 .....143 F7
Great La CB25 ....129 C1
Great N Fen Dro CB4 ..125 C6
Great N Rd
 Alconbury PE28 .....150 E4
 Buckden PE19 ....117 A5
 Eaton Socon PE19 ...74 B2
 Peterborough PE2 ...185 A4
 St Neots PE19 ....74 C7
 Sibson cum Stibbington
 PE8 ....183 E8
 Southoe & Midloe PE19 ..95 F4
 Wothorpe PE9 ......244 A2
Great Northern St
 PE29 ....141 D5
Great Parlow Cl PE19 ..97 E7
Great Paxton CE Prim Sch
 PE19 ....96 E5
Great Staughton Prim Sch
 PE19 ....93 F6
Great Whyte PE26 ...172 A8
Great Wilbraham CE Prim
 Sch CB1 ....67 F8
Great Wilbraham Rd
 CB1 ....86 F1
Greater Foxes CB1 ...66 F5
Greatford Rd PE9 ...230 C6
Greatlands PE28 ....163 B4
Grebe Cl
 Mildenhall IP28 .....239 D3
 Whittlesey PE7 ......190 A8
Grebe Ct PE7 ....190 A8
Grebe Way **3** PE19 ...75 B7
Green Acres SG19 ...41 C5
Green Bank Rd CB5 ..108 B2
Green Butts CB2 ....32 D5
Green Cl PE19 ....94 A6
Green Drift SG8 ....5 B6
Green Dro
 Coveney CB6 ....217 D4
 Crowland PE6 ....232 D8
 Elm PE14 ....236 D2
 Northside PE6 ....200 F4
 Thorney PE6 ....233 A6
Green End
 Comberton CB3 ....62 C6
 Fen Ditton CB5 ....84 B8
 Gamlingay SG19 .....41 C5
 Landbeach CB4 ......105 D8
 Little Staughton MK44 ..93 A3
 Little Stukeley PE28 ..152 A1
 Sawtry PE28 ....168 B2
 Stretham CB6 ....210 F4
Green End Rd
 Cambridge CB4 ....84 B6
 St Neots PE19 ....75 A5
 Sawtry PE28 ....168 B3
Green Farm PE1 ....195 E2
Green Head Rd CB5 ..108 C4
Green Hedges Sch The
 CB2 ....49 C4
Green Hill CB2 ....211 B7
Green How PE27 ....143 E6
Green La Ashwell SG7 ...2 E5
 8 Benwick PE15 ....222 A5
 Brampton PE28 .....140 D2
 Christchurch PE14 ..229 D3
 Ellington PE28 ......138 F4
 Everton SG19 ....40 C3
 Great Staughton PE19 ..93 F6
 Hail Weston PE19 ....95 A1
 Leverington PE13 ...237 F2
 Linton CB1 ....35 C2
 Peterborough PE4 ...198 A4
 St Ives PE28 ....143 A5
 Stamford PE9 ....244 B7
 Upton & Coppingford
 PE28 ....160 C2
 Walsoken PE14 .....245 F4
 Yaxley PE7 ....181 D6
Green Leys PE27 ....143 F5
Green Man La CB2 ...47 E3
Green Pk Brinkley CB8 ..70 D2
 Cambridge CB4 ....84 B6
 Chatteris PE16 ....241 E5
Green Rd
 Newborough PE6 ....205 F3
 Newmarket CB8 .....111 B3
 Upwell PE14 ....229 E8
Green Rd The CB2 ....33 A8
Green Side CB6 ....106 B7
Green St
 Cambridge CB2 ......246 A3
 Duxford CB2 ....32 D1
 March PE15 ....243 E3
 Royston SG8 ....5 D8
 Willingham CB4 ......209 A1
Green The Ashley CB8 ...91 F8

Green The continued
 Beck Row, Holywell
 Row & Kenny Hill IP28 ..213 C7
 Bluntisham PE28 ....140 D2
 Cambridge CB4 ....84 B5
 Castor PE5 ....195 E2
 Foxton CB2 ....30 B5
 Glinton PE6 ....203 E8
 Great Staughton PE19 ..93 F7
 Haddenham CB6 ....210 A6
 Kingston CB3 ....61 B3
 Kirtling CB8 ....72 C5
 Lolworth CB3 ....101 F5
 Peterborough PE4 ...204 C3
 Royston SG8 ....5 D6
 Snailwell CB8 ....132 A3
 Somersham PE28 ...215 C1
 Steeple Morden SG8 ..11 C1
 6 Thorney PE6 .....233 A3
 Whittlesey PE7 .....181 E5
Green Tiles Cl PE29 ..132 E1
Greenacres Duxford CB2 ..32 D1
 Peterborough PE4 ...204 A4
Greenbanks SG8 ......14 C5
Greenbury Cl SG8 .....6 F1
Greendale PE29 .....141 A6
Greenend Cl SG8 ......5 B7
Greenfield Cl CB2 ....49 D4
Greenfields
 Earith PE28 ....208 E6
 Elltsley PE19 ....77 E4
 Hemingford Grey PE27 ..143 F1
 Newmarket CB8 .....111 C3
 1 St Neots PE19 ......75 A6
Greenfields Way CB9 ..23 F6
Greenford Cl SG8 ....28 D8
Greengage Cl SG8 ...14 C4
Greengage Rise SG8 ..14 C5
Greengarth PE27 ....144 A5
Greengate Ct PE1 ...198 C4
Greenham PE3 ....197 A4
Greenhaze La CB3 ....79 B3
Greenhill Rd PE8 ....178 F8
Greenhills CB7 ....212 C3
Greenlands CB2 ....65 B3
Greenleas CB4 ....104 B5
Greenlow SG8 ....14 A4
Green's Rd CB4 ......83 E4
Greenside Cl CB4 ...122 C6
Greenstock La PE13 ..238 A6
Greensward La PE13 ..119 B4
Greenwood Cl
 1 Haverhill CB9 .....23 E7
 Ramsey PE26 ....172 A5
Greenwood Way **18**
 PE15 ....223 B7
Gregory Rd PE28 ...239 A6
Grenadier Dr PE16 ..241 C6
Grenadier Rd CB9 ....23 C8
Greneway Sch The SG8 ..5 E7
Grenfell Rd PE28 ...172 A5
Grenville Way PE19 ..74 B2
Gresham Rd CB1 ....246 C1
Gresley Dr PE9 ......244 B4
Gresley Way
 March PE15 ....243 B6
 Peterborough PE3 ..197 C6
Gretton Ct PE2 ......186 C7
Greville Rd CB1 ....65 B7
Greville Starkey Ave
 CB8 ....110 F5
Greys SG8 ....5 A4
Greys The PE15 .....243 E2
Greystoke Ct **1** CB1 ..65 E5
Greystoke Rd CB1 ....65 E5
Grieve Ct CB4 ....84 C5
Griffins Cl PE6 ....207 D1
Griffiths Ct PE2 ......185 E5
Grimeshaw Wood Nature
 Reserve* PE3 ....197 E7
Grimmer's Rd **6** PE13 ..245 E7
Grimshaw Rd PE1 ...198 B6
Grip The CB1 ....35 B1
Groat La SG19 ....41 C8
Grosvenor Gdns PE19 ..74 E6
Grosvenor House Ct **6**
 IP28 ....239 B5
Grosvenor Rd PE13 ..245 D7
Grosvenor Yd CB8 ...111 A3
Grounds Ave PE15 ...243 F4
Grounds Way PE7 ...191 A8
Grove Cl CB3 ....80 B1
Grove Ct
 Little Paxton PE19 ...95 F2
 St Ives PE27 ....144 A4
Grove End PE28 .....120 C1
Grove Gdns CB7 .....212 C2
Grove La
 Brampton PE28 .....140 D3
 Cambridge CB1 .....246 B1
 Peterborough PE3 ..197 A2
Grove Pk CB2 ....212 E2
Grove Prim Sch The
 CB4 ....83 F6
Grove The
 Cambridge CB4 ....84 B6
 Chatteris PE16 .....241 C5
 Huntingdon PE29 ..142 B6
 Linton CB1 ....35 B3
 Mildenhall IP28 ....213 D8
 Orwell SG8 ....39 E4
 St Neots PE19 ....74 E6
 1 Stretham CB6 ...210 F5
 Whittlesey PE7 .....189 F6

Grove The continued
Wistow PE28 ....163 F6
Grove Way PE26 ......172 A4
Grovelands PE3 ....197 E2
Grovemere Ct PE28 ...114 B7
Grunty Fen Rd CB6 ...210 F8
Guanockgate Rd PE12 .234 C8
Guash Way PE9 ....244 D7
Guelder Rose CB7 ......240 F5
Guest Rd CB1 ....246 C2
Guild Rd PE13 ....245 E6
Guilden Morden CE Prim Sch
SG8 ....10 F5
Guildenburgh Cres
PE7 ....190 A7
Guildhall Pl 8 CB1 ....246 A2
Guildhall St 5 CB1 ....246 A2
Guilsborough Rd PE6 ..232 B2
Guineas Cl CB8 ....110 E6
Guise La SG8 ....12 D6
Gull Bank PE13 ....234 E3
Gull Dro PE13 ....233 D3
Gull La PE13 ....238 A3
Gull Rd PE13 ....234 F3
Gull Way
Chatteris PE16 ....241 C6
Whittlesey PE7 ......190 A8
Gullymore PE3 ....196 F8
Gunhill Cl CB1 ....65 C5
Gunhild Ct CB1 ....65 C5
Gunhild Way CB1 ....65 C5
Gunnell Cl CB4 ....105 D2
Gunning Rd CB6 ....240 E8
Gunnings Way CB4 .....83 C6
Gunnings Way PE28 ...143 C1
Gunthorpe Prim Sch
PE4 ....204 E2
Gunthorpe Rd
Newborough PE6 .....204 F4
Peterborough PE4 ....204 E2
Gunthorpe Ridings
PE4 ....205 A2
Guntons Rd PE6 ....205 C6
Guntons Cl CB7 ....212 B4
Gurlings Cl CB9 ....39 A2
Gurnard Leys PE3 .....204 A1
Gurney Way CB4 ....83 E4
Guthlac Ave PE4 ......204 D1
Guyatt Ct CB5 ....130 B2
Guyhirn CE Prim Sch
PE13 ....235 A2
Guyhirn Gull PE13 ....234 E3
Gwydir St CB1 ....65 A8
Gypsy Cnr PE28 ....150 B6
Gypsy La PE13 ....238 C4

H

Hacke Rd PE3 ....197 D3
Haddenham End Field
CB6 ....210 A7
Haddenham Rd CB6 ...217 A1
Haddon Cl PE2 ....187 E5
Haddon Rd
Haddon PE7 ....180 C6
Peterborough PE3 ....197 E3
Haddon Way PE7 .....187 B2
Haddow's Cl CB4 .....123 F2
Haden Way Over CB4 .208 F1
Willingham CB4 ......123 F8
Hadleigh Ct CB5 ......84 E4
Hadley Rd PE4 ....204 D1
Hadrian Cl CB9 ....24 D7
Hadrians Ct PE2 ......187 B8
Hadstock Rd CB1 .....35 B1
Hagbech Hall PE14 ...236 D6
Hagger's Cl SG8 ......14 C6
Haggis Gap CB1 ......66 F5
Haig Ct CB4 ....84 A4
Haigh's Cl PE16 ......241 B4
Hake's Dro PE15 .....227 A2
Halcyon Ct PE29 .....141 C6
Hale Ave CB4 ....83 D4
Hale Cl SG8 ....14 D6
Hale Dro CB6 ....225 E6
Hale Fen CB6 ....242 C8
Hale Fen La CB6 .....217 A4
Hale Fen Rd CB6 .....225 E4
Haley Cl
Hemingford Grey PE28 143 B1
Wisbech PE13 ....245 C8
Half Acre Dro CB7 ...211 C7
Half Acre La CB7 ....211 D8
Halfpenny La PE14 ...245 D1
Halfpenny Toll Rd
PE14 ....229 E4
Halifax Rd
Cambridge CB4 ......83 B4
Mildenhall IP28 ......213 E8
Halifax Way CB8 .....110 E5
Hall Bank PE13 ......237 E7
Hall Barn Rd CB7 ....212 F4
Hall Bridge Rd PE14 .236 D1
Hall Cl Bourn CB3 ...60 C5
Foxton CB2 ....30 B6
Huntingdon PE29 ....142 A6
Little Paxton PE19 ...95 F2
Hall Cres CB2 ....33 A7
Hall Dike PE14 ....236 F4
Hall Dr Hardwick CB3 .80 F3
Highfields CB3 ....80 F2
Hall End CB4 ....105 D2
Hall Farm La SG19 ..58 C4
Hall Farm Rd 2 CB4 ..83 D5
Hall Gate Rd PE12 ...234 B8
Hall Gn La PE28 .....121 B6

Hall La
Abbots Ripton PE28 ..152 D8
Brinkley CB8 ....70 E2
Burwell CB5 ....130 B1
Great & Little Chishill SG8 .7 F2
Peterborough PE4 ....204 C4
Tilbrook PE28 ....113 C8
Wittering PE8 ....230 B1
Hall Rd Outwell PE14 .236 F3
St Neots PE19 ....74 E3
Hall St CB7 ....212 B5
Hallards The 6 PE19 .74 C6
Hallaton Rd PE1 .....198 D8
Hallcroft Rd PE7 ....189 C8
Hallfields La PE4 ....204 E1
Hallkeys Gdns CB8 ...110 F2
Haistead Cl 2 PE13 ..245 E5
Ham La PE2 ....158 A5
Hamden Way CB3 ....99 B3
Hamerton Rd
Alconbury Weston PE28 .150 C7
Buckworth PE28 .....149 D6
Winwick PE28 ....158 C6
Hamerton Zoo Pk*
PE28 ....159 B5
Hamilton Cl CB8 .....110 E2
Hamilton Rd
Cambridge CB4 ......246 B4
Ely CB6 ....240 B4
Newmarket CB8 .....110 E3
Hamiltons The CB8 ...110 E3
Hamlet Cl PE7 ....150 C7
Hamlet Rd PE8 ......24 B7
Hamlet The CB6 .....218 C6
Hammond Cl
Newmarket CB8 .....110 E6
Pampisford CB2 .....33 B5
Wittering PE8 ....230 C1
Hammond Way PE28 .208 C8
Hampden Rd 2 PE13 .245 D5
Hampden Rise SG8 ..5 D4
Hampden Way PE19 ..75 A3
Hampshire Rd PE28 ..143 B8
Hampstead Ave IP28 .239 B6
Hampton Cl PE2 .....121 C6
Hampton Ct PE3 .....197 C6
Hampton Hargate Prim Sch
PE7 ....186 C2
Hanaper Dr SG8 .....6 F1
Hanbury PE2 ....185 F3
Hanchet End CB9 ....38 B1
Hankey St PE1 ....197 F4
Hanmer Ave IP28 ....239 C5
Hannath Rd PE14 ...238 B8
Hannington Cl PE7 ..189 C8
Hanover Cl
Bar Hill CB3 ....102 B3
Eaton Socon PE19 ...74 D5
Hanover Ct
Brampton PE28 ......140 D3
Cambridge CB1 ......246 B1
Peterborough PE3 ...197 A8
Hansell Rd PE28 .....140 B3
Hanson Ct CB4 ......83 E7
Harbins La PE19 ....57 C6
Harbour Ave CB3 ....62 D6
Harbour Sch The CB6 .210 C6
Harcombe Rd CB1 ...65 E6
Harcourt PE29 ....142 A2
Harding Cl 1 PE5 ....106 A7
Harding Way
Cambridge CB4 ......83 C5
Histon CB4 ....104 B4
St Ives PE27 ....144 B5
Hardman Rd CB2 ....30 C5
Hardwick Com Prim Sch
CB3 ....81 A3
Hardwick Ct PE3 ....197 B2
Hardwick La PE19 ...117 A5
Hardwick Rd
Haverhill CB9 ....24 B8
St Neots PE19 ....74 E3
Toft CB3 ....61 E6
Hardwick St CB3 ....64 C7
Hardwicke Cl CB6 ...242 C5
Hardwick Fields CB6 .210 A6
Hardwicke La PE19 ..58 F6
Hardwicke Rd SG19 .58 F6
Hardy Cl PE29 ....141 F6
Hardy Dr SG8 ....5 D8
Hardy Pl 1 PE19 .....74 D6
Hardy's La PE7 ......189 E6
Harebell Cl
Cambridge CB1 ......66 A5
Huntingdon PE29 ....141 D6
Peterborough PE1 ...205 B1
Harecroft Rd PE13 ..245 B5
Harefield Rise CB1 ..35 E2
Harewood Gdns PE1 .197 E2
Hargate Way PE7 ...186 D3
Hargood Ct 3 PE19 ..74 B3
Hargreaves Rd 6 SG8 .5 D5
Harland Rd PE19 ....74 E4
Harlech Ct 5 PE19 ..74 F2
Harlech Grange PE3 .197 B1
Harlestones Rd CB4 .125 D4
Harley Ind Pk PE19 ..96 D2
Harlton Ct PE2 ......187 E5
Harlton Rd
Great Eversden CB3 .45 F7
Haslingfield CB3 .....46 F5
Harold Heading Cl
PE16 ....241 B3
Harold's Bank PE13 .237 B1
Harper's Dro PE26 ..170 F7
Harradine Cl PE29 ...155 B5
Harrier Cl PE29 .....142 A8
Harrington Dr PE6 ..232 C8

Harris Cres PE27 ....208 A2
Harris La PE28 ......163 E6
Harris Rd CB4 ....83 D6
Harris St PE1 ....197 F6
Harrison Cl PE13 ...196 F3
Harrison Way PE27 ..144 B3
Harrison's Dro
Burwell CB5 ....129 A8
Swaffham Prior CB7 .128 D7
Harris's La PE28 ....163 E7
Harrolds Cl 5 PE14 ..238 F1
Harrow Rd CB9 ......5 F7
Harry Palmer Cl CB7 .212 E1
Harry Scott Ct CB4 ..83 E7
Harrys Way PE13 ...245 C2
Harston & Newton CP Sch
CB2 ....47 D2
Harston Mill CB2 ....47 D2
Harston Rd
Haslingfield CB3 .....47 C4
Newton CB2 ....31 B8
Hart Cl CB9 ....38 F1
Hart Rd PE26 ....171 E3
Hartfield Cl CB8 ....70 E4
Hartford Com Jun & Inf Sch
PE29 ....141 F5
Hartford Cl PE2 .....187 D6
Hartford Rd PE29 ...141 E4
Hartington Gr CB1 ..65 A5
Hartlands PE7 ....190 E8
Hartley Cl CB5 ......197 C5
Hartwell Cl PE7 ....197 C5
Hartwell Way PE3 ..197 B5
Harvest Cl PE7 .....175 F8
Harvest Ct PE27 ...144 A4
Harvest Way CB1 ...84 A2
Harvester Way
Crowland PE6 ....232 B8
Peterborough PE1 ..198 C1
Harvey Cl CB8 .....230 B1
Harvey Dr 5 PE28 ..201 E4
Harvey Goodwin Ave
CB4 ....83 D4
Harvey Goodwin Gdns
CB4 ....83 D4
Harvey Rd CB1 .....246 C1
Harvey St 3 PE19 ..74 E4
Haselburst Cl PE15 .243 F4
Haslingfield Prim Sch
CB3 ....47 A5
Haslingfield Rd
Barrington CB2 ......29 F8
Barton CB3 ....46 E6
Harlton CB3 ....46 E6
Hasse Rd CB7 ......212 C8
Hassock Hill Dro
PE3 ....237 D3
Hassock Way 1 PE15 .243 F7
Hastings Rd PE4 ...204 C2
Hatchet La CB9 ....114 B2
Hatfield Rd PE28 ..168 A4
Hathaway Cl PE19 ..74 C3
Hatherdene Cl CB1 ..65 E8
Hatley Cl CB8 ......110 F5
Hatley Dr CB5 .....84 C3
Hatley Pk* SG19 ...42 F7
Hatley Rd
Gamlingay SG19 ....41 F4
Wrestlingworth &
Cockayne Hatley SG19 .25 B7
Hatton Pk Prim Sch
CB4 ....123 F2
Hatton's Pk CB4 ...123 F2
Hatton's Rd CB4 ...102 D6
Hautboy La PE8 ...178 B3
Hauxton CP Sch CB2 .48 C4
Hauxton Rd
Cambridge CB2 .....48 C8
Great Shelford CB2 .48 A5
Havelock Cl SG19 ..41 C5
Havelock Dr PE2 ...187 E6
Haven The CB1 ....66 F5
Haverhill Arts Ctr*
CB9 ....24 A7
Haverhill Bsns Pk CB9 .24 A5
Haverhill Leisure Ctr
Thriplow CB2 ....8 A7
Haverhill Rd
Castle Camps CB1 ..22 E4
Horseheath CB1 ....37 A3
Little Wratting CB9 .39 F3
Stapleford CB2 .....24 D5
Steeple Bumpstead CB9 .24 B1
Havenswater Cl 1 PE4 .204 E2
Haviland Way CB4 ..83 F6
Hawcrofts La CB4 ...208 D2
Hawe's La CB7 .....211 E2
Haweswater PE29 ..141 C5
Hawk Dr PE29 ......142 B7
Hawkes End PE28 ..140 E2
Hawkes La PE27 ...208 B4
Hawkesden Rd PE19 .75 B6
Hawkesford Way PE19 .74 F7
Hawkins Dr PE18 ..115 D3
Hawkins Rd CB4 ...123 E5
Hawkins's Dro PE7 .242 F13
Hawkshead Way 2 PE7 .204 F5
Hawthorn Ave
Hauxton CB2 ....48 B4
Sawston CB2 ....32 F6
Hawthorn Cl
Little Paxton PE19 ..95 F2
Littleport CB6 ......242 E3
Newborough PE6 ...207 C1
Royston SG8 ....5 F7
Hawthorn Dr PE29 ..141 D5
Hawthorn End 1 PE28 .150 F5

Hawthorn Rd
Emneth PE14 ....236 D5
Folksworth PE7 ....175 D8
Haverhill CB9 ....38 D1
Peterborough PE1 ..198 C6
Ramsey PE26 ....171 F7
St Neots PE19 .....74 E6
Yaxley PE7 ....181 F5
Hawthorn Way
Burwell CB5 ....130 C3
Cambridge CB4 .....83 F4
Royston SG8 ....5 F7
St Ives PE27 ....144 A5
Sawtry PE28 ....168 B3
Hawthorn Wlk 4 PE28 .213 F8
Hawthorne Ave PE15 .243 D5
Hawthorne Dr PE7 ..189 F6
Hawthorne Gr PE15 .243 C5
Hawthorne Rd CB2 ..49 B4
Hawthorns The PE16 .241 C5
Hay Cl CB1 ....53 B1
Hay Fen Cl 6 CB6 ...210 F5
Hay St SG8 ....11 B2
Haycocks Rd CB9 ...29 D8
Haycraft Cl PE28 ...116 A7
Haycroft The PE19 ..117 F2
Haydock Rd SG8 ...5 F5
Hayes Wlk PE28 ...178 D8
Hayfield Ave CB2 ...32 F7
Hayland Dro PE28 ..213 B7
Hayley Wood Nature
Reserve* CB3 ......43 C6
Hayling Ave PE19 ..96 A2
Hayling Cl 4 PE29 ..118 F7
Hayman's Way CB3 ..99 A2
Haymarket Rd 7 CB3 .83 C3
Hayster Dr CB1 ....65 E6
Hayter Cl CB1 .....53 F4
Haywardsfield PE3 ..197 A1
Haywoods La SG8 ..5 C7
Hayzen Cl PE2 .....29 F8
Hazel Cl Chatteris PE16 .241 D4
Haverhill CB9 ....23 E7
Mildenhall IP28 ....239 E4
Hazel Croft PE4 ....204 A4
Hazel Ct 7 CB6 ....210 F5
Hazel Gdns 8 PE13 .245 D6
Hazel La CB1 ......79 C5
Hazel Rd CB4 ......83 D6
Hazel Way PE27 ...144 B4
Hazelwood Cl CB4 ..83 D6
Hazelwood Wlk PE29 .141 F7
Head Fen Dro CB6 ..224 F3
Headford Cl CB5 ...84 D4
Headington Cl CB1 ..65 F5
Headington Dr CB1 ..65 F5
Headlake Dro CB6 ..128 E1
Headland Ave CB4 ..23 E7
Headlands
Fenstanton PE28 ...121 C5
Huntingdon PE29 ...141 C3
Headlands Way PE7 .189 D8
Headley Gdns CB2 ..49 B4
Headley's La CB4 ...217 A2
Heasman Cl CB8 ...110 F5
Heath Ave SG8 .....5 C5
Heath Farm Rd IP28 .213 F1
Heath House CB4 ...84 A5
Heath La PE28 ......163 A4
Heath Rd Bottisham CB1 .87 B4
Burwell CB5 ....109 D5
Exning CB8 ....110 B6
Gamlingay SG19 ....41 C4
Helpston PE6 ....231 C2
Mildenhall IP28 ....239 E5
Newmarket CB8 ...111 C3
Swaffham Bulbeck CB5 .108 B2
Swaffham Prior CB5 .109 A3
Warboys PE28 .....165 C6
Heath Row PE1 ....197 F6
Heathbell Rd CB8 ..111 C3
Heathcote PE15 ...243 F4
Heather Ave PE1 ..198 A8
Heatherdale Cl PE7 .187 C5
Heatherset Way 1 PE28 .213 F1
Heathersett Cl CB8 .110 E7
Heathfield Royston SG8 .5 C5
Thriplow CB2 ....8 A7
Heaton Cl Ely CB6 ..240 F7
Peterborough PE3 ..197 B3
Heaton Dr CB6 ....240 F7
Hectare The CB2 ...48 F7
Heddon Way PE27 ..144 B6
Hedgelands
Peterborough PE4 ..204 C5
Wisbech PE13 .....245 C8
Heffer Cl CB2 ......49 C4
Heights Dro Rd PE6 .170 D6
Helen Cl 3 CB5 ....84 E4
Helens Cl PE26 ....171 B1
Helions Bumpstead Rd
CB9 ....23 F5
Helions Pk Ave CB9 .24 A7
Helions Pk Glade CB9 .24 A7
Helions Pk Gr CB9 ..24 A7
Helions Service Rd
CB9 ....24 A7
Helions Wlk CB9 ...24 A7
Helmsdale Gdns PE4 .204 B2
Helmsley Cl PE7 ...187 F5
Helpston Rd
Castor PE5 ....195 D2
Etton PE6 ....203 C8
Heltwate PE3 ......197 C7
Heltwate Sch PE3 ..197 B7
Hemingford Cres PE7 .187 E6
Hemingford Grey Prim Sch
PE28 ....143 D2

Hemingford Rd
Cambridge CB1 .....65 B8
Hemingford Grey PE27 .143 F2
Hemington Cl 10 CB4 .208 D1
Hemlocks The CB3 ..47 B5
Hemmerley Dr PE7 ..189 E8
Hempfield Pl CB6 ...242 D4
Hempfield Rd CB6 ..242 D4
Hempsals 12 PE19 ..74 C6
Hempsals Rd or Mdw Dro
CB4 ....209 C1
Hempstead Rd
1 Haverhill CB9 ....38 C1
Peterborough PE7 ..186 C1
Hen Brook PE19 ...74 F4
Henderson Cl CB9 ..38 C1
Henford Gdns PE15 .243 D5
Henley Rd CB1 ....84 B2
Henley Way CB7 ...240 F6
Henry Cl CB9 ......23 D6
Henry Crabb Rd CB6 .242 A6
Henry Morris Rd
Histon CB4 ....104 C3
Sawston CB2 ....33 A8
Henry Orbell Cl 3 PE13 .243 E4
Henry St
Peterborough PE1 ..198 A4
Wisbech PE13 .....245 C5
Henry Warby Ave 9
PE14 ....236 A5
Henshaw PE1 .....198 E6
Henson Cl PE13 ...245 C8
Henson Rd PE15 ...243 C5
Herbert Human Cl 3
CB7 ....212 B4
Herbert St CB4 ....83 E4
Herbert Twinn Ct CB5 .84 D4
Hercules Cl 5 CB4 ..83 E8
Hereford Cl 7 PE28 .208 C8
Hereward PE2 .....208 E6
Hereward Ave IP28 .239 C5
Hereward Cl
Haddenham CB6 ...209 E4
Histon CB4 ....104 C3
Peterborough PE1 ..198 B2
Hereward Com Coll
PE1 ....198 D5
Hereward Rd
Peterborough PE1 ..198 B2
1 Wisbech PE13 ...245 D5
Hereward St Ely CB6 .240 B4
March PE15 ....243 D5
Hereward Way PE4 .231 F8
Herewood Cross Sh Ctr
PE1 ....198 A2
Heritage Pk Prim Sch
PE7 ....187 F5
Hermitage Rd PE28 .208 E6
Herne Rd PE26 ....220 D4
Heron Cl
Peterborough PE7 ..187 D6
1 St Neots PE19 ...75 B6
Heron Pk PE1 .....198 F6
Heron Rd PE13 ....245 D2
Heron Way PE27 ..143 F7
Heron Wlk PE15 ...243 F5
Heronry Dr PE6 ...172 B1
Herons Cl CB6 ....65 D4
Herons Cl 5 Ely CB6 .240 B5
Tallington PE9 .....230 F6
Heronshaw PE16 ..241 C6
Herrick Cl PE1 ....197 E8
Herring's Cl CB5 ..85 F5
Herringswell Rd
Herringswell IP28 ..214 B2
Kentford CB8 ......134 B4
Herschel Rd CB3 ..83 B1
Hertford Cl CB3 ...240 A3
Hertford St CB4 ...246 A4
Hervey Cl CB6 ....240 B3
Hethersett Cl CB8 .110 E8
Hetley Rd PE2 ....142 A6
Hexham Ct 8 PE3 ..198 D3
Heydon La Elmdon CB11 .8 F4
Heydon SG8 ....9 E1
Heydon Rd SG8 ...7 E2
Heyford Ct PE4 ...204 F2
Heyford Ct 5 IP28 .239 B5
Hickling Wlk PE4 ..204 E3
Hicks La Girton CB3 .102 B8
Peterborough PE7 ..186 F5
Hicks Way 8 CB9 ..24 E5
Hide Cl CB2 ....32 F6
High Barns CB7 ...240 E6
High Broadgate PE13 .237 F7
High Cl SG8 ....8 A5
High Cswy PE7 ....189 E7
High Ct Wray PE7 ..181 D8
High Ditch Rd CB5 ..85 A4
High Fen Crooked Dro
PE28 ....215 B5
High Fen Straight Dro
PE28 ....215 B6
High Flyer Cotts CB7 .240 F7
High Gn Abington PE19 .57 B6
High Gn Shelford CB2 .48 A4
High Haden Rd PE28 .175 B1
High Leys PE27 ...143 F5
High Mdw Harston CB2 .47 F3
Ramsey PE26 ......172 A3
High Piece Cres CB4 .208 C1
High Pk Cnr CB7 ..132 D5
High Rd Downham CB6 .217 F6

High Rd continued
Gorefield PE13 . . . .**237** E3
Newton PE13 . . . .**238** A5
Tydd St Giles PE13 . . . .**237** F6
Wisbech St Mary PE13 . . . .**235** A6
High Sch CI PE15 . . . .**243** D6
High Side PE13 . . . .**235** A8
High St Abbotsley PE19 . . .**57** B6
Abington Pigotts SG8 . . . . . .**11** F5
Alconbury PE28 . . . .**150** F4
Alconbury Weston PE28 . . . .**150** D6
Ashley CB8 . . . .**91** F8
Ashwell SG7 . . . .**2** D4
Babraham CB2 . . . .**33** D8
Balsham CB1 . . . .**216** D1
Barley SG8 . . . .**6** F2
Barrington CB2 . . . .**29** E8
Barton CB3 . . . .**63** B4
Bassingbourn SG8 . . . .**12** F4
Benwick PE15 . . . .**222** A5
Bluntisham/Colne PE28 . . . .**208** C5
Bottisham CB5 . . . .**86** F5
Bourn CB3 . . . .**60** C6
Boxworth CB3 . . . .**101** B5
Brampton PE28 . . . .**140** E2
Brinkley CB8 . . . .**70** D2
Buckden PE19 . . . .**117** A4
Burwell CB5 . . . .**109** B8
Cambourne CB3 . . . .**79** B3
Castle Camps CB1 . . . .**222** F1
Castor PE5 . . . .**195** F2
Catworth PE28 . . . .**136** D7
Chatteris PE16 . . . .**241** C5
Cherry Hinton CB1 . . . .**66** A7
Cheveley CB8 . . . .**91** C7
Chippenham CB7 . . . .**132** E8
Chrishall SG8 . . . .**8** D3
Conington CB3 . . . .**121** C1
Coton CB3 . . . .**82** D6
Cottenham CB4 . . . .**125** E4
Croxton PE19 . . . .**76** F4
Croydon SG8 . . . .**27** A7
Doddington/Wimblington
PE15 . . . .**223** A5
Dry Drayton CB3 . . . .**102** B1
Earith PE28 . . . .**200** D5
Ellington PE28 . . . .**139** A4
Ely CB7 . . . .**240** D4
Eye PE6 . . . .**232** A1
Eyeworth SG19 . . . .**10** A8
Fen Ditton CB5 . . . .**84** E5
Fen Drayton CB4 . . . .**121** F5
Fenstanton PE28 . . . .**121** A6
Fowlmere SG8 . . . .**15** E8
Foxton CB2 . . . .**30** B5
Fulbourn CB1 . . . .**66** F5
Girton CB3 . . . .**103** E1
Glinton PE6 . . . .**203** E8
Grantchester CB3 . . . .**64** A4
Graveley PE19 . . . .**97** F5
Great & Little Abington
CB1 . . . .**34** C6
Great Chesterford CB10 . . . .**18** E2
Great Eversden CB3 . . . .**45** E8
Great Paxton PE19 . . . .**96** D4
Great Shelford CB2 . . . .**48** E3
Great Wilbraham CB1 . . . . . .**67** F7
Guilden Morden SG8 . . . .**10** F4
Haddenham CB6 . . . .**209** E4
Hail Weston PE19 . . . .**74** B8
Harlton CB3 . . . .**46** D5
Harston CB2 . . . .**47** F3
Haslingfield CB3 . . . .**47** B5
Hauxton CB2 . . . .**48** C5
Haverhill CB9 . . . .**24** A7
Hemingford Abbots
PE28 . . . .**143** A3
Hemingford Grey PE28 . . . .**143** C2
Hildersham CB1 . . . .**34** E5
Hilton PE28 . . . .**120** B1
Hinxton CB10 . . . .**18** B7
Histon CB4 . . . .**123** D8
Holywell-cum-Needingworth
PE27 . . . .**144** F5
Horningsea CB5 . . . .**106** A1
Huntingdon PE29 . . . .**141** D4
Kimbolton PE28 . . . .**113** F4
Knapwell CB3 . . . .**100** E3
Landbeach CB4 . . . .**105** D6
Linton CB1 . . . .**35** C5
Little Paxton PE19 . . . .**95** F2
Little Staughton MK44 . . . . . .**93** B1
Little Wilbraham CB1 . . . .**86** E1
Littleport CB6 . . . .**202** D1
Lode CB5 . . . .**107** C2
Longstanton CB4 . . . .**123** F3
Longstowe CB3 . . . .**59** F2
Madingley CB3 . . . .**81** F5
Manea PE15 . . . .**224** C4
March PE15 . . . .**243** D3
Market Deeping PE6 . . . . . .**231** D8
Maxey PE6 . . . .**231** C7
Melbourn SG8 . . . .**14** C5
Meldreth SG8 . . . .**14** B8
Mepal CB6 . . . .**216** E3
Mildenhall IP28 . . . .**239** C4
Milton CB4 . . . .**105** D2
Needingworth PE27 . . . .**208** A3
Newmarket CB8 . . . .**110** F3
Oakington CB4 . . . .**103** C6
Offord Cluny PE19 . . . .**96** F8
Orwell SG8 . . . .**45** E1
Over CB4 . . . .**208** D1
Pampisford CB2 . . . .**33** B5
Peterborough PE2 . . . .**187** A6

High St continued
Pidley cum Fenton PE28 . . .**155** E8
Rampton CB4 . . . .**124** E5
Ramsey PE26 . . . .**172** A6
Royston SG8 . . . .**5** D6
St Neots PE19 . . . .**74** E5
Sawston CB2 . . . .**32** F6
Sawtry PE28 . . . .**168** B4
Shepreth SG8 . . . .**22** E4
Soham CB7 . . . .**212** B4
Somersham PE28 . . . .**208** C8
Spaldwick PE28 . . . .**137** F6
Stamford PE9 . . . .**244** B5
Stetchworth CB8 . . . .**90** A2
Stilton PE7 . . . .**176** A7
Stourbridge Common CB4 . . .**84** A4
Stretham CB6 . . . .**210** F5
Sutton CB6 . . . .**216** D1
Swaffham Bulbeck CB5 . . . .**108** B1
Swaffham Prior CB5 . . . . . .**108** D5
Swavesey CB4 . . . .**122** E6
Tadlow SG8 . . . .**26** A3
Teversham CB1 . . . .**66** C8
Tilbrook PE28 . . . .**113** B6
Toft CB3 . . . .**61** D4
Tuddenham IP28 . . . .**214** D2
Upwood PE26 . . . .**171** B2
Warboys PE28 . . . .**164** F5
Waterbeach CB5 . . . .**106** B8
West Wickham CB1 . . . .**37** A7
West Wratting CB1 . . . .**53** F5
Whittlesford CB2 . . . .**32** C5
Wicken CB7 . . . .**110** C8
Wilburton CB6 . . . .**210** C5
Willingham CB4 . . . .**209** A1
Wisbech PE13 . . . .**245** C5
Witcham CB6 . . . .**217** A3
Wrestlingworth SG19 . . . . . .**25** B4
Yelling PE19 . . . .**98** C1
High St Back 2 CB7 . . . . .**240** D4
High St Pas CB7 . . . .**240** D4
High St St Martin's
PE9 . . . .**244** C4
Higham Rd IP28 . . . .**214** E1
Highbury St PE1 . . . .**198** A5
Highclere Rd PE7 . . . .**186** D3
Highdene Rd CB1 . . . .**66** A6
Highfield Ave
Alconbury Weston PE28 . . . .**150** D6
Cambridge CB4 . . . .**83** E5
Highfield CI CB2 . . . .**17** D8
Highfield Cotts SG8 . . . .**4** B7
Highfield Gate CB1 . . . .**66** F6
Highfield Rd
Histon CB4 . . . .**104** C1
March PE15 . . . .**243** D3
Highfield Sch CB6 . . . .**240** C5
Highfields Rd CB3 . . . .**80** C2
Highgate Gn PE8 . . . .**178** D8
Highlands SG8 . . . .**5** E6
Highlands The CB8 . . . . . .**110** D8
Highlees Prim Sch
PE3 . . . .**197** C6
Highsett CB1 . . . .**246** C1
Hightown Dro CB3 . . . . . .**129** C4
Highway The PE19 . . . .**94** A6
Highworth Ave CB4 . . . .**83** F5
Hilda Clarke CI 1 PE14 . . .**241** C3
Hilda St CB4 . . . .**83** D4
Hildersham Mill CB1 . . . . . .**34** F5
Hildersham Rd CB1 . . . .**34** D7
Hill CI
Brington & Molesworth
PE28 . . . .**147** C5
Little Stukeley PE28 . . . .**151** F1
Newmarket CB8 . . . .**110** E3
Peterborough PE1 . . . .**198** D5
Sawtry PE28 . . . .**168** B3
Hill Cres CB8 . . . .**39** A1
Hill Est Ramsey PE26 . . . .**172** B4
St Ives PE28 . . . .**143** B5
Hill Farm Rd CB2 . . . .**32** B3
Hill Farms CB1 . . . .**66** C2
Hill La CB9 . . . .**24** F3
Hill Rd Over CB4 . . . .**208** E1
Wistow PE26 . . . .**164** A8
Hill Rise St Ives PE27 . . . .**143** E7
St Neots PE19 . . . .**72** A4
Hill Row CB6 . . . .**209** E6
Hill Row Cswy CB6 . . . . . .**209** A6
Hill St 5 PE13 . . . .**245** C5
Hill View
Dry Drayton CB3 . . . .**102** D1
Lidgate CB8 . . . .**73** F8
Hillary CI PE9 . . . .**244** D6
Hillburn Rd PE13 . . . .**245** B4
Hillcrest CB3 . . . .**129** C4
Hillcrest Ave PE7 . . . .**181** E5
Hillcrest Dr PE13 . . . .**235** A2
Hillfield Alconbury PE28 . .**150** F5
Foxton CB2 . . . .**30** C5
Hillfield Rd CB3 . . . .**62** D6
Hills Ave CB1 . . . .**65** B5
Hills La CB6 . . . .**240** B4
Hills Rd CB2 . . . .**246** C1
Hills Rd Sixth Form Coll
CB1 . . . .**65** A6
Hillside Orwell SG8 . . . .**45** E2
Royston SG8 . . . .**5** D5
Sawston CB2 . . . .**32** F8
Sutton CB6 . . . .**216** D1
Hillside CI
Ellington PE28 . . . .**138** F4
Ufford PE9 . . . .**230** F2
Hillside Cotts PE28 . . . . . .**146** A4
Hillside La CB8 . . . .**44** C4
Hillside Mdw CB7 . . . .**212** F1

Hillside Rd PE15 . . . .**243** B5
Hillstead CB2 . . . .**49** D7
Hillward CI PE2 . . . .**186** C6
Hillway CB1 . . . .**35** C2
Hilsdens Dr PE29 . . . .**142** A1
Hilton Rd PE28 . . . .**120** E3
Hilton St CB4 . . . .**208** D1
Hinchcliffe PE2 . . . .**185** E2
Hinchinbrooke Rd
PE28 . . . .**117** D8
Hinchinbrooke Ctry Pk*
PE29 . . . .**140** F4
Hinchingbrooke Dr
PE16 . . . .**241** B4
Hinchingbrooke Hospl
PE29 . . . .**141** B5
Hinchingbrooke House*
PE29 . . . .**141** B3
Hinchingbrooke Sch
PE29 . . . .**141** A4
Hines CI CB3 . . . .**63** A4
Hines La CB3 . . . .**62** C5
Hinkins CI SG8 . . . .**14** D6
Hinton Ave CB1 . . . .**65** C5
Hinton CI PE7 . . . .**189** D8
Hinton Rd CB1 . . . .**66** D5
Hinton View CB6 . . . .**210** A6
Hinton Way
Great Shelford CB2 . . . .**49** C6
Wilburton CB6 . . . .**210** C6
Hinxton Rd CB2 . . . .**17** E8
Hinxworth Rd SG7 . . . .**2** B4
Histon & Impington Inf Sch
CB4 . . . .**104** B3
Histon & Impington Jun Sch
CB4 . . . .**104** C4
Histon Rd
Cambridge CB4 . . . .**83** C4
Cottenham CB4 . . . .**104** B4
Histon Sch CB4 . . . .**104** B4
Histon St 6 CB6 . . . .**242** D4
Hitherford CB4 . . . .**208** E1
Hive Rd CB6 . . . .**217** A4
Hives The PE19 . . . .**74** D4
Hoadly Rd CB3 . . . .**83** B5
Hobart Ct CB1 . . . .**243** C5
Hobart Rd CB1 . . . .**65** C7
Hobbledods CI CB4 . . . . . .**122** E6
Hobson CI CB1 . . . .**66** A7
Hobson St CB2 . . . .**246** B3
Hockland Rd PE13 . . . .**237** F7
Hockley CI CB1 . . . .**22** B5
Hod Fen Dro
Denton & Caldecote PE7 . . .**177** A7
Yaxley PE7 . . . .**181** F2
Hod Hall La CB6 . . . .**210** A5
Hodgson Ave PE4 . . . .**200** B6
Hodley Pl CB3 . . . .**99** B1
Hodney Rd 2 PE29 . . . . . .**232** A1
Hodson's Dr PE29 . . . .**141** E5
Hodwell SG7 . . . .**2** D4
Hog Fen Dro PE7 . . . .**182** A5
Hogarth CI PE27 . . . .**144** A7
Hogarth Pl 2 PE19 . . . .**74** D5
Hogens La PE13 . . . .**238** A5
Hogherd's La 3 PE13 . . . .**226** F5
Hoghill Dro CB6 . . . .**209** F3
Hog's La SG8 . . . .**8** D3
Holbein Rd PE27 . . . .**144** A7
Holben CI CB3 . . . .**63** B3
Holborn Ave PE28 . . . .**239** B6
Holbrook Rd
Cambridge CB1 . . . .**65** B4
Haverhill CB9 . . . .**23** C6
Holburn View CB6 . . . .**168** B2
Holcroft PE2 . . . .**186** B3
Holden End CB10 . . . .**21** B2
Holdfield PE3 . . . .**197** B6
Holdich St PE3 . . . .**197** C2
Holdsworth Valley CP Sch
CB8 . . . .**110** F3
Holgate La CB4 . . . .**204** B7
Holkham Mead CB5 . . . . .**130** C2
Holkham Rd PE1 . . . .**185** D3
Holland Ave PE4 . . . .**204** D1
Holland Pk CB8 . . . .**91** C7
Holland Rd PE4 . . . .**204** C6
Hollands Bsns Ctr CB9 . . . .**24** B6
Hollands Rd CB9 . . . .**24** A6
Hollands Road Ind Est
CB9 . . . .**24** A6
Hollesley Ave CB9 . . . .**23** C8
Holliday's Rd PE28 . . . . . .**208** D5
Hollies CI SG8 . . . .**5** E6
Hollies The PE15 . . . .**243** E7
Hollmans CI CB1 . . . .**66** F4
Hollow Hill CB9 . . . .**38** B4
Hollow La PE26 . . . .**172** E6
Hollow Rd Chrishall SG8 . . . .**8** D1
Elmdon CB11 . . . .**9** C4
Ramsey Forty Foot PE26 . . .**221** C2
Hollow The PE7 . . . .**122** B6
Holly Ave PE14 . . . .**236** A5
Holly CI
Newborough PE6 . . . .**207** C1
Red Lodge IP28 . . . .**213** F1
Holly Dr 4 PE15 . . . .**223** A6
Holly Way 7 PE6 . . . .**231** E8
Holly Wlk Ely CB7 . . . .**240** F5
3 Mildenhall IP28 . . . .**213** F8
Peterborough PE7 . . . .**186** D3
Hollybush Way CB1 . . . .**35** D3
Hollycroft PE14 . . . .**236** D5
Hollycroft Rd PE14 . . . .**84** A2
Hollymount 2 CB1 . . . .**84** B2
Hollytrees CB3 . . . .**102** C3
Holme CE Prim Sch
PE7 . . . .**177** A4

Holme CI Castor PE5 . . . . .**195** D2
Oakington/Longstanton
CB4 . . . .**103** C5
Holme Dro PE28 . . . .**208** E7
Holme Fern Dro PE28 . . . .**208** D7
**Holme Fen National Nature
Reserve*** PE7 . . . .**177** C7
Holme La CB6 . . . .**218** A6
Holme Rd
Market Deeping PE6 . . . . . .**220** C3
Yaxley PE7 . . . .**181** E4
Holme Way CB2 . . . .**32** F8
Holmehill PE29 . . . .**118** F8
Holmes Dr PE13 . . . .**245** E5
Holmes La CB7 . . . .**212** B5
Holmes Rd PE6 . . . .**203** F7
Holmes The CB6 . . . .**242** E4
Holme Way PE4 . . . .**204** E2
Holmewood PE7 . . . .**186** B6
Holmewood Cres PE7 . . . .**176** F4
Holmsey Gn PE28 . . . .**213** F8
Holmsey Gn Gdns 2
IP28 . . . .**213** F8
Holt CI 8 PE8 . . . .**230** B1
Holt Fen CB6 . . . .**211** B7
Holyrood CI CB4 . . . .**83** C6
Holywell CE Prim Sch
PE27 . . . .**208** A2
Holywell CI PE3 . . . .**197** A1
Holywell Ferry Rd
CB4 . . . .**121** F6
Holywell Front PE27 . . . . .**144** F2
Holywell Way PE3 . . . .**196** F2
Holywell Rd Graham PE28 .**116** A6
Histon CB4 . . . .**104** B4
Home End PE27 . . . .**144** F2
Home Farm CI
Abbotsley PE19 . . . .**57** B6
Hilton PE28 . . . .**120** B1
Rampton CB4 . . . .**124** F4
Home Farm Rd PE28 . . . . .**143** B5
Home Pasture PE4 . . . . . .**204** B5
Homefield CI CB4 . . . .**84** E5
Homefield Rd CB9 . . . .**23** F5
Homefield Rd Units
CB9 . . . .**23** F5
Homerton Coll CB2 . . . .**65** A5
Homerton St CB2 . . . .**65** A5
Homestall Cres CB9 . . . . . .**38** B4
Homestead 8 PE28 . . . . . .**215** C1
Homestead Dr 4 IP28 . . . .**213** F8
Homing The CB5 . . . .**84** E3
Honey Dro PE15 . . . .**223** E4
Honey Hill
9 Cambridge CB3 . . . .**83** C3
Fen Drayton CB4 . . . .**122** A4
Fenstanton PE28 . . . .**121** B6
Gamlingay SG19 . . . .**41** D4
West Wratting CB1 . . . .**53** C5
Honey Hill Mews CB3 . . . . .**83** C3
Honeydon Ave PE19 . . . . . .**74** B5
Honeyhill PE4 . . . .**205** A1
Honeyhill Com Prim Sch
PE4 . . . .**205** A1
Honeyhill Rd PE13 . . . .**237** C2
Honeymead Rd PE15 . . . . .**223** B6
Honeysome Rd PE16 . . . . .**241** A5
Honeysuckle CI
Haverhill CB9 . . . .**38** E1
Red Lodge IP28 . . . .**134** A8
2 Soham CB7 . . . .**212** B4
Honeysuckle Ct PE2 . . . . .**186** D7
Hoo CI PE15 . . . .**117** B4
Hood CI CB6 . . . .**242** D3
Hook Dro PE15 . . . .**228** B1
Hook La PE15 . . . .**223** C7
Hook Rd PE15 . . . .**223** C7
Hook's Dro PE13 . . . .**234** C4
Hook's Mill CB8 . . . .**111** D6
Hooper St CB1 . . . .**84** A1
Hop Row CB6 . . . .**210** A6
Hopbine Ct PE29 . . . .**171** F5
Hope St CB1 . . . .**65** B8
Hopkins CI CB4 . . . .**84** A6
Hopton Rise CB9 . . . .**38** B1
Horn La Kirtling CB8 . . . .**72** B5
Linton CB1 . . . .**35** B2
Hornbeam Rd PE28 . . . .**84** F6
Horningsea Rd
Fen Ditton CB5 . . . .**84** F6
Horningsea CB5 . . . .**85** A8
Horse and Gate St
CB4 . . . .**121** F5
Horse Comm CI PE29 . . . .**141** E5
Horse Comm La PE29 . . . .**141** E5
Horse Dro PE26 . . . .**221** A1
Horse Fair Sh Ctr
PE13 . . . .**245** A5
Horse Ware CB4 . . . .**208** D2
Horsegate
Market Deeping PE6 . . . . . .**231** D8
Whittlesey PE7 . . . .**189** D7
Horsegate Gdns PE6 . . . . .**241** C5
Horsegate Dro PE14 . . . . .**229** F4
Horseheath Gn CB1 . . . .**37** C1
Horseheath Pk CB1 . . . .**37** D3
Horseheath Rd
Linton CB1 . . . .**35** D2
Withersfield CB9 . . . .**38** A4
Horsehill Dro
PE16 . . . .**241** B1
Horsemoor Rd PE15 . . . . .**223** D8
Horseshoe CI
Balsham CB1 . . . .**53** C2

Horseshoe CI continued
Elmdon CB11 . . . .**9** B4
Horseshoe La
4 Haverhill CB9 . . . .**23** E7
4 Stamford PE9 . . . .**244** B5
Horseshoe Terr PE13 . . . .**245** B7
Horse-shoe Terr
PE13 . . . .**245** A7
Horseshoes La CB1 . . . .**54** D5
Horseshoes Way PE7 . . . .**186** D1
Horseshows Way PE28 . . .**140** D2
Horseway PE16 . . . .**222** A4
Horsey Hill (Civil War Fort)*
PE7 . . . .**188** A4
Horsham CI 3 CB9 . . . .**38** C1
Horsley Hale CB6 . . . .**242** D6
Horton Wlk PE3 . . . .**197** D5
Hospital Rd PE15 . . . .**222** C6
Hostmoor Ave PE15 . . . . .**243** A7
Hotel La PE28 . . . .**151** F3
Houghton Ave PE2 . . . . . .**187** F5
Houghton Gdns PE28 . . . .**240** B4
Houghton Grange
PE28 . . . .**143** C5
Houghton Hill Rd
PE28 . . . .**143** B5
**Houghton Mdws Nature
Reserve*** PE28 . . . .**143** C4
Houghton Mill* PE28 . .**143** C4
Houghton Prim Sch
PE28 . . . .**143** B5
Houghton Rd PE27 . . . . . .**143** E5
Houghtons La CB7 . . . .**213** B5
Houldsworth Terr CB8 . . . .**110** F3
Housman Ave SG8 . . . .**5** C8
How Hill (Tumulus)*
IP27 . . . .**214** F7
Howard CI CB5 . . . .**84** D4
Howard Ct CB5 . . . .**84** D4
Howard De Walden Way
CB8 . . . .**111** A4
Howard Rd
Cambridge CB5 . . . .**84** E4
Eaton Socon PE19 . . . .**74** C1
Meldreth SG8 . . . .**14** A8
Howard Rd Ind Est
PE19 . . . .**74** C1
Howard's La CB1 . . . .**37** A2
Howe Rd CB9 . . . .**38** F1
Howes PE7 . . . .**183** A5
Howgate Rd CB4 . . . .**83** D7
Howitt's Gdns PE19 . . . . . .**75** A2
Howitt's La 5 PE19 . . . .**74** F3
Howitts La PE19 . . . .**74** F4
Howland PE2 . . . .**186** A3
Howlett Way CB5 . . . .**86** E6
Howletts CI PE15 . . . .**243** C4
Hoylake Dr PE7 . . . .**245** C4
Huddleston Way CB2 . . . . . .**33** A7
Hudpool PE29 . . . .**118** F7
Hudson CI 1 CB9 . . . .**24** C6
Hudson Leisure Ctr
PE13 . . . .**245** A5
Hulatt Rd CB1 . . . .**65** C4
Humber Dr PE7 . . . .**181** E6
Humber Rd PE29 . . . .**141** F7
Humberdale Way
PE28 . . . .**164** F5
Humberley CI 1 PE19 . . . . .**74** F3
Humberstone Rd CB4 . . . .**246** C4
Humphreys Rd CB4 . . . .**83** E6
Humphries Way CB4 . . . . .**105** D3
Humphrys St PE2 . . . .**186** D8
Hunchback La PE14 . . . . . .**238** E2
Hundon Rd CB9 . . . .**24** A3
Hundred Rd PE15 . . . .**243** C8
Hundreds Rd PE6 . . . .**232** C6
Hungarton Ct PE21 . . . . . .**198** D7
Hungate Rd PE14 . . . .**236** D6
Hunsbury CI PE7 . . . .**189** F6
Hunters Chase PE15 . . . . .**243** E2
Hunters CI PE16 . . . .**241** D5
Hunters Way
Kimbolton PE28 . . . .**113** F5
Royston SG8 . . . .**5** E6
Sawtry PE28 . . . .**168** B3
Hunting Ave PE2 . . . .**186** F7
Hunting Gr CB3 . . . .**101** B5
Huntingdon Boat Club
PE29 . . . .**141** D5
Huntingdon Jun & Inf Sch
PE29 . . . .**141** E6
Huntingdon Leisure Ctr
PE29 . . . .**141** D6
Huntingdon Racecorse
PE28 . . . .**140** C5
Huntingdon Rd
Boxworth CB3 . . . .**101** E7
Brampton PE28 . . . .**141** A2
Cambridge CB3 . . . .**83** A5
Chatteris PE16 . . . .**241** B4
Fen Drayton CB4 . . . .**121** D4
Houghton & Wyton PE28 . . .**142** F5
Lolworth CB3 . . . .**102** B5
Ramsey PE26 . . . .**171** C2
St Neots PE19 . . . .**75** A8
Sawston CB2 . . . .**32** F8
Huntingdon St PE29 . . . . .**141** E6
Huntingdon Sta PE29 . . . .**141** C4
Huntingdonshire Coll
Huntingdon PE29 . . . .**141** B6
St Neots PE19 . . . .**74** F6
Huntings Dr PE28 . . . .**168** B4
Huntly CI CB4 . . . .**84** B7
Huntly Gr PE1 . . . .**198** B4
Huntly Rd PE1 . . . .**186** E7
Hunts CI 4 PE15 . . . .**222** F5
Hunts End PE19 . . . .**117** B4

Hunt's Gate PE12 ......237 F8
Hunts La CB10 ......18 B7
Hunts Rd CB2 ......17 D8
Huntsmans Gate PE3 ..196 F3
Huntsmill CB1 ......66 E4
Hurdle Dro IP28 ......213 D8
Hurdleditch Rd SG8 ..28 B8
Hurdles Way CB2 ......31 E1
Hurn Rd PE6 ......203 E3
Hurrell Rd CB4 ......83 C6
Hurrell's Row CB2 ....47 E2
Hurricane Cl PE29 ..141 B8
Hurrys Cl CB2 ......32 E7
Hurst Ave 1 PE15 ..243 E4
Hurst La CB6 ......240 A6
Hurst Pk Ave CB2 ....47 D3
Hurstingstone PE27 ..144 A5
Hurts Croft CB7 ......212 E1
Hut Field La CB3 ......99 A3
Hutchinson Cl PE15 ..224 A4
Huttles Gn SG8 ......29 E4
Hyholmes PE3 ......196 F7
Hyll Cl CB10 ......16 D8
Hyperion Way CB8 ..110 D8
Hythe Cl CB5 ......130 A3
Hythe La Burwell CB5 ..130 A3
  Ely CB7 ......240 D4
Hythe The CB6 ......242 D5
Hythegate PE4 ......204 D4

I

Ibberson's Dro PE15 ..221 F4
Ibbott Cl PE2 ......187 E5
Ibbott Cres 7 PE28 ..215 C1
Iceni Way CB8 ......110 B8
Icewell Hill CB8 ......111 A4
Ickleton Grange CB10 ..17 A1
Ickleton Cl CB9 ......24 B8
Ickleton Rd Duxford CB2 ..17 E7
  Elmdon CB11 ......9 A4
  Great Chesterford CB10 ..18 C2
  Hinxton CB10 ......18 B6
Icknield Cl Cheveley CB8 ..91 C5
  Ickleton CB10 ......17 A1
Icknield Prim Sch The
  CB3 ......33 A8
Icknield Wlk SG8 ......5 F6
Icknield Wlk Fst Sch
  SG8 ......5 F7
Ida Darwin Hospl CB1 ..66 D5
Ihlee Cl PE4 ......204 E1
Ilex Cl PE7 ......186 C3
Ilex Rd PE27 ......144 B6
Illing's La La PE28 ..164 A1
Illingworth Way CB2 ..30 C5
Illston Pl PE1 ......198 D7
Impala Dr CB1 ......66 A7
Imperial War Mus*
  CB2 ......31 F1
Impett's La CB1 ......67 A4
Impington La CB4 ..104 C3
Impington Village Coll
  CB4 ......104 D3
India La CB2 ......151 F2
Infield Rd PE28 ......167 C7
Ingham Hall Gdns
  PE13 ......234 D7
Ingham Rd CB9 ......24 A8
Ingle Rd PE14 ......236 B5
Ingleborough PE1 ......198 A5
Ingleborough Mill
  PE14 ......238 E5
Ingle's La 14 PE15 ..223 A5
Ingoldsby Cl 3 PE15 ..243 D2
Ingram St 8 PE29 ..141 E4
Inham's Rd PE7 ......189 E6
Inhams Cl PE13 ......234 D5
Inhams Ct PE2 ......187 E4
Inhams Way PE26 ....116 A7
Inkerman Rise PE19 ..74 C5
Inley Dro PE2 ......237 A8
Innovation Way PE2 ..185 B5
Institute of Astronomy
  CB3 ......83 A3
Institute of Public Health
  CB2 ......65 B2
Interchange Ind Est The
  PE29 ......141 C8
International Extension Coll
  CB1 ......65 A8
Inverness Cl CB4 ......84 A5
Iram Dro CB4 ......209 B1
Irchester Pl PE3 ......197 D4
Ireton Cl PE19 ......74 F3
Ireton Way PE15 ......243 D2
Ireton's Way
  Chatteris PE16 ......241 F2
  Mepal PE16 ......216 C6
Irnham Rd PE9 ......244 C7
Ironmonger St 8 PE9 ..244 C5
Irving Burgess Cl PE7 ..189 C8
Isaacson Rd CB5 ......109 C8
Isham Rd PE3 ......197 D4
Isherwood Cl SG8 ......5 C8
Isinglass Cl CB8 ......111 E2
Isis Way PE2 ......185 B5
Isle Bridge Rd PE14 ..236 F2
Isle Coll Chatteris PE16 ..241 C5
  Wisbech PE13 ......235 D4
Isle of Ely Way
  Chatteris PE16 ......241 C7
  March PE15 ......243 A4
Isleham CE Prim Sch
  CB7 ......213 A5
Isleham Marina IP28 ..213 B6
Isleham Rd CB7 ......212 F2

Isons Cl SG8 ......15 E8
Itter Cres PE4 ......197 E8
Ivan Clark's Cnr CB1 ..34 C7
Ivatt St CB4 ......125 E5
Ivatt Way PE3 ......197 C7
Ivel Cl PE19 ......74 C4
Ivelbury Cl PE19 ......117 A3
Iver Cl CB1 ......65 F7
Ives Dro PE7 ......189 A2
Ivesdyke Cl 4 PE13 ..238 B2
Ivett's Cl CB3 ......45 E7
Ivy Field CB3 ......63 B4
Ivy Gr PE4 ......204 D2
Ivy Way PE28 ......138 A6
Ivydene CB5 ......128 A2
Ixworth Cl 8 PE6 ....232 A1
Ixworth Rd 5 CB9 ....23 E6
Izaak Walton Way PE6 ..204 A8
Izzard Rise PE19 ......96 E4

J

Jack Haws La 4 PE9 ..230 D4
Jack Hunt Sch PE3 ..197 B3
Jack Hunt Swimming Pool
  PE3 ......197 B3
Jack Jarvis Cl 5 CB8 ..111 A3
Jack Warren Gn CB5 ..84 F3
Jack's Cnr Dro PE26 ..172 E3
Jackson Cl CB2 ......48 C5
Jackson's La CB10 ....18 D3
Jackson's Sq CB10 ....18 D3
Jackson's Way SG8 ....15 E8
James Carter Rd IP28 ..239 A6
James Ct PE19 ......74 F2
James Essex Dr CB6 ..240 E7
James Gage Ct PE16 ..241 B3
James Gdns PE7 ......189 E7
James Nurse Cl CB1 ..66 A6
James St CB5 ......246 C3
James Cl CB9 ......24 D6
Jarman Way SG8 ......5 B7
Jarman's La IP28 ......213 D7
Jarvis Way CB3 ......110 E5
Jasmin Cl PE13 ......245 F7
Jasmine Ct
  Cambridge CB1 ......65 C5
  Peterborough PE2 ....185 E2
Jasmine Way PE7 ......181 F6
Jay Cl CB9 ......24 C7
Jaywick Rd CB8 ......24 A8
Jeavons La 6 CB3 ......79 C3
Jedburgh St 3 CB4 ....82 F8
Jefferson St 22 PE6 ..230 B1
Jeffery Ave 8 PE13 ..245 C3
Jeffrey Cl SG8 ......5 C8
Jellicoe Pl PE19 ......74 A2
Jenkins Cl PE19 ......74 B2
Jennings Ave PE19 ....74 B2
Jenyns Cl CB5 ......86 E7
Jepps La SG8 ......5 D6
Jermyn Cl CB4 ......83 D6
Jerusalem Dro CB4 ..217 A5
Jesus Coll CB5 ......246 B3
Jesus La CB5 ......246 C3
Jesus Terr CB1 ......246 C3
Jetty The PE13 ......235 C7
Jew House Dro PE14 ..236 D5
Jim Mollison Cl 2 IP28 ..239 B5
Jj Thompson Ave CB3 ..82 F7
Job's La PE15 ......243 C1
John Amner Cl CB6 ..240 D6
John Breay Cl SG8 ....29 D4
John Clare Prim Sch
  PE6 ......231 B4
John Clarke Ct CB4 ..185 B4
John Conder Ct CB1 ..65 C7
John F Kennedy Ct 2
  PE13 ......245 D4
John Falkner Com Inf Sch
  CB2 ......32 E7
John Impey Way SG8 ..14 D6
John Mansfield Sch
  PE1 ......198 A3
John Paxton Jun Sch
  CB2 ......32 F8
John Sale Cl SG7 ......2 C4
John St Cambridge CB1 ..246 C2
  Royston SG8 ......5 D6
John Thompson Rd 3
  PE13 ......245 D4
Johnson Way PE16 ....241 C6
Johnson Wlk PE1 ......197 F7
Johnson's Dro PE13 ..234 B7
Joiner's Cl CB1 ......35 B2
Joiner's Rd CB1 ......35 B2
Jolley Way CB1 ......35 A8
Jones Cl PE15 ......243 B3
Jones Ct PE26 ......172 E7
Jones Dr CB3 ......99 A3
Jones La PE7 ......190 C7
Jones's Dro PE27 ......221 F8
Jopling Way CB2 ......48 C4
Jordan Mews 2 PE1 ..198 B3
Jordans Yd CB1 ......246 A3
Jorose St CB4 ......197 A3
Jorose Way PE3 ......197 F3
Joscelynes CB2 ......49 C4
Joshua Cl 2 PE16 ....241 C5
Josiah Ct CB5 ......105 C8
Joyce's Cl CB2 ......32 F6
Jubilee Ave PE28 ......164 D6
Jubilee Cl Isleham CB7 ..213 A5
  Little Paxton PE19 ....95 F2
  Waterbeach CB5 ......106 A8
Jubilee Ct CB8 ......90 A1

Jubilee End SG8 ......11 B2
Jubilee St PE2 ......186 F8
Jubilee Terr CB7 ......240 D3
Jubilee Way SG8 ......11 B2
Jubilee Wlk
  Haverhill CB9 ......24 A7
  Wisbech PE13 ......245 D8
Judson Ct 8 PE29 ....141 F8
Julian Cl CB9 ......24 D2
Julius Martin La CB2 ..212 A4
Junc The 2 PE15 ......243 D7
Junction Rd PE20 ....239 B5
Juniper Cl IP28 ......239 E5
Juniper Cres PE3 ......197 A2
Juniper Dr
  Chatteris PE16 ......241 D5
  Ely CB7 ......240 F5
Jupiter Cl 2 CB9 ......24 C6
Jury Rd PE7 ......181 C8
Justinian Cl CB9 ......24 D6
Jutland Rise PE19 ....74 C5

K

Kaldor Ct CB4 ......83 E7
Kathleen Elliot Way
  CB1 ......65 F7
Kay Hitch Way CB4 ..104 B2
Keates Rd CB1 ......66 A5
Keats Cl SG8 ......5 C8
Keats Gr PE19 ......74 C6
Keats Way PE1 ......197 D7
Keble Cl PE9 ......244 A7
Keble Ct PE9 ......244 A7
Kedleston Rd PE7 ....187 F6
Keep The CB9 ......23 E7
Keeton Rd PE1 ......197 E7
Kefford Cl SG8 ......5 A1
Kellers Cl PE13 ......245 A7
Kelful Cl PE7 ......190 D7
Kelsey Cres CB1 ......35 B8
Kelsey Kerridge Sports Ctr
  CB1 ......246 C1
Kelsey Way PE15 ......243 D2
Kelvin Cl PE4 ......204 C1
Kelvin Cl CB1 ......65 D5
Kemmann La CB3 ......75 A5
Ken Stimpson Comp Sch
  PE6 ......204 B4
Kendal Cl PE4 ......204 F2
Kendal Way CB4 ......84 A6
Kendrick Cl PE7 ......187 D6
Kenilworth Ave PE7 ..188 A5
Kenilworth Cl 3 PE7 ..194 D4
Kenilworth Ct PE19 ..74 A3
Kennedy Croft CB4 ..126 A7
Kennedy Rd PE7 ......213 A5
Kennels Rd PE6 ......196 D4
Kennet Gdns PE4 ......204 E1
Kennetside CB8 ......73 D1
Kennett Com Prim Sch
  CB8 ......133 F5
Kennett Rd or Moulton Road
  CB8 ......112 F7
Kennett Sta CB8 ......133 F3
Kennulphs Cl 3 PE6 ..232 C8
Kent Cl Ely CB6 ......240 B5
  St Ives PE27 ......143 F7
Kent Rd
  Huntingdon PE29 ....141 E8
  Peterborough PE3 ....197 E2
Kent Way CB4 ......83 F7
Kentings CB3 ......62 B5
Kentmere Pl 1 PE4 ..204 F2
Kents La CB7 ......212 B4
Kentwell Pl CB5 ......130 C2
Kenwood Gdns CB1 ....35 E2
Kerridge Cl CB1 ......84 A1
Kespar CB8 ......73 D6
Kesters Cl CB1 ......81 B2
Kesteven Cl 6 PE6 ....231 E8
Kesteven Rd PE4 ......244 B7
Kesteven Wlk PE1 ....198 B2
Kestrel Cl
  Cottenham CB4 ......125 C5
  Huntingdon PE29 ....142 A7
Kestrel Ct PE14 ......190 F7
Kestrel Dr 2 PE14 ..245 D2
Kestrel Rd PE1 ......75 B7
Kestrel Rd CB9 ......24 C7
Kestrel Way 7 SG8 ....5 B7
Keswick Cl PE4 ......204 F3
Kettering Rd PE7 ......244 B2
Kettlefields CB8 ......89 F1
Kettlefields Prim Sch
  CB8 ......89 F1
Kettles Cl CB4 ......103 C5
Kettle's Yd* CB1 ......246 A4
Key Theatre* PE1 ....198 A1
Keynes Rd CB5 ......50 A4
Keyston Rd PE28 ......135 D2
Kidmans Cl Hilton PE28 ..148 A8
Kigezi Int Sch of Medicine
  CB2 ......246 B2
Kildare Dr CB4 ......197 C4
Kilham PE2 ......186 F8
Kilkenny Ave CB4 ....240 E7
Killem's Gn CB11 ....14 E4
Kilmaine Cl CB4 ......83 E8
Kiln Cl
  2 Little Downham CB6 ..218 A7
  St Ives PE27 ......143 E6
Kiln House Yd SG8 ....5 D6
Kiln La CB4 ......240 F5
Kilverstone PE2 ......186 A4
Kim Rd PE28 ......114 A7

Kimberley Rd CB4 ....246 C4
Kimbolton Ct PE1 ....197 F3
Kimbolton Prep Sch
  PE28 ......113 E5
Kimbolton Rd
  Hail Weston PE19 ......74 A8
  Pertenhall MK44 ......113 D1
  Wisbech PE28 ......113 F4
Kinderley Com Prim Sch
  PE13 ......237 F6
Kinderley Rd PE13 ..245 C8
King Cob CB6 ......210 F5
King Edgar Cl CB6 ..240 D7
King Edward Rd PE14 ..241 C5
King Edward VII Rd
  Doddington/Wimblington
  PE15 ......223 B7
  Mildenhall IP28 ......239 C4
  10 Over CB4 ......200 D1
  1 Peterborough PE1 ..198 A2
  Rampton CB4 ......124 E4
King George Ave CB4 ..110 B8
King Hedges Prim Sch
  CB4 ......83 F7
King James Way SG8 ....5 B5
King St Cambridge CB1 ..246 B3
  Huntingdon PE29 ......141 F4
  Peterborough PE1 ......197 F2
Kingdon Ave CB7 ......219 B5
Kingfisher Cl Bourn CB3 ..60 C6
  Chatteris PE16 ......241 C6
  Haverhill CB9 ......24 C8
  Little Paxton PE19 ....96 A2
  March PE15 ......243 E5
  Sawston CB2 ......32 E6
  Yaxley PE7 ......181 D5
Kingfisher Dr
  Elmdon CB11 ......9 A3
  St Neots PE19 ......75 A5
Kingfisher Rd PE27 ..143 F7
Kingfisher Way PE29 ..141 A6
Kingfishers PE2 ......185 D6
Kings Cl
  Huntingdon PE29 ....142 A7
  Mildenhall IP28 ......239 D5
Kings Coll CB2 ......246 A2
Kings Coll Sch CB3 ....83 C1
Kings Cts CB8 ......110 B8
Kings Delph PE7 ......188 C5
Kings Dr CB8 ......111 B1
Kings Dyke Cl PE7 ....187 E6
Kings Gr CB3 ......63 B4
Kings Hedges Rd CB4 ..83 D7
Kings La Cambridge CB1 ..246 A2
Kings Mead CB8 ......110 B8
Kings Mill La
  Great Shelford CB2 ....48 F4
  2 Stamford PE9 ......244 B4
Kings Par CB7 ......212 B3
Kings Rd
  Eaton Socon PE19 ....74 B3
  Peterborough PE2 ....187 E6
  St Ives PE27 ......144 A4
  St Neots PE19 ......74 F6
  Stamford PE9 ......244 B6
Kings Sch The CB6 ....240 C5
Kings Wk 3 PE13 ....245 C4
Kingsbridge Ct PE4 ..204 A5
Kingsbrook PE27 ......144 A5
Kingsfield Prim Sch
  PE16 ......241 B5
Kingsland Way SG7 ....2 D4
Kingsley Ave PE13 ....245 B4
Kingsley Cl 1 PE9 ....230 D3
Kingsley Rd PE1 ......198 C4
Kingsley St PE15 ......243 D5
Kingsley Wlk CB6 ....240 A4
Kingsline Cl PE6 ......233 A3
Kingsmead Ct CB6 ....242 E4
Kingsmead Cl PE2 ....187 E5
Kingston Pas 2 CB8 ..111 A3
Kingston Rd CB3 ......61 D1
Kingston St CB1 ......65 A8
Kingston Vale SG8 ....5 E5
Kingsway Arbury CB4 ..31 F1
  Duxford Airfield CB2 ..31 F1
  Leverington PE13 ......245 F7
  Mildenhall IP28 ......239 C4
  Newmarket CB8 ......110 F4
  Royston SG8 ......5 D8
Kingswood Rd PE15 ..243 C3
Kinnaird Way CB1 ....65 C4

Kinnears Wlk PE2 ....185 F2
Kinross Rd CB4 ......84 A5
Kintbury CB2 ......17 D8
Kipling Ct PE1 ......197 E8
Kipling Pl 1 PE19 ....74 E5
Kipling Rd 1 SG8 ....5 C8
Kirby Cl CB4 ......83 F5
Kirby Cross Ave CB6 ..242 B5
Kirby Rd CB5 ......127 C1
Kirby Terr CB5 ......127 B1
Kirby Wlk PE3 ......197 C5
Kirby's Cl 12 CB4 ....208 D1
Kirk Ogden Cl PE15 ..243 D3
Kirkgate PE13 ......237 F7
Kirkgate St PE13 ....245 E7
Kirkham's La PE14 ..236 C4
Kirkmeadow PE3 ......197 A8
Kirk's La PE14 ......235 E5
Kirkstall PE2 ......186 B3
Kirkton Gate PE3 ....197 A1
Kirkwood Cl PE3 ....197 F2
Kirkwood Rd CB4 ......83 F7
Kirtling Pl 5 CB9 ....24 B8
Kirtling Rd Kirtling CB8 ..72 D7
  Woodditton CB8 ......90 E1
Kisby Ave PE29 ......142 A1
Kite Cl PE29 ......142 A7
Kitson Gdns PE3 ......210 F5
Knapp Rise CB3 ......47 A5
Knapp The CB2 ......47 A5
Knaresborough Ct 10
  PE19 ......74 F1
Knarr Fen Rd PE6 ....202 D8
Knaves Acre Dro CB7 ..212 E5
Kneesworth House (Hospital)
  SG8 ......13 C5
Kneesworth Rd SG8 ....13 F8
Kneesworth St SG8 ....5 C7
Knight Mews PE2 ......187 A6
Knight's End Rd PE15 ..223 A5
Knight's End Rd PE15 ..243 C1
Knighton Cl PE7 ......186 D1
Knights Cl
  Eaton Socon PE19 ....74 B4
  18 Leverington PE13 ..238 B2
Knights Ct CB9 ......23 E7
Knights Way CB4 ....105 D3
Knipe Cl PE29 ......141 B7
Knole Wlk PE3 ......197 B3
Knowle Ct CB6 ......242 B5
Knowles Ave PE28 ....164 C5
Knowles Ct PE28 ......164 C5
Knox End CB10 ......21 A2
Knutsford Rd SG8 ....12 E4
Kooreman Ave CB2 ..245 D7
Kyle Cres PE28 ......140 D2
Kym Rd PE19 ......74 C4

L

Laburnum Gr PE1 ....198 B8
Laburnum Ave
  Mildenhall IP28 ......239 E5
  Yaxley PE7 ......181 F6
Laburnum Cl
  Cambridge CB1 ......83 F4
  Red Lodge IP28 ......213 C5
  5 Wisbech PE13 ......245 E7
Laburnum Ct PE15 ....243 C6
Laburnum La CB5 ......130 A3
Laburnum Way PE27 ..144 A5
Lacey's La CB8 ......110 B7
Lacks Cl CB4 ......125 D3
Laddus Bank PE14 ....236 C1
Laddus Dro PE14 ......229 B8
Lady Adrian Sch The
  CB4 ......83 E5
Lady Charlotte Rd
  PE7 ......186 D3
Lady Jermy Way PE1 ..85 B1
Lady Lodge Dr PE2 ..186 A5
Lady Margaret Rd 1
  CB3 ......83 C3
Lady Romayne Cl PE9 ..244 C4
Lady Smith Ave PE7 ..189 F8
Lady Way PE19 ......74 B4
Ladybower Way PE4 ..204 E3
Ladygate 1 CB9 ......23 E6
Lady's Dro PE14 ......236 D6
Lady's Wood Nature
  Reserve* PE20 ......170 E2
Ladywalk CB4 ......123 F3
Lake Ave PE14 ......229 F3
Lake Ct PE13 ......245 D4
Lake Dro PE14 ......190 E6
Lake Way PE29 ......141 C5
Lakefield Ave PE19 ..96 A2
Lakes Dro CB6 ......209 F3
Lakeside
  Hamilton Hargate PE7 ..186 C2
  Peterborough PE4 ....204 D4
Lakeside Cl
  Little Paxton PE19 ....96 A2
  Perry PE28 ......115 D3
Lakeside Leisure Ctr
  PE2 ......186 A5
Lakeview Way PE7 ....186 C2
Lakeway 8 PE14 ......215 C1
Lamb Fair Ct CB1 ......35 D2
Lambert Mews PE9 ..244 C4
Lambeth Wlk PE9 ......244 A6
Lamble Cl PE14 ......213 F8
Lambourn Cl 1 CB2 ....64 D3

Lambourne Rd CB3 ....81 A3
Lambs' Cross CB4 ...103 F8
Lambs Hill Dro PE15 .228 B1
Lamb's La
  Cottenham CB4 ....125 D3
  Glatton PE28 ....175 D2
Lamb's Pl PE15 ....243 D4
Lammas Field **4** CB3 ...64 C7
Lammas Gdns PE29 ...141 D5
Lammas Rd PE1 ....198 A7
Lammas Way
  St Ives PE27 ....143 F4
  St Neots PE19 ....74 E6
Lamport Dr PE29 .....141 F8
Lancaster Cl
  Old Hurst PE28 ....154 D6
  Warboys PE28 ....164 F4
Lancaster Ct PE7 .....181 F6
Lancaster Dr PE27 ...144 A6
Lancaster Rd
  Mildenhall IP28 ....213 E8
  Ramsey PE26 ....171 E3
  10 Stamford PE9 ......244 B6
Lancaster Way Ely CB6 .217 F1
  Godmanchester PE29 ..141 F2
  Huntingdon PE29 ......141 B8
  Yaxley PE7 ....181 F6
Lancaster Way Bsns Pk
  CB6 ....217 F1
Lancelot Way PE28 ...121 C5
Lancing Cl PE4 ....204 C3
Landau Way PE15 .....243 E6
Landbeach Rd CB4 ...105 D3
Landcliffe Cl PE27 ...144 B5
Lander Cl CB4 ....105 C3
Landseer Ct CB9 ....23 F6
Landwade Rd
  Exning CB8 ....131 B4
  Fordham CB8 ....131 D5
Lane End CB9 ....38 B1
Lane The Easton PE28 .138 B4
  Hauxton CB2 ....48 B4
  Old Hurst PE28 ....154 E6
  Stow Longa PE28 .....137 B2
  West Deeping PE6 ....231 B7
Lanes The
  Great Wilbraham CB1 ...67 E8
  Over CB4 ....208 D1
  St Ives PE28 ....143 A5
Langdale Cl CB1 ....66 A7
Langdyke PE1 ....198 F6
Langford Rd PE2 .....133 F1
Langham Rd CB1 ....65 C6
Langham Way Ely CB7 .240 E7
  Haverhill CB9 ....38 B1
Langley PE3 ....197 B8
Langley Cl PE27 ......144 A4
Langley Ct PE27 ......144 A4
Langley Lawn CB11 ....1 D2
Langley Way PE25 ...143 B1
Langton Rd PE1 ....198 D7
Langwood Cl **7** PE19 ...74 C6
Langwood Fen Dro
  PE16 ....216 D8
Langwood Hill Dro
  PE16 ....216 B7
Lankester Rd SG8 ......5 C5
Lansbury Cl **4** PE19 ...74 E4
Lansdowne Cl CB6 ...240 B3
Lansdowne Rd
  Cambridge CB3 ....82 F3
  Yaxley PE7 ....181 F6
Lansdowne Rd PE2 ...186 D7
Lansdowne Wlk PE2 ..186 D7
Lantree Cres CB2 ......64 D1
Lanwades Pk CB8 .....133 F1
Lapwing Cl IP28 ....239 D4
Lapwing Dr PE7 ......190 A8
Lapwings Cl PE1 ....85 B1
Larch Cl PE7 ....181 F6
Larch Gr PE1 ....198 C6
Larham Way PE16 ....241 B5
Lark Cl IP28 ....213 F4
Lark Cres PE1 ....142 A6
Lark End PE19 ....117 B3
Lark Grange CB7 .....219 D4
Lark Hill CB8 ....112 C5
Lark Rd IP28 ....239 D4
Lark Rise CB3 ....80 F3
Lark Way PE3 ....150 E4
Larkfield Rd CB7 .....240 E6
Larkhall Rd CB7 .....212 D1
Larkin Cl Cambridge CB4 .84 A6
  Royston SG8 ....13 D1
Larkin Pl SG8 ....13 D1
Larkins Rd SG8 ....26 F6
Larklands PE3 ....197 B1
Larks Cl CB9 ....24 C7
Larksfield PE3 ....245 C3
Larkspur Cl **4** IP28 ...213 F1
Larkspur Wlk PE4 ....204 D3
Larmor Dr CB3 ....83 B3
Latham Ave PE2 ......186 C6
Latham Cl CB2 ....64 D6
Latham Rd
  Cambridge CB2 ....64 D6
  Huntingdon PE29 .....141 C8
Latimer Cl CB5 ....84 E3
Latin Cl PE19 ....118 A2
Lattersey Cl PE7 .....189 F7
Lattersey Nature Reserve*
  PE7 ....190 B6
Laundress La CB2 ....246 A2
Laundry La CB1 ....65 D5
Laureate CP Sch CB8 .110 E6

Laureate Gdns CB8 ...110 E6
Laureate Paddocks
  CB8 ....110 E6
Laureate Sch Rd CB8 .110 E6
Laurel Cl Haverhill CB9 ..38 D2
  Mepal CB6 ....216 E3
  9 Red Lodge IP28 ...214 A1
Laurel Dr Elm PE14 ..236 A5
  Thorney PE6 ....232 F3
Laurels Cl PE19 ....74 F4
Laurels The PE15 .....243 E7
Lauriston Pl **1** CB4 ....83 E8
Lavender Cl
  8 Red Lodge IP28 ...213 F1
  Yaxley PE7 ....181 F6
Lavender Cres PE1 ...198 B8
Lavender Ct **4** PE7 ..141 F7
Lavender Field CB9 ....23 D8
Lavender Rd CB4 ......84 A7
Lavender Way PE27 ..144 A6
Lavenham Ct PE2 ....186 D7
Lavington Grange PE1 .198 E6
Law Cl CB6 ....242 D3
Law's Cl PE6 ....206 F1
Law's Lawn PE8 ......192 C2
Lawn Ave PE1 ....198 A7
Lawn La
  Little Downham CB6 ...218 A7
  Sutton CB6 ....216 E1
Lawn The CB2 ....32 C5
Lawns Cres CB8 ......218 A7
Lawns Ct SG8 ....5 D6
Lawns The
  Cambridge CB3 ....83 A2
  Everton SG19 ....40 C3
  Melbourn SG8 ....14 C5
  Wisbech PE13 ....243 B1
Lawrance Lea CB2 .....47 F2
Lawrence Ave PE7 ...187 C2
Lawrence Cl CB3 ......82 D8
Lawrence Rd
  Eaton Socon PE19 ....74 C5
  Ramsey PE26 ....172 C7
  Wittering PE8 ....230 B1
Lawrence Way CB4 ...83 C7
Laws Cres SG19 ....40 C4
Lawson Ave PE7 ......187 D6
Laxton Ave CB3 ....81 A3
Laxton Cl PE19 ....74 C4
Laxton Grange PE28 .208 C5
Laxton Way CB4 ....84 C6
Layer Rd PE7 ....23 E7
Layston Pk SG8 ....5 D5
Layton Cres PE28 ....140 D2
Lea Brooks Cl PE28 ..164 F4
Lea Gdns PE3 ....197 F1
Lea Rd PE28 ....143 C1
Leach Cl PE13 ....245 C2
Leaden Hill SG8 ....28 D8
Leaden's La PE19 ....117 C3
Leader's Way CB8 ...110 E4
Leading Dro PE7 ......181 E4
Leaf Ave PE7 ....186 D3
Leafere Way **1** PE13 .238 B2
Leam The PE14 ......236 A4
Leather La CB9 ....23 E7
Lebanon Dr PE13 ....245 F7
Ledbury Rd PE3 ......197 C3
Ledger Cl PE27 ......144 A6
Ledham PE3 ....185 D4
Ledo Rd PE3 ....31 F2
Lee Cl Cottenham CB4 .125 D3
  Hanchet End CB9 ......38 F2
Lee Rd PE7 ....181 E4
Leechcroft PE4 ....121 C6
Lees La PE19 ....95 E5
Lees Way CB3 ....133 A1
Leete Pl SG8 ....5 C7
Leete Rd CB1 ....65 F5
Leete's La CB3 ....46 A8
Leeway Ave CB2 ....49 B5
Legg Rd **21** PE8 ......230 B1
Legge-bourke Ct
  PE13 ....245 F6
Legion Ct CB4 ....83 E7
Legion Way PE29 ....142 B1
Leicester Cl PE3 .....240 A3
Leighton PE2 ....186 C4
Leighton Prim Sch
  PE2 ....186 C4
Leinsters Cl PE13 ....197 D3
Leiston Ct PE6 ....232 A1
Leiston Rd CB7 ....212 D6
Lemur Dr CB1 ....66 B7
Lensfield Rd CB2 ....246 B1
Lenton Cl PE2 ....140 D2
Lents Way CB4 ....84 C5
Leofric Sq PE1 ....198 E3
Leonard Cl **2** CB5 .....84 E4
Leopold Wlk CB4 ....125 E3
Leverow Rd PE13 ....245 C2
Les Baux Pl **8** PE13 ..245 E3
Leslie Gn Rd PE28 ..143 B5
Lessingham PE2 ......185 D4
Lester Dr CB6 ....210 A6
Lester Piggott Way
  CB8 ....110 F6
Lethbridge Rd PE4 ..204 E2
Lettice Martin Croft
  CB2 ....32 D5
Levellers La PE19 ....74 F3
Leverington Comm
  PE13 ....235 B8
Leverington Prim Sch
  PE13 ....238 B2

Leverington Rd PE13 .245 A6
Leverington Rd Ind Est
  PE13 ....245 B7
Levers Wr PE29 ......141 C5
Levitt's Dro PE6 .....200 C4
Lewes Gdns PE4 .....204 C3
Lewis Cl
  Great & Little Abington
  CB1 ....34 C5
  March PE15 ....243 B3
Lewis Cres CB1 ....34 C5
Lexington Cl **3** CB4 ..83 C5
Ley Rd CB8 ....90 A1
Leyburn Cl CB1 ....66 A7
Leys Ave CB4 ....83 C5
Leys Rd Cambridge CB4 .83 F5
  St Neots PE19 ....74 E6
Leys Rectory PE19 ..117 F2
Leys Sch The CB2 ...246 B1
Leys Sports Ctr The
  CB2 ....64 E7
Leys The
  Alconbury PE28 ....150 F4
  Little Gransden SG19 .58 E3
  Peterborough PE1 ....197 A1
  Sawtry PE28 ....168 C3
Leys Wlk CB2 ....48 C4
Leyton Ave IP28 ......239 B6
Liberator Rd PE26 ...171 E3
Lichfield Ave PE4 ....204 B3
Lichfield Rd CB1 ......65 B6
Licking's Dro PE13 ..245 A2
Lidgate Cl PE2 ....186 C7
Lidgate Rd CB8 ....92 E7
Lilac Cl Haslingfield CB3 .47 B5
  Wisbech PE13 ....245 F7
Lilac Ct CB1 ....65 C5
Lilac End CB3 ....47 B4
Lilac Rd PE13 ....245 F7
Lilac Way PE27 ......144 B6
Lilley Cl CB4 ....84 B5
Lilyholt Rd PE15 .....222 A5
Lime Ave PE13 ....245 C7
Lime Cl Burwell CB5 .130 C1
  Mildenhall IP28 ....239 C5
Lime Gr March PE15 .243 C6
  Royston SG8 ....5 C8
  St Neots PE19 ....74 F6
Lime Kiln Cl PE3 .....197 E4
Lime Rd PE26 ....172 A8
Lime Tree Ave PE1 ..197 F4
Limekiln Cl SG8 ....5 E5
Limekiln Rd CB1 ......65 E3
Limes Ave **1** PE14 ..236 A5
Limes Cl
  Bassingbourn SG8 ....12 E5
  Littleport CB6 ....242 C4
Limes Ct PE27 ....143 F1
Limes Pk Rd PE27 ...143 F1
Limes Rd CB3 ....81 A3
Limes The
  Bassingbourn SG8 ....12 E5
  Castor PE5 ....195 F1
  Harston CB2 ....47 F2
  Sawston CB2 ....32 F8
  5 Wittering PE8 .....230 B1
Limestone Cl **7** CB7 .213 A5
Limetree Cl
  3 Cambridge CB1 ....65 D5
  Yaxley PE7 ....181 F7
Limlow Sch 4 B8
Linclare Pl **7** PE13 ....74 C4
Lincoln Ave PE27 ....143 F7
Lincoln Cl PE19 ......117 A5
Lincoln Rd
  Deeping Gate PE6 ....231 E7
  Mildenhall IP28 ......213 E8
  Peterborough PE4 ....197 C8
  Ramsey PE26 ....171 C1
  Stamford PE9 ....244 D7
  Wyton Airfield PE28 .143 A8
Linden Cl
  Cambridge CB4 ....83 C4
  Haddenham CB6 .....210 A5
Linden Dr PE16 ......241 C4
Linden End CB6 ......210 A5
Linden Gr PE29 ......141 F2
Linden Way CB6 .....210 A5
Lindens Cl PE13 .....234 A2
Lindeth Cl PE29 .....141 A7
Lindisfarne Cl **9** PE19 .74 F1
Lindisfarne Rd PE4 ..232 A1
Lindridge Wlk PE3 ..197 A2
Lindsay Cl SG8 ....13 C1
Lindsells Wlk PE3 ...241 C5
Lindsey Cl PE4 ....204 D1
Lindsey Rd
  Stamford PE9 ....244 C6
  9 Uffington PE9 ....230 C6
Ling Garth PE1 ......198 B8
Lingfield Rd CB8 ....5 E6
Lingholme Cl **2** CB4 .83 C5
Lingmoor PE29 ......141 A7
Lingrey Ct CB2 ....64 D2
Lingwood Pk PE2 ...197 A1
Link Dr PE28 ....140 C3
Link La CB6 ....216 E1
Link Rd
  Peterborough PE1 ....197 F3
  Sawston PE8 ....32 F8
Links The CB8 ....89 D8
Links Way PE27 .....143 F4
Linkside PE3 ....204 B1
Linley Rd St Neots PE19 .74 F3
  Whittlesey PE7 ......189 E6
Linlithgow Cl PE3 ....99 A3
Linnet PE2 ....185 D6

Linton CE Inf Sch CB1 ...35 C2
Linton Cl CB8 ....110 F5
Linton Hts Jun Sch
  CB1 ....35 D2
Linton Liby CB1 ....35 C2
Linton Pl CB9 ....24 B8
Linton Rd Balsham CB1 .52 F2
  Great Abington CB1 ..34 D6
  Hadstock CB1 ....20 B8
  Horseheath CB1 ......36 F3
Linton Village Coll CB1 .35 B2
Linton Zoological Gdns*
  CB1 ....35 B1
Linwood La PE15 ....223 A8
Lion Cl PE26 ....220 D3
Lion Ct CB6 ....210 A6
Lion Wlk PE26 ....172 A5
Lion Yd PE26 ....172 B6
Lion Yd Sh Ctr CB1 ..246 B2
Lionel Walden Prim Sch
  PE15 ....223 A5
Lions Cross PE29 ....119 A8
Lisburn Rd CB8 ......111 B3
Lisle Cl CB7 ....240 E5
Lisle La CB7 ....240 E4
Lisle Wlk CB1 ....66 A6
Lister Rd PE1 ....197 F7
Lister's Rd PE14 ....236 E1
Litchfield Cl PE7 ....181 F5
Litlington Rd SG8 ...11 E1
Little Back La The
  CB5 ....129 C1
Little Bowsers CB10 ..20 D3
Little Casterton Rd
  PE9 ....244 A6
Little Chilfords CB1 ..35 B4
Little Chishill Rd SG8 .1 C6
Little Church St **2**
  CB3 ....245 C5
Little Cl PE6 ....232 A1
Little Dowgate PE13 .245 A7
Little End Rd PE19 ...74 B1
Little End Rd Ind Est
  PE19 ....74 B1
Little Farthing Cl
  PE27 ....144 B4
Little Fen Dro
  Burwell CB5 ....129 C6
  Swaffham Prior CB5 .129 A1
Little Fendyke La
  PE14 ....236 E5
Little Gn Cheveley CB8 .91 C5
  Guilden Morden SG8 .11 A7
Little Gransden La
  SG19 ....58 D4
Little Hasse Dro CB7 .212 C6
Little Heath SG19 ...41 C4
Little How PE27 .....143 E6
Little Johns Cl PE3 ..196 F3
Little La Ely CB6 .....240 B4
Little London CB4 ...212 C5
Little London Dro CB7 .212 C5
Little London La PE7 .212 C5
Little Marefen Cl
  CB6 ....242 A7
Little Mdw CB3 ......102 B2
Little Moor PE28 ....121 C5
Little Northfields **3**
  PE29 ....230 D4
Little Paddocks CB10 .19 A4
Little Paxton La PE19 .95 F2
Little Paxton Prim Sch
  PE19 ....95 F1
Little Ramper PE13 ..245 B7
Little Setchel Dro CB4 .209 F2
Little St CB6 ....218 B6
Little St Mary's La
  CB2 ....246 A1
Little Thetford CE Prim Sch
  CB6 ....211 B7
Little Whyte PE26 ..172 B7
Little Wilbraham Rd
  CB1 ....86 D4
Littlechild Dr **5** PE13 .238 B2
Littlecotes Cl PE28 ..137 F7
Littlefield Cl
  Godmanchester PE29 .118 F8
  Wilburton CB6 ......210 C6
Littlemeer PE2 ......185 F4
Littleport Com Prim Sch
  CB6 ....242 B4
Littleport Sta CB6 ..242 E6
Littleworth Dro PE12 .233 F8
Littleworth End PE19 .118 A1
Livermore Gn PE4 ..204 A2
Loch Fyne Cl PE2 ..185 C4
Lock Lomond Way
  PE2 ....185 C4
Locks Cl PE6 ....206 B7
Locks La PE28 ....183 A8
Lockspit Hall Dro
  Cottenham CB4 ......125 F8
  Ottenham CB4 ....209 A5
Lode Ave Outwell PE14 .236 F1
  Waterbeach CB5 ....106 C6
Lode Cl PE14 ....212 B3
Lode La CB7 ....211 E1
Lode Rd Bottisham CB5 .86 D7
  Lode CB5 ....109 D1
Lode Way
  Chatteris PE16 ......241 C6
  Haddenham CB6 ....210 A6
Loder Ave PE1 ....196 F3
Lodes End Dro PE26 .220 F2
Lodge Cl PE29 ....141 C4

Lodge Gdns CB6 .....210 A6
Lodge Rd SG8 ....31 A1
Loftsteads **3** PE28 ..215 C1
Logan's Way CB4 .....84 A3
Loire Ct PE1 ....197 E4
Lomax Dr PE28 ......140 C3
Lombardy Dr PE1 ...198 B8
London La PE3 ....96 E4
London Rd Barley SG8 ..6 F1
  Chatteris PE16 ......241 C2
  Fenstanton PE28 ....120 E7
  Fowlmere SG8 ....15 D5
  Godmanchester PE29 .141 F1
  Great Chesterford CB10 .18 C2
  Harston CB2 ....49 B4
  Hemingford Grey PE27 .143 F1
  Kimbolton PE28 .....114 A4
  Peterborough PE7 ...186 F3
  Royston SG8 ....5 D4
  Sawston PE9 ....32 F5
  Stamford PE9 ....244 C2
  Whittlesey PE7 ......194 B2
  Yaxley PE7 ....181 C5
London St
  Godmanchester PE29 .141 F1
  Whittlesey PE7 ......189 D6
Lone Tree Ave CB4 ...83 C8
Lone Tree Gr CB4 ....83 C8
Long Cswy
  Peterborough PE1 ...198 A2
  Witcham CB6 ....217 C2
Long Dolver Dro CB7 .212 B6
Long Dro Bury PE26 .172 F5
  Cottenham CB4 ......125 F3
  Downham CB6 ....224 F3
  Elm PE14 ....235 B1
  Feltwell PE38 ....226 F6
  Haddenham CB6 ....210 A4
  Holme PE7 ....177 D5
  Over CB4 ....208 D3
  Parson Drove PE13 .234 B5
  Ramsey PE26 ....221 D2
  Somersham PE28 ...215 D2
  Waterbeach CB5 ....106 D8
  Whittlesey PE7 ......200 F3
Long Furlong CB4 ...208 C3
Long Holme Dro CB4 .208 E3
Long La Coveney CB6 .217 C4
  Fowlmere SG8 ....15 D8
  Gamlingay SG19 ......41 F6
  Hemingford Grey PE28 .120 C8
  Linton CB1 ....35 C1
  Over CB4 ....208 D3
  Spaldwick PE28 .....137 F5
  Willingham CB4 ....124 A8
Long Lots PE14 ......236 F8
Long Mdw Field PE13 .237 F2
Long Mdw Rd CB5 ..107 F2
Long N Fen Dro CB6 .212 C6
Long Nightlayer's Dro
  PE16 ....241 E8
Long Pasture PE4 ...204 B5
Long Rd Cambridge CB2 .64 E6
  Comberton CB23 .....81 D2
Long Rd Sixth Form Coll
  CB2 ....64 F3
Long Reach Rd CB4 ..84 C6
Longchamp Dr CB7 ..240 F6
Longfellow Ave **5** PE7 .74 D5
Longfield Gate PE2 ..186 A6
Longfield Rd CB6 ...242 B5
Longfields CB6 ......240 A3
Longhead La PE14 ..238 D3
Longhill Rd PE15 ...228 B6
Longholme Rd PE26 .171 A4
Longmere La CB7 ...212 A5
Longsands Com Coll
  PE19 ....75 A6
Longsands Par **3** PE19 .75 A6
Longsands Rd PE19 ..75 A5
Longstaff Way PE29 .142 A6
Longstanton Rd
  Oakington/Longstanton
  CB4 ....103 B6
  Over CB4 ....123 B7
Longthorpe Ct PE3 ..197 A2
Longthorpe Gn PE3 .197 B2
Longthorpe House Mews
  PE3 ....196 F2
Longthorpe Parkway
  PE3 ....197 A2
Longthorpe Prim Sch
  PE3 ....197 A2
Longueville Ct PE2 ..197 A1
Longview CB6 ....216 D1
Longwater PE2 ......186 B6
Longwood CB3 ....81 B8
Longworth Ave CB4 ...35 E2
Lonsdale CB1 ....35 E2
Lonsdale Terr PE13 .245 C3
Loop Rd PE28 ....146 A4
Loose La PE13 ....234 B7
Lord's Croft La CB9 ..24 A7
Lord's Gr CB5 ....128 C2
Lords La PE13 ....235 D6
Lord's La PE13 ......235 D6
Lordship Cl Orwell SG8 .45 E1
  Willingham CB4 .....209 A1
Lordship Dr SG8 .....14 C7
Lordship End PE2 ...233 E8
Loris Ct CB1 ....66 A7
Lorna Ct PE27 ....143 F6
Lornas Field PE7 ...186 D2
Losecoat Cl PE9 ....244 D7
Lotfield St SG8 ....45 E1
Lottings Way PE19 ...74 C6

Loughborough Univ of
Peterborough PE1 ....198 A3
Loughrigg Cl PE29 ....141 B7
Loughton Ct CB5 ....84 E4
Louthe Way PE28 ....168 C3
Love La Ashwell SG7 ....2 A5
Houghton & Wyton PE28 ...143 A5
Wisbech PE15 ....245 C4
Lovell Rd CB4 ....84 A7
Lovells The PE14 ....236 D6
Lovers La PE5 ....194 F2
Love's Cl CB4 ....104 C2
Love's Hill PE5 ....195 F1
Low Cl PE7 ....189 E8
Low Cross PE7 ....189 D8
Low Fen Dro Way CB5 ....85 B4
Low Gate PE13 ....237 F8
Low Harthay PE28 ....139 F4
Low Pk Cnr CB7 ....133 A6
Low Rd Burwell CB5 ....130 B2
Crowland PE6 ....207 F7
Fenstanton PE28 ....121 A7
Hemingford Grey PE27 ...144 A1
Little Stukeley PE28 .....151 D3
The Stukeleys PE28 ......140 C7
Wisbech PE14 ....245 E1
Low Side PE14 ....236 E2
Lowbury Cres CB4 ....103 B6
Lowburyholme Rd
CB4 ....208 C1
Lower Downs Slade
CB9 ....24 A8
Lower Dro CB4 ....211 D3
Lower End CB5 ....108 E5
Lower Gn CB11 ....1 F1
Lower Gower Rd SG8 ......5 D8
Lower King St SG8 ....5 D6
Lower Pk St CB5 ....246 A3
Lower Rd Croydon SG8 ....20 D1
Ely CB7 ....218 D1
Wicken CB7 ....211 E2
Lower St SG8 ....31 B1
Lower Wood Nature
Reserve* CB8 ....54 C6
Lower Yd CB8 ....132 A2
Lowerfield SG8 ....6 D5
Loweswater PE29 ....141 C5
Lowfields CB3 ....44 F8
Lowick Gdns PE3 ....197 C5
Lowndes Dro PE7 ....148 B7
Lowry Cl Haverhill CB9 ...38 D1
St Ives PE27 ....144 A7
Lowry Rd PE19 ....74 C6
Lowther Gdns PE4 ....204 D2
Lowther St CB8 ....110 F3
Loxley PE4 ....204 A4
Loxley Gn PE28 ....142 F5
Luard Cl CB2 ....65 A4
Luard Rd CB2 ....65 A4
Lucas Ct PE29 ....141 F7
Lucas La SG7 ....2 E4
Lucerne Cl
Cambridge CB1 ....66 A6
Red Lodge PE28 ....213 F1
Lucketts Cl CB4 ....104 B5
Luck's La PE19 ....117 A4
Lucombe Dr PE14 ....245 F7
Lucy Cavendish Coll
CB3 ....83 C3
Luddington Cl PE19 ....96 E4
Luddington Rd
Great Gidding PE28 ......166 C3
Peterborough PE4 ....204 D1
Ludlow La CB1 ....67 A5
Lug Fen Droveway
CB5 ....107 A5
Luke St PE19 ....74 E4
Lulworth Dr CB9 ....23 E8
Lumen Rd SG8 ....5 D7
Lumley Cl CB4 ....240 E8
Lundy Cl CB9 ....24 D7
Lutton Gate Rd PE12 .....234 A8
Lutton Gr PE3 ....197 C6
Lye Cl PE19 ....94 A6
Lyles Rd CB4 ....125 D4
Lymage Rd PE28 ....115 D3
Lyme Wlk PE3 ....197 C6
Lynch La SG8 ....15 E8
Lynchwood PE2 ....185 C5
Lyndale Rd CB1 ....185 C6
Lyndewode Rd CB1 ......246 C1
Lyndhurst Cl CB4 ....105 C2
Lynfield La CB4 ....84 A4
Lynn Rd Ely CB6 ....240 D6
Littleport CB6 ....242 F6
Wisbech PE13 ....245 C6
Lynton Cl CB6 ....240 D6
Lynton Dr CB6 ....240 D6
Lynton Rd PE11 ....197 F6
Lynton Way CB2 ....33 A8
Lynx The CB1 .... 66 A7
Lyons Ct PE16 ....241 C4
Lyon's Dro PE15 ....223 F4
Lysander Cl PE27 ....143 F7
Lythemere PE2 ....186 C4
Lyvelly Gdns PE1 ....198 E6

M

Macaulay Ave CB2 ....49 B6
MacBeth Cl PE29 ....141 F6
Mace Rd PE2 ....187 D5
MacFarlane Cl CB4 ....104 C2
MacKenzie Rd [5] CB1 .....84 A1
MacKerel Hall SG8 ....5 B6
MacPherson Robertson Way
IP28 ....239 A5

Maddingley Way CB6 .....210 A7
Madecroft PE28 ....165 A5
Madeley Ct PE28 ....143 C2
Madingley Hall* CB3 .....81 E5
Madingley Rd
Cambridge CB3 ....83 B3
Dry Drayton CB3 ....102 B1
Madingley Sch CB3 ....81 F5
Madingley Wood CB3 .....82 A4
Madras Rd CB1 ....65 C7
Maffit Rd PE5 ....195 D3
Magazine Cl PE13 ....245 A4
Magazine La PE13 ....245 A4
Magdalene Cl CB4 ....123 F2
Magdalene Coll CB4 .....246 A4
Magdalene St CB2 ....246 A3
Magee Rd PE4 ....204 C1
Magistrates Rd PE7 .....181 D8
Magna Cl CB1 ....34 C6
Magnolia Ave CB4 ....197 A2
Magnolia Cl
Cambridge CB1 ....65 B5
[2] Maldon La PE20 ......213 F1
Magrath Ave CB4 ....246 A4
Maida La PE9 ....244 C5
Maid's Cswy CB5 ....246 C3
Mailes Cl CB3 ....63 B4
Main Dro CB6 ....225 A2
Main Rd Etton PE6 ......203 B8
Little Gransden SG19 .....58 D3
Parson Drove PE13 ......234 E7
Uffington PE9 ....230 D6
Upwell PE14 ....229 F7
Wisbech PE14 ....236 A3
Main St Ailsworth PE5 ...195 D2
Barnack PE9 ....230 D3
Bythorn & Keyston PE28 ..114 F6
Caldecote CB3 ....61 B6
Castor PE5 ....195 D3
Coveney CB6 ....217 B5
Dunton CB6 ....217 D8
Ely CB7 ....217 A3
Farcet PE7 ....187 C2
Great Gidding PE28 ......166 D3
Hardwick CB3 ....81 A1
Hatley SG19 ....43 A3
Huntingdon PE29 ....142 A6
Little Downham CB6 .....218 A6
Littleport CB6 ....218 D8
Old Weston PE28 ....147 F7
Shudy Camps CB1 ....21 F6
Southorpe PE9 ....230 E1
Stow cum Quy CB5 ....85 F5
Thetford PE28 ....211 B7
Ufford PE9 ....230 F3
Welney PE14 ....225 A8
Wentworth CB6 ....217 B1
Witchford CB6 ....217 E1
Yarwell PE8 ....183 A8
Yaxley PE7 ....181 E5
Maio Rd CB4 ....83 F5
Maitland Ave CB4 ....84 B6
Malborne Way PE4 ......186 B4
Malcolm St CB1 ....246 B3
Malcolm Way CB8 ....111 B5
Malden Cl CB5 ....85 D4
Malden Way PE19 ....74 D2
Maldon Rd PE13 ....245 E5
Malecoff PE29 ....118 F7
Males Ct CB4 ....125 C5
Malin Cl CB4 ....24 D7
Mallard Cl
Chatteris PE16 ....241 C5
Whittlesey PE7 ....189 F8
Mallard Ct PE9 ....244 B4
Mallard La PE19 ....75 A4
Mallard Rd
Peterborough PE3 ......204 A1
Royston SG8 ....5 C6
Mallard Rise CB6 ....210 A6
Mallard Way PE15 ....243 F5
Mallards The
Peakirk PE6 ....206 B1
St Ives PE27 ....143 F7
Mallett Cl PE15 ....243 F4
Malletts Rd CB1 ....66 A5
Mallory La [11] PE19 .....244 B5
Mallory Rd PE1 ....198 C2
Mallow Cl PE14 ....175 D8
Mallow Wlk
Haverhill CB9 ....23 C8
[1] Royston SG8 ....5 E5
Mallows Cl [2] CB3 ......62 D6
Malory Pl CB3 ....99 A3
Malt Dr CB3 ....245 B3
Malta Rd CB1 ....63 B7
Maltby Cl [7] PE8 ....230 B1
Malthouse Cl PE29 ......141 D4
Malthouse La PE26 ......171 F5
Malthouse Way CB2 ......29 F8
Malting End CB8 ....72 D4
Malting La
Cambridge CB3 ....64 C8
Ellington PE28 ....139 A4
Eynesbury PE19 ....74 C5
Isleham CB7 ....213 A5
Lillington SG8 ....12 A2
Malting The PE26 ....171 F5
Maltings Cl
Moulton CB8 ....112 E5
Royston SG8 ....5 C7
Maltings La SG8 ....7 D2
Maltings Pl SG19 ....41 D5
Maltings The
Alconbury PE28 ....150 E5
Cambourne CB3 ....80 B2
Eaton Socon PE19 ....74 C5
Gamlingay SG19 ....41 D6

Maltings The continued
St Martin's Without PE9 ..244 C2
Sawtry PE28 ....168 B4
[3] Thorney PE6 ....233 A3
Maltmas Dro PE14 ......235 F2
Malton La SG8 ....29 B4
Malton Rd SG8 ....45 F1
Malvern Cl CB8 ....111 B2
Malus Cl PE7 ....186 C3
Malvern Rd
Cambridge CB1 ....65 C6
Peterborough PE4 ......204 C2
Manasty Rd PE2 ....185 D2
Mancetter Sq PE4 ......204 B1
Manchester Rd PE28 ...117 D8
Manchester Way
PE27 ....144 A8
Mandene Gdns SG19 .....58 E4
Mander Way CB1 ....65 C5
Manderston Rd CB8 .....110 E4
Mandeville
Burwell CB5 ....109 B8
Peterborough PE2 ......185 F4
Mandrill Cl CB1 ....66 A7
Manea Com Prim Sch
PE15 ....224 C4
Manea Rd PE15 ....223 D6
Manea Sta PE15 ....224 B6
Maners Way CB1 ....65 C4
Mangers La CB22 ....32 D1
Manhattan Dr CB4 ......246 C4
Manners Ct CB4 ....64 E8
Manor Ave PE2 ....187 B7
Manor Cl
Brampton PE28 ....140 E2
Buckden PE19 ....117 A3
Graveley PE19 ....98 A5
[2] Great Staughton PE19 ..93 F6
Harston CB2 ....29 A2
Little Paxton PE19 ....95 F2
Little Wilbraham CB1 .....86 D1
Ramsey Forty Foot PE26 ..221 A3
St Ives PE28 ....142 F5
[18] Somersham PE28 ...215 C1
Witchford CB6 ....217 E1
[1] Wittering PE8 ....230 B1
Yaxley PE7 ....181 D5
Manor Com Coll CB4 ......83 F6
Manor Cres CB3 ....81 A1
Manor Ct CB3 ....64 B8
Manor Ct Rd CB6 ....217 E1
Manor Dr
Fenstanton PE28 ....121 B6
Peterborough PE6 ......205 A3
Sawtry PE28 ....168 C4
Manor East [5] PE15 ....223 A5
Manor Farm Cl
Haverhill CB9 ....24 B7
Oakington & Westwick
CB24 ....103 C6
Manor Farm Ct PE28 ....115 D2
Manor Farm La PE5 .....195 E2
Manor Farm Rd
Beck Row, Holywell
Row & Kenny Hill PE28 ..213 D7
Girton CB3 ....103 E2
St Neots PE19 ....75 A5
Waresley SG19 ....57 E2
Manor Gdns
Buckden PE19 ....117 A4
Peterborough PE2 ......187 C7
Wisbech PE13 ....245 C5
Manor Gr PE19 ....75 A5
Manor House Cl [1] PE19 ..74 C2
Manor House St PE1 ....198 A3
Manor La
Alconbury PE28 ....150 F5
Boxworth CB3 ....101 C6
Great Chesterford CB10 ...91 E7
Great Gransden SG19 .....58 D4
Manor Leisure Ctr
PE7 ....189 E6
Manor Pk CB4 ....104 A4
Manor Pl CB4 ....246 B3
Manor Rd
Folksworth PE7 ....180 D1
Gamlingay SG19 ....57 D6
[8] Haverhill CB9 ....24 B7
Hemingford Grey PE28 ..143 B1
Little Shelford CB2 ....48 E4
Meldreth SG8 ....29 A1
Mildenhall IP28 ....239 B4
Sutton PE5 ....194 F2
Whittlesey PE7 ....189 D2
Witchford CB6 ....217 E2
Manor St
Cambridge CB1 ....246 B3
Wistow PE28 ....164 A7
Manor View
Barton Mills IP28 ....239 D2
Whittlesey PE7 ....189 D6
Manor Way
Hail Weston PE19 ....95 A1
Market Deeping PE6 ....231 F8
Manor Wlk CB4 ....84 A6
Manor Dr CB4 ....125 C3
Mansel Ct CB4 ....83 E6
Mansel Way CB4 ....83 E6
Mansell Rd CB13 ....245 D3
Mansfield Cl CB4 ....105 C2
Mansfield Rd CB1 ......185 C6
Manton PE3 ....197 F4
Maple Ave Sawston CB2 ..32 F5
Wisbech PE13 ....245 C7
Maple Cl
Bluntisham/Colne PE28 ..208 C6
Bottisham CB5 ....86 F5

Maple Cl continued
[4] Bourn CB3 ....79 C3
Cambridge CB4 ....83 F5
Linton CB1 ....35 B3
Sawtry PE28 ....168 A3
Maple Ct
Gamlingay SG19 ....41 C5
Yaxley PE7 ....181 F6
Maple Dr
Huntingdon PE29 ....141 E8
Little Stukeley PE28 .....151 E3
Stilton PE7 ....176 A7
Maple End PE28 ....150 F4
Maple Gr March PE15 ...243 C5
Peterborough PE2 ......198 C7
Maple Gr Inf Sch
PE15 ....243 C5
Maple Rd March PE15 ...243 D5
Maple Way
Melbourn SG8 ....14 C5
Royston SG8 ....5 E8
Maple Wlk PE7 ....186 C2
Maples The
Fulbourn CB1 ....66 E5
Peterborough PE1 ......198 F5
March & District Mus*
PE15 ....243 D4
March La CB1 ....65 F8
March Rd
Coates/Eastrea PE7 ....191 A8
Elm PE13 ....227 F8
Coldham PE14 ....235 F2
Guyhirn PE13 ....235 A6
Welney PE14 ....229 F1
Whittlesey PE7 ....191 D7
Wimblington PE15 ......223 B7
March Riverside PE14 ...229 C8
March Sta PE15 ....243 D6
March Trad Est PE15 ....243 B7
Marchioness Way [8]
PE19 ....74 B4
March's Cl CB1 ....66 E5
Marconi Dr PE7 ....181 D6
Marcus Cl CB9 ....24 D7
Mardale Gdns PE4 ......204 F2
Mare Fen Nature Reserve*
CB4 ....122 F8
Marefen Dro CB6 ....225 C3
Marfleet Cl CB2 ....48 F7
Margett St CB4 ....125 E4
Margholm Rd PE13 ......143 D1
Marholm Rd
Castor PE6 ....196 B3
Peterborough PE6 ......204 B1
Ufford PE9 ....231 A2
Marian Way PE16 ....241 C2
Marigold Dr PE28 ....133 F8
Marina Dr PE15 ....243 A5
Mariner's Way CB4 ......84 A3
Marion Cl CB3 ....83 B4
Maris Gn CB2 ....49 A6
Maris La CB2 ....64 C2
Markby Cl CB2 ....17 D8
Market Hill
Cambridge CB2 ....246 A2
Chatteris PE16 ....241 C5
Haverhill CB9 ....24 A8
[2] Huntingdon PE29 ....141 D4
Royston SG8 ....5 D6
St Ives PE27 ....144 A3
Market La Linton CB1 ....35 B2
St Neots PE19 ....144 A3
Market Pas CB2 ....246 B2
Market Pl [5] Ely CB7 ...240 B4
Little London PE15 ......243 D4
Mildenhall IP28 ....239 C4
St Neots PE19 ....74 E5
Whittlesey PE7 ....189 E7
Wisbech PE13 ....245 C5
Market Rd PE7 ....144 B3
Market Sq
Cambridge CB2 ....246 A2
[8] Ely CB7 ....240 B4
St Neots PE19 ....74 E5
Market St
Cambridge CB2 ....246 A2
Ely CB7 ....240 D4
Fordham CB7 ....206 A4
Mildenhall IP28 ....239 C4
[2] Newmarket CB8 .....111 A3
[2] Soham CB7 ....212 B4
Swavesey CB4 ....122 E6
Whittlesey PE7 ....189 D7
Wisbech PE13 ....245 C5
Market Way CB4 ....217 A2
Markfield Rise CB6 ......84 A7
Markham Cl CB4 ....84 A7
Markham Ret Pk PE7 ...244 D7
Markhams Cl [3] CB9 .....38 E1
Mark's Way CB1 ....103 E1
Marlborough Cl
St Ives PE27 ....143 F7
Yaxley PE7 ....181 E5
Marlborough Ct
[1] Haverhill CB9 ....23 E7
Wisbech PE13 ....245 A4
Marley Rd PE27 ....143 F8
Marlowe Ct [2] PE19 ....74 D6
Marlowe Gr PE4 ....197 F8
Marlowe Rd CB3 ....64 C7
Marmora Rd CB4 ....84 D8
Marne Ave CB4 ....204 C1
Marne Rd PE7 ....189 F5
Marquis Cl [4] PE19 .....74 B4
Marriott Ct PE1 ....198 E5
Marriott Dr CB6 ....240 C4

Lou – Mea 263
Marriott's Dro PE26 ....221 A4
Marriotts Cl PE26 ......221 A4
Marritt Cl PE16 ....241 B6
Marroway La [4] CB6 ...217 D1
Marsh Cl PE15 ....243 F6
Marsh La CB28 ....143 D1
Marsh Rd Outwell PE14 ..236 F4
Walpole PE14 ....238 F8
Marsh The PE14 ....238 F8
Marsh Wlk [5] PE13 ....245 D5
Marshall Rd CB1 ....65 A5
Marshall's Bank PE13 ...234 D8
Marshall's Cl CB1 ......85 A1
Marshall's Ct CB14 .....218 B6
Marshall's Way [7] PE2 ..187 C2
Marsham PE2 ....185 F3
Marshfields Sch PE1 ....198 D7
Marshland High Sch
PE14 ....238 E4
Marston Rd PE19 ....75 A3
Martin Ave PE15 ....243 A7
Martin Cl
Godmanchester PE29 ...119 A8
Mildenhall IP28 ....239 D3
Soham CB7 ....212 A5
Martin Ct
Peterborough PE4 ......204 C4
Whittlesey PE7 ....189 F7
Martin Rd CB5 ....130 B3
Martin's La CB6 ....218 A6
Martindale Way CB2 .....32 E8
Martingale Cl [3] CB4 ....83 C6
Martingale Rd [4] SG8 ....5 E6
Martins La Linton CB1 ...35 E2
Witcham CB6 ....217 A3
Martins Mews CB9 ......38 C1
Martins Way PE2 ....185 F5
Martinsbridge PE1 ......198 F8
Marwick Rd PE15 ....243 D7
Mary Armyne Rd PE2 ...186 B5
Mary Walsham Cl PE2 ...187 E5
Maryland Ave
Huntingdon PE2 ....141 F8
Swaffham Bulbeck CB5 ..108 B2
Marylebone Rd PE15 ...243 C4
Masefield Ave PE19 ......74 C6
Masefield Way SG8 ......13 D1
Maskew Ave PE1 ....197 E6
Mason Gdns IP28 ......213 D6
Mason Rd CB5 ....130 B5
Master Dike PE7 ....237 D8
Masterton Cl PE9 ......244 D7
Masterton Rd PE9 ......244 C7
Matilda Way PE2 ....185 C5
Matley Prim Sch PE2 ...185 E5
Matt Dawson Cl CB8 ...110 F6
Matthew Parker Cl
CB4 ....105 D7
Matthew Wren Cl CB6 ..218 A6
Matthews La CB6 ....55 F6
Maule Cl
Huntingdon PE29 ....141 E6
St Neots PE19 ....74 E1
Maurice Cl CB2 ....113 F5
Mawson Cl CB6 ....240 B3
Mawson Rd CB1 ....246 C1
Maxey Rd Helpston PE6 ..231 C5
Northborough PE6 ......231 D7
Maxey View [10] PE6 ...231 E8
Maxham's Gn Rd PE6 ...205 B6
Maxwell Rd PE2 ....186 D6
May St SG8 ....7 E2
Mayfair Gdns PE13 .....235 C7
Mayfield PE19 ....117 A3
Mayfield Cl [2] CB6 .....240 B5
Mayfield Cres PE29 .....141 F6
Mayfield Prim Sch CB4 ..83 C5
Mayfield Rd
Coates/Eastrea PE7 ....190 F7
Girton CB3 ....82 F8
Huntingdon PE29 ....141 F6
Peterborough PE1 ......198 A6
Mayflower Rd [1] PE13 ..245 E3
Mayfly Cl PE16 ....241 B3
Maynards CB2 ....32 C5
Mayne's Dike PE12 .....237 F8
Mayor's Wlk PE3 ....197 E3
Mayors Cl PE15 ....243 D7
Maypole Croft CB1 ......37 C8
Maypole La CB8 ....90 E3
May's Ave CB1 ....53 A2
May's La PE13 ....238 A2
May's Way CB4 ....84 C5
Maysfield Dr [8] PE13 ...243 B4
Maytrees PE2 ....143 F1
Maze Rd PE26 ....120 C1
McCalmont Way CB8 ...111 E2
Mead Cl PE3 ....204 B1
Mead The PE4 ....204 B1
Mead View CB4 ....103 B5
Meadenvale PE1 ....198 F5
Meadlands Main Dro
CB6 ....215 F1
Meadow Bsns Ctr The
PE27 ....144 B2
Meadow Cl
Chatteris PE16 ....241 C3
Little Paxton PE19 ......95 F2
St Ives PE27 ....144 A4
Soham CB7 ....212 B3
Stilton PE7 ....175 F8
Witchford CB6 ....217 E2
Meadow Ct CB6 ....242 B5
Meadow Dr PE15 ....243 F3
Meadow Drift CB3 ......100 B5

Meadow Dro PE28 ... 208 E6
Meadow Farm Cl CB4 ... 103 D6
Meadow Gr PE1 ... 205 B1
Meadow How PE27 ... 143 F6
Meadow La
Earith PE28 ... 208 E6
Hemingford Abbots PE28 ... 142 F3
Hemingford Grey PE28 ... 143 D3
Houghton & Wyton PE28 ... 143 B4
Linton CB1 ... 35 B2
Newmarket CB8 ... 111 D1
Offord Darcy PE19 ... 117 F2
Over CB4 ... 208 D1
Ramsey PE26 ... 172 B4
St Ives PE27 ... 144 C3
Thornhaugh PE8 ... 193 F5
Meadow Prim Sch The CB1 ... 53 B2
Meadow Rd
Great Chesterford CB10 ... 18 D3
Great Gransden SG19 ... 58 B5
Newborough PE6 ... 204 D8
Peakirk PE6 ... 206 C1
Ramsey PE26 ... 171 B1
Willingham CB4 ... 209 B1
Meadow Rise CB3 ... 60 C6
Meadow View PE19 ... 77 E4
Meadow Way
Doddington/Wimblington PE15 ... 223 B7
Earith PE28 ... 208 E6
Godmanchester PE29 ... 142 A2
Great Paxton PE19 ... 96 E4
Harston CB2 ... 48 A3
Mepal CB6 ... 216 E3
Warboys PE28 ... 164 F5
Meadow Way S 7 PE15 ... 223 B7
Meadow Wlk CB1 ... 34 C6
Meadowbrook CB6 ... 209 E4
Meadowcroft CB6 ... 210 F5
Meadowcroft Way SG8 ... 28 E8
Meadowfield Rd CB2 ... 32 E6
Meadowgate PE9 ... 230 F5
Meadowgate La PE14 ... 245 E2
Meadowgate Sch PE13 ... 245 E3
Meadowground PE28 ... 116 A7
Meadowlands
Burwell CB5 ... 130 B1
March PE15 ... 243 A6
Meadowlands Rd CB5 ... 84 E3
Meadows Cl 5 PE19 ... 74 F5
Meadows The
Haslingfield CB3 ... 47 B5
Worlington IP28 ... 213 F4
Meadowsweet PE19 ... 74 B6
Meadowsweet Cl
2 Cambourne CB3 ... 79 A4
Haverhill CB9 ... 38 E1
Meals Gate PE4 ... 204 F2
Medallion Ct 1 PE19 ... 74 F5
Medbourne Gdns PE1 ... 198 C8
Medcalfe Way SG8 ... 14 D6
Medeswell PE2 ... 186 C4
Medieval Village of Clopton (site of)* SG8 ... 26 E6
Medieval Village of Croydon (site of)* SG8 ... 27 B8
Medieval Village of Great Childerley (site of)* CB3 ... 80 D8
Medieval Village of Landbeach (site of)* CB4 ... 105 C7
Medieval Village of Papley (site of)* PE8 ... 174 B7
Medieval Village of Sawtry (site of)* PE28 ... 169 B2
Medieval Village of Sibberton (site of)* PE8 ... 193 E5
Medieval Village of Wintringham* PE19 ... 75 F4
Medland Gr 6 PE19 ... 75 A5
Medway Cl PE13 ... 245 E4
Medway Rd PE29 ... 141 E7
Medway The CB6 ... 240 D6
Medworth PE2 ... 185 F3
Meeting La
Litlington SG8 ... 12 A2
Melbourn SG8 ... 14 C6
Meeting Wlk CB9 ... 24 B8
Megans Way 4 PE16 ... 241 C5
Meggan Gate PE3 ... 197 A1
Megg's Dro PE26 ... 221 D2
Megs Cl PE28 ... 208 D5
Melbourn Bury SG8 ... 14 B5
Melbourn Prim Sch SG8 ... 14 C6
Melbourn Rd SG8 ... 5 D7
Melbourn Science Pk SG8 ... 14 D7
Melbourn St SG8 ... 5 D6
Melbourn Village Coll SG8 ... 14 C7
Melbourne Ave PE15 ... 243 B7
Melbourne Dr IP28 ... 239 B5
Melbourne Pl CB1 ... 246 C2
Melbourne Rd PE9 ... 244 D6
Meldon Pl CB6 ... 240 D5
Meldreth Manor Sch & Orch House SG8 ... 29 A1
Meldreth Rd
Shepreth SG8 ... 29 D4
Whaddon SG8 ... 28 C1
Meldreth Sta SG8 ... 14 B7
Meldrith Prim Sch SG8 ... 14 B8
Melford Cl Burwell CB5 ... 130 C2
Peterborough PE3 ... 197 A2
Mellis Cl CB9 ... 38 B1
Mellows Cl PE1 ... 198 C3
Melrose Dr PE2 ... 187 A7
Melrose Gdns CB8 ... 110 E4
Melton Cl 1 CB8 ... 111 B2
Melvin Way CB4 ... 104 A4
Memorial Ct CB3 ... 83 C1
Mendip Gr PE4 ... 204 E2
Mepal & Witchem CE Prim Sch CB6 ... 216 D3
Mepal Long Highway CB6 ... 216 C4
Mepal Outdoor Ctr PE16 ... 216 C6
Mepal Rd CB6 ... 216 E2
Mepal Short Highway CB6 ... 216 C5
Mercers Row CB5 ... 84 B4
Mercian Ct PE2 ... 187 D7
Mere Cl PE26 ... 221 A4
Mere Dro Ramsey PE26 ... 221 D4
Yaxley PE7 ... 181 F4
Mere Mill Dro CB6 ... 210 F4
Mere Side CB7 ... 212 A4
Mere Side Dro PE26 ... 221 B4
Mere View PE7 ... 182 A5
Mere View Ind Est PE7 ... 182 A6
Mere Way
Cambridge CB4 ... 83 E6
Hemingford Grey PE28 ... 120 B5
Houghton & Wyton PE28 ... 143 A6
Merelade Gr PE4 ... 204 B5
Meridian Cl 22 PE28 ... 215 C1
Meridian Prim Sch CB3 ... 62 C5
Meridian Sch SG8 ... 5 E7
Meriton PE2 ... 185 F3
Merle Way CB3 ... 79 A4
Merlin Cl
Huntingdon PE29 ... 142 B7
St Neots PE19 ... 75 B7
Merlin Dr 4 CB6 ... 240 B5
Merritt St PE29 ... 141 C5
Merton Grange SG19 ... 41 F5
Merton Rd CB4 ... 104 B3
Merton St CB3 ... 64 C7
Mertoun Paddocks CB8 ... 90 A8
Metcalfe Rd CB4 ... 83 D5
Metcalfe Way CB6 ... 210 A5
Metro Ctr The PE2 ... 186 D6
Mewburn PE3 ... 204 A1
Mews Cl PE26 ... 172 B7
Meynell Gdns CB8 ... 111 A5
Meynell Wlk PE3 ... 197 B3
Michael's Cl CB3 ... 103 E1
Mickle Gate PE3 ... 197 A1
Mickle Hill PE28 ... 135 D7
Mid Career Coll CB1 ... 67 B4
Mid Fetter PE26 ... 221 B3
Middle Broad Dro PE13 ... 237 D5
Middle Cl 5 CB6 ... 210 F5
Middle Drift SG8 ... 5 C6
Middle Dro
Newton PE13 ... 237 E3
Ramsey PE26 ... 171 A7
Soham CB7 ... 211 F3
Wimblington PE15 ... 223 C5
Middle Pasture PE4 ... 204 B5
Middle Rd
Crowland PE6 ... 207 E7
March PE15 ... 227 E4
Newborough PE6 ... 205 C7
Middle St Elton PE8 ... 178 D8
Farcet PE7 ... 187 C2
Great Gransden SG19 ... 58 E4
Litlington SG8 ... 12 A2
Thriplow SG8 ... 31 B1
Middle Watch CB4 ... 122 E5
Middle Way CB2 ... 50 A1
Middlefield PE7 ... 186 D3
Middlefield Com Prim Sch PE19 ... 74 F2
Middlefield Rd PE28 ... 168 B3
Middleham Cl PE7 ... 187 F5
Middlemiss View PE29 ... 118 F8
Middlemoor Rd
Ramsey PE26 ... 220 D3
Whittlesford CB2 ... 32 A5
Middleton PE3 ... 197 A4
Middleton Prim Sch PE3 ... 197 A4
Middleton Way CB4 ... 121 E4
Middletons Rd PE7 ... 181 E5
Midfield CB4 ... 103 D4
Midgate PE1 ... 198 A2
Midhurst Cl CB4 ... 84 A5
Midland Rd PE3 ... 197 E3
Midloe Grange PE19 ... 95 A6
Mikanda Cl PE14 ... 245 C2
Milburn Dro CB8 ... 112 E5
Mildenhall Airfield IP28 ... 239 B8
Mildenhall Coll of Tecnology IP28 ... 239 E4
Mildenhall Ind Est IP28 ... 239 B6
Mildenhall Mus* IP28 ... 239 C4
Mildenhall Pl CB9 ... 24 B8
Mildenhall Rd
Barton Mills IP28 ... 239 C2
Mildenhall Rd *continued*
Beck Row, Holywell Row & Kenny Hill IP28 ... 239 C8
Ely CB7 ... 219 E8
Fordham IP28 ... 213 A2
Freckenham IP28 ... 213 D3
Icklingham IP28 ... 214 E4
Littleport CB7 ... 242 F6
Mildenhall Swimming Pool IP28 ... 239 C4
Mildmay Rd PE4 ... 197 D8
Mile Dro Glinton PE6 ... 231 F5
Yaxley PE7 ... 182 B5
Mile End Rd CB7 ... 219 C6
Mile Rd CB2 ... 50 C4
Mile Tree La PE13 ... 235 E7
Miles Hawk Way IP28 ... 239 A5
Milford St CB1 ... 84 A1
Military Rd CB7 ... 212 C2
Militia Way CB7 ... 240 C4
Milk and Wr Dro PE7 ... 188 A4
Milk and Wr Dro Ramsey Rd PE7 ... 188 A2
Milking Hills Dro CB4 ... 209 B2
Milking Nook Rd PE6 ... 206 E1
Milking Slade Rd PE28 ... 167 A4
Mill Cl Burwell CB5 ... 130 B1
Exning CB8 ... 110 B8
Hemingford Grey PE28 ... 143 D2
Huntingdon PE29 ... 142 A6
Murrow PE13 ... 234 D5
The Stukeleys PE28 ... 151 D3
Wisbech PE13 ... 245 C6
Mill Cnr CB7 ... 212 A4
Mill Comm PE29 ... 141 C3
Mill Cres PE2 ... 185 E4
Mill Croft CB7 ... 212 B3
Mill Cswy SG8 ... 8 C5
Mill Ct CB2 ... 49 A5
Mill Dro Crowland PE6 ... 207 F7
Lode CB5 ... 128 A1
Ramsey PE26 ... 221 A2
Soham CB7 ... 212 A3
Southery PE38 ... 226 E8
Mill End SG19 ... 25 A4
Mill End Cl CB1 ... 65 F5
Mill End Rd CB1 ... 65 E6
Mill Field 3 CB6 ... 216 E2
Mill Field Cl PE6 ... 231 C4
Mill Gn PE28 ... 165 A5
Mill Hill Conington PE7 ... 177 C1
Downham CB6 ... 217 F7
Glatton PE28 ... 175 E1
Haverhill CB9 ... 23 F7
Newmarket CB8 ... 111 A4
Royston SG8 ... 5 E4
Swaffham Prior CB5 ... 108 E5
Weston Colville CB1 ... 54 C6
Mill Hill End PE28 ... 120 B1
Mill Hill Rd 7 PE19 ... 74 D5
Mill Hole CB2 ... 33 E8
Mill La Arrington SG8 ... 44 C3
Barrington CB2 ... 29 E8
Bassingbourn SG8 ... 12 D5
Bluntisham/Colne PE28 ... 208 D5
Burwell CB5 ... 130 B1
Cambridge CB2 ... 246 A2
Castor PE5 ... 184 F7
Duxford CB2 ... 32 E1
Exning CB8 ... 110 B8
Fordham CB7 ... 212 F1
Gorefield PE13 ... 235 B8
Hauxton CB2 ... 48 A6
Hemingford Grey PE28 ... 143 D3
Hinxton CB10 ... 18 A7
Histon CB4 ... 104 D6
Ickleton CB10 ... 18 B4
Impington CB4 ... 104 D5
Linton CB1 ... 35 C2
Little Paxton PE19 ... 95 E1
Newton PE13 ... 237 F5
Peterborough PE7 ... 185 A5
Potton SG19 ... 40 D1
Ramsey PE26 ... 172 B8
St Neots PE19 ... 74 F8
Sawston CB2 ... 32 E7
Shingay cum Wendy SG8 ... 27 B4
Stetchworth CB8 ... 89 F1
Swaffham Bulbeck CB5 ... 108 B3
Tallington PE9 ... 230 F7
Toft CB3 ... 61 D5
Water Newton PE8 ... 184 C7
West Walton PE14 ... 238 F4
Whittlesford CB2 ... 32 D5
Mill Pit Furlong CB6 ... 242 D3
Mill Rd Alconbury PE28 ... 150 E4
Ashley CB8 ... 91 F8
Buckden PE19 ... 117 C3
Cambridge CB1 ... 246 C2
Emneth PE14 ... 236 D6
Fen Drayton CB4 ... 121 D5
Glatton PE28 ... 175 E1
Great Gidding PE28 ... 166 E3
Great Wilbraham CB1 ... 67 F7
Harston CB2 ... 47 D2
Haverhill CB9 ... 24 A7
Histon CB4 ... 104 B1
Huntingdon PE29 ... 142 A6
Kirtling CB8 ... 72 E5
Little Gransden SG19 ... 58 E4
Little Stukeley PE28 ... 151 D4
Little Wilbraham CB1 ... 86 D1
Lode CB5 ... 107 C2
Maxey PE6 ... 231 C7
Nassington PE8 ... 183 A7
Oakington/Longstanton CB4 ... 103 D6
Mill Rd *continued*
Royston SG8 ... 5 D7
Stilton PE7 ... 175 F8
Walpole PE14 ... 238 F6
Waterbeach CB5 ... 106 A7
West Walton PE14 ... 238 D4
West Wickham CB1 ... 36 E8
West Wratting CB1 ... 53 F2
Whittlesey PE7 ... 189 E6
Wisbech St Mary PE13 ... 234 C5
Wistow PE28 ... 163 F6
Mill Reef Cl CB8 ... 110 D7
Mill St Ashwell SG7 ... 2 D4
Cambridge CB1 ... 246 C1
Gamlingay SG19 ... 41 D5
Isleham CB7 ... 213 A5
Mildenhall IP28 ... 239 B3
St Ives PE28 ... 143 A5
Mill View March PE15 ... 243 D4
Peterborough PE7 ... 185 A5
Sawtry PE28 ... 168 A4
Mill View Ct PE19 ... 74 C2
Mill Way
Grantchester CB3 ... 64 A3
Holywell-cum-Needingworth PE27 ... 144 F3
Stretham CB6 ... 210 E6
Swavesey CB4 ... 122 C6
Wisbech PE14 ... 236 A4
Mill Yd PE29 ... 141 E2
Millards La CB5 ... 107 D2
Millbank CB8 ... 110 F4
Miller Cl
2 Doddington/Wimblington PE15 ... 222 F5
Godmanchester PE29 ... 118 F8
Offord Cluny PE19 ... 118 A2
Miller Way
Brampton PE28 ... 140 C3
Cambourne CB3 ... 79 B3
Miller's Rd CB3 ... 61 D5
Miller's Way PE28 ... 173 C3
Millers Cl CB1 ... 35 D3
Millfield Littleport CB6 ... 242 C3
Upwell PE14 ... 236 E2
Willingham CB4 ... 124 A8
Millfield Cl PE16 ... 241 B2
Millfield La CB6 ... 210 C5
Millfield Pl CB6 ... 210 D5
Millfield Prim Sch The CB6 ... 242 C3
Millfield Rd
Market Deeping PE6 ... 231 F8
Maxey PE6 ... 231 D8
Millfield Way PE7 ... 189 F6
Millfields Ramsey PE26 ... 172 B8
Stetchworth CB8 ... 89 F1
Millfields Way CB9 ... 24 B8
Millington Rd CB3 ... 64 C7
Mills La
Longstanton CB4 ... 124 A1
Witchford CB6 ... 217 D1
Millstone La PE9 ... 230 D3
Millyard CB6 ... 210 A6
Milner Cl March PE15 ... 243 D5
Sawston CB2 ... 32 E7
Milner Rd
Comberton CB3 ... 62 D6
Wisbech PE13 ... 245 C4
Milners Row 15 PE9 ... 244 C5
Milnyard Sq PE2 ... 185 C2
Milton Ave PE19 ... 74 C6
Milton CE Prim Sch CB4 ... 105 C2
Milton Cl
Huntingdon PE29 ... 141 E6
Ramsey PE26 ... 171 F5
Royston SG8 ... 13 C1
St Ives PE27 ... 143 F6
Milton Ctry Pk* CB4 ... 105 D1
Milton Dr PE13 ... 238 B1
Milton Rd
Cambridge CB4 ... 246 B4
Impington CB4 ... 104 F4
Peterborough PE2 ... 187 A7
Milton Rd Prim Sch CB4 ... 83 E4
Milton Way PE3 ... 196 E3
Mina Cl PE2 ... 187 D4
Minden Ct 8 PE19 ... 74 C5
Minerva Cl CB9 ... 24 D6
Minerva Way CB4 ... 83 E8
Mingle La CB2 ... 49 B5
Minster Pl 4 CB7 ... 240 D4
Minster Precincts PE1 ... 198 B2
Minster Rd
Haverhill CB9 ... 39 A1
Royston SG8 ... 5 C8
Mint La PE19 ... 96 E4
Minter Cl CB5 ... 86 A5
Minton Ent Pk CB8 ... 110 F7
Missleton Ct CB1 ... 65 C5
Misterton PE2 ... 185 E3
Misty Mdws CB5 ... 84 D4
Mitchell Cl PE1 ... 198 C2
Mitchells CB10 ... 20 B1
Mitchells Cotts CB10 ... 20 B1
Moat La
Abbots Ripton PE28 ... 152 C8
Melbourn SG8 ... 14 D7
Perry PE28 ... 115 D1
Moat Way CB4 ... 122 E6
Moat Wlk CB9 ... 23 E8
Moats' Way PE28 ... 119 E7
Mobb's Hole SG7 ... 10 C4
Moggswell La PE2 ... 186 B4
Mole Dro PE12 ... 233 F8
Molewood Cl CB4 ... 83 C6
Molls Dro PE14 ... 236 C3
Monarch Ave PE2 ... 187 A6
Monarch Rd PE19 ... 74 B4
Moncrieff Cl 1 CB4 ... 83 E7
Mondela Pl PE7 ... 176 A7
Monet Cl PE27 ... 144 A7
Money Bank PE13 ... 245 E4
Money Hill (Tumulus)* CB3 ... 47 B3
Moneypiece Cl 1 CB9 ... 38 F1
Monk Dr CB3 ... 79 C4
Monkfield La CB3 ... 79 C3
Monkfield Pk Prim Sch CB3 ... 79 B4
Monks Cl PE7 ... 189 D8
Monks Dr 17 PE6 ... 232 A1
Monks Gr PE4 ... 204 A5
Monks Hardwick PE19 ... 75 E8
Monks Mdw PE6 ... 232 B8
Monks Way PE28 ... 168 B2
Monks Wood National Nature Reserve* PE28 ... 161 B4
Monkswell CB2 ... 64 D3
Monkswood CB6 ... 242 C5
Montagu Ct 2 PE19 ... 74 E4
Montagu Gdns PE28 ... 113 E5
Montagu Rd
Huntingdon PE29 ... 141 E4
Little Stukeley PE28 ... 151 F2
Peterborough PE4 ... 197 D8
Montagu Sq PE19 ... 74 E4
Montagu St PE19 ... 74 E4
Montague Rd PE28 ... 117 D8
Monte Long Cl PE15 ... 243 E1
Montford Cl CB5 ... 130 C4
Montfort Ct 9 CB9 ... 23 F7
Montfort Way CB4 ... 83 E6
Montgomery Rd CB4 ... 83 E6
Montreal Rd CB1 ... 65 C7
Montrose Cl CB4 ... 83 E7
Monument St PE1 ... 198 A3
Monument View PE15 ... 243 D1
Moon Hall La CB9 ... 24 A6
Moonhall Bsns Pk CB9 ... 24 A5
Moor End SG8 ... 29 D3
Moor Pasture Way CB9 ... 39 B4
Moor Rd
Great Staughton MK44 ... 93 B1
Newborough PE6 ... 206 E2
Moor The SG8 ... 14 C7
Moore Cl CB4 ... 84 A6
Moore's La 4 PE6 ... 232 A1
Moores Wlk PE19 ... 74 F5
Moorfield PE6 ... 206 F3
Moorfield Rd
Duxford CB2 ... 32 E3
Peterborough PE3 ... 197 D3
Moorfield Way PE28 ... 151 F2
Moorhen Rd PE7 ... 201 A1
Moorhouse Dr PE29 ... 141 E7
Moory Croft Cl PE19 ... 94 A6
Moot Way PE28 ... 155 A5
Morborne Cl PE2 ... 187 D6
Morborne La PE7 ... 180 D4
Morborne Rd PE7 ... 180 C2
Morden Rd CB3 ... 99 B3
More's Mdw CB2 ... 48 F6
Moreton Cl PE7 ... 189 F8
Moretons Cl PE7 ... 190 A8
Morgan Cl PE7 ... 181 E6
Morgans CB4 ... 125 D4
Morland Way PE27 ... 144 A7
Morley Cl 7 IP28 ... 213 F8
Morley Meml Prim Sch CB1 ... 65 B5
Morley Way
17 Eastwood End PE15 ... 223 B7
Peterborough PE2 ... 186 D5
Morpeth Cl PE2 ... 186 C6
Morpeth Rd PE3 ... 197 C3
Morrice Gn SG8 ... 1 A3
Morris Cl PE19 ... 117 A3
Morris Ct PE7 ... 181 E6
Morris St PE1 ... 198 B3
Mortimer La IP28 ... 213 C3
Mortimer Rd
Cambridge CB1 ... 246 C2
Royston SG8 ... 5 E6
Mortimers La CB2 ... 30 C5
Mortlock Ave CB4 ... 84 B6
Mortlock Cl SG8 ... 14 C6
Mortlock Gdns CB1 ... 34 C5
Mortlock St SG8 ... 14 C6
Morton Ave PE15 ... 243 E3
Morton Cl CB6 ... 240 E8
Morton St SG8 ... 5 D7
Morton Way 6 PE15 ... 223 B7
Morton's Leam* PE7 ... 200 C1
Mosquito Rd PE26 ... 171 E3
Moss Bank CB4 ... 84 C5
Moss Cl PE26 ... 171 B1
Moss Dr CB3 ... 47 C5
Mostyn Cl 2 CB6 ... 216 E1
Motocross Circuit CB3 ... 78 F8
Moules La CB1 ... 20 C6
Moulton Ave CB8 ... 134 A2
Moulton CE VC Fst Sch CB8 ... 112 E6
Moulton Gr PE3 ... 197 C6
Moulton Paddocks CB8 ... 111 F6
Moulton Rd
Ashley CB8 ... 112 D1
Cheveley CB8 ... 91 D8
Newmarket CB8 ... 111 D4
Moulton Road or Kennett Rd CB8 ... 112 F7
Mount Dr PE13 ... 245 E4

Mount Pleasant
3 Cambridge CB3 . . . . .83 C3
Great Paxton PE19 . . . . . . .96 E4
Peterborough PE2 . . . . . . .187 C7
Spaldwick PE28 . . . . .137 E6
Mount Pleasant Pl
PE13 . . . . .245 C7
Mount Pleasant Wlk 2
CB3 .83 C3
Mount Rd CB9 . . . . .24 A7
Mount The Barley SG8 . . . . . .6 E1
Toft CB3 . . . . .61 D5
Mountbatten Ave
Stamford PE9 . . . . .220 A3
Yaxley PE7 . . . . .181 D5
Mountbatten Ct 6 PE7 . . . .74 C4
Mountbatten Dr 3 PE13 . .245 A7
Mountbatten Way
Peterborough PE3 . . . . . . .197 B6
Whittlesey PE7 . . . . .190 A6
Mounteagle 2 SG8 . . . . . . .5 D5
Mountford Cl CB2 . . . . .48 C4
Mountfort Cl 3 PE19 . . . . .74 F3
Mountsteven Ave PE4 . . . .204 C1
Mouth La PE13 . . . . .235 B4
Mowbray Cl 4 PE13 . . . . .235 B7
Mowbray Rd
Bretton PE3 . . . . .203 F1
Cambridge CB1 . . . . .65 C4
Mowfen Rd CB6 . . . . .242 D5
Mowlam Cl CB4 . . . . .104 C2
Moyne Cl CB4 . . . . .83 D7
Moyne Rd PE28 . . . . .168 C3
Moyse's Bank PE14 . . . . . .236 F6
Muchwood La PE26 . . . . . .221 B1
Mudd's Dro PE14 . . . . .229 F6
Mugglestons La PE26 . . . .172 B6
Mulberry Cl
Bottisham CB5 . . . . .86 F6
Cambridge CB4 . . . . .83 F5
Mildenhall IP28 . . . . .239 E4
Whittlesey PE7 . . . . .189 F5
Yaxley PE7 . . . . .182 A5
Mulberry Way CB7 . . . . . .240 E5
**Mullard Radio Astronomy
Obsy*** CB3 . . . . .46 E7
Mullein Cl 4 PE7 . . . . .74 C5
Mumby's Dro PE14 . . . . . .229 E6
Mumford Theatre*
CB1 . . . . .246 C2
Muncey Wlk CB4 . . . . .104 C5
Munday Way 10 PE13 . . . .238 B2
Munnings Cl CB9 . . . . .38 D1
Muntjac Cl 2 PE19 . . . . . . .74 B5
Murfitt Way SG19 . . . . .41 D6
Murfitt's La CB7 . . . . .212 E2
Muriel Cl CB3 . . . . .99 B2
Murrell Cl PE19 . . . . .74 F7
Murrell Ct PE19 . . . . .74 F7
Murrow Bank PE13 . . . . . .234 D6
Murrow La PE13 . . . . .234 F5
Murrow Prim Sch
PE13 . . . . .234 D6
Murton Cl PE13 . . . . .130 A3
**Museum of Archaeology &
Anthropology*** CB2 . . . .246 B2
**Museum of Bronze Age at
Flag Fen The*** PE6 . . . . .199 B2
**Museum of Classical
Archaeology*** CB3 . . . . . .64 C8
Museum of Technology*
CB5 . . . . .84 B3
Museum Sq 2 PE13 . . . . .245 C5
Musgrave Way
Fen Ditton CB5 . . . . .84 F6
7 St Neots PE19 . . . . .74 F5
Musker Pl CB3 . . . . .99 B1
Muskham PE3 . . . . .196 F4
Musticott Pl PE13 . . . . . . .245 F6
Mustill's La CB4 . . . . .123 B8
Muswell Rd PE3 . . . . .197 E4
Mutlow Hill (Tumulus)*
CB1 . . . . .67 F1
Myles Way PE13 . . . . .245 C8
Myrtle Ave PE1 . . . . .198 C7
Myrtle Ct PE1 . . . . .198 C7
Myrtle Gn PE27 . . . . .144 A5
Myrtle Gr PE1 . . . . .198 C7
Myrtle House Cvn Pk
PE1 . . . . .198 E5
Myrtle Way PE27 . . . . . . .144 A5

N

Nansicles Rd PE2 . . . . . . .186 D6
Napier Pl PE2 . . . . .185 C6
Napier St CB1 . . . . .246 C3
Narrow Dro
Yaxley PE7 . . . . .188 C5
Yaxley PE7 . . . . .182 C5
Narrow La CB4 . . . . .104 B4
Naseby Cl PE3 . . . . .197 C5
Naseby Gdns PE19 . . . . . . .75 A4
Nash Rd 7 SG8 . . . . .5 D5
Nat Flatman St CB8 . . . . .111 B3
Natal Rd CB1 . . . . .65 C7
Nathan Cl PE3 . . . . .197 B2
National Extension Coll
CB2 . . . . .64 F7
National Horse Racing Mus*
CB8 . . . . .111 A3
Navigation Wharf 6
PE19 . . . . .74 E5
Nayland Rd CB9 . . . . .23 E6
Neale Cl CB1 . . . . .65 F7
Neale-wade Com Coll
PE15 . . . . .243 D1

Neaverson Rd PE6 . . . . . .203 F7
Nedderworth Rd . . . .
Doddington/Wimblington
PE15 . . . . .222 F5
Needham Bank PE14 . . . . .236 C4
Needingworth Rd
PE27 . . . . .144 B4
Nelson Gdns PE13 . . . . . .245 D6
Nelson Rd
Eaton Socon PE19 . . . . . . .74 B3
Huntingdon PE29 . . . . . . .142 A6
Nelson's La CB6 . . . . .210 A5
Nene Cl Wansford PE8 . . .194 A3
Whittlesey PE7 . . . . .189 F6
7 Wittering PE8 . . . . .230 B1
Nene Par March PE15 . . . .243 E4
Wisbech PE13 . . . . .245 B2
Nene Parkway PE3 . . . . . .196 F1
Nene Pk* PE2 . . . . .185 C7
Nene Quay PE13 . . . . .245 C5
Nene Rd
Eaton Socon PE19 . . . . . . .74 C4
Ely CB6 . . . . .240 C6
Huntingdon PE29 . . . . . . .141 E8
Kimbolton PE28 . . . . .114 A7
Whittlesey PE7 . . . . .189 E6
Nene Sch The PE13 . . . . . .245 D4
Nene St PE1 . . . . .198 B2
Nene Way St Ives PE27 . . .144 A7
Sutton PE5 . . . . .194 F2
Neneside 1 PE16 . . . . . . .222 A5
Neptune Cl CB4 . . . . .83 E7
Ness Rd CB5 . . . . .130 C3
Nether Gr CB4 . . . . .123 F7
Netherhall Sch The
CB1 . . . . .65 E4
Netherhall Way CB1 . . . . . .65 E4
Nettle Bank PE14 . . . . . . .235 C4
Neve Gdns IP28 . . . . .213 E6
Neville Rd CB1 . . . . .65 C6
New Barn Dro PE28 . . . . . .173 D4
New Barns Ave CB7 . . . . .240 D6
New Barns Rd CB7 . . . . . .240 D5
New Bridge La
Elm PE14 . . . . .235 F6
8 Wisbech PE14 . . . . . . .245 A1
New Bridge Rd PE14 . . . .236 E1
New Broadpool PE28 . . . .173 F1
New Cangle CP Sch
CB9 . . . . .38 F1
New Cheveley Rd CB8 . . . .111 C2
New Cl SG8 . . . . .12 B2
New Cl Rd CB6 . . . . .211 A7
New Cross Dro CB8 . . . . . .216 B3
New Cross Rd PE7 . . . . . .244 B5
New Cut
Newmarket CB8 . . . . .111 A3
Thorney PE6 . . . . .233 D5
New Dro Soham CB7 . . . . .211 E4
3 Wisbech PE13 . . . . . . .245 D2
Wisbech St Mary PE13 . . .235 C5
New England PE28 . . . . . .120 B2
New Farm Cl SG8 . . . . .15 E8
New Farm Cotts CB1 . . . . .20 E7
New Fen Dike PE12 . . . . . .237 A8
New Fen Rd La PE26 . . . . .171 C8
New Field
Gorefield PE13 . . . . .237 D2
Newton PE13 . . . . .237 F4
New Hall CB3 . . . . .83 C3
New Hall La CB3 . . . . .79 C4
New La PE14 . . . . .183 C8
New Long Dro PE7 . . . . . .177 F6
New Mdw Dro PE7 . . . . . .187 D1
New Orch Pk CB6 . . . . . . .242 E4
New Path CB7 . . . . .212 E1
New Pk St PE15 . . . . .243 E5
New Pk St CB5 . . . . .246 A4
New Rd Barton CB3 . . . . . . .63 A4
Burwell CB5 . . . . .130 B3
Chatteris PE16 . . . . .241 E5
Cottenham CB4 . . . . .125 E4
Eynesbury PE19 . . . . .110 B8
13 Eye PE6 . . . . .232 A1
Great & Little Chishill SG8 . .15 B1
Guilden Morden SG8 . . . . . .11 A5
Haddenham CB6 . . . . .210 A6
Harston CB2 . . . . .47 D4
Haslingfield CB3 . . . . .47 B5
Hemingford Abbots
PE28 . . . . .143 A4
Hinxton CB10 . . . . .18 B6
Histon CB4 . . . . .104 C3
Littleport CB6 . . . . .242 D5
March PE15 . . . . .243 C4
Melbourn SG8 . . . . .14 E4
Mepal CB6 . . . . .216 E3
Offord Cluny PE19 . . . . . . .118 A2
Outwell PE14 . . . . .236 E1
Over CB4 . . . . .208 D1
Peterborough PE2 . . . . . . .185 E4
Ramsey PE26 . . . . .172 B7
St Ives PE27 . . . . .144 B3
Sawston CB2 . . . . .32 E8
Shudy Camps CB1 . . . . .22 C7
Upwell PE14 . . . . .229 E8
Warboys PE28 . . . . .165 A4
Whittlesey PE7 . . . . .189 F6
Wood Walton PE28 . . . . . .161 E7
Woodston PE2 . . . . .186 F7
New Rd Prim Sch PE7 . . . .189 F5
New River Bank CB7 . . . . .242 F5
New River Gn CB8 . . . . . . .110 B8
New Row 8 PE6 . . . . .231 E8
New Sch Rd CB4 . . . . .104 B3
New Sq CB1 . . . . .246 B3
New St Cambridge CB1 . . . .84 A2
Chippenham CB7 . . . . .132 E6

New St continued
Doddington/Wimblington
PE15 . . . . .222 F5
Godmanchester PE29 . . . .141 F1
Huntingdon PE29 . . . . . . .239 C4
St Neots PE19 . . . . .74 E5
Stamford PE9 . . . . .244 C6
New Town Rd CB6 . . . . . .209 F6
Newark Ave PE1 . . . . .198 C6
Newark Cl SG8 . . . . .5 C8
Newark Hill Prim Sch
PE1 . . . . .198 C6
Newark Rd PE1 . . . . .198 F4
Newbey Cl PE3 . . . . .197 B3
Newbolt SG8 . . . . .5 D8
Newborn Cl PE2 . . . . .187 E5
Newborough Prim Sch
PE6 . . . . .207 C1
Newborough Rd PE4 . . . . .205 C2
Newboults La PE9 . . . . . .244 A5
Newcastle Dr PE2 . . . . . . .186 D6
Newcomb Ct PE9 . . . . . . .244 B5
Newcombe Way PE2 . . . . .185 D2
Newell Cl SG8 . . . . .44 D1
Newell Wlk CB1 . . . . .65 F7
Newgate Rd PE13 . . . . . . .237 F6
Newgate St PE15 . . . . . . .222 F5
Newgates 1 PE9 . . . . . . .244 C5
Newghant Dro PE15 . . . . .223 F4
Newham Rd PE7 . . . . .244 A7
Newington CB4 . . . . .124 B8
Newlands PE15 . . . . .243 D5
Newlands Bldgs SG19 . . . .42 D4
Newlands Rd
Chatteris PE16 . . . . .241 E6
Parson Drove PE13 . . . . . .234 D7
Peterborough PE7 . . . . . . .190 A8
Newman Ave SG8 . . . . .5 F6
Newman Cl 10 PE8 . . . . .230 B1
Newman Rd 1 PE1 . . . . . .198 B6
Newmarket Hospl
CB8 . . . . .111 A5
Newmarket Leisure Ctr
CB8 . . . . .110 F4
Newmarket Rd
Ashley CB8 . . . . .91 E8
Barton Mills IP28 . . . . .239 D1
Burwell CB5 . . . . .130 C1
Cambridge CB5 . . . . .246 C3
Cheveley CB8 . . . . .91 C8
Cowlinge CB8 . . . . .73 D3
Fen Ditton CB1 . . . . .85 D3
Fordham CB7 . . . . .111 A2
Great Chesterford CB10 . . . .18 C3
Lidgate CB8 . . . . .73 C6
Moulton CB8 . . . . .112 E5
Royston SG8 . . . . .5 F6
Snailwell CB8 . . . . .132 B2
Stow cum Quy CB5 . . . . . . .85 F4
Stretham CB6 . . . . .211 A3
Newmarket Sports Ctr
CB8 . . . . .110 F4
Newmarket Sta CB8 . . . . .111 A2
Newmarket Swimming Pool
CB8 . . . . .110 F4
Newmarket Upper Sch
CB8 . . . . .110 F4
Newnham Cl
Huntingdon PE29 . . . . . . .142 A7
Mildenhall IP28 . . . . .239 D5
Newnham Coll CB3 . . . . . . .64 C8
Newnham Croft Prim Sch
CB3 . . . . .64 D8
Newnham Croft St 2
CB3 . . . . .64 C7
Newnham Dro CB5 . . . . . .129 C5
Newnham La CB5 . . . . . . .130 B3
Newnham Rd CB3 . . . . .64 C7
Newnham St 7 CB4 . . . . . .64 C7
Newnham Terr
Cambridge CB1 . . . . .246 A1
Newnham CB3 . . . . .64 C8
Newnham Way SG7 . . . . . . .2 B2
Newnham Wlk CB3 . . . . . . .64 D8
Newport Ave CB7 . . . . . . .213 A1
Newstead Cl PE6 . . . . .232 A2
Newstead La PE9 . . . . . . .244 F8
Newstead Rd PE9 . . . . . . .230 A8
Newton Cl PE15 . . . . .237 E4
Newton Pl 9 PE13 . . . . . . .24 B8
Newton Prim Sch The
PE19 . . . . .77 C3
Newton Rd
Cambridge CB2 . . . . .64 E5
Great Shelford CB2 . . . . . . .48 D3
Harston CB2 . . . . .47 F1
Newton CB2 . . . . .31 A8
Sawtry PE28 . . . . .168 C4
Newton Way PE2 . . . . . . .198 D2
Newtons Ct PE29 . . . . . . .141 E4
Newton
Hail Weston PE19 . . . . .74 B8
Kimbolton PE28 . . . . .113 F5
Stamford PE9 . . . . .244 C4
Newton La PE28 . . . . .113 F5
Newtown Rd PE26 . . . . . . .172 B7
Next Odsey SG7 . . . . .3 C3
Nicholas Taylor Gdns
PE3 . . . . .196 F3
Nicholls Ave PE3 . . . . . . .197 E3
Nicholson Way CB4 . . . . . .83 C6
Nigel Rd CB6 . . . . .240 E8
Nightall Dr PE15 . . . . .243 D7
Nightall Rd CB7 . . . . .212 A4
Nightingale Ave
Bassingbourn SG8 . . . . .13 A5
Cambridge CB1 . . . . .65 C3
Nightingale Cl IP28 . . . . . .239 D4

Nightingale Ct PE4 . . . . . .205 A2
Nightingale Dr PE7 . . . . . .181 D6
Nightingale Way
Royston SG8 . . . . .5 E8
1 St Neots PE19 . . . . .75 B7
Nightingale Wlk PE15 . . . .224 B4
Nimbus Way CB8 . . . . . . .110 E8
Nine Chimneys La CB3 . . . .53 B2
Nipcut Rd PE6 . . . . .232 C2
Nixhill Rd PE15 . . . . .223 B6
Noahs Way CB6 . . . . .242 B5
Noble Gdns PE15 . . . . . . .243 E3
Nobles Cl PE7 . . . . .190 B8
Nobles La PE28 . . . . .208 C5
Noel Murless Dr CB8 . . . .110 F5
Nook The PE6 . . . . .231 C4
Norburn PE3 . . . . .197 B8
Norfolk Ave CB8 . . . . .110 C5
Norfolk Cl Ely CB6 . . . . . .240 A3
Huntingdon PE29 . . . . . . .141 E8
St Ives PE27 . . . . .144 A8
Wyton Airfield PE28 . . . . . .143 B8
Norfolk St 3 PE9 . . . . . . .244 B6
Norfolk St
Cambridge CB1 . . . . .84 A1
Doddington/Wimblington
PE15 . . . . .223 B7
Peterborough PE1 . . . . . . .197 F4
Wisbech PE13 . . . . .245 C4
Norfolk Terr CB1 . . . . .84 A1
Norgett's La SG8 . . . . .14 D6
Norham Ct PE7 . . . . .188 A5
Norico Bay PE15 . . . . .243 E2
Norman Dr PE7 . . . . .189 E8
Norman Dr PE15 . . . . .175 F8
Norman Pk CB3 . . . . .102 C4
Norman Rd PE1 . . . . .198 C4
Norman Way
3 Doddington/Wimblington
PE15 . . . . .223 B7
Over CB4 . . . . .123 B7
Norman's Cl 8 SG8 . . . . . . .5 D5
Normanton Rd PE1 . . . . . .198 D7
Normanton Way CB4 . . . .104 B5
Normoor Dro PE16 . . . . . .223 B2
Nornea La CB7 . . . . .211 F8
Norris Mus* PE27 . . . . . . .144 A3
Norris Rd PE27 . . . . .144 A4
North Ave CB9 . . . . .23 E8
North Bank PE6 . . . . .199 D1
North Bank Rd 4 PE1 . . . .198 D3
North Brink PE13 . . . . . . .245 A4
North Brook End SG8 . . . . .11 B6
North Cambridgeshire Hospl
PE13 . . . . .245 D5
North Cl SG8 . . . . .5 C8
North Cotts CB2 . . . . .64 D4
North Dr March PE15 . . . . .243 E4
Newmarket CB8 . . . . .110 F5
Soham CB7 . . . . .212 B5
North End Rd CB10 . . . . . . .18 A8
North Fen Dro CB6 . . . . . .218 B8
North Fen Rd PE6 . . . . . . .231 F5
North La SG19 . . . . .42 B7
Nobles Lodge Dr CB3 . . . . .99 B2
North Pl IP28 . . . . .239 C4
North Rd
Alconbury Weston PE28 . . .150 D5
Brampton PE28 . . . . .140 D1
Great Abington CB1 . . . . . . .33 F5
Wetherley CB22 . . . . .31 C5
Whittlesford CB2 . . . . .32 B6
North Side PE6 . . . . .200 F5
North St Burwell CB5 . . . . .130 B4
Cambridge CB4 . . . . .83 C4
Folksworth & Washingley
PE7 . . . . .181 A1
Freckenham IP28 . . . . .213 C3
Huntingdon PE29 . . . . . . .141 D5
March PE15 . . . . .243 D5
Peterborough PE1 . . . . . . .198 A2
Stamford PE9 . . . . .244 B5
Stilton PE7 . . . . .176 A8
Wicken PE7 . . . . .211 E1
Wisbech PE13 . . . . .245 C5
North Terr
Cambridge CB1 . . . . .246 C3
Mildenhall IP28 . . . . .239 C4
Peterborough PE1 . . . . . . .198 E7
Sawston CB2 . . . . .32 F5
Northam Cl PE6 . . . . .232 A2
Northampton Cl CB6 . . . . .240 A3
Northampton St CB3 . . . . . .83 C2
Northborough Prim Sch
PE6 . . . . .231 F6
Northey Rd PE6 . . . . .199 C2
Northfield Fulbourn CB1 . . . .67 A5
Girton CB3 . . . . .103 E2
Northfield Cl SG19 . . . . . . .41 C6
Northfield Pk CB7 . . . . . . .212 A5
Northfield Rd
Ashwell SG7 . . . . .2 C7
Peterborough PE1 . . . . . . .198 D7
Soham CB7 . . . . .212 A5
Wyboston PE19 . . . . .74 A1
Northfields Ave CB4 . . . . . .83 E7
Northfields La PE9 . . . . . .244 C6
Northfields Rd CB5 . . . . . .107 D2
Northgate PE6 . . . . .199 D8
Northgate Cl PE7 . . . . .189 D8
Northminster PE1 . . . . . . .198 A3

Northumberland Ave 4
PE9 . . . . .244 A6
Northumberland Cl 2
CB4 . . . . .83 D6
Northumbria Cl CB6 . . . . .210 A7
Northwold CB6 . . . . .240 C5
Norton Cl
Cambridge CB5 . . . . .84 D3
Papworth Everard CB3 . . . . .99 A2
Norton Rd Haverhill CB9 . . .23 E6
Peterborough PE1 . . . . . . .197 F6
Norwalde St PE15 . . . . . . .243 C6
Norwich Rd PE13 . . . . . . .245 D5
Norwich St CB2 . . . . .64 E7
Norwood Ave PE15 . . . . . .243 D5
Norwood Cres PE15 . . . . .243 C6
Norwood La PE4 . . . . .205 B2
Norwood Prim Sch
PE4 . . . . .204 F3
Norwood Rd
10 Somersham PE28 . . . .215 C1
Notley Dr CB9 . . . . .38 C1
Nottingham Way PE1 . . . .198 C6
Nuffield Cl CB4 . . . . .84 B7
Nuffield Rd
Cambridge CB4 . . . . .84 B6
St Ives PE27 . . . . .144 C6
Nunns Way 4 CB6 . . . . . .216 E1
Nun's Orch CB4 . . . . .104 B4
Nuns Way CB4 . . . . .83 F7
Nursery Cl Isleham CB7 . . .212 F4
Mildenhall IP28 . . . . .239 D4
Peterborough PE1 . . . . . . .198 A4
Nursery Dr March PE15 . . .243 B5
Wisbech PE13 . . . . .245 E8
Nursery Gdns
Little Paxton PE19 . . . . . . .96 A2
St Ives PE27 . . . . .144 B5
Whittlesey PE7 . . . . .189 F6
Nursery La 1 PE19 . . . . . .198 D2
Nursery Rd
Huntingdon PE29 . . . . . . .141 E4
St Neots PE19 . . . . .74 F4
Nursery Way 2 CB3 . . . . . .62 C5
Nursery Wlk
Brampton PE28 . . . . .140 C3
Cambridge CB4 . . . . .83 C5
Nutholt La CB6 . . . . .240 D5
Nutters Cl CB3 . . . . .64 A4
Nuttings Rd CB1 . . . . .84 D1

O

O Furlong Dro CB6 . . . . . .224 F1
Oak Cl PE19 . . . . .75 A5
Oak Dr Brampton PE28 . . .140 C4
Little Stukeley PE28 . . . . . .151 F3
Mildenhall IP28 . . . . .213 F8
Outwell PE14 . . . . .236 F3
Oak End PE28 . . . . .150 F4
Oak Farm Cl PE7 . . . . .176 A7
Oak La Cheveley CB8 . . . . . .91 C4
Littleport CB6 . . . . .242 A2
Oak Rd Glinton PE6 . . . . . .231 E5
Stilton PE7 . . . . .176 A7
Oak Tree Ave CB4 . . . . .83 F5
Oak Tree Cl
March PE15 . . . . .243 C5
St Ives PE27 . . . . .143 F5
Oak Tree Way CB4 . . . . . .104 B3
Oak View PE4 . . . . .196 F2
Oak Way PE26 . . . . .220 D3
Oakdale Ave PE2 . . . . .187 D4
Oakdale Prim Sch
PE7 . . . . .187 C4
Oakery The CB7 . . . . .240 D6
Oakington Barracks
CB4 . . . . .124 B1
Oakington CE Prim Sch
CB4 . . . . .103 C5
Oakington Rd
Cottenham CB4 . . . . .125 B1
Dry Drayton CB3 . . . . .102 D2
Girton CB3 . . . . .103 C3
Oakington & Westwick
CB4 . . . . .103 E7
Oaklands
Fenstanton PE28 . . . . .121 B5
Peterborough PE1 . . . . . . .198 B4
Oaklands Ave PE28 . . . . . .163 F7
Oaklands Dr PE13 . . . . . . .245 F7
Oakleaf Rd PE1 . . . . .198 C6
Oakleigh Cres PE29 . . . . .141 F1
Oakleigh Dr PE2 . . . . .186 C6
Oakley Cl PE13 . . . . .245 E4
Oakroad Prim Sch
PE7 . . . . .187 C4
Oakrits SG8 . . . . .14 B8
Oakroyd Cres PE13 . . . . . .245 C6
Oaks Bsns Pk The
CB8 . . . . .110 E7
Oaks Dr CB8 . . . . .110 F7
Oaks The Milton CB4 . . . . .105 C2
Soham CB7 . . . . .212 B3
Oaktree Cl PE15 . . . . .222 F5
Oaktree Rd CB4 . . . . .121 D6
Oasthouse Way PE26 . . . .172 C4
Oates' La CB5 . . . . .90 F2
Oates Way PE26 . . . . .172 C7
Oatlands Ave CB3 . . . . . . .102 B4
Occupation Rd
Cambridge CB4 . . . . .84 A2
Peterborough PE1 . . . . . . .197 E6
Ockendon Cl PE19 . . . . . . .74 B3

Octagon Dr PE13 .....245 A6
Octavia Cl PE13 .....245 F6
Octavia Hill Birthplace Mus
The* PE13 ....245 B5
Odecroft PE3 ....197 C7
Offa Lea CB2 ....33 A7
Offord Prim Sch PE19 ..118 A2
Offord Rd PE19 ......97 F6
Ogden Cl SG8 ....14 D6
Old Mill La PE13 ....245 B5
Oilmills Dro PE26 ...220 F4
Oilmills Rd PE26 ....220 E6
Old Auction Yd PE16 ..241 C5
Old Bailey Rd PE7 ...181 C8
Old Bank CB7 ....219 B4
Old Brewery Cl CB7 ..240 E4
Old Broadpool PE28 ..173 D2
Old Church La PE28 ..208 C7
Old Clements La **7** CB9 ..23 F7
Old Ct Hall PE13 ....141 E1
Old Farm Cl
  Histon CB4 ....104 B5
  3 Needingworth PE27 ..208 A3
Old Fen Dike PE12 ...237 B8
Old Field PE13 ......237 F4
Old Fletton Prim Sch
  PE2 ....186 F6
Old Ford La PE19 ....114 B2
Old Forge Way CB2 ...32 E8
Old Glebe PE28 ......150 E5
Old Great N Rd
  St Martin's Without PE9 ..244 C3
  Sibson cum Stibbington
  PE8 ....194 C2
Old Haverhill Rd CB9 ..39 E4
Old Houghton Rd
  PE29 ....142 B6
Old House Rd CB1 ....53 C2
Old Knarr Fen Dro
  PE6 ....233 C2
Old Leicester Rd PE8 ..194 A3
Old Lynn Dro CB6 ....217 C7
Old Lynn Rd PE13 ....245 E7
Old Mill Ave PE28 ...165 A5
Old Mill Cl CB2 .....29 D7
Old Mill La IP28 ....239 F2
Old Mkt PE13 ....245 C5
Old N Rd
  Bassingbourn cum Kneesworth
  SG8 ....13 B4
  Longstowe CB3 ......60 A3
  Royston SG8 ....5 C7
  Sawtry PE28 ....168 A4
  Wansford PE8 ....194 A3
Old Orch The PE15 ...222 A5
Old Oundle Rd PE8 ...193 A6
Old Pinewood Way CB3 ..99 B4
Old Pond La PE5 .....195 E2
Old Pools Dro CB6 ...225 C4
Old Pound Cl PE23 ...143 D2
Old Ramsey Rd
  St Ives PE28 ....143 E8
  Woodhurst PE28 ....154 E2
Old Rectory Dr
  Dry Drayton CB3 ....102 B1
  4 Tallington PE9 ...230 F7
  Thornhaugh PE8 .....194 A6
Old Rly Ind Est PE27 ..144 D4
Old Rope Wlk CB9 ....23 E7
Old Rorge Gdns PE16 ..241 C5
Old Sch Cl Burwell CB5 ..130 C3
  Littleport CB6 .....242 D5
  1 Soham CB7 ......212 B5
Old Sch Gdns **3** PE19 ..74 C2
Old Sch La Brinkley CB8 ..70 E1
  Milton CB4 ....105 D2
  Wicken CB7 ....211 B1
Old Sta Rd CB8 .....111 B4
Old Stable Wlk PE26 ..172 A4
Old W Est PE15 .....222 A5
Old Weston Rd PE28 ..158 A5
Oldbrook PE3 ....200 A4
Oldeamere Way PE7 ...190 A7
Oldfield Ave PE13 ...236 B5
Oldfield Gdns PE7 ...189 D7
Oldfield La PE13 ....245 B4
Oldforge Gdns PE16 ..241 C5
Oldhurst Rd PE28 ....155 E8
Olive Rd PE1 ....198 C7
Oliver Cl PE26 .....172 A6
Oliver Cromwell's House*
  CB7 ....240 C4
Oliver Rd PE27 .....144 B3
Olivers Way PE15 ...243 D2
Olivia Rd PE28 .....140 C3
Ollard Ave PE13 ....245 D7
Ongar Cl CB5 ......84 F4
Onyx Cl **0** PE13 ..245 C5
Open Univ The CB2 ...246 C1
Opportune Rd PE13 ...245 C6
Orange Gr **1** PE13 ..245 C4
Orchard Ave CB4 ....83 E5
Orchard Cl Balsham CB1 ..52 F3
  Bassingbourn SG8 ...13 A5
  Cottenham CB4 .....125 C3
  Eaton Socon PE19 ...74 C4
  Elsworth CB3 ......100 A4
  Girton CB3 ....103 E1
  Hail Weston PE19 ..95 A1
  Haverhill CB9 .....23 F7
  Lidgate CB8 ....72 F7
  Little Wilbraham CB1 ..86 E2
  Littleport CB6 ....242 D4
  Manea PE15 ....224 B4
  March PE15 ....243 E3

Orchard Cl *continued*
  9 Market Deeping PE6 ..231 E8
  Peterborough PE3 ...197 D3
  Stamford PE9 ......244 B5
  Stilton PE7 ....176 A7
  Warboys PE28 ......178 B3
  Warmington PE8 ....178 B3
  9 Wisbech PE14 ...236 A5
  13 Wisbech PE13 ..238 B2
Orchard Cres PE28 ...208 E6
Orchard Ct PE6 .....232 F3
Orchard Dr Girton CB3 ..82 E7
  Waterbeach CB5 ....127 B1
  Wisbech PE13 ......245 E4
Orchard End
  Bluntisham/Colne PE28 ..208 C5
  Rampton CB4 ....124 E4
Orchard Est
  Cambridge CB1 .....65 F7
  1 Little Downham CB6 ..218 B7
Orchard Gate SG8 ...14 C6
Orchard Gdns PE28 ...121 B5
Orchard La
  Brampton CB4 ......140 E3
  Huntingdon PE29 ...141 E4
Orchard Mews PE2 ...186 F8
Orchard Pightle CB1 ..20 B6
Orchard Rd
  Barnack PE9 ....230 E4
  Eaton Socon PE19 ...74 C4
  Great Shelford CB2 ..49 B6
  Haslingfield CB3 ...47 B5
  Histon CB4 ....104 C5
  March PE15 ....243 E3
  Melbourn SG8 ......14 C5
  Royston SG8 ....5 B7
  Sawston CB2 ....32 E7
  Stamford PE9 ......244 B5
Orchard Rd S PE15 ...243 E3
Orchard Row PE2 ....212 C2
Orchard St
  Cambridge CB1 .....246 B3
  Peterborough PE2 ...186 F7
  Stow cum Quy CB5 ..85 F5
  Whittlesey PE7 ....189 D7
Orchard Terr
  St Ives PE27 ....144 A4
  Whittlesford CB2 ...32 C4
Orchard The Ashley CB8 ..91 F7
  Fen Drayton CB4 ....121 F5
  Little Paxton PE19 ..95 F2
  Peterborough PE4 ...204 C3
Orchard View CB5 ....127 B1
Orchard Way
  Burwell CB5 ....130 B3
  Cambourne CB3 .....79 A3
  4 Doddington/Wimblington
  PE15 ....223 B7
  Godmanchester PE29 ..141 F2
  Haddenham CB6 .....210 A5
  Histon CB4 ....104 B5
  14 Somersham PE28 ..215 C1
  Stamford PE9 ......244 A5
Orchards Prim Sch
  PE13 ....245 D8
Orchards The
  Cambridge CB4 .....65 F5
  Chatteris PE16 ....241 D5
  Great Shelford CB2 ..49 B6
  Peterborough PE2 ...185 F4
  Sutton CB6 ....216 E2
  11 Wilburton CB6 ..210 C6
  Witcham CB6 ....217 A2
Orchid Cl
  18 Eaton Socon PE19 ..74 C6
  Yaxley PE7 ....181 F7
Orchid Fare CB3 ....80 C2
Orford Rd CB3 ......23 F6
Orkney Cl CB9 .....24 D7
Orme Rd PE3 ....197 D4
Orthwaite PE2 ......186 A7
Orton Ave PE3 ......186 E7
Orton Dr CB6 ......217 D1
Orton Longueville Sch
  PE2 ....186 A5
Orton Mere PE2 ....186 B7
Orton Parkway PE2 ...185 D4
Orton Wistow Foundation
  Prim Sch PE2 ......185 C6
Orwell Cl PE27 ....144 A6
Orwell Dr PE15 ....243 B5
Orwell Furlong CB4 ..84 C7
Orwell Gr PE4 .....204 F1
Orwell Rd CB2 .....29 C8
Osborn Cl CB4 .....209 A1
Osborne Pk CB13 ...245 C8
Osborne Rd PE13 ...245 C5
Osbourne Cl PE4 ...204 F1
Osier Cl CB7 ......240 E4
Osier Ct **4** PE19 ..74 C6
Osier Holt PE28 ...208 D6
Osier Way CB3 .....79 C5
Osiers The PE19 ...117 A3
Oslar's Way CB1 ...66 E5
Osprey Cl PE7 .....189 C7
Osprey Ct PE19 ....142 A7
Osprey Rd CB9 .....24 C7
Osric Ct PE1 ......198 C5
Otago Cl PE7 ......189 F8
Otago Rd PE7 ......189 E8
Othello Cl PE7 ....142 A7
Otter Cl CB3 ......102 B4
Otter Way **9** PE19 ..74 B5
Otterbrook PE2 ....185 D5

Oundle Rd Elton PE8 ..183 F1
  Peterborough PE2 ...185 E6
Ouse Fen Rd Or Bank
  CB4 ....208 D3
Ouse Rd
  Eaton Socon PE19 ...74 C4
  Kimbolton PE28 ....114 B7
  St Ives PE27 ....144 A7
Ouse Valley Way PE19 ..117 E4
Ouse Washes Nature
  Reserve* CB6 ......224 D2
Ouse Wlk PE29 .....141 E4
Outfield PE3 ......204 A1
Outwell Rd
  Boyces Bridge PE14 ..236 D4
  Elm PE14 ....236 C5
  Outwell PE14 ......236 C5
Over Hall La CB10 ..21 D2
Over Prim Sch CB4 ...208 D1
Over Rd Swavesey CB4 ..122 F8
  Willingham CB4 ....208 F1
Overchurch Cl CB9 ...23 F7
Overcote La PE27 ...208 B2
Overcote Rd CB4 ...208 D1
Overend PE8 ....178 D8
Overhall Gr Nature Reserve*
  CB3 ....100 F3
Overhills Prim Sch
  PE28 ....113 F5
Overstone Ct PE3 ...197 C6
Overstone Rd **1** PE14 ..235 D1
Overstone Rd **2** PE14 ..235 D1
Overton Way PE2 ...185 F4
Overwater Cl PE29 ..141 A6
Ovington Pl **3** CB9 ..24 B8
Owall Wlk **8** SG8 ..5 E8
Owen Cl **3** PE9 ..230 D3
Owen Dr SG8 ......13 D1
Owl End
  The Stukeleys PE28 ..151 F2
  Yaxley PE7 ....181 D5
Owl Way PE29 ......142 B7
Owls End PE26 .....172 A4
Oxborne Rd CB3 ....64 C7
Ox Cl PE3 ....197 A8
Ox Field PE13 .....237 F3
Oxbow Cres PE15 ...243 C4
Oxburgh Cl
  Peterborough PE7 ...187 F5
  Wisbech PE13 .....245 A7
Oxford Cl
  Bassingbourn SG8 ...12 F7
  Mildenhall IP28 ...239 A5
  Wyton PE29 ....143 B8
Oxford Rd
  Cambridge CB4 ....83 B4
  Peterborough PE1 ...197 F5
  St Ives PE27 ......144 A4
  Stamford PE9 .....244 A7
Oxford St CB8 .....110 B8
Oxholme Dro CB4 ...209 F1
Oxney Rd PE1 .....198 D5
Oyster Row CB5 ....84 B3

P

Pacific Cl PE15 ...243 C6
Paddock Cl CB4 ....104 C4
Paddock Row CB3 ...100 B4
Paddock St CB7 ....212 B4
Paddock The
  Eaton Socon PE19 ...74 C4
  Ely CB6 ....240 D5
  Harston CB2 ....47 F2
  Huntingdon PE29 ..141 E5
  18 Somersham PE28 ..215 C1
  Stamford PE9 .....244 A5
Paddock Way
  Haddenham CB6 ....210 A6
  Sawston CB2 ....32 F7
Paddocks Chase PE19 ..118 A3
Paddocks CP Sch CB8 ..110 E4
Paddocks Dr CB8 ...111 A1
Paddocks The
  Alconbury PE28 ....150 F5
  Burwell CB5 ....130 B1
  Cambridge CB1 ....84 C1
  Folksworth PE7 ...175 D8
  Hilton PE28 ....120 B2
  Little Wilbraham CB8 ..68 F6
  Peterborough PE4 ...204 A5
  Whittlesey PE7 ....189 C7
  Woodhurst PE28 ...155 B4
  Worlington IP28 ...213 F4
Padgett's Rd PE14 ..229 C3
Padgetts Cl PE28 ..165 A5
Padholme Rd PE1 ...198 C3
Padholme Rd E PE1 ..198 E3
Padlock Rd CB1 ....84 C1
Padnal Bank CB7 ...219 B6
Padnal Dro CB6 ....242 E3
Padney Dro CB7 ....211 D5
Page Cl CB7 ....240 D6
Pages Way **3** PE28 ..140 C3
Paget Cl CB2 ......64 E3
Paget Pl CB8 ......111 A6
Paget Rd CB2 ......64 D2
Painter's La CB6 ..226 D5
Pakenham Cl CB4 ...84 A5
Pakenham Pl CB9 ..24 B7
Palace Gdns SG8 ...5 C6
Palace La CB7 .....132 D8
Palace St CB5 .....246 B3
Palisade Ct **2** CB6 ..211 B7
Palm Ct PE1 ....198 B8
Palmer Cl PE7 .....189 F6

Palmers Cl CB1 ....35 B3
Palmers La
  Alconbury PE28 ...150 F4
  Chrishall SG8 .....8 C4
Palmers Rd PE1 ....198 F5
Palmers Way SG8 ...14 D6
Palmers Wlk CB1 ...246 C2
Palmerston Rd PE2 ..186 F7
Pamment's La PE28 ..213 D6
Pampisford Rd CB1 ...34 C5
Pamplin Ct **1** CB1 ..65 F6
Panswell La PE13 ..235 C8
Panther Way CB1 ..66 A7
Pantile La CB5 ....130 A3
Pantiles CB1 ......20 B7
Panton St CB2 .....246 B1
Papley Gr Farm Cotts
  PE19 ....77 E2
Papley Hollow PE19 ..77 F8
Papworth Hospl CB3 ..99 C2
Papworth Rd
  Graveley PE19 .....98 A5
  March PE15 ....243 F4
Papworth's Cl PE28 ..208 D1
Papyrus Rd PE4 ....203 F3
Papyrus Way PE28 ..168 B4
Parade La CB7 .....219 D2
Paradise Ctr & Pool
  CB7 ....240 D5
Paradise La
  Northborough PE6 ...231 F6
  3 Whittlesey PE7 ..189 D6
Paradise Nature Reserve*
  CB1 ....246 A1
Paradise St CB1 ...246 C5
Paragon Rd PE27 ..144 A4
Parcel Wlk PE29 ...118 F8
Parish Bush Dro CB7 ..219 C1
Park Ave Histon CB4 ..104 A4
  Little Paxton PE19 ..95 F1
  Newmarket CB8 ....111 B3
  St Ives PE28 ....144 B4
  Wisbech PE13 .....245 C6
Park Cl
  Bassingbourn SG8 ...12 E5
  Holme PE7 ....176 F4
  Little Paxton PE19 ..95 E1
  Moulton CB8 ......112 F5
  Thorney PE6 ......233 B3
  Yaxley PE7 ....181 F5
Park Cotts CB8 ....111 B3
Park Cres
  Bassingbourn SG8 ...95 F2
  Peterborough PE1 ...198 B5
  Thorney PE6 ......233 B3
  Waterbeach CB5 ...106 C8
Park Dr Histon CB4 ..104 C3
  Little Paxton PE19 ..95 F1
Park End CB5 ......87 B8
Park Farm Cl PE6 ...231 F8
Park Farm Cotts CB10 ..18 F6
Park Farm Cres PE7 ..187 A5
Park Farm Dr IP28 ..214 A2
Park Farm La SG8 ...1 A2
Park Farm Rd PE6 ...196 E5
Park Farm Way PE7 ..187 A8
Park Hill CB1 .....37 C2
Park Home Rd PE7 ..186 D1
Park La Brampton PE28 ..117 D8
  Castle Camps CB1 ..22 E3
  Dry Drayton CB3 ...81 C8
  Fen Drayton CB4 ...121 F6
  Godmanchester PE29 ..141 F2
  Histon CB4 ....103 F4
  Kimbolton PE28 ...113 F2
  Langley CB11 ......1 F2
  Leverington PE13 ..238 A3
  Little Downham CB6 ..217 F6
  Longstowe CB3 .....59 F3
  Madingley CB3 ....81 F6
  Newmarket CB8 ....111 B3
  Newton PE13 ......237 F3
  Peterborough PE1 ...198 C4
  Stamford PE9 .....244 C4
  Whittlesey PE7 ...189 C7
Park La Prim Sch PE7 ..189 C6
Park Par CB5 ......246 A4
Park Rd Brampton PE28 ..140 C2
  Buckden PE19 ......117 B4
  Burwell CB5 ......130 B2
  Cheveley CB8 .....91 C6
  Great Chesterford CB10 ..13 E5
  Haverhill CB9 .....23 D8
  Manea PE15 ....224 B4
  Market Deeping PE6 ..231 E8
  Peterborough PE1 ...198 A3
  Ramsey PE26 ......171 F6
  St Ives PE27 .....144 A4
  St Neots PE19 ....74 F6
  Sawston CB2 ......32 F7
  Sawtry PE28 ......168 B5
  Sutton CB6 ....216 E2
  Tydd St Giles PE13 ..237 D7
  Wisbech PE13 .....245 D7
Park Side
  Little Paxton PE19 ..95 E1
  St Ives PE27 ......144 B4
Park St Cambridge CB5 ..246 A3
  Chatteris PE16 ...241 C4
  Dry Drayton CB3 ..102 C1
  Peterborough PE1 ...186 F7
  2 Wisbech PE13 ...245 D5
Park St CE Prim Sch
  CB5 ....246 A3
Park Terr
  Cambridge CB1 ....246 B2
  Peterborough PE1 ...198 A6

Park View
  Bassingbourn SG8 ...12 E5
  Little Stukeley PE28 ..151 F1
  Needingworth PE27 ..208 A2
Park View E PE15 ..243 C4
Park View W PE15 ..243 C4
Park Way
  Little Paxton PE19 ..95 F1
  Offord Cluny PE19 ..118 A2
  St Neots PE19 ....74 F7
Parker Cl PE19 ....74 E2
Parker Rd PE8 .....230 B1
Parkers Cl CB1 ....246 B2
Parker's Ct PE16 ..241 B5
Parker's Dro IP28 ..213 D6
Parker's Terr **2** CB1 ..84 A2
Parkers Wlk CB8 ...110 E8
Parkfield La PE15 ..223 B6
Parkgate PE29 ....141 C6
Parkhall Rd PE28 ..215 C2
Parkinson's La **1** PE7 ..189 D6
Parklands SG8 ....5 E6
Parkside
  Cambridge CB1 ....246 C2
  Chatteris PE16 ...241 D4
  Chippenham CB7 ...132 E8
  Haverhill CB9 ....23 F6
  Mildenhall IP28 ..214 A8
  Peterborough PE2 ...186 B6
Parkside Foundation Coll
  CB1 ....246 C2
Parkside Pools CB1 ..246 C2
Parkway St Ives PE27 ..144 B4
  Shudy Camps CB1 ..22 C6
  The Stukeleys PE29 ..141 A5
Parkway Mid Sch CB9 ..23 D8
Parliament St PE1 ..197 F5
Parlour Cl CB4 ....104 B5
Parnwell Prim Sch
  PE1 ....198 F2
Parnwell Way PE1 ..198 F6
Parr Cl CB4 ....104 C3
Parr Rd CB9 ......23 D6
Parrens Rd PE28 ...208 E6
Parr's Dro La PE13 ..238 B2
Parsonage Barns CB5 ..86 F5
Parsonage Cl
  Burwell CB5 ......130 B2
  Duxford CB2 ......17 E8
Parsonage Farm La
  CB8 ....90 F2
Parsonage Gdns **2** CB9 ..23 E7
Parsonage St
  Cambridge CB5 ....246 C3
  Wistow PE28 ......163 F6
Parsonage Way CB1 ..35 C2
Parson's Ct CB2 ...246 A2
Parson's Dr PE28 ..139 A4
Parson's La CB6 ...242 C4
Parson's Land Dro
  PE15 ....222 D6
Parsons Gn PE27 ..144 C4
Parthia Cl CB3 ....5 E6
Partridge Cl PE7 ..181 D5
Partridge Dr CB3 ..102 B3
Partridge Gr PE4 ..204 A5
Partridge Hill **5** CB7 ..2 C3
Passage The **8** CB7 ..240 D4
Paston La PE4 .....197 D8
Paston Parkway PE4 ..204 E4
Paston Ridings PE4 ..204 E1
Paston Ridings Prim Sch
  PE4 ....204 F1
Pasture Cl PE28 ...165 A5
Pasture La PE6 ....233 C4
Pasture The **2** PE28 ..208 B8
Pastures The CB3 ..81 A1
Pates Cl CB3 ......47 A6
Pathfinder Way
  Ramsey PE26 ......171 F5
  Warboys PE28 .....164 F4
  Wyton PE28 ....143 A8
Patterdale Dr PE4 ..205 A2
Patterdale Rd PE4 ..205 A2
Paulsgrove PE2 ....185 D5
Pavement The PE27 ..144 A3
Pavilion Ct Haverhill CB9 ..24 B7
  7 Kings Hedges CB4 ..83 E8
Paxton Cl CB4 ....125 E3
Paxton Hill PE19 ..96 D2
Paxton Pitts Nature
  Reserve* PE19 ....96 A3
Paxton Rd
  Offord Darcy PE19 ..96 F7
  Peterborough PE2 ...185 D4
Payne Ave PE13 ...245 D7
Payne Prim Sch PE13 ..234 D7
Paynells PE2 ......186 A3
Paynes Mdw CB5 ...130 A3
Paynesholm PE4 ...205 A1
Payton Way CB5 ...130 A3
Peacock Dr CB5 ...86 F7
Peacock Way
  Littleport CB6 ....242 E4
  Peterborough PE3 ...196 F2
Peacocks CB2 .....49 A4
Peaks Cl PE6 ......235 E6
Peakes Dr PE7 ....201 F1
Peakes Dr PE7 ....201 F1
Peakirk cum Glinton Prim
  Sch PE6 ....203 E8
Peakirk Rd
  Deeping Gate PE6 ...231 F8
  Glinton PE6 ......203 F8
  Northborough PE6 ...206 A4
Peakirk Wildfowl Trust*
  PE6 ....206 B2

Peaks Ct PE29 . . . . .141 A5
Pear Tree PE13 . . . . .234 C2
Pear Tree Cl
  Fenstanton PE28 . . . . .121 A5
  Haddenham CB6 . . . . .210 A5
Pear Tree Cres PE13 . . . .238 A2
Pearce Cl CB3 . . . . .64 B8
Pearces Rd PE6 . . . . .199 B5
Pearl Leisure Ctr PE5 . . .195 E1
Pearmain Ct CB4 . . . . .84 C5
Pearmains Cl SG8 . . . . .45 E1
Pearson Cl Milton CB4 . . .105 D1
  St Neots PE19 . . . . .74 E2
Peartree Way 10 PE14 . . .236 A5
Peas Hill CB2 . . . . .246 A2
Peas Hill Rd PE15 . . . . . . .243 A5
Pease Way CB4 . . . . .103 F4
Peate Cl PE29 . . . . .141 F1
Peatlings La PE13 . . . . . .245 A7
Peckover Cl PE7 . . . . .187 F5
Peckover Dr PE13 . . . . . . .245 E4
Peckover House*
  PE13 . . . . .245 B5
Peckover Prim Sch
  PE13 . . . . .245 B6
Pecks Cl CB3 . . . . .120 C1
Pecks Yd PE16 . . . . .241 C5
Peddars Way PE3 . . . . . . .197 A2
Pedley La PE13 . . . . .245 A6
Peer Rd PE19 . . . . .74 B4
Pegler Ct CB4 . . . . .209 A1
Peldon Dr PE13 . . . . .245 C5
Pelham Cl
  Cottenham CB4 . . . . .125 D3
  Peterborough PE3 . . . . . . .196 F2
Pelham Ct CB4 . . . . .83 C6
Pelham Way CB4 . . . . .125 D3
Pelican Prep Sch CB1 . . . . .65 B4
Pemberton Terr CB2 . . . .246 B1
Pembroke Ave
  Peterborough PE2 . . . . . . .185 F5
  9 St Neots PE19 . . . . .74 F2
  Waterbeach CB5 . . . . .105 F8
Pembroke Cl
  Huntingdon PE29 . . . . .141 F7
  Mildenhall IP28 . . . . .239 C5
  2 Newmarket CB8 . . . . . . .111 B2
Pembroke Coll CB2 . . . . .246 A2
Pembroke Dr PE6 . . . . . . .203 F8
Pembroke La CB1 . . . . .35 E2
Pembroke Rd PE9 . . . . . . .244 A7
Pembroke St CB2 . . . . . . .246 A2
Pembroke Way CB1 . . . . . .85 B1
Pen Cl CB1 . . . . .66 A6
Pen Hills Nature Reserve*
  SG8 . . . . .27 A8
Penarth Pl CB3 . . . . .64 A8
Pendleton PE3 . . . . .197 B6
Pendragon Com Prim Sch
  CB3 . . . . .99 A3
Pendragon Hill CB3 . . . . . .99 A4
Pendula Rd PE13 . . . . .245 E7
Pennine Way PE4 . . . . . . .204 D2
Pennington PE2 . . . . .186 E3
Pennington Rd PE8 . . . . . .142 A7
Pennway 11 PE28 . . . . . . .215 C1
Penrith Gr PE4 . . . . .205 A2
Penrose Gdns PE13 . . . . .245 E4
Penrwyn Ct 5 PE19 . . . . . .74 F1
Pentelowes The PE28 . . . .135 D2
Pentland Way PE15 . . . . . .243 B5
Pentlands Cl CB4 . . . . . . .243 B5
Pentlands Cl CB4 . . . . . . .246 C4
Pentlands The PE4 . . . . . .204 E2
Pentlow Hawke Cl CB4 . . . .24 B7
Penwald Cl 7 PE6 . . . . . . .232 B8
Penyale PE3 . . . . .197 A1
Pepper Cl SG8 . . . . .12 F4
Peppercorn Cl PE1 . . . . . .197 E6
Peppercorns La 2 PE19 . . .74 C2
Pepperslade CB2 . . . . .31 F1
Peppin Brown Gall The*
  CB2 . . . . .32 C5
Pepys House* PE28 . . . . . .140 F2
Pepys Rd
  Brampton PE28 . . . . .140 F2
  St Neots PE19 . . . . .75 A4
Pepys Terr CB4 . . . . .104 C1
Pepys Way CB3 . . . . .82 E8
Percheron Cl CB4 . . . . . . .104 D3
Percheron Dr PE15 . . . . . .243 E2
Percival St PE1 . . . . .197 E2
Peregrine Cl PE29 . . . . . . .142 A7
Perkins La 7 PE6 . . . . . . .231 C7
Perne Ave CB1 . . . . .65 C6
Perne Rd CB1 . . . . .65 C5
Pernys Cl PE7 . . . . .186 D3
Perowne St CB1 . . . . .84 A1
Perry Cl CB6 . . . . .210 A6
Perry Ct CB3 . . . . .83 A2
Perry Dr SG8 . . . . .5 E7
Perry Rd Buckden PE19 . . .116 F3
  Leverington PE13 . . . . .238 B2
Perse Boys Sch The
  CB2 . . . . .65 A4
Perse Girls 6th Form Coll
  CB1 . . . . .246 C1
Perse Prep Sch CB2 . . . . .246 B1
Perse Sch For Girls The
  CB2 . . . . .246 B1
Perse Way CB3 . . . . .83 D5
Pershore Rd CB3 . . . . .81 A3
Pershore Way PE3 . . . . . . .232 B2
Persimmon Wlk CB8 . . . . .110 E8
Peter Goodin Cl CB4 . . . .105 C2
Peterborough Airport
  (Conington) PE7 . . . . . . .176 F3

Peterborough Bsns Pk
  PE2 . . . . .185 C5
Peterborough Cath (St
  Peter's)* PE1 . . . . .198 A2
Peterborough Coll of Adult
  Ed PE1 . . . . .198 B3
Peterborough District
  PE3 . . . . .197 E2
Peterborough Dr
  Bretton PE3 . . . . .196 E2
  Castor PE6 . . . . .196 D3
Peterborough High Sch
  PE3 . . . . .197 D2
Peterborough Mus & Art
  Gall* PE3 . . . . .197 F2
Peterborough Rd
  Castor PE6 . . . . .195 E1
  Crowland PE6 . . . . .232 B8
  Eye PE6 . . . . .205 F1
  Newborough PE6 . . . . .205 D8
  Peterborough PE7 . . . . . . .187 C3
  Wansford PE8 . . . . .194 A3
  Warmington PE8 . . . . .174 A6
  Whittlesey PE7 . . . . .189 B7
Peterborough Regional Coll
  Peterborough PE1 . . . . . . .198 B5
  Woodston PE2 . . . . .186 D6
Peterborough Sta PE3 . . .197 F2
Petergate 1 PE9 . . . . .244 B4
Peterhouse CB2 . . . . .246 A1
Peterhouse Cl
  Milden PE8 . . . . .239 D4
  Stamford PE9 . . . . .244 B7
Peterhouse Cres PE15 . . .243 E6
Peterhouse Dr CB8 . . . . . .111 A2
Peterhouse Tech Pk
  CB1 . . . . .66 A4
Petersfield 3 CB1 . . . . . .246 C2
Petersfield CE Sch SG8 . .28 D8
Petersfield Rd CB2 . . . . . . .17 D8
Petersfield St CB5 . . . . . . .86 C5
Petingo Cl CB8 . . . . .110 D7
Pettis Rd PE27 . . . . .143 E6
Pettis Wlk PE27 . . . . .143 F7
Pettit Rd PE29 . . . . .142 A1
Pettits Cl CB1 . . . . .66 F4
Pettitt's Cl CB3 . . . . .103 C2
Pettitt's La CB3 . . . . .102 C1
Petts Cl 3 PE13 . . . . .245 E7
Petts La CB10 . . . . .19 E1
Petty Cury CB2 . . . . .246 B2
Petworth St CB1 . . . . .84 A2
Peverel Cl CB5 . . . . .84 D3
Peverel Rd CB5 . . . . .84 D3
Peveril Rd CB1 . . . . .197 F6
Peyton Ave PE15 . . . . .243 B6
Peyton Cl CB3 . . . . .223 A5
Pheasant Gr PE4 . . . . .204 A5
Pheasant Rise CB3 . . . . . .102 A3
Pheasant Way PE7 . . . . . .181 D5
Philip Gdns PE19 . . . . .74 F2
Philippa Cl CB8 . . . . .240 E7
Philipps Cl CB8 . . . . .110 D4
Phillips Ave SG8 . . . . .5 C8
Phillips Chase PE15 . . . . .243 C4
Phillips Ct PE9 . . . . .244 C4
Phillips' Fen Dro CB7 . . . .219 B6
Phoenix Rd CB9 . . . . .25 A5
Phoenix Sq PE19 . . . . .74 E6
Phorpres Cl PE7 . . . . .186 D3
Phorpres Way PE7 . . . . . .186 E4
Pickards Way PE13 . . . . . .245 A6
Pickle Fen Dro PE15 . . . . .215 E6
Picknage Rd SG8 . . . . .7 A2
Pidley Hill PE28 . . . . .208 A8
Pidley Sheep La PE28 . . .155 F7
Pieces La CB5 . . . . .106 B8
Pieces Terr CB5 . . . . .106 B7
Pierce Cres PE8 . . . . .178 C3
Pig La CB6 . . . . .66 F5
Pig La PE27 . . . . .144 B5
Pigeons Cl SG8 . . . . .31 C2
Pightle Cl Harston CB2 . . .47 D2
  Royston SG8 . . . . .5 C7
Pightle The
  Bottisham CB5 . . . . .86 E6
  Grafham PE28 . . . . .138 A7
  Haverhill CB9 . . . . .24 A8
Pikes Wlk CB1 . . . . .246 B3
Piketts Cl PE7 . . . . .189 D7
Pilgrims Cl CB10 . . . . .11 A2
Pilgrims Way CB6 . . . . . . .240 A3
Pilton Cl 4 PE4 . . . . .204 F2
Pinder Cl PE29 . . . . .118 F7
Pine Gr CB4 . . . . .122 A3
Pine Tree Cl PE11 . . . . . . .198 B8
Pine Trees Ave PE28 . . . . .239 E4
Pine View CB4 . . . . .126 A7
Pines Ind Est The CB8 . . .131 F4
Pinewood Ave
  Whittlesey PE7 . . . . .189 C7
  Wittering PE8 . . . . .230 B1
Pinfold La
  Godmanchester PE29 . . . . .141 F7
  1 Somersham PE28 . . . . . .208 B8
  Stamford PE9 . . . . .244 C3
Pinfold Rd PE14 . . . . .236 E1
Pingle Bank PE7 . . . . .177 A4
Pingle Cl PE7 . . . . .189 C7
Pingle Dro PE6 . . . . .216 E6
Pingle La PE6 . . . . .231 F6
Pingle Wood & Cutting
  Nature Reserve*
  PE28 . . . . .165 A8
Pinhoe Dr PE19 . . . . .23 C8
Pinkeneys SG8 . . . . .8 D5
Pinza Cl CB8 . . . . .110 E8
Pipe La PE1 . . . . .198 B2

Piperell Way CB9 . . . . .24 A5
Pipers Cl CB9 . . . . .24 C7
Pipers La PE29 . . . . .141 F1
Pipistrelle Cl PE19 . . . . . . .96 A2
Pipistrelle Ct 6 PE4 . . . . .204 C3
Pippin Cl
  Offord Darcy PE19 . . . . . . .117 F1
  4 Girton CB4 . . . . .208 D1
Pippin Dr CB4 . . . . .84 C6
Pippin Gr SG8 . . . . .5 C7
Pippin Pk CB8 . . . . .73 E8
Pippin Wlk CB3 . . . . .81 A3
Pitfield Cl PE28 . . . . .121 C5
Pits La PE15 . . . . .243 D1
Pits The CB7 . . . . .213 A4
Pitsdean Rd PE19 . . . . .57 A4
Pittneys PE4 . . . . .204 F1
Pius Dro PE14 . . . . .236 E2
Place Farm Com Prim Sch
  CB9 . . . . .23 F8
Plains La CB6 . . . . .225 C3
Plaistow Way SG8 . . . . .7 E2
Plane Tree Cl SG19 . . . . . .41 C6
Plank Dro PE6 . . . . .232 B8
Plantation Gate CB6 . . . .210 F5
Plantation Rd CB2 . . . . . . .33 A7
Plantwater Dro PE15 . . . .227 D5
Plash Dro PE13 . . . . .234 F4
Playles Yd SG8 . . . . .12 E5
Plough Cl SG8 . . . . .3 B8
Plough Cres PE7 . . . . .189 C8
Plough La PE6 . . . . .207 D1
Plough Rd PE7 . . . . .189 D8
Plover Cl CB6 . . . . .241 C5
Plover Dr PE15 . . . . .243 F5
Plover Rd PE7 . . . . .189 F8
Ploverly PE4 . . . . .204 C4
Plowright Cl PE15 . . . . . . .243 B3
Plum Tree Cl 8 CB4 . . . . .83 F2
Plumian Way CB2 . . . . .53 C2
Plumpton Ave IP28 . . . . . .239 C5
Polecat La PE6 . . . . .150 E5
Poles Ct PE7 . . . . .189 D7
Pollards La PE28 . . . . .213 D7
Pond Cl
  Eastwood End PE15 . . . . . .223 B6
  Pidley cum Fenton PE28 . .165 D1
  The Stukeleys PE29 . . . . . .140 F5
Pond Gn CB7 . . . . .211 E1
Pond La CB6 . . . . .218 A6
Pond The CB6 . . . . .210 A7
Pont's Hill CB6 . . . . .242 D5
Pooley Way PE7 . . . . .181 D6
Pools Rd CB6 . . . . .210 D8
Poor's Land CB6 . . . . .6 D4
Poorsfield Rd 8 CB5 . . . .106 A7
Pope Rd PE19 . . . . .74 E4
Pope Way PE1 . . . . .197 E8
Popes Ct 3 CB9 . . . . .24 E5
Pope's La PE13 . . . . .238 A2
Popes La Thetford CB6 . . .211 F7
  Warboys PE28 . . . . .159 F5
Popham Cl PE19 . . . . .74 A3
Pophams Eau* PE14 . . . . .229 C7
Poplar Ave PE1 . . . . .198 C8
Poplar Cl
  Great Gransden SG19 . . . . .58 D4
  Great Shelford CB2 . . . . . . .49 A5
  Haverhill CB9 . . . . .38 D1
  Huntingdon PE29 . . . . .141 E7
  March NG15 . . . . .243 C5
  Royston SG8 . . . . .5 E7
Poplar Dr SG8 . . . . .5 E7
Poplar Dro CB6 . . . . .242 F8
Poplar Farm Cl SG8 . . . . . .12 D4
Poplar Rd CB4 . . . . .104 B3
Poplar Way CB2 . . . . .49 C4
Poplars Cl CB5 . . . . .130 B2
Poplars The PE28 . . . . . . .208 C6
Popple Dro PE13 . . . . .235 A8
Poppy Fields 7 PE7 . . . . .212 B5
Poppyfields Ave PE15 . . .224 B4
Porch Cl PE29 . . . . .141 F1
Porson Cl CB2 . . . . .64 E4
Porson Rd CB2 . . . . .64 D5
Port La PE5 . . . . .195 E1
Porthester Cl PE2 . . . . . . .187 F5
Porters Yd PE16 . . . . .241 C6
Portland Ave PE1 . . . . . . .197 F7
Portland Gn CB3 . . . . .110 E3
Portland Pl
  Cambridge CB1 . . . . .246 C3
  Whittlesey PE7 . . . . .189 E6
Portland Rd CB8 . . . . .110 E3
Portman Cl PE3 . . . . .197 C4
Portobello La CB2 . . . . .32 E7
Portugal Pl CB2 . . . . .246 A3
Portugal St CB5 . . . . .246 A3
Portway SG8 . . . . .14 F7
Portway Rd CB3 . . . . .71 B6
Post Office La 10 PE13 . . .245 C5
Post Office Terr CB2 . . . . .246 B2
Post St PE29 . . . . .141 E2
Pot Hall Rd IP28 . . . . .213 E6
Potter's La CB7 . . . . .240 D3
Potters Way PE1 . . . . .198 B1
Potton End PE19 . . . . .74 B3
Potton Rd Everton SG19 . . .40 C3
  Fenstanton PE28 . . . . .120 D3
Gamlingay SG19 . . . . .41 D3
Gamlingay Great Heath
  SG19 . . . . .40 F3
  Guilden Morden SG8 . . . . . .10 F6
  Hilton PE28 . . . . .99 B8
  St Neots PE19 . . . . .74 E6
  Wrestlingworth SG19 . . . . .25 A4
Potton Wood* SG19 . . . . . .25 A8

Poulter Ave PE2 . . . . .187 D5
Poulter's Dro PE14 . . . . . .229 D5
Pound Cl Bottisham CB5 . . .86 E7
  Burwell CB5 . . . . .130 B2
  Hail Weston PE19 . . . . .95 B1
  Spaldwick PE28 . . . . .137 F6
Pound Gn SG8 . . . . .10 F5
Pound Hill CB3 . . . . .83 C3
Pound La Isleham CB7 . . .213 A5
  Kimbolton PE28 . . . . .113 F4
  Sutton CB6 . . . . .216 E2
Pound Rd
  Chatteris PE16 . . . . .241 B6
  Hemingford Grey PE28 . . .143 D1
  Ramsey PE26 . . . . .172 A4
Pound The PE27 . . . . .144 A5
Pound Way CB5 . . . . .108 B2
Powell Cl CB3 . . . . .61 D5
Powis Pl 2 PE19 . . . . .74 F1
Pratt Ave PE4 . . . . .204 F2
Pratt St PE27 . . . . .212 B4
Prentice Cl CB4 . . . . .123 F2
Prescott Cl PE28 . . . . .208 C5
Preston Cl CB3 . . . . .61 D5
Pretoria Rd CB4 . . . . .246 C4
Priam's Way CB2 . . . . .49 E6
Prickwillow Drainage Engine
  Mus* CB7 . . . . .219 B5
Prickwillow Rd
  Ely CB7 . . . . .240 F5
  Isleham CB7 . . . . .212 F7
  Soham CB7 . . . . .219 D3
Priest La CB4 . . . . .209 A1
Priestgate 4 PE1 . . . . . . .198 A2
Priests Mdw Ct CB6 . . . .240 C5
Primary Ct CB4 . . . . .84 B5
Prime Cl SG8 . . . . .14 C6
Primes Cl CB2 . . . . .29 D7
Primrose Cl
  Cambridge CB1 . . . . .66 A5
  Peterborough PE1 . . . . . . .198 A8
  Ramsey St Mary's PE26 . . .220 D3
Primrose Dr PE7 . . . . .181 F7
Primrose Farm Rd CB1 . . .36 E2
Primrose Hill
  Doddington PE15 . . . . .222 E5
  Haverhill CB9 . . . . .23 F7
  Little Gransden SG19 . . . . .58 E3
Primrose La
  Huntingdon PE29 . . . . .141 E5
  5 Soham CB7 . . . . .212 B5
  Waterbeach CB5 . . . . .106 A8
Primrose St CB4 . . . . .83 D4
Primrose View SG8 . . . . . . .5 F5
Prince Andrew's Cl 1
  SG8 .5 D5
Prince Cl PE14 . . . . .59 F1
Prince of Wales Cl
  PE13 . . . . .245 D8
Prince S Rd PE13 . . . . . . .245 C4
Prince's Cl PE13 . . . . .245 D5
Prince William Cl CB4 . . .83 C4
Prince William Way
  CB2 . . . . .32 F6
Prince's St
  Huntingdon PE29 . . . . .141 D4
  Peterborough PE1 . . . . . . .198 A4
  Ramsey PE26 . . . . .172 A4
Princes Cl CB1 . . . . .53 C1
Princes Dr PE19 . . . . .75 A6
Princes Gate PE1 . . . . . . .198 B4
Princes Gdns PE1 . . . . . . .198 B4
Princes Mews SG8 . . . . . . .5 C6
Princes Rd
  Peterborough PE2 . . . . . . .187 A4
  Stamford PE9 . . . . .244 B6
Princess Ave PE15 . . . . . .243 C2
Princess Ct CB1 . . . . .246 B1
Princess Dr CB2 . . . . .49 F1
Princess of Wales Hospl
  CB6 . . . . .240 E7
Princess Way
  Haverhill CB9 . . . . .23 E8
  Newmarket CB8 . . . . .110 E4
Pringle Cl PE7 . . . . .189 C7
Pringle Ct PE7 . . . . .151 D4
Prins Ave PE13 . . . . .245 D7
Prins Ct 8 PE13 . . . . .245 D7
Prior Cl CB4 . . . . .104 B4
Prior's Ct 6 CB6 . . . . .216 C2
Priors Cl CB6 . . . . .240 B5
Priors Gate PE4 . . . . .204 A4
Priory Cl CB9 . . . . .125 D7
Priory Gdns
  Peterborough PE7 . . . . . . .184 F3
  Stamford PE9 . . . . .244 D5
  Waterside CB7 . . . . .213 A5
Priory Gr PE29 . . . . .141 E5
Priory Hill PE19 . . . . .75 B7
Priory Hill Rd PE19 . . . . . .75 B7
Priory Inf Sch PE19 . . . . . .75 A6
Priory La
  Huntingdon PE29 . . . . .141 E5
  Royston SG8 . . . . .5 D5
  St Neots PE19 . . . . .74 E6
Priory Mews
  St Ives PE27 . . . . .144 A3
  St Neots PE19 . . . . .74 E6

Pea - Que 267

Priory Pk Inf Sch PE19 . . .74 F6
Priory Rd
  Cambridge CB5 . . . . .84 A3
  Holywell-cum-Needingworth
  PE27 . . . . .208 A3
  Horningsea CB5 . . . . .106 A1
  Huntingdon PE29 . . . . .141 E5
  Needingworth PE27 . . . . . .144 F5
  Peterborough PE3 . . . . . . .197 E3
  St Ives PE27 . . . . .144 A2
  St Neots PE19 . . . . .74 E6
  Stamford PE9 . . . . .244 D5
Priory St 3 CB4 . . . . .83 C4
Priory The PE19 . . . . .74 E5
Priory Wlk CB3 . . . . .79 C3
Proby Cl PE7 . . . . .181 D5
Prospect Pl PE13 . . . . . . .245 C3
Prospect Rd PE15 . . . . . . .243 B5
Prospect Row
  Cambridge CB1 . . . . .246 C2
  3 St Neots PE19 . . . . .74 F5
Prospect Way PE16 . . . . .241 C6
Prospero Cl PE22 . . . . . . .186 F6
Prospero Way PE29 . . . . .141 F7
Provence Pl 2 PE13 . . . . .245 E3
Provence Rd PE29 . . . . . .141 A6
Providence Ct 16 PE28 . . .175 F7
Providence Pl PE15 . . . . .224 B4
Providence Way CB5 . . . .127 A1
Pryor Cl CB4 . . . . .105 D2
Pudding Bag La PE9 . . . . .230 C4
Pudding La SG8 . . . . .7 A1
Puddock Hill PE28 . . . . . . .165 A8
Puddock Rd
  Ramsey PE28 . . . . .221 F1
  Warboys PE28 . . . . .165 A8
Pudgell The SG8 . . . . .7 E2
Puffin La PE7 . . . . .181 D8
Pump La 2 Hardwick CB3 .81 A3
  4 Stretham CB6 . . . . .210 F5
Purbeck Rd CB2 . . . . .65 A5
Purl's Bridge Dro
  PE15 . . . . .224 B3
Purls Rd 1 CB3 . . . . .79 A4
Purls Bridge PE15 . . . . . .224 B2
Putney Hill Rd CB7 . . . . . .219 B4
Pye Terr 84 A4
Pyecroft PE1 . . . . .198 B6
Pyhill PE3 . . . . .197 B8
Pymore (Pymoor) La
  CB6 . . . . .224 C1
Pyrecroft CB3 . . . . .79 A3
Pyrethrum Way CB4 . . . . .209 A1

Q

Quadrangle The PE28 . . .208 D7
Quadrant The
  Royston SG8 . . . . .5 C8
  St Ives PE27 . . . . .144 B3
Quail Wlk 8 SG8 . . . . .5 E8
Quainton Cl CB3 . . . . .84 D3
Quaker Cl PE28 . . . . .153 C6
Quaker La PE13 . . . . .245 C3
Quaker Way PE16 . . . . . . .241 C5
Quaker's Dro PE7 . . . . . . .191 F5
Quaker's La CB7 . . . . .24 A7
Quakers' Rd IP28 . . . . . . .239 F5
Quanea Dro CB7 . . . . .239 A3
Quarry La
  Haslingfield CB3 . . . . .47 B4
  Maxey PE6 . . . . .231 C6
  Swaffham Bulbeck CB5 . . .108 B1
Quay Ct PE27 . . . . .144 A3
Quay Hill CB6 . . . . .242 E4
Quay The PE27 . . . . .144 A3
Quayside
  Cambridge CB1 . . . . .246 A3
  Chatteris PE16 . . . . .241 C6
  Ely CB7 . . . . .240 E3
Queen Adelaide Way
  CB7 . . . . .240 E3
Queen Edith Com Prim Sch
  CB1 . . . . .65 D4
Queen Edith's Way CB1 . .65 D4
Queen Eleanor Cl PE7 . . .176 A8
Queen Eleanor Sch
  PE9 . . . . .244 B6
Queen Elizabeth Dr
  PE13 . . . . .245 D3
Queen Emma Wlk
  CB6 . . . . .240 E6
Queen Mary Cl PE26 . . . .172 A6
Queen St Cowlinge CB8 . . .73 C1
  Haverhill CB9 . . . . .24 A8
  Newmarket CB8 . . . . .111 B3
  2 Peterborough PE1 . . . . .198 A2
  Whittlesey PE7 . . . . .189 C3
  Yaxley PE7 . . . . .181 F6
Queen's Cl Holme PE7 . . .176 F4
  1 Over CB4 . . . . .208 D1
Queen's Dr
  Mildenhall IP28 . . . . .239 B4
  Wisbech PE14 . . . . .236 A3
Queen's Dr Inf Sch
  PE1 . . . . .198 A5
Queen's Dr W PE1 . . . . . .198 A5
Queen's Gdns PE1 . . . . . .198 A5
Queen's Mdw CB1 . . . . . . .65 F7
Queen's Rd CB3 . . . . .64 C8
Queen's Wlk PE9 . . . . . . .244 A5

Q

Queenholme Way
CB4 ....209 C2
Queens Cl Balsham CB1 ...52 F2
Harston CB2 ....48 A3
St Ives PE27 ....144 A5
Queens Coll CB3 ......246 A2
Queens Ct
Eaton Socon PE19 ......74 B3
7 Haverhill CB9 ....23 E8
Queens Dr PE29 ......141 F5
Queens Gdns PE19 ....74 B4
Queens' La CB2 ......246 A2
Queens Rd
Littleport CB6 ....242 B5
Peterborough PE2 ....187 B7
Royston SG8 ....5 D7
Somersham PE28 .....215 C1
Wisbech PE13 ....245 C4
Queens Sch The PE13 ...245 D3
Queens Sq CB4 ....241 A8
Queens St March PE15 ..243 D6
Stamford PE9 ....244 B6
Withersfield CB9 ......38 C4
Queens St Cl PE15 ....243 D6
Queens View CB4 ....110 A8
Queens Way CB4 ......103 D6
Quince Rd CB3 ....241 A8
Queensberry Rd CB8 ..111 A3
Queensgate Ctr PE1 ..198 A2
Queensway
Cambridge CB1 ....64 E6
Chatteris PE16 ......241 D5
Exning CB8 ....110 B8
Haverhill CB9 ....23 E8
Mildenhall IP28 ......239 B4
Royston SG8 ....5 D7
St Neots PE19 ....74 F7
Sawston CB2 ....32 F8
Soham CB7 ....212 B4
Quendon Pl CB9 ......24 B8
Quickset Rd CB11 ......9 B5
Quidditch La CB3 ......79 A4
Quince Rd CB3 ....241 A8
Quinion Cl PE7 ....189 F6
Quinton Garth PE2 ...197 C5
Quorn Cl PE6 ....205 C8
Quy Rd CB5 ....86 B8

R

Racey's Cl PE14 ......236 D6
Raceys Cl PE14 ......236 D6
Rachel Cl **1** CB5 .....84 E4
Rackham CE Prim Sch The
CB6 ....217 E1
Rackham Cl CB4 ....83 C4
Radcliffe Cl **1** PE9 ..244 B5
Radcliffe Rd PE2 ....244 A5
Radegund Rd CB1 .....60 D7
Radegunds CB2 ....32 C5
Radford Cl PE8 ......230 C1
Radwinter Rd CB10 ....21 B1
RAF Molesworth PE28 .147 C8
RAF Witchford Display of
Memorabilia* CB6 ...217 F1
RAF Wyton PE28 .....143 A8
Ragdale Cl PE1 ....198 E7
Railway Cl CB5 ......109 B8
Railway La PE16 .....241 C5
Railway Rd CB1 ......245 C3
Railway St CB1 ....65 F7
Railworld Mus* PE2 ...197 F1
Raine Ave CB9 ....23 D8
Raleigh Cl PE19 ......74 A2
Raleigh Way PE1 ....197 B6
Ramnoth Jun Sch
PE13 ....245 D4
Ramnoth Rd PE13 ....245 D4
Rampart The CB8 .....210 A6
Ramper Rd CB4 ......123 A3
Rampley La PE19 ......95 F2
Rampleys The PE28 ..143 D2
Ramply Cl PE19 ....95 F1
Rampton Drift CB4 ...124 B2
Rampton End CB4 ....209 A1
Rampton Rd
Cottenham CB4 ......125 B4
Longstanton CB4 .....124 A2
Oakington/Longstanton
CB4 ....123 F1
Willingham CB4 .....124 B7
Ramsden Sq CB4 ......84 A7
Ramsey Abbey Gatehouse*
PE26 ....172 C7
Ramsey Abbey Sch
PE26 ....172 C7
Ramsey Hollow Dro
PE26 ....173 B7
Ramsey Hts Nature Reserve*
PE26 ....170 E6
Ramsey Jun Sch PE26 .172 A7
Ramsey Leisure Ctr
PE26 ....172 C7
Ramsey Rd
Benwick PE15 ....221 F4
Ely PE7 ....240 E6
Kings Ripton PE28 ...172 E5
Old Hurst PE28 .....154 D6
Ramsey PE26 ....221 C2
St Ives PE27 ....143 F7
Upwood & The Raveleys
PE26 ....171 Q2
Warboys PE28 ....164 E6
Whittlesey PE7 .....220 E7

Ramsey Rural Mus*
PE26 ....172 D7
Ramsey Way PE2 .....187 F6
Ramshill Cotts PE6 ...203 A2
Randalls La CB4 .....208 D1
Range The CB7 ......240 C4
Rangefield PE2 ......185 E4
Ransome's Cl PE14 ...236 E2
Ransonmoor Dro
PE15 ....222 D7
Ransonmoor Grange
PE15 ....222 F8
Raptor Foundation The*
PE28 ....155 C4
Ras Ct **2** PE1 ......198 D3
Ratcliffe Ct PE1 ....198 D7
Ratfords Yd CB1 .....68 A8
Rathmore Cl CB1 .....65 A6
Rathmore Rd CB1 .....65 A6
Raveley Fen Rd PE28 .162 D8
Raveley Rd PE28 ....161 F6
Raven Cl
Mildenhall IP28 .....239 D4
St Neots PE19 ....75 B7
Ravenhill Dr PE15 ...243 C3
Ravens Ct CB6 ......240 C5
Ravenscourt **6** PE27 ..208 A3
Ravensdale PE7 .....175 F7
Ravensthorpe Prim Sch
PE3 ....197 C7
Ravensworth Gdns CB1 ..65 A7
Rawlyn Cl CB5 ....84 D3
Rawlyn Ct CB5 ....84 D3
Rawlyn Rd CB5 ......84 D3
Ray's Dro PE26 ......220 B1
Rayes La CB8 ......111 A4
Rayleigh Cl CB2 ......64 E5
Raymond St **14** PE13 ..245 C4
Rayner Ave PE2 .....187 E5
Rayner's Cl SG8 ....30 D1
Rays Ct PE15 ....223 B6
Rayson Way CB5 .....84 D3
Reach Dro PE7 ....189 B5
Reach Rd Burwell CB5 ..109 B8
Reach CB5 ....129 F1
Reaches The PE6 ....232 C3
Read's St CB6 ......210 F5
Ream Cl PE19 ....74 E2
Recreation Cl CB4 ...105 D1
Recreation Gd Rd PE6 .244 B6
Recreation Rd CB9 ...23 F7
Recreation Way IP28 ..239 C4
Rectory Cl
Brampton PE28 ......140 E2
Great Paxton PE19 ....96 E4
Oakington/Longstanton
CB4 ....123 F1
Sawtry PE28 ....168 C5
Rectory Farm Rd CB1 ...86 F2
Rectory Fields CB6 ..216 E3
Rectory Gdns
Glinton PE6 ....203 E8
Godmanchester PE29 ..141 F2
Peterborough PE2 ....187 B7
Wisbech PE13 ......245 E6
Rectory La Ashdon CB10 ...21 A1
Etton PE6 ....231 E5
Fowlmere SG8 ....15 E8
Glinton PE6 ....203 E8
Kingston CB3 ....65 C1
Peakirk PE6 ....206 B2
St Ives PE28 ....142 F5
Somersham PE28 ....215 B1
Southoe & Midloe PE19 ...95 D6
Rectory Rd
Bluntisham/Colne PE28 ..208 D5
Duxford CB2 ....17 E8
Newton PE13 ....233 B5
Outwell PE14 ......236 F2
Rectory Way PE7 ....175 F7
Red Barn PE7 ......191 E6
Red Cross La CB2 .....63 B3
Red Dock La CB8 .....73 F1
Red Fen Rd CB6 ....210 F7
Red Hill Cl CB2 ......48 E8
Red Hill La CB2 ......48 E8
Red Lion Cl PE28 ...150 F4
Red Lion La **6** CB6 .216 E1
Red Lion Sq **5** SG8 ...84 B5
Red Lion St **12** PE9 .244 B5
Red Roofs CB6 ......210 B8
Redbridge PE4 ......204 A6
Redcaps La CB6 .....217 E6
Redcot Gdns **8** PE9 ..244 B6
Redcott Gdns PE9 ...244 B5
Redebourne La PE26 ..171 F4
Redfern Cl PE14 .....83 E6
Redgate Ct PE1 .....198 E7
Redgate Rd Girton CB3 ...82 E8
Tydd St Giles CB13 ..238 C8
Redhouse Gdns **3** CB7 .212 B3
Redit La CB7 ....211 C1
Redlands SG8 ....8 E8
Redlands Rd CB3 ....101 E5
Redman Cl CB7 .....240 F7
Redmile Wlk PE1 ....198 D8
Redmoor Bank PE14 ..235 F4
Redmoor Cl PE27 ...144 B7
Redmoor La PE26 ...235 F5
Redroofs CB6 ....211 B7
Redshank Cl
Haverhill CB9 ....24 C7
Whittlesey PE7 ......201 A1
Redwell Cl PE27 ....143 E5
Redwing Cl PE27 ...187 E7
Redwing Dr Royston SG8 ...5 E8
9 Wisbech PE14 ....245 D2

Redwing Pl **2** PE19 ...75 B7
Redwing Rise SG8 ....5 E8
Redwongs Way PE29 .141 D7
Reed Cl Cambridge CB2 ...64 E1
Chatteris PE16 ......241 C3
Reed Way PE14 .....236 A4
Reedland Way PE7 ..186 C1
Reedmace Cl PE4 ...205 C8
Reeds La CB9 ....24 A8
Reepham PE2 ....185 D4
Rees Thomas Sch CB4 ...83 F6
Reeve Hill SG8 ....8 A6
Reeves Pightle SG8 ....7 F3
Reeves Way PE1 ....198 D5
Regal Dr CB7 ....212 D3
Regal La CB7 ....212 C3
Regal Rd PE13 ......245 B2
Regatta Ct CB5 ......84 B4
Regency Sq CB1 .....65 A7
Regency Way PE3 ...197 E1
Regent Ave PE15 ...243 D5
Regent Ct PE19 ......74 B4
Regent Pl **11** CB7 ...212 B3
Regent St CB2 ......246 B1
Regent Terr CB2 ....246 B1
Regents Ct CB8 .....110 F3
Regional Swimming Pool
PE1 ....198 B1
Reilly Way CB1 ......65 F8
Rembrandt Way PE27 .144 A7
Renoir Cl PE27 ......144 A7
Resbury Cl CB2 ......50 A1
Retreat The **8** PE6 ..231 C7
Reubens Rd CB4 ....105 C7
Reynold's Cl CB1 .....38 D1
Reynolds Cl PE27 ...144 A7
Reynolds Dr PE19 ....95 F1
Reynolds' Cro CB4 ..124 B2
Rhee Lake Dro PE28 .208 E8
Rhees The PE28 ....208 D6
Rhonda Pk PE15 ....223 C7
Rhone Pl **3** PE13 ..245 E3
Rhugarve Gdns CB1 ..35 D2
Rhymers Gate PE28 .142 F5
Ribble Cl PE27 ......144 B6
Ribe Ct CB6 ....240 C4
Ribes Cl PE7 ....186 D3
Ribston Way CB4 ....84 C6
Richard Young Cl
PE13 ....245 C8
Richards Cl PE15 ...243 B5
Richardson Way PE7 .189 E7
Richmond Ave
March PE15 ....243 C3
Peterborough PE4 ...204 C2
Richmond Cl
Huntingdon PE29 ...141 E8
7 St Neots PE19 ....74 F1
Richmond Ct PE13 ..245 A4
Richmond Field PE13 .237 E2
Richmond Rd CB4 ....83 B4
Richmond Terr CB1 ..246 A4
Richmond Way **8** PE13 .238 B2
Rickard Cl CB1 ....65 E6
Rickwood Cl CB6 ...216 C5
Rickyard The CB2 ....2 D3
Riddiford Cres PE28 .140 C2
Riddy Cl CB2 ....209 A6
Riddy La CB3 ....60 C5
Rideaway PE28 .....119 F8
Ridge Way PE2 .....187 B8
Ridgefield Prim Sch
CB1 ....65 C7
Ridgeway
Papworth Everard CB3 ...99 A4
Perry PE28 ....115 D2
St Neots PE19 ......74 F2
Ridgeway The CB1 ...35 E2
Ridley Hall Rd CB3 ...64 C8
Rigg Cl PE13 ....245 B3
Rightwell PE3 ......197 A6
Rightwell E PE3 ....197 A5
Rightwell W PE3 ...197 A5
Riley Cl PE7 ....181 D6
Ringers La PE13 ....238 B2
Ringstead Rd PE4 ..204 F1
Ringwood PE3 .....196 F3
Ringwood Cl PE26 ..172 A4
Ripon Cl PE4 ......204 B3
Rippons Dro PE4 ...231 F7
Risby PE4 ....204 B3
Riseholme PE2 .....185 E3
Rivar Pl CB1 ....84 A1
Rivendale PE4 .....204 B2
River Bank CB7 ....212 B3
River Cl **2** Benwick PE15 .222 A5
Little Paxton PE19 ...95 F1
Mepal CB6 ....210 E6
River Dr PE15 .....243 E4
River Dro PE7 .....174 A1
River End PE8 .....178 C8
River La Brampton PE28 .178 C8
Cambridge CB5 ......84 A3
Elton PE8 ....178 C8
Fordham CB7 ......212 E1
Great Paxton PE19 ...96 D3
Haslingfield CB3 ....47 C5
Peterborough PE2 ..197 F2
River Mdw PE28 ...142 F3
River Terr
3 St Neots PE19 ....74 E5
Little Paxton PE19 ...95 F2
8 Newmarket CB8 ...111 A3
Riverbank Cl **12** PE6 .231 F8

Riverdown PE15 .....243 F5
Rivergate **3** PE1 ...198 A1
Rivergate Sh Ctr PE1 .198 A1
Rivermill Gall* PE19 ..74 C2
Riverside Cambridge CB5 ...84 B3
11 Market Deeping PE6 ..231 F8
Riverside Cl Ely CB7 ..219 B5
Mildenhall IP28 ....239 B4
Whittlesey PE7 ....189 D6
Riverside Ct CB1 ...246 B4
Riverside Gdns
Parson Drove PE13 ..234 C7
Peterborough PE3 ..197 D1
Riverside Mead PE7 .187 B8
Riverside Mid Sch
PE13 ....239 A4
Riverside Rd PE29 ..141 E4
Riverside Spinney
PE8 ....194 A3
Riverside Way PE13 .245 B3
Riverside Wlk CB7 ..240 E3
Rivermead PE19 .....74 E6
Rivers Cl CB1 ....35 D3
Rivey Way CB1 ......35 D2
Roan Wlk **8** SG8 ....5 E6
Robbs Wlk PE27 ...144 A3
Robden Ct PE2 .....197 E1
Robert Arkenstall Prim Sch
The CB6 ....210 A3
Robert Ave
Peterborough PE1 ..197 F8
4 Somersham PE28 ..215 C1
Robert Jennings Cl
CB4 ....84 A6
Robert May Cl CB1 ...65 D7
Robert Rayner Cl PE2 .186 D6
Roberts Cl PE19 .....74 B2
Robertson Way PE29 .152 E1
Robin Cl Bar Hill CB3 ..102 C4
Haverhill CB9 ....24 C7
Mildenhall IP28 ....239 D4
Robin Goodfellow's La
PE15 ....243 D5
Robin Hood Cl PE19 .196 F2
Robin Mews **4** PE14 .245 D2
Robingoodfellow's La
PE15 ....243 C6
Robins Cl **5** Ely CB6 ..240 B5
8 Isleham CB7 .....213 A5
Peterborough PE2 ..186 E8
Robins End PE28 ...194 A4
Robins' La CB3 .....101 F5
Robins Wood PE4 ...84 B6
Robinson Coll CB3 ...83 B1
Robinson Way CB2 ...65 A3
Robinson Cl **4** PE15 ..243 E4
Rocester Way SG8 ....5 D8
Rochford Wlk **5** PE13 .245 E5
Rochfort Ave PE15 ..110 E5
Rock Rd Cambridge CB1 ...65 A6
Peterborough PE1 ..197 F6
Royston SG8 ....5 C8
Stamford PE9 ......244 B5
Rock Cl CB9 ....22 D7
Rockingham Rd PE28 .168 B3
Rockingham Rd PE28 .168 B3
Rockingham Yd CB8 ...90 D8
Rockmill End CB4 ..209 A1
Rodham Rd PE15 ...228 F5
Rodings The CB5 ....88 E4
Roe Green Rd PE29 .142 A6
Roe Gn PE19 ....74 B5
Roedeer Cl CB1 ......65 A7
Roe's Cl PE2 ....32 F8
Roger's Cl CB3 ....100 B4
Rogers End CB10 ....21 B1
Rogers Rd CB5 .....108 E6
Rogues La CB3 ......99 D5
Roland Cl CB4 ....83 E5
Rolleston Garth PE1 .198 C8
Rollys La SG7 ....2 D4
Roman Bank
Newton PE13 ....238 B4
Stamford PE9 ......244 A4
Roman Cl Burwell CB5 ..130 A2
Whittlesey PE7 ....189 F8
Roman Courts CB4 ...83 B4
Roman Dr PE8 .....194 D2
Roman Drift CB8 ....80 C1
Roman Hill CB3 ......63 C4
Roman Way
Haverhill CB9 ....24 D7
March PE15 ....243 E6
Perry PE28 ....115 D2
Stilton PE7 ....176 A8
Roman Way Fst Sch SG8 ...5 D8
Romany Gdns PE2 ..187 D5
Romney Cl PE27 ...144 A7
Romney Ct **2** PE19 ...74 C5
Romsey Mews CB1 ...65 B7
Romsey Rd CB1 .....65 B7
Romsey Terr CB1 ....65 B7
Ronalds Way CB4 ....65 B7
Ronaldsway **5** PE25 .222 F5
Rook Gr CB4 ....209 A1
Rookery Cl
Great Chesterford CB10 ..18 D3
St Ives PE27 ......144 C4
Waterbeach CB5 ...106 A8
Rookery Pl PE28 ...121 C5
Rookery Sh Ctr The
CB8 ....111 A4
Rookery The
Balsham CB1 ....53 A2
Little Paxton PE19 ...95 F2
8 Newmarket CB8 ..111 A3
Peterborough PE2 ..185 C7

Rookery The continued
Yaxley PE7 ....181 D5
Rookery Way PE28 ..121 B5
Rooks St CB4 ......125 E4
Rookswood Rd PE15 ..243 C4
Rookwood Cl CB9 ....24 A6
Roscrea Terr PE29 ..141 D4
Rose and Crown Rd
CB4 ....122 C3
Rose Ave PE2 ......187 C7
Rose Cres CB2 .....246 A3
Rose Croft PE28 ...115 E2
Rose Ct **8** PE19 ....74 C4
Rose Gn La **10** IP28 .213 F8
Rose Hill CB2 ....38 D5
Rose La **4** Elm PE14 ..236 A5
Great Chesterford CB10 ..18 E2
Melbourn SG8 ......14 C6
Rose Wlk Royston SG8 ...5 C7
Wisbech PE13 .....245 A6
Rosebay Gdns **6** CB7 .212 B5
Roseberry Rd PE14 .236 B5
Rosebery Way CB8 .110 C5
Rosedale PE14 ....236 B8
Rosedene Dr PE15 ..243 D3
Rosefinch Cl CB9 ....24 C7
Roseford Rd CB4 ....83 D6
Roselea CB2 ....4 C3
Rosemary Cl **7** IP28 ..214 A1
Rosemary Gdns PE1 .197 F8
Rosemary Greene Cl
CB3 ....78 C2
Rosemary La
Cambridge CB1 ......65 C7
Chatteris PE16 .....241 B4
Sutton CB6 ....216 C1
Rosemary Rd CB5 ..106 B7
Rose's Cl PE15 .....243 D2
Rosewood Cl PE7 ..181 E5
Rosie Hospl CB2 .....65 A3
Rosie Cl PE22 ....65 A3
Ross Piers Sports Ctr The
CB7 ....212 B3
Ross St CB1 ....65 B8
Roswell View CB7 ..240 E5
Rosyth Ave PE2 ....185 D3
Rotherby Gr **4** PE1 ..198 D7
Rotherwick Way CB1 ..65 C3
Rothleigh Rd **2** CB2 .65 C5
Rothwell Way PE2 ..186 C7
Round Church St CB2 .246 A3
Round Hills Way PE28 .168 A5
Round House Dro
PE28 ....222 A1
Roundhills View PE28 .167 E8
Roundhouse La PE19 ..74 C3
Roundhouse Dr PE28 .115 D3
Rous Rd CB8 ......111 B3
Row The CB6 ......216 E1
Rowan Ave
Peterborough PE1 ..198 C5
Sawston CB2 ....32 F6
Rowan Cl Bottisham CB5 ...86 F6
Hanchet End CB9 ...38 E1
Huntingdon PE29 ..141 E8
Wisbech PE13 .....245 F7
Rowan Wlk IP28 ....239 E5
Rowans The
2 Doddington/Wimblington
PE15 ....223 A6
Milton CB4 ....105 C1
Rowe Ave PE2 .....186 C7
Rowell Cl CB9 ....39 A2
Rowell Wlk PE1 ....172 A4
Rowells The CB4 ...125 C3
Roxburgh Rd CB4 ...83 C5
Royal Anglian Regiment Mus
The* CB7 ....16 F3
Royal Ct **2** PE19 ....74 B4
Royal Oak La PE28 .143 A2
Royal Pal Cl CB8 ...110 D7
Royal Pl **2** PE13 ..245 C4
Royce Cl PE7 ......181 E6
Royce Ct PE27 ....144 B7
Royce Rd Alwalton PE7 .185 A4
Eastfield PE1 ......198 D3
Royle Cl PE2 ......186 C5
Royse Gr SG8 ....5 D4
Roysia Mid Sch SG8 ...5 C7
Royston Ave
Peterborough PE2 ..186 C6
Spaldwick PE28 ...137 F6
Royston Hospl SG8 ...5 D4
Royston La
Comberton CB23 ...62 C3
Elmdon CB11 ....9 C6
Royston Mus* SG8 ...5 D4
Royston Outdoor Pool
SG8 ....5 D6
Royston Rd Barley SG8 ...5 C6
Carlton CB8 ....59 F7
Duxford CB2 ....17 C2
Foxton CB2 ....30 A5
Harston CB2 ....47 D1
Litlington SG8 ......12 B1
Royston Sta SG8 ....5 C7
Rubens Way PE27 ..144 A2

Ruddles La PE28 ....142 E6
Rudlands Cl 3 CB7 ....213 A5
Rudyard Gr PE4 ....204 E3
Ruffles Rd CB9 ....24 C7
Rupert Brooke Mus*
  CB2 ....64 A3
Rush Gr CB1 ....66 A6
Rushbrook Cl CB3 ......59 F3
Rushmere Cl PE27 ....144 B5
Rushmere PE2 ....185 F6
Rushton Ave PE4 .....204 A4
Ruskin Cl 2 CB9 ....38 D1
Russell Ave PE15 ....243 B6
Russell Cl
  Cambridge CB2 ....64 E7
  St Neots PE19 ....74 F6
Russell Hill PE8 ......193 F6
Russell St
  Cambridge CB2 ....246 C1
  Peterborough PE1 ....197 F3
  St Neots PE19 ....74 C6
  Wisbech PE13 ....245 C6
Russet Cl PE27 ......144 B5
Russet Ct CB4 ....84 C6
Russet Way SG8 ....14 D6
Russet Wlk 3 CB3 ......81 A3
Russets The PE14 ....236 E2
Russett Ave PE27 ....208 A3
Rustat Ave CB1 ....65 A7
Rustat Rd CB1 ....65 A6
Rustons Rd PE14 ....236 F7
Rustons The CB2 ......32 D1
Rusts La PE28 ....150 F4
Rutherford Rd CB2 ...64 E4
Rutland Cl
  Cambridge CB4 ....83 D6
  St Ives PE27 ....143 F7
Rutland Ct 1 CB9 .....23 E7
Rutland Gn PE28 ....120 B1
Rutland Rd PE9 .....244 D7
Rutland Terr PE9 ....244 A4
Rutland Way PE15 ...224 B4
Rutner Cl PE2 ....186 D8
Rycroft Ave
  3 Deeping St James PE6 .231 F8
  St Neots PE19 ....74 E6
Rydal Cl PE27 ....141 B6
Rydal Ct PE4 ....204 E3
Rye Cl 4 PE19 ....74 F1
Rye Ct 10 CB9 ....23 E7
Ryecroft La SG8 ......15 E8
Ryhall Rd PE9 ......244 D6

S

Sable Cl CB1 ....66 A7
Sackville Cl CB4 ......83 E7
Sackville St CB8 .....111 B4
Sackville Way CB3 ....79 C4
Sacred Heart RC Prim Sch
  PE3 ....197 A5
Sacrewell Farm & Crty Ctr*
  PE8 ....194 C5
Saddle Cl PE4 ....197 E8
Saddlers Cl PE6 .....203 E8
Saddlers Pl SG8 ......5 C7
Sadlers Cl Coton CB3 ..82 B2
  Hardwick CB3 ....81 A1
Sadlers Way PE28 ...143 D1
Saffron Cl CB4 .....242 C2
Saffron Piece 3 CB6 .216 E1
Saffron Rd Histon CB4 .104 B3
  Sawston CB2 ....33 A8
Saffron St SG8 ....5 F5
Sage's La PE4 ......197 C8
Saggers Cl SG8 ......12 D6
Sainfoin Cl CB2 .....33 A8
Sainsfons CB2 ....48 F1
St Alban's Dr 20 PE1 .232 A1
St Alban's RC Prim Sch
  CB2 ....246 B1
St Albans CB8 ......111 A4
St Albans Rd CB4 ...83 D6
St Andrew CB8 .....111 A4
St Andrew's CE Com Jun Sch
  CB4 ....84 C6
St Andrew's Dr
  CB7 ....212 B3
St Andrew's Cl CB2 ..49 C4
St Andrew's Hill CB5 .106 B7
St Andrew's Pk CB4 .104 B5
St Andrew's Pl PE7 .189 D6
St Andrew's Rd CB4 ..84 A3
St Andrew's CE
  Cambridge CB2 ......246 B2
  Mildenhall IP28 ....239 C4
St Andrew's La CB6 .240 B6
St Andrews Cl 1 CB7 .213 A5
St Andrews Hill CB5 .106 B7
St Andrews La 2 PE28 .113 F4
St Andrews Rd 4 PE6 .231 F7
St Andrews Way
  Histon CB4 ....104 E4
  Sawtry PE28 ....168 C4
St Ann's La PE29 ...141 F1
St Annes CE Prim Sch
  PE29 ....118 F8
St Anns Dr PE29 ...239 B4
St Anselm Pl 1 PE19 .74 E5
St Anthony 2 CB8 ...111 A4
St Anthonys Wlk CB2 .64 E7
St Audleys La PE27 .144 A5
St Audrey Cl
  Peterborough PE2 ...187 D6

St Audrey Cl continued
  St Ives PE27 ....144 B5
St Audrey's Cl CB4 .104 A4
St Audrey's Way CB6 .240 D6
St Augustine's Jun Sch
  PE2 ....186 F8
St Augustine's Wlk
  PE2 ....186 E8
St Augustines Inf Sch
  PE13 ....245 D8
St Augustines RC Prim Sch
  PE9 ....244 C7
St Augustines Rd
  PE13 ....245 C5
St Barnabas Ct 3 PE29 .141 F7
St Barnabas Rd CB1 .65 A8
St Bartholomew's Ct
  CB5 ....84 B3
St Bede's Cres CB1 ..65 E6
St Bede's Gdns CB1 .65 E6
St Bede's Inter Church Comp
  Sch CB1 ....65 D6
St Bee's Dr 16 CB6 ..216 E6
St Benedict's Cl PE6 .203 F7
St Benedict's St 5 PE29 .141 D4
St Benet's Gdns 6 PE6 .232 A1
St Botolph La PE2 ..186 C6
St Botolph's Gn PE8 .178 E7
St Botolph's Prim Sch
  PE2 ....186 B6
St Botolph's Way
  Haverhill CB9 ......23 F8
  Thorney PE6 ....233 A2
St Botolphs Pl CB9 ..23 E7
St Catharine's Coll
  CB2 ....246 A2
St Catharines Hall CB2 .82 C2
St Catharines Sq CB4 .83 C7
St Catherine's CB6 .240 C5
St Catherines CE IP28 .239 D6
St Catherines Prep Sch
  CB2 ....64 E7
St Christophers Ave 2
  CB4 ....83 C4
St Clement Cl PE14 .236 F2
St Clement's PE29 ..141 A5
St Clements Gdns
  CB1 ....246 A3
St Clements Pas PE29 .141 E4
St Colettes Prep Sch
  CB1 ....64 F7
St David CB8 ....111 A4
St David's Sq PE1 ..198 D1
St David's Way CB8 .168 C4
St Denys 3 CB8 ....111 A4
St Edmunds Coll CB3 .83 C3
St Edmunds Dr PE14 .236 D5
St Edwards Pas 4 CB1 .246 A2
St Ethelwolds CB6 ..240 B4
St Fabians Cl CB8 ..110 F5
St Faiths Sch CB2 ..64 E6
St Felix CE VC Mid Sch
  CB8 ....110 F6
St Felix Cl CB7 ....212 B5
St Felix RC Prim Sch
  CB9 ....23 D7
St Felix Rd PE26 ..221 C2
St George 1 CB8 ...111 A4
St George Ave PE2 .187 E6
St George's Rd
  St Ives PE27 ....144 A4
  4 Wittering PE8 ...230 B1
St George's Sq 5 PE9 .244 C5
St George's St PE1 .244 D5
St Georges Ave PE9 .244 D6
St Georges Cl CB4 .140 E1
St Georges Ct 3 PE29 .141 D4
St Georges Sch
  Peterborough PE1 ...198 A7
  Stamford PE9 ......244 C7
St Georges Way CB4 .104 E4
St Germain St PE29 .141 C4
St Germain Wlk 8
  PE29 ....141 D4
St Gilberts Sch PE9 .244 B5
St Giles Cl PE7 ....176 F4
St Giles Gr PE14 ...236 B6
St Helena Farm IP28 .239 F6
St Helena Wlk IP28 .239 C7
St Helen's Prim Sch
  PE28 ....208 A6
St Hugh's Rd PE19 .117 A4
St Ives Rd Eltisley PE19 .77 E6
  Hemingford Grey PE28 .143 D2
  Old Hurst PE28 ....154 D6
  Papworth Everard CB3 .98 F2
  5 St Ives PE28 ....143 A5
  Somersham PE28 ...208 B8
St Ivo Leisure Ctr
  PE27 ....143 F4
St Ivo Sch PE27 ...143 F5
St James CB8 ......111 A4
St James Ave PE1 ..197 F7
St James Ct
  Newton PE13 ......238 A5
  8 Stretham CB6 ...210 F5
St James Ct 9 CB9 ..23 E8
St James Rd PE19 ..95 F3
St John Fisher RC Sch
  PE1 ....198 C4
St John's CE Prim Sch
  PE29 ....141 E7
St John's Chase PE15 .243 D5
St John's Cl
  Mildenhall IP28 ....239 C4
  7 Needingworth PE27 .208 A3
  Waterbeach CB5 ...106 B7
St John's Coll CB2 .246 A3

St John's La CB5 ...106 A2
St John's Pl
  Cambridge CB4 ......83 C3
  Wistow PE28 ....163 F7
St John's Rd
  Cambridge CB5 .....246 A4
  Coton CB3 ....82 B2
  Ely CB6 ....240 A4
  March PE15 ....243 D5
  18 Wittering PE8 ..230 B1
St John's St
  Beck Row, Holywell
  Row & Kenny Hill IP28 .214 A8
  Cambridge CB2 .....246 A3
  Duxford CB2 ....32 D1
  Mildenhall IP28 ...213 F8
  Peterborough PE1 ..198 B2
St Johns Ave CB8 ..111 A1
St Johns Church Sch (Aided)
  PE2 ....185 E3
St Johns Cl PE28 ..155 B5
St Johns Coll Sch CB3 .83 C2
St Johns Innovation Ctr
St Johns La CB3 ....99 B2
St Johns Mews PE19 .96 E4
St Johns Rd PE2 ...187 B7
St Johns St PE19 ..141 D5
St Johns Way CB3 ..79 A4
St Judes Cl PE13 ..197 C4
St Judith's La PE28 .160 B6
St Kilda Ave CB4 ...84 A7
St Laurence Rd CB2 ..30 C5
St Laurence's RC Prim Sch
  CB4 ....83 D7
St Lawrence Way 2
  PE9 ....230 F7
St Leonard's La 4 PE13 .238 B2
St Leonard's St 4 PE9 .244 C5
St Louis RC VA Prim Sch
  CB8 ....111 A4
St Luke's CE Prim Sch
  CB4 ....83 C4
St Lukes Cl PE29 ..141 D5
St Lukes Mews CB4 .83 D4
St Lukes St CB4 ....246 A4
St Margaret's Rd CB3 .82 F4
St Margaret's Sq CB1 .65 B5
St Margarets Pl PE2 .186 F6
St Margarets Rd PE2 .186 F6
St Margarets Way
  PE29 ....141 C6
St Mark's Ct 3 PE1 .198 A3
St Mark's Cl CB4 ...83 C4
St Marks Rd PE13 ..237 E3
St Marks St PE1 ...198 A3
St Martin's Cl
  Chatteris PE16 ....241 D5
  Exning CB8 ....110 C7
  Stamford PE9 ......244 C4
St Martin's Rd
  Chatteris PE16 ....241 D4
  Newborough PE6 ...205 B8
  Wisbech PE13 .....245 E7
St Martin's St PE1 .197 F5
St Martins Wlk CB7 .240 D5
St Mary's Earith PE28 .208 E6
  Gamlingay SG19 ....41 E5
St Mary's Ave PE8 .230 B1
St Mary's CE Prim Sch
  PE19 ....75 A5
St Mary's Cl
  Bainton PE9 ....230 F5
  Bluntisham PE28 ..208 D5
  Farcet PE7 ....187 C2
  Peterborough PE1 ..198 B4
  Thorney PE6 ......233 A2
  Wisbech St Mary PE13 .235 C7
St Mary's Dr
  PE15 ....243 C5
  Peterborough PE2 ..185 F4
St Mary's Gn PE28 .164 E6
St Mary's Hill 9 PE9 .244 C5
St Mary's Pas CB2 .246 A2
St Mary's RC JMI Sch
  ....5 D7
St Mary's Rd
  Bluntisham/Colne PE28 .208 C5
  Ramsey PE26 ......220 E2
  Sawston CB2 ....33 A7
  Stilton PE7 ....175 F8
  West Walton PE14 .238 E4
St Mary's St
  1 Cambridge CB1 ..246 A2
  Ely CB7 ....240 C4
  Farcet PE7 ....187 C2
  St Neots PE19 ....74 E4
  Stamford PE9 ......244 C5
  Whittlesey PE7 ...189 D6
St Mary's Wlk
  Everton SG19 ......40 C3
  Fowlmere SG8 ......15 E8
St Marys Ct Ely CB7 .240 C4
St Marys Pas CB1 ..246 A2
St Marys Pk SG8 ...5 D2
St Marys Sch CB2 ..64 E7
St Marys Sq 4 PE29 .141 D4
St Marys St 5 PE13 .141 D4
St Matthew's Ct 5 CB1 .84 A2
St Matthew's Gdns CB1 .84 A2
St Matthew's Prim Sch
  CB1 ....246 C2
St Matthew's St CB1 .84 A2

St Michael's Ave PE13 .245 C7
St Michael's Gate PE1 .198 F7
St Michael's Rd 12 PE8 .230 B1
St Michaels CB4 ...103 A8
St Michaels La
  Longstanton CB4 ..124 A1
  Oakington/Longstanton
  CB4 ....103 A8
St Neots Comm Nature
  Reserve* PE19 .....74 E2
St Neots Leisure Ctr
  PE19 ....74 E2
St Neots Mus* PE19 .74 E5
St Neots Rd
  Abbotsley PE19 ....57 A7
  Comberton CB23 ...81 D3
  Coton CB23 ....82 B3
  Eaton Socon PE19 .74 C4
  Eltisley PE19 .....77 D4
  Hardwick CB3 ......80 E4
  Knapwell CB3 ......79 D5
  Madingley CB3 .....81 A6
St Neots Sta PE19 .75 B6
St Olave's Dr PE19 .232 A1
St Ovins Gn CB6 ...240 B5
St Patrick 4 CB8 ..111 A4
St Paul's CE Prim Sch
  CB2 ....246 B1
St Paul's Cl
  Gorefield PE13 ....237 C2
  8 Wisbech PE13 ...245 C4
St Paul's Rd
  Cambridge CB1 .....246 C1
  Peterborough PE1 ..197 F7
St Paul's St PE9 ..244 C5
St Pauls Dr PE16 ..241 D6
St Pauls Wlk CB1 ..246 C1
St Pega's Rd PE6 ..204 A8
St Peter's CE Junn Sch
St Peter's Dr 10 PE15 .223 B7
St Peter's Hill 8 PE9 .244 B5
St Peter's Rd Coton CB3 .82 B2
  Huntingdon PE29 ..141 D7
  March PE15 ....243 D3
  4 Wisbech PE13 ...245 C4
St Peter's Sch PE29 .141 D6
St Peter's Sch
  Cambridge CB3 .....83 C3
  Caxton CB3 ....59 E8
  Duxford CB2 ....17 D8
  Stamford PE9 ......244 B4
St Peter's Vale PE9 .244 B4
St Peter's Way
  Ellington PE28 ....139 A4
  Thorney PE6 ......233 A2
St Peters Ave CB8 .112 F4
St Peters Cl CB8 ..112 F5
St Peters Ct 9 PE9 .244 B5
St Peters Dr PE16 .241 D5
St Peters Pl CB7 ..212 F1
St Peters Rd
  Outwell PE14 ......236 C1
  Peterborough PE1 ..198 A2
St Peters Terr CB1 .246 B1
St Philip's CE Prim Sch
  CB1 ....84 C1
St Philip's Rd CB1 .65 B8
St Philips Rd
  Cambridge CB1 .....65 C8
  Newmarket CB8 ....110 E4
St Regis CB4 ....83 F4
St Stephen's Dr PE16 .241 C6
St Stephen's Pl 1 CB4 .83 C4
St Thomas PE19 ....77 E4
St Thomas Cl CB3 ..62 D6
St Thomas Dr PE15 .243 C3
St Thomas Moore RC Prim
  Sch PE1 ....198 D4
St Thomas' Dr CB7 .240 C2
St Thomas's Sq CB1 .65 D6
St Tibb's Row CB2 .246 B2
St Vigor's Rd CB1 .66 F4
St Vincent's Cl CB3 .82 E8
St Wendreda's Dr
  PE15 ....243 C1
St Wendreda's Way
  CB8 ....110 B7
Salcott Dr PE13 ..245 C5
Salem Ct PE16 ....241 C4
Salisbury Cl PE27 ..143 F8
Salisbury Ct 1 CB9 .23 F7
Salisbury Rd PE4 ..204 B3
Salisbury Villas CB1 .64 F7
Sallowbush Rd PE26 .141 D6
Sallows PE28 ......121 C6
Sallows Rd PE1 ...198 B6
Salmon La CB4 ....246 C3
Salon Way PE29 ..141 B7
Saltergate PE1 ....198 E7
Salters Way
  Sawtry PE28 ....168 B5
  Wisbech PE13 ....245 A2
Saltergate PE1 ....198 F7
Saltmarsh PE1 ....186 C4
Salts Rd PE14 ....238 F4
Sambar Cl 3 PE19 .74 F1
Sames Ct CB4 .....125 E5
Samian Cl CB3 ....80 C2
Samuel Pepys Sch
  PE19 ....75 A4
Samuel Ward Upper Sch
  CB9 ....39 B1
Samuels Way CB6 .240 C4
Samworths Cl PE5 .195 F2

Sancton Wood Sch
  CB1 ....246 C1
Sand Acre Cl IP28 .239 D5
Sand Bank PE13 ..235 A7
Sand Dro CB8 .....127 C8
Sand La CB6 ......209 E4
Sand Rd SG19 .....58 F5
Sand St CB7 ......212 B3
Sandall Rd PE13 ..245 C3
Sanderling Cl IP28 .239 D4
Sanderlings The PE6 .206 B1
Sanders Cl CB23 ..151 D3
Sandfields Rd PE19 .74 F4
Sandford PE3 .....197 B5
Sandhill CB6 .....242 F3
Sandhurst Rd PE7 .186 C1
Sandown Rd PE13 .245 A2
Sandpiper Cl
  Haverhill CB9 .....24 B7
  Whittlesey PE7 ...190 A8
Sandpiper Dr PE2 .187 E6
Sandpit Rd PE6 ..233 A3
Sandringham Ave
  PE13 ....245 D6
Sandringham Cl PE9 .244 B7
Sandringham Dr PE26 .221 C2
Sandringham Rd PE4 .197 C8
Sandwich Cl
  Huntingdon PE29 ..141 C7
  St Ives PE27 ......143 F8
Sandwich Rd
  Brampton PE28 ....140 D1
  St Neots PE19 ....75 A5
Sandwick Cl 2 CB4 .83 E8
Sandy Dro PE19 ..214 D3
Sandy Gate PE12 .237 A7
Sandy La Cambridge CB4 .83 F4
  Kimbolton PE28 ...113 C6
  Tydd St Giles PE13 .238 B7
  Wisbech PE13 ....245 E4
Sandy Rd Everton SG19 .40 B2
  Lode CB5 ....107 C6
Sandyland PE13 ..245 B5
Sandys Cres CB4 ..212 A3
Sanfoin Cl 5 IP28 .214 A1
Sapcote Way PE28 .168 B3
Sapley Pk PE29 ...141 F8
Sapley Rd PE29 ...152 F1
Sapley Spinneys Nature
  Reserve* PE28 ....152 E1
Sapley Sq PE29 ...141 E7
Sapperton PE4 ....204 B6
Sargent's Ct PE9 .244 A6
Sascombe Vineyard*
  ....72 F3
Saunders Cl
  Huntingdon PE29 ..141 D6
  Peterborough PE2 ..186 E8
Saunders Ct CB3 ..79 B3
Savile Way SG8 ...15 E8
Savile's Ct PE17 ..54 F4
Saville Rd PE3 ....197 D5
Saville Rd Ind Est PE3 .197 D5
Savory Rd PE13 ..245 B7
Sawpit La PE28 ...159 A4
Sawston Rd CB22 ..33 D8
Sawston Village Coll
  CB2 ....32 E8
Sawtry Com Coll PE28 .168 C4
Sawtry Jun & Inf Sch
  PE28 ....168 B3
Sawtry Leisure Ctr
  PE28 ....168 B3
Sawtry Rd
  Conington PE28 ...167 F8
  Sawtry PE28 ......168 A6
Sawtry Way PE29 .168 F2
Sawtry Way Cotts
  PE28 ....143 C6
Saxby Gdns PE1 ..198 C8
Saxham Ct CB9 ...38 B1
Saxon Cl Ely CB6 .240 C5
  Exning CB8 ....110 D8
  Godmanchester PE29 .141 F1
Saxon Ct SG8 .....168 C3
Saxon Dr CB5 .....130 B1
Saxon Pl PE19 ....74 F4
Saxon Rd
  5 Barnack PE9 ....230 D3
  Cambridge CB5 ....84 A3
  Peterborough PE1 ..198 C4
  Whittlesey PE7 ...189 C7
Saxon St CB8 .....246 B1
Saxon St Rd CB8 ..91 D4
Saxon Way Bar Hill CB3 .102 B2
  Melbourn SG8 .....14 C4
  3 Waterbeach CB5 .106 A7
Sayer Ct PE2 .....185 F2
Sayer St PE29 ....141 C5
Sayers Ct PE28 ...208 C5
Scaldgate PE7 ....189 E6
Scalesgate Rd PE12 .237 A8
Scalford Dr PE2 ..198 C8
Scaltback Cl CB8 .110 E6
Scaltback Mid Sch
  CB8 ....110 E6
Scarfield La PE14 .236 C6
Scargill's La PE15 .243 D3
Scarlett's La CB8 .53 D4
Scarsdale Cl CB4 .84 B6
Sch of Clinical Medicine
  CB2 ....65 B3
Schlumberger Laboratories
  CB3 ....82 E3

Scholars Ave PE29 ....141 C4
Schole Rd CB4 ....209 A1
School CI Cheveley CB8 ...91 C6
　Gamlingay SG19 ....41 D5
　5 Maxey PE6 ....231 C7
　Peterborough PE3 ....197 A5
　2 Wisbech St Mary PE13 ..235 B7
School Dro PE26 ....171 A7
School Farm Dro
　PE26 ....171 E8
School Hill CB4 ....104 B4
School La
　Alconbury PE28 ....150 F5
　Barley SG8 ....7 A1
　Barton CB3 ....63 B4
　Bourn CB3 ....79 B3
　Boxworth CB3 ....101 B5
　Buckden PE19 ....117 B4
　Burwell CB5 ....130 B1
　Bythorn & Keyston PE28 ..146 D4
　Conington CB3 ....122 C1
　Coveney CB6 ....217 D5
　Downham CB6 ....218 A7
　Pymore CB6 ....224 D1
　Eaton Socon PE19 ....74 C2
　Elton PE8 ....178 D8
　Fenstanton PE28 ....121 B6
　Fulbourn CB1 ....66 F4
　Glinton PE6 ....203 E8
　Haslingfield CB3 ....47 B5
　Haverhill CB9 ....23 D8
　Histon CB4 ....104 C3
　Kings Ripton PE28 ....153 C6
　Little Paxton PE19 ....96 A2
　Longstanton CB4 ....123 F1
　Longstowe CB3 ....60 A3
　Manea PE15 ....224 B4
　4 Maxey PE6 ....231 C7
　Mepal CB6 ....216 E3
　Ramsey PE26 ....172 B7
　St Neots PE19 ....74 E4
　Swavesey CB4 ....122 E6
　Thriplow SG8 ....31 B2
　Toft CB3 ....61 D4
　3 Uffington PE9 ....230 C6
　Warmington PE8 ....178 B3
　Waterbeach CB5 ....127 B8
　Wilburton CB6 ....210 C5
　1 Wisbech PE13 ....245 C5
School Rd
　5 Barnack PE9 ....230 D4
　Broughton PE28 ....153 F8
　Earith PE28 ....208 E6
　Great Wratting CB9 ......39 E5
　Moulton CB8 ....112 F6
　Newborough PE6 ....205 D8
　Outwell PE14 ....229 D8
　Warboys PE28 ....164 F5
　West Walton PE14 ....238 E4
　Woodditton CB8 ....91 A3
School St CB10 ....108 D7
School Wlk CB3 ....99 A2
Scolding Dro PE6 ....233 E5
Scorney PE28 ....121 C6
Scotendon PE2 ....185 E3
Scotenoon PE2 ....185 E3
Scotgate PE9 ....244 A5
Scotland CI CB4 ....84 B5
Scotland End CB7 ....213 C1
Scotland Rd
　Cambridge CB4 ....84 A5
　Dry Drayton CB3 ....81 A6
Scotney St PE1 ....197 E7
Scotney Way PE28 ....168 C3
Scotred CI CB5 ....109 B8
Scotsdowne Rd CB2 ......64 D3
Scott Ave PE28 ....239 C5
Scott CI
　Peterborough PE2 ....187 E6
　Royston SG8 ....13 D1
Scott Polar Research Institte
　CB2 ....246 B1
Scott's Rd PE14 ....229 C2
Scotts CI PE28 ....120 B1
Scotts Cres PE28 ....120 B1
Scotts Gdns CB2 ....32 C5
Scotts Rd PE6 ....203 F8
Scotts Yd CB3 ....47 B5
Scrolans PE27 ....143 E6
Seabank Rd PE13 ....245 F6
Seadyke Bank PE13 ......235 A7
Seadyke Rd PE13 ....234 F6
Seafield Rd **2** PE13 ...238 B2
Sealey's La PE13 ....234 D8
Sealodes Rd CB2 ....211 E5
Seargeants CI PE6 ......207 C1
Searjeant St PE1 ....197 E5
Searle St CB4 ....83 D4
Searles Ct PE7 ....189 D8
Searles Mdw CB3 ....102 B1
Sears CI PE29 ....158 F6
Searson CI PE9 ....230 F7
Seathwaite PE29 ....141 B6
Seaton CI PE7 ....181 D6
Sebrights Way PE3 .....196 F3
Second Ave
　Warboys PE28 ....164 E6
　Wisbech PE13 ....245 D4
Second Broadpool Dro
　PE28 ....165 F8
Second Drift PE9 ....244 B2
Second Dro
　Downham CB6 ....218 A8
　Littleport CB6 ....225 B1
　Ely CB7 ....218 F5

Second Dro continued
　Peterborough PE1 ....198 D1
　St Ives PE27 ....144 C2
Second Dro Ind Est
　PE1 ....198 D1
Second Marsh Rd
　PE14 ....238 C3
Sedge Fen Rd PE38 .....226 E7
Sedge Way CB6 ....217 D2
Sedgwick Mus of Earth
　Sciences* CB2 ....246 B2
Sedgwick St CB1 ....65 B8
Sedley Inf Sch CB1 ....65 C7
Sedley Taylor Rd CB2 ...64 F4
Sefton Ave PE13 ....245 E6
Sefton CI CB2 ....64 D3
Sefton Way CB8 ....110 D5
Selby CI **3** PE29 ....141 F7
Sellers Grange PE2 .....186 B4
Selsingen Way CB2 ......32 F7
Selwyn CI
　Great Shelford CB2 ....49 A5
　Mildenhall IP28 ....239 D6
　Newmarket CB8 ....111 A1
Selwyn Coll CB3 ....64 B8
Selwyn Gdns CB3 ....64 B8
Selwyn Rd
　Cambridge CB3 ....64 B7
　Stamford PE9 ....244 A7
Senate House Pas
　CB2 ....246 A2
Senes Cakls **6** PE27 ..208 A3
Seppings CI **2** CB6 ...210 C6
Serby Ave SG8 ....5 C8
Serjeants CI PE28 ....172 A6
Serlby Gdns PE3 ....197 B3
Serpentine Gn Sh Ctr
　PE7 ....186 D3
Setchel **1** PE19 ....74 C6
Setchel Dro CB4 ....125 F7
Setcheli CI PE19 ....97 F5
Setchfield PI PE2 ....186 F7
Seven Rides SG8 ....5 D3
Sevenacres PE2 ....185 E5
Seventh Ave PE13 ......245 E4
Seventh Dro CB6 ....225 A3
Severn CI PE4 ....204 E1
Severn PI CB1 ....84 A2
Severne Dr CB9 ....23 D7
Seymour CI CB8 ....111 C3
Seymour Ct CB1 ....65 C8
Seymour PI PE4 ....205 B2
Seymour St CB1 ....65 C8
Seynory Dro PE7 ....177 F7
Shade The CB7 ....212 A5
Shadowbush CI **2** CB9 ...38 F1
Shady Wlk **2** PE19 .....74 F5
Shaftenhoe End Rd SG8 ..7 A1
Shaftesbury Ave
　March PE15 ....243 E5
　St Neots PE19 ....74 F5
Shaftesbury Ct **17** CB1 ..23 E7
Shaftesbury Rd CB2 .....64 F6
Shaftesbury Way SG8 ....5 E5
Shaftesbury Ct PE15 ...243 E3
Shakespeare SG8 ....5 D8
Shakespeare Ave PE1 ...197 F7
Shakespeare Rd
　Eaton Socon PE19 ....74 C3
　St Ives PE27 ....143 F6
Shamrock CI PE2 ....187 C7
Shannon CI CB9 ....24 D7
Shardlow CI **1** CB9 .....58 B1
Sharma Leas PE4 ....204 A3
Sharman's Rd CB7 ......212 E1
Sharnbrook Ave PE7 ....186 C1
Sharps La PE19 ....150 F3
Shaw Dr PE15 ....243 C3
Shawley Rd PE28 ....168 A4
Shearling Dr CB3 ....79 A4
Shearwater PE2 ....185 D6
Sheep Mkt
　St Ives PE27 ....144 B3
　6 Stamford PE9 ....244 B5
Sheep St PE28 ....148 D3
Sheepfold PE27 ....144 C5
Sheepfold La CB3 ....79 B5
Sheepwalk PE4 ....205 A1
Sheldrick's Rd CB7 .....213 B5
Shelford Mill CB2 ....48 F4
Shelf PA Ave CB2 ....49 A5
Shelford Rd
　Cambridge CB2 ....48 E8
　Fulbourn CB1 ....66 C3
　Harston CB2 ....48 C3
　Whittlesford CB2 ....32 A6
　Shelford Sta CB2 ....49 B5
Shelford's Rd CB4 ......209 A4
Shelley CI
　Huntingdon PE29 ....141 F6
　Peterborough PE1 ....197 E8
　Royston SG8 ....13 D1
Shelley PI **5** PE19 ......74 D6
Shelly Gdn CB3 ....83 C3
Shelly Row **4** CB3 ......83 C3
Shelton Rd PE2 ....187 D6
Shepherd CI SG8 ....5 E5
Shepherd Dr PE19 ....74 E2
Shepherd's CI
　Cambridge CB1 ....66 A6
　Fen Ditton CB5 ....84 F5
Shepherd's Dro CB7 ....226 B2
Shepherds CI PE4 ......204 B6
Shepherds CI **3** CB9 ...23 E7
Shepherds Gr **1** SG1 ...85 B1
Sheppard's Dro PE6 ....232 D8
Sheppersons Gr **2**
　PE15 ....243 E4

Shepreth L-Moor Nature
　Reserve* SG8 ....29 D3
Shepreth Rd
　Barrington CB2 ....29 D7
　Foxton CB2 ....30 A4
　Shepreth SG8 ....30 B3
Shepreth Sta SG8 ....29 E5
Shepreth Wildlife Pk*
　SG8 ....29 C5
Sheralds Croft La SG8 ...31 A2
Sherborne Rd PE1 ......198 D6
Sherbourne CI CB4 ......84 B6
Sherbrooke CI PE15 ....243 D1
Sheridan Rd PE1 ....197 F8
Sheriffs Ct CB8 ....70 F3
Sheringham Way PE2 ..186 C6
Sherlock CI CB3 ....83 B4
Sherlock Ct CB3 ....83 B4
Sherlock Rd CB3 ....83 B5
Sherwood Ave
　Peterborough PE2 ....186 F7
　Wisbech PE13 ....245 D7
Shetland Rd CB9 ....24 D8
Shillow Hill PE26 ....172 B1
Shinngay La CB2 ....29 D7
Ship Gdns IP28 ....239 B3
Ship La CB7 ....240 D3
Shippea Hill Rd IP28 ...213 E8
Shirdley Rd PE19 ....74 F4
Shire Ct **7** CB9 ....23 E7
Shire Gr PE1 ....198 C5
Shires The
　Bluntisham/Colne PE28 ..208 C5
　March PE15 ....243 E2
　Royston SG8 ....5 E6
Shirley CI CB4 ....105 E2
Shirley Gr CB4 ....84 B5
Shirley Inf Sch CB4 ......84 B5
Shirley Rd CB4 ....104 B3
Shooter's Hollow
　PE19 ....116 D3
Shores CI IP28 ....213 C3
Short CI PE8 ....178 B3
Short Cswy CB4 ....217 C4
Short Dr PE15 ....224 B5
Short Dro
　Cottenham CB4 ....125 F2
　Little Downham CB6 ....217 F5
　Pymore CB6 ....217 C8
　Downham CB6 ....224 F3
　Earith PE28 ....208 F6
　Holme PE7 ....177 A4
　Ramsey PE26 ....221 A2
　Somersham PE28 ....215 D3
Short La
　Bluntisham/Colne PE28 ..208 C5
　Coveney CB6 ....217 C4
　Willingham CB4 ....209 A1
　Wisbech PE13 ....238 A1
Short Nightlayer's Dro
　PE16 ....241 C6
Short Rd Exning CB8 ...131 F2
　Snailwell CB8 ....132 A3
　Stretham CB6 ....210 E5
Short St Bourn CB3 ......60 D5
　Cambridge CB1 ....246 B3
Shortacres Rd PE2 .....186 F7
Shortfen PE2 ....186 C4
Shortland **6** PE28 .....215 C1
Shortsands Yd **3** PE19 ..75 A5
Shrewsbury Ave PE2 ...186 D5
Shropshire PI PE1 ......198 B2
Shrub House CI IP28 ...213 F8
Shrub Rd PE7 ....186 C1
Shrubberies The CB8 ...111 D1
Shrubbery Gr SG8 ....5 D4
Shrubbery The PE16 ...241 D4
Shrublands IP28 ....239 C4
Shudy Camps Pk CB1 ...22 C6
Sibson Aerodrome
　PE8 ....183 E6
Sidgwick Ave CB3 ....64 C8
Siding Dro PE28 ....215 C5
Sidney Farm Rd CB1 ....65 E6
Sidney Gdns CB3 ....47 B6
Sidney St CB2 ....246 A3
Sidney Sussex Coll
　CB1 ....246 B3
Siggin's La CB1 ....10 D6
Silhalls CI CB8 ....91 F7
Silt Rd Littleport CB6 ...242 D5
　March PE15 ....243 F4
　Upwell PE14 ....229 F5
Silver Birch Ave PE27 ...143 F6
Silver Birch CI PE29 ...141 E7
Silver Hill PE7 ....186 D3
Silver La PE27 ....208 A3
Silver Lodge IP28 ....239 F3
Silver St Ashwell SG7 ....2 D4
　Buckden PE19 ....117 B4
　Burwell CB5 ....130 B4
　Cambridge CB3 ....246 A1
　Ely CB7 ....240 C4
　Godmanchester PE29 ...118 E8
　Guilden Morden SG8 .....14 D7
　Litlington SG8 ....12 A2
　March PE15 ....243 C7
　Peterborough PE7 ......186 F7
　Ramsey PE26 ....172 B7
　St Neots PE19 ....74 E4
　Willingham CB4 ....209 A1
　Wisbech PE13 ....245 C6
　Witcham CB6 ....212 A8
　Wittersfield CB9 ....38 A4
Silverdale Ave CB3 ......82 B2
Silverdale CI CB3 ....82 A2
Silverley Way CB8 ....91 F7
Silver's La PE13 ....234 E7

Silverweed PE19 ....74 C5
Silverwood CI CB1 ......84 B2
Silverwood Rd PE1 .....197 F5
Silvester Rd PE5 ....195 E2
Simeon CI CB6 ....240 F7
Simmer Piece PE28 .....121 C5
Simpkin CI PE19 ....74 B2
Singerfire Rd PE5 ......195 D2
Sir Harry Smith Com Coll
　PE7 ....189 F7
Sir James Black Rd
　CB7 ....240 C2
Siskin CI SG8 ....5 E8
Sissley PE2 ....185 E2
Six Bells **14** PE28 ....215 C1
Six Mile Bottom Rd
　CB8 ....69 A1
Sixteen Foot Bank
　Christchurch PE14 .....229 C4
　Wimblington PE15 .....223 E5
Sixth Ave PE13 ....245 E4
Skaters Way PE4 ....204 C4
Skeels Ct PE29 ....141 F7
Skeggles CI PE29 ......141 B5
Skeleton Dro PE14 .....217 A5
Skelton PI PE27 ....144 B5
Skelton's Dro IP28 .....213 F8
Skipper's La
　West Wickham CB1 ......37 F8
　West Wratting CB1 ......54 E1
　Withersfield CB9 ....38 A5
Skiver CI CB2 ....32 F6
Skylark PI **11** SG8 ......5 E8
Skylarks CI PE7 ....186 D3
Slade CI PE26 ....172 A7
Slade The
　Witcham CB6 ....217 A2
　Wrestlingworth
　Cockayne Hatley SG19 ..25 B3
Slade Way SG8 ....241 C5
Slateborn Dro PE7 .....221 C8
Sleaford St CB1 ....84 A1
Sleford CI CB1 ....53 B2
Sleights Dr **4** PE14 ...238 F1
Slid La CB2 ....29 F8
Slipe Cotts PE28 ....146 A6
Small Lode PE14 ....236 F1
Smallwood PE3 ....197 B5
Smeefield PE28 ....99 B8
Smeeth Rd
　Emneth PE14 ....236 E6
　Marshland St James
　PE14 ....236 F7
Smith Dr PE19 ....117 B3
Smith St CB3 ....100 A4
Smith's Dr PE15 ....243 F3
Smith's Dro PE28 ......226 F4
Smith's End La SG8 ......6 F1
Smithey Fen Engine Dro
　CB4 ....209 E2
Smithfield PE6 ....233 B3
Smiths Chase PE15 .....243 B5
Smiths Yd PE19 ....94 A6
Snail Croft PE13 ....238 A2
Snailwell Rd
　Fordham CB8 ....131 F5
　Newmarket CB8 ....111 B6
Snailwell Short Rd
　CB8 ....131 E1
Snoots Rd PE7 ....189 B7
Snowberry Way **3** CB7 .212 B5
Snowden CI **1** PE6 ....232 C8
Snowden CI CB9 ....23 E6
Snowdonia Way PE29 ...141 A4
Snowley Pk PE7 ....189 B8
Snowy Way PE29 ....142 B6
Soham Mere CB7 ....211 F4
Soham Rd Ely CB7 .....211 D8
　Fordham CB7 ....212 D2
Soham Village Coll
　PE28 ....215 C1
Soham Village Coll
　CB7 ....212 B3
Soke Parkway PE3 .....197 A3
Soke Rd PE6 ....207 B1
Sokemans Way PE28 ...117 D8
Somerby CI PE19 ....94 A6
Somerby Garth **1** PE1 .198 D7
Somers Rd PE13 ....245 B4
Somerset CI CB4 ....83 D7
Somerset Ct **16** CB9 ...23 E7
Somerset Rd
　Histon CB4 ....104 A3
　Wyton Airfield PE28 ....143 B8
Somersham Prim Sch
　PE28 ....215 C1
Somersham Rd
　Bluntisham PE28 ....155 C2
　Colne PE28 ....208 C8
　Holywell-cum-Needingworth
　PE27 ....144 C7
Somervell Ct **5** CB4 ...83 E7
Somerville PE4 ....204 A5
Somerville Rd **1** PE9 ..244 A6
Somes CI **1** PE9 .....230 C6
Sorbus CI PE7 ....186 D3
Sorrel Rd CB9 ....59 F5
Sorrel Wlk CB9 ....38 D1
Sorrell CI SG8 ....5 F5
South Brink Elm PE14 ...235 B4
　Wisbech PE13 ....245 A3
South CI SG8 ....5 B7
South Dr March PE15 ...243 E4
　Newmarket CB8 ....110 F4
South End SG8 ....12 E3
South End Rd CB6 ......64 C7
South La **3** CB3 ....60 C5
South Par PE7 ....197 E3
South Pk Dr CB3 ....99 B1
South Pk St PE16 ......241 C4

South Rd
　Brampton PE28 ....117 D8
　Great Abington CB1 .....33 F4
　Histon CB4 ....104 B1
South St Comberton CB3 ..42 A6
　Great Chesterford CB10 ..18 D2
　Huntingdon PE29 ......141 F5
　Litlington SG8 ....12 A2
　Peterborough PE1 ......198 B2
　5 St Neots PE19 ....74 E5
　Woodhurst PE28 ....155 A4
South Terr CB2 ....32 F5
South View PE2 ....186 F7
South View Rd PE4 .....197 D8
Southacre CI CB2 ....64 E6
Southacre Dr CB2 ......64 E6
Southampton PI PE16 ..241 C3
Southbrook Field CB3 ...99 A2
Southbrooke CI **2** CB2 ..64 E3
Southcourts 48 F3
Southdown Rd PE7 ......64 F3
Southerns The **7** CB6 ..216 E1
Southey Wood* PE9 ....231 A1
Southfield CB10 ....18 A3
Southfields Ave PE2 ...187 D5
Southfields CI
　Newmarket CB8 ....110 E4
　Wisbech PE13 ....245 E7
Southfields Dr PE2 .....187 D6
Southfields Jun & Inf school
　PE2 ....187 D5
Southgate Ave IP28 ....239 F7
Southgate Way PE2 ....185 C2
Southlands Ave PE1 ....198 A6
Southoe Rd PE7 ....187 D2
Southorpe Mdw Nature
　Reserve* PE9 ....230 E2
Southorpe Paddock Nature
　Reserve* PE9 ....230 E1
Southside Ct CB4 ....84 A5
Southwell Ave PE4 .....204 A4
Southwell Rd PE13 ....245 C8
Southwick CI PE4 ......204 E1
Sovereign CI PE13 .....245 A6
Sovereign PI PE3 ......197 E2
Sovereign Way CB4 .....125 E3
Spalding Way CB1 ....65 D4
Spaldings La CB4 ......104 C3
Spaldwick Prim Sch
　PE28 ....137 F5
Spaldwick Rd PE28 ....137 C3
Sparkes CI **2** CB7 ....213 A5
Sparrow CI PE2 ....141 E5
Sparrow Dr PE28 ....150 E4
Sparrow Rd PE7 ....186 D1
Sparrow Way PE28 .....120 B1
Sparrowgate Rd PE14 ..238 F1
Sparrowwk Way
　PE29 ....142 B7
Sparrows CI PE28 .....117 D8
Speechley Rd PE7 .....181 F6
Speechley's Dro PE6 ...207 F2
Speed La CB7 ....212 B4
Speedwell CI CB1 ....66 A6
Spencer Ave PE7 ......187 D5
Spencer CI
　3 Eaton Socon PE19 ...74 C6
　West Walton PE14 .....238 E4
Spencer Croft CB7 .....240 E6
Spencer Dr
　Melbourn SG8 ....14 D6
　St Ives PE27 ....144 A7
Spencer Dro
　Guyhirn PE13 ....235 A2
　Soham CB7 ....212 A4
Spencer Rd CB10 ....18 D3
Spens Ave CB3 ....64 B8
Spenser CI SG8 ....13 D1
Speyside Ct **1** PE2 ....185 D4
Spiggots CI CB4 ....123 E2
Spindle Rd CB9 ....38 D1
Spinney Abbey CB7 ....211 D2
Spinney CI
　Brampton PE28 ....140 D3
　Warboys PE28 ....164 F5
　Warmington PE8 ....178 B2
Spinney Dr CB2 ....49 A4
Spinney Field PE28 ....138 F3
Spinney Fields PE7 ....176 F4
Spinney La PE28 ....150 F5
Spinney Prim Sch The
　CB1 ....65 C6
Spinney The
　Bar Hill CB3 ....102 B3
　Cottenham CB4 ....125 C5
　Huntingdon PE29 ......142 B6
Spinney Way
　18 Needingworth PE27 ..208 A3
　St Ives PE27 ....143 F6
Spinning Inf Sch PE26 ..172 B6
Spires End PE28 ....150 D6
Spitfire CI PE29 ....141 B8
Spittals Way
　Huntingdon PE29 ......141 C7
　The Stukeleys PE28 ....152 C1
Splash La Castor PE5 ..164 E8
　St Ives PE28 ....142 F6
Split Dro CB5 ....129 A4
Spong Dro CB4 ....209 B1
Spooners CI CB8 ....70 F8
Sprignall PE3 ....196 F4
Spring CI Burwell CB5 ..130 B1
　Histon CB4 ....104 C4
　Peterborough PE7 .....141 E6
Spring Comm Sch
　PE29 ....141 F6
Spring Dr PE7 ....187 B2
Spring Hill MK44 ....93 A3

Spring La
Bassingbourn SG8 . . . . .12 F3
Bottisham CB5 . . . . .86 F6
Spring Mdw Inf Sch
CB7 . . . . .240 E6
Spring PI PE19 . . . . .95 A1
Springbrook PE19 . . . . . .74 F4
Springfield
Huntingdon PE29 . . . . .141 E5
Peterborough PE2 . . . . .187 A7
Somersham PE28 . . . . .215 C1
Springfield Ave PE15 . .243 C2
Springfield Cl
Buckden PE19 . . . . .117 A3
2 St Neots PE19 . . . . . . .75 A5
Springfield Rd
Alconbury Weston PE28 . . .150 D5
Cambridge CB4 . . . . .83 E4
1 Parson Drove PE13 . . .234 D7
Peterborough PE1 . . . . .197 F5
Sawston CB2 . . . . .32 F5
Yaxley PE7 . . . . .181 F5
Springfield Terr 1 CB4 . .83 E4
Springfields PE1 . . . . . . .190 C7
Springhead SG7 . . . . .2 D4
Springhead La CB7 . . . . .240 E5
Springhill Rd CB4 . . . . . .121 E6
Spruce Dr PE28 . . . . .151 F2
Spurgeons Ave CB5 . . . .106 B8
Spurgeon's Cl CB11 . . . . .85 B1
Spurling Cl CB8 . . . . .91 C5
Square The
6 Barnack PE9 . . . . .230 D4
Stow cum Quy CB5 . . . . . . .86 A6
Squire's Dr PE14 . . . . . . .229 F7
Squire's Field The CB7 . .67 F7
Squires Cl 17 PE28 . . . . .215 C1
Squires Ct
5 Eaton Socon PE19 . . . .74 B4
Haverhill CB9 . . . . .23 E7
Squires Gate PE4 . . . . . .204 F3
Squires The PE2 . . . . . . .186 F8
St Johns Bsns Pk
PE29 . . . . .141 C8
Stable Yd CB3 . . . . .79 B3
Stables Ct PE13 . . . . .238 B2
Stackyard The
Ickleton CB10 . . . . .18 A3
Peterborough PE2 . . . . .185 E5
Stafford Rd PE7 . . . . . . .189 F6
Staffordshire Gdns 8
CB1 . . . . .84 A1
Staffordshire St CB1 . . . .84 A2
Stagsden PE2 . . . . .185 F4
Stagshaw Dr PE2 . . . . . .187 B8
Stained Glass Mus*
PE9 . . . . .240 D4
Staithe Rd PE28 . . . . .245 E5
Stake Piece Rd SG8 . . . . . .5 C5
Stakings The CB2 . . . . . . .32 D7
Stallebrass Cl PE7 . . . . . .187 E5
Stamford & Rutland Hospl
PE9 . . . . .244 D6
Stamford Arts Ctr
PE9 . . . . .244 C5
Stamford Ave SG8 . . . . . . .5 D7
Stamford Cl SG8 . . . . .5 D7
Stamford Coll PE9 . . . . .244 D6
Stamford Endowed Sch
PE9 . . . . .244 C5
Stamford High Sch
PE9 . . . . .244 C4
Stamford High Sch Juns
PE9 . . . . .244 B4
Stamford Jun Sch
PE9 . . . . .244 B3
Stamford La PE28 . . . . . . .178 B3
Stamford Leisure Ctr
PE9 . . . . .244 D6
Stamford Lodge Rd
PE6 . . . . .196 D4
Stamford Mus* PE9 . . . .244 C5
Stamford Rd
Barnack PE9 . . . . .230 C4
Easton on the Hill PE9 . . . .244 A1
Helpston PE6 . . . . .231 C1
Marholm PE6 . . . . .203 B2
Market Deeping PE6 . . . . . .231 D8
Tallington PE9 . . . . .231 A8
Stamford Ret Pk PE9 . . .244 D6
Stamford Sch PE9 . . . . . .244 C5
Stamford St 3 CB8 . . . . .111 B2
Stamford Sta PE9 . . . . . .244 B4
Stamford Theatre*
PE9 . . . . .244 C5
Stamford Wlk 16 PE9 . . .244 C5
Stamford Yd SG8 . . . . .5 C6
Stamfords Artists Gall
PE9 . . . . .244 C5
Stamper St PE2 . . . . .196 F3
Stan Rowing Ct PE2 . . . .187 C7
Stanbury Cl CB4 . . . . .84 E6
Stanch Hill Rd PE28 . . . .168 C3
Standish Ct PE2 . . . . .186 D8
Stanegate 3 PE28 . . . . .168 C2
Stanesfield Rd CB6 . . . . .84 D3
Stanford Bus Pk PE9 . . .244 D6
Stanford Wlk PE3 . . . . . .197 C7
Stanground Coll PE7 . . .187 C5
Stanground Newt Ponds
Nature Reserve***
PE7 . . . . .187 C4
Stanground St John's Prim
Sch PE1 . . . . .187 C7
Stanground Wash Nature
Reserve* PE2 . . . . .187 D7
Staniland Way PE4 . . . . .204 B5
Stanley Ct CB5 . . . . .84 B3

Stanley Rd
Cambridge CB5 . . . . .84 B3
Great Chesterford CB10 . . .18 E3
Newmarket CB8 . . . . .111 C3
Peterborough PE1 . . . . .198 A3
Stanley St PE9 . . . . .244 C5
Stanpoint Way PE27 . . . .144 A5
Stansfield Gdns CB1 . . . .66 F5
Stansgate Ave CB2 . . . . . .65 B3
Stanton Mere Way
CB4 . . . . .124 A6
Stanton Sq PE7 . . . . .186 D2
Stanwick Ct PE3 . . . . . . .197 F2
Stapledon Rd PE2 . . . . . .185 D2
Stapleford Com Prim Sch
CB2 . . . . .49 C4
Staples La CB7 . . . . .212 B3
Star And Garter La CB8 . .91 C7
Star Cl PE1 . . . . .198 B2
Star La Ramsey PE26 . . . .172 A8
Stamford PE9 . . . . .244 C5
Star Mews PE1 . . . . .198 C2
Star Rd PE1 . . . . .198 C2
Stargoose Cl CB3 . . . . . . .80 B1
Starling Cl
Alconbury PE28 . . . . .150 E4
Milton CB4 . . . . .105 D3
Starlock Cl CB6 . . . . .210 E4
Stathern Rd PE1 . . . . .198 D7
Station App
March PE15 . . . . .243 D6
Newmarket CB8 . . . . .111 A4
Somersham PE28 . . . . .208 C8
Station Ave PE13 . . . . . . .234 D5
Station Dr
Wisbech PE13 . . . . .245 C4
Wisbech St Mary PE13 . . . .235 C7
Station Gate CB5 . . . . . . .109 B8
Station Gdns PE26 . . . . . .172 A8
Station La PE19 . . . . .117 F3
Station Rd
Abbots Ripton PE28 . . . . . .162 B1
Ailsworth PE5 . . . . .184 C8
Ashwell SG7 . . . . .2 A8
Barnack PE9 . . . . .230 E4
Bluntisham PE28 . . . . .208 C4
Cambridge CB1 . . . . .64 F7
Catworth PE28 . . . . .136 D5
Chatteris PE16 . . . . .241 C4
Deeping St James PE6 . . . .206 E6
Ely CB7 . . . . .89 C2
Elm PE14 . . . . .235 C2
Ely CB7 . . . . .240 D3
Fordham CB7 . . . . .131 A8
Foxton CB2 . . . . .30 B6
Fulbourn CB1 . . . . .67 A5
Gamlingay SG19 . . . . .41 E5
Gedney Hill PE12 . . . . .233 F8
Great Shelford CB2 . . . . . . .49 A5
Haddenham CB6 . . . . .210 A6
Harston CB2 . . . . .47 F2
Haverhill CB9 . . . . .24 A8
Histon CB4 . . . . .104 C3
Holme PE7 . . . . .177 A4
Isleham CB7 . . . . .213 A4
Kennett CB8 . . . . .133 F5
Linton CB1 . . . . .35 B2
Littleport CB6 . . . . .242 E4
Lode CB5 . . . . .107 C2
Longstanton CB4 . . . . .123 F4
Manea PE15 . . . . .224 B5
March PE15 . . . . .243 D5
Meldreth SG8 . . . . .14 B6
Mildenhall IP28 . . . . .239 B3
Oakington & Westwick
CB4 . . . . .103 D7
Over CB4 . . . . .122 F8
Pampisford CB2 . . . . .33 F6
Peterborough PE3 . . . . .197 F2
Ramsey PE26 . . . . .172 A7
St Ives PE27 . . . . .144 B3
St Neots PE19 . . . . .75 B5
Shepreth SG8 . . . . .29 E5
Soham CB7 . . . . .212 B4
Stamford PE9 . . . . .244 B4
Steeple Morden SG8 . . . . . .3 B7
Stow cum Quy CB5 . . . . . .106 E1
Sutton CB6 . . . . .216 F1
Swaffham Bulbeck CB5 . . .108 A2
Swaffham Prior CB5 . . . . . .108 C5
Swavesey CB4 . . . . .122 C7
Thorney PE6 . . . . .233 A4
Tilbrook PE28 . . . . .113 B7
Walsoken PE14 . . . . .236 E8
Warboys PE28 . . . . .164 F7
Waterbeach CB5 . . . . .106 B7
Whittlesey PE7 . . . . .189 E5
Wilburton CB6 . . . . .210 C7
Willingham CB4 . . . . .120 A7
Wisbech St Mary PE13 . . . .235 C7
Yaxley PE7 . . . . .182 A7
Station Rd E CB2 . . . . . . .32 E3
Station Rd W CB2 . . . . . .32 E3
Station St PE16 . . . . .241 B4
Station Yd PE19 . . . . .239 B3
Staughton Pl PE19 . . . . . .74 C4
Staunch Hill PE28 . . . . . .148 C3
Staverton Rd PE4 . . . . . .204 A3
Staxton Cl PE6 . . . . .203 C1
Steam Brewery Mus*
PE1 . . . . .244 B5
Stearne's Yd CB3 . . . . . . .47 B5
Steeple Morden CE Prim Sch
SG8 . . . . .11 B2
Steeple View PE15 . . . . .243 C1
Stephen Cl CB9 . . . . .23 F8
Stephens Way 15 PE6 . .231 F8

Stephenson Cl
1 March PE15 . . . . .243 D7
Royston SG8 . . . . .5 B7
Yaxley PE7 . . . . .181 D6
Stephenson Ct PE1 . . . . .198 B2
Stephenson Rd PE27 . . . .144 B6
Stepping Stones PE28 . . .143 D1
Stepping Stones Sch
PE4 . . . . .197 D8
Stermyn St 8 PE13 . . . . .245 C5
Sterndale Cl CB3 . . . . . . .82 E8
Sterne Cl CB1 . . . . .65 B6
Sternes Way CB2 . . . . . . .49 C4
Stetchworth Rd
Dullingham CB8 . . . . .70 F8
Stetchworth CB8 . . . . .71 C8
Stevens Cl CB4 . . . . .125 D4
Stevens Way PE15 . . . . .243 D6
Stevenson Cl
Cambridge CB1 . . . . .84 A3
Eaton Socon PE19 . . . . . . .74 D6
Steward Cl CB7 . . . . .211 D8
Steward's La CB6 . . . . . .216 E1
Stewart Cl PE28 . . . . .140 C2
Steynings The PE4 . . . . .204 C3
Stickle Cl PE29 . . . . .141 B7
Stile Plantation SG8 . . . . .5 E6
Stiles The PE27 . . . . .144 C2
Still The PE13 . . . . .238 B1
Stuart Cl
Godmanchester PE29 . . . . .142 A1
Peterborough PE2 . . . . .187 C6
Stuart Ct PE1 . . . . .198 B4
Stuart Dr SG8 . . . . .5 D8
Stubbs Cl 3 Haverhill CB9 .38 D1
St Ives PE27 . . . . .144 A7
Studlands Pk Ave
CB8 . . . . .110 D6
Studlands Rise 5 E6
Studlands Rise Fst Sch
SG8 . . . . .5 E5
Stukeley Cl
Cambridge CB4 . . . . .64 A8
Peterborough PE2 . . . . .187 D5
Stukeley Mdws Ind Es
PE29 . . . . .141 C8
Stukeley Mdws Prim Sch
PE29 . . . . .141 C6
Stukeley Pk PE28 . . . . . .152 A2
Stukeley Rd PE29 . . . . . .141 C6
Stulp Field Rd CB3 . . . . . .64 A4
Stump Cross CB10 . . . . . .18 C5
Stumpacre PE3 . . . . .197 A8
Stumpcross 4 PE28 . . . .168 C2
Stuntney Cswy CB7 . . . . .240 E2
Sturmer Cl 6 CB4 . . . . . .83 C7
Sturmer Dr CB9 . . . . .24 B7
Sturmer Road Ind Est
CB9 . . . . .24 B7
Sturrock Way PE3 . . . . . .197 C8
Sturton St CB1 . . . . .84 A1
Sudbury Ct
Peterborough PE7 . . . . .187 F5
Whittlesey PE7 . . . . .189 C8
Sudeley Gr CB3 . . . . .81 A3
Suet Hills Dro PE7 . . . . . .188 E1
Suez Rd CB1 . . . . .65 C7
Suffolk Cl Ely CB6 . . . . . .240 A3
Huntingdon PE29 . . . . .141 E6
Peterborough PE7 . . . . .197 B2
St Ives PE27 . . . . .144 A8
Suffolk Rd 5 SG8 . . . . .5 E6
Suffolk Way
March PE15 . . . . .243 C2
Newmarket CB8 . . . . .243 C2
Sugar Way PE2 . . . . .186 D8
Sulehay Rd PE8 . . . . .193 C1
Sumerling Way PE28 . . .208 C6
Summerfield CB3 . . . . . . .64 C8
Summerfield Cl PE13 . . .245 A6
Summerfield Rd PE1 . . . .197 F4
Summerhayes CB7 . . . . .240 F6
Sun Hill SG8 . . . . .5 C5
Sun La CB6 . . . . .110 C8
Sun St 9 Cambridge CB1 . .84 A2
Isleham CB7 . . . . .213 A5
Sunderland Ave CB2 . . . . .33 A8
Sundew Cl PE11 . . . . .74 B6
Sunfield Rd PE26 . . . . . . .172 A4
Sunflower St CB4 . . . . . . .83 D7
Sunmead Wlk CB1 . . . . . .66 A6
Sunningdale Cl CB8 . . . . .185 E6
Sunningdale Ave PE28 . .237 A8
Sunnybank 1 PE19 . . . . . .75 A5
Sunnymead PE4 . . . . .204 A6
Sunnyside CB6 . . . . .84 E2
Sunnyville Rd PE7 . . . . . .190 F8
Sunset Gdns PE13 . . . . . .245 E2
Sunset Sq 2 CB2 . . . . .83 D7
Surrey Rd PE27 . . . . .141 E8
Sussex Rd
Stamford PE9 . . . . .244 B6
Wyton Airfield PE28 . . . . . .143 B8
Sussex St CB2 . . . . .246 B3
Sutcliffe Rd PE8 . . . . .193 D8
Sutton CE Prim Sch
CB6 . . . . .216 E5
Sutton Cl CB4 . . . . .105 D3
Sutton Ct 6 CB6 . . . . . . .216 E2
Sutton Gate PE12 . . . . . .237 D8
Sutton Mdws PE26 . . . . .216 E2
Sutton Pk CB6 . . . . .216 E2
Sutton Rd
Eyeworth SG19 . . . . .10 A8
Haddenham CB6 . . . . .210 A8
Mepal CB6 . . . . .216 A6
Newton PE13 . . . . .233 B6
Wentworth CB6 . . . . .217 C1
Wisbech PE13 . . . . .245 A7

Street The continued
Dalham CB8 . . . . .92 E8
Freckenham IP28 . . . . .213 C3
Great Bradley CB8 . . . . .55 F7
Great Wratting CB9 . . . . . . .39 E6
Kirtling CB8 . . . . .72 D6
Lidgate CB8 . . . . .73 D8
Mildenhall IP28 . . . . .213 E8
Moulton CB8 . . . . .112 F5
Snailwell CB8 . . . . .132 A4
Westley Waterless CB8 . . . .70 C5
Woodditton CB8 . . . . .91 D3
Worlington CB8 . . . . .213 F4
Streetly End CB1 . . . . .37 B5
Streetways CB8 . . . . .68 E7
Stretham Com Prim Sch
CB6 . . . . .210 F5
Stretham Old Engine*
CB6 . . . . .210 F4
Stretham Rd
Wicken CB7 . . . . .211 D2
Wilburton CB6 . . . . .210 D5
Stretten Ave CB4 . . . . .83 D4
Stretton Ave CB8 . . . . . . .111 B2
Stricklands Dr 5 PE6 . . .232 B8
Strollers Way CB8 . . . . . . .90 A2
Stroud Hill PE28 . . . . .165 E2
Strympole Way CB3 . . . . .80 B1

Swaffham Bulbeck CE Prim
Sch CB5 . . . . .108 B1
Swaffham Heath Rd
CB5 . . . . .108 C1
Swaffham Prior CE Prim
Sch CB5 . . . . .108 D5
Swaffham Rd
Bottisham CB5 . . . . .107 E1
Burwell CB5 . . . . .109 A7
Reach CB5 . . . . .108 E2
Swain Ct PE2 . . . . .186 F8
Swain's Dro PE13 . . . . . .238 C8
Swale Ave PE14 . . . . .204 E1
Swallow Cl PE7 . . . . .201 A1
Swallow Ct PE2 . . . . .186 A3
Swallow Dr 3 PE19 . . . . . .75 B6
Swallow La CB13 . . . . . . .238 B8
Swallow Way PE15 . . . . .243 F5
Swallows Cl CB4 . . . . .84 A4
Swan Cl St Ives PE27 . . . .143 F7
Whittlesey PE7 . . . . .189 F8
Swan Ct PE15 . . . . .243 D6
Swan Dr PE16 . . . . .241 D5
Swan End PE19 . . . . .117 B4
Swan Gdns
Fenstanton PE28 . . . . .121 B5
Parson Drove PE13 . . . . . .234 C7
Peterborough PE1 . . . . .198 E6
Swan Gr CB8 . . . . .110 B8
Swan La Exning CB8 . . . . .110 B8
Guilden Morden SG8 . . . . . .10 F4
Haverhill CB9 . . . . .24 A8
Swan Rd
Fenstanton PE28 . . . . .121 B5
Peterborough PE7 . . . . .189 F8
Swan St SG7 . . . . .2 D4
Swanhill 8 CB4 . . . . .194 A4
Swann Rd CB5 . . . . .84 C4
Swann's Cl CB5 . . . . .84 B4
Swann's Rd CB5 . . . . .84 B4
Swann's Terr 4 CB1 . . . . .65 A8
Swansley La CB3 . . . . .79 A4
Swanspool PE3 . . . . .197 B6
Swanton Cl PE15 . . . . . . .223 F5
Swasedale Dro CB2 . . . . .219 A5
Swavesey Prim Sch
CB4 . . . . .122 C6
Swavesey Rd CB4 . . . . . .122 A4
Swavesey Village Coll
CB4 . . . . .122 C5
Swayne's La CB23 . . . . . . .62 C5
Sweetbriar La PE4 . . . . . .204 B6
Sweeting Ave PE19 . . . . . .95 F1
Sweetings Rd PE19 . . . . .118 F8
Swift Cl March PE15 . . . . .243 F5
Market Deeping PE6 . . . . . .231 E8
Royston SG8 . . . . .13 C1
Swifts Cnr CB1 . . . . .66 F5
Swinburne Cl SG8 . . . . . . .13 B5
Swinnell Cl SG8 . . . . .13 A5
Sybil Rd PE13 . . . . .245 C6
Sycamore Ave PE1 . . . . .198 C6
Sycamore Cl
4 Cambridge CB1 . . . . . .65 D5
March PE15 . . . . .243 C3
Sycamore Dr PE29 . . . . .141 E8
Sycamore La CB7 . . . . . . .240 F5
Sycamore Pl CB6 . . . . . . .242 D4
Sycamore Rd PE7 . . . . . .189 F6
Sycamores The
Bluntisham/Colne PE28 . . .208 C6
Little Paxton PE19 . . . . .95 F2
Milton CB4 . . . . .105 C2
Sydney Rd PE7 . . . . .187 D5
Syers La PE7 . . . . .187 D5
Sylton Cl PE29 . . . . .141 F1
Sylvden Dr PE13 . . . . . . .245 F6
Sylvester Rd CB3 . . . . . . .83 B1
Symmington Cl PE2 . . . .186 F8
Symonds Cl CB4 . . . . . . .104 B4
Symonds La CB5 . . . . .35 B3
Sywell Gr 5 PE14 . . . . . .236 A5

T

Tabrum Rd CB3 . . . . .63 F4
Tadlow Rd SG19 . . . . .25 C3
Taggart Tile Mus*
PE13 . . . . .93 E6
Tait Cl PE1 . . . . .198 C5
Talbot Ave PE2 . . . . .186 D6
Talbot Cl PE7 . . . . .175 F8
Tall Trees 3 SG8 . . . . .5 B4
Tallington Dry Ski Slope
PE9 . . . . .230 F8
Tallington Lakes Leisure Pk*
PE9 . . . . .231 A8
Tall's La PE28 . . . . .121 B6
Tamar Cl PE27 . . . . .144 B6
Tamarin Gdns CB4 . . . . . .66 A6
Tan House La CB5 . . . . . .109 B8
Tan Yd PE19 . . . . .74 E5
Tanglewood
Alconbury Weston PE28 . . .150 E6
Peterborough PE4 . . . . .204 B6
Tanhouse PE2 . . . . .186 C5
Tanners La CB7 . . . . .212 B3

Tannersfield Way CB8 ..110 F4
Tannery Cl SG8 ....5 C6
Tannery Drift SG8 ......5 C7
Tannery Drift Sch SG8 ..5 C6
Tannery Rd CB2 ....32 F6
Tansor Garth PE2 .....197 C5
Tansor Grange PE8 ...178 A1
Tansur Ct PE19 ....74 F8
Tansy Cl 2 PE19 ......74 B5
Tantallon Ct PE3 .....197 B1
Tanyard The SG8 ......12 E4
Tarrant PE4 ....204 A6
Tasman Rd CB9 ....24 C7
Tates Field CB3 ....59 E8
Tatwin Dr 8 PE6 .....232 B8
Taunton Cl CB1 ....65 D7
Taverners Dr PE26 ...171 F5
Taverners Rd PE1 ....197 F4
Tavistock Cl 8 PE6 ..233 A3
Tavistock Rd
  Cambridge CB4 ......83 C6
  Wisbech PE13 ......245 D5
Tavny Cres PE29 .....142 B7
Tay Cl PE27 ....148 B7
Taylor's Dro PE12 ...237 C8
Taylor's La CB4 ......122 D6
Taylors Field CB8 .....70 F8
Taylors Gn PE8 ......178 A2
Taylors La PE19 .....116 F5
Taymor Pl PE14 .....225 A8
Tea Kettle La CB8 .....89 F1
Teal Cl Chatteris PE16 .241 C6
  St Ives PE27 ......143 F7
Teal Rd PE7 ....189 F8
Teanby Ct PE3 ....196 F3
Teasdale Cl SG8 ......13 D1
Teasel Cl
  1B Eaton Socon PE19 .74 C6
  2 Royston SG8 ....5 E5
Teasel Dr CB6 ....240 B5
Teasel Way CB1 ....66 A5
Tebbutts Rd PE19 ....74 E5
Tedder Way CB4 ......83 C6
Telegraph St CB4 ...125 E4
Telford Dr PE7 ......181 D6
Templars Ct CB9 .....23 E7
Temple Cl Duxford CB2 .32 D1
  Huntingdon PE29 ..141 E4
Temple Ct 4 CB4 .....83 E7
Temple End
  Great Wilbraham CB1 ..68 A8
  Little Thurlow CB9 ....55 F2
Temple Grange PE4 ..204 B6
Temple Rd CB7 ......212 F4
Templemore Cl CB1 ..65 B4
Temples Cl PE6 .....231 B4
Tempsford Rd SG19 ..40 A4
Ten Acre Dro PE7 ...220 C8
Ten Bell La 8 CB7 ..212 B4
Ten Mile Bank CB6 ..242 F6
Tenby Cl CB1 ....66 A6
Tenby Way 8 PE19 ...74 F1
Tenison Ave CB1 .....64 F7
Tenison Manor CB4 ..125 D4
Tenison Rd CB1 ......65 A8
Tennis Ct Ave PE29 .141 E5
Tennis Ct Rd CB2 ...246 B1
Tennis Ct Terr CB2 ..246 A1
Tennyson Ave PE27 .143 F6
Tennyson Cl
  Huntingdon PE29 ..141 F6
  Royston SG8 ....13 D1
Tennyson Pl
  Eaton Socon PE19 ..74 D6
  Ely CB6 ....240 A5
Tennyson Rd PE1 ....197 F7
Tenter La PE9 ......244 C5
Tenterleas PE27 ....144 B3
Tern Cl CB9 ....24 C7
Tern Gdns PE16 ....241 C6
Tern Way 4 PE19 ....75 B6
Terr The CB4 ....111 A3
Terrington Cl PE14 ..236 D6
Tetworth Hill SG19 ..41 A7
Teversham CE Prim Sch
  CB1 ....85 B2
Teversham Drift CB1 ..66 A7
Teversham Rd CB1 ...66 D6
Teversham Way CB2 ..50 A1
Teynham Cl CB1 .....65 D7
Thackeray Cl SG8 ...13 D1
Thackers Cl PE8 ....194 A4
Thackray Cl PE29 ...141 E7
Tharp Way CB7 .....213 C1
Thatcher Stanfords Cl
  SG8 ....14 C7
Thatchers Cl PE26 ..171 B2
Thatchers Wood CB4 .123 C1
Thatchwood Ave PE14 .236 C6
Thetford Cnr CB6 ...211 A7
Thetford Rd CB4 ...123 C1
Thetford Terr CB5 ...84 E2
Thicket Rd PE28 ...143 B4
Thickwillow 2 PE29 .118 F8
Third Ave
  Warboys PE28 ....164 E6
  Wisbech PE13 ....245 E5
Third Dro
  Downham CB6 .....225 B1
  Peterborough PE1 .198 E2
Third Marsh Rd PE14 .238 C3
Thirlby Gdns CB7 ...240 E7
Thirleby Cl CB4 .....83 D5

Thirlemere Gdns PE4 .204 E3
Thirlmere PE29 ....141 B6
Thirlmere Gdns 3 PE4 .204 E3
Thirlwall Dr CB7 ...213 A1
Thistle Cnr CB7 ...218 D4
Thistle Dr PE2 ....187 C7
Thistle Gn CB4 ....122 E6
Thistlemoor Rd PE1 .197 E7
Thoday St CB1 .....65 B8
Thodays Cl CB4 ...209 A1
Thomas Christian Way
  CB5 ....86 E7
Thomas Cl PE3 ....196 F3
Thomas Eaton Prim Sch The
  PE15 ....223 B7
Thomas King Dr PE29 .141 C6
Thomas Parsons Sq
  CB2 ....240 C4
Thomas Rd CB1 .....66 D5
Thomas Way SG8 ...13 D1
Thomas Wlk CB11 ....9 F1
Thompsons Gd PE7 ..186 D3
Thompson's La CB2 ..246 A3
Thompsons Mdw SG8 .11 A4
Thongsley PE29 ....141 F7
Thongsley Fields Prim Sch
  PE29 ....141 F7
Thorby Ave PE15 ...243 A7
Thorley Cres PE2 ..186 D8
Thorleye Rd CB5 ....84 C2
Thorn Cl CB7 ......212 A4
Thorn Rd PE7 .....186 C2
Thorndown Cl PE27 .143 E6
Thorndown Com Jnr Sch
  PE27 ....143 E6
Thorndown Com Jun Sch
  PE27 ....143 E6
Thorney Dyke PE6 ..201 C6
Thorney Heritage Mus*
  PE6 ....233 A3
Thorney Rd Eye PE6 .232 B1
  Newborough PE6 ..206 E2
  Wisbech St Mary PE13 .234 C2
Thornham Way PE7 .190 C6
Thornhill Pl CB4 ...123 F2
Thornleigh Dr PE2 .186 C6
Thornmead PE4 ....204 D4
Thornton Cl Girton CB3 .82 F6
  Peterborough PE4 .204 E3
Thornton Rd Girton CB3 .82 F7
  March PE15 ......243 D6
Thornton Way CB3 ...83 A6
Thorolds Way PE5 ..195 D2
Thoroughfare La CB1 .218 F1
Thoroughfare Way
  CB6 ....242 E4
Thorpe Ave PE3 ...197 C2
Thorpe Lea Rd PE3 .197 F1
Thorpe Mdws PE3 ..197 D7
Thorpe Pk Rd PE3 .197 C3
Thorpe Prim Sch PE3 .197 B3
Thorpe Rd PE3 ....197 B1
Thorpe The PE28 ..143 B1
Thorpe Way CB5 ....84 F4
Thorpe Wood PE3 ..196 F1
Thorpe Wood Nature
  Reserve* PE3 ....196 F1
Thoresby Cl PE3 ..197 B3
Thrapston Rd
  Brampton PE28 ..140 B4
  Catworth PE28 ...147 C2
  Kimbolton PE28 ..113 F5
  Spaldwick PE28 ..137 F6
Three Cups Wlk CB7 .240 D4
Three Hills CB1 .....21 A7
Three Shires Way
  PE28 ....135 E4
Thrifts Wlk CB4 .....84 A4
Thriplow CE Prim Sch
  SG8 ....31 B2
Thriplow Rd SG8 ....30 F1
Throckmorton PE14 .164 E5
Throckmorton Rd
  PE28 ....117 D8
Throstlenest PE7 ..187 C3
Thruffle Way CB3 ..102 C3
Thulborn Cl CB1 ....85 B1
Thurland's Dro PE14 .229 C8
Thurlaston Cl PE14 .197 B2
Thurley Cl PE19 ....95 E5
Thurlow Cl PE13 ..245 C2
Thurlow Rd CB9 ....39 C6
Thurnall Ave SG8 ....5 D5
Thurning Rd PE28 .157 F7
Thuro Gr PE2 .....186 A3
Thursfield PE4 ....204 C4
Thurston Gate PE2 .141 F8
Tiberius Cl CB1 ....24 D7
Tilbrook Mill* MK44 .113 A7
Tilbrooks Hill CB8 ..73 C1
Tillyard Way CB1 ...65 D4
Tilton Ct PE1 ......198 C8
Tindall Cl PE13 ...245 C8
Tinker's Dro PE13 .245 D8
Tinker's La CB3 ....61 C2
Tinkers La PE28 ...168 B4
Tintagel Ct
  Peterborough PE3 .197 B1
  2 St Neots PE19 ..74 F2
Tintern Rise 3 PE6 .232 A1
Tinwell Rd PE9 ....244 A4
Tipplers' Rd CB4 ..122 E2
Tiptree Cl CB5 .....84 F4
Tirrington PE3 ....197 A3
Tithe Ave IP28 ....213 F8

Tithe Cl PE28 .....120 B2
Tithe Rd PE16 ....241 C2
Tithe Way CB3 .....79 C3
Tiverton Rd PE3 ..197 C3
Tiverton Way CB1 ...65 C7
Toates Cl CB6 ....210 C6
Toft La CB1 ....67 F7
Toftland PE2 .....186 D5
Tointons Rd PE14 .229 F8
Tolethorpe Sq 5 PE9 .244 B6
Toll Bar La PE6 ...146 B5
Toll Dro PE15 ....224 A3
Toll House Rd PE2 .186 C7
Toll Rd PE7 ......188 A5
Tollfield PE28 ....113 F4
Tollgate PE3 .....197 A5
Tom Jennings Cl CB8 .110 F5
Tomlinson Ct PE29 .141 F8
Toneham La PE6 ...232 F1
Top La PE19 ....57 B5
Top St CB6 ....210 F5
Topcliffe Way CB1 ..65 C3
Topham Cres 9 PE6 .233 A3
Topham Ct PE14 ...74 F7
Topham Way CB4 ...83 D6
Topmoor Way PE4 .204 F1
Torkington Gdns 3
  PE9 ....244 B5
Torpel Way 2 PE6 .231 C7
Tort Hill PE28 ...168 C5
Toseland Rd PE19 ..97 E4
Tothill Rd CB5 ...108 D4
Touthill Cl PE1 ...198 A2
Tower Cl
  Bassingbourn SG8 .12 F5
  Cottenham CB4 ..125 D3
  Huntingdon PE29 .141 D8
  11 Over CB4 .....208 D1
  Ramsey PE26 ....171 B4
  Whittlesey PE7 ..189 B8
Tower Ct Ely CB6 ..240 B3
  Haverhill CB9 ....23 E7
  Peterborough PE2 .186 F8
Tower Rd
  Downham CB6 ....217 F7
  Elm PE14 ....245 A3
  Ely CB7 ....240 B3
  Sawston CB2 ......33 A8
  Sutton CB6 ......216 E2
Tower Sq PE29 ...152 D1
Tower St PE2 .....186 F8
Tower View CB1 ...35 D3
Towgood Way PE19 .96 D4
Towler St PE1 ....198 A3
Town Bridge PE13 .245 B5
Town Cl CB2 ......32 E7
Town End Cl CB9 ...38 F1
Town Farm Cl SG8 .14 B3
Town Gn Rd SG8 ...28 D8
Town La CB2 ....33 B5
Town Orch PE19 ...95 E5
Town St Newton CB2 .31 B7
  Outwell PE14 ....236 E1
Town The PE19 ....93 E6
Towne Rd SG8 ......5 D5
Townley Prim Sch
  PE14 ....229 D3
Townsend CB7 ....212 A5
Townsend Cl CB4 ..105 D3
Townsend Rd
  Needingworth PE27 .208 A3
  Upwell PE14 .....229 E7
  Wittering PE8 ...230 A1
Townsend Way PE27 .175 D8
Townshend Rd PE13 .245 D6
Toyse Cl CB5 .....130 C4
Toyse La CB5 .....130 B4
Trafalgar Rd
  Cambridge CB4 ..246 B4
  Eaton Socon PE19 .74 C5
Trafalgar Terr PE9 .244 B6
Trafalgar Way CB3 .102 B5
Trafford Est PE14 .238 F4
Trafford Pk 1 PE13 .245 E6
Trafford Rd PE13 .245 D5
Tram Sta La PE14 .236 B6
Tramar Dr 2 PE6 .216 E2
Trap Rd SG8 ......11 A2
Treading Bank PE13 .237 C4
Treading Field PE13 .237 C4
Tredegar Cl CB4 ...83 E6
Tredgold La CB1 ..246 C3
Treeway PE16 ....241 B5
Trefoil Ct 2 CB9 ..23 F7
Trent Cl PE27 ....144 A7
Trent Rd PE8 ....195 D8
Tresham Rd PE2 .185 D3
Trevone Pl CB4 ....65 D7
Tribune Cl PE16 ..241 D3
Tribune Cl CB4 ....83 E7
Trienna PE2 .....186 B5
Trigg Way SG8 ....14 D6
Trinity Ave PE28 .239 C5
Trinity Cl Balsham CB1 .53 B7
  Bottisham CB5 ...86 F6
  Ely CB6 ....240 C5
  Fordham CB7 ....212 F1
  Great Paxton PE19 .96 E4
  Haslingfield CB3 ..47 B5
Trinity Coll CB2 ..246 A3
Trinity La CB2 ...246 A2
Trinity Link CB9 ...39 A1
Trinity Pl PE29 ..141 E4
Trinity Rd
  Stamford PE9 ...244 A6

Trinity Rd continued
  Wisbech PE13 ...245 E6
Trinity St
  Cambridge CB2 ..246 A2
  3 Peterborough PE1 .198 A2
Triplow Mdws Nature
  Reserve* SG8 ....31 B2
Troughton Way 12 PE13 .238 B2
Troutbeck Cl PE4 .204 F3
Truman Ave PE15 .243 A5
Trumpington Gall*
  CB4 ....83 E4
Trumpington High St
  CB2 ....64 D3
Trumpington Rd CB2 .64 E5
Trumpington St CB2 .246 A2
Trundle Mere PE7 .182 B2
Trundle Rd PE28 .215 C1
Trundley Cl CB9 ...38 D1
Tucker's Yd PE2 ..187 C7
Tuckers Nook 1 PE6 .243 A7
Tuddenham Rd IP28 .239 F2
Tuddenham VC Sch
  IP28 ....214 E2
Tudor Ave PE7 ...186 C1
Tudor Cl PE4 ....204 E2
Tudor Ct
  Bassingbourn cum Kneesworth
  SG8 ....13 B4
  Kimbolton PE28 ..113 F5
Tudor Rd PE29 ...141 F2
Tulyar Wlk CB8 ..110 E8
Tunbridge Cl
  Bottisham CB5 ...86 E6
  Burwell CB5 .....130 B2
Tunbridge La CB5 ..86 E6
Tunkers La PE28 ..171 F4
Tunwells Cl CB2 ...49 A5
Tunwells La CB2 ...49 A5
Turberville Ct PE28 .143 C1
Turf Dro PE7 ....191 C5
Turf Fen La PE15 .222 F5
Turf Fen Rd PE26 .170 F3
Turf Lot Dro PE14 .229 E1
Turf Maze* PE28 .120 C1
Turnbull Rd PE15 .243 B3
Turner Cl CB9 ....38 D1
Turner Rd
  Eaton Socon PE19 .74 C5
  St Ives PE27 ....144 A7
Turners La PE7 ..189 D6
Turningtree Rd PE7 .190 A3
Turnpike Cl 2 PE13 .245 E6
Turnpike Hill CB9 ..38 C4
Turnpike La PE18 .133 E8
Turnpike Rd IP28 .133 E8
Turnpike The CB7 .240 B3
Turnstone Cl PE29 .244 D7
Turnstone Ct 4 PE28 .239 D4
Turnstone Way PE2 .187 D7
Turpin's Ride
  4 Royston SG8 ....5 D5
  Stilton PE7 .....176 A7
Turpyn Ct CB4 ....83 E6
Turvers La PE26 ..172 B7
Turves Rd PE6 ...232 A2
Tuyar Wlk CB8 ...110 E8
Tweed Cl CB8 ....112 F6
Tweedale CB1 .....64 F5
Twelvetree Ave PE4 .204 A5
Twenty Foot Rd PE15 .227 F8
Twenty Pence Rd
  Cottenham CB4 ..125 F6
  Wilburton CB6 ...210 B3
Two Pole Dro
  Farcet PE7 ......187 F1
  Soham CB7 ......211 E2
Two Tree Hundred Dro
  PE15 ....228 A6
Twyford Gdns PE1 .198 D7
Tydd St Giles Golf & Leisure
  Ctr PE13 ....238 A7
Tyesdale PE3 ....197 A4
Tylers Mews PE4 .204 B3
Tyrrell Pk PE1 ...198 D2
Tythe Piece PE28 .121 C5

U

UCLES CB1 ....246 C1
Uffen Way CB10 ...32 E8
Uffington Rd
  11 Barnack PE9 ..230 D4
  Stamford PE9 ...244 D5
Uffington Sch PE9 .230 C6
Ufford Pl 7 CB9 ...24 B8
Uldale Way PE4 ..204 F2
Ullswater PE29 ..141 C5
Ullswater Ave PE4 .204 D2
Underwood Cl PE7 .190 D7
Union La CB4 .....83 A5
Union Pl CB2 ....246 B1
Union Rd CB2 ...246 B1
Union St 12 PE13 .245 C5
Univ Arts Scits Caf*
  CB2 ....246 A2
Univ Museum of Zoology*
  CB2 ....246 B2
Univ of Cambridge
  Cambridge CB1 ...84 A2
  Madingley CB3 ...81 E6
University Concert Hall
  CB3 ....83 C1
University Music Sch
  CB3 ....83 C1
Unwin's La 15 CB4 .208 D1
Uphall Rd CB1 ....84 D1

Upherd's La CB6 ..240 C5
Uplands PE4 .....204 C5
Upper Delph Dro CB6 .209 A5
Upper Gatley End SG8 ..3 D6
Upper Gwydir St 1 CB1 .84 A1
Upper King St SG8 ..5 D6
Upton Cl
  Stanground PE2 ..187 E5
  Longthorpe PE3 ..197 A2
Upton Hill PE28 ..160 C1
Upton La CB4 ....242 D4
Upton Pl CB6 ....242 C4
Upware Rd
  Swaffham Prior CB7 .128 D8
  Wicken CB7 .....211 C1
Upwell Pk PE15 ..243 F3
Upwell Prim Sch
  PE14 ....229 D8
Upwell Rd
  Christchurch PE14 .229 C4
  March PE15 .....243 E3
Upwood Airfield
  Polebrook PE8 ...174 A2
  Ramsey PE26 ....171 D4
Upwood Mdws National
  Nature Reserve*
  PE26 ....171 A2
Upwood Prim Sch
  PE26 ....171 D3
Upwood Rd PE26 .171 B5

V

Valarian Cl 14 PE19 .74 C6
Vale Dr PE2 .....186 C1
Valence Rd PE2 ..185 F4
Valerian Ct CB1 ...66 A5
Valiant Rd PE27 ..143 F7
Valiant Sq PE26 ..171 F3
Valley Rise SG8 ....5 E6
Valley Rd Cambridge CB3 .62 D6
Valley Way CB8 ..110 E4
Valparaiso Univ CB3 .83 C3
Van Diemans Way
  PE28 ....116 A7
Van Dyke Pl PE27 .144 A7
Van Gogh Pl PE27 .144 A7
Vange Pl CB9 .....24 B8
Vanners Rd PE29 ..24 A7
Varrier Jones Dr PE7 .99 A3
Varrier Jones Pl CB3 .99 A3
Veasey Rd PE29 ..142 A7
Velos Wlk CB8 ....84 E4
Vence Cl PE9 ....244 A5
Ventress Cl CB1 ...65 D5
Ventress Farm Ct CB1 .65 C5
Verdun Rd PE13 ..245 B5
Vere Rd PE1 .....197 F7
Vergette Rd PE6 ..203 F8
Vergette St PE1 ..198 B4
Vermont Gr PE3 ..197 E1
Vermuyden PE28 .208 C6
Vermuyden Gdns 5
  CB6 ....216 E2
Vermuyden Way CB4 .121 F5
Vernalam Way CB4 ..83 C6
Vester's Hill Dro PE26 .171 B7
Vetch Wlk CB9 ....38 D1
Vetchfield PE2 ...185 E5
Vicarage Ave CB7 ..32 F7
Vicarage Cl
  Chatteris PE16 ..241 D3
  Dullingham CB8 ..89 C1
  Holme PE7 ......177 A4
  Melbourn SG8 ....14 C6
  Oakington/Longstanton
  CB4 ....103 D6
  Swaffham Bulbeck CB5 .108 A1
  Waterbeach CB5 ..106 A7
Vicarage Dr CB3 ...64 A3
Vicarage Farm Rd 5
  PE1 ....198 B3
Vicarage Farm Yd PE19 .57 B6
Vicarage La
  Swaffham Prior CB5 .108 D4
  Whittlesford CB2 ..32 B5
  Woodditton CB8 ...90 D3

Vicarage Rd
  Newmarket CB8 ..111 B3
  Waresley SG19 ....58 A2
Vicarage Terr CB1 ..84 A1
Vicarage Way PE7 .181 D5
Vicarage Wlk PE19 .93 F6
Viceroy Ct PE3 ....74 A3
Victor Cl PE27 ...144 A7
Victoria Ave CB3 .246 B3
Victoria Cres
  Royston SG8 ......5 D7
  St Ives PE28 ....143 A5
Victoria Gdns 3 CB6 .242 D4
Victoria Gn 3 CB6 .217 D1
Victoria Pk CB4 ...83 D4
Victoria Pl
  Peterborough PE1 .197 F4
  5 Wisbech PE13 .245 C4
Victoria Rd
  Cambridge CB4 ...83 D4
  Haverhill CB9 ....23 D7
  Stamford PE9 ...244 B6
  Wisbech PE13 ...245 C4
Victoria Sq PE29 .141 E4
Victoria St
  Cambridge CB1 ..246 B2
  Chatteris PE16 ..241 C4
  Ely CB7 ....240 D3
  Littleport CB6 ...242 E4

Victoria St *continued*
Old Fetton PE2 .... 186 F6
Peterborough PE1 .... 198 A5
Victoria View CB4 ...... 125 F7
Victoria Way CB8 .... 110 E7
Victory Ave PE7 .... 189 F7
Victory Rd PE13 .... 245 B3
Victory Way CB4 .... 125 D4
Victory Wlk 7 SG8 .... 5 E5
Viersen Platz PE1 ...... 198 A1
Viking Cl CB1 .... 53 E5
Viking Way
Bar Hill CB3 .... 102 B4
Whittlesey PE7 .... 189 E8
Villa Ct CB4 .... 83 E8
Villa Pl CB4 .... 104 C2
Villa Rd CB4 .... 104 C2
Village The PE2 .... 186 B5
Vincent Cl CB8 .... 110 E7
Vinces Ct CB6 .... 240 C4
Vine Cl
Great Shelford CB2 .... 49 C4
Hemingford Grey PE27 .... 143 E2
Vine St PE9 .... 244 C5
Vine Wlk PE3 .... 197 B4
Vinegar Hill PE28 ...... 150 E7
Vinery Ct PE26 .... 172 B7
Vinery Pk CB1 .... 84 C1
Vinery Rd CB1 .... 65 C8
Vinery Way CB1 .... 84 C1
Viney Cl PE1 .... 198 D5
Vineyard Rd PE1 .... 198 B2
Vineyard The PE28 ..... 208 D7
Vineyard Way
Buckden PE19 .... 117 B3
Ely CB7 .... 240 E5
Vineyard Wlk CB5 .... 86 F6
Vineyards The CB7 ..... 240 D4
Vintner Cl CB3 .... 99 A3
Vintners Cl PE3 .... 197 D3
Violet Cl CB1 .... 66 A5
Violet Way PE7 .... 181 F7
Virginia Cl PE3 .... 197 A2
Virginia Rd IP28 .... 213 E8
Virginia Way PE27 ...... 143 E6
Viscount Ct PE19 .... 74 B3
Viscount Rd PE2 .... 187 A6
Vixen Cl PE7 .... 181 F6
Vokes St PE2 .... 186 D8
Vulcan Way PE19 .... 74 B1

W

Wadbury's Folly PE27 ... 208 B4
Waddelow Rd CB5 ..... 106 A8
Wade Pk Ave 4 PE6 ..... 231 E8
Wadloes Rd CB5 .... 84 D4
Waggoners Way 15
PE15 .... 223 B7
Wagstaff Cl CB4 .... 83 F7
Wainman Rd PE2 ...... 186 D5
Wainwright PE4 .... 204 A5
Waits The PE27 .... 144 A3
Wake Ave IP28 .... 239 C5
Wake Rd March PE15 .... 243 C6
Peterborough PE1 .... 198 B2
Wakefield Cl CB10 .... 18 D3
Wakelin Ave CB2 .... 49 F1
Wakelyn Rd PE7 .... 189 C7
Wakerley Dr PE2 .... 186 C7
Walcot Rd PE9 .... 230 E2
Walcot Wlk PE3 .... 197 B3
Walden Cl 17 PE15 ...... 223 A5
Walden Gr PE29 .... 141 D4
Walden Rd
Great Chesterford CB10 .... 18 E3
Hadstock CB1 .... 20 B6
Huntingdon PE29 .... 141 D4
Walden Way CB2 .... 48 F6
Wales Bank PE14 .... 236 A5
Walgrave PE2 .... 186 B4
Walker Ct CB4 .... 83 E6
Walker Rd PE6 .... 203 F7
Walkers Way PE3 .... 196 F3
Walkling Way CB4 ...... 105 D1
Walks E The 7 PE29 .... 141 D4
Walks N The PE29 ...... 141 D4
Wallace Ct PE29 .... 142 A8
Wallace's Dro PE6 ..... 233 D4
Waller's Cl SG8 .... 7 F2
Wallman's La CB4 ...... 122 E6
Walnut Cl
Newborough PE6 .... 205 C8
Royston SG8 .... 5 D6
Walnut Gr IP28 .... 213 E4
Walnut Tree Ave CB5 .... 84 A3
Walnut Tree Cl
Bassingbourn SG8 .... 12 E5
Little Downham CB6 ...... 218 A6
8 Stretham CB6 .... 210 F5
Walnut Tree Cres
PE28 .... 121 B5
Walnut Tree Dr PE29 ... 141 C6
Walnut Tree Gr PE28 ... 140 D3
Walnut Tree Way CB4 .... 83 C7
Walnut Way PE7 .... 175 F7
Walpole Bank PE14 ..... 238 F7
Walpole Ct CB7 .... 240 C4
Walpole Rd CB1 .... 65 D6
Walsingham Ct PE13 .... 245 A7
Walsingham Way
Ely CB6 .... 240 B5
10 Eye PE6 .... 232 A1
Walsoken Rd PE14 ...... 236 E7
Waltham Cl PE1 .... 198 D8
Walton Cl CB7 .... 212 E1
Walton Com Sch PE4 ... 204 C1
Walton Hill PE28 .... 161 D5
Walton J & I Sch PE4 ... 204 C1
Walton Pk PE4 .... 204 C1
Walton Rd
9 Leverington PE13 ..... 238 B2
Marholm PE6 .... 203 E1
Wisbech PE13 .... 245 E7
Waltons CB10 .... 21 C3
Wamil Rd IP28 .... 213 F5
Wamil Way IP28 .... 239 B4
Wandlebury Ctry Pk*
CB2 .... 50 B8
Wansford Pasture Nature
Reserve* PE8 .... 193 F3
Wansford Rd
Elton PE8 .... 183 D5
Wansford PE8 .... 194 A3
Yarwell PE8 .... 193 F2
Wantage Gdns PE19 ..... 96 A2
Warbon Ave PE1 .... 197 F7
Warboys Airfield Ind Est
PE28 .... 164 D2
Warboys Cl CB3 .... 61 D5
Warboys CP Sch PE28 .. 164 E5
Warboys Rd PE28 ...... 155 E8
Ward Cl
Peterborough PE1 .... 198 B3
Ramsey PE26 .... 172 A5
St Ives PE28 .... 143 A5
Ward Rd CB1 .... 65 D6
Ward Way CB6 .... 217 D1
Warden Hill SG19 .... 40 C3
Ware La PE28 .... 142 F5
Ware Rd PE19 .... 74 E6
Wareley Rd PE2 .... 197 F1
Waresley & Gransden Woods
Nature Reserve*
SG19 .... 58 C2
Waresley Rd
Gamlingay SG19 .... 41 D6
Great Gransden SG19 ...... 58 B3
Warkworth St CB1 ...... 246 C2
Warkworth Terr CB1 .... 246 C2
Warmington Sch PE8 ... 178 B3
Warner's Dro
Pidley cum Fenton PE28 .. 215 B3
Somersham PE28 .... 215 C2
Warners Gr PE27 .... 144 A4
Warren Cl St Ives PE28 .. 142 F6
Wilburton CB6 .... 210 C5
Warren Croft PE28 ..... 168 B5
Warren Ct 6 CB9 .... 23 E7
Warren La
Bythorn & Keyston PE28 .. 146 D4
Titchmarsh PE28 .... 156 F1
Warren Pl CB8 .... 111 F5
Warren Rd
Cambridge CB4 .... 84 A6
Herringswell CB8 .... 134 A7
Red Lodge IP28 .... 214 A1
St Ives PE27 .... 144 B4
Wothorpe PE9 .... 244 B1
Warren The
3 Royston SG8 .... 5 D5
Witchford CB6 .... 217 E1
Warren Twrs CB8 .... 111 E4
Warrenne Keep PE9 .... 244 B4
Warrington St CB8 ..... 111 A2
Warwick Ct
Eaton Socon PE19 .... 74 C3
2 Haverhill CB9 .... 23 E8
Warwick Dr CB6 .... 240 A3
Warwick Rd
Cambridge CB4 .... 83 C5
Peterborough PE4 .... 204 C1
Wasdale Gdns PE4 ..... 205 A2
Wash La PE7 .... 189 E8
Wash Rd PE14 .... 225 B8
Washbank Rd PE19 .... 74 E4
Washingley La PE7 ..... 175 B7
Washingley Rd
Folksworth PE7 .... 175 D8
The Stukeleys PE29 ...... 141 C8
Washington Cl CB6 .... 242 D5
Washington St IP28 .... 213 E8
Washpit La CB3 .... 46 D7
Washpit Rd CB3 .... 82 C8
Wastwater PE29 .... 141 B6
Water End
Alwalton PE7 .... 185 A5
Marholm PE6 .... 203 D1
Peterborough PE3 .... 197 D2
Wrestlingworth SG19 ...... 25 B3
Water La Bourn CB3 ...... 60 D6
Cambridge CB4 .... 84 B5
Castor PE5 .... 195 F1
Cottenham CB4 .... 126 A7
Great Bradley CB8 .... 55 F8
Histon CB4 .... 104 C3
Melbourn SG8 .... 14 C5
Oakington/Longstanton
CB4 .... 103 C5
Sturmer CB9 .... 24 F5
Water St Cambridge CB4 .. 84 B4
Stamford PE9 .... 244 C4
Waterbeach CP Sch
CB5 .... 106 B8
Waterbeach Rd CB4 .... 105 E7
Waterbeach Sta CB5 .... 106 C6
Watercourse The CB8 .. 111 A4
Waterfall Gdns PE6 .... 207 C1
Waterfields PE16 .... 241 B3
Waterfurlong PE9 ...... 244 A4
Watergall PE3 .... 197 B8
Watergall Prim Sch
PE3 .... 197 A8
Watergate 6 PE9 .... 244 C5
Waterlees Rd 2 PE13 ... 245 E7
Waterloo Cl
Brampton PE28 .... 140 D3
Newmarket CB8 .... 110 D8
Waterloo Dr 2 PE19 ...... 74 F3
Waterloo Rd PE1 .... 198 A5
Watermead CB3 .... 102 C3
Watermead Cres CB3 .... 79 A3
Waterside Ely CB7 ...... 240 E4
Isleham CB7 .... 213 A5
Waterside Gdns
March PE15 .... 243 E5
Whittlesey PE7 .... 189 D8
Waterslade Rd PE7 ..... 181 C4
Watersmead PE19 ...... 117 E3
Waterton Cl 6 PE6 ..... 231 F8
Waterwick Hill CB11 .... 1 F1
Waterworks La PE6 .... 203 D6
Waterworks Rd IP28 ... 213 E8
Watsons La 1 CB6 ...... 211 B7
Watt Cl PE4 .... 204 E2
Wattle Cl CB3 .... 79 A4
Wavell Way CB4 .... 83 E6
Waveney Dr PE15 ...... 243 B5
Waveney Gr PE4 .... 204 E2
Waveney Rd PE27 ...... 144 A7
Waveney Terr CB9 .... 24 B7
Waverley Cl PE13 ...... 235 A3
Waverley Gdns 3 PE9 .. 244 A6
Way Head Dro CB6 ..... 217 C6
Way La
Waterbeach CB5 .... 106 B8
Wicken CB7 .... 211 D2
Way The Fowlmere SG8 .... 15 E8
Fowlmere SG8 .... 30 E1
Wayford Cl PE3 .... 197 A2
Weasenham La 1 PE13 . 245 D2
Weatheralls Cl 4 CB7 ... 212 B4
Weatheralls Prim Sch The
CB7 .... 212 B4
Weatherthorn PE2 ..... 186 C5
Weavers Field CB3 .... 82 E7
Webbs Mdw SG19 .... 58 D4
Webb's Rd CB1 .... 36 F5
Webster's Way CB4 ..... 208 D1
Websters Cl PE6 .... 203 F8
Weddell Rd CB9 .... 24 C6
Wedgewood Dr CB1 .... 65 F6
Wedgwood Dr PE13 .... 245 D5
Weedon Cl PE4 .... 204 F2
Weir Cl Buckden PE19 .... 117 A3
Hemingford Grey PE28 .... 143 D1
Weir Rd PE28 .... 143 D1
Weirs Dro CB5 .... 129 F1
Welbeck Rd PE13 .... 245 E4
Welbeck Way PE2 .... 186 D7
Welbourne PE4 .... 204 C4
Welbourne Prim Sch
PE4 .... 204 C4
Welby Cl PE28 .... 115 D3
Welches Dam Visitor Ctr*
CB6 .... 217 A8
Well Bottom CB8 .... 112 B8
Well Creek Rd PE14 .... 236 F2
Well End PE14 .... 236 A3
Welland Bank PE6 ...... 207 D7
Welland Cl
Peterborough PE1 .... 198 A7
St Ives PE27 .... 144 A7
Welland Ct 9 PE19 .... 74 C4
Welland Mews PE9 ..... 244 C4
Welland Pl CB6 .... 240 D6
Welland Prim Sch
PE1 .... 198 C8
Welland Rd
Peterborough PE1 .... 198 B8
Wittering PE8 .... 230 B1
Welland Way 5 PE6 ..... 231 F8
Wellbrook Way CB3 ...... 82 F7
Wellcome Trust Genome
Campus CB10 .... 18 B6
Wellingly Ct CB3 .... 79 A3
Wellington Ave PE27 ... 143 F7
Wellington Cl
Old Hurst PE28 .... 154 E7
Thistley Green IP28 ..... 213 D6
Warboys PE28 .... 164 F4
Waterbeach CB5 .... 106 B7
Wellington Ct 3 CB1 ..... 84 A2
Wellington Pl SG8 .... 13 B5
Wellington Rd Ely CB6 .. 217 F1
Mildenhall IP28 .... 213 E8
Wellington St
4 Cambridge CB1 .... 84 A2
Littleport CB6 .... 242 D4
4 Newmarket CB8 .... 111 A3
Peterborough PE1 .... 198 B2
St Ives PE27 .... 144 A3
Wellington Terr
15 Haverhill CB9 .... 23 E7
20 Wisbech PE13 .... 245 C5
Wells Bridge PE26 ...... 221 C3
Wells Cl Haslingfield CB3 .. 47 A5
Peterborough PE4 .... 204 B3
Wells Ct
Mildenhall IP28 .... 239 B5
Peterborough PE2 .... 187 D6
Wells Way PE7 .... 177 A5
Wellsfield PE29 .... 141 E6
Wellum Cl 18 CB9 .... 23 E7
Welmore Rd PE6 .... 203 F8
Welstead Rd CB1 .... 66 A6
Wenny Ct PE16 .... 241 C4
Wenny Est PE16 .... 241 D3
Wenny Rd PE16 .... 241 E3
Wenny Severals PE16 .. 216 B7
Wensum Cl PE27 .... 144 B6
Wentworth Dr IP28 .... 239 B4
Wentworth Rd CB4 .... 83 C4
Wentworth St 1 PE1 ... 198 A1
Wentworth Terr 6 CB9 ... 23 E8
Wenvoe Cl CB1 .... 65 F6
Werrington Bridge Rd
PE6 .... 204 E7
Werrington Gr PE4 ..... 204 B2
Werrington Gr Cvn Pk
PE4 .... 204 B2
Werrington Mews 5
PE4 .... 204 C3
Werrington Parkway
PE6 .... 203 E5
Werrington Pk Ave 2
PE4 .... 204 C3
Werrington Prim Sch
PE4 .... 204 C3
Werrington Sports Ctr
PE4 .... 204 B4
Wertheim Way PE29 .... 141 B6
Wesley Dr PE16 .... 241 D5
Wesley House CB5 ...... 246 B3
Wesleyan Rd PE1 ...... 198 A7
Wessex Cl PE2 .... 187 D7
West Ave PE26 .... 171 F6
West Brook PE28 .... 120 B2
West Brook Cl PE28 .... 120 B2
West Cl
Alconbury Weston PE28 ... 150 D6
March PE15 .... 243 B6
Waresley SG19 .... 57 F2
West Delph PE7 .... 189 D8
West Dr
Friday Bridge PE14 ...... 236 A4
Highfields CB3 .... 80 C2
March PE15 .... 243 F4
Mildenhall IP28 .... 239 B4
Soham CB7 .... 212 B4
West Dr Cres CB7 ...... 212 A4
West Dr Gdns CB7 ..... 212 A4
West Dro S PE12 .... 233 E8
West End Ashwell SG7 ..... 2 C3
Brampton PE28 .... 140 C3
Ely CB6 .... 240 C4
Gorefield PE13 .... 237 E3
Haddenham CB6 .... 209 F6
March PE15 .... 243 B4
Somersham PE28 .... 208 B8
Whittlesey PE7 .... 189 C7
Whittlesford CB2 .... 32 B4
Wilburton CB6 .... 210 B5
Woodditton CB8 .... 71 D8
Yaxley PE7 .... 181 D4
West End Cl PE16 ...... 241 B4
West End La CB9 .... 38 E8
West End Rd
Fenstanton PE28 .... 121 A5
Maxey PE6 .... 231 C7
West End Villas PE9 .... 244 A5
West Fen Dro
Downham CB6 .... 218 A6
March PE7 .... 227 A1
Whittlesey PE7 .... 191 F3
West Fen Rd
Coveney CB6 .... 217 E4
Ely CB6 .... 240 B5
Willingham CB4 .... 208 F2
Witchford CB6 .... 218 A3
West Field CB1 .... 34 B7
West Field Rd PE15 ..... 224 A3
West Gn CB2 .... 29 D7
West Hill Rd CB2 .... 30 B4
West Leys PE27 .... 143 F4
West Lodge La CB6 .... 216 D1
West Meadowgate
PE14 .... 245 E2
West Moor Ave CB2 ...... 32 E8
West Newlands 3 PE28 . 208 B8
West Par
Peterborough PE3 .... 197 D3
Wisbech PE13 .... 245 B7
West Perry PE28 .... 115 D2
West Pk St PE16 .... 241 C4
West Rd Cambridge CB3 ... 83 C1
Gamlingay SG19 .... 41 C4
Histon CB4 .... 104 B3
3 Tallington PE9 .... 230 F7
Tydd St Giles PE13 ...... 238 B8
West Row Prim Sch
IP28 .... 213 D7
West Row Rd
Beck Row, Holywell
Row & Kenny Hill IP28 ... 213 F6
Mildenhall IP28 .... 239 A5
West St Chatteris PE16 .. 241 B3
Godmanchester PE29 .... 141 E1
Great Gransden SG19 ...... 58 D4
Helpston PE6 .... 231 B4
Huntingdon PE29 .... 141 E5
Isleham CB7 .... 212 F5
Over CB4 .... 123 A8
St Ives PE27 .... 144 A4
St Neots PE19 .... 74 E5
Stamford PE9 .... 244 B4
Toft CB3 .... 62 B5
Wisbech PE13 .... 245 C4
West St Gdns PE9 ...... 244 A5
West Stonebridge
PE2 .... 186 C5
West Town Prim Sch
PE3 .... 197 E3
West View
Cambridge CB3 .... 64 C7
Little Stukeley PE28 ..... 151 F1
West Way Meldreth SG8 ... 28 F1
Sawston CB2 .... 50 A1
West Wickham Rd
Balsham CB1 .... 53 C1
Horseheath CB1 .... 37 A3
West Wlk CB5 .... 86 F6
West Wr Cres PE7 ...... 186 C1
West Wratting Rd CB1 ... 53 B2
Westberry Ct CB3 .... 64 B8
Westbourne Cl PE16 .... 241 B3
Westbourne Ct CB9 ...... 24 A8
Westbourne Dr PE6 .... 203 E8
Westbourne Rd PE16 ... 241 B4
Westbrook Ave PE2 ..... 186 F7
Westbrook Cl
1 Brampton PE28 .... 140 C3
Steeple Morden SG8 .... 3 B8
Westbrook Pk Cl PE2 ... 186 F7
Westbrook Pk Rd PE2 .. 186 F7
Westbury Rd PE27 ...... 143 F4
Westcombe Sq PE1 .... 198 D4
Westcott House Theological
Coll CB1 .... 246 B3
Westcroft 4 CB3 .... 62 B4
Westering The CB5 .... 84 E2
Westerley Cl PE3 .... 197 C4
Westerman Cl PE28 .... 168 B5
Western Ave
Haverhill CB9 .... 38 E1
Peterborough PE1 .... 198 B7
Westfield CB4 .... 124 A6
Westfield Com Prim Sch
CB9 .... 24 B7
Westfield Jun Sch
PE27 .... 144 A4
Westfield La CB4 .... 83 C4
Westfield Rd
Fowlmere SG8 .... 15 D8
Great Shelford CB2 .... 48 E7
Newton PE13 .... 237 F5
Peterborough PE3 .... 197 E4
Ramsey PE26 .... 171 F7
Sawtry PE28 .... 168 B4
Wisbech PE13 .... 245 E7
Yaxley PE7 .... 181 D5
Westfields CB3 .... 99 A2
Westgate Cambridge CB1 .. 65 E5
Peterborough PE1 .... 197 F2
Westhawe PE3 .... 196 F7
Westhorpe CB5 .... 130 B4
Westlake Ave PE7 ...... 186 C1
Westlands
Comberton CB3 .... 62 B4
Littleport CB6 .... 225 B3
Westley Bottom Rd
CB8 .... 69 B8
Westmead Ave PE13 .... 245 E2
Westmeadow Cl CB4 ... 208 F1
Westminster & Cheshunt
Colleges CB3 .... 83 C3
Westminster Gdns 16
PE6 .... 232 A1
Westminster Pl PE1 .... 198 F5
Westmoor Comm CB6 .. 217 E8
Westmoor Dro
Chatteris PE16 .... 222 D2
Littleport CB6 .... 225 B4
Westmoreland Gdns
PE1 .... 198 B2
Weston Ave SG8 .... 5 C7
Weston Cl PE19 .... 95 A1
Weston Colville Rd
CB8 .... 70 D1
Weston Ct PE19 .... 74 C4
Weston Gr CB1 .... 66 E5
Weston Miller Dr
PE13 .... 245 C7
Weston Rd PE13 .... 245 C3
Weston Way CB8 .... 110 F6
Westry Ave PE15 .... 243 A7
Westry Cl 3 PE14 .... 238 F1
Westway Pl CB6 .... 217 A2
Westwick Hall* CB4 .... 103 E7
Westwood PE3 .... 197 C8
Westwood Ave PE15 .... 243 C5
Westwood Com Jun Sch
PE15 .... 243 C5
Westwood Ind Est
PE3 .... 197 D7
Westwood Pk Cl PE3 ... 197 C3
Westwood Pk Rd PE3 .. 197 D2
Westwood Rd PE27 ..... 144 A4
Wetenhall Rd CB1 .... 65 B8
Wetherby Way 1 PE1 ... 198 D3
Weymouth Way PE1 .... 198 D6
Whaddon Gap SG8 .... 28 A1
Whaddon Rd SG8 .... 28 E2
Whaddons The PE29 .... 141 F6
Whalley St PE1 .... 198 B3
Wharf Rd PE9 .... 244 C4
Wheat Croft CB1 .... 35 D3
Wheatdole PE2 .... 186 A3
Wheatfield Cres 2 SG8 ..... 5 E6
Wheatfield Dr PE26 .... 171 F5
Wheatfield Jun & Inf Sch
PE27 .... 144 A6
Wheatfields PE27 ...... 144 A6
Wheatley Bank PE14 .... 238 F2
Wheatley Cres PE28 ... 208 C6
Wheats Cl 1 CB6 .... 217 D1
Wheatsheaf Cl CB6 ..... 240 A3
Wheatsheaf Dro PE14 .. 229 C3
Wheatsheaf Rd
Alconbury Weston PE28 ... 150 D6
Eaton Socon PE19 .... 74 C3
Woodhurst PE28 .... 155 D4
Wheatsheaf Way CB1 .... 35 D3
Wheatsheaves 2 PE28 .. 168 C2
Wheel Ctr The PE15 .... 243 D4
Wheel Yd PE1 .... 198 A2

Wheeler St CB2 ......246 A2
Wheeler's Cl CB3 ......46 A7
Wheeler's Way CB3 ......46 A7
Wheelers CB7 ......49 B6
Wheelwright Way CB5 ...86 A5
Wellhams Yd PE26 ......172 C7
Wherry Cl PE15 ......243 D4
Whetstone Ct 3 PE1 ...198 D7
Whichcote Rd PE6 ......206 E6
Whines La CB4 ......123 B8
Whinfell Cl PE29 ......141 A7
Whipple Mus of the History
  of Science* CB1 ......246 A2
Whipplefree Rd CB2 ...32 A5
Whistler Rd 5 PE19 ...74 C5
Whistlers The PE27 ....144 A7
Whiston Cl
  Peterborough PE4 ....204 F2
  4 Somersham PE28 ..208 C8
Whitacre PE1 ......198 E6
Whitby St 3 PE13 ....245 C5
White Acres PE7 ......189 E8
White Cross PE3 ......197 B6
White Cross Hill CB6 ..210 D6
White Cross Rd CB6 ...250 C5
White Droveway CB5 ..108 A3
White Fen Droveway
  CB5 ......107 B5
White Field Way CB2 ...32 D8
White Hall Cl 21 PE28 .215 C1
White Hart Ct PE27 ...144 A3
White Hart Dr 6 PE15 .222 A5
White Hart La
  Godmanchester PE29 ..142 A1
  6 Littleport CB6 ....242 D4
  St Ives PE27 ......144 A3
  13 Soham PE7 ......212 B4
White Horse La CB6 ...218 A6
White House Rd CB7 ..226 C2
White Lion Cl 1 PE15 .243 D2
White Rose Wlk 6 CB4 .83 D7
Whitecroft Rd SG8 ....14 A8
Whitecross PE27 ......144 A4
Whitefriars CB4 ......84 B5
Whitegate Cl Girton CB3 .82 E8
  Swavesey CB4 ......122 D6
Whitegates CB8 ......111 C3
Whitehall Gdns CB2 ...31 E1
  Whitehall Sch PE28 ..215 B1
Whitehall Way PE28 ..115 D2
Whitehall Wlk PE19 ...74 F4
Whitehill Cl CB1 ......84 D2
Whitehill Rd CB5 ......84 C2
Whitehouse La CB3 ...83 A5
Whitemill Rd PE28 ....168 A4
Whitemoor Rd PE15 ...241 C3
Whitepost Rd
  Borough Fen PE6 ....207 F1
  Newborough PE6 ....205 F6
Whitewater PE2 ......185 D6
Whiteway Dro CB5 ....107 F8
Whiteway PE2 ......185 D6
Whitfield Cl CB4 ......83 E7
Whitgift Rd CB1 ......85 B1
Whitlocks CB2 ......64 D2
Whitman Rd 7 PE9 ...230 D3
Whitmore St PE7 ......189 D7
Whitmore Way CB5 ...106 B6
Whitsed Rd PE6 ......207 D1
Whitstof St PE1 ......198 B8
Whittets Cl SG19 .....58 D4
Whittington PE1 ......198 E7
Whittlesea Sta PE7 ...189 F5
Whittlesey Mus* PE7 .189 D7
Whittlesey Rd
  Benwick PE15 ......221 E6
  March PE15 ......243 A5
  Peterborough PE2 ....187 B7
  Thorney PE6 ......200 F7
Whittlesford Rd
  Little Shelford CB2 ...48 F2
  Newton CB2 ......31 D7
Whittlesford Sta CB2 ..32 E3
Whitton Cl CB4 ......122 E5
Whitwell PE4 ......205 A2
Whixall St CB3 ......82 A2
Whybrows La PE28 ...208 E6
Whydale Rd 4 SG8 ...5 E5
Whyefield Rd PE26 ...172 A7
Whytford Cl CB4 ......84 A3
Wicken Fen National Nature
  Reserve* CB7 ......211 D1
Wicken Rd CB7 ......212 B1
Wicken Way PE2 ......197 C6
Widgham Gn CB8 ....71 D3
Wiggin Cl PE29 ......239 D2
Wigmore Cl PE4 ......141 E1
Wigmore Dr PE7 ......187 F5
Wigstone's Rd PE15 ..243 E5
Wilberforce Rd
  Cambridge CB3 ......83 B2
  Peterborough PE1 ....197 E7
  Wisbech PE13 ......245 D5
Wilbraham Rd
  Bottisham CB1 ......86 F3
  Fulbourn CB1 ......67 C7
Wilbraham Temple
  CB1 ......68 A8
Wilburton CE Prim Sch
  CB6 ......210 C6
Wilburton Rd CB6 ....210 A6

Wild Acres CB5 ......130 B1
Wild Goose Leys PE28 .152 D5
Wildbar Cl PE19 ......74 F4
Wilderness The PE27 ..144 B3
Wilderspin Cl CB3 ....82 F6
Wilding Wlk CB4 ......84 A5
Wildlake PE1 ......186 C5
Wildmere La IP28 .....214 A8
Wiles Cl Cambridge CB4 .84 A7
  Waterbeach CB5 ....106 A8
Wilff Cl PE20 ......152 E1
Wilford Dr CB7 ......240 E6
Wilford Furlong CB4 ..209 A1
Wilkin St 1 CB1 ......65 A8
Wilkins Rd CB4 ......236 D7
Wilkinson Cl
  Eaton Socon PE19 ....74 B3
  March PE15 ......243 E5
Willan Ct PE2 ......186 F8
Willesden Ave PE4 ....197 D8
William Blake Ct CB9 ..38 E1
William de Yaxley CE Jun
  Sch
  Yaxley PE7 ......181 F6
  Yaxley PE7 ......181 E6
William Dr 8 PE19 ...74 F1
William Law Prim Sch
  PE4 ......204 B5
William Rd PE13 .....245 C5
William Smith Cl CB1 ..65 A7
William Westley CE Prim Sch
  CB2 ......32 D5
William's Way IP28 ...213 D6
Williams Cl
  Brampton PE28 ......140 C3
  Ely CB6 ......240 E7
  Newborough PE6 ....207 C1
Williams Way PE15 ...224 B4
Williamson Ave PE3 ..197 E3
Willie Snaith Rd CB8 ..110 F6
Willingham Gn Rd CB8 .54 D8
Willingham Prim Sch
  CB4 ......209 A1
Willingham Rd CB4 ...208 E1
Willis Rd CB1 ......246 C2
Willmott Rd SG8 ....12 F5
Willock La PE13 ......235 A5
Willonholt PE3 ......197 C7
Willoughby Ct PE1 ...198 E8
Willoughby Rd PE9 ...244 C7
Willow Ave PE1 ......198 B7
Willow Cl
  Beck Row, Holywell
  Row & Kenny Hill IP28 .214 A8
  Brampton PE28 ......140 C2
  Doddington PE15 ....222 A5
  Haverhill CB9 ......38 D1
  Little Paxton PE19 ...95 F1
  St Neots PE19 ......74 F3
  Stilton PE7 ......175 F7
Willow Cres
  Milton CB4 ......105 D2
  Newmarket CB8 .....111 B2
Willow Ct CB6 ......242 E4
Willow Dr PE15 ......243 B3
Willow End PE26 ......150 F4
Willow Farm Cl PE28 ..150 D7
Willow Gn PE27 ......208 A3
Willow Gr Ely CB7 ...240 E4
  Lode CB5 ......107 C2
Willow Hall La PE6 ...199 D6
Willow Holt PE7 ......186 C3
Willow La CB3 ......79 C3
Willow Rd PE7 ......182 A6
Willow Row Farms
  CB6 ......226 A5
Willow Way
  Bottisham CB5 ......86 F6
  Hauxton CB2 ......48 B4
  Ramsey PE26 ......172 B7
  St Ives PE27 ......144 C4
  Wisbech PE13 ......245 D3
Willow Wlk
  Cambridge CB1 ......246 B3
  Ely CB7 ......240 E4
Willowbrook Dr PE2 ..201 F1
Willows The
  Glinton PE6 ......203 F8
  Great Chesterford CB10 ..18 D3
Willowside Way SG8 ..5 C8
Wilson Cl CB4 ......84 A7
Wilson Way
  Brampton PE28 ......117 E8
  Milton CB4 ......105 D2
Wilson's Rd CB4 ......103 A8
Wilsons La SG7 ......2 C4
Wilthorne PE28 ......165 A5
Wilton Cl PE13 ......197 C4
Wilton Dr PE3 ......197 C4
Wilton Gdns CB6 ....216 E3
Wiltshire Rd PE28 ...154 B1
Wimbish Rd CB3 ......99 A2
Wimblington Rd
  Doddington/Wimblington
  PE15 ......223 A5
  March PE15 ......243 C1
  Wimblington PE15 ...223 E6
Wimborne Dr PE1 ....198 E7
Wimpole Ave* SG8 ...27 F5
Wimpole Hall* SG8 ...44 F3
Wimpole Home Farm*
  SG8 ......44 F3

Wimpole Pk* SG8 ....44 E3
Wimpole Rd Barton CB3 .63 A2
  Great Eversden CB3 ..45 E7
Wimpole St PE16 ....241 B4
Winchester Way PE3 .197 E1
Winchfield SG19 .....58 E5
Winchmore Dr CB2 ...64 C3
Winderemere Cl CB1 ..66 A7
Windermere PE29 ....66 A6
Windermere Way PE4 .204 E3
Winders La CB4 ......104 B5
Windgate Way PE4 ...194 A6
Windlesham Cl CB4 ...83 E6
Windmill Cl
  Ellington PE28 ......138 F4
  Ely CB6 ......240 B3
  Sawston CB2 ......32 F8
  Shanton CB7 ......212 C2
Windmill Hill CB8 ....110 C8
Windmill La
  Fulbourn CB1 ......66 E4
  Histon CB4 ......104 B4
  8 Sutton CB6 ......216 E1
Windmill Sch The CB1 ..66 D5
Windmill St
  Peterborough PE1 ...197 F5
  Whittlesey PE7 ......189 D8
Windover Rd PE29 ...141 D7
Windrush Dr PE4 ....204 F1
Windsor Ave PE4 ....197 C8
Windsor Cl
  Chatteris PE16 ......241 E5
  St Ives PE27 ......143 F8
  10 St Neots PE19 ...74 F2
  Stamford PE9 ......244 B7
Windsor Dr
  March PE15 ......243 B5
  Peterborough PE2 ...187 D6
  Ramsey PE26 ......221 C2
  Wisbech PE13 ......245 D8
Windsor Gdns 9 PE28 .208 C8
Windsor Pl PE7 ......190 A7
Windsor Rd
  Cambridge CB4 ......83 C5
  Godmanchester PE29 .142 A1
  Newmarket CB8 ....110 E4
  Royston SG8 ......168 B3
  Sawtry PE28 ......168 B3
  Yaxley PE7 ......181 F6
Windsor Terr CB9 ....23 D8
Windsors The PE15 ..243 A5
Winfold Rd CB1 ......106 A8
Wingate Cl CB2 ......64 D3
Wingate Way CB2 ...64 D3
Wingfield PE2 ......185 F3
Winhills Prim Sch
  PE19 ......75 A4
Winship Rd CB4 ......104 C1
Winslow Rd PE3 ......197 C3
Winston Way PE7 ...187 C2
Wintringham Rd 8 PE19 .74 F5
Winwick Pl PE2 ......186 A3
Winwick Rd PE28 ....158 B8
Winyates PE2 ......185 F3
Winyates Prim Sch
  PE2 ......186 A3
Wisbech Castle*
  PE13 ......245 C4
Wisbech Gram Sch
  PE13 ......245 B6
Wisbech Rd
  Littleport CB6 ......242 A6
  Manea PE15 ......224 C5
  March PE15 ......243 A7
  Outwell PE14 ......236 F3
  Thorney PE6 ......233 A3
  Walsoken PE13 ......245 E8
  Welney PE14 ......229 E2
  Whittlesey PE7 ......191 C8
  Wisbech St Mary PE13 .234 A2
Wisbech St Mary CE Prim
  Sch PE13 ......235 B7
Wisbech Yacht Harbour*
  PE13 ......245 C6
Wissey Way CB6 .....240 C6
Wistaria Rd PE13 ....245 F7
Wisteria Rd PE14 ....181 D4
Wistow Ct 3 PE19 ...74 C6
Wistow Fen Dro PE28 .173 B4
Wistow Fen La PE28 ..164 C8
Wistow Way PE7 ....185 D6
Wistow Wood Nature
  Reserve* PE28 ....172 D1
Witcham Bridge Dro
  CB6 ......217 A5
Witcham Rd CB6 .....216 E3
Witchford Rd CB6 ....240 A3
  Witchford CB6 ......217 F1
Witchford Village Coll
  CB6 ......217 E2
Witham Cl PE9 ......244 C6
Witham Way PE4 ....204 F1
Withers Pl CB7 ......212 E1
Withersfield Rd
  Haverhill CB9 ......38 E1
  Withersfield CB9 ....38 F7
Withering Ave PE18 ..230 A2
Wittering Prim Sch
  PE8 ......230 B1
Wittering Rd PE9 ....230 D3
Woburn Cl
  Cambridge CB4 ......83 E7
  Peterborough PE1 ...197 A1
Woburn Ct PE7 ......176 A7

Woburn Dr PE6 ......233 A2
Woburn Pl CB2 ......31 F1
Wolf La Gorefield PE13 .237 F1
  Wisbech PE13 ......235 C8
Wolfson Coll CB3 ....64 B8
Wollaston Rd
  Cambridge CB1 .....246 C1
  Peterborough PE3 ...197 C6
Wolseley Cl PE7 .....181 E6
Wolsey Gdns PE19 ..117 A5
Wolsey Way CB1 .....65 F7
Wood End
  Bluntisham/Colne PE28 .208 C6
  Pertenhall MK44 ....113 D1
Wood La
  Abbots Ripton PE28 .162 E2
  Broughton PE28 ....163 A2
  Papworth Everard CB3 .99 A4
  Ramsey PE26 ......172 C8
  Stretham CB6 ......210 F5
Wood St Littleport PE16 .241 C4
  Doddington/Wimblington
  PE15 ......223 A6
  Huntingdon PE29 ...141 E4
  Wisbech PE13 ......245 B6
Wood View PE26 .....140 B4
Woodbine St PE2 ....187 A8
Woodbryth Rd PE1 ..198 A6
Woodcock Cl
  Haverhill CB9 ......24 C7
  Histon CB4 ......104 A4
Woodcote Rd 10 SG8 ..5 E8
Woodcote Cl PE1 ...198 A7
Woodcote La PE15 ..245 A4
Woodcroft Castle*
  PE6 ......203 C5
Woodcroft Rd
  Etton PE6 ......203 B7
  Glinton PE6 ......203 C3
  Marholm PE6 ......203 D1
Wooditton Rd
  Kirtling CB8 ......72 B5
  Newmarket CB8 ....111 A1
  Woodditton CB8 ....90 B8
Woodfen Rd CB8 ....242 A2
Woodfield Ave PE26 .172 A4
Woodfield Dr PE28 ..168 A3
Woodfield La CB3 ...79 A3
Woodfield Rd PE7 ...193 D3
Woodfoode Cl SG7 ..2 E4
Woodgate PE6 ......231 C4
Woodgate La PE6 ...231 D7
Woodgate Rd 3 PE23 .238 B2
Woodhall La PE7 ....189 F1
Woodhall Rise PE4 ..204 B6
Woodhead Cl PE7 ...244 D7
Woodhead Dr CB3 ..83 F6
Woodhead Pl CB3 ...99 B3
Woodhurst Rd PE2 ..187 D6
Woodland Lea PE6 ..231 B4
Woodland Rd CB3 ...32 F8
Woodland Wlk 2 CB3 .79 C3
Woodlands 1 Royston SG8 .9
  St Neots PE19 9
  Warboys PE28 9
Woodlands Ave CB5 .243 D2
Woodlands Cl
  Girton CB3 ......103 D1
  Great Shelford CB2 ..49 A4
Woodlands Ct PE13 ..245 F7
Woodlands Dr SG8 ...14 B8
Woodlands Pk CB3 ..103 D1
Woodlands Rd CB3 ..103 D1
Woodlands The
  Linton CB1 ......35 B4
  Peterborough PE1 ...198 D5
  Woodlands Way IP28 .239 F5
Woodlark Dr CB4 ....125 D4
Woodlark Rd CB3 ....83 D5
Woodlands Way CB4 .105 D2
Woodroffe Rd PE8 ..193 D8
Woods Cl PE29 ......24 E5
Woodside
  Chatteris PE16 ......241 C4
  Oakington/Longstanton
  CB4 ......123 F1
Woodside Way PE27 .144 B5
Woodson Ind Est PE2 .186 C6
Woodson Prim Sch
  PE2 ......186 F7
Woodwalton Fen National
  Nature Reserve*
  PE26 ......170 B6
Woodwalton Marsh Nature
  Reserve* PE26 .....161 E7
Woodward Cl PE7 ...176 A8
Woodyshield 2 PE15 ..223 B7
Woolcroft Cl PE13 ...238 A1
Woolfellhill Rd PE6 ..205 F3
Woolgard PE3 ......197 A3
Woollards La CB2 ...49 A4
Woolley Cl PE28 ....140 D3
Woolley Hill PE28 ...128 B3
Woolpack Way SG8 ..149 B3
Woolpack La
  St Ives PE27 ......144 A3
  2 Whittlesey PE7 ...189 D6
Woolpack Way SG8 ..29 B1
Woolthwaite La CB3 ..79 A4
Wooton Field SG19 ..41 D4
Woottens Cl CB3 ....62 C5
Wootton Ave PE26 ..186 F6
Wootton Way CB3 ...64 A8

Worboys Ct SG8 ......10 F5
Worcester Ave CB3 ...81 A4
Worcester Cres 2 PE9 .244 B6
Worcester Rd PE13 ..245 C7
Worcester Way SG8 ..14 E6
Wordsworth Ave PE19 .74 D6
Wordsworth Cl
  Peterborough PE4 ...197 E8
  Wisbech PE13 ......13 D1
Wordsworth Gr CB3 ..64 C8
Workhouse La PE14 ..229 D8
Worlington Rd
  Barton Mills IP28 ...214 C3
Worlington Rd
  Worlington IP28 ....239 A3
Worsley PE2 ......186 A4
Worsey Chase PE15 ..243 D2
Wortham Pl 2 CB9 ..24 B8
Wortham Rd SG8 ....5 E4
Worthington Cl PE7 ..176 A7
Worts' Cswy CB1 ....65 C2
Wothorpe Hill PE9 ...244 A1
Wothorpe Mews 5 PE9 .244 B4
Wothorpe Rd PE9 ...244 B4
W Gdns The PE13 ...245 A5
Wragg Dr CB8 ......111 A6
Wrating Rd
  Great Thurlow CB9 ...39 B8
  Haverhill CB9 ......24 A8
Wren Cl IP28 ......239 D4
Wren Pk CB2 ......32 B4
Wrens Cl CB6 ......240 A5
Wrestlingworth Lower Sch
  SG19 ......25 B3
Wrexham Terr SG8 ...5 D7
Wright Ave PE2 ....187 D5
Wright's Cl CB5 ....84 E6
Wrights Dro PE6 ....232 B7
Wrights Dro PE7 ...220 B8
Wrights Gr CB1 ....66 F6
Wroe The PE14 ....236 C5
Wulfric Sq PE3 ....197 C8
Wulfstan Cl CB1 ...65 C4
Wulfstan Way CB1 ..65 A4
Wyatt Cl PE26 ....172 B6
Wyboston Cl 1 PE19 .74 C4
Wycliffe Gr PE4 ...204 A5
Wycliffe Rd CB1 ...65 C8
Wydham Pk PE2 ...185 D6
Wye Pl PE4 ......204 E1
Wykes Dr 3 PE13 ...235 B7
Wykes Rd PE7 ....181 D4
Wyman Way PE2 ...185 F5
Wynborne Cl CB4 ...83 E5
Wyndham Way CB4 ..111 A6
Wynford Way CB4 ...83 F7
Wype Dr PE7 ......191 A5
Wype Rd PE7 ......190 C7
Wysing Arts Ctr* CB3 .60 C3
Wytches The CB6 ...211 A7
Wyton Airfield PE28 .153 F2
Wyton Prim Sch PE28 .143 B4

Y

Yardy Cl PE15 ......243 B4
Yarmouth Pl 1 CB9 ..24 A8
Yarrow Cl PE15 .....243 B5
Yarrow Rd CB1 ......66 A5
Yarwell Cl PE2 ......186 D7
Yarwells Headlands
  PE7 ......189 D8
Yarwells Wlk PE7 ...189 D8
Yaxley Inf Sch PE7 ..181 E4
Yaxley Rd PE7 ......177 B4
Yeats Cl SG8 ......13 D1
Yeldham Pl CB9 ....24 A8
Yeomans Cl PE28 ...136 D7
Yerril Gdn 3 CB9 ...23 E7
Yew Tree Wlk PE4 ..197 A2
York Cl
  Godmanchester PE29 .141 F1
  Mildenhall IP28 ....213 D8
York Gdns CB1 ......84 A1
  Wisbech PE13 ......245 C6
York Way Royston SG8 ..5 B7
  St Ives PE27 ......144 A8
Yorke Way CB6 ....240 B3
Young St CB1 ......84 A2
Youngman Ave CB4 ..104 C5
Youngman Cl CB4 ...104 C5

Z

Zetland Wlk CB1 ....65 D7

Name and Address	Telephone	Page	Grid reference

Any feature in this atlas can be given a unique reference to help you find the same feature on other Ordnance Survey maps of the area, or to help someone else locate you if they do not have a Street Atlas.

The grid squares in this atlas match the Ordnance Survey National Grid and are at 500 metre intervals. The small figures at the bottom and sides of every other grid line are the National Grid kilometre values (**00** to **99** km) and are repeated across the country every 100 km (see left).

To give a unique National Grid reference you need to locate where in the country you are. The country is divided into 100 km squares with each square given a unique two-letter reference. Use the administrative map to determine in which 100 km square a particular page of this atlas falls.

The bold letters and numbers between each grid line (**A** to **F**, **1** to **8**) are for use within a specific Street Atlas only, and when used with the page number, are a convenient way of referencing these grid squares.

Example   The railway bridge over DARLEY GREEN RD in grid square B1

Step 1: Identify the two-letter reference, in this example the page is in **SP**

Step 2: Identify the 1 km square in which the railway bridge falls. Use the figures in the southwest corner of this square: Eastings **17**, Northings **74**. This gives a unique reference: **SP 17 74**, accurate to 1 km.

Step 3: To give a more precise reference accurate to 100 m you need to estimate how many tenths along and how many tenths up this 1 km square the feature is (to help with this the 1 km square is divided into four 500 m squares). This makes the bridge about **8** tenths along and about **1** tenth up from the southwest corner.

This gives a unique reference: **SP 178 741**, accurate to 100 m.

Eastings (read from left to right along the bottom) come before Northings (read from bottom to top). If you have trouble remembering say to yourself "Along the hall, THEN up the stairs"!

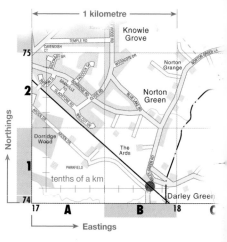

PHILIP'S MAPS

the Gold Standard for drivers

◆ **Philip's street atlases cover every county in England, Wales and much of Scotland**

◆ Every named street is shown, including alleys, lanes and walkways

◆ Thousands of additional features marked: stations, public buildings, car parks, places of interest

◆ Route-planning maps to get you close to your destination

◆ Postcodes on the maps and in the index

◆ Widely used by the emergency services, transport companies and local authorities

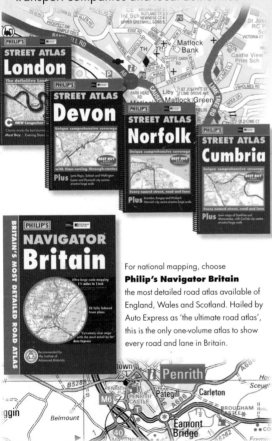

For national mapping, choose **Philip's Navigator Britain** the most detailed road atlas available of England, Wales and Scotland. Hailed by Auto Express as 'the ultimate road atlas', this is the only one-volume atlas to show every road and lane in Britain.

Street atlases currently available

England	
Bedfordshire	East Sussex
Berkshire	West Sussex
Birmingham and West Midlands	Tyne and Wear
Bristol and Bath	Warwickshire
Buckinghamshire	Birmingham and West Midlands
Cambridgeshire	Wiltshire and Swindon
Cheshire	Worcestershire
Cornwall	East Yorkshire Northern Lincolnshire
Cumbria	North Yorkshire
Derbyshire	South Yorkshire
Devon	West Yorkshire
Dorset	
County Durham and Teesside	**Wales**
Essex	Anglesey, Conwy and Gwynedd
North Essex	Cardiff, Swansea and The Valleys
South Essex	Carmarthenshire, Pembrokeshire and Swansea
Gloucestershire	
Hampshire	Ceredigion and South Gwynedd
North Hampshire	
South Hampshire	Denbighshire, Flintshire, Wrexham
Herefordshire Monmouthshire	
Hertfordshire	Herefordshire Monmouthshire
Isle of Wight	Powys
Kent	
East Kent	**Scotland**
West Kent	Aberdeenshire
Lancashire	Ayrshire
Leicestershire and Rutland	Dumfries and Galloway
	Edinburgh and East Central Scotland
Lincolnshire	
London	Fife and Tayside
Greater Manchester	Glasgow and West Central Scotland
Merseyside	
Norfolk	Inverness and Moray
Northamptonshire	Lanarkshire
Northumberland	Scottish Borders
Nottinghamshire	**Northern Ireland***
Oxfordshire	County Antrim and County Londonderry
Shropshire	County Armagh and County Down
Somerset	
Staffordshire	Belfast
Suffolk	County Tyrone and County Fermanagh
Surrey	
	*Publishing autumn 2006